INSIGHT GUIDES
UNITED STATES
ON THE ROAD

AMIGO'S CAFE

Discovery CHANNEL

APA PUBLICATIONS L
Part of the Langenscheidt Publishing Group

INSIGHT GUIDE
UNITED STATES
On The Road

Editorial
Editor
Martha Ellen Zenfell
Editorial Director
Brian Bell

Distribution

UK & Ireland
GeoCenter International Ltd
Meridian House, Churchill Way West
Basingstoke, Hampshire RG21 6YR
Fax: (44) 1256 817988

United States
Langenscheidt Publishers, Inc.
46–35 54th Road, Maspeth, NY 11378
Fax: 1 (718) 784 0640

Australia
Universal Publishers
1 Waterloo Road
Macquarie Park, NSW 2113
Fax: (61) 2 9888 9074

New Zealand
Hema Maps New Zealand Ltd (HNZ)
Unit D, 24 Ra ORA Drive
East Tamaki, Auckland
Fax: (64) 9 273 6479

Worldwide
Apa Publications GmbH & Co.
Verlag KG (Singapore branch)
38 Joo Koon Road, Singapore 628990
Tel: (65) 6865 1600. Fax: (65) 6861 6438

Printing

Insight Print Services (Pte) Ltd
38 Joo Koon Road, Singapore 628990
Tel: (65) 6865 1600. Fax: (65) 6861 6438

CONTACTING THE EDITORS
We would appreciate it if readers
would alert us to errors or out-
dated information by writing to:
**Insight Guides, P.O. Box 7910,
London SE1 1WE, England.
Fax: (44) 20 7403 0290.**
insight@apaguide.co.uk

www.insightguides.com
In North America:
www.insighttravelguides.com

ABOUT THIS BOOK

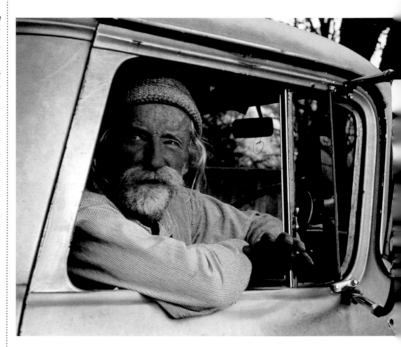

The first Insight Guide pioneered the use of creative full-color photography in travel guides in 1970. Since then, we have expanded our range to cater for our readers' need, not only for reliable information about their chosen destination but also for a real understanding of the history, culture and workings of that destination. Now, when the internet can supply inexhaustible (but not always reliable) facts, our books marry text and pictures to provide those much more elusive qualities: knowledge and discernment. To achieve this, they rely heavily on the authority of locally based writers and photographers

This book is carefully structured to convey an understanding of the United States and its unique, on-the-road culture, as well as to guide readers through the country's variety of sights and activities:

◆ The **History and Features** section, indicated by a yellow bar at the top of each page, covers the history and travel culture of the country in a series of informative essays.

◆ The main **Routes** section, indicated by a blue bar, is a complete guide to all the sights and areas worth visiting. We sent out four writers to travel five east-west or north-south routes, which together cover the very best of the USA. Each route begins, and some end, in a major "hub" city, as we believe most visitors start a journey from a large city, and then hit the road in earnest after that.

Because this book is a celebration of rural areas and small-town life, we have given both the hub cities and the major towns along the routes special treatment, condensing the information into easy-to-assimilate, bite-size features. This leaves the body of the book to stand as free-wheeling, on-the-road narrative text, fun to read but even more rewarding to follow on a cross-country trip of your own.

♦ The **Travel Tips** listings section, with an orange bar, provides a handy point of reference for practical information. The section begins with general travel, hotel and cultural tips on the country as a whole, then follows the same geographical breakdown as the Routes section, giving suggestions, first in the hub city, then town-by-town, on where to stay, where to eat, and where to shop.

The contributors

The guiding hand behind this book was that of **Martha Ellen Zenfell**, a London-based American who has been the project editor of most of Insight Guides' North American titles; she was also responsible for selecting the pictures for the book. The first of our highwaymen to be commissioned were ace writers and photo snappers **Greg Ward** (Southern Route) and **Paul Karr** (Atlantic and Northern Routes). The Central Route was undertaken by Insight Guides stalwart **John Wilcock**, together with **Teresa Machan**, who did not know each other until meeting up in Washington, DC, the hub city for that 3,000-mile (4,800-km) journey; we await with interest the *real* story of what it is like to travel across the country with a perfect stranger. Wilcock also tackled the Pacific Route, with help from Zenfell, who drew on a trip through Big Sur on a Harley-Davidson to supply that bugs-in-the-teeth realism.

Paul Taylor was our first and only choice to write the feature on Route 66; as publisher of *Route 66 Magazine* he *has* to be the favored son of the Mother Road. All copy was processed through **Jason Mitchell** in London, then sent to Arizona to **Barbara Balletto** who refined the narrative flow. Texan **Alyse Williams** compiled the massive Travel Tips section. **Catherine Karnow** was only one of the many photographers whose images helped to shape this book, which is based on the 1980s original *Insight Guide: Crossing America*. Particular thanks to **Adam Liptak**, **Robert Seidenberg** and **Rich Taskin** for producing such a timeless title. **Laura Martone** updated the text.

Map Legend

▬ ▪ ▬ ▪ ▬	International Boundary
▬ ▬ ▬ ▬	State Boundary
⊖	Border Crossing
▬ • ▬ ▬	National Park/Reserve
═══	Highway
════	Other Multi-lane Highway
═══	Principal Highway
───	Through Highway
──	Other Road
⑤	Interstate Highway
⑴ ㉙	US Highway
㊿ ㉳⑨	Other Highway
→	On the Road Routes
✈ ✈	Airport: International/Regional
★	Place of Interest

The main places of interest in the guide section of the book are coordinated by number with a full-color map (e.g. ❶). A symbol at the top of every right-hand page tells you where to find the map.

INSIGHT GUIDE
UNITED STATES
On The Road

CONTENTS

The beginning and the end of the road, Florida Keys

Travel Tips

◆ **Full Travel Tips index is on page 385**

Hub Cities

WE'RE ON THE ROAD TO SOMEWHERE

*Americans are always on the move. A French explorer in the 1800s
identified this unique trait and called it "restlessness amidst prosperity"*

The most basic images of American life – the heavy wagon train rumbling across the prairie, a railroad car speeding through the night, the arrival of immigrants at Ellis Island – are powerful symbols of the United States' timeless obsession with movement. In fact, in a nation where change is the only constant, movement and travel have established the ever quickening tempo of American history, from Lewis and Clark's exploration of the territories west of the Mississippi River, to Neil Armstrong's historic walk on the moon.

If the exploration and colonization of America is an example of travel, is there any real connection with the day-trip into the countryside? Is it possible to seriously suggest that the 17th-century Puritan seeking refuge in Boston has anything in common with the 22-year-old computer whiz who moves from Lexington, Massachusetts, to Seattle, Washington, in search of a higher paying job? Do Lewis and Clark have any common bond with vacationers of the 1950s rolling down Route 66?

Epic adventure

Every one of these travelers believed that movement might bring prosperity, discovery and renewal. The difference lies in the purpose of the journey. Travel in pre-modern America was a very serious affair: an essential part of discovering and populating the continent. While a few wealthy Americans embarked on European *wanderjahrs*, and some even traveled for pleasure to Newport and Saratoga Springs, we do not associate such ease and comfort with the days of old. Rather, we recall Daniel Boone leading pioneers through the Cumberland Gap; young men heeding Horace Greeley's advice

---

PRECEDING PAGES: vintage surf car, Southern California; friends on good form, the Southwest; biker with "rat bike," Florida; taking a call, Northern California.
LEFT: on the road up in the hills.
RIGHT: hitching a ride on Route 66.

and going West to grow up with the country; the Mormons' perilous flight across the Great Plains; or the stagecoach company that warned its riders not to "point out where murders have been committed, especially if there are women

passengers." Given the harsh landscape, we think of travel in early America as a dangerous and epic adventure.

In the early 21st century, when we take a trip there is little heroic about it, nor much physical discomfort. Yet, Americans still migrate for economic reasons, particularly to the Sunbelt states in the South, or to the Pacific Northwest. But this anonymous and isolated movement of people lacks the drama of the pioneers, or the great "Dust Bowl" migration of the 1930s, immortalized in the ballads of Woody Guthrie and John Steinbeck's novel *The Grapes of Wrath*. Still, it is very likely that an American historian in the next century will judge this movement to be as significant a force during these millennium years as it was in past times.

The sheer number of automobiles in America today suggest that the experience of travel is now available to almost everyone. Travel has been democratized, and plays no small role in contributing to the American tendency to view cars, boats and planes as symbols of equality, if not distinction. For better or worse, to be an American is to believe that personal liberty and the freedom to travel, be it on an errand or in search of Utopia, are inseparable.

Is there any truth in this belief? Is there a vital link between the uniquely democratic culture

of the United States and the transportation revolution of the past two centuries? Michael Chevalier thought so. Chevalier, a French aristocrat sent to the United States in the 1830s to study its public works, and author of a report on its political and social machinery, believed that improved means of travel would hasten the collapse of the old order and play an important role in the emergence of "modern society." During his tour, he was amazed by the readiness with which Americans embraced new means of travel: first (after initial disinterest), roads had been constructed with passionate intensity, then canal building had become a national mania. And Chevalier bore witness to

the birth of the age of the railroad, for which he rightly forecast a glorious future.

Riding a steamboat into New Orleans, Chevalier noted that "formerly it was possible only for a patrician to travel, and the great bulk of mankind were then attached to the globe, chained to the soil by the difficulty of locomotion." But as avenues of economic exchange opened to increasing numbers of people, both ideas and populations were transmitted hither and yon along with pelts, peppers and teas. Travel became, in Chevalier's words, a catalyst "to equality and liberty," and he was convinced that modern transportation would "increase the rights and privileges of the greatest number as truly and as amply as could be done by electoral laws."

Restless spirits

Chevalier wrote at the beginning of the Industrial Revolution in America, and believed deeply in the 19th-century maxim of progress through science. We now know all too well the mixed blessing of living in a world of rapid transit and rapid deployment systems; but also how those technological achievements have routinized experience while eliminating labor and opening up new paths to the multitudes. And even though the pursuit of freedom and adventure at the end of the road is now much easier, the allure of crossing America has lost little of its appeal to restless spirits.

For, as Alexis de Tocqueville – author of the quote about "restlessness amidst prosperity" – observed two centuries ago: "An American will build a house in which to pass his old age and sell it before the roof is on; he will plant a garden and rent it just as the trees are coming into bearing; he will clear a field and leave others to reap the harvest; he will take up a profession and leave it, settle in one place and soon go off elsewhere with his changing desires. If his private business allows him a moment's relaxation, he will plunge at once into the whirlpool of politics. Then, if at the end of a year crammed with work he has a little spare leisure, his restless curiosity goes with him traveling up and down the vast territories of the United States. Thus he will travel 500 miles in a few days as a distraction from his happiness." ❑

LEFT: modern roadsign in the antebellum South.
RIGHT: a man, his best friend and his dog.

Decisive Dates in American History

1492 Tierra! Tierra! Explorer Christopher Columbus reaches America, landing at San Salvador.
1585 Sir Walter Raleigh founds the soon-to-be-lost colony of Roanoke, in Virginia.
1607 Jamestown, Virginia settled by the British.
1619 First African slaves sold in Jamestown.
1620 The Plymouth Company finances 66 Puritans to establish a permanent settlement in North America. They found Plymouth Colony, on Cape Cod Bay.

1773 In the "Boston Tea Party," 60 men in disguise dump tea crates over the railings of three ships in the harbor in protest against taxes.
1774 On September 5, the First Continental Congress convenes at Philadelphia.
1775 Paul Revere rides from Boston warning Minutemen of the impending arrival of British troops. The following day the "shot heard 'round the world" begins a battle leaving eight Minutemen dead and beginning the American Revolution.
1776 On July 4, the Continental Congress, meeting in Philadelphia, adopts the Declaration of Independence, penned by Thomas Jefferson.
1787 Philadelphia's Constitutional Convention convenes for the first time.

1789 George Washington takes the first presidential oath at New York's Federal Hall.
1792 An open-air money market is founded beneath a tree on New York's Wall Street.
1804 Lewis and Clark set out on their 8,000-mile (13,000-km) expedition to the Pacific Coast.
1814 Francis Scott Key pens the national anthem, "The Star Spangled Banner."
1825 The Erie Canal, known as the "Big Ditch," connects the Hudson River with the Great Lakes.
1836 Siege of the Alamo in San Antonio, Texas, results in the death of all 189 American defenders.
1838 New Orleans' first Mardi Gras parade.
1848 Gold is discovered at Sutter's Fort, California, bringing over 200,000 prospectors within the next three years. The Chicago Board of Trade, the world's oldest and largest futures exchange, is established.
1858 After a 25-day journey, John Butterfield's Overland Stage delivers its first sack of mail to the West Coast.
1860 South Carolina secedes from the Union, and the Confederate states are born.
1862 Confederates open fire on Fort Sumter, in the first shots of the Civil War. Abraham Lincoln legally frees all slaves by issuing the Emancipation Proclamation.
1864 The transcontinental telegraph connects Seattle, Washington, with the rest of the US.
1865 With the surrender of Robert E. Lee to Ulysses S. Grant in Virginia, the Civil War ends. President Abraham Lincoln is assassinated in Washington, DC.
1869 The Central Pacific and Union Pacific railroads meet in Ogden, Utah, completing the first transcontinental railroad. Major John Wesley Powell leads an expedition through the Grand Canyon.
1871 The Great Chicago Fire kills 300 people and destroys 18,000 buildings.
1876 General George A. Custer leads his 264 men into battle at LIttle Bighorn Creek. All are wiped out in "Custer's Last Stand."
1881 Wyatt Earp and Doc Holiday kill cattle rustlers at the "Gunfight at the OK Corral" in Arizona.
1886 In a ceremony on Ellis Island, Grover Cleveland presents France's gift to honor America: the Statue of Liberty.
1890 A US Army regiment attacks a camp near Wounded Knee Creek in South Dakota's Pine Ridge Reservation, killing 300 Indians.
1906 A massive earthquake measuring 8.2 on the Richter Scale, followed by a devastating fire, flattens San Francisco.
1907 Neiman-Marcus store opens in Dallas, Texas.

1908 Henry Ford begins mass production of the Model T car. Filmmaker William Selig completes *The Count of Monte Cristo*, California's first commercial movie.

1915 Thomas Watson, a resident of San Francisco, receives the first transcontinental phone call from Alexander Graham Bell. New Orleans music is introduced to Chicago. It is called "jazz."

1919 Eighteenth Amendment to the Constitution outlaws alcoholic beverages.

1920 Nineteenth Amendment to the Constitution guarantees women's right to vote.

1921 Margaret Sanger founds the American Birth Control League.

1925 The Grand Ole Opry opens its doors in Nashville, Tennessee.

1927 60-year-old sculptor Gutzon Borglum begins work on South Dakota's Mount Rushmore.

1929 Wall Street crashes, and with it comes the beginnings of the Great Depression.

1930 An oil find outside Dallas initiates the East Texas Oil Field, the largest petroleum deposit known to the world at that time.

1930s Because of misuse of land and years of water shortages, the "Dust Bowl" forces thousands from farmlands around Oklahoma on a migrant trek west to California in search of work.

1931 The Empire State Building opens.

1934 Depression-era bank robbers Bonnie Parker and Clyde Barrow meet a hail of bullets, ending a 102-day manhunt by Texas Rangers.

1937 Golden Gate Bridge opens in San Francisco.

1941 Japan attacks Pearl Harbor, and the United States enters World War II.

1945 First atomic bomb detonates in New Mexico; bombs dropped on Hiroshima and Nagasaki. United Nations charter drafted in San Francisco.

1955 Rev. Martin Luther King, Jr leads the Montgomery (Alabama) Bus Boycott.

1963 President John F. Kennedy is assassinated while touring Dallas, Texas.

1967 Hippies, leftists and idealists, drawn to San Francisco's Haight-Ashbury district, celebrate the Summer of Love.

1968 Division over the Vietnam War bursts into street violence, culminating with a "police riot" against demonstrators at Chicago's Democratic National Convention. James Earl Ray kills Martin Luther King, Jr in Memphis, and Robert F. Kennedy is assassinated in Los Angeles.

1969 *Apollo 11* commander Neil Armstrong communicates with Houston from the moon.

1974 Richard M. Nixon, 37th president, resigns after facing impeachment proceedings due to a 1972 break-in and cover-up at the Watergate Hotel.

1980 Mount St Helens in Washington erupts, devastating the surrounding region.

1986 Seattle's Bill Gates takes Microsoft public, becoming one of the richest men in the world.

1989 An earthquake (7.1 on the Richter Scale)

collapses a freeway and causes chaos and destruction in the San Francisco area.

1993 Agents storm a cult compound near Waco, Texas, resulting in more than 80 deaths.

2000 Hanging chads cause rage in Florida as George W. Bush becomes president.

2001 Four passenger jets hijacked by suicide bombers destroy New York City's World Trade Center.

2002 Utah's Salt Lake City hosts the winter Olympics.

2005 Hurricane Katrina causes major flooding and destruction in New Orleans and along the Gulf Coast, killing thousands of residents.

2006 Gerald Ford, the 38th President of the US, dies in California, aged 93. ❏

PRECEDING PAGES: the joining of the Central and Pacific railroads in 1869 linked the East and West coasts.
LEFT: President Thomas Jefferson paid $15 million in 1803 for the land between the Mississippi River and the Rocky Mountains, doubling the size of the US.
RIGHT: Neil Armstrong, astronaut and moon walker.

THE TRANSPORTATION REVOLUTION

From wagon trains to the iron horse to today's superhighways,
travel is at the heart of America's history

During the 17th and 18th centuries, white settlers in early America followed the network of paths that Native Americans had carved out for themselves, and travel conditions were notoriously wretched. During the time of colonization with Great Britian, it cost less to transport goods across the Atlantic Ocean from London to Philadelphia than to carry those same goods 100 miles to Lancaster, Pennsylvania. In 1776, news of the Declaration of Independence took 29 days to reach the people of Charleston, South Carolina. No wonder New England delegates at the Constitutional Convention in 1787 had more things in common with their brethren in Britain than with their fellow countrymen down South in the Carolinas and Georgia.

Fifty years later, when Alexis de Tocqueville, Michael Chevalier and a host of European travelers *(see page 16)* examined the American experiment of self-government, conditions on dry land were little improved. Whereas the Roman Empire made the construction of great roads an important function of its central government, in 19th-century America *laissez-faire* attitudes predominated, leaving the construction of highways a state and local responsibility. Often, farmers and laborers who were unable to meet their tax obligations ended up doing the little road work that was done.

Tolerance of mud

As a direct consequence of the American belief in "the less government the better," roads suffered from neglect and disrepair. Pioneers, such as Abraham Lincoln's father, Thomas, had to possess courage, physical strength and an incredible tolerance of mud. William Herndon, Lincoln's law partner and biographer, described the Lincoln family's move from Indiana to Illinois in March of 1830 as one which "suited the roving and migratory spirit of Thomas Lincoln." With the "obscure and penniless"

LEFT: pioneers on wagon trains faced harsh conditions.
RIGHT: explorer Meriwether Lewis.

21-year-old Abe commanding a wagon drawn by two oxen, "the journey was a long and tedious one." Basing his literary account of the trip on Lincoln's recollections, Herndon memorably evokes the experience of thousands of similar travelers. "The rude, heavy wagon," he wrote, "with its primitive wheels, creaked and groaned as it crawled through the woods and now and then stalled in the mud. Many were the delays."

In antebellum America, geography created a formidable barrier to migration. Even as late as the 1830s, approximately 80 percent of the American population still continued to reside east of the Allegheny Mountains. One might have been inclined to agree with Thomas Jefferson's earlier prediction that it would take close to 1,000 years to settle the entire vastness of the North American continent.

As it turned out, Jefferson was wrong by about 910 years. Indeed, his decision to send those two intrepid travelers, Captain Meriwether Lewis and Lieutenant William Clark, to explore the territories west of the Mississippi River charted the way for settlement of the vast, important region. President Jefferson dispatched Lewis and Clark shortly after the Louisiana Purchase in 1803. His motives for asking for a $2,500 appropriation from Congress to finance the expedition were mixed. Even at this late date, it appears Jefferson had not abandoned all hope that a passage to Asia might be found. He was also confident that the explorers would discover trade routes to benefit fur traders. Nor was Jefferson without hope of further expanding what he liked to call the "empire of liberty." But this is not to say that the president was prevaricating when he explained to the Spanish Minister that the purpose of the mission was the "advancement of science." Jefferson, a child of the Enlightenment Era, saw the active study of the physical universe as an important chapter in the life of the mind.

Lewis and Clark did not disappoint Jefferson. Their voluminous journals provided detailed descriptions of what eventually became the Oregon Trail. Perhaps what is remembered most from sampling their writings are the descriptions of the geology, fauna and wildlife of the West. Their wide range of learning, courage displayed in the face of physical

THE PONY EXPRESS

One of the 19th century's most romantic enterprises, the Pony Express, galloped across the western landscape and into the history books in just over 18 months. From April 1860 through October 1861, Express horsemen formed a record-setting, trans-Mississippi relay team that won over the hearts of Americans, if not the pocketbooks of the US Congress. The daring young mail carriers braved rain, snow, sleet, dead of night and Indian attacks between St Joseph, Missouri, and Sacramento, California, to deliver 35,000 letters, telegrams and newspapers. The riders tallied up 650,000 miles (1 milllion km) on the 1,966-mile-long (3,164-km) Pony Express Trail. And they lost only one mailbag.

Newspaper ads for Express riders did not mince words: "WANTED – Young, skinny, wiry fellows not over 18. Must be expert riders willing to risk death daily. Orphans preferred." Eighty riders, almost all weighing less than 125 pounds (57 kg), were hired initially, including a fatherless 15-year-old named William F. Cody, later known as Buffalo Bill. The pay was attractive, at least $50 a month, plus free lodging and food. Each rider took an oath, agreeing not to use profane language, not to get drunk and not to fight with other employees. Each horseman also received a copy of the Bible, plus two Colt revolvers, a knife and a carbine. The journey took 10 days each way.

deprivation, and eloquence are inspiring. Lewis and Clark prepared the way for the invasion of the West that is still in progress today.

By the mid-19th century, poets and orators matched hyperboles in an effort to describe what one person called the "untransacted destiny of the United States." One orator even forecast that the American lamp of liberty would be visible from Tierra del Fuego to the Aurora Borealis.

In the 1840s, the journalist John O'Sullivan popularized the phrase "manifest destiny" to

A PRESIDENT PREDICTS

Thomas Jefferson thought it would take close to a thousand years to settle the lands west of the Mississippi River; he was mistaken by more than 900 years.

Age of the iron horse

Before the Union could be linked by rail, the United States was plunged into the Civil War. It took four weeks for the news of the opening volley at Fort Sumter to reach San Francisco, but, by the end of the war, the nation was forging the bonds of union. The age of the turnpike, steamboat and canal had been overtaken by the iron horse; it is widely conceded that the North's superior transportation system played a crucial role in crushing the Southern rebels. In 1863, the

describe this widespread expansionist ideology.

Western politicians such as Stephen Douglas based their political fortunes on promoting the future greatness of the West as the ultimate destination and demanded the construction of a transcontinental railroad in order to link the nation's rapidly expanding economy. Douglas repeatedly argued during the 1840s and '50s that the West was not only the stage for the nation's future, but that it would also be an effective alternative to the increasingly nasty bickering between the North and the South.

LEFT AND ABOVE: the Pony Express lasted only 18 months, but inspired countless stories.

North was able to transport 25,000 troops by rail from Washington, DC, to Chatanooga, Tennessee, to turn the tide in a major battle.

Mark Twain and Charles Dudley Warner dubbed the final third of the 19th century "the Gilded Age," an era of conspicuous consumption and corruption. Perhaps the age might better be thought of as being the age of the railroad. The railroad barons – the Goulds, Huntingtons and Vanderbilts – all understood that the railroad was the lubricant of both a booming economy and sleazy politics.

The railroad also made long-distance travel for pleasure a realistic possibility for middle-class Americans. The creation of the Pullman

Palace Car Company in 1868 reflected the growing number of Americans interested in taking vacations. Although a period of rest and relaxation did not sit well with those devoted to work ("the sum of wisdom" according to Emerson, is that "the time is never lost that is devoted to work"), so publicists for the new leisure ethic stressed that Americans were growing unhealthy – both physically and spiritually – as a result of their obsession with success. Regeneration through contact with the great outdoors and the vigorous life was a stock promise from popularizers of the West.

In 1893, the year of the Chicago World's Fair,

two bicycle mechanics, Charles and J. Frank Duryea, successfully tested the first automobile on the streets of Springfield, Massachusetts, and a new age began.

Car crazy

Public roads were among the initial benefactors of the age of the automobile. The movement to upgrade the quality of American highways had begun during the 1880s when bicycling organizations like the League of American Wheelmen led the call for improved roads. When automobiles began to appear in the streets and villages in greater numbers after 1900, the drive for surfaced roads attracted increasing support. The instinctive American distrust of Federal intrusion into the lives of its citizens was overcome by the politically popular demand that the US Mail ought to be delivered directly to rural Americans over improved roads. In 1916, President Woodrow Wilson signed a Federal Aid Road Act which was the first of a series of occasions when Federal intrusion into the nation's transportation system met with widespread public approval.

The constituency for such governmental action grew larger with each passing decade. And the person who probably deserves the greatest share of credit for democratizing the automobile and travel is Henry Ford, who introduced to the industry the assembly line which revolutionized the production and sale of cars; by 1922, he was selling an astonishing 1.3 million Model Ts. And while their uniformity would soon render them obsolete, the Tin Lizzie had made the automobile a badge of social distinction as well as a necessity.

The impact of the widespread ownership of cars upon travel cannot be overstated. It was probably the single most important factor in the opening of American life not only to travelers seeking remote scenes, but also to 20th-century movers and migrants.

What would the 1930s have been like, after all, if John Steinbeck's literary Tom Joad and his fellow wandering poor could not have climbed into a car and headed for California where, as a Jimmie Rodgers song promised, the "water tastes like cherry wine?" The increased mobility the automobile offered underscores the judgement of George F. Pierson, who in his book *The Moving American* describes this freedom as "the great American permit to be both more free and more equal than our contemporaries could manage to become in the more static societies of Europe."

In the early years of the new millennium, people are traveling faster and farther than ever before in ever-increasing numbers. The Frenchman de Tocqueville's American of the 1800s who traveled "500 miles in a few days as a distraction from his happiness" has been replaced by a far-reaching, highly mobile globe-trotter pursuing equally elusive dreams. ❏

LEFT: cycling the steps of the Capitol, Washington, DC. Cyclists were responsible for improving highways.
RIGHT: the West is seen as the ultimate destination.

AMERICAN ARTISTS AND THE ROAD

Novelists, poets, musicians, film-makers – the
romance of the open road seduces them all

American artists are perpetually on the run. Their work epitomizes the wanderlust of the American people: the belief in movement for movement's sake. "The sound of a jet," John Steinbeck wrote in 1961, "an engine warming up, even the clopping of shod hooves on pavement brings an ancient shudder, the dry mouth and vacant eye, the hot palms and the churn of stomach high up under the rib cage."

A century before Steinbeck, Herman Melville depicted travel as a balm to a depressed soul. "Whenever I find myself growing grim about the mouth," he mused in the famous first paragraph of *Moby Dick*, "whenever it is a damp, drizzly, November in my soul; …whenever my hypos get such an upper hand of me, that it requires a strong moral principle to prevent me from deliberately stepping into the street, and methodically knocking people's hats off – then, I account it high time to get to sea as soon as I can." In the classic American fiction of Melville, Edgar Allan Poe, James Fenimore Cooper and Mark Twain, we encounter characters fleeing the inertia of polite society for a jaunt into the wild.

A change of place

"I wish for a change of place," J. Hector St John de Crevecoeur wrote in *Letters from an American Farmer*. "The hour is come at last, that I must fly from my home and abandon my farm!" Crevecoeur's threat to flee into the Indian territory "and revert into a state approaching nearer to that of nature, unencumbered either with voluminous laws, or contradictory codes" was pure fiction.

As unlikely to occur as Mark Twain hooking up with Huck Finn a century later when Huck threatened to "light out for the territory." Still, Crevecoeur is only one of many

LEFT: Marlon Brando as *The Wild One*, one of the first anti-heroes of the silver screen.
RIGHT: Tom Hanks as *Forrest Gump*, who runs across America and participates in much of its recent history.

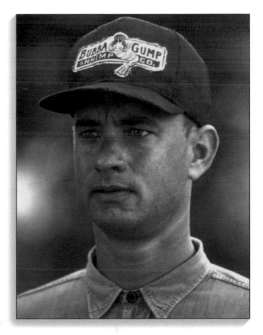

writers who celebrated the movement away from complex modern life.

Indeed, the great writers of 19th-century America viewed travel as a "stay against confusion" in a society committed to material gain. Melville, Nathaniel Hawthorne and Cooper felt alienated from the climate of the times and sought refuge in foreign travel.

Their despair with the democratic masses stands in marked contrast to one of the greatest American poets of the open road, Walt Whitman. A journey along the open highway suited his desire to comprehend the whole of life: the casual meeting, the encounter between the eye of the seer and the landscape and the timelessness of nature. Whitman saw the open road as the passage to wisdom and fraternity.

The act of traveling itself is a democratic gesture to the poet, a source of inspiration and a symbol of his personal liberty. Not only were the "American people the greatest poem," but the American environment itself was an incubator of freedom and unity. As he wrote in his acclaimed "Song of the Open Road:"

I think all heroic deeds were all conceiv'd
in the open air, and all free
poems also,
I think I could stop here myself
and do miracles,
I think whatever I shall meet
on the road I shall like, and
whoever beholds me shall like
me.
I think whoever I see must be happy.

Mark Twain used the voyage as a metaphor for change. In his novel *The Adventures of Huck-*

> **LONESOME ROAD BLUES**
>
> *I'm going down that long,*
> *lonesome road*
> *And I ain't gonna be*
> *treated this a-way.*
> *–Going Down the Road Feelin' Bad.*

Since World War II, the accelerated pace of travel has produced a literature equally frenetic. The most famous road book has been Jack Kerouac's *On the Road*, the definitive statement of Beat culture and the cultural radicals of the 1960s and '70s. Kerouac's prose may impress less now, but his celebration of finding spiritual truths while racing across the continent makes the work transcend conventional literary canons.

Kerouac's work continued the tradition of writer as pathfinder and spiritual voyager;

leberry Finn, he made it clear that the voyage was a learning experience and a rebellion against conventional morality. Some of the book's most moving passages are Huck's accounts of life on the river. Each time Huck and the escaped slave Jim encounter people on shore, trouble, trickery and cruelty predominate. The book ends with Huck's famous vow to flee civilization and its hypocrisy. But, of course, the old-fashioned frontier was disappearing when Twain was writing in the 1880s, so Huck's dream of flight belonged to a vanishing world. Still, Huck's words at the close of *Huckleberry Finn* bring to mind another characteristic of American literature: loneliness, and the traveler as a solitary figure.

William Least Heat Moon's *Blue Highways* picked up that tradition. Moon traversed the nation in his van "ghost dancing." His report is both a rumination on travel literature and a revealing study of the state of the nation. Richard Grant, a British journalist, fell in love with the American nomadic lifestyle. His *Ghost Riders* tells the story of nomads present (in their own words from boxcar slang to cowboy drawl) and past.

Whereas Kerouac filtered all experience through his ahistorical frame of mind, Moon and Grant, by letting people speak for themselves, capture the diversity of the landscape that often overwhelms the trans-American traveler.

Music to their ears

It is not just literary artists who have sung of the loneliness and vagaries of the open road. Country music in particular often focuses on that "lonesome guy" Hank Williams sang about on "the lost highway." Cowboys, singing at night to fight off despair and keep cattle from stampeding, often reworked old Irish and English ballads about murder and betrayal. Much of the music produced under such circumstances was often grim and filled with resignation. In the 1940s and

BORN TO RUN

Baby, this town rips the bones from your back/It's a death trap, it's a suicide rap/We gotta get out while we're young/'Cause tramps like us, we were born to run.

cops and anything that might get in the way.

The theme of the open road extends to rock music and blues as well. Is it any wonder that one of the rock anthems of the 1970s was Bruce Springsteen's "Born to Run?"

Or that avant garde New York performance artist and musician Laurie Anderson chose Melville's travel-as-balm *Moby Dick* to reinterprete and take on a world tour in the year 2000?

Ace bluesman Robert Johnson evoked the road as a haunting meeting place. In his highly

'50s, cowboy singers such as Roy Rogers evoked the nostalgia of the open range for listeners confined by harsh economic circumstances to lives of poverty and loneliness.

Not all country music is downbeat, however. A whole genre of music has arisen devoted to the lives of the modern riders of the open range: truckdrivers. These contemporary folk figures form a loyal audience for country music, and songs like the admired and much-recorded "Six Days on the Road" are pure Walt Whitmanesque whoops of triumph over the law, the

influential song "Crossroads" (recorded by Eric Clapton and others), it is hard to say exactly why "he got down on his knees and prayed" – perhaps because the crossroad is where suicides are buried? Or because Johnson sold his soul to the devil in exchange for playing the guitar? Whatever the reason, what is most clear is the musician's anguish and fear.

If Walt Whitman is the most boyant celebrator of the open road and Robert Johnson the most serious habituate of the dark side of the street, surely Woody Guthrie is the "bard of the open road." Even a simple listing of some of his songs – "Dust Bowl Refugees," "I Ain't Got No Home," "Walkin' Down the Railroad Line"

LEFT: Jack Kerouac and Woody Guthrie.
ABOVE: John Steinbeck and Walt Whitman.

– suggests the prominence he assigned to "walkin' down the line." Like Whitman, he attempted to capture the whole of America in the verses of "This Land is Your Land." In songs like "The Great Historical Bum," he even laughed at his persona as the roustabout poet:

> *I'm just a lonesome traveler, the great*
> *historical bum.*
> *Highly educated from history I have come,*
> *I built the Rock of Ages, it was in the*
> *year of one*
> *And that's about the biggest thing that*
> *man has ever done.*

Guthrie lived the life he wrote about after his family was wrecked by tragedy and disease. His best work is timeless – not surprisingly, many of his tunes borrow heavily from hymns and ballads – and will live as long as there are roads to walk and people to sing.

Sagas of the silver screen

The great road films of Hollywood are the best visual sagas of the open plains. People all over the world think of the United States as a land of wide open spaces, thanks to the images they receive from the films of directors John Ford and other Western movie-makers. Again we encounter solitary figures in an uncomfortable

ON THE ROAD MOVIES

About Schmidt (Alexander Payne, 2002)
American Graffiti (George Lucas, 1973)
Badlands (Terrence Malick, 1973)
Down by Law (Jim Jarmusch, 1986)
Duel (Steven Spielberg, 1971)
Electra Glide in Blue (James William Guercio, 1973)
Five Easy Pieces (Bob Rafelson, 1970)
The Grapes of Wrath (John Ford, 1939)
It Happened One Night (Frank Capra, 1934)
Joy Ride (John Dahl, 2001)
Leningrad Cowboys Go America (Aki Kaurismaki, 1989)
Little Miss Sunshine (Jonathon Dayton and Valerie Faris, 2006)

Natural Born Killers (Oliver Stone, 1994)
The Outlaw Josey Wales (Clint Eastwood, 1986)
North by Northwest (Alfred Hitchcock, 1959)
Paris, Texas (Wim Wenders, 1984)
Rain Man (Barry Levinson, 1988)
The Sugarland Express (Steven Spielberg, 1974)
The Searchers (John Ford, 1956)
Two Lane Blacktop (Monte Hellman, 1971)
Vanishing Point (Richard C. Sarafian, 1971)
Wild at Heart (David Lynch, 1990)
Wild Hogs (Walt Becker, 2007)
The Wizard of Oz (Victor Fleming, 1939)

relationship with polite society. Ready to right wrong wherever they find it, the cowboy must move along in the last reel.

Anti-heroes

Clint Eastwood's *Pale Rider* attempted to revive this formula in the 1980s, but, since the '60s, motor-driven outlaws have replaced the cowboy as the stars of mythic road films. From Marlon Brando in the *The Wild One* to Mel Gibson in *The Road Warrior*, films set on the road have focused on wandering anti-social, anti-heroes alienated from society. Robert Zemeckis's *Forrest Gump* (1994) added a twist:

make their getaway to the sound of rebellious country music.

Bonnie and Clyde brought the road film skidding into the tumultuous 1960s, but few films of the recent past inspired more real-life voyages than *Easy Rider* (Dennis Hopper, 1969). Those who see the film as a period piece and high camp have no idea how its original viewers saw it. *Rider* was probably the most powerful advertisement for the counter-culture to appear in movie houses throughout the heartland of the nation. To this day, there are middle-aged workers who dream of throwing away their cell phones, mounting a Harley motorcycle and

the main character is too simple to know if he is hero or anti-hero, or to realize the significance of the events he witnesses.

Bonnie and Clyde (Arthur Penn, 1967) is an example of the perfect tragi-comic road picture. Viewed through the counter-cultural lens of the 1960s, the story of Clyde Barrow and Bonnie Parker seems like a folk tale of the Depression-era '30s. Bonnie and Clyde rob banks that rob the poor of their dreams and

LEFT: Dennis Hopper and Peter Fonda hit the open road in *Easy Rider.*

ABOVE: Faye Dunaway and Warren Beatty as runaway bank robbers in *Bonnie and Clyde.*

setting off for Mardi Gras in New Orleans.

Thelma and Louise (Ridley Scott, 1991) updated this story, using cars and women to illustrate the hi-jinks and low life of on-the-road escapism. The final scene, when the women decided to end it all, is in the tradition of the best Westerns of the 1950s.

The swoop of history follows us down every highway, and the traveler has many teachers to choose from before embarking on an adventure. For William Moon, Walt Whitman served as the model. For Ridley Scott, John Ford was the inspiration. As you head out on the highway, listen to these voices, but be aware that there is no experience like an original one. ❑

ROUTE 66:
AMERICA'S MAIN STREET

Quirky motels, mom 'n' pop diners, drive-in movie theaters:
in its heyday, many thought this was the most magical road in the world

In 1926, US Highway 66 put down its roots near Lake Michigan at the corner of Michigan Avenue and Jackson Boulevard in Chicago, Illinois. With its catchy double-six road markers, it stretched its 2,448 miles (3,940 km) of asphalt and concrete westward through three time zones, across eight states – Illinois, Missouri, Kansas, Oklahoma, Texas, New Mexico, Arizona and California – to the shores of the Pacific Ocean at Santa Monica. Route 66 was one of the country's first continuous spans of paved highway, linking the eastern part of America with the west.

A stroll on wheels

US Highway 66, with undisputed certainty, reigns as the most storied highway in the United States. A recurring theme in American literature, Route 66 has been the star of more stories, books, songs, movies and television shows than any other. The road is more popular than Route 1 from Maine to Key West. From the mid-1920s to the mid-1970s, it was more traveled than Highway 101 on the Pacific Coast, and better known than the Pennsylvania Turnpike or the Alcan Highway. And before the advent of the interstate systems, US 66 came closer than any other highway to becoming the National Road. Route 66 was soon known as "the most magical road in all the world." A legend was in the making.

And what a legend it would be. During its glory days, authors, songwriters and movie moguls all seemed to be headed west on Route 66. Nobody could possibly know how many Americans – from the Dust Bowl famine victims in Oklahoma to the flower children headed for California's Haight Ashbury – would consider Route 66 to be first, and foremost, an invi-

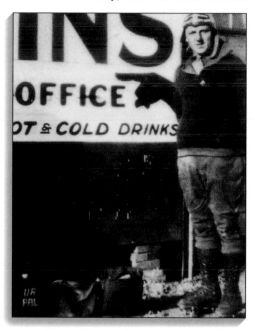

tation for an extended stroll on four wheels.

The nation first became aware of US Highway 66 when the 1928 International Transcontinental Foot Marathon (affectionately known as the Bunion Derby) followed Route 66 from Los Angeles to Chicago, then on to Madison Square Garden in New York, a distance of 3,448 miles (5,548 km). The winner was handed $25,000. Andy Payne, a part-Cherokee Indian from Oklahoma, won the purse.

Three decades later, for a fee of $1,500, Peter McDonald walked on stilts from New York City to Los Angeles, a distance of 3,200 miles (5,150 km). From Chicago to Los Angeles, his way out west was Route 66. Pete was neither the first nor the last to place the road in the public eye – wild, weird and wondrous celebrants were to follow. Two such celebrities were Happy Lou Phillips and his friend Lucky Jimmy Parker. The pair of intrepid travelers

---

LEFT: family outings along Route 66 were common in the 1940s and '50s.
RIGHT: Happy Lou Phillips made headlines by roller-skating from Washington, DC, to San Francisco.

strapped on skates and rolled their way along America's Main Street, as it was called, during their cross-country journey from Washington, DC, to San Francisco. Through the state of Arizona, a newspaper reported, "They walked a great deal, since at that time (1929) Route 66 was only paved through towns."

"Hobo" Dick Zimmerman routinely walked Route 66 from California to Michigan, pushing a wheelbarrow, to visit his 101-year-old mother. Dick was 78.

Another student of perambulating the old

SING IT LOUD

If you ever plan to motor west; travel my way, take the highway that's the best. Get your kicks on Route Sixty-six!

National magazines called Route 66 "America's worst speed trap," naming the tiny hamlets where cops and judges had their palms outstretched for bribes. The American Automobile Association reported on towns that should be avoided, unless drivers were prepared to sweeten the police treasury. Route 66 was a highway of flat tires, overheated radiators, motor courts, cars with no air conditioning, tourist traps, treacherous curves, narrow lanes and detour signs.

In the Roaring Twenties, desperadoes and

highway was "Shopping Cart" Doughtery, who, sporting a white beard and turban, traveled 9 to 16 miles (14 to 26 km) a day on Route 66 with all his worldly possessions in a shopping cart. History doesn't tell us the final destination of Doughtery.

Joggers and baton twirlers

In 1972, John Ball, a 45-year-old South African, jogged from California to Chicago on Route 66, and then became a hero on the East Coast. The journey took 54 days.

The Mother Road has also seen its share of high school baton twirlers, who have marched along Old 66 setting dubious records.

bootleggers – the likes of John Dillinger, Al Capone, Bugs Moran, Bonnie and Clyde and Ma Barker and her god-fearing boys – lurched down Old 66, using it as an escape route. Occasionally, the Associated Press warned travelers of the dangers of "the criminally few who mix with the tourist throng."

Route 66 was Burma Shave signs, neon signs, full-service gas stations, mom 'n' pop diners, blue-plate specials, homemade pies and waitresses who called everybody "honey," winked at the kids and yelled at the cook. Hitchhiking was safe, and billboards along the highway were legal. People guzzled Grape Nehi, and summer lasted longer because of drive-in movies, miniature golf and slow-pitch softball under the lights. Motels didn't take reservations. And doctors didn't mind making house calls.

Through good times and hard times, the highway became a symbol of faith for the future. Novelist John Steinbeck set the tone of the highway in his Pulitzer Prize-winning book *The Grapes of Wrath*, when he found a nurturing quality in Route 66 and called her "The Mother Road." It was the "Road of Second Chance." To some, like the immigrants of the

> ### SING IT PROUD
> *It winds from Chicago to L.A.*
> *More than two thousand miles*
> *all the way.*
> *Get your kicks on Route Sixty-six!*

Trail, Wire Road, Postal Highway, Grand Canyon Route, National Old Trails Highway, Ozark Trail, Will Rogers Highway and, because it went through the center of so many towns, the Main Street of America.

All-night radio

Route 66 was hundreds of locally improved and maintained lanes going from one town to the next. In Vega, Texas, a story – probably sprinkled with a little local folklore – is told of the town's baseball team. They wanted to play the team in

Dust Bowl, it was the "Glory Road." To architect Frank Lloyd Wright, it was the chute of a tilting continent, on which everything loose seemed to be sliding into Southern California. And to travel agencies it was the chosen thoroughfare of the growing numbers of discriminating American tourists.

Route 66 was to carry a sundry of names at different locations throughout her history – names like the Pontiac Trail, Osage Indian

LEFT: whimsical motels like the Iceburg in Albuquerque, New Mexico, have been demolished.
ABOVE: DJ Wolfman Jack was the voice on the radio accompanying most long-distance drives.

a nearby community but there was no connecting road. So the ambitious folks in this small Texas town built one. Today, that former deep-rutted path is said to be Route 66.

Route 66 was all-night radio out of Del Rio Texas, Continental Trailways and Greyhound buses, lemonade stands, family reunions, 25¢ haircuts and a 5¢ cup of coffee. Kids counted telephone poles on the road, waved at engineers on trains, slept in a wigwam in Holbrook, Arizona, and signs in New Mexico promised "Tucumcari Tonight."

"Route 66," Bobby Troup's hit song of 1946, became a highway national anthem. Originally crooned by Nat "King" Cole, the simple tune

Burma Shave

The Burma Shave company was founded by an imaginative insurance salesman to provide a speedy, brushless shave for the businessman on the go. Clinton Odell, father of the company's former CEO, collaborated with pharmacist Carl Noren to produce an item that became one of the most famous in America by virtue of being seen along every highway.

"By the start of the year we were getting the first repeat orders in the history of the company – all from druggists serving people who traveled these

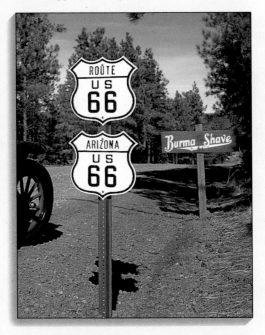

roads," Odell told Frank Rowsome, Jr, who wrote the history of the company.

Does Your Husband/Misbehave/Grunt and Grumble/Rant and Rave/Shoot the Brute Some/ Burma Shave was one of the earliest signs, its lines spaced 100 paces apart – like most of the thousands that followed. In his book, *the verse by the side of the road*, Rowsome explained that, traveling at 35 mph, the sequence took 18 seconds to read – "far more time and attention than a newspaper or magazine advertiser could reasonably expect from the casual viewer." Alexander Woollcott maintained that it was as difficult to read a single sign as it was to eat one salted peanut.

In those very early days, rival advertisers soon became jealous. Many of them had been spending thousands on marketing their product, only to see a perky upstart impress its name on the consumer in a way that was remembered long after the signs ceased to exist. Sensing their annoyance, the signs cheekily responded by rubbing it in: *Let's Give the/Clerk a Hand/Who Never/ Palms Off/Another Brand.* Burma Shave also knew how to needle the latest electric competition: *A Silky Cheek/Shaved Smooth/And Clean/Is Not Obtained/With a Mowing Machine.*

There were once 35,000 Burma Shave signs, but by 1963 they were removed. By this time, they were costing the company almost a quarter of a million dollars a year and clearly were having a diminishing effect on sales. *Our Fortune/Is Your/Shaven Face/It's our Best/Advertising Space,* the company had once boasted.

"The commercial fortunes of the Burma-Vita Company can be read like tea leaves in the jingles themselves," wrote Rowsome. There were many reasons for the downturn in sales: people were driving too fast, superhighway rights of way frequently banned commercial signs, and possibly the fact that people were becoming too sophisticated to regard them as anything more than corny relics.

Most people were sad to see the Burma Shave signs disappear, as their growing insignificance proved to be just one more nail in the coffin of the vibrant Mother Road. As early as 1930, the company had been spending $65,000 a year (prompting $3 million in annual sales), but it was not only passing drivers that enjoyed them: friendly relations had been established with hundreds of farmers on whose land the red-and-white signs appeared. Although rentals rarely topped $25 per year, many farmers were so proud of the signs that they made their own repairs when necessary. Incidentally, horses found them to be perfect backscratchers – until the company got wise and raised the height of the signs.

There was never a chance that Burma Shave would run out of slogans. An annual contest offering $100 for each jingle used drew more than 50,000 entries. These would be whittled down to the best 1,000 stanzas. Of course, there were thousands of entries that were not considered "appropriate" and hence were never used: *Listen, Birds/These Signs Cost Money/So Roost a While/But Don't Get Funny.* ❑

LEFT: once upon a time there were 35,000 Burma Shave signs marching down American highways.

went on to be immortalized by Bing Crosby, Chuck Berry, The Rolling Stones and a host of other recording artists – at last count over 100 of them. Nothing captured America's love affair with the road more than this song.

It celebrated the end of World War II, and the end of gas and food rationing. The lyrics invited Americans to get their kicks on Route 66, and millions of motoring adventurers, addicted to the smell of gasoline and the drone of rubber on the pavement, took Bobby's suggestion to heart.

NAME GAME

Route 66 has had many names over the years. Three of them are the Mother Road, the Glory Road and the Road of Second Chance.

Mom wrote "Wish you were here" messages on picture postcards. The kids bought rich, gooey Pecan Logs at Stuckeys mini-mart while Dad filled the gas tank at 17¢ a gallon and bought the entire family sticky, orange-flavored popsicles out of the freezer.

The toll fare at the Chain of Rocks Bridge over the mighty Mississippi River was 35¢ per automobile, and brightly colored signs on the outskirts of St Louis, Missouri, advertised "the Greatest Show under the Earth" at the nearby Merimac Caverns.

Itchy Feet

Americans with itchy feet were ready to hit the road. They removed the musty canvas that had covered and protected the Plymouth ragtop and the Oldsmobile Woody since the outbreak of the war. And although the cars had been stored on blocks, folks replaced the pre-war tires with a set of six-ply Allstate clinchers at a total cost of $43.80. Vacationers shined up their new postwar sedans and thumbed through state maps and plotted a course on the road to adventure – Route 66.

ABOVE: the 1960s weekly series sold more Corvette sports cars than any TV commercial.

Now you go thru Saint Looey and
*   Joplin, Missouri*
And Oklahoma City is mighty pretty.

The 1950s saw Route 66 reach genuine celebrity status. Families could leave their homes in the East and Midwest and drive to the Painted Desert or Grand Canyon. They could drive all the way to the Pacific Ocean on a highway that passed through towns where the young outlaw Jesse James robbed banks, where Abraham Lincoln practiced law, and cross the great river Mark Twain wrote about. Tourists could see snake pits and caged wild critters and mysterious caverns and real live cowboys and

Indians, and visit Mickey's Magic Kingdom in Disneyland, California.

Won't you get hip to this timely tip,
When you make that California trip.
Get your kicks on Route Sixty-six!

Route 66 reached even greater popularity when a nomadic pot-boiler of a book by the same name as the highway became a hit TV show during 1960–64. *route 66* (yes, the 'r' was not capitalized in the show title) was the story of two young adventurers, Buz (George Maharis) and Tod (Martin Milner), getting their

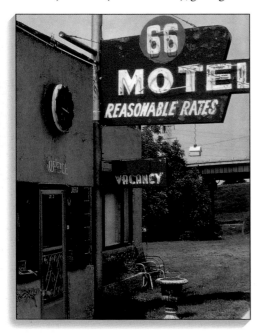

kicks on Route 66 in a Corvette. Among its 116 episodes, few were actually filmed on Route 66. Sponsored in part by Chevrolet, it is probably the only show that sold more Corvettes than any TV commercial, and established the Vette as an American icon.

When the Federal Highway Act of 1956 called for the construction of interstate systems throughout the United States, it looked as if the bright lights of fame and fortune that had shined on Route 66 for so many years was beginning to dim.

Little by little, here and there, pieces of Route 66 were replaced by the interstate. Bypassing of the towns that the fabled highway served was a task that took five different superhighways to achieve – Interstate 55 from Chicago to St Louis, Interstate 44 from St Louis to Oklahoma City, Interstate 40 from Oklahoma City to Barstow, Interstate 15 from Barstow to San Bernardino and Interstate 10 from San Bernardino to Santa Monica.

The last stretch of Route 66 was bypassed in 1984 at Williams, Arizona, when the old highway was replaced by Interstate 40. There was a ceremony, almost a wake. The late Bobby Troup was there to give a speech. As tears streamed from his eyes, he called the occasion "a very sad day."

Wurlitzer jukeboxes

In 1985, US Highway 66 was decertified, giving way to superhighways of diesel fumes and fast-food chains. Because the road is no longer classified as a federal highway, some folks will tell you the road is no longer there.

But progress does not necessarily conquer all. Beyond the endless, blandness of the interstates, there is a powerful rhythm in an old two-lane highway that still rises and twists and turns across rolling hills, the mountains and the deserts. Slowing through quiet towns, then rushing on and up again to the next ridge, you'll find the road waiting to be discovered in each of the eight Route 66 states.

Cafés and roadside attractions have been revived, restored and reopened. Vintage Wurlitzer jukeboxes blare out old road songs. Folks in classic cars cruise into a drive-in for a hamburger and shake. Service station attendants offer to check under the hood and wash the windshield. Family-owned restaurants serve homemade pie, and a waitress in a starched pink uniform still calls you "Hon!" and yells at the cook. The old road still beckons pilgrims not only from across the US, but from nearly every compass point of the world.

With the car open to the wind, and an AM station riddled with static from a thunderstorm on the horizon, memories flicker in the sweetness of the moment. The miles themselves dissolve every question except the one that matters. What lies waiting, there, just over the next rise of Route 66? ❑

LEFT AND RIGHT: bypassing the towns that Route 66 served was a task that took five different superhighways to achieve.

Routes across America

Atlantic Route
Northern Route
Central Route
Southern Route
Pacific Route

N

| 0 | 200 miles |
| 0 | 200 km |

THE ATLANTIC ROUTE

A detailed guide to the attractions of the eastern seaboard, with principal sites cross-referenced by number to the maps

The systematic colonization by the British of America's East Coast was only accomplished once settlers had learned to use its waterways: the Atlantic coastline's bays, the long rivers running out of the Appalachian Mountains and the languid tidal inlets so vital to inland transport in the flat but densely foliated southern states. It was at the mouths of rivers and ports that virtually every important Eastern city sprang up.

Appropriately, then, our route south will rarely stray very far from water. Beginning in New York City, undisputed king of America's cities, we will then pass through a close succession of two more important cities, each with its own distinct personality: Philadelphia, cradle of American independence, and Baltimore, originally a fishing town and one still largely dependent on port activities.

From there, we will move inland to make two exceptionally scenic drives in Virginia, passing at last into North Carolina and examining one of the South's most pleasant states. We will cut east through tobacco fields to the coastline and ride along water once again through South Carolina and Georgia, each time stopping to linger over a beautiful old city or a small half-forgotten town.

Once in Florida, the weather – and the temperature of the water – will turn steadily warmer as we zigzag south from the nation's oldest settlement, St Augustine on the Atlantic Ocean, to Orlando's lakes, Tampa's mild Gulf of Mexico waters, and past the edge of south Florida to the vast (and moist) natural area known as the Everglades. At long last, we will emerge at the Atlantic coast once more, skimming past Miami and its attached beaches – in order to come back later – to continue on to the Florida Keys, a place where water is more influential and obvious than it is anywhere else, probably, in North America. ❏

PRECEDING PAGES: Highway 1, Big Sur, California; winding through the Badlands, South Dakota; heat haze on the highway, Nevada.
LEFT: Kawasaki fan, Florida.

A SHORT STAY IN NEW YORK CITY

New York is the city that never sleeps; it has energy and confusion, culture and great charm. Here's a list of the not-to-be-missed attractions:

◆ Dubbed the Crossroads of the World, Times Square used to be dirty and dangerous, but clean-up campaigns have made it the icon of New York. You can buy Broadway tickets here, too.

◆ The Statue of Liberty, a gift from France and once the symbol of America for immigrants, still draws the crowds. Catch a boat to Staten Island from downtown Manhattan.

◆ The Ellis Island Immigration Museum provides a visual history of the port that 40 percent of all Americans can trace their roots to, and documents the migration from the world to the United States from the 1850s to the mid-20th century.

◆ New York's Museum of Modern Art (MoMA) houses the greatest collection of modern art in the US. Founded in 1929, the world-class institution has recently been doubled in size, with the help of architect Yoshio Taniguchi.

◆ Famous for the Rockettes, Radio City Music Hall hosts spectacular music and theater shows. Tours are also available during the day of this Art Deco institution.

◆ The hub of much of New York City's night life, Greenwich Village is still a center for musicians, artists, the eccentric and the shoppers.

◆ SoHo and Tribeca, with their art galleries and watering holes, are perfect for Saturday strolling. Chinatown is just a walk away if you're hungry.

◆ More than just the center of global capitalism, Wall Street in historic downtown New York is lined with beautiful architecture.

△ **CENTRAL PARK**
Ice skating in the wintertime, outdoor concerts in the summertime – the tree-filled park in the center of the city keeps New Yorkers sane.

◁ **CHRYSLER BUILDING**
The shimmering, Art Deco Chrysler Building was the tallest building in the world in 1930, until it was surpassed by the Empire State Building one year later.

For visitors interested in staying longer in the Big Apple, pick up a copy of *Insight Guide: New York*. A companion to the present volume, it is packed with insightful text and stunning pictures.

◁ PANORAMA OF THE CITY
Star of stage, screen and countless photographs, the panorama of Manhattan from the Empire State Building never fails to impress.

△ GUGGENHEIM MUSEUM
Designed by Frank Lloyd Wright and opened in 1959, the spiral ramp inside allows for constant viewing of the priceless art collection.

▷ EMPIRE STATE BUILDING
When the Empire State was completed in 1931, it was the tallest building in the world.

THE BIG APPLE

There is a mix of fantasy and foreignness in New York that is unsurpassed anywhere. You want to have a cocktail on a level with the clouds? Go dancing when the moon is high and the mood overtakes you? Want to go in-line skating, ice skating, or take in that Broadway show? You've come to the right town. New York's skyline is instantly recognizable; its attractions the best in the world. Its cultural life is matched only by its culinary awareness; there are over 15,000 eating places. If there are more ways of making it here, there are also more ways of spending it, so bring a fat wallet and lots of stamina.

▽ Red arrows on the map indicate routes from the city detailed in this book

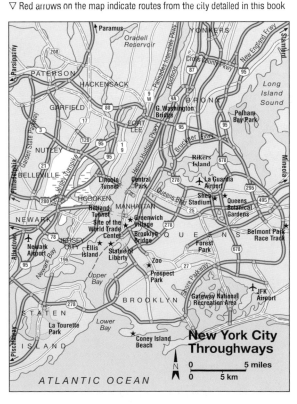

New York City Throughways

0 — 5 miles
0 — 5 km

Important Information

Population:
8 million
Dialing codes: 212,
646, 347, 718, 917
Website:
www.nycvisit.com

Tourist information:
810 Seventh Avenue,
NY 10019
Tel: 212-484-1222;
freephone 1800-
NYCVISIT

NEW YORK TO VIRGINIA

*Just beyond the frenzy of New York City lie
national historic sites and cities of colonial interest,
as well as the green, green hills of Virginia*

Map
on page
56

T his first leg of the Atlantic route takes in some of the most historic sites in the United States – places where the Revolutionary and Civil Wars were fought, and where the brash, new nation was conceived. But in order to take this cruise through history, a bit of contemporary, behind-the-wheel negotiation is required first. There are three ways to leave **New York City ❶** *(see page 53)* and cross the Hudson River into the neighboring state of New Jersey. Although all – depending on the time of day – can be unnervingly congested (and all charge a toll), the northernmost of these "escapes" from Manhattan is probably also the least unpleasant: across the **George Washington Bridge**. The simplest way to find it, from wherever you are in Manhattan, is to head towards the mighty Hudson until you hit SR 9A (the Henry Hudson Parkway), and head north until it intersects with I-95 and the bridge. If you don't feel like driving north to eventually go south in New Jersey, then your only option is to go *under* the river via the extremely tedious **Lincoln** or **Holland tunnels**, both located more at the southern end of Manhattan.

Whichever way you choose, eventually you'll be steered onto the New Jersey Turnpike (I-95). New Jersey's nickname, the Garden State, seems a cruel joke at first: the early miles reveal nothing more than bleak industrial landscape. Past the factories, warehouses and landfills, however, you pass into a more diverse region of some natural beauty and historical significance.

LEFT: hanging out over the green fields of Virginia. **BELOW:** the Blue Ridge Parkway.

Slower pace

If you've taken the Lincoln Tunnel out of Manhattan, head south on the New Jersey Turnpike. If you have opted for the Holland Tunnel, then head north for a short stretch: your aim is to cut west on I-280 toward the Oranges. Here, the harsh landscape begins to soften. Luxurious greenery replaces the endless drab scrub along the turnpike, and the smoke-belching factories give way to white churches and comfortable middle-class homes.

Only 15 minutes out of the Big Apple, small-town life already begins to take the place of the urban crush, and the pace of day-to-day life slows considerably. Get off the freeway at either exit 9 or 10 and head east to connect with Main Street, heading north through the town of **West Orange** past the town hall. You will arrive at the **Edison National Historic Site** (tel: 973-736-0550; www.nps.gov/edis; open Fri–Sun).

This lab complex, sometimes described as "the cradle of American industry," is maintained by the National Park Service, which offers an excellent tour by well-informed guides.

The tour begins in a chemistry lab filled with antique burettes and beakers, then continues through the experimental machine shop in which Thomas Edison and his associates fabricated the parts necessary for the construction of products that have altered irrevocably the course of modern life: the light bulb, the phonograph and the motion picture camera, to name only three important inventions. A gorgeous library is on display in the building, lined with thousands of leather-bound volumes in numerous languages.

On the walls hang portraits of Edison, as well as various placards inscribed with sayings of which he was fond: "There is no expedient to which a man will not resort in order to avoid the real labor of thinking" (Sir Joshua Reynolds), and Edison's own famous description of genius as "1 percent inspiration and 99 percent perspiration." Edison supposedly claimed that Reynolds' quotation served as his 1 percent inspiration.

First film studio

Included on the tour is a walk by a reconstructed version of Black Maria, the world's first film studio, preceded by a screening of *The Great Train Robbery*, the first feature film to be produced at Edison Studios. You may well leave the complex filled with a powerful sense of wonder at Edison's artistic vision and technical prowess.

Before leaving West Orange, don't forget to visit **Glenmont** (tel: 973-736-0550), Edison's beautiful Victorian residence, located a half-mile from the Laboratory Complex in the private residential community of Llewellyn Park. Although Glenmont is now open to the public, the Edison National Historic Site is currently closed for major structural repair.

Jog south a bit, then turn west onto State 510 through enclaves of great wealth to reach **Morristown**, home to a constellation of Revolutionary War sites. At 230 Morris Street stands the lovely **Jacob Ford Mansion**, the colonial house that General George Washington used as headquarters during the bitter winters of 1777 and 1780.

It is part of the **Morristown National Historical Park** (tel: 973-539-2085; www.nps.gov/morr; open daily) as are – 6 miles (10 km) southwest of Morristown proper in the Fort Nonsense unit of the park

– **Jockey Hollow**, where the Revolutionary army encamped under Washington, and **Wick House**, an 18th-century farmhouse rich with the smell of firewood. On weekends, women and children dressed in colonial garb cook in the kitchen.

Map on page 56

Cloistered wealth

Head south on US 202 to get more of the country flavor of the Garden State; the road here is verdant and calming. Just after Bridgewater, US 202 continues with a sharp turn to the southwest, but you want to continue due south on US 206. You soon arrive at **Princeton ❷**, home to elegant **Princeton University** – which possesses one of the most beautiful campuses in the Northeast. A Gothic architectural style dominates, although there are a few modern structures thrown in for good measure as well – and you'll also find a fine collection of outdoor sculpture scattered about the grounds. **Nassau Hall**, the oldest building on campus, played host to the Continental Congress in 1783 when mutinous soldiers forced Congress to leave Philadelphia.

Princeton has one of the most beautiful campuses in the East.

Princeton remains a bastion of cloistered wealth, with preppie college kids browsing in the rich boutiques of Nassau Street as they have always done, but it is also one of the nation's finest educational institutions. Author F. Scott Fitzgerald was one famous alumnus who walked its halls, typifying a mixture of privilege and skill that still characterizes its students today.

From Princeton, you've got several options. You can shoot straight down busy US 1 or I-295 to Philadelphia, or – with time on your hands – sidetrack through the lovely **Delaware River Valley**.

To do that, backtrack north up US 206 to State 518, then head west. At the river, you'll pass through quiet **Lambertville** with old inns, antique shops and a narrow

BELOW: Cleveland Tower, Princeton University.

bridge connecting it to **New Hope**, Pennsylvania. Both **Washington Crossing State Park** (tel: 609-737-0623), where General George Washington landed on Christmas Eve, 1776, and the state capital of **Trenton ❸**, where Washington's army captured Hessian soldiers in battle that night, sit directly downriver and can be reached via twisting Route 29. It's a fitting colonial and historical introduction to what awaits in the "City of Brotherly Love," Philadelphia, just beyond (Route 29 will connect with I-95 just as you get into Trenton; take that south).

Philadelphia

At the time of the American Revolution, **Philadelphia ❹** was the economic and political center of the fledgling United States. During the early years of the Republic, however, the nation's economic heart was transplanted north to New York City while governmental power traveled south to the new city of Washington, DC. This left the city with a bit of an identity crisis. An interesting ethnic mix has sustained the place ever since, however, making it today one of America's most vibrant – and low-profile – large cities.

The nation's fifth most populous city, this is for tourists and historians – along with Boston – an American city *par excellence*. Film buffs cannot help but feel a swell of emotion, either, when viewing the Art Museum stairs Sylvester Stallone ran up to Bill Conti's soaring score in the film *Rocky*. Stallone wasn't a local, but his choice of Philly for the *Rocky* screenplay – which sent him to stardom – was apt: this is a gritty, lively and fascinating place.

Situated at the conjunction of the Schuylkill (pronounced *skoo-kill*) and Delaware rivers, the city was founded in 1682 by the English Quaker William Penn. Penn envisioned a colony in which the right to freedom of religious expression would not be quashed, so it's not surprising that when representatives of the 13 colonies convened to sign the Declaration of Independence, they did so here on July 4, 1776, thereby giving birth to the United States of America.

BELOW: architectural detail in Philadelphia's Elfreth's Alley, the oldest continuously occupied street in America.

A nation is born

At **Independence National Historical Park** (tel: 215-965-2305; www.nps.gov/inde; open daily), which extends from Second to Sixth streets between Walnut and Chestnut, the extraordinary sequence of events that led to the founding of the United States becomes palpable. The Declaration of Independence and the Constitution were signed in elegant **Independence Hall**, (timed entry tickets available in advance). The **Assembly Room**, which contains the inkstand used by the signers of the Declaration as well as the chair in which George Washington supposedly sat during the drafting of the Constitution, should not be missed.

Not far away is **Congress Hall**, where the US Congress convened between 1790 and 1800 when Philadelphia was briefly the nation's capital. On 6th Street between Market and Chestnut streets, stands the Liberty Bell Center. It was constructed in 2003 at a cost of $12.6 million to provide a better space for the ironic icon of freedom and more room for educational exhibitions. It is still invariably packed with tourists.

On Independence Mall, between Race and Arch

streets, is the new National Constitution Center (tel: 215-409-6600, www.constitutioncenter.org; open daily). Using interactive exhibits and live actors, the museum tells the story of the constitution – its creation in early America, its application in history and its continuing impact on the lives of Americans today.

On Market Street toward the Delaware River, you'll find **Franklin Court**, site of Ben Franklin's residence. His home no longer exists but is commemorated by an evocative outline of painted white steel beams. Beneath the courtyard, a museum features displays and a film about Franklin's life as an author, traveler, scientist, gastronome and colonial mover and shaker. **Christ Church**, at Second Street just above Market, was built in 1695 and was the preferred house of worship for the men of the Continental Congress. Plaques mark pews once occupied by George Washington, Ben Franklin and Betsy Ross. Nearby, **Betsy Ross House** was the place where Ross stitched the new nation's first flag.

High Society

From Independence Hall, wend your way toward South Street via the cobblestone streets and garden paths of **Society Hill**, Philly's original residential district and a place of elegant 300-year-old Federalist style homes.

During the late 1970s, Philadelphia's waterfront – like that of many eastern seaboard cities – underwent considerable rehabilitation. **Penn's Landing**, between Market and Lombard streets along the Delaware River, is where William Penn came ashore in 1682. Today, the area features the **Independence Seaport Museum** (tel: 215-413-8615; www.phillyseaport.org; open daily) – several historic ships moored in the harbor – and views of **Camden**, New Jersey, (home to the American poet Walt Whitman) across the river. One block below

The Liberty Bell, cast in England in 1752, is the emblem of Philadelphia.

BELOW: reenacting the American Revolution in Trenton, NJ.

Map on page 56

BALTIMORE: CHARM CITY

Baltimore is a big city with a small-town feel – the home of good food, great baseball and "The Star Spangled Banner"

The favorite food on most Baltimore tables is the local Maryland blue crab, also found in abundance on the menus of the seafood restaurants of the town's Inner Harbor. The sports equivalent of the blue crab, in popularity at least, is the city's beloved baseball team, the Orioles. Baseball addicts will enjoy visiting the Babe Ruth Birthplace (tel: 410-727-1539; www.baberuthmuseum.com; open daily) on Emory Street. Babe Ruth, a native of the city, still casts a huge shadow over the game even in death; his mighty home-run swats at Yankee Stadium changed the way the game was played forever.

Afterward, get a look at the bigger picture

of the town as seen from the Top of the World observation deck, located on the 27th floor of the pentagonal World Trade Center.

Not far away at Pratt Street is the fine National Aquarium (tel: 410-576-3800; www.aqua.org; open daily), one of the nation's best, complete with a simulated Amazon rainforest, coral reef display and 220,000-gallon (830,000-liter) open ocean tank.

Fell's Point, Baltimore's first ship-building and maritime center, still has the charm of an old port town. Among the cobbled streets stand more than 350 original Colonial homes, many in perfect condition. Interspersed are old pubs, antique shops and, of course, great places to eat. You can also take a stroll through the original wooden Broadway Market.

The best-known attraction on the waterfront is Fort McHenry (tel: 410-962-4290; www.nps.gov/fomc; open daily). During the war of 1812, this fort withstood a 25-hour bombardment from the British fleet, later prompting Francis Scott Key to pen the lyrics that were to eventually become America's national anthem, "The Star Spangled Banner."

Mount Vernon Place, designated a National Historic Landmark, features many of Baltimore's oldest and most elegant townhouses, churches and cultural institutions. At the center of the district stands the Washington Monument, the first formal monument to George Washington. Climb the 228 stairs of this 178-foot (54-meter) white marble column for another unobstructed view of the city.

Head up Charles Street to Johns Hopkins University, which since the late 19th century has been a major force in medical research. Right next door stands the respected Baltimore Museum of Art (tel: 443-573-1700; www.artbma.org; closed Mon–Tues), which contains works by Picasso and Matisse, art from Africa and a beautiful modern sculpture garden. ❏

LEFT: National Aquarium; Federal Hill area.
ABOVE: ships and entertainment complexes are common around Baltimore's Inner Harbor.

Lombard at **South Street**, you will find a stimulating array of punk haberdashers as well as chic boutiques.

City Hall, at Broad and Market streets, is the largest municipal building in the US. It was patterned after the Louvre, though it more resembles Paris's Hôtel de Ville. The 37-foot (11-meter) high rooftop statue of William Penn is the tallest atop any building in the world. Until recently, the Philadelphia skyline was capped by an ordinance declaring no structure could exceed the height of Penn's hat.

The **Benjamin Franklin Parkway**, built in the 1920s, was modeled after the Champs-Elysées in Paris. This broad road cuts diagonally through Philly's square grid from City Hall to Fairmount Park. On the parkway at 20th Street, visit the **Franklin Institute** (tel: 215-448-1200; www2.fi.edu; open daily), a science museum that is also a memorial to Franklin containing many of his personal possessions. Four floors of science exhibits are sure to amuse and educate all ages. In addition, the **Fels Planetarium** offers several shows daily.

Art in the city

Two blocks away is the **Rodin Museum** (tel: 215-568-6026; www.rodin museum.org; closed Mon), with an excellent collection of casts and originals by the great French sculptor. Among them is *The Thinker*, one of the most beloved statues in the world. At the end of the parkway stands the Rodin Museum's "parent," the **Philadelphia Museum of Art** (tel: 215-763-8100; www.philamuseum.org; closed Mon), one of the great American art museums. Among the works in its collection are Breughel's *Village Wedding* and Picasso's *Three Musicians*, as well as an extraordinary collection of art and artifacts from the Middle Ages.

After hours spent walking the streets of Philly's historic districts and visiting its museums, the greenery of **Fairmount Park** – the country's largest municipal park – rejuvenates even the most exhausted traveler. In addition to grassy meadows and acres of woodland, the park features a horticultural center, zoo, Japanese house, tea garden and several historic homes along the banks of the Schuylkill. If you're roadweary, bring a picnic lunch and spend a full day taking in the pleasures of this gorgeous park before taking to the road again toward **Baltimore ❺** *(see page 60)*. From Philadelphia, it's no more than an hour's drive down either I-95 or the somewhat quieter US 1 to Maryland: a journey that travels across the Mason-Dixon line which separates, many say, the North from the South.

ON TOWARD VIRGINIA

Leaving Baltimore, take State Route 2 south to Annapolis. As you cross the Severn River, you might well get a view of sailboats crisscrossing a sparkling expanse of water.

Annapolis ❻ sparkles, too, in a way particular to towns built on and sustained by the sea. At dusk, its elegant Georgian houses and winding narrow streets shimmer in the dying light of day. Walking is an easy way to see the town, starting at the top where the **Maryland State House** sits. It was here that the Continental Congress ratified the Treaty of Paris, which officially ended the War of Independence.

Wind your way toward the beautifully preserved

Map on page 56

BELOW: Calder sculpture and the Philadelphia Museum of Art.

During four Civil War battles in the Fredericksburg area, 110,000 people died – the site is called the "bloodiest ground" in North America.

BELOW:
Fredericksburg and Spotsylvania, the largest military park in the world.

18th-century waterfront to the **US Naval Academy** and its museum at **Preble Hall** (tel: 410-293-2108; www.usna.edu/Museum; open daily), with exhibits on maritime life and the history of this venerable institution. You'll be feeling suitably red, white and blue by the time you climb back into your car and drive the short 30 miles (48 km) west along US 50 towards America's capital, **Washington, DC** *(see "Central Route," page 180)*. For our purposes on this route, we'll bypass the city using the I-495 loop; take the highway south to connect up with I-95 (or the slower, but more interesting, highway US 1 that runs parallel to it). You're on your way to the heart of the Confederate South.

Confederate South

Only 52 miles (84 km) outside of Washington, DC, and midway between it and the once-opposing capital of Richmond *(see page 63)*, it is not surprising that **Fredericksburg ❼** was a major battleground during the Civil War. In fact, with 110,000 casualties occurring during the four major battles fought in the vicinity of the city, it has been said that it is the "bloodiest ground" on the North American continent.

In recognition of the men who died during those battles, in 1927 the US Congress established the 8,400-acre (3,400-hectare) **Fredericksburg and Spotsylvania County Battlefields Memorial National Military Park** (tel: 540-373-6122; www.nps.gov/frsp), the largest military park in the world. The park lies just west of the city on either side of Route 3. Both the Fredericksburg Battlefield and the Chancellorsville Battlefield have visitor centers that are open daily and feature exhibits and slide programs; historians are also on hand to answer questions. The park includes several important historic structures, including

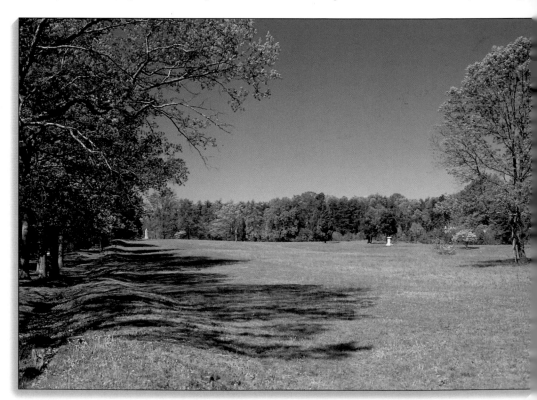

Chatham Manor (open daily), which served as Union headquarters during the battle of Fredericksburg and where Clara Barton and Walt Whitman joined in the efforts to treat hundreds of wounded soldiers. Fredericksburg was also the home of George Washington. **Ferry Farm** (tel: 540-370-0732; www.kenmore.org; open daily), where he grew up, is just across the Rappahannock River on Route 3 – it was here that young George allegedly uttered that line, "I cannot tell a lie," and came clean about chopping down a certain cherry tree. The nation's fifth president, James Monroe, also hailed from here; the **James Monroe Museum and Memorial Library** (tel: 540-654-1043; www.umw.edu/jamesmonroe museum; open daily) on Charles Street contains a collection of the personal possessions, furnishings and papers of Monroe and his wife, Elizabeth.

18th-century tavern life

Today's Fredericksburg still remains rooted in the past, helped along considerably by its large (40-block) **Historic Kenmore** containing not only historic attractions, but antique shops and restaurants. Some buildings, like the elegant **Kenmore Plantation and Gardens** (tel: 540-373-3381; www.kenmore.org; open daily*) on Washington Avenue, give a taste of how the city's elite lived in bygone days. But everyday life is also represented at places like the **Hugh Mercer Apothecary Shop** (tel: 540-373-3362; www.apva.org/hughmercerapothecary; open daily) – where visitors can hear about how to treat a lady's hysteria – and the **Rising Sun Tavern** (tel: 540-371 1494; www.apva.org/risingsuntavern; open daily), which provides an interpretation of 18th-century tavern life. Both are on Charles Street.

Head back down I-95 (or US 1) for another 55 miles (88 km) to what locals consider to be the "birthplace of America," **Richmond ❽**. It was here – at

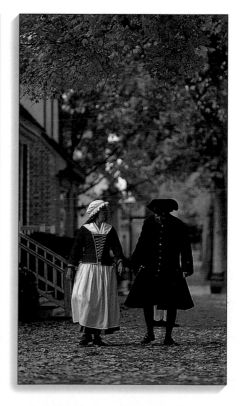

BELOW: patriots set the pace in colonial Williamsburg.

DETOUR: WILLIAMSBURG

A 54-mile (87-km) drive from Richmond along SR 60 ends at colonial Williamsburg, which does more than just revive buildings, streets and gardens: it recreates the everyday life of the nation's infancy. Established in 1633, Williamsburg grew into an outpost of culture, fashion and festive living. After the state government moved to Richmond in 1780, the city languished until the Rev. W.A.R. Goodwin approached John D. Rockefeller, Jr, in 1926 for funds to save those historic buildings still standing and rebuild others. Using original blueprints and materials, Goodwin resurrected the entire town, from the Congress – where George Mason's Declaration of Rights to the House of Burgesses laid the foundation for the Constitution – to the Raleigh Tavern, where George Washington plotted military strategy in the revolt against Great Britain. Nearly 2,000 "residents" recreate the original Williamsburg community. The blacksmith pounds away at glowing iron as visitors look on; the cabinetmaker carves chair legs while clad in knee breeches and powdered wig; a maid in bonnet and hooped skirt weaves linen at a 200-year-old loom. The baker, the printer and the glass-blower are all represented, too. For tour information, tel: 757-220-7645.

Map on page 56

pretty **St John's Church** on Broad Street – where the 2nd Virginia Convention was held in 1775, a stirring event that culminated in Patrick Henry's famous "Give Me Liberty, or Give Me Death" speech. Discovered by British explorers in 1607 and named after a borough of London, the city of Richmond wasn't founded until 1737. Laid out on the fall line of the James River, its location made it a natural center for commerce. By 1779, this more centrally located city had replaced colonial Williamsburg as the capital of Virginia.

Thomas Jefferson designed the striking neoclassical **State Capitol**, which is home to Jean-Antoine Houdon's full-size statue of George Washington, one of America's most valuable pieces of sculpture. During the Civil War, Richmond became the capital of the Confederacy, and about two blocks away from the State Capitol – at 12th and Clay streets in the city's historic **Court End** neighborhood – is the **Museum of the Confederacy** (tel: 804-649-1861; www.moc.org; closed Wed), consisting of a modern museum and the restored White House of the Confederacy. If it's Civil War artifacts you're interested in, this is the place: it has the world's largest and most comprehensive collection.

Civil War buffs can also fuel their interest in this ever-interesting subject by visiting the **Hollywood Cemetery** on Cherry Street (final resting place of Confederate president Jefferson Davis, US presidents James Monroe and John Tyler, and more than 18,000 Confederate soldiers); **Monument Avenue** (home to – surprise! – a wealth of monuments to various key Civil War figures); and strings of battlefield parks and trails in the area.

Despite its huge historic neighborhoods and attractions, Richmond remains surprisingly untouristy, and also has a pleasant dash of modernity in its skyline and its cosmopolitan atmosphere. The city is renowned for its symphony, opera and ballet, as well as for the **Virginia Museum of Fine Arts** (tel: 804-340-1400; www.vmfa.state.va.us; closed Mon–Tues) on Grove Avenue.

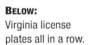

BELOW:
Virginia license
plates all in a row.

Land of Jefferson

From Richmond, take I-64 or US 250 west for 74 miles (119 km) to **Charlottesville ❾**, site of the University of Virginia and the home of Thomas Jefferson. Although the city now has its fair share of chain restaurants and hotels, it has still managed to retain something of a countrified splendor.

Jefferson designed the original buildings and campus of the **University of Virginia** in the 1820s and claimed, late in life, that it was of this achievement that he was most proud. His architecture is based on European classical style, adapted to local materials such as red brick and painted wood. Daily tours of the university leave from the **Rotunda**, which is modeled after the Roman Pantheon. Looking out from the elevated walkway of the Rotunda, you will see the splendid swath of grass known as "**The Lawn**," bordered by columned pavilions. Originally, these were the residences of all the students and professors of Jefferson's "academic villages" – now they are inhabited by school officials and honor-grade students. **West Range** is on McCormack Road, where Edgar Allan Poe lived during his unsuccessful undergraduate tenure here. His former room is open to visitors

Continue down University Avenue to "**The Corner**," a collection of restaurants and shops catering to students, tourists and local residents, if you want to see the modern-day beneficiaries of Jefferson's dream – a university consistently ranked near the top in lists of public universities in the United States.

Map on page 56

Colonial gadgetry

Even before you arrive at **Monticello** (tel: 434-984-9800; www.monticello.org; open daily), the "little mountain" estate of Thomas Jefferson, you will be familiar with its shape; its image adorns the tail side of the US nickel. This elegant, dome shape is particularly Jeffersonian, for not only does it appear on the Rotunda at the University of Virginia, but also as the roof of the Jefferson Memorial building in Washington, DC. Jefferson designed every aspect of Monticello, and the imprint of his active mind is everywhere apparent.

Try to arrive early, as the wait for the mandatory tour is known to extend up to two hours at midday. The walk takes you through the ground floor of the residence; afterward you're free to wander about the lovely grounds of the mansion. The house's gadgetry is particularly endearing, especially the seven-day clock by the entrance, the double writing machine in Jefferson's study and the dumbwaiter in the dining room. Be sure and ask about the home's extraordinary toilet system. Library walls are lined with leather-bound books, many written by the philosophers of the French Enlightenment who so strongly influenced Jefferson. The former president's grave is visible as you leave the grounds to return to the parking lot.

Every aspect of Thomas Jefferson's home, Monticello, was designed by the inventive president.

Jefferson's good friend James Monroe, fifth president of the United States, lived nearby at attractive **Ash Lawn-Highland** (tel: 434-293-9539; www.

BELOW:
Jefferson's Rotunda at the University of Virginia.

Map on page 56

ashlawnhighland.org; open daily). Though not nearly as stately as Monticello, Monroe's residence has a friendly charm of is own. As you drive back toward I-64 to continue south, you will pass by **Michie Tavern**, once a pre-Revolutionary watering hole but now a museum filled with colonial furniture and artifacts.

The road to Natural Bridge

Take I-64 west to Rockfish Gap, where the breath-taking 459-mile (739-km) **Blue Ridge Parkway** begins. Cutting through the **George Washington National Forest**, the Parkway was – like its nearby counterpart, the Skyline Drive *(see page 184)* – cut into the side of the Blue Ridge Mountains. However, as this is not a national park, you'll note one big difference: this drive is filled not only with forest and flowers but also with working farms. Trees carpet the surrounding mountains, which seem bluer and bluer as they recede in the distance. If you're driving alone, don't allow the superb views to lure your eyes too far from the road or you'll end up tumbling over the edge of a cliff.

If you want to experience a questionable slice of Americana, get off the Parkway at Mile 61 (Km 98) via State 130 west to **Natural Bridge** – and prepare yourself for some of the crassest come-ons in the whole grand tour. Billboards blare "See the Natural Bridge!" and offer to throw a wax museum and cavern into the bargain. In order to get down to the Natural Bridge, which is an extraordinary 215-foot (66-meter) high rock formation, you are forced to pass through a knick-knack shop as big as a department store, which is absolutely packed with junky tourist paraphernalia. Descend the stairs, walk past the electronic game room and begin the short hike down to the main attraction.

The Monocan Indians called this "The Bridge of God," and no doubt the enormous limestone arch must have been a place of great wonder in the past. By the time you arrive there, however, you may be so queasy from the overload that it becomes difficult to conjure up the requisite awe; loudspeakers on high blare recordings of church bells. Things get even worse after dark, when the concern that owns Natural Bridge goes so far as to audaciously project a nightly religious film right onto the stone side of the bridge.

BELOW: Natural Bridge, Virginia.
RIGHT: rocky mountain view in the Blue Ridge.

End of the line

Back on the Parkway, gratefully continue south toward North Carolina. Below the pretty town of **Roanoke** ❿ *(see page 187)* the road continues to climb and dip, winding through attractive farmlands where the hay is gathered and neatly rolled into picturesque bales. Wooden fences turned silver-gray by time line the road, keeping the cows right where they are – grazing languidly in green pastures.

Just before the North Carolina border, the Blue Ridge Parkway ends and you begin to pass through a stretch of farmers' markets selling local produce and religious curios at bargain prices. The accent of the people is now very heavy, you will notice, almost incomprehensible to an ear accustomed to Northerners. If you are beginning to feel you are entering another country altogether, you are right. You are entering the Deep South. ❑

NORTH CAROLINA TO SAVANNAH

*Pine-scented mountains, sandy beaches,
plantation homes and antebellum cities –
the Deep South begins here*

Map on page 56

All that remains of the first-known settlement in present-day North Carolina is one word. That word – Croatan – has kept etymologists and philologists busy for centuries, ever since it was found scraped into a tree in the vanished colony of Fort Raleigh on Roanoke Island. Nothing else was left of the "lost colony," which was founded in 1587.

Today, the state is experiencing rapid transformation from a country backwater to a manufacturing and educational power. Jobs and suburbs are sprouting up all along the Interstate 85 corridor, particularly in light industrial trades. Charlotte has become the banking power of the South. And the Raleigh-Durham area contains a very high concentration of quality universities. It's a measure of this success that you can now watch ice hockey in a state where it rarely snows, and professional football, too; both have recently arrived along with the new jobs. Strains of folk and bluegrass music can still be heard in the mountainous Appalachian third of the state, but you've got to hunt a bit for them now.

New York

Miami

LEFT: Great
Smoky Mountains
and the bears.
BELOW: rustic living
in North Carolina.

Weeping willow trees

US 52 takes you over the border from Virginia's Blue Ridge Parkway through trim **Mount Airy ⓫** – birthplace of Carolina hero Andy Griffith, and the model town for his wildly popular classic TV program *Mayberry RFD* – then on down to Winston-Salem *(see page 188).* Take the "King and Tobaccoville" exit and follow the back roads to **Bethania**, a town founded by Moravians who came to the New World to escape religious persecution.

The road is lined with graceful weeping willow trees and leads past fields covered, as you'd expect, with tobacco plants; visit in summer, and they'll be high and big-leafed, but come back in autumn and they'll be a mess of tangled vines burned black.

State 67 east (continue on US 52 if you did not detour to Bethania) leads on to **Winston-Salem ⓬**, home of the R.J. Reynolds tobacco factory, which produces more than 450 million cigarettes daily. The odor of tobacco wafts throughout the town, a constant reminder of the second-largest industry in North Carolina (textiles are first). The Reynolds plant is located, naturally, on Reynolds Boulevard and it's open to visitors during the week. This is also stock-car racing country, an area where many NASCAR greats were reared and still live.

The Salem half of Winston-Salem was founded by Moravians in 1766. The name is derived from the Hebrew word "shalom," meaning peace. In 1913, it

North Carolina is moving away from agriculture and into technology and big banking.

was incorporated with its neighbor Winston, and when its old buildings fell into disrepair, a restoration project during the 1930s saved them. The success of this effort can be seen in **Salem Old Town**, which is entered from the Old Salem Road near the center of town. Particularly interesting are the **Mikisch Tobacco Shop**, thought to be the oldest tobacco shop still standing in America; the **Winkler Bakery**, a restored Moravian bakery that produces lovely bread Monday through Saturday; and the **Salem Tavern** with its **Barn and Farm Museum**. **God's Acre**, a Moravian graveyard nearby, possesses 4,000 graves, many graced with flat marble markers symbolizing the equality of the deceased. *(For more information on Winston-Salem, see page 188.)*

Busy four-lane US 421 leads east through undistinguished country toward growing **Greensboro**, once the home of short story master O. Henry (William Sydney Porter) and long a major producer of textiles; white-collar jobs are now springing up here as well. A Woolworth's store in the central downtown area, now closed, unfortunately, was the site of one of the very first civil rights actions in the South – a sit-in at a soda fountain by local black activists.

The Research Triangle

BELOW:
tobacco drying
in the sun.

Continue along either US 70 or Interstate 40 east to the town of **Durham** ⑬, home of **Duke University**. Along with **Chapel Hill** and **Raleigh**, Durham is part of the Research Triangle, a liberal oasis in the middle of North Carolina which claims to have more Ph.D.'s per capita than any other area in the nation. This is also the place to come for top-quality college basketball in winter: North Carolina is a hoops-crazy state, and its Duke Blue Devils, North Carolina Tar Heels and North Carolina State Wolfpack – all playing in the Triangle – do the

DETOUR: OUTER BANKS

A leisurely 193-mile (311-km) drive along SR 64 from Raleigh leads to the Outer Banks, which emerge like the head of a whale breaching into the Atlantic. Two national seashores, Cape Hatteras and Cape Lookout, preserve 120 miles (190 km) of these beaches on Bodie, Hatteras and Ocracoke islands, and Core and Shackleford banks. While most coastal islands lie within 10 miles (16 km) of shore, the Outer Banks belong to the realm of the sea; in places, 30 miles (48 km) of water separate Hatteras Island from the mainland. The National Seashores of the Outer Banks have personalities unique to the rest of North Carolina. The islands have wide, water-thrashed beaches, while scattered patches of sea oats and beach grasses bind low dunes behind them. Clumps of shrubby marsh elder and bayberry dot the swales. The mainland side of each island hosts extensive tidal marshes of swaying cordgrass. Distinctly patterned lighthouses mark the shores for passing ships, in particular the spiral-painted Cape Hatteras lighthouse. The lighthouse now stands less than 200 ft (61 meters) from the shore, although it was built 1,500 ft (460 meters) away. Due to Hurricane Isabel, you should contact the Chamber of Commerce, tel: 252-441-8144, for current information.

state proud. Duke's campus is among the most beautiful in the South, filled with Gothic and Georgian buildings filling neat quadrangles and plenty of nice botanical gardens and lawns for picnicking. Figure out a legal place to park, then head for the Duke University Chapel to see the **Benjamin N. Duke Memorial Flentrop Organ**, a 5,000-pipe extravaganza. The **Duke Woods**, nearby, provides a short walk through the pines if you're wanting to get outside.

Map on page 56

Southern summer evenings

The city is also interesting for its lively mixture of tobacco warehouses and chic restaurants, working-class mill hands and college professors, old Southerners and new Yankee up-starts. **Ninth Street** is the place to go for youth, with plenty of good record shops, bookstores, coffee shops and eateries.

Also make a point of finding the Durham Bulls' minor-league ballpark, one of the nation's finest and the perfect spot to spend a warm summer evening watching future stars play baseball the way it was meant to be played. Note the outfield bull, which snorts steam when a home run is hit. The Bulls' former ballpark, El Toro Field, was even more authentic – one side consisted of tobacco warehouses, and the steam-snorting bull made its debut here during the filming of the baseball film *Bull Durham* – though the place has lately fallen into disuse; you can still take a look, though, as it is easily walkable from Downtown.

Just to the southwest of Durham, smaller **Chapel Hill** is the home of the pleasant **University of North Carolina** campus. UNC is said to have been the first state university chartered in the US. Fans of astronomy will enjoy the **Morehead Planetarium**, while sports fans will take joy in the fact that the great, all-around athlete Michael Jordan played college ball here.

BELOW:
Winston-Salem was settled by Moravians.

Toward the coast

Continue along US 15-501 (also known as the Jefferson Davis Highway) south through residential Chapel Hill toward **Sanford** 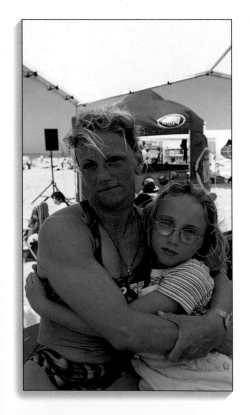, where pottery has become a popular cottage industry. At Sanford, change onto US 421, a road lined with fast-food shops, and angle southeast. You are now on the way to Wilmington, principal deep-water port on the North Carolina coast and a refreshing change from this hot and dusty road, where roadside fields are again densely covered with tobacco plants and the occasional weeping willow or algae-covered pond does little to dispel summer's oppressive heat.

At **Dunn**, turn south on State 301 toward **Fayetteville**. This smaller road runs through farm country, through corn and tobacco fields extending for acres back from the highway. There are innumerable small churches along the road, the majority of which are Baptist; you are truly in the South now.

Use the I-95 to get around Fayetteville, exiting shortly to continue south on State 87, a scenic route to the coast taking you deep into the heart of southeast Carolina. Along the way, you'll pass through the tiny settlements of **Tar Heel** and **Dublin,** but little else of size.

By the time you reach **Elizabethtown** ⑮, you may be so tuckered out from driving that a swim will seem a tantalizing idea. Follow State 41 east to **White Lake**, an oasis in the middle of the Cape Fear region. On the eastern side of the lake is **Goldston's Beach**, a public beach with the requisite tourist shops and thrill rides. The water is warm and soothing, though, and the sandy beach might well prove a haven to muscles weary of driving. The small amusement park nearby has pinball machines from the 1960s and old skee-ball games, which lend an anachronistic air to the place, as though it had been bypassed by 40 years of history. Many of the small towns of the Deep South, you will find, have just this same feeling to them: frozen in another era.

BELOW:
North Carolina has both mountains and beaches.

Cape Cod in Carolina

Continue on State 87 to **Wilmington** ⑯, NBA great Michael Jordan's hometown. It's interesting to note that the town's good looks and extremely savvy marketing campaign have created a recent film boom. A number of popular television programs and movies are filmed and produced here in a huge studio lot – with Wilmington standing in for the likes of Cape Cod, California and so forth.

For sightseeing, why not think about visiting the *USS North Carolina* **Battleship Memorial** (tel: 910-251-5797; www.battleshipnc.com; open daily)? Nicknamed "The Showboat," the ship was commissioned in 1941 and was considered at the time to be the greatest fighting vessel the United States had yet produced. In town, many historic houses are to be seen, among them the **Zebulon Latimer House** at 126 South Third Street and the **Burgwin-Wright House** at Third and Market streets. None appear affected by the high flooding from recent tropical storms and hurricanes.

The Southern grace of Wilmington's finer homes will pique your interest, and prepare you for the even more splendid homes of Charleston and Savannah that lie just to the south.

SOUTH CAROLINA

On December 20, 1860, South Carolina became the first state to secede from the Union. John C. Calhoun's efforts to combat federal laws had not been enough to keep the South's economic and social order – built as it was on the institution of slavery – intact. Knowing its way of life was threatened, South Carolina insisted in 1860 on the right of states to disavow the Federal union. That one step plunged the nation into one of its bloodiest wars: a war with itself.

Even after the Civil War ended in defeat, South Carolina refused to grant the right to vote to its newly freed blacks – a situation that led to the imposition of martial law for a time. This refusal to change with the times kept the state mired in an economic backwater until after World War II, when the state's economy began to switch from an agricultural one to a newly developing industrial base. Textiles, furniture and chemical industries began to flourish. (Agriculture remains strong, however: this is America's top peach producer and its only producer of tea.)

In succeeding years, the modern industry of tourism also began to gather steam here. Nowhere can this burgeoning industry be better seen – for better and worse – than along the Carolina coast, from Myrtle Beach and the Grand Strand down to Charleston and beyond.

Take US 17 south from Wilmington into South Carolina, and you will have entered the 55-mile (88-km) stretch of beach resort known as the **Grand Strand**. The first oddity you will encounter is the ubiquity of fireworks shops. This is the only East Coast state to have legalized the sale of fireworks, and throughout the area they are big business, hawked perhaps a little too enthusiastically at dozens of roadside stands.

Map on page 56

Southerners are great storytellers. In Wilmington, ask about the unsolved murder of 1760, which involved a man, a snake ring and a riderless horse on a rainy night.

BELOW: an off-the-road alternative: the Intracoastal Waterway.

Myrtle Beach's coastal position and leisure activities makes it one of the most popular resorts on the East Coast.

Myrtle Beach ⑰ is the third most popular tourist resort on the East Coast, after Disney World and Atlantic City. The extraordinary commercialization of the area may well overwhelm you, as the grandly named King's Highway (US 17) consists of mile after mile of high-rise condominium developments, miniature golf courses and honky-tonk shops dispensing the accessories that go with beach culture. The city's **Boardwalk**, with amusement parks, fast-food stands and hordes of tourists, is a typical slice of American beach excess. If you must have excitement, try the Corkscrew, a harrowing roller coaster that turns you upside down at oblique angles and over death-defying humps.

For swimming, you're best advised to eschew the crowded strand at Myrtle Beach in favor of less spoiled beaches to the north or south. **Pawley's Island ⑱** has one particularly beautiful beach where you can enjoy the warm waters and good body-surfing of the Carolina coast minus the throngs and relax in one of the hammocks for which the island is famous.

South of Myrtle Beach on US 17, across the Pee Dee River, lies quieter and more genteel **Georgetown ⑲**. An early failed attempt by the Spanish to settle this coast, it today consists mostly of museums, churches, old homes and plantations. The **Rice Museum** (tel: 843-546-7423; www.ricemuseum.org; closed Sun) gives a look at the crop that sustained this area for much of its early history.

Historic Charleston

BELOW: by carriage is an appropriate way to view elegant Charleston.

South again along US 17, you pass over a steep and narrow double set of bridges over the Cooper River before touching down in **Charleston ⑳**. Located on the peninsula formed where the Cooper meets the Ashley River, this was the first permanent settlement in the Carolinas. The prosperity of the city's early days is

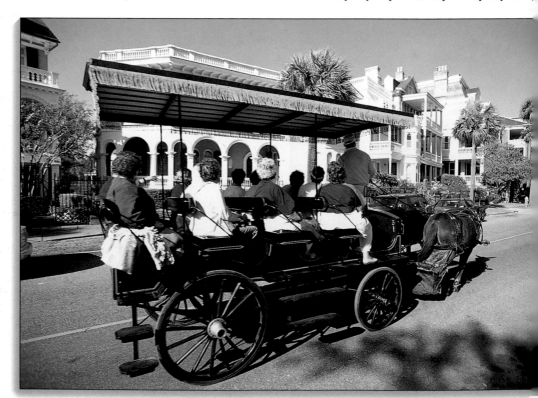

reflected in elegant 18th-century homes that fill the residential area south of Broad Street. In fact, this is one of America's top walking cities (more compact Savannah, just to the south, is another). Charleston suffered massive damage when Hurricane Hugo raged onto its shore in 1989, but fortunately the historic district was spared heavy damage. Amble about the cobbled streets at your leisure, taking in the many museums and monuments here.

Map on page 82

Moss-draped walks

The palmetto-lined **Battery** faces Charleston Harbor and is a good place to begin a walking tour of town. In **White Point Gardens,** you can see gorgeous live oak trees with languid Spanish moss hanging from them. At Number 21 East Battery sits the **Edmondston-Alston House**, built around 1828 by a wealthy wharf owner and decorated in Greek Revival style; it offers an unobstructed view of the harbor. Be sure to sit on the "**joggling board**" located behind the house. This board is 16 feet (5 meters) long and works as a kind of rocking chair; once thought to have therapeutic properties in the cure of rheumatism, the joggling board is also said to prevent spinsterhood – though scientific studies have never been made to test this theory.

The **Nathaniel Russell House,** at 51 Meeting Street, is also worth a visit – quite elegant, with an impressive flying staircase spiraling unsupported to the top. Both these homes are maintained by the Historic Charleston Foundation (tel: 843-723-1623; www.historiccharleston.org), a non-profit restoration agency founded in 1947 to protect Downtown's architectural treasures. Informative tours given by the foundation explain the intricacies of design of each home, as well as the histories and customs of the families that have lived in them.

BELOW: the palmetto-lined Battery faces Charleston Harbor.

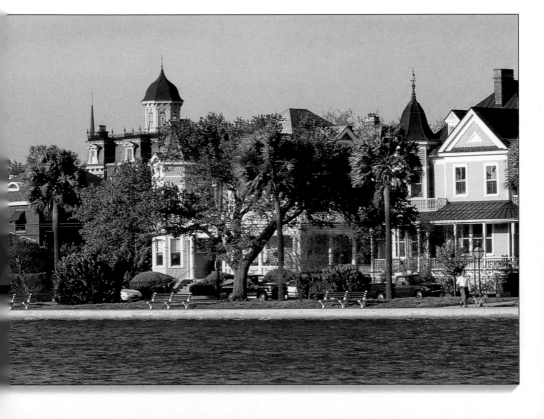

In addition, the Charleston Museum (tel: 843-722-2996; www.charleston museum.org; open daily) administers tours of the very handsome **Heyward-Washington House** (87 Church Street) and the **Joseph Manigault House** (350 Meeting Street), both highly regarded as architectural attractions. The best way to see Charleston's historic homes in one fell swoop is to visit the city during early spring, when the annual Festival of Houses opens many normally private homes to public walking tours. Watch for classic examples of the "Charleston single house" – long, narrow homes with side piazzas and a marked West Indian influence.

Slave market

At the **Old Slave Mart Museum** on Chalmers Street, you can see, among other items, facsimiles of bills of sale used in the slave trade. "A prime gang of 25 negroes accustomed to the culture of Sea Island Cotton and Rice," reads one placard advertising the upcoming sale of 25 human beings into bondage. It is a startling and sobering museum, especially so when one realizes this heinous practice was still in full swing just a century and a quarter ago. The self-contented opulence south of Broad suddenly appears quite different after a long, thoughtful visit to the slave market.

Charleston is chock-full of historic churches, as well as all its other cultural and social attractions. Two of the more interesting are the **Huguenot Church**, a Gothic structure built by French Protestants, and **St Michael's Episcopal Church** with its 186-foot (57-meter) high steeple. Nearby **Fort Sumter** (tel: 843-883-3123; www.nps.gov/fosu; open daily), site of the Confederate attack on Union forces that touched off the Civil War, is accessible from Charleston Harbor: a 2½-hour tour leaves several times daily from the Municipal Marina.

BELOW:
18th-century slave cabins at Boone Hall Plantation.

Plantations a'plenty

Three plantations in the vicinity of Charleston are also worth a visit if you have the time. **Magnolia Plantation and Gardens** (tel: 843-571-1266; www.magnoliaplantation.com; open daily) on Ashley River Road (State Route 61) has beautiful gardens, a children's petting zoo, an 18th-century herb garden and a 16th-century horticultural maze to lose yourself in. At **Middleton Place** (tel: 843-556-6020; www.middletonplace.org; open daily), farther up the road, you can see the oldest landscaped gardens in the country – the result of nearly 10 years' labor by 100 slaves. Just north of Charleston on US 17 is **Mount Pleasant**, and the achingly beautiful avenue of live oak trees featured in the movie version of *Gone With the Wind*. At the end of the drive lies **Boone Hall**, most people's idea of the perfect antebellum residence. In fact, the house was rebuilt only in 1935, but the nine slave cabins are authentic.

After Charleston, follow US 17 south through the so-called "Low Country" toward the Georgia border. Turn onto State 174 for a ride beneath a canopy of oaks, and in 24 miles (39 km) you arrive at **Edisto Island**, a resort community whose commercialism has not yet eliminated its rustic charm. Farther south, turning east onto US 21 from US 17 is **Beaufort** (pronounced *bew-ford*), the second oldest town in South Carolina and one that's still quite compact and attractive. Hollywood movie producers come calling to use the gorgeous antebellum waterfront homes as set pieces. Indigo and rice cultivation brought wealth during the 18th century, when most of these houses (some are inns) were constructed. The best way to experience this town is to wander about, enjoying the friendly talk of residents at any one of the seafood restaurants before moving on south again into Georgia and that beautiful "Southern belle" of a city, **Savannah** ㉑ *(see page 78)*. ❑

Map on page 82

The slave cabins at Boone Hall were built of bricks made on the premises; among several other industries, the plantation had a working brick and tile yard.

BELOW:
the gardens at Magnolia Plantation date from the 16th century.

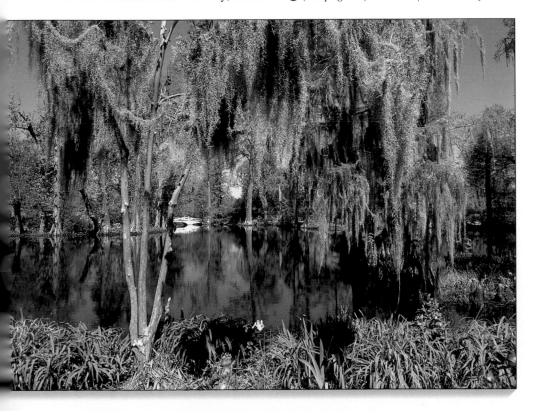

SAVANNAH: FIRST CITY OF GEORGIA

The port of Savannah is a strange, seductive place – equal parts history, treachery, revelry and oddity

Best known for its gorgeous, moss-draped live oaks, cobblestone streets and light, pastel-colored buildings, an air of mystique still hovers over Georgia's original settlement. Savannah is a strange, seductive place – equal parts history, treachery, revelry and oddity.

The saucy, best-selling book *Midnight in the Garden of Good and Evil* made this city a household name, with a corresponding increase in the city's tourism. Today, a visit is likely to consist of a horse-drawn carriage ride through stately squares, lunch in an outdoor café – and a roaring evening in a gay bar where transvestites waltz across stage.

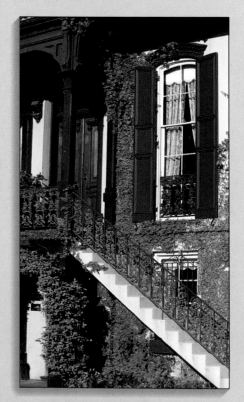

Founding father James Edward Oglethorpe must be turning in his grave.

In 1733, Oglethorpe received a royal charter to establish "the colony of Georgia in America" – and protect the coast from Spanish Florida while producing wine and silk for the Crown. Oglethorpe laid out a grid of broad thoroughfares, punctuated at regular intervals with two dozen spacious public squares. The 20 that remain have been refurbished, forming the nucleus of Savannah's Historic District – one of the largest urban national historic landmark districts in the United States, and probably the most beautiful. The district is bounded by the Savannah River to the north and Forsyth Park to the south, covering a 2½-mile (4-km) radius in all.

Each square has a distinctive character; Bull Street, running the length of the district north to south, links some of the most beautiful squares to each other. These squares excel in Savannah's most characteristic details: fancy ironwork and atmospheric Spanish moss. They are also enlivened with daily activity – art vendors, hot dog stands and street performers. Summer brings free jazz concerts to John Square near the river, but early spring is the best time to visit, when the city's azaleas are in full blossom.

The Historic Savannah Foundation has preserved many of the city's treasures. Anyone interested in history or architecture should see the Owens-Thomas House (124 Abercorn Street), the Hamilton-Turner Mansion at Lafayette Square and the Cathedral of St John the Baptist, also by Lafayette Square. One of the nation's most beautiful synagogues is located here. Yet another notable structure is Juliette Gordon Low's birthplace at 142 Bull Street, a handsome home that is associated with the founder of the Girl Scouts of America.

Horticulturists should seek out Trustees' Garden on East Broad Street, planted in the 1700s as Georgia's first experimental garden; it is now filled with exotic plants from around the world. Afterward, join a jovial crowd upstairs at Hannah's East, where Emma Kelly, a real-life character from the *Midnight* novel, used to play each evening before her death in January 2001.

Several historic buildings in the next few blocks were designed in Regency style by

English architect William Jay on his arrival in 1817, most notably the Alexander Telfair home (121 Barnard Street) – once the official residence of visiting state governors – and the William Scarbrough house (41 West Broad Street), which once hosted President James Monroe.

But the most talked-about residence in recent memory is Mercer Williams House, located on Monterey Square and built by composer Johnny Mercer's grandfather. This was the home of the late antique dealer Jim Williams, an eccentric millionaire who shot his 22-year-old male companion in 1981. Convicted twice of murder, he was later acquitted; today, his sister occupies the house, a magnificent antique-filled structure that is not open to the hordes of tourists drawn to it.

For lunch, stop by Mrs Wilkes' Boarding House on Jones Street. Tucked away between stately homes, her Southern-style restaurant serves up fried chicken, bowls overflowing with fresh vegetables and bottomless cups of sweet iced tea. Mrs Wilkes' round tables comfortably seat 10 to 12 diners at a time; you'll sit elbow-to-elbow with locals and other Savannah fans.

The Historic District's procession of squares ends nicely in beautiful Forsyth Park, a 31-acre (13-hectare) setting of constant outdoor activity. At the center of the park stands an elaborate fountain.

Savannah's harborside of old brick warehouses and shipping offices have become tourist attractions, reached by a series of steep steps; these are now inns, pubs, restaurants and gift shops that run the length of River Street.

Walking is the best way to see the city, unless the heat is oppressive, in which case, the Hyatt Regency Hotel and the Savannah Visitor Center are your best bets for catching a tour bus. You can choose from a wide selection of transportation, from modern mini-buses to horse-drawn carriages.

Leave Downtown by heading east on Victory Drive in the direction of the coastal islands to visit Bonaventure Cemetery, a

luxurious final resting place for Savannah's most distinguished citizens. A former plantation, Bonaventure is wistfully beautiful, dripping with moss and overflowing with azaleas, jasmine, magnolias and live oak trees. The images on several of the gravestones have become synonymous with both the *Midnight* book and the city itself.

Thunderbolt, 6 miles (10 km) east of Downtown on US 80, is a shrimping and fishing village on the banks of the Intracoastal Waterway. Continue east along US 80 over more bridges to Skidaway and Tybee islands, where the breeze is as fresh as the seafood in the restaurants alongside the water. ❑

LEFT: detail on River Street; one of Savannah's beautifully preserved buildings.
RIGHT: tomb statuary from the cover of *Midnight*; Oglethorpe monument; Mercer Williams House.

GEORGIA TO THE FLORIDA KEYS

*Small-town ambiance, a tropical paradise,
alligators in the Everglades and the southernmost point
in the US highlight the end of the Atlantic Route*

Map on page 82

The Georgia coast is one of the Southeast's most interesting natural regions, a string of marshes, largely undeveloped islands and good beaches rarely sought out by the traveler focused solely on getting through the state via Interstate 95 as quickly as possible. No wonder this region is known locally as the Golden Isles. The inattentive traveler's loss, however, has been others' gain: a number of unusual birds live secreted along this coast, and there are also vestiges of African culture from the dark days when slaves were shipped across the Atlantic to work the plantations of the South.

From Savannah, take Victory Drive (US 17) west out of town, where it shortly becomes Ogeechee Road – and also becomes much more rural in character. About 25 miles (40 km) along, stop in **Midway** ㉒ for a look at the small, whitewashed village church, a copy of the original church erected here in the late 1700s by displaced New Englanders. Get its key from the gas station just beside and take a look around, noting the eerie presence inside a section that was designated specifically for slaves and a gracefully kept cemetery outside. Adjacent to the church stands the small **Midway Museum** (tel: 912-884-5837; closed Mon), with a collection of period items.

LEFT: just in time for dinner.
BELOW: barbershop pole in a small Southern town.

Small town life

Past Riceboro, home to an agricultural research station, the highway passes beneath I-95 again and crosses a bridge over a tidal inlet into McIntosh County. To learn more about the politics, poverty and small-town intrigue of the county, look for the biting nonfiction book *Praying for Sheetrock*, which won awards for its clear-eyed portrait of local life.

If you make a left just after the bridge onto unnumbered Harris Neck Road, you can find **Harris Neck National Wildlife Refuge**, a pocket of wilderness that was saved from development because a former military airstrip occupied the land. Fishing is the most popular activity here, but you can also drive a one-way dirt loop road for a look at the waterfowl in their natural environs. Just offshore sits St Catherines Island, an off-limits island used as a breeding ground for rare birds and animals by the Brooklyn Zoo.

South again on US 17, make a brief detour onto Georgia 99, which reveals some truly old-fashioned towns and dwellings – shacks, mostly, many of them occupied by the modern-day descendants of freed slaves. These small communities – Crescent, Valona, Meridian, Carnigan and Ridgeville – are fishing and shellfishing communities now.

At **Darien**, rustic Georgia 99 rejoins US 17 again.

South Carolina to Key West

↑ Wilmington

North Carolina
South Carolina

17 — Myrtle Beach **17**

Pawley's Island **18**

Georgetown **19**

Charleston **20**

17 — 174 Edisto Island

South Carolina
Georgia

17 — Junc 35 / Junc 21 — 21 Beaufort

Savannah **21**

17 — Midway **22** — Harris Neck N.W.R

Darien — 99

Fort King George State Historic Site
Hofwyl-Broadfield Plantation State Historic Site

17 — Brunswick **23** — Sea Island / St Simons Island

Cumberland Island

Georgia
Florida

17 — Yulee

Jacksonville 24

95 — Castillo de San Marcos National Monument

St. Augustine **25**

207 — Junc 94

26 — Gainesville **26**

Paynes Prairie — Micanopy — Cross Creek

441 — 346

27 / 441 — Ocala **27**

Junc 289

28 Orlando — Walt Disney World

Junc 272 — 4

50 — Citrus Tower

98

50 — Weeki Wachee **29**

Bayport

50 — 19

60 — Tarpon Springs **30**

Clearwater Beach

60 — **Tampa 31** — Busch Gardens

St Petersburg

Ruskin

Bradenton

Sarasota — 75

Venice

32 Fort Myers

Sanibel Island — 41

80 Lake Okeechobee

33 Naples

75 Fort Lauderdale

34
The Everglades — 41 — Tamiami Canal

◉ **Miami 35**

1 — Homestead

John Pennekamp Coral Reef State Park

Key Largo **36**

Islamorada

★ Long Key State Park

Marathon **37**

No Name Key — ★ Bahia Honda State Park

1 — Key West **38**

The **Fort King George State Historic Site** (tel: 912-437-4770; closed Mon) here re-creates a Colonial-era blockhouse; this is where the British first settled Georgia and for a brief period administered to the area.

Five miles (8 km) south, at the mouth of the Altamaha River, sits the **Hofwyl-Broadfield Plantation** (tel: 912-264-7333; closed Mon) – prettifying the story of slavery somewhat as it demonstrates how the know-how of slaves imported from Africa was crucial to the successful cultivation of rice on these islands.

Hold your nose as you enter industrial **Brunswick 23**, a major center for paper and chemical production. Despite its industrial character, Brunswick's Down-town is surprisingly slow-paced and old-Southern, with an attractive grid of streets, homes and moss-draped live oak trees. One such oak tree, the so-called Lover's Oak, is believed to have stood for hun-dreds – possibly even close to one thou-sand – years.

The city is also set on a wide, beautiful (if not exactly pure) marsh immortalized by poet Sidney Lanier as the **"Marshes of Glynn"** (for Glynn County). A turnout facing the marshes has information explaining their formation, which pro-vides an opportunity to stretch your legs, take some snapshots and pick up lots of tourist information.

Lush islands

From the marshes, turn east and cross the toll bridge for a look at lush, though some-what exclusive, **St Simons Island**. Palm fronds, live oak trees and flowers cover both sides of the road in perpetual green as you drive through the road to the single attractive harborfront, and you might con-sider staying the night in these restful envi-rons. A museum in the former lighthouse tells the history of coastal Georgia, and there's a good beach out beyond the main settlement. **Sea Island**, an even more exclusive resort reached via another series of roads on the island, possesses beautiful beaches and a world-class golf course.

South again on US 17, you cross more bridges and then pivot inland through tiny towns. At Kingsland, you can make turnoff to catch the ferry for elegant **Cumberland Island**, one of the most attractive islands in the Georgia chain. Once the exclusive domain of wealthy families, it is now mostly owned by the US government as a "national seashore," meaning there are a small number of rudimentary campsites available to the public. Spirited jockeying for these few camping spots begins well in advance, however, so don't expect to just waltz in and secure one at the last moment.

Map on page 82

FLORIDA

Crossing the St Marys River, really little more than a tidal inlet, you're greeted with a double row of palm trees and, possibly, the presence of police cars: you have reached Florida. The first town you reach is **Yulee**, named for legislator and entrepreneur David Yulee. Yulee built a railroad from coast to Florida coast, and it thrived for a short time, but politics and the Civil War soon did it in and the town is of little consequence today. It isn't very long afterward that the rural roads give way to sprawl, announcing the outskirts of **Jacksonville ㉔**.

"Tree spirit" on St Simons Island, Georgia.

Once a crime-ridden backwater, Jacksonville is trying hard to remake itself over as a new urban destination, and corporate headquarters are relocating here to take advantage of the excellent weather and pristine beaches. And there are cultural attractions, too – the town is justly proud of its **Riverwalk** and the associated **Museum of Science and History** (tel: 904-396-6674; www.the-mosh.org; open daily), for example, while the **Cummer Museum of Art and Gardens** (tel: 904-356-6857; www.cummer.org; open daily) stands amid lush gardens right on the St Johns River.

Still, it's not a place to spend much time. Move on southward on I-95, instead, to the indisputable jewel of northern Florida, a town small enough to explore in

BELOW:
wild horses and
Dungeness ruin,
Cumberland Island.

Map
on page
82

a day: **St Augustine** ㉕. This town, founded by Spanish explorers in 1565 and later occupied by the British, lays claim to being America's oldest continuously occupied city. Most of downtown's buildings aren't nearly so ancient, but a pleasantly Mediterranean atmosphere has been preserved with narrow alleys, flowers, shops and Spanish architecture. A number of museums and attractions compete for the traveler's attention – some boasting rather dubious "oldest this" or "oldest that" claims – and there's also a good set of beaches and state parks just across the Lions Bridge, which can be crossed from the center of town.

Several attractions are of special note, including the star-shaped **Castillo de San Marcos** fort (tel: 904-829-6506; www.nps.gov/casa; open daily), right on the water, which defended the Spanish town from invaders. **The Spanish Quarter** interprets 18th-century Spanish life with blacksmiths, woodworkers and the like. A series of buildings constructed by oil and railroad magnate Henry Flagler are notable, particularly the **Memorial Presbyterian Church** that Flagler built as a memorial to his daughter. Finally, note the huge round **zero milestone** across the road from the visitors' center: this stone marks the endpoint in a string of Spanish missions that once stretched to San Diego.

Sweet potatoes and greens

From St Augustine, head southwest out of town on Florida 207, passing beneath the interstate and then through fields of sweet potatoes, cabbages and greens – you are back in deep-southern farm country – across the broad St Johns River the highway becomes Florida 20. The route passes Newnans Lake and comes directly into **Gainesville** ㉖, home to the University of Florida. As a result, there are gardens and nature trails, not to mention a good choice of restaurants and cultural offerings, within city limits.

US 441 exits the city south, shortly cutting right through the middle of **Paynes Prairie State Preserve**, a huge expanse of marsh and grassland bridged by the four-lane highway. The preserve is home to rare bison and cranes, among other creatures, and you can get a glimpse at some of them from a high wooden viewing tower. Or take one of the park-sponsored tours. Just south is tiny **Micanopy**, a town of dirt roads and simple buildings – an anomaly, something like what the old Florida must have looked.

For an even closer look at the state's recent past take State Route 346 a few miles east, then follow signs south along Route 325 for a look at **Cross Creek** – a tiny town, not even a town, really, but rather a place strongly identified with Florida author Marjorie Kinnan Rawlings. You can tour Rawlings former home, where she penned *The Yearling* and endured a tough life of farming and ranching, then dine, if you like, in a fine upscale restaurant on the premises. Highway 441 continues south through horse country to **Ocala** ㉗, a small Southern market town with a square and old-fashioned eateries. From Ocala US 441 gets busy and inches through quiet lake towns, lush citrus groves and sharp-smelling juice processing plants. Soon enough, you enter the extensive suburbs announcing the most improbable Florida success story of all, **Orlando** ㉘ *(see page 85)*.

BELOW: Castillo de San Marcos, St Augustine, Florida.

ORLANDO: THE WORLD'S BEST PLAYGROUND

Not long ago, Orlando was just another agricultural town. Now it's Florida's best success story, a transformation made possible by a cartoon mouse

The most obvious attraction at Orlando is just southwest of the city. Walt Disney World (tel: 407-934-7639; www.disneyworld.com; open daily), with its four enormous complexes of entertainments, is thronged year-round by American and international tourists alike.

The Magic Kingdom is Mickey Mouse's domain and the original facility. It still remains the most popular with visitors of all ages, and is divided into four distinctive theme areas – Tomorrowland, Adventureland, Fantasyland and Frontierland.

Introduced by a glittering "geospherical" dome, the Future World exhibits at EPCOT Center, the second part of the Disney complex, provide an invigorating look at science past, present and future. The other half of EPCOT is its World Showcase, where you can "travel the world" in less than a day through a variety of cultural (and culinary) attractions.

Rides and tours in the Disney-MGM Studios portion of the Disney World experience give a closer look at "show business," with perspectives as seen from both sides of the cameras. Disney's Animal Kingdom, the most recent addition to the Mickey Mouse empire, invites visitors to explore the world of animals on a safari, in a prehistoric world and at special stage shows held throughout the day.

Not far from Disney World – but a completely separate entity – is Universal Orlando Resort (tel: 407-363-8000; www.universalstudios.com; open daily). Opened the same year as Disney-MGM's facility, this attraction offers a similar experience: a chance to learn more about live television and film production, with a number of exciting movie-themed

rides thrown in as well. Look for the spotlights just west of Interstate 4.

There are dozens of similar amusements scattered about the greater Orlando area. Water slides, weird museums and amusement park rides are especially prevalent, and kids will go crazy with joy as parents just go crazy.

The most intriguing non-Disney or movie-related spot in the area, however, isn't within the city limits at all, but is worth traveling the few extra miles to see. About 40 miles (64 km) to the east, on a sandy stretch known as Cape Canaveral, the Kennedy Space Center (tel: 321-452-2121; www.kennedyspacecenter.com; open daily) provides a fascinating up-close look at the workings of America's space program. If you're lucky, your visit will coincide with a space shuttle or rocket launch. When it doesn't, you can still tour the same runways, training areas, assembly buildings and launch pads that NASA uses to prepare the crafts – and their crews – for flight. ❑

LEFT: Mickey's Kingdom; NASA space exhibit.
RIGHT: EPCOT Center; Universal Studios, Florida.

Marmalade from local oranges makes a great gift.

BELOW:
locally caught
sponges for sale,
Tarpon Springs.

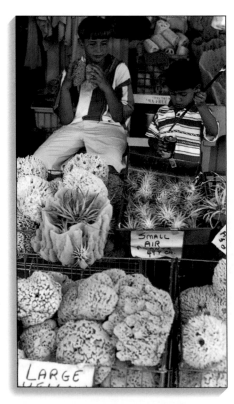

SOUTH FLORIDA

The vast majority of those travelers heading out from Orlando use the interstates and toll roads, but for more of the real Florida take the state highways awhile longer. Florida 50 (also called West Colonial Drive) leaves Orlando's city center and cuts due west, shedding the suburbs. In about 15 miles (24 km), you come to Clermont, singular for its drab but undeniably tall **Citrus Tower** – a slightly odd testament to the oranges, grapefruits, lemons and limes for which this state is so well known. You can pay to ride an elevator 23 stories to the top if you fancy a view of the surrounding lakes and hills.

Florida 50 now passes through the limestone spine of central Florida – a land of scrubby trees and prickly plants, sand dunes, citrus groves heavy with fruit in mid-winter, golf courses, even cowboys working cattle herds. Backroad stands sell everything from bovine medicine to boiled peanuts, a local specialty that makes a starchy, salty mess and is definitely an acquired taste.

The route continues west, brushing the edge of Withlacoochee State Forest before arriving at whimsically named **Weeki Wachee ㉙**, a town famous with tourists for its natural warm-water spring – and the water park, cruise facility, zoo and other attractions that have "sprung" up around it. It all requires a certain sense of humor and tolerance for excess to enjoy properly.

If you're in a hurry to get a glimpse of the **Gulf of Mexico**, press west a few additional miles to tiny **Bayport** with its picnic area overlooking the water. Otherwise, turn south down US 19 and prepare for a spell of thick four-lane traffic and plenty of stoplights. During early spring, this area is home to the training grounds for a number of major league baseball teams.

It's 30 miles (48 km) down US 19 to the junction with Alt-19. Take Alt-19 to **Tarpon Springs ㉚**, a harbor community that is fascinating not for its physical appearance but its population: the town is largely Greek. Greeks originally settled this area to dive for the sponges that live abundantly in the warm surrounding seas, and today local shops and restaurants continue to reflect this heritage.

Past Dunedin, take Florida 60 west across the causeway to **Clearwater Beach**, a relaxed town of seafood restaurants and beach homes. It's a fine place to swim in warm water and lie on the beautiful – and public – white sand beaches.

Turn south down the beach road (which eventually becomes Florida 699), crossing several short toll bridges linking the various sandbars. You will pass through more waterfront towns, most with excellent sand but some too overdeveloped for their own good. The finest beach on the entire string is probably the southernmost one, **Passe-a-Grille Beach**, some 20 miles (32 km) of slow driving onward from Clearwater. Gawk at the huge and expensive pink **Don Cesar Hotel**, an Art Deco masterpiece right beside the blue Gulf waters, then hit the sand.

Downtown **St Petersburg** is strangely vacant for stretches, with long blocks of cheap package stores and adult dance clubs, but in the central downtown district on Third Street you will find the interesting **Salvador Dalí Museum** (tel: 727-823-3767; www.salvadordali museum.org; open daily), which displays dozens of the

Map on page 82

artist's paintings – without question the central cultural attraction of the city. East across Tampa Bay via either I-275 or US 92, and set right on the water facing St Pete, is **Tampa ㉛**. This city's Cuban influence is nowhere clearer than in **Ybor City**, with its concentration of Cuban diners and cigar manufacturers. Ybor City was built on empty scrub by a local cigar maker in the late 1800s, and soon became not just a manufacturing center but also the city's most swashbuckling quarter; while yuppies have clearly discovered the place, converting many former factories into brewpubs and the like, Spanish is still the language of the streets.

Be a little bit careful here if you come after dark, but be sure to sample the extremely vibrant nightlife and good restaurants. Other city attractions include a full February slate of events, kicked off by a wild Mardi Gras-like parade, and Tampa Bay itself – best viewed during a stroll along the sidewalk arcing around upscale Bayshore Boulevard.

Frolicking manatees

Most visitors to Tampa also make a visit to **Busch Gardens** (tel: 888-800-5447; www.buschgardens.com; open daily), a slightly strange amusement park with an African-exploration theme that seems contrived. The park does feature heart-dropping roller coasters, water slides and simulated rapids, however, not to mention world-famous performances of water ballet, waterskiing skills and the like.

Take US 41 south out of Tampa, stopping a moment outside **Ruskin** where the Little Manatee River empties into the bay. As you'd expect from the name, you can sometimes find manatees frolicking at this inlet in winter, when they swim here to enjoy the warm water.

US 41 plunges due south through strings of heavily built-up towns and cities, many catering to elderly retirees. A much faster route would take the parallel Interstate 75.

Bradenton and **Sarasota** are next, twin cities on the Gulf of Mexico, offering very favorable weather, spring baseball and more good sandy beaches with warm ocean water. The beaches continue, in fact, through Siesta Key and Casey Key to **Venice** and beyond. The highway circles around Charlotte Harbor and crosses the Caloosahatchee River into well-known **Fort Myers ㉜**. The mild climate has made this a popular winter resort town for a very long time; Northerners Thomas Edison and Henry Ford were neighbors on the riverfront, for example, and you can tour both their adjacent winter homes on one combined ticket. The highlight is a museum collecting some of Edison's inventions. If you're in a mood to do some seashell collecting (known here as "shelling"), follow signs over the toll bridge to **Sanibel Island.**

Sanibel may offer the finest shell collecting in all of America. Devotees come out here so often that someone coined a phrase to describe the parade of hunched-over collectors inspecting the backwash of each wave for new finds: they call this posture the "Sanibel stoop." You can expect to find a number of brightly colored shells here in the balmy surf, not to mention fossilized shark's teeth as well.

The route continues south to exclusive **Naples ㉝**, haunt of the rich and the beautiful. Now, you have a

BELOW: head over heels in Busch Gardens, Tampa.

choice of routes east between **Alligator Alley**, as the high-speed toll route of Interstate 75 is known, or else older US 41 farther south, cutting alongside the **Tamiami Canal** that connects the Atlantic Ocean with the Gulf of Mexico.

The Everglades

US 41 goes on for miles and miles through the quiet heart of Florida, passing no towns at all save the occasional gas station. There are no towns because you are slowly penetrating the **Everglades ❹**, a vast pocket of swampland partially protected by law and difficult, in any case, to build on.

This strange landscape is home to alligators, poisonous snakes, sinuous blackwater creeks overhung by lush vegetation and probably a few desperado-like characters too; it also supplies the bulk of the drinking water to greater Miami. Authors, including Marjory Stoneman Douglas and Peter Matthiessen, have written about the unique people and creatures here in books like *River of Grass* and *Killer Mister Watson*, but the place to this day remains somewhat inscrutable. Bear in mind carefully all warnings about the sun, snakes, stinging insects, reptiles, navigation and other potential troubles: it's a tricky place to spend a few days, but intensely rewarding, too.

Midway through the 'Glades you encounter a sliver of the **Miccosukee Indian Reservation**, a bit depressing for its hawking of cheap goods and casino gambling; there is no sign at all of heroic Seminole warriors like Osceola, who outfoxed Federal troops in these endless swamps for more than a year rather than surrender to a government that had broken treaties and promises and spilled his people's blood. Just a few miles east, the National Parks Service has constructed a loop road at **Shark Valley** that can only be

TIP

The best way to explore the Everglades is to rent a canoe or boat, or get in touch with one of the licensed outfitters who also provide guides. Seeing this exotic place only from land does not do justice to its mystery.

BELOW: fish, coral and sponges taking over a ship's hull.

LAKE OKEECHOBEE

A 58-mile (93-km) drive along SR 80 from Fort Myers brings you to Lake Okeechobee and its 750 sq miles (1,940 sq km) of crystal waters. Florida's largest lake is as beautiful as it is sad; the lake reflects the damage being done to the sensitive Everglades environment by the booming population of Florida. The water from Lake Okeechobee once fed the wide shallow river of the Everglades, but dikes, pumping stations and canals were constructed to tame this dramatic lake and its flooding waters. While this has made the surrounding area an agricultural paradise (the area produces enough sugar to supply 15 million Americans' sweet tooth for an entire year), the projects have brought ecological hardship to the surrounding environment. Both the Everglades and South Florida's cities have been threatened with drought by the dwindling water level of the lake. Excessive pumping of the Everglades' mother waters for the booming population along the Gold Coast is also sucking it dry. Still a popular destination for anglers, fish camps punctuate the lake's perimeter. Okeechobee, the largest town on the north shore of the lake, is the best base if you want to explore the area. Boat trips can be easily arranged.

toured by bicycle or tram. The tour terminates at an observation tower that allows unhindered views out over miles of the southern Everglades. Sitting here in the humid silence, it's a bit odd to consider how you're a mere half-hour's drive from the hustle, bustle and danger of downtown; you somehow feel safer here, among the vines and snakes, than you will there.

Map
on page
82

FLORIDA KEYS

If you want to hold off diving into downtown **Miami** ㉟ *(see page 92)* – or are already there and want to make an escape to another type of landscape altogether – by all means get yourself down to the **Florida Keys**. This 100-mile (160-km) string of islands forms the end of the line for the north-to-south traveler, and they are one of the most distinctive places in the USA. The Keys' tropical climate and physical isolation mean you will find birds and fish here that live nowhere else in the land, plus a landscape in which water is never far away and a system of good state parks from which to enjoy it all. Even the light is different here, a mysterious, turquoise shade of blue that reflects off everything it touches. It is a wonder, really, that these disparate islands are connected to each other or the mainland at all. Yet a series of 42 highway bridges does indeed bridge the many gaps between land and water.

From Miami, US 1 proceeds south through **Homestead**, a quiet community that was demolished by the winds of Hurricane Andrew in August 1992 – one of the most powerful hurricanes to strike North America, although loss of life was low. A branch road here, Florida 9336, leads through a wild section of Everglades National Park that terminates on Florida Bay, but it's a long side trip down and back. Skip it if you're hurrying to see the Keys.

BELOW: the Overseas Highway, Florida Keys.

Key information

US 1 enters the Keys as the Overseas Highway at **Key Largo** ㊱, immortalized in the Humphrey Bogart/Lauren Bacall film of the same name (which wasn't actually filmed here), and right away you get an opportunity to view the sea up-close. At **John Pennekamp Coral Reef State Park** (tel: 305-451-6300; www.pennekamppark.com; open daily), one of the most popular parks in Florida, you can gaze through glass-bottomed boats at the most incredible formations of coral reef under the sea. Equally compelling are the fish and shellfish swimming and living throughout this delicate ecosystem. Snorkelling and diving are a must. Key Largo is also home to what is probably the world's only undersea lodge, Jules'.

If this reef is the best place to see the nature of the Keys, the next park, **Long Key State Park**, some 30-odd miles (48 km) farther along US 1, is your best bet for a swim or reclining in the sun before proceeding west. Stop midway between the two parks for a bite at **Manny and Isa's**, a longstanding, popular Cuban diner in **Islamorada** that is famous for its Key Lime pie.

For a lesson on what made the Keys into such a unique place, journey 20 more miles (32 km) beyond Long Key to the best museum in the region, the **Crane Point Museum** (tel: 305-743-9100; www.cranepoint.org; open daily) in the resort town of **Marathon** ㊲. Marathon itself is more like a big town than an island paradise, and is best used for stocking up on supplies.

The mangrove forests thicken beyond here, and the touristic accoutrements begin to slip away as nature begins reclaiming the westernmost islands. You'll get plenty of water views on both sides of the car now as you cross **Seven Mile Bridge**, landing briefly on beautiful **No Name Key** and its **Bahia Honda State Park** – yet another wonderful state-run park.

Florida wildlife is not for feeding.

BELOW: Jules' Undersea Lodge, Key Largo.

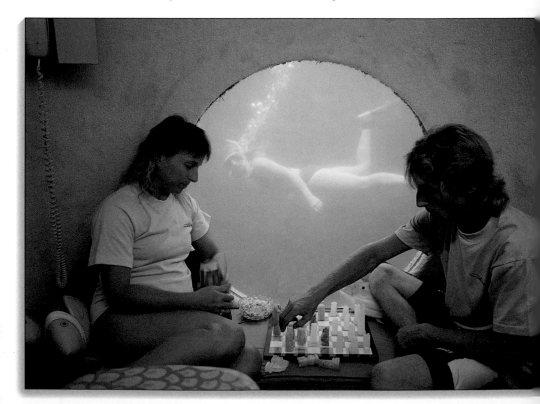

Key West

You cross more bridges still, landing on **Big Pine Key**, **Sugarloaf Key** and **Looe Key**, each with its own personality and laid-back eateries. The pace, too, down-shifts almost to a crawl as you meet former stockbrokers owning T-shirt shops and the like. Eventually, the highway comes to rest upon balmy **Key West 38**, last island in the chain – and also the name of the town here that has been drawing interesting characters for a very long time. Today, it's a mixture of fishermen, retirees, Cubans and tourist tack, as well as a thriving gay and lesbian population.

The writer Ernest Hemingway lived here, and purveying "Papa's" image has become one of the town's hottest cottage industries. To get a taste of how he lived, visit the **Ernest Hemingway Home and Museum** (tel: 305-294-1136; www.hemingwayhome.com; open daily), where Hemingway wrote for a decade; notable are the gardens he personally tended and the cats that overrun the place. As tour guides will tell you, they are all descendants of the writer's own cats. The bars lining **Duval Street**, including several once frequented by Hemingway, are a lively refreshment spot, and the Hemingway look-alike contest held every year is a highlight of a noisy social season that is busy to begin with.

The two most popular sights in town, however, are both free. The first is **Mallory Square Dock**, where residents and tourists alike have been turning out every night for decades to cheer the beautiful sunsets over the water. The other free attraction is also a good one: the brightly colored buoy that marks the **southernmost point** in the continental 48 states, which is near the aptly named Southernmost Hotel and Southernmost House (an old private home converted to a quirky museum and guest house). Locals claim that on a very clear night you can even faintly make out the lights of Cuba, lying less than 100 miles (160 km) away. ❑

Map on page 82

Help a turtle cross the street by slowing down in your car.

BELOW:
Key West
guest house.

A SHORT STAY IN MIAMI

Sensual and warm, spicy and seductive, Miami appeals to the visitor who is longing for escape. Here's a list of the not-to-be-missed attractions:

◆ Coral Gables is an enchanting Mediterranean-style city, home to the glorious Biltmore Hotel (1926) and the Venetian Pool, sometimes called "the most beautiful swimming hole in the world."

◆ The largest tropical garden in the US, Coral Gables' Fairchild Tropical Botanic Garden maintains an outstanding collection of tropical flowering trees, and more than 5,000 ferns, plants and orchids.

◆ Coconut Grove is a vibrant, eclectic neighborhood of funky houses, dense natural greenery and good shopping at Coco Walk.

◆ I.M. Pei designed the futuristic International Place, a 47-story building in downtown Miami that changes color at the flick of a switch.

◆ Bayside Marketplace is a flashy outdoor arcade full of neon signs and impulse items.

◆ Lummus Park combines the oldest structures in Miami (the William English Slave Plantation House and the William Wagner House) with a white-sand beach stretching along the coastline.

◆ Little Haiti is home to immigrants from the Caribbean island of Haiti. The area offers great food and an encounter with a rich culture.

◆ Key Biscayne, an island paradise connected by bridge, offers many water-related recreations, like jet-skiing, windsurfing and, of course, lying on your back under the sun.

◆ Metrozoo has lots of tropical wildlife, with wild animals from Africa, Asia and Australia. The zoo area is divided into little animal kingdom islands connected by bridges.

For visitors interested in staying longer in the big city, pick up a copy of *Insight Guide: Miami*. This is a companion to the present volume, and is packed with insightful text and stunning pictures.

▷ **ART DECO DISTRICT**
Stars, models and wannabes flock to the pastel-colored fantasy buildings in South Beach, which have now been converted into hotels, restaurants, bars and shops.

△ **DECO DETAIL**
In 1979, the 500 playful buildings with their colorful frills constructed in the 1930s became the youngest historic district in the United States.

△ **SEAQUARIUM**
Dolphins, porpoises, sea lions and a killer whale are among the mammals that perform at the Miami Seaquarium, a bay-front marine park dedicated to the preservation of sea life.

▷ **CUBAN CIGAR FACTORY**
Visit a cigar factory, brush up on your Spanish, eat spicy Caribbean food and stroll through Little Havana, the US's most highly concentrated neighborhood of Cubans.

CITY OF FANTASY

Miami is everything other cities are not – pastel colors, swaying palms and Art Deco balconies are not only easy on the eye, but also kind to the disposition: it's impossible to fret when there's a fizzy cocktail on the table, a pink plastic flamingo on the counter and a three-piece band playing loud and sassy salsa in your eardrums. If you're staying in South Beach, you can also leave your car behind and stretch those weary legs before getting them tanned on the sandy beach across the street. Miami has a lot of things worth discovering. But don't forget the sunscreen.

△ VIZCAYA MUSEUM
It may look like an old Italian country villa, but Vizcaya and its fantastic gardens are only about 100 years old.

▷ MIAMI BEACH
The beaches and bronzed, beautiful people of Miami have been attracting tourists since the 1920s.

▽ Red arrows on the map indicate routes from the city detailed in this book

Miami Throughways

Important Information

Population:
400,000
Dialing code:
305, 786
Website:
www.gmcvb.com

Tourist information:
Convention & Visitors Bureau, 701 Brickell Avenue, Suite 2700, FL 33131
Tel: 305-539-3000

THE NORTHERN ROUTE

*A detailed guide from east to west, with principal sites
clearly cross-referenced by number to the maps*

This northern route across the US is framed on either side by one of the nation's most interesting cities and some of its most unspoiled lands. On the road between Boston and Washington state's Olympic Peninsula, you will encounter a collage of farmlands, ranches, wilderness, port towns, declining industrial cities, reborn urban centers and constant reminders of the nation's history.

The first half of the journey is largely marked and guided by water. From Boston, you follow the Atlantic coast through the best of New England up to Maine; later, from the Albany area, your route will swing west alongside the once-busy, now-dormant Erie Canal.

The Great Lakes dominate the next portion of the trip, including Chicago, the great Midwestern crossroads, and a city of marvelous architecture at the southern tip of Lake Michigan. From here to the thriving twin cities of Minneapolis and St Paul, the tour is never far from water, most significantly when it runs right beside the mighty Mississippi for a beautiful, scenic stretch.

Once you reach western Minnesota, however, the character of the land begins to change and water becomes scarce indeed. As you cut across South Dakota, the geography overwhelms: rising out of the prairie are the otherworldly Badlands, the Black Hills and Wounded Knee, a reminder of the nation's brutal treatment of Native Americans. Along a legendary stagecoach route, come towns of the notorious Wild West that were once inhabited by the likes of Wild Bill Hickok, Calamity Jane and Buffalo Bill Cody. The sky here is huge and the land seems vast, populated mainly by small buttes, sagebrush, cattle and deer. The route through Wyoming and Montana passes the site of General Custer's last stand against the Indians.

From here, the tour passes into the northern portion of the Rocky Mountains, where the main attractions are the gorgeous national parks. Crossing the Continental Divide on paths previously traveled by mountain tribes, gold prospectors and homesteaders, the route cuts through the forests, lakes and buffalo reserves of Montana, the Idaho panhandle and into the state of Washington, where the land modulates between deserts, canyons and irrigated farmland.

The final portion of the route runs westward toward the Pacific Ocean like a river, west to Seattle and the Olympic Peninsula. Suddenly, water is abundant again, almost pervasive, as you enter America's only rainforest. This is among the nation's most remote and wildly beautiful spots, an ideal place to reflect upon your just-completed trans-American journey. ❑

PRECEDING PAGES: Grand Teton National Park, Wyoming; covered bridge and grazing cattle, Vermont.
LEFT: ready to hit the open range.

A SHORT STAY IN BOSTON

The many colleges in this historic and attractive city ensure it retains a youthful, vibrant outlook. Here's a list of the not-to-be-missed attractions:

◆ A full-scale replica of the *Brig Beaver II* sits in the harbor at the Boston Tea Party Ships and Museum, commemorating the 1773 dunking of taxed tea from Britain, an incident that fueled the flames of the American Revolution. Undergoing a full renovation, it will reopen in fall 2008.

◆ Built in 1676, the Paul Revere House is the oldest residence in downtown Boston; Revere lived here from 1770 to 1800. Exhibits include the saddlebags the patriot used on his famous midnight ride to warn of a British attack.

◆ On July 4, 1795, Massachusetts Governor Samuel Adams and Paul Revere laid the cornerstone for the "new" State House. The building overlooks Boston Common and can be explored on a (free) guided tour.

◆ The oldest botanical garden in America, the Public Garden is Boston's prettiest green space. The focus is the lagoon, surrounded by willow trees and crossed by a mock suspension bridge.

◆ Constructed in 1826, Quincy Market (now called the Faneuil Hall Marketplace) served for almost 150 years as a distribution center for meat and produce. Now restored, it houses foodstalls, restaurants, shops and a flower market.

◆ Opened in 1895, the Boston Public Library is designed in the Renaissance Revival style. The interior includes murals by John Singer Sargent; the courtyard is reminiscent of 16th-century Italy.

◆ The Isabella Stewart Gardner Museum has many architectural elements, from Venetian window frames to Roman mosaic floor tiles. The galleries hold paintings by Titian, Raphael, Degas and Rembrandt.

For visitors interested in staying longer in the big city, pick up a copy of *Insight Guide: Boston*. This is a companion to the present volume, and is packed with insightful text and stunning pictures.

▷ **CHARLES RIVER BASIN**
The Back Bay, with the Salt and Pepper Bridge, named for its four recognizable towers. The cleaning and greening of the basin changed the area.

△ **TRINITY CHURCH**
Designed by H.H. Richardson in 1872, the church is one of the finest ecclesiastical buildings in the US. Stained-glass windows are by La Farge.

◁ **THE OLD STATE HOUSE**
The lion and unicorn on the facade, symbols of British royalty, recall the days when th first governors resided here.

▽ *USS CONSTITUTION*
Known as "Old Ironsides," the ship emerged victorious from all 40 of the battles she fought. She is now berthed in Charlestown Navy Yard.

◁ **JOHN HANCOCK TOWER**
At 740 feet (226 meters), the tower is Boston's tallest building. There's a rooftop observatory and great views of the city from the top.

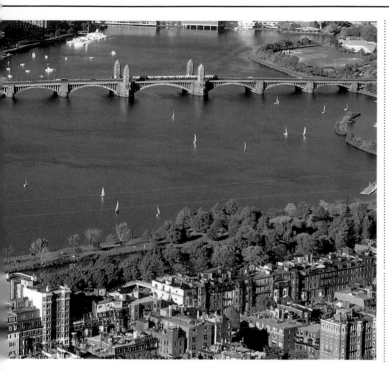

THE BACK BAY CITY

"I have learned never to argue with a Bostonian," said poet Rudyard Kipling in the early 1900s, and that is still true now. By American standards, Boston is old. Cobbled streets lit by gas-lamps; National Historic Landmarks; individual buildings of great stature and charm. A couple of decades ago, Boston was in danger of becoming a museum of living history, forever trapped in its 1700s and 1800s heyday. Then a change took place: the basin was cleaned, the buildings washed and, due to the high-tech industries of nearby Cambridge, businesses began to flock back. Boston is booming again, so go check it out. And no arguing.

> **MUSEUM OF FINE ARTS**
The permanent collection includes works from Asia and Egypt, along with American and European fine art.

WITCHES CROSS HERE
The nearby town of Salem is famous for its witch trials of 1692. Salem was also a busy port in the 1700s.

Important Information

Population:
560,000
Dialing code:
617, 857
Website:
www.bostonusa.com

Tourist information:
Greater Boston C&VB
2 Copley Place, Suite
105, MA 02116
Tel: 888-SEE-BOSTON
Fax: 617-424-7664

▽ Red arrows on the map indicate routes from the city detailed in this book

Boston Throughways

BOSTON TO BUFFALO

Take a drive through the prettiest parts of New England before beginning a coast-to-coast trek to the West, starting with the old route of the Erie Canal

Map on page 104

Beginning in downtown **Boston ❶** *(see page 100)*, the Northern route across the United States starts out by visiting "suburban Boston." This is accomplished by crossing the Charles River into busy **Cambridge ❷**. Cambridge's combination of old-fashioned leafy streets, active squares and buzzing student life make it one of Greater Boston's most interesting areas. The activity focuses around triangular **Harvard Square** and more rough-and-tumble but no less vibrant **Central Square**. While here, explore the brick buildings and carefully manicured greens of **Harvard University**, the second-oldest educational institution in the land; it was chartered back in 1636 and remains one of the finest universities in America, with a number of good museums on the quiet campus.

The city's beautifully kept **Mount Auburn Cemetery** is worth seeing, as well; its peaceful grounds harbor the remains of such artistic luminaries as Henry Longfellow, Oliver Wendell Holmes and Winslow Homer.

Keep following signs for 2A, a scenic route that leads out from Massachusetts Avenue into quieter towns. You soon come to **Arlington**, now suburban and high-tech but once a textile community where retreating British soldiers skirmished with local residents known as "Minutemen" – they were said to have been ready at a minute's notice to fight – in April of 1775 as the British backtracked along this road.

LEFT: New England pumpkin patch dressed for Halloween. **BELOW:** fall in Vermont.

Paul Revere's ride

At **Lexington**, about 10 miles (16 km) outside Boston proper, turn off 2A into the downtown area for a look at the town green, the main stage of the Battle of Lexington on that fateful April night. A number of statues and monuments commemorate this spirited American defense of their town, considered critical in turning the tide of the American Revolution; silversmith Paul Revere rode his horse here from Boston under cover of night to warn the residents of a British attack. There are also several old taverns in the area, one of which – Munroe Tavern – served as the makeshift British hospital and command center during the battle.

Continue west along 2A, where American Revolution events are further cataloged in the now-peaceful **Minute Man National Historical Park** (tel: 978-369-6993; www.nps.gov/mima; open daily), which occupies both sides of the highway in a green patch just northwest of the village green.

Concord, the next town, is another significant site. This town was a center of literature and philosophy during the 19th century, as evidenced by such prominent residents as Ralph Waldo Emerson, Henry David Thoreau and Louisa May Alcott, among others. Alcott's former home, **Orchard House** (tel: 978-369-4118; www.louisamayalcott.org; open daily), where she wrote

Little Women, is first as you approach town, on the right. **Emerson House** (tel: 978-369-2236; closed in winter) comes next, less than half a mile beyond on the left, with items from the life and work of the influential Transcendentalist thinker.

From the center of town, take Walden Street south a short distance to visit **Walden Pond State Reservation** (tel: 978-369-3254), a testament to Henry Thoreau's life, work and unique viewpoint. Thoreau built a simple cabin beside this pond in 1845 and lived there for a time, later writing *Walden* about the experience. "I went to the woods because I wished to live deliberately," he proclaimed, emerging with a view of nature as teacher – rather than slave – of man, and though the book sold poorly in his time, it has since become one of the enduring classics of American literature. The pond isn't nearly as peaceful as it was in his time, but you can still get a sense of what Thoreau must have felt.

ENTERING NEW ENGLAND

Before leaving Boston bound for the wild West, it's worth a short detour north first through the splendors of back-road New England, where America began and a delightful small-town neighborliness can still be felt today.

Begin, then, by heading north from downtown Boston on State Route 1A (North Street from Downtown) towards **Salem ❸**. This sea town was one of the earliest capitals of the Massachusetts Bay Colony, and is filled with period captain's homes and the like. It's more famous, though, for the **Salem Witch Trials** that began in 1692, an attempt to root out suspected witchcraft among local women and children; nearly two dozen were killed during the height of the frenzy – a symbol, ever after, for misplaced persecution. (The term "witch hunt," broadly applied to political activities, remains in the American lexicon today.) The **Salem Witch Museum** (tel: 978-744-1692; www.salemwitch museum.com; open daily), beside the city's large central green, offers an explanation of the trials. Writer Nathaniel Hawthorne was born in one of the houses on the **House of the Seven Gables Historic Site** (tel:

Map on page 104

978-744-0991; www.7gables.org; open daily), on the city waterfront nearby; the famed gabled house about which he later penned the well-known novel is also there; its "official" name is the Turner-Ingersoll Mansion.

Route 1A heads due north from Salem and continues on a scenic track through salt marshes, small drawbridges, farmland and little fishing and commuter towns such as Ipswich, Rowley and Newbury. Along the way, you may wish to detour east to **Gloucester**, the entrance to lovely Cape Ann and home port to large numbers of fishing and whale-watching boats.

NEW HAMPSHIRE AND MAINE

After entering **New Hampshire**, 1A frees itself from ticky-tacky beach development to reveal the Atlantic itself at **Rye Beach** – your first true glimpse of the open ocean on this tour. Continue a few miles to **Portsmouth ❹**, New Hampshire's most attractive city and one with a salty taste.

Originally known as Strawberry Banke for the wild fruits covering the ground, Portsmouth was ideally situated at the meeting place of a river mouth and the ocean; founded in 1630, it has been a fishing and shipping center ever since. Fine old seamen's homes still crowd the downtown area, and while designer coffeeshops and microbreweries are rapidly crowding out the old salts – this is only an hour's commute from Boston, remember – you can still find good clam chowder in the local diners.

North across the Piscataqua River and its bridges lies **Maine**, the "Pine Tree State." Pull off busy US 1 after 6 miles (10 km) to visit **York ❺**, Maine's first settlement, which possesses a clutch of old buildings (including an old jail) by the waterfront, all connected by a coastal walking track. Most visitors come,

The Massachusetts port of Gloucester was the setting for The Perfect Storm, *the best-selling book and movie of the same name. The story was based on a real-life tragedy, when several local fishermen died at sea.*

BELOW: night-time in a small New England town.

however, for the long stretch of good beach known as **Long Sands**, framed at one end by a much-photographed lighthouse, the Cape Neddick Light Station, known locally as **Nubble Light**. Buy exceptional homemade ice cream in the summer months from a long-running family business just uphill of the famous beacon; choose between apple pie, checkerberry (a New England berry tasting of wintergreen) or Danish cream flavors if they're in stock.

North again on US 1, **Wells** is a fairly forgettable beach town, but just north lies the **Wells Estuarine Reserve** – a protected section of marshland on the sea. Its presence commemorates scientist Rachel Carson, whose books about the ocean, songbirds and ecology changed the way Americans thought about the natural world.

Upper crust

Farther north, you hit the Kennebunks, two towns physically joined at the hip by a bridge but quite different in character. **Kennebunk** is more workaday, with an exclusive beach several miles east, while **Kennebunkport** is a slice of quaint, upper-crust New England – all gift shops, designer beers and fish houses, a bit rich for the blood. Former president George Bush Sr's family compound stands among dramatic shore rocks and crashing waves east of Downtown.

It's 20 more slow miles (32 km) north along US 1 (or you can pay to take Interstate 95) to **Portland ❻**, the state's largest city and cultural center, if rather a humdrum place. At least there's a good collection of beaches, parks and restaurants to sample before moving along.

Eastern Promenade Park makes a good first stop, with its panoramic view of islands in the bay and part of the city's working waterfront. The **Old Port**

Lobsters 2 go.

BELOW: Cape Neddick Light Station, also known as Nubble Light, in York, Maine.

district, once a maze of rough streets frequented by sailors, has now been entirely taken over by gift shops, overpriced restaurants and cut-rate bars aimed at day-trippers; avoid it and go instead for the residential **West End**, where the **Victoria Mansion** (also known as the Morse-Libby House; tel: 207-772-4841; www.victoriamansion.org; open May–Oct) on Danforth Street stands as an excellent example of Victorian architecture. Or take a ferry to tranquil little **Peaks Island** for a closer look at the sea. Back in the center of town, the **Portland Museum of Art** (tel: 207-775-6148; www.portlandmuseum.org; open Tues–Sun year-round, also Mon Oct–May) sometimes hangs good exhibits and has a gallery devoted to Winslow Homer. Just watch the time on your parking meter: ticketers around town are needlessly ruthless.

From Portland, quieter Route 25 cuts swiftly west through suburbs and then rolling farmland. The town of **Gorham** is little more than a four-way intersection and the rural main campus of the University of Southern Maine; stay on Route 25, proceeding through more small towns. At Limington, the bridge crosses the slow Saco River, a superb canoeing river that winds from deep in western Maine to the sea. A free park on the left-hand side of the road here provides a scenic little picnic and swimming spot; rocks make for good sunning, and a pathway leads downriver to a wider place in the river, out of the sometimes-swift current.

Farther west, the route passes through more countryside to **Cornish** ❼, one of western Maine's very handsome towns. The activity here is focused around a small triangular green space lined with small shops and a hardware store, most in typical whitewashed New England fashion. Each September, an annual apple festival showcases local pies, cider and other apple products on the town common – and the winner gets a night for two at the venerable Cornish Inn that stands beside the green. The best part comes after the judging, when all pies – winners and losers – are auctioned off to lingering spectators.

Windy heights

Keep to Route 25 as it jogs west into New Hampshire, the "Granite State," then briefly north; if you kept going north on Route 16, you would soon pass **Mount Washington,** at 6,288 ft (1,917 meters) the tallest peak east of the Mississippi – and home to the highest recorded winds on the planet.

At West Ossipee, however, make a turn inland again and follow Route 25 through Moultonborough, **Center Harbor** – whose little general store features old-fashioned wooden iceboxes of cola – and finally **Meredith**, a resort town with a doll museum set on big, pretty **Lake Winnipesaukee** ❽, New Hampshire's largest body of water.

Head south a short while on Route 3 as the road passes right beside the lake. Going uphill as you leave the town, bear right to take state Route 104 through small, typically New Hampshire towns. At Danbury, cut south on US 4 a short distance to Route 11, and then turn west again just after **Potter Place**.

It's only 10 miles (16 km) more to the prim town of **New London** ❾ (turn onto Route 114 just past Elkins), which has a fine central green and good views of the surrounding hills and mountains. This is known

BELOW: the Maine tools for local fishermen.

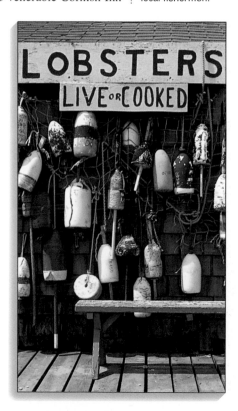

Map on page 104

locally as a college town, with attractive Colby-Sawyer College located right next to the village green. This former women's college was long one of America's few remaining single-sex institutions of higher education, and became co-educational only in recent years. Connecting with Route 11 from Route 114, the road passes through the hamlets of Georges Mills (a general store, coves on either side of the road and little more) and the lake town of Sunapee, with a pretty harbor on **Lake Sunapee** – reputedly one of the cleanest lakes in America, and one circled by hills of hardwoods.

Six more miles (10 km) east on Route 11, **Newport** ❿ spreads out in the Sugar River Valley, a small textile and arms manufacturing town with an old opera house, wooden covered bridge and the handsome rectangular "town common" so typical of older New England towns. These green pastures once served as common grazing spaces for local livestock, but today serve mostly as the settings for soccer matches, carnivals, bake sales and picnics.

Newport is perhaps best known for Sarah Josepha Buell Hale (1788-1879). Despite early tragedies including the loss of her mother, sister and husband, Hale rose to prominence in Boston and Philadelphia as one of America's early feminists and female editors. She advocated education and equal opportunity for women, convinced President Abraham Lincoln to create Thanksgiving Day and penned the popular children's nursery rhyme "Mary Had a Little Lamb." Her birth home is on Route 11 a few miles before you enter town, across the street from a once-famous woolen mill.

Bridge to the past

For a look at the **Corbin Covered Bridge**, drive through Newport's main street and continue north on Route 10 for a mile or so, then turn left, passing the town airport and driving through a corridor of pine trees. The bridge at the edge was constructed as a copy to replace the original jewel, which was burned by a thoughtless arsonist during the 1990s. Such bridges are sprinkled throughout New England, their distinctive design both a shield from poor weather and, some say, a method of keeping horses drawing carriages from being spooked by rushing rivers below.

The craftsman who built this particular bridge was such a perfectionist for detail that he copied the original design and then hauled the bridge to its Sugar River home with an oxen team – both to transport it undamaged and to preserve a sense of history.

From central Newport, Route 103 proceeds west through **Claremont**, a fading mill city that nevertheless still possesses an impressive old block of central buildings known as Tremont Square and a fine Opera House with a good summer program of folk and orchestral concerts. Just west of the city, the highway crosses the broad and picturesque Connecticut River dividing New Hampshire from its similar-sized (but very different-thinking) cousin, Vermont.

At **Ascutney**, on the far side of the river, the antenna-topped peak of Mount Ascutney fills the eye; Vermont 5 keeps it to one side and the broad Connecticut River to the other as it heads due north.

The distinctive roof of a New England covered bridge served two purposes: first, as a shield against poor weather; and also as a method of keeping horses that were pulling carriages from being spooked by the river waters rushing below.

BELOW:
covered bridges are found all over New England.

Shortly thereafter, the road arrives in **Windsor ⓫** – a town that rightly claims itself the "Birthplace of Vermont." In Elijah West's tavern on Main Street, now known as **Old Constitution House** (tel: 802-672-3773; open Wed–Sun late May–mid-Oct), Vermont's Constitution was drafted and signed in 1777, making it for a time an independent republic that was neither British nor American. This independent streak still marks Vermonters today – in the 1990s, they elected and re-elected the only Socialist sitting in the US House of Representatives.

Map on page 104
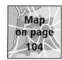

The **Simon Pearce** glassblowing shop, also in Windsor, may be one of the nation's finest such shops. (The establishment also operates a restaurant on Main Street in **Quechee**, serving meals on the glass. "Don't wash just *any* dishes" says a help-wanted advertisement.)

Still heading north on Vermont 5, you dip and curve riverside and soon enough come to **Norwich**, a tiny, typical Vermont town with its classic general store – the first of many you'll see on this drive. Near the interstate, the local **King Arthur Flour Baker's Store** sells the company's superior stone-milled flour, plus some top-grade cooking supplies and cookbooks, at a picturesque store on Vermont 5. Outside town, the **Montshire Museum of Science** (tel: 802-649-2200; www.montshire.net; open daily) provides children with a terrific hands-on look at ecology and nature amid riverside fields.

Ivy-clad Dartmouth

Cross the Connecticut River into New Hampshire once more on Route 120 to **Hanover**, an attractive town largely thanks to the elegant, ivy-clad presence of **Dartmouth College**. Dartmouth was founded in 1769 by the Reverend Eleazer Wheelock to educate (and, of course, convert) local Indian children. Now, it is one of America's finest private colleges, with especially strong programs in the sciences, humanities and Native American studies. The pleasing Dartmouth Green is a center of town life, surrounded on all sides by college buildings, including the **Hopkins Center** performing arts space – designed by the same architect who later went on to plan New York's Metropolitan Opera House.

The downtown district also features the excellent Dartmouth Bookstore, as well as one of New England's most-beloved natural food cooperatives. It isn't unusual to see haggard, unshaven hikers lugging huge backpacks tramping through town, either, as the bridge from Norwich and downtown Hanover form one of the most civilized stretches of the entire Appalachian Trail *(see page 110)*.

For a little more of New England character before moving west, continue farther north on Route 5, which snuggles between the interstate and the river, mostly passing through dairy pastures and cornfields. Several of the small towns have interesting gathering spots, such as the Fairlee Diner in **Fairlee**, Vermont. Across a small bridge from Fairlee, in **Orford**, New Hampshire, beautiful white wooden and red brick homes from the 1900s – not to mention the Orford Social Library and a general store full of local characters – line the town's main street. It was from here that local car salesman Mel Thompson rose to become a multi-

BELOW: Dartmouth College in Hanover, New Hampshire, dates from 1769.

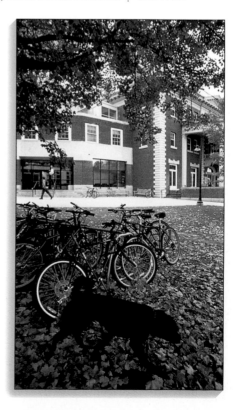

term governor of the state, never straying from his extremely Republican view of things. On summer weekends, the **Mount Cube Sugar House**, in the hills east of Orford down Route 25A, serves huge breakfasts with their own maple syrup: a delicious taste of the region that should not be missed if you are in the area. Locals swear by them.

From Hanover, cross back to Vermont and proceed a short distance south before turning west on US 4. You soon come to little Quechee, nondescript but for deep **Quechee Gorge**. This 165-foot (50-meter) cut in the rock, made by the Ottauquechee River, is accessible from several viewpoints; you can't hike down the steep, narrow walls, but you can hike the woods and camp in a state park across the street. Unfortunately, a small tourist complex has sprung up right beside the gorge.

Leaf-peepers

Ten miles (16 km) beyond, compact **Woodstock ⑫** sits prettily among trees, ridges and river. On an autumn afternoon, the town is jammed tightly with leaf-peepers crowding the streets, but early October is the time to come – an annual chili cook-off and apple festival and other autumn events compete with the stunning foliage. From Downtown, it is just a few paces to the handsome **Middle Bridge** covered bridge, which is located beside a row of exceptionally fine homes surrounding the village green.

The Woodstock Historical Society leads tours of some of these homes that encircle the central common, and two outstanding museums nearby – the **Billings Farm and Museum** (a look at 19th-century dairy farming; open daily Apr–Oct) and the **Vermont Institute of Natural Science** (tel: 802-457-2779;

BELOW: the Appalachian Trail stretches from Maine to Georgia.

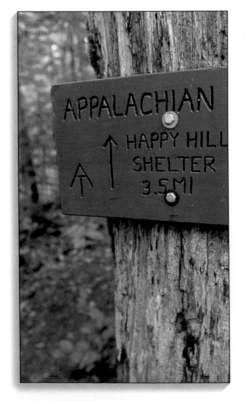

APPALACHIAN TRAIL

A pleasant 19-mile (31-km) drive along SR 100 from the town of Bridgewater Corners, Vermont, leads to one of the longest marked footpaths in the world, winding a total of 2,135 miles (3,435 km) from Maine to Georgia. Benton MacKaye, who proposed the trail in 1921, wrote about his great project: "The ultimate purpose? There are three things: 1) to walk; 2) to see; 3) to *see* what you see... Some people like to record how speedily they can traverse the length of the trail, but I would give a prize for the ones who took the longest time." His idea was for a super-trail running the length of the industrialized East Coast. This would be a trail that was wild, yet within reach of major urban centers and the throngs of workers who were alienated from outdoor life. He felt the trail would grace all who spent time on it with the healing tonic of wilderness. Winding from north to south, it traverses the many distinct ranges that make up the Appalachian chain, touching the tops of many of the states it enters. Though not the first of its kind, the Appalachian Trail remains a favorite with outdoors people, enjoying celebrity status among the great hikes of the world. For more information, call the Appalachian Trail Conservancy at 304-535-6331.

www.vinsweb.org; open daily; closed Mon–Tues Nov–Apr), with its good record of nursing birds of prey back to health – provide additional diversion. Just 2 miles (3 km) west of town via US 4, the community of **West Woodstock** already has a slightly less manicured feel. The White Cottage Snack Bar serves up fried clams, ice cream and similar summertime snacks, while the Woodstock Farmers' Market purveys gourmet foods and produce next door. You pass a llama farm, dipping with the steepening terrain, and go several more miles to **Bridgewater Corners**, home of the Long Trail Brewing Company and its locally popular Long Trail Ale.

Turn left onto Vermont 100A for a beautiful little detour through some of the state's nicest scenery – past haybales and syrup signs, red barns, spotted cows and grazing horses: pure Vermont. The stretch is particularly beautiful when leaves are changing color. About 6 miles (10 km) along, take a right onto the dirt drive for a look at the **President Calvin Coolidge State Historic Site** (tel: 802-672-3773; open daily from end of May to mid-Oct), the farm homestead where "silent Cal" was raised and periodically returned.

When President Warren G. Harding died in office in 1923, Coolidge was sworn into office on the spot here by his father, a notary public. He remains to this day a hero to Vermonters, symbol of a kind of taciturn, humanistic work ethic that still drives Vermont farmers and politicians alike.

Kids love the tour of Ben & Jerry's ice cream plant in Waterbury, Vermont.

Famed footpaths

Continue on Route 100A until it ends at Vermont 100, making a right and driving north. You pass numerous B&Bs in the agreeable small towns; if you're in a hurry to get west, turn at **Killington** and cut through the scenic mountains to Rutland. With time to spare, however, you should continue north on Route 100 to the junction of routes 4 and 100. This is the spot where two of America's famous hiking trails – the **Appalachian Trail** ⑬ and Vermont's **Long Trail** – diverge. Making a right on 100 north, you can park and take a short stroll on the trail to the left (through Gifford Woods State Park) or the right, around the shore of Kent Pond.

BELOW:
ice cream for all.

Stay on Vermont 100 through little **Stockbridge** until it connects with Route 125, then make a choice: food or nature? If you are hungry, continue north up 100 to **Waterbury** and take a tour of the Ben & Jerry's ice cream plant. We, however, suggest a left turn onto Vermont 125 to begin 13 gorgeous miles (21 km) of national forest land. You'll discover why it's been designated a state scenic route as you wind through **Green Mountain National Forest**. Partway along, just before **Ripton**, pull over for a peek at several Robert Frost-related sites.

Frost, one of America's best-loved poets, moved to this area and wrote his finest poetry in a farmhouse here. **Bread Loaf**, the complex of yellow buildings on the right, is a campus of Middlebury College that becomes an internationally famous school of writing each summer; the yellow Bread Loaf Inn offers lodging on-site. The **Robert Frost Interpretive Trail**, on the left, combines passages from his writing with the typical elements – stone walls, maple trees – that inspired it. There are also a number of impressive hikes off the main road, clearly sign-posted, although to reach them requires driving some rough gravel and dirt roads. The twisty final miles of Route 125 snake down the western slope of the Green Mountains beside the Middlebury River and must be driven carefully, but they are rewarded at last with a stunning view of the misty stacks of the Adirondacks as the route coasts down into the village of East Middlebury. At US 7, turn right and enter **Middlebury**, a college town with its own handsome buildings and microbrewery.

The illustrator Norman Rockwell (1894–1918) was known for his realistic and humorous scenes of small-town life. His best work appeared as covers for the magazine The Saturday Evening Post.

Now, we head south on Vermont 30, which angles almost due south. It's delightful driving through classic Vermont scenes of grazing spotted cows, rivers, red barns and the like. You pass several quiet lakes with good camping grounds, then through **Pawlet**, which possesses one of Vermont's best country stores, now called Mach's: among the wooden iceboxes of beer and stacks of rakes and rubbers, you can actually see the river running beneath the store through a grate. It was once a hotel, and there's a sepia 1900s photograph of dapper men with mustaches who once stayed at the place.

Next comes East Rupert, and then **Dorset ⓮**, an attractive town with a down-town golf course close beside classic New England homes, many of which are now characteristic bed-and-breakfast establishments.

Rockwell country

Crowds begin appearing again in **Manchester**, a tourist-filled town nestled on the **Battenkill River**, itself one of the world's finest fly-fishing rivers. You can learn more at the **American Museum of Fly Fishing** (tel: 802-362-3300; www.amff.com; open daily), which displays the rods and gear of famous fishermen

BELOW: shopping for arts and crafts.

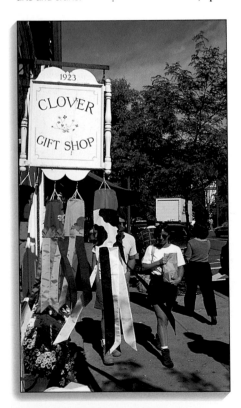

like Hemingway and Eisenhower, among others. Not surprisingly, this is also home to the outdoor equipment and clothing manufacturer Orvis and loads of other shops – no longer the real Vermont, despite the presence of Norman Rockwell memorabilia everywhere.

Breeze right through town and continue south down Vermont 7A, here known as "Historic 7A," as it passes Robert Todd Lincoln's former home, **Hildene** (tel: 802-362-1788; www.hildene.org; open Thur–Mon Nov–May, daily June–Oct). This beautiful Georgian Revival mansion features a huge pipe organ, and just after Christmas tour guides lead walks through the home by candlelight; the rest of the year, you can tour it by day. The road then takes in the pleasing ridge of **Mount Equinox**, especially stunning in fall. A toll road rises to the top, if you wish to drive it. Apple orchards, meadows and cows continue to be the prevailing themes along 7A.

At **Arlington ⓯**, you can have a look at the famed **Norman Rockwell Exhibit** (tel: 802-375-6423 closed Tues), a collection of the artist's work. The artist lived in two homes in this area, and locals often served as models for his so-American portraits.

Turn west onto Vermont 313, and as you leave town and Vermont, there's one final treat: just before the New York border you pass by the covered **Arlington Bridge**, a small bridge over the Battenkill with plain, typical New England church behind – a com position Rockwell himself was said to have especially loved. As these are a local specialty, this is the last one you'll see on this cross-country trip. Linger awhile contemplating the river – and the New England – you have seen.

Map on page 104

NEW YORK STATE

As you greet the sign welcoming you to **New York** state, you have not only crossed a line on a map separating one state from another. You have also crossed an imaginary, but no less real, boundary where yard sales at once become tag sales, tonic becomes soda, beef-on-*wick* replaces grinders for lunch and where the clipped, shorthand speech of New Englanders becomes the louder, more persistent one of New Yorkers.

Entering on State Route 313, you arrive shortly to a pleasant picnic spot beside the Battenkill River. Then you pass through **Cambridge**, a small town with antiques and an attractive little general store, more form than function these days. You'll also pass the Cambridge Hotel, built in 1885, self-proclaimed "home of pie à la mode." Change to Route 372, join State 29 and continue driving west. Ten or 12 miles (16–19 km) on, the road crosses the **Hudson River** at Schuylerville, unimpressive here since it's split up into so many parts; in fact, the great river seems tame indeed – there is no hint yet of the power and beauty that will soon fill a great valley and inspire countless artists.

It was only a few miles downstream from these banks that the two Battles of Saratoga were fought in 1777, resulting in a crushing defeat of British troops – a crucial momentum swing in the Revolution. A turnoff leads to the **Saratoga National Historical Park** (tel: 518-664-9821; www.nps.gov/sara; open daily), commemorating the battles, where you can drive or be guided through the fields.

BELOW: Arlington, Vermont, is the home of the Norman Rockwell Exhibit. The artist often used local people for his rural portraits.

Continue to **Saratoga Springs** ⓰, long a resort town due to the mineral springs that bubble up from beneath it and more recently a popular weekend town. It is also home to Skidmore College students and faculty, and thus a fair number of coffeehouses, ice-cream shops and bookstores speckle the downtown district. The Saratoga Performing Arts Center, within a green park on the southern edge of town, frequently hosts big-name concerts. Summertime also brings crowds to the harness track here, where horse racing is king – witness the presence here of the **National Museum of Racing and Hall of Fame** (tel: 518-584-0400; www.racingmuseum.org; open daily). Finally, don't miss **Caffé Lena**, an upstairs joint on a central street which is said to have been the first American coffeehouse to host regular folk music performances. It still does.

Oh, the Er-i-ee is arisin' / And the gin is agettin' low / And I scarcely think we'll get a drink / 'Til we get to Buffalo –
OLD ERIE CANAL SONG

Erie Canal

Route 50 brings you south through Ballston Spa, home of the eccentric **National Bottle Museum** (tel: 518-885-7589; www.nationalbottlemuseum.org; open daily in summer; closed weekends in winter), to the Mohawk River and the Erie Canal. Tracing this great inland water route west to Buffalo is not the shortest way to get from here to there, but it is a route that runs rich with American history.

The idea of a canal connecting the port cities of Albany (on the Hudson River) and Buffalo (on Lake Erie) was greeted with skepticism and derision at first. Detractors called it "Clinton's Ditch" after DeWitt Clinton, champion of the project. Completed in 1825, and eventually bypassed in the early 20th century, the Erie Canal was responsible for the settling of the Midwest and the rise of the state of New York. The old canal towns, once the sites of boisterous activity, are quiet now, many down on their luck.

BELOW: father, son and the family business.

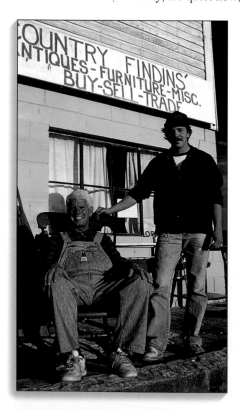

Begin tracing the route in **Schenectady** ⓱. A plaque in this town sums up its early history: "Settled by Van Curler 1661. Burned by French and Indians Feb 8, 1690."

Because it was the farthest west of all Dutch settlements in the New World, the town's settlers built a stockade around the land, which was bounded by the Mohawk River and the Binne Kill. The stockade is now gone, dismantled during the American Revolution, but the area it protected is still known as the **Stockade** and is now a historic district containing an eclectic array of buildings that spans over three centuries of American life.

Schenectady's strategic riverfront location has historically made it an important center for commerce and transportation. The city supplied Revolutionary troops battling in the Mohawk Valley, and in the 19th century it was a major port. In 1931, it became the terminus of the nation's first passenger steam train, the "DeWitt Clinton," an innovation stimulated by the protracted process of traversing the 23 locks between Albany and Schenectady.

Schenectady has not been exempt from the exodus of industry out of the Northeast. In the 19th century it progressed from being a center for the manufacture of brooms, to "the city that lights and hauls the world." The Schenectady Locomotive Works (later the American Locomotive Company) opened in 1851

Map on page 104

followed by Edison and his Machine Works – which later became General Electric. The Locomotive Company pulled out of town in 1970, but the lights are still switched on at GE.

Leatherstocking trails

New York's heartland is generally considered to begin west of the industrial triangle of Albany, Troy and Schenectady. This essentially rural area north of the Catskill Mountains and south of the Adirondacks is also known as the **Leatherstocking District**, after the protective garb once worn by trailblazers. Native son James Fenimore Cooper immortalized the region in his *Leatherstocking Tales* and other works. And the numerous Revolutionary War battles that took place throughout the Mohawk River Valley are the subject of Walter D. Edmonds' historical novel, *Drums Along the Mohawk*.

Schenectady's Broadway leaves town in a southwesterly direction (State 7). It passes through Rotterdam and Duanesburg, where State 7, US 20 and I-88 converge. From there, US 20 travels to **Esperance** on Schoharie Creek. This pleasant town features old houses, antique shops and the obligatory country store. About 8 miles (13 km) south of here along State 30, which follows the creek, is the town of **Schoharie**, the third oldest village upstate. Its **Old Stone Fort Museum Complex** (tel: 518-295-7192; May–Oct daily) started as a church in 1722, became a fort during the Revolution, and has served as museum and library specializing in early Americana since 1889.

An interesting chapter out of Schoharie's past includes the Middleburg and Schoharie Railroad, built in the late 1860s. This short, 6-mile (10-km) run down the Schoharie Creek Valley transported hops and other local products. The railroad's president was fond of pointing out that although it wasn't as long as other railroads, it was just as wide. In its last days, the line's single locomotive faltered physically and financially, and operation was finally stopped in 1936.

Take me out to the ballgame

US 20 west of Sharon and Sharon Springs is one of the loveliest stretches of road in central New York, providing a panoramic view of **Cherry Valley**, the site of an infamous massacre in 1778, now crimson only in autumn.

It would be a mistake not to detour 10 miles (16 km) south down State 80 to visit **Cooperstown ⓲**, a charming town with several important attractions. James Fenimore Cooper's house and museum is one, but the main draw is the **National Baseball Hall of Fame** (tel: 607-547-7200; www.baseballhalloffame.org; open daily) – a tremendous experience of the history of the sport, which has inspired countless novels, films and even poems. Make time for a visit to the monuments, biographies and collections here.

Past **Richfield Springs**, known for its sulfur springs and fossil-hunting grounds, State 167 travels north toward **Little Falls**. Not far up this road stands the **Russian Orthodox Holy Trinity Monastery**, starting to the eye in a land of colonial history, 19th-century buildings and rustic farm houses. Little Falls'

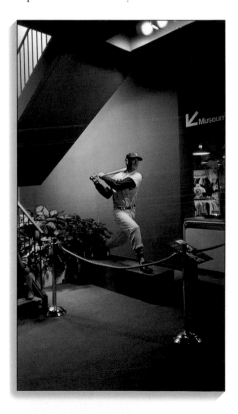

BELOW: the National Baseball Hall of Fame is located in Cooperstown, New York.

Herkimer Home, former residence of Revolutionary War hero Brigadier General Nicholas Herkimer, provides a glimpse of colonial life, with maple sugar gathering, sheep shearing and other exhibitions. This canal town once had the world's highest lock, at 41 feet (12.5 meters).

West along State 5 is Herkimer, named after the general whose statue still commands attention. The **Herkimer County Courthouse** was the site of the Gillette murder trial, which inspired Theodore Dreiser to write *An American Tragedy*, depicting the dark side of the American dream. George Stevens' film version, *A Place in the Sun*, featured Montgomery Clift, Shelley Winters and Elizabeth Taylor.

Christmas all year-round

Between Herkimer and **Mohawk ⑲**, along State 5S, stands the **Fort Herkimer Church**, built in 1730. Mohawk's most unusual attraction, however, is **Dorothea's Christmas**, an estate overlooking the Mohawk Valley that harks back to 1790. The front parlor and ballroom of the 23-room house contain 20 Christmas trees decorated with European glass ornaments and antique miniatures. This fanciful indoor forest is open from May Day to Christmas Eve.

Ilion, a small industrial pocket, is located just beyond Mohawk. The interesting **Remington Firearms Plant and Museum** (tel: 315-895-3200; closed Sun) here is devoted to the great guns made by Remington Arms Company, past and present. Continuing west, the road terminates in **Utica ⑳**, the only city of any size you'll have seen since Schenectady.

Utica, once named Fort Schuyler, is rich in colonial and revolutionary history. But the biggest attraction here is the **Munson-Williams-Proctor Arts**

BELOW: boat rides on the Erie Canal are a good way to see the sights.

Institute (tel: 315-797-0000; www.mwpai.edu; closed Mon), reputed to have one of the finest collections of 18th- through 20th-century American and European art in the northeast, housed in a building designed by Philip Johnson. On a much less cultural note, Utica's **Matt Brewery** serves its beer up in a Victorian-era tavern built in 1888. It's all part of a brewery tour that culminates in a trolley ride to the tavern.

State 69 leaves Utica for **Rome ㉑**, best known for its crucial role in the building of the Erie Canal. Beyond this point, there were no continuous natural water routes westward. This is where excavation began. Commemorating this important chapter in its history is the **Erie Canal Village** (tel: 315-337-3999; www.eriecanalvillage.net; open Wed–Sun Memorial Day–Labor Day), a reconstructed 1840s village near a refurbished section of the old canal. The biggest tourist attraction here is the ***Independence***, a packet boat towed down the canal by horses for a half-hour ride. When the snow flies, the village also features sleigh rides, a pleasant experience on a crisp, clear day.

The canal brought industry to Rome, some of which remains. There is also a military presence here – the Strategic Air Command's 416th Bombardment Wing at Griffiss Air Force Base. Tours of the base are available throughout the summer months. Rome has always been serious about America: this, after all, is where native son Francis Bellamy wrote the famous "Pledge of Allegiance" that every American school child learns by heart.

State 46 takes you from Rome to **Oneida**, still home to the Oneida Indians. The Oneida Community, associated with this town but actually just southeast in Sherrill, was established in the mid-19th century by John Humphrey Noyes and his followers. Calling themselves perfectionists, they adhered to a strict sexual code as part of a community-determined system of selective breeding. In their spare time, they produced high quality silver-plated flatware. The community was dissolved in 1881, but the silver-plate business continues to thrive.

From Oneida, **Chittenango** is a short drive along State 5. Don't be surprised, in town, to see a yellow brick sidewalk, for this is "**Oztown, USA.**" The sidewalk is a tribute to L. Frank Baum, author of the beloved *Wizard of Oz*. Stay on State 5 and it will lead right into Syracuse, the biggest city for miles around in these parts.

Finger Lakes

Busy **Syracuse ㉒** is the urban gateway to the Finger Lakes. State 5 becomes Erie Boulevard as it cuts through the heart of the city along a path carved by the Erie Canal. The **Weughlock Building**, built in 1849 in Greek-Revival style, once weighed canal boats for the purpose of toll collection. At the turn of the 19th century, it was converted into an office building, while in its most recent reincarnation it serves as the **Erie Canal Museum** (tel: 315-471-0593; www.eriecanalmuseum.org; closed Mon).

Thanks to the canal, this was once a center for the salt trade, and some still refer to it as "Salt City." The town boomed during the 19th and early 20th centuries on the back of salt and other industries, and its well-preserved architecture testifies to former prosperity.

Map on page 104

Ride a bike along the Seneca Lake Wine Trail that winds around Seneca Lake.

BELOW: Finger Lakes vineyards produce wine for the East Coast.

TIP

In Auburn, New York, be sure to visit the Harriet Tubman home. Tubman was an escaped slave who coordinated a network called the Underground Railroad to spirit other slaves out of the South.

BELOW: the former mansion of George Eastman, who founded Kodak, now houses the International School of Photography.

The **Landmark Theatre**, an ornate "fantasy palace" built in the 1920s, now functions as a multi-dimensional entertainment center. But the main draw here today is **Syracuse University**, elevated on a hill above the city, which brings crowds of students, sports fans and other audiences to its huge **Carrier Dome**. Basketball games are especially well-attended, though football games and rock concerts follow a close second. For the more sedate, the campus also offers the **Joe and Emily Lowe Art Gallery**. Those same art lovers also should not miss the **Everson Museum of Art** (tel: 315-474-6064; www.everson.org; closed Mon), designed by renowned architect I.M. Pei. State 5 leaves Syracuse on its way to **Camillus**, where you can canoe to your heart's content along 7 miles (11 km) of navigable canal in the **Camillus-Erie Canal Town Park**. Farther along, State 5 merges with US 20, a route that strings together the northern tips of the largest **Finger Lakes**.

Following close on the heels of the Leatherstocking region, this series of 11 watery depressions was created by scraping glaciers. The region is characterized by vineyards, gracious inns, water pursuits and hot-air ballooning. The area's vines look especially beautiful when their leaves begin to turn coppery red in late summer, and the colorful balloons are also an attractive sight. The small city of **Auburn**, on US 20/Route 5, isn't quite set on the lakes but does have one site to visit: the **home of Harriet Tubman** (tel: 315-252-2081) on South Street.

Seneca Lake

After Auburn, US 20/Route 5 then passes Cayuga Lake and follows the Seneca River to **Seneca Falls** ㉓, where the First Women's Rights Convention was convened. The site has been developed into a National Historic Site and includes the **National Women's Hall of Fame** (tel: 315-568-8060; www.greatwomen.org; open daily May–Sept; closed Sun–Tues from Oct–Apr). **Waterloo**, also in between fingers, prides itself on being the birthplace of Memorial Day. The road through here passes by the old Scythe Tree, upon which local farm boys planted their scythes on their way to wars past.

Seneca Lake follows, the town of **Geneva** ㉔ its jewel, replete with elegant inns and mansions. This town is also the gateway to a circuit round the lake known as the Seneca Lake Wine Trail; the drive takes in several dozen vintners, including two specializing in champagne and mead (honey wine). It is very pretty in fall, when the grape and maple leaves are changing color. Seneca Lake may seem small and thin, but it's actually one of the deepest freshwater lakes in the world – going down and down to a depth of more than 600 feet (180 meters). The US Navy used the lake to test depth charges during World War II.

Approximately 20 miles (32 km) west of Geneva on US 20/Route 20 is **Canandaigua**, at the northern tip of Canandaigua Lake. Of particular interest here is the Federal-style **Granger Homestead** ㉕ (tel: 585-394-1472; www.grangerhomestead.org; open late May–late Oct Tues–Fri plus Sat–Sun from June–Aug) built in 1816, with its collection of 40 horse-drawn vehicles. North of town – take State 21 – are the **Sonnenberg Gardens** (tel: 585-394-4922; www.sonnenberg.org

Map on page 104

open daily May–Oct), acres of Victoriana with a mansion incorporating the Wine Center, a collection of gourmet foods and wines from the Finger Lakes region.

Remain on State 21 and you will pass through Shortsville on the way to **Palmyra**, a pilgrimage site for Mormons. This was the home of Joseph Smith who, according to Mormon belief, received and translated ancient records in the Book of Mormon, buried them here and subsequently founded the Church in the 1820s. Religious sites and a replica of Smith's farm homestead are open to the public, as is the **Martin Harris Landmark Cobblestone House**. Built in 1850, the house is typical of the farmers' homes that sprang up along the Erie Canal.

It's about 20 miles (32 km) from Palmyra to Rochester along State 31. The names of the towns along the way are perhaps more exotic than the towns: after Palmyra comes Macedon and then Egypt, where the New York State Barge Canal stands in for the Nile.

Pretty as a picture

Like other upstate cities, **Rochester** ㉖ thrived during the canal era and suffered economically with the advent of alternative modes of transportation. But it has adjusted to change better than its siblings and is on the upswing as a center for high-tech industries, while still preserving much of its 19th-century architectural ambiance. Eastman Kodak is the big name in Rochester, so big they still call it "Picture City." Kodak offers tours of its facilities.

The former mansion of George Eastman, who founded Kodak, now houses the **International Museum of Photography and Film** (tel: 585-271-3361; www. eastmanhouse.org; closed Mon), devoted to the history of this art and science. The **Eastman School of Music** sponsors musical events, from jazz to rock to folk to

BELOW: U-pick all U-like at this strawberry farm near Seneca Lake.

Map on page 104

symphonic works, while the **Eastman Theatre** is the home of the Rochester Phil-harmonic. For those who still enjoy childish things, the **Strong National Museum of Play** (tel: 585-263-2700; www.strongmuseum.org; open daily) has one of the most extensive collections of dolls in the western world, as well as many exhibits relating to life in early America. Winters are severe in Rochester, thanks to its northern location on Lake Ontario, the easternmost Great Lake. But in late May, **Highland Park** is abloom during the Lilac Festival – featuring the world's largest display of these blossoms – when Rochester really is "pretty as a picture."

On to the falls

State 31 continues along the path of the Erie Canal from Rochester to Niagara Falls. The names of the towns along this route, including Spencerport, Brock-port, Middleport and Gasport, continue to remind the traveler of the canal's former importance. But there are other reminders as well. **Medina 27** has cobblestone buildings and Culvert Road, which passes beneath the canal. **Lock-port** also has its share of cobblestone houses, though it is best known for its magnificent flight of five locks.

From Lockport, State 31 (here called Saunders Setara Settlement Road) travels directly to **Niagara Falls 28**. Once known as America's "Honeymoon Capital," the town is fond of referring to itself as an international tourist desti-nation. And, indeed, this remains one of the top tourist draws in all the US despite its endless tackiness. Quite simply, the 700,000 gallons (3 million liters) of water plummeting from top to bottom each second here are a wondrous assault on the senses, something that must be experienced while in America. The magnetic draw of these falls has even inspired some visitors to attempt cross-ing them on a tightrope or riding them in a barrel with sometimes-tragic results; both activities are now illegal, though daredevils still occasionally try.

The natural beauty of the site might have been irreparably compromised had it not been for the efforts of landscape architect Frederick Law Olmsted, landscape painter Frederic Church and others. Their "Free Niagara" (from commercialism) campaign resulted in the establishment of the Niagara Reservation in 1875. One of the best ways to experience the falls today is by donning the provided foul-weather gear and taking a boat ride on the *Maid of the Mist*. Alter-natively, you might drive across the river to Canada and enjoy what many consider to be a superior view.

River Road hugs the eastern branch of the Niagara River, past the falls and through industrial landscape to **Buffalo 29**. Like other industrial giants past their prime, New York's second-largest city has acquired a somewhat bad reputation. As the 19th-century ter-minus of the Erie Canal, Buffalo once served as a fun-nel through which raw materials, cash, pioneers and immigrant labor flowed into the Midwestern states. Today, it's a bit ragged. Still, there are reasons to stop for a visit; you can eat well and cheaply here. A local specialty is spicy chicken wings, which anywhere else are called "Buffalo wings," but here are "wings." You might like to go to the source, the Anchor Bar, whose owner is said to have invented the dish.

BELOW: late afternoon in the summertime.
RIGHT: Niagara Falls and the *Maid of the Mist* boat tour: weatherproof gear is provided.

BUFFALO TO THE BADLANDS

Map on page 124

Follow the shores of Lake Erie though New York, Pennsylvania and Ohio, then continue through the Midwest and the Great Lakes for the bleak, beautiful hills of the Badlands

Buffalo was an important point of departure for 19th-century settlers heading for the Midwest. From Buffalo, they traveled to major ports of the Great Lakes in order to start their new life. Today, the road from Buffalo to the Midwestern states follows the shore of Lake Erie through New York, Pennsylvania and Ohio. Although known primarily as an industrial area, there are still some unspoiled stretches of coastline that are remarkable for their beauty. At Toledo, the highway diverges from the shoreline on its way to big, busy, beautiful Chicago.

South of Buffalo along US 62 is the town of **Hamburg**, where the hamburger – perhaps America's greatest contribution to world cuisine – was purportedly invented in 1885. In celebration of the centennial of this event, J. Wellington Wimpy came to town and was honored as the undefeated hamburger-eating champion of the world. Essentially a rural town, Hamburg has been host to America's largest county fair since 1868. It's only about 5 miles (8 km) from here to Lake Erie, where you can pick up State 5, a lakeside road that takes you to Ohio.

LEFT: heading to the home of the urban blues: Chicago.
BELOW: buy homemade crafts to take home.

Antique trail

Lake Erie has suffered more than its sister Great Lakes at the hands of industry, yet miles of its beautiful, sandy, ocean-like shoreline are still unspoiled. The stretch from Silver Creek, New York, to the Pennsylvania border has been called an "antique trail" for the abundance of antique shops located just off the road. But more importantly, it cuts directly across a region devoted to the gentle art of viniculture.

State 5 takes you past terrain blanketed with grape vines and other fruit trees. In **Silver Creek**, go straight to the site of the **Skew Arch Railroad Bridge** on Jackson Street. Built on an angle in 1869, it is one of only two such bridges in the world.

Dunkirk and Fredonia follow, in the heart of the Concord Grape Belt (the world's largest) which extends into Pennsylvania. **Dunkirk**, with its natural harbor, is also a center for boating and the "Chautauqua (County) wine trail." **Fredonia**, to the south, is home of Grange Number One, America's first such farmers' organization.

Continuing along the lake, the road passes pretty **Lake Erie State Park ㉚** in **Brocton**, where campers will find a pleasant place to pitch their tents. **Westfield** follows, calling itself "The Grape Juice Capital of the World" and dominated by the various production facilities of a popular grape jelly. Combined with peanut butter and two pieces of bread, it vies with Hamburg's hamburgers as *the* American food.

There is no obvious transition between New York and its westerly neighbor other than a town named State

Buffalo to Badlands

62	Buffalo **29**
75	Hamburg
	Silver Creek
5	Dunkirk
	Brocton
	Lake Erie State Park **30**
	New York
5	North East
	Pennsylvania

Pennsylvania / Ohio — Presque Isle State Park — Erie **31** — Junc 1

90

Cleveland **32**

90	Junc 174B	77	Peninsula
			Cuyahoga Valley N.R.A.
2			Canton

Marblehead — 163 — 2 — Junc 7

Detroit — 75 — Toledo **33** — Junc 19

20

Ohio / Indiana

Limberlost State Hist. Site — 9 — 6 — 69 — Junc 148 / Junc 134 — Chain O'Lakes State Park

9

Ligonier — 5 — Nappanee

34 Topeka — ★ Amish Acres

6 — Westville — 2

130 Valparaiso

Indiana / Illinois — 90

94 — Chicago **35**

Illinois / Wisconsin

50 — Lake Geneva

12 — Kettle Moraine State Forest

18 — Madison **36**

10 — Mount Horeb
12 — Dodgeville
23 — ★ House on the Rock

★ Taliesin **37**

Richland Center

14

Wisconsin / Minnesota — 90 — Coon Valley **38**

61

Red Wing **39**

40 Minneapolis, St Paul — 61

19 — New Prague **41**

Le Sueur

169

Mankato

14
68

14

23 — Pipestone **42**

Minnesota / South Dakota — Jasper — 269 — ★ Devil's Gulch **43**

Garretson

Sioux Falls **44**

90

Mitchell **45**
★ Corn Palace

Junc 212

83

Pierre **46**

14

240 — Cottonwood

Black Hills — Badlands National Park **47**

Line, Pennsylvania. The landscape remains the same – a sparkling lake on one side and lush vineyards on the other. In season, roadside stands sell the local grapes in every imaginable form. Only 63 miles (101 km) of Lake Erie shoreline prevent Pennsylvania from being a landlocked state (an economic decision to do with lake access), and it knows just what to do with it. Past State Line is the town of **North East**, center of the state's tiny wine industry. Several wineries do fairly good business here and all offer tours and tastings.

About 15 miles (24 km) west of wine country on State 5 sits the city of **Erie** ❸, off whose shores Commander Oliver Hazard Perry's fleet defeated the British in the Battle of Lake Erie during the War of 1812. Despite his motto – "Don't give up the ship!" – the flagship *Niagara* was left to sink in what later became known as **Misery Bay**. That bay is now a quiet fishing cove off Presque Isle, and the ship was rescued a century later. A reconstructed *Niagara* now sits high and dry along the Erie waterfront.

On the other side is Erie's finest physical feature, **Presque Isle**, a claw of land – almost an island, really – reaching out into the lake. You can drive its length, pass Presque Isle Lighthouse, and then loop around along the southern end going past Misery Bay. You'll find lovely sand beaches, wooded trails, fishing holes and lazy lagoons.

THE TOP OF OHIO

Before you can say "knee high by the Fourth of July," you're in Ohio. Interstate 90 cuts through the gently rolling farmland of this part of the state past Ashtabula, Geneva and Euclid before reaching the **Cleveland** ❸ area. Cleveland has its share of high culture – the Cleveland Orchestra and the **Cleveland Museum of Art** (tel: 216-421-7340; www.clevelandart.org; closed Mon) – and pop culture – the **Rock and Roll Hall of Fame** (tel: 216-781-ROCK, www.rockhall.com; open daily). The latter covers everyone from Louis Jordan to John Lennon, with exhibits including report cards and Jim Morrison's Cub Scout uniform. Hungarian food is a particular specialty of Cleveland, so try some dishes before leaving town.

It's well worth a short detour south from Cleveland to explore the green **Cuyahoga Valley**. The valley's ridges were settled during the late 18th century by the New Englanders who first surveyed its boundaries, and their influence remains today. The town of **Peninsula**, reached by Interstates 77, 80 and 271, is a prime example – all Cape Cod-style whitewashed houses fronted by maple trees. A scenic small-gauge railroad line runs upriver to the even smaller Boston, and a cycling path runs along the Ohio & Erie canal towpath.

Map on page 124

Football Hall of Fame

Sport fans will want to make a brief detour south down I-77, through the smoky industrial city of Akron – tire and rubber capital of America – to the city of **Canton**. Here, the **Pro Football Hall of Fame** (tel: 330-456-8207; www.pro-footballhof.com; open daily) offers a look at the heroes of American football. Things peak in late August, when an annual game is played here to kick off each season and to celebrate the new class of inductees.

State 2 leaves Cleveland on its way west, diverging from I-90 and running closer to Lake Erie. At Ceylon, it comes right to the lake, loops around Sandusky, then bridges Sandusky Bay to arrive on the Marblehead Peninsula. State 163 takes you out to land's end and reveals the peninsula as a slightly rundown but refreshingly unpretentious place, full of lively harbors, the Prehistoric Forest, orchards and fruit stands. At its rocky tip is **Marblehead Lighthouse**, which has been in continuous use since 1821, longer than any other beacon on the Great Lakes. It protects ships and boats from this, the most treacherous outcropping along Lake Erie. Looking back south across the bay, you'll see the

Time for lunch: both hamburgers and peanut butter and jelly sandwiches have claims to this part of the US.

BELOW: go slow whenever you see a school bus.

roller coasters and other thrill rides of **Cedar Point** (tel: 419-627-2350; www.cedarpoint.com; open daily mid-May–Aug; weekends Sept–Oct), a popular 364-acre (147-hectare) amusement park located on the tip of a peninsula accessible from Sandusky. Off the Marblehead Peninsula, State 2 proceeds toward Toledo. This region was once part of the **Black Swamp**, a refuge for wildlife which extended from Sandusky to Detroit. Small remnants of the swamp have managed to survive along this route.

Famous hot dogs

The road emerges from the swamp and continues straight as an arrow to the town of **Toledo** ㉝, past bait shops, drive-through liquor stores and drive-in movie theaters. The "Toledo Strip" was once the subject of a border dispute between Ohio and Michigan. When Ohio got the Strip, Michigan got its Upper Peninsula from Wisconsin Territory as compensation – a swap in which Michigan probably made out like a bandit.

At first glance, Toledo seems like an industrial wasteland. Still, there are signs of rejuvenation and redevelopment in the downtown riverfront area along the Maumee. If you've got the time, drop into Tony Packo's Cafe – made famous by Corporal Max Klinger in the long-running TV series *M*A*S*H* – a fun restaurant known for its "Hungarian hot dogs" and quirky collection of hot dog buns autographed by celebrities.

Leaving Toledo and Lake Erie behind at last, US 20 heads due west, cutting straight through Ohio farm country to the Indiana border, a distance of about 60 miles (100 km). The road here parallels the Michigan border, which is just a few miles to the north.

BELOW:
Detroit, Michigan's
Fox Theatre was
built in 1928; the
style is described
as "Siamese
Byzantine."

DETOUR – DETROIT

A 45-mile (72-km) drive beside Lake Erie on I-75 leads from Toledo, Ohio, to Detroit, Michigan – the Motor City. Henry Ford was the single most influential American in motoring history, forming the Ford Motor Company in 1903. Six years later, he had 10,000 orders for his newest car, the Model T, and, by 1919, was selling close to a million cars. His innovations bolstered Detroit's economy, increased the automobile's popularity and gave more people jobs; the city still revolves around his industry. The 260-acre (105-hectare) Henry Ford Museum and Greenfield Village complex in the nearby town of Dearborn is the world's largest indoor/outdoor museum, commemorating Ford's contribution to the city. The Ford Museum holds Henry's collection of wheeled technology and decorative arts, including early automobiles, while the Village houses recreations of famous businesses and residences, including Thomas Edison's Menlo Park laboratory. Detroit is also the home of Motown records, created by former Ford assembly line worker Berry Gordy, Jr, in 1958, which produced stars of the Detroit Sound such as Smokey Robinson and Diana Ross. The Motown Historical Museum charts the label's influence from the 1960s to the present. The Detroit Visitors Bureau is at 800-338-7648 or www.visitdetroit.com.

INDIANA

They call **Indiana** the Hoosier state, and native Indianans Hoosiers. Some say the name comes from a common inquiry from the pioneer days, "who's yer?" Others say the nickname comes from a canal-builder named Samuel Hoosier, who liked to hire Indiana men over other workers; the workers became known as Hoosiers, and the name stuck. Other versions exist as well, and the question may never be properly settled. Whatever the case, this state has produced such high-profile celebrity residents as basketball star Larry Bird, singer John Mellencamp and television personality David Letterman.

Meanest man in the world

Ten miles (16 km) inside the state at Angola, leave US 20 for I-69 south; you'll immediately note a proliferation of stands selling fireworks, which are illegal in adjoining states but freely available here. Fifteen miles (24 km) later, cut over to US 6, which will carry you westward through northern Indiana to Illinois. Fields of golden grain (mostly corn) and silos announce it: you are solidly in the Midwest now. At Brimfield, detour a few miles north up Indiana 9 to the **Limberlost State Historic Site** (tel: 260-368-7428; open Wed–Sun Apr–Dec), a log cabin where the writer lived and wrote her well-loved books and essays about Midwestern nature. It's a peaceful spot among trees on a lake, perfect for a picnic.

On the other side of Brimfield, south on Indiana 9, sits another fine park – **Chain O'Lakes State Park**, a refreshing string of oases in the middle of Noble County. This county was once home of the "meanest man in the world," according to Indiana's contribution to the 1930s WPA American Guide Series. Legend

Map on page 124

At the same time as fans the world over were hysterical with grief over the sudden death of James Dean, the 1950s Hollywood heartthrob was being laid to rest in his Indiana hometown of Fairmount.

BELOW: sunset over golden grain, the Midwest.

has it that this man divorced his wife, after which she landed in the poorhouse. In order to get funds, the institution would farm people out to the highest bidders, and when his ex-wife was put on the auction block, the "meanest man" purchased her to do the housework that his second wife had refused to do.

Back on US 6, tiny towns punctuate a landscape of corn in this region, known for the productivity of its land and for its considerable Amish population. The Amish have been in this area for more than a century. These inventive, industrious and deeply religious people go about their business while shunning worldly things such as buttons, zippers, electricity and motor vehicles. Cut north up Indiana 5 for a look at their farms, homes and horse-drawn buggies.

The Amish splintered off from Swiss Anabaptists in 1693 and settled in Pennsylvania. Now nearly half the states in the US have communities, and the number of followers is growing.

Life in the past lane

First, you pass through **Ligonier**, a real find of a small town complete with a single main street – which, for some reason, boasts a surprising number of Mexican eateries. The interesting town clock here was erected by John Cavin, son of local pioneer Isaac Cavin, in memory of the father who laid the town out in 1835. Also have a look at the **Indiana Historic Radio Museum**, with its collection of old radio memorabilia.

Continue north on State 5 and then turn right at a gas station to reach **Topeka ㉞**, a tiny town whose slogan is "Life in the Past Lane." It's the kind of place where Amish buggies line up in parking lots, and hardware and feed stores outnumber banks three-to-one. Amish ride cycles around town, work the counter at restaurants and just generally blend into life in this farming community. For a more intimate experience, inquire locally about the Amish Bed and Breakfast network, or just drive one of the many other county roads in this area. White

BELOW:
the horse is the prime symbol of the Amish identity.

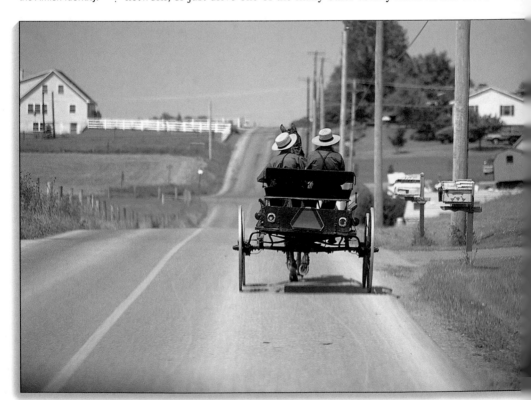

farmhouses with full clotheslines and empty driveways are usually Amish, though you should always check ahead with tourism offices before attempting to visit a private home.

Now, retrace your steps back to US 6 and continue west. **Amish Acres** in **Nappanee** (tel: 800-800-4942; www.amishacres.com; open daily; closed Jan–Feb), a historic farm homestead which interprets the Amish lifestyle for visitors, is fun though a bit over-commercialized. The round red barn hosts theater performances.

Beyond that, it's more lovely country driving through more fields of corn and occasional stands of maple trees. Drifting along US 6 like the "Windiana winds" through the last of rural Indiana before Chicago's industrial fringe, the route takes you over the Kankakee River (a good fishing stream) and on to **Westville**, home of an annual Pumpkin Festival that brings a carnival – and piles of orange pumpkins, of course – to town early each October.

Old-fashioned atmosphere

If you're hungry, make a quick swing down to US 30, on Indiana 2, and the town of **Valparaiso**, where Al's Diner serves up old-fashioned atmosphere in the form of open-faced sandwiches, "Green River" sodas and thick malts beneath walls decked out with pictures of James Dean, Marilyn and Elvis. The town was also the home of bow-tied popcorn magnate Orville Redenbacher, and you'll still find occasional popcorn stands in these parts of northern Indiana. In fact, this is a region of America that sometimes appears permanently frozen in 1950 – you'll encounter plenty of classic cars, crew cuts and friendly folks. Make the most of it before you reach the sensory assault – and very different pace – of **Chicago** ㉟ *(see page 130).*

Map on page 124

The Amish shun worldliness for small-scale values, with emphasis on the community.

BELOW: the Amish have been in Indiana for over 100 years.

CHICAGO:
THE WINDY CITY

Broad-shouldered and big-hearted,
Chicago has a long a list of aliases:
Chitown and Second City are just two

Although a few people might well dispute the authenticity of some of Chicago's various nicknames, one in particular will remain forever true: Crossroads of the Midwest. Chicago's railroad yards are the largest in the world. O'Hare claims to be the world's busiest airport. Even the famed Art Institute of Chicago straddles train tracks. Visitors get around by a light railway known as the El, for "elevated," because it usually is.

The site, at the confluence of the Midwestern prairie, the Chicago River and Lake Michigan, was an obvious place for a town to spring up. With the building of a canal in

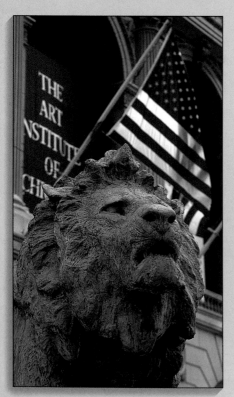

the 1840s – essentially linking the Great Lakes with the Mississippi River drainage system – followed by the advent of railroading, Chicago spread like the proverbial wildfire as commerce and masses of immigrants descended upon it.

Then, in 1871, wildfire became a reality. As the story goes, a certain Mrs O'Leary's cow knocked over a certain lantern, starting a disastrous blaze known as the "Great Chicago Fire." The fire signified the beginning of a new era in Chicago. The city became the workshop of architects like William LeBaron Jenny (the father of the skyscraper), Louis H. Sullivan, Frank Lloyd Wright and later Ludwig Mies van der Rohe.

From the Chicago Water Tower and Pumping Station, the only public building to survive the Great Fire, to the Sears Tower, tallest building in America, the city's buildings and skyline are built to impress.

A few remnants of the 19th century have managed to survive, particularly in the Prairie Avenue Historic District. Once known as the "Avenue of Avenues," the area experienced a mass exodus during the early part of the 20th century. However, the buildings that remain are now being restored and lovingly protected.

Chicago has made the most of its magnificent lakeshore. A huge front yard encompasses 29 miles (47 km) of beaches, wonderful parks with distinct personalities and some of the nation's finest cultural institutions: open daily are the Museum of Science and Industry (tel: 773-684-1414; www.msichicago.org) on the South Side; the Field Museum (tel: 312-922-9410; www.fmnh.org), the excellent Shedd Aquarium (tel: 312-939-2438; www.sheddaquarium.org) and the Art Institute of Chicago (tel: 312-443-3600; www.artic.edu), all in Grant Park. The Art Institute is known for its collection of French Impressionists, and is also the home of that famous stoic couple staring out of Grant Wood's painting *American Gothic*.

Chicago is crazy about outdoor sculpture. All the big names are represented – including Oldenburg, Calder, Picasso, Miro and Dubuffet. Chicago is the ultimate *film noir* set piece. Never has a place been so closely associated with gangsters and political corruption, the latter almost an institution. Eternally proud of those things that set it apart, the city has made little attempt to dispel these images even if they are quite unrealistic today. The real life of Chicago is a bit different. Politics are one face of it: black activist Jesse Jackson started his political career here and former mayor Richard J. Daley – gone but never forgotten – pulled the town's strings for so long that time is now measured in years AD ("After Daley").

This is also a writer's town, as articulate as it is brash. A steady stream of writers have interpreted their hometown for the rest of the world, everyone from James T. Farrell and Richard Wright to Saul Bellow, Studs Terkel, David Mamet and the columnist Mike Royko.

Dark, smoky blues clubs have long been part of the Chicago scene, ever since players and singers from fields in the rural South relocated and invented "electric blues" here. You can hear all about it at B.L.U.E.S. on North Halsted or at the Checker Board Lounge on the city's rougher South Side, where generations of University of Chicago undergraduates have learned about the important things in life from bluesman Muddy Waters.

There's a new brightness to the hip North Side of Chicago, although some locals never wanted the lights to shine – the lights of ivy-walled Wrigley Field, that is. After a long and impassioned debate, the home of the Chicago Cubs was the last Major League baseball park to get lights, thereby facilitating night games. Cub fans are fanatics.

The communities flanking Chicago have become part of the silver screen in a number of films poking fun at suburbia. Glencoe, to the north, is familiar to many as the home of Joel, the fictional teenager played by Tom Cruise in the movie *Risky Business* who submerges his father's Porsche in Lake Michigan. Aurora was the setting for the wacky comedy *Wayne's World*. And Joliet's penitentiary briefly housed John

Belushi in *The Blues Brothers*.

Landlocked Oak Park is west of Chicago's Loop via I-290, on the other side of the city limits. Ernest Hemingway grew up here, and Frank Lloyd Wright lived and worked in Oak Park during the early part of his career before moving to Wisconsin. He left behind 25 buildings, making this the world's largest repository of his work. Wright's home and studio, built in 1889, is most revealing of his personality and genius: every touch,

from the distinctive and renowned streamlined Prairie Style to the Scottish proverb that's carved over a fireplace, bears his characteristic imprint. ❑

LEFT: Marshall Field's department store clock; lions in front of the Art Institute of Chicago.
RIGHT: Chicago Theatre; sculpture by Miro; Chicago Bulls statue on North Michigan Avenue.

Wisconsin's rural road sign is in the shape of the state.

THE WINDY CITY TO THE TWIN CITIES

Leaving Chicago, take Lake Shore Drive straight north out of the city and follow either US 41 or hop onto I-94 for a spell. Soon enough, you're in **Wisconsin**, the unofficial Cheese Capital of America, a friendly place settled by blond Scandinavians still very much in evidence today.

A few miles inside the state, turn west on Wisconsin 50 to make a lovely country drive past orchards, fruit stands and small lake towns – one of which is called **Lake Geneva**, attractive if not exactly a match for its counterpart in Switzerland. Turn north on US 12, passing plenty of maple trees, small cafés, burger joints and rustic roads (so marked by state road signs). You'll also come through **Kettle Moraine State Forest**, named for unusual features of the landscape – ridges of rock and silt, and circular ponds – produced here by the last great glaciation of North America. Rent a cycle to explore the area at your leisure.

At Whitewater, a small university town, you'll note a preponderance of custard stands serving burgers and frozen custard – a concoction invented in nearby Milwaukee. By state law, custard must contain a certain percentage of cream and a certain number of eggs. It's like ice cream, but sinfully richer; a spoon is barely adequate to pry it from the cup.

US 12 brings you to **Madison** ㊱, Wisconsin's capital and one of the Midwest's most agreeable cities. The city boasts a splendid downtown grid of streets with a capital building at its center, a university district to match and miles of lake frontage popular with joggers, boaters, skiers and skaters – depending on the season. Snack on "brats" (short for bratwurst, local sausages of German origin) and beer, or enjoy the open-air market that takes over the university's main square in summer, a market purveying everything from Turkish food to African food to tofu dogs. There are also a number of museums here.

From Madison, take US 18 west through green pastures and roadcuts revealing the limestone underlying the countryside. This area is an anomaly in the normally flat Midwest, with numerous ridges popping up between you and the horizon; farms top distant hilltops like ships on sea swells. At the little town of **Mount Horeb**, exit onto County Road ID – in Wisconsin, unusually, minor roads are lettered instead of numbered – for a look at two attractions. The National Natural Landmark, **Cave of the Mounds** (tel: 608-437-3038), provides a scenic look below ground; **Little Norway** (tel: 608-437-8211; www.littlenorway.com; open daily May–Oct) is a somewhat tacky attraction celebrating the Norwegian immigrants who largely settled this state.

Get back onto US 18 and continue to County Road BB, where a short detour south brings you to the **Folklore Village** (tel: 608-924-4000; www.folklorevillage.org; closed Mon), a small complex of period buildings. The highlight is a one-room 1882 church, very simple but nicely restored; it was jacked up and moved from a nearby town. There is also a schoolhouse and working well pump on the property, which is often booked up by school groups.

Dodgeville, home to clothier Land's End, is just a few miles on. Take Wisconsin 23 north past the headquarters. On the way out of town you will pass the

Don Q Inn – an eccentric lodge. Themed rooms include an igloo built for two, a hot air balloon gondola and many other options suitable for all levels of taste.

More dips and rises in the road lead to the **House on the Rock** (tel: 608-935-3639; open daily mid Mar–Oct), Wisconsin's quirkiest must-see attraction. This absolutely unique complex of buildings on top of an odd rock formation was built up over a period of decades by inveterate collector Alex Jordan, Jr. Its many attractions include rooms and rooms of art, antiques and oddities, an "Infinity Point" glass bridge with views down a gorge, a huge assemblage of dolls and a large collection of remote-controlled airplanes. It's well worth the expensive admission price, if only for a look at the fruits of a single man's manic obsession – you could easily spend the better part of a day roaming around this kitschy complex. If you don't have time for a long visit, there's an attractive spot just north of the entrance to park, walk a spell and get a distant glimpse of the house.

Frank Lloyd Wright's Wisconsin

Wisconsin 23 soon comes to the sandy banks of the Wisconsin River, where you'll be surprised to suddenly come upon Frank Lloyd Wright's **Taliesin** ㊲ (tel: 608-588-7900; www.taliesinpreservation.org; open daily May–Oct; weekends in Nov) The modern main building here, designed by the architect, contains research and exhibit facilities, but you must take a bus tour to get to Wright's actual former home. The setting is peaceful and lovely.

The route continues to the pretty little town of Spring Green, turns west onto US 14 and abruptly flattens before passing through **Richland Center**, the humdrum county seat renowned for being Wright's birth town. Then the road begins climbing and wrinkling again, indicating the approach of the Mississippi River.

Map on page 124

BELOW: farm stand in rural Wisconsin.

At **Coon Valley** ⓸, neatly tucked within a surprisingly deep valley, you'll marvel at the surroundings and the town's solid Lutheran church. The **Norskedalen** (tel: 608-452-3424; www.norskedalen.org; open daily May–Oct; closed Sat rest of year) complex outside town provides a pleasant look at Norwegian heritage in a quiet natural setting. Speed right through industrial La Crosse, hop onto I-90 and take the big bridge across the Mississippi; get off again on the other side at signs for Bob Dylan's Highway 61. You have entered **Minnesota** and are now following the **Great River Road** toward the river's source. The route north clings to the bluffs of the Mississippi River, revealing spectacular colors in fall and outstanding river views at any time of the year. Patrons once rode steamboats all the way upriver from St Louis to gaze upon these high, beautiful bluffs.

US 61 is mostly grand views and plain towns from here to the Twin Cities, but there are a few worthy stops along the way. **Pepin**, back across the great river on the Wisconsin side, is famous for being the birthplace of Laura Ingalls Wilder of *Little House on the Prairie* fame. There's a copy of the cabin just north of town, and a small museum (open daily, mid-May–mid-Oct) as well.

North again, **Red Wing** ⓹, with an especially good vista of the valley, makes a good place for a picnic and a photograph. There's an Indian reservation close by, as well, and it's good to have a look round before plunging into the suburban ring of towns and highways that have replaced what, until very recently, were cornfields but now serve as the suburban bases for legions of commuters into Minneapolis and St Paul.

The Twin Cities

SLOW!! BUSY STREET AHEAD

Highways have replaced cornfields in many parts of Minnesota.

BELOW: Minneapolis.

Because of their proximity, **Minneapolis** and **St Paul** ⓺, on opposite sides of the Mississippi, will eternally be known as Minnesota's "Twin Cities." Fraternal rather than identical, they are like sides of the same coin: different, yet inseparable. St Paul, the more conservative, ethnic and parochial of the two, presents an earthier and more weatherbeaten appearance. There's a more neighborly feel, too, and malt shops, health-food stores and homes are more common here than the apartments, condos and skyscrapers across the river.

Minneapolis, more competitive and cosmopolitan, dresses for success while living and breathing the concept of quality time. Local radio humorist Garrison Keillor puts it this way: "The difference between St Paul and Minneapolis is the difference between pumpernickel and Wonder Bread."

Yet together they are responsible for an urban success story, the envy of every overcrowded and crime-ridden metropolis. Minnesota pioneers were forced by circumstances to cooperate with one another, and a genuine spirit of friendliness toward strangers prevails to this day.

People here put a lot of stock in politics and have developed a rather civic, populist bent: this state nourished the careers of Hubert Humphrey and Walter Mondale. More recently, the late Senator Paul Wellstone – and, outrageously, Governor Jesse "The Body" Ventura, a former professional wrestler – have continued this populist tradition, if in very different ways.

MINNESOTA: LAND OF 10,000 LAKES

It always comes back to the lakes. Without its waters, Minnesota wouldn't even be Minnesota; the name itself comes from the Sioux, meaning "sky-blue water." The shore of **Lake Superior** marks the border of its northeast corner and the **Mississippi River** courses down its eastern flank. State license plates affirm "Land of 10,000 Lakes," but there are even more than that in the state.

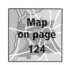

During the 18th century, French explorers stumbled onto this region and named it *L'Etoile du Nord*, the Star of the North. Over the next 150 years, the Sioux and Ojibwa Indians who originally occupied the territory were frequently set upon by hundreds of white settlers, and violent clashes between the two Indian groups escalated.

In order to protect the early settlers and establish a secure trading station, **Fort Snelling** was built in 1819, high on river bluffs at the site of what is now Minneapolis. As rampaging Indians crossed the plains, white farmers fled to the fort for refuge; thus was the city born. Today, Fort Snelling has been reconstructed and staffed with actors who give visitors a first-hand glimpse of frontier life, *circa* 1827.

An increase in commerce along the river gave birth to the towns of St Paul and Minneapolis. The former sprang up as a local center of navigation and was originally known as Pig's Eye, after "Pig's Eye" Parrent, proprietor of a riverfront saloon. Seeking a better image, its residents renamed it St Paul.

Ever-industrious Minneapolis, "the city of water," evolved upstream around **St Anthony Falls**, source of power for sawmills and gristmills. Both towns were flooded with a wave of immigrants, mostly northern Europeans, on their way to harvest the bounty of the Great North Woods: lumber and iron ore. In the wake of the Homestead Act, more settlers then poured in to help cultivate a sea of wheat.

BELOW: St Paul.

The Twin Cities' status in the world of agriculture, in fact, is never far from the minds of Minnesotans. Reports from the Minneapolis Grain Exchange, the nation's largest cash market, monopolize the local airwaves; General Mills and Pillsbury are headquartered here. Magnificent grain elevators, standing tall above the Mississippi, vie for attention with the likes of Minneapolis's **Investors Diversified Services** (IDS) building – the tallest one between Chicago and San Francisco – **St Paul's Cathedral** and the handsome **Capitol Building**.

Weather watchers

Characterized by stable neighborhoods and superbly planned public places and open spaces, the Twin Cities runs smoothly even in cold weather. They've given a lot of thought to the weather here, after all, and over the years have refined methods of dealing with a winter that is typically cruel and unrelenting. Glass-enclosed skywalks radiate from the Crystal Court of the IDS building, as they do in downtown St Paul, and the **Hubert H. Humphrey Metrodome** (enclosed) hosts sports events and concerts year-round – including two World Series titles for baseball's Minnesota Twins and success for the football team, the Vikings.

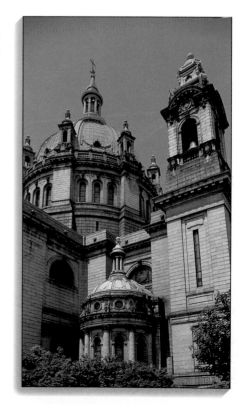

Yet people here are also perversely proud of their ability to withstand record-cold temperatures, and they celebrate the ice and snow at the St Paul's Winter Carnival, an annual event since 1886.

Culture is well-endowed and thriving, particularly in Minneapolis. The **Walker Art Center** is a forum for contemporary visual and performing arts that *The New York Times* called "one of the best contemporary art exhibition facilities in the world." The Center incorporates the **Guthrie Theatre**, indisputably one of the premier repertory theaters. The **Northrup Dance Season** puts together one of the most impressive dance series. The **American Swedish Institute** archives and the European collections of the **Minneapolis Institute of Arts** (tel: 612-870-3131; www.artsmia.org; closed Mon) are within a short distance of each other; both are terrific.

And there's still more to be found – avante-garde films, classical music, art galleries, jazz. At **Mendota**, a tiny riverfront community just west of the Mississippi, you'll find the **Hall Bros**. **Emporium of Jazz**, said to be the oldest jazz club in town.

Famous state fair

BELOW:
the town of Blue
Earth, in some of
the most productive
farmland in the US.

The annual **Minnesota State Fair**, the nation's second-largest (behind New York's) should not be missed if you're coming through in late summer. Held at the State Fairgrounds, it's a week-long stream of fishing and farming demonstrations, folk and country music performances and carnival rides – accompanied by every sort of meat or cheese one can imagine, placed onto a stick and fried. It's a huge dose of Midwestern popular culture, a little overwhelming but absolutely authentic.

Map on page 124

THE MISSISSIPPPI TO THE BADLANDS

The region extending from the Mississippi River in Minnesota to the Missouri River in South Dakota marks the transition from the Midwestern to the Western states – geographically, culturally and spiritually.

The transition can be subtle. If you listen to the car radio, up-to-the-minute reports from the floor of the Minneapolis Grain Exchange will be heard with progressively less frequency. Western idioms begin to turn up in small farm towns. The changes in geography are more abrupt, as the Missouri River serves as a sharp boundary between the Grain Belt and the true West.

Pipestone, Minnesota, is only a few miles short of being halfway between the Atlantic and the Pacific oceans.

Sodbusters

The region of Minnesota southwest of "The Cities" is unmistakably farm country. This land was settled by European and Scandinavian immigrants during the latter half of the 19th century. Some called them "sodbusters" as they indiscriminately cleared land and penetrated virgin sod, exposing the rich soil of the Midwestern prairie. Many of their grandchildren and great-grandchildren still farm the land here, an occupation known these days as agribusiness.

The founders of **New Prague 🜔**, a town dominated by **St Wenceslaus Church,** clearly had no desire to hide their Eastern European heritage. West of the town, along State 19, are peculiarly medieval-looking buildings with domed roofs, looking incongruous in the midst of all-American corn country.

Those who believe the Valley of the Jolly Green Giant to be a mythical place created by television advertising executives are mistaken. At **Le Sueur,** renowned for its peas, US 169 intersects the Minnesota River and passes through this lush, green valley, marked by the Green Giant himself sprouting from the top of a billboard.

BELOW: man on fire at the Minnesota State Fair: don't miss it.

Branching southwest toward **Mankato,** the road enters Blue Earth country across the **Blue Earth River**. This is some of the most productive farmland in the state, a green expanse interrupted only by lakes. Modern farming is still a family business here, and it isn't unusual to see an entire family out in the fields working various pieces of machinery.

From Mankato, take US 14 west as far as tiny Florence, passing many more farms along the way, and then turn south onto Minnesota 23 for a more scenic stretch. In **Pipestone 🜔**, near the South Dakota border, the strong suit is Sioux quartzite rather than agriculture. Buildings constructed from this local, pinkish stone appear up and down historic Main and Hiawatha streets; significant not only because they are lovely to look at, but because they are among the last of their kind. The use of Sioux quartzite is no longer considered cost-effective.

But for a period of less than 20 years before the turn of the 19th century, Pipestone went to town with it – the **County Courthouse,** the **Public Library,** the **Bank Building,** the **Calumet Hotel** and, most impressively, **Moore Block** (*circa* 1896) are all made of this material. L.H. Moore embellished the block bearing his name with fanciful images of the sun, angels, gargoyles, a jester and the devil.

Underlying and veining Sioux quartzite is a material called pipestone, which gave the town its name. Longfellow's *The Song of Hiawatha* tells of "the great Red Pipestone Quarry," and the quarries in Pipestone and the land that surrounds them are still sacred ground of the Sioux and other Native Americans today – a land of legend and tradition, and now also a national monument.

To see more, take the **Circle Trail**, a mile loop through the prairie surrounding the quarries. It goes past **Hiawatha Lake**, **Winnewisa Falls**, quartzite cliffs and wind-carved formations known as **Old Stone Face** and the **Oracle**. A stone inscription along the trail documents the past presence of the Nicolet expedition, members of which traveled through here in 1836 while exploring the lands of the isolated Upper Mississippi region.

Continue south from Pipestone along Minnesota 23, passing through **Jasper** (which also has its share of quartzite buildings). Angle onto Route 269, and in a few miles you will have crossed another state line – and you will be poised exactly halfway between the Atlantic and the Pacific oceans.

THE PINK ROAD TO SOUTH DAKOTA

The South Dakota Department of Highways chose to make use of the locally plentiful quartzite, and so a pink road unfolds at the border of their state. It takes you to **Garretson**, known for its **Devil's Gulch** . The gulch is a sliver in the quartzite cliffs that loom above **Split Rock Creek**. According to one legend, the rocks were split by the Great Spirit's tomahawk. According to another, outlaw Jesse James jumped across the gap while being pursued by a posse. Fortunately for modern travelers, they can now cross the gap over a short, non-threatening bridge. Devil's Gulch lends Garretson an Old West image, but it is primarily a small farming community.

BELOW: the Corn Palace, Mitchell, South Dakota.

The prairies of eastern South Dakota and the pioneers who settled this land have been immortalized both on canvas and in popular literature. The paintings of Harvey Dunn, son of homesteaders and sodbusters, depict the reality and the dignity of these people. These same themes are mirrored in the work of Laura Ingalls Wilder, author of the beloved *Little House on the Prairie* and other books concerning life in the pioneer era before it was changed by modern times. (The books have now become an enormous industry, with over 50 million volumes having been sold. With the aid of some of Ingalls' descendants, ghostwriters have been employed to continue the series.)

To save time through this stretch of the Great Plains, get onto I-90, which cuts through eastern South Dakota in a nearly straight line through terrain that becomes a bit hillier and less green as rainfall becomes scarcer and the cultivation of hay and wheat mingles with that of corn.

These crops will eventually be taken to busy and industrious **Sioux Falls** , the state's commercial center, a city of little interest although it can claim the headquarters of the Gateway computer company – a firm started by two Iowa brothers whose computers are now shipped in distinctive, cow-spotted black-and-white boxes.

Farther west, in **Mitchell** , they have created a

monument to and with all the amber-colored grains: the **Corn Palace** (tel: 866-273-2676; www.cornpalace.org; closed weekends in winter). It's one good reason to stop in Mitchell – the other being to take a much-needed break from the interstate. The Corn Palace is most certainly the world's only Byzantine structure decorated with murals of corn and other grains; each year, the patterns change according to local whim. It is a slice of quintessential Americana.

As I-90 approaches the Missouri River, which divides South Dakota into "East River" and "West River," a very different type of terrain lies ahead.

Where the West begins

Western South Dakota is unquestionably where the West begins. Visually, the Badlands and the Black Hills rise out of the prairie and hit you with a one-two punch; they are equally unexpected and stunning. But there is more to these regions than just their bleak beauty. They have been witnesses to some pretty tumultuous history.

If you're hurrying, stay on I-90 through to these twin wonders, but if you've got the time and inclination to explore rural South Dakota, then meander west instead along US 14, which you can pick up at the rather ordinary state capital of **Pierre** , reached on US 83 north from Vivian. After crossing the banks of the Missouri River, set your watch back an hour and prepare to traverse mound after mound of prairie grass. This route also coincides with a section of the **Old Deadwood Trail**, a legendary wagon-train and stagecoach route.

The wagon-trains and stagecoaches were destined for uncivilized parts of the expanding nation; nevertheless, they had certain rules. "If you must drink, share the bottle," was one. Chewing tobacco was permitted, though it was requested the chewer spit "with the wind, not against it." And specified topics of conversation were forbidden: stagecoach robberies and Indian uprisings, to name but two.

US 14 cuts due south and then west again toward **Cottonwood**, foretold by grove after grove of cottonwood trees – the almost magical tree with the ability to find water in an arid landscape, and then reproduce in small communities. This tree was the single most useful tool the prairie settlers had: they could build a fence with it, sit under its shade, even cut into its bark to drink a bit of watery pulp in an emergency. Whenever you see the cottonwood's big-toothed leaves in a valley, you know there is water nearby, whether it be in the form of river, stream or some other hidden source.

Continuing west, the motorist is besieged by a growing number of signs imploring him to stop at Wall Drug, located in Wall on the northern edge of the Badlands (see page 143). Depending on your degree of thirst, hunger, illness or defiance, you can continue west and arrive at Wall in no time at all, or turn south at Cottonwood directly into the Badlands.

This area is also known as the Dakota by the Sioux Indians, which roughly translates as "land bad." French trappers in the early part of the 19th century described it as "a bad land to cross." Many contemporary travelers bypass the Badlands (rarely visible

Map on page 124

TIP

After crossing the Missouri River, set your watch back by one hour; Central time gives way to Mountain time here.

BELOW: these boots were made for walking; buy custom-made in South Dakota.

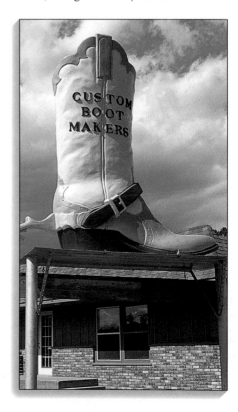

from the interstate) while rushing to the Black Hills and the stone faces of Mount Rushmore, but it is an absolutely unique landscape and one certainly worth seeing – even if it can be a brutally hot place in summer.

Sand castles and canyon walls

This constantly eroding landscape has often served as a metaphor of youthful malaise and rootlessness: Terence Malick used it as a title for an acclaimed film (*Badlands*, 1973), and Bruce Springsteen later sang about "Badlands" on his 1978 album "Darkness at the Edge of Town." Despite all the discouraging words, there is a rare and striking beauty to be found here – it's well worth a detour off the interstate and the $10 per vehicle charge that it costs to enter the national park.

The region has been described as "Hell with the fires burned out," but fire has played no part in it; it has been shaped chiefly by wind and water. Spires, turrets and ridges comprise a silent skyline, which changes with each gust of wind and torrential (though infrequent) downpour. **Badlands National Park** ❹ (tel: 605-433-5361; www.nps.gov/badl) is not a single piece of land, but rather several chunks of territory loosely strung together and carved out of **Buffalo Gap National Grassland** and the **Pine Ridge Indian Reservation**.

It is possible to be driving through rolling grasslands and suddenly be confronted without warning with Badlands terrain: huge sand castles and canyon walls. A 40-mile (64-km) loop road traverses the park and provides access to points of geological and paleontological interest, including a number of hikes through the strange terrain.

This was once the stomping ground of ancient camels, three-toed horses and saber-toothed tigers, whose fossilized remains continue to be uncovered by the elements. Many of these fossils, dating back to the Oligocene Epoch, 25 to 35 million years ago, have been preserved by the **South Dakota School of Mines and Technology** and are exhibited at their **Museum of Geology** (tel: 800-544-8162; open daily) in Rapid City. The largest of the Oligocene mammals was the titanothere, known in Sioux mythology as the Thunderhorse. It was believed by the Sioux that this creature descended from the heavens during thunderstorms and killed buffalo.

Enthusiasts were well on their way toward cleaning out the Badlands of its fossil treasures before the government and Federal protection intervened, and the abundant wildlife that once roamed here was also largely gone by the 1890s – depleted by the throng of humanity *en route* to the Black Hills in search of "the devil's metal" – gold.

Antelope and buffalo

Thanks to reintroduction and protection, however, the park is today a sanctuary for pronghorn antelope and buffalo. Prairie dogs also thrive here in their own metropolis. These peculiar rodents employ an elaborate system of tunnels, entry holes and sentries; a shrill "barking" rings throughout the prairie if anyone ventures too closely.

These dogs are not especially well-liked by ranchers,

BELOW: a Sioux artist paints a teepee, Badlands National Park.

as cattle can be severely injured by stepping into their holes – nor is the weather, which here is as severe as it is unpredictable. Old-timers still talk about the blizzard of May 1905, when the weather progressed from balmy to icy. Thousands of head of cattle and horses drifted south with the wind and eventually fell to their death by pitching over the north wall of the Badlands.

Comparatively few people visit the Badlands, and those who do keep their visits short. Even fewer call this inhospitable landscape home. Two of those who do are Ansel Woodenknife and Lavanne Green, proprietors of the **Woodenknife Drive-Inn** in **Interior**. You can't miss the Woodenknife. Its neon signs beam across the barren landscape, addressing the most primal of needs: "EAT" and its companion, "FOOD."

Map on page 124

Life in the Badlands

Lavanne grew up in Interior and says she "couldn't wait to get out." Get out she did, roaming around for a while, seeing the world, having adventures, only to return in 1975, after many years. Now she and son-in-law Ansel fix delicious and authentic Indian tacos, fry bread and buffalo burgers for weary travelers passing through the area who eventually find their colorfully painted little café. Once in a while, they even make a special dish: *wojapi* (whoa-jah-pee), a seasonal fruit soup made with local chokecherries or wild plums. The soup is usually served at powwows, Ansel says, but can be whipped up on request if the fruits are ripe and available.

The café is not just a living but also a passport to meet people from across the United States and around the world – something the two clearly enjoy as much as they do the cooking. ❑

The Badlands have "a rare and striking beauty." For the visual evidence, see pages 44–45.

BELOW: branding cattle.

THE BADLANDS TO YELLOWSTONE

*Drive through the land of Buffalo Bill, Wild Bill Hickok,
Calamity Jane and the Sundance Kid to see
Mount Rushmore and the tragic sites of the Indian Wars*

eaving the **Badlands** ⓧ behind and heading west through South Dakota on Route 44, you'll come upon tiny **Scenic**, a ramshackle place named by someone with an extremely wry sense of humor; in exactly the same spirit, a sign along the main road ("Business District") signals your arrival. There's a tiny church here, a few abandoned shacks, several vintage mobile homes, a hole-in-the-wall US Post Office, a heap of junked cars and, on the edge of town, the place people come here to see: the **Longhorn Saloon**.

The Longhorn was established in 1906, and the ankle-deep sawdust on the floor has been collecting ever since, as have the bullet holes and cattle brands on the ceiling. In its heyday, it was always the site of a recent shootout, and even now discomfort pervades the atmosphere. Tractor seats mounted on metal barrels serve as bar stools. Its façade features longhorn skulls and a weatherbeaten sign that says "no Indians allowed." But, actually, this is an anachronism; the staff are often Oglala Sioux from the nearby Pine Ridge Reservation, and Native American customers are more than welcome. Route 44 will take you on to Rapid City.

LEFT: make friends with a llama at Custer State Park, South Dakota. **BELOW:** fresh eggs for breakfast.

Wounded Knee

The **Pine Ridge Reservation** surrounds the southern tier of Badlands National Park and coincides with Shannon County, which has the lowest per capita income in the United States. On this bleak land, **Wounded Knee Creek** bleeds off from the White River to the site of the infamous massacre of December 29, 1890 – when 250 Sioux, mostly unarmed, were slaughtered by the army. Chief Sitting Bull was a casualty of this skirmish – the last tragic episode of the Indian Wars – and the name "Wounded Knee" has become an enduring symbol of unfathomable loss.

Wall Drug, in the town of Wall (located on Interstate 90), is a one-of-a-kind roadside stop – though it can't possibly live up to the miles of repeated advertising painted onto abandoned trucks and wooden signs as you come west. Never has there been a more elaborate drugstore: located on the northern wall of the Badlands alongside the interstate, it is difficult to pass through this part of South Dakota without dropping in.

Apothecary Ted Hustead began posting the ubiquitous signs along the highway in the early 1930s, inspired by the old Burma Shave signs. By the time drivers hit the Missouri River, even the most stoic of travelers perceives a need for a glass (or maybe even a jug) of Wall Drug's famous ice water – although it

Badlands to the Olympic Peninsula

- Badlands National Park ❹❼
- 90 Wall
- 44 Scenic
- *Junc 110*
- Rapid City
- *Junc 60* — Black Hills ❹❽
- 385 Lead — 385 Mt Rushmore Nat'l Mem. ❹❾
- 85 Deadwood ❺⓿ — Crazy Horse Memorial
- 90 Spearfish — Jewel Cave Nat'l Monument
- South Dakota — Wind Cave National Park
- Wyoming — Sundance
- Devils Tower ❺❶ National Monument — *Junc 185*
- 14 — Moorcroft
- *Junc 153*
- Wyoming — Gillette
- Montana — Garryowen — 90 Buffalo ❺❷ — 25 Denver
- Little Bighorn Battlefield National Monument
- Crow Agency — Fort Phil Kearny State Historic Site
- Old Fort C.F. Smith — *Junc 9*
- Sheridan ❺❸
- Ranchester
- Montana — 90 — Connor Battlefield State Historic Site
- Wyoming — Alt 14 — Burgess Junction
- Bighorn Canyon National — 37 — Medicine Wheel National Historic Landmark
- Recreation Area — Lovell ❺❹
- ❺❺ Cody — Buffalo Bill Historical Center
- Buffalo Bill Dam
- Alt 14 — Shoshone — National Elk Refuge
- ● National — Grand Teton National Park
- Forest — Kelly
- 89 Jackson
- Wyoming — ★ Yellowstone ❺❻
- 89 — National Park
- Montana — Gallatin National Forest
- 89 — ●
- Livingston ❺❼
- 90 — Bozeman ❺❽
- Three Forks
- 287 — Lewis & Clark Caverns State Park
- Townsend
- Canyon Ferry — ★ Helena ❺❾
- 12 — *Junc 174*
- 90
- Missoula ❻⓿
- *Junc 96*
- ★ National Bison Range ❻❶
- St Ignatius
- Polson
- 2 89
- 93 — Kalispell — Hungry Horse
- Glacier National Park ❻❷
- Browning
- 2 — Libby
- Troy
- Montana — Bonners Ferry
- Idaho — 2 95 — Sandpoint
- ❻❸ Coeur d'Alene — *Junc 12*
- Idaho — Salt Lake City — 95 — 90 Kingston
- Washington — 90 — *Junc 277*
- 2 — Spokane ❻❹
- 174 — Grand Coulee Dam ❻❺
- 155 — Grand Coulee
- 2 — Coulee City
- Orondo
- Wenatchee — Leavenworth ❻❻
- National Forest ● — 2
- *Junc 178* — *Junc 194*
- Puget Sound — Edmonds — 5 ▶ Seattle ❻❼
- 104 — Kingston ❻❽
- Port Gamble
- Olympic National Forest
- ❻❾ Port Townsend — 20 — Sequim
- 101 — Port Angeles
- ● Olympic
- Sappho — National Park ❼⓿
- 113 — ★ Makah — 101 Forks
- 112 — Indian Reserve
- Cape Flattery — Neah Bay

does sell other drinks as well. Hence, what began as the only drugstore in a small, dusty town became famous as the "Ice Water Store" and now takes up most of Main Street.

Wall Drug has, among other things, a chapel for those in need of solace; a clothing and boot shop for those in need of Western duds; a fine bookstore; a harness shop for serious riders; an art gallery; and a staggering assortment of Western "attractions," from a replica of Mount Rushmore (for those tired of driving) to a mythical 6-ft (2-meter) "jackalope," a mounted buffalo and life-sized carvings of Butch Cassidy and the Sundance Kid. Donuts and coffee are free for hunters, skiers, honeymooners, missile crewmen and drivers of 18-wheelers. Approximately 20,000 folks stop by Wall Drug on a good day. It's the archetypal American success story, and Ted Hustead defines the lesson of his success in this way: "there's absolutely no place on God's earth that's godforsaken."

The ride from Wall to **Rapid City** along I-90 is approximately 50 miles (80 km) of rolling, treeless prairie and wheat fields. You'll note black cattle dotting the grasslands, rolling hills slowly increasing in elevation and occasional patches of sunflowers. Rapid City, settled by prospectors in 1876 and slowly becoming a sophisticated place, is the gateway to the Black Hills.

The Black Hills

These words, taken together, summarize the course of late 19th-century history in the **Black Hills** ❹❽, indeed throughout the West. It was an era characterized by greed, deception and bloodshed. The Sioux were "granted" eternal rights to this land that held little interest for the white man until the discovery of gold. After that, of course, it was a different story.

George Armstrong Custer led an army reconnaissance expedition through here in 1874. The presence of gold was barely confirmed before a deluge of humanity swept through the hills, leaving the treaty of 1868 shredded in its wake. Years of bloodshed followed, and the Sioux would never regain exclusive rights to their sacred *Paha Sapa*. A steady stream of travelers continues to flow through the Black Hills today – mostly past Mount Rushmore, the "shrine of democracy" that was never completed.

Going on past Rapid City and all the rampant commercialism of US 16, you'll encounter a road of another color, a 17-mile (27-km) corkscrew known as the **Iron Mountain Road**. It is one of the spectacular, specially engineered Black Hills highways built in the 1930s and intended for pleasure driving. The inspiration of Highway Commissioner Peter Norbeck, the roads are characterized by hairpin turns, switchbacks, granite tunnels (which are placed to provide remarkable vistas) and pigtail bridges using native pine columns in place of steel.

Map on page 144

Heads above the rest

Rather than sashaying around the mountain, Iron Mountain Road heads straight for the top. It passes by **Mount Rushmore National Memorial** ❹❾ (tel: 605-574-2523; www.nps.gov/moru; open daily), which first appears framed at the end of a tunnel. This sight is akin to watching Hitchcock's *North by Northwest* (1959) on television from across the room. You may find yourself squinting to see if those specks up there are actually Cary Grant and Eva Marie Saint escaping across the six-story, granite faces.

Rushmore, the (uncarved) mountain, was purportedly named for Charles E. Rushmore, a New York attorney who visited here in 1885. When he asked a local about the name of the (then-nameless) peak, the fellow is said to have obligingly replied, "It is called Mount Rushmore." In the 1920s, Doane Robinson, the official historian of South Dakota, was considering various projects aimed at attracting visitors to the Black Hills. He decided on the concept of a

Twins and friends forever.

BELOW: sculptor Gutzon Borglum began work on Mount Rushmore in 1927, at the age of 60.

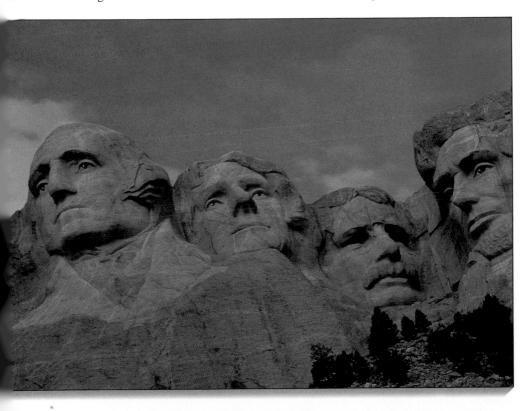

colossal mountain carving, envisioning statues of legendary mountain men such as Jim Bridger, John Colter and Kit Carson. But the more universally admired presidential subjects (George Washington, Thomas Jefferson, Abraham Lincoln and, later, Theodore Roosevelt) were finally chosen.

In 1927, sculptor Gutzon Borglum (then 60 years old) was commissioned to do the work. The enormous endeavor took him the remainder of his life, and work on the mountain came to a permanent halt following Borglum's death and then the Japanese attack on Pearl Harbor. It's interesting to note that Borglum had intended the figures to be carved to the waist, and had he begun from the bottom rather than the top, the US would have been left with a rather peculiar shrine of democracy.

The project was always plagued by controversy and a lack of funding, largely as a result of Borglum's artistic temperament and egotism. Some say he pushed for the inclusion of Roosevelt because he considered the president's spectacles to be a particular challenge to his skills, for instance. He also planned a 500-word chiseled inscription to be written by President Calvin Coolidge – an idea aborted following a ruthless and undiplomatic edit by Borglum. But the sculptor's ambition and talent were of the highest order, even if he was a difficult man to work with. The stone memorial is a testament to his own peculiar genius, and

BELOW: scale model of the Crazy Horse Memorial, with rock and the work-in-progress in the background.

must be seen simply because it is unique to the United States.

Crazy Horse

Mount Rushmore is not the only mountain carving in the Black Hills. There is also the **Crazy Horse Memorial** (tel: 605-673-4681; www.crazyhorse.org; open daily), a work-in-progress by the late Korczak Ziolkowski. Whereas Mount

Rushmore remains incomplete, Crazy Horse, even more ambitious in scale, is still in its infancy. Ziolkowski left detailed plans and instructions behind, and the grounds – the town of Crazy Horse now – are literally abuzz with workers.

Ziolkowski was engaged to carve this depiction of the great Sioux warrior by Chief Henry Standing Bear so that the white man might know that "the red man had great heroes, too." Although some 8 million tons of rock have been blasted off the mountain since 1949, it is still difficult to visualize a figure on horseback without the aid of a 1/34th scale plaster model. Still, the figure is gradually taking shape. Come for a look at the mountain and also to visit the ever-expanding **Indian Museum of North America**, as well as Ziolkowski's studio. Learning about the sculptor, his life and his ambitions for this place is time well spent. Ziolkowski was a fascinating giant of man, as a father, artist and humanitarian. He liked to think of himself as a "storyteller in stone," and these are words he personally inscribed on the door of his tomb.

South of Mount Rushmore and Crazy Horse is **Wind Cave**, the first cave to be named a National Park. Wind Cave and **Jewel Cave** (its sister to the west) are the eighth- and fourth-largest caves in the world, respectively. They are characterized by calcite crystals and honeycomb formations known as "box-work," found more extensively here than anywhere else in the world.

Supernatural highway

North of Wind Cave in the direction of Lead is **Needles Highway**, another Black Hills driving experience. The road was built to show off the Needles, granite spires which reach for the sky. Frank Lloyd Wright called it "an endless supernatural world more spiritual than Earth, but created out of it." The highway meanders and climbs several miles up into the firmament, at times through tiny granite tunnels. You must sound your horn before proceeding and don't let your attention stray too far.

Past Needles Highway, continuing north toward Lead on US 385, the aroma of pine pervades the atmosphere as the road passes through thick, dark stands of ponderosa pine. The appearance of these trees from afar gave the Black Hills its name. Lead (pronounced *leed*), named for a lode or vein of ore, is the site of **Homestake Mine**, which today produces more gold than any other gold mine in the Western Hemisphere. It's still a company town of pickup truck-driving roughnecks, though tourists now mix curiously with them on the patchwork main street. Although all mining here now takes place underground, the town's main tourist attraction is the old "**Open Cut**" – a gash in the side of the mountain where gold was originally discovered in 1876. Locals are proud of their rough-hewn town, and like to point out that it's a mile high, a mile long, a mile wide – and a mile deep.

Deadwood ㊿, three miles (5 km) northeast of Lead on US 14A, is the other Black Hills town built by gold. In fact, this was the original center of local gold mining activity – immortalized in the Eric Taylor/Nanci Griffith song "Deadwood, South Dakota" – before Lead overtook it. During the 1870s, Deadwood gained

The best driving experience in the Black Hills is to meander along Needles Highway through huge granite spires. Frank Lloyd Wright called the spires "an endless, supernatural world."

BELOW: Cathedral Spires – Needles Highway was built to show them off.

Old-style saloon in Deadwood, the "town built by gold." Calamity Jane and Wild Bill Hickok are buried in a cemetery near here.

BELOW: South Dakota is full of Indian reservations.

a reputation as the quintessential Wild West town thanks to local characters like "Wild Bill" Hickok, Calamity Jane and others. Wild Bill and Calamity are buried beside each other in **Mount Moriah Cemetery** high above Deadwood, in accordance with Jane's last wishes, but today the place is rather tame and highly overdeveloped, its every nook devoted either to perpetuating a faux-"Wild West" image or to milking tourists out of their cash at one of the several gambling casinos.

If you must, visit **Saloon No. 10**, where Wild Bill was fatally shot by Jack McCall – but you have to find it first, as several bars claim the location. The real one is billed as "Home of the Deadman's Hand" and "The Only Museum in the World With a Bar," but the most interesting attractions of this area lie outside the town as you head further west. Descend from the hills via spectacular **Spearfish Canyon**, reached by driving north from Deadwood on US 385 for just a few miles. You can turn off onto a still rougher Forest Service road at the town of **Savoy** to glimpse the landscape where part of the movie *Dances With Wolves* was filmed.

Last green oasis

Back on 14A, the canyon, threaded by the highway, winds down and down right alongside the cool, shaded Spearfish River. You'll have plenty of motorcycles and recreational vehicles for company, but there are a number of pull-offs where you can park and hike up or down the canyon in some solitude, noting the striking high cliffs of sandy-colored rock topped with aspen and pine trees. As this is the last green oasis before some very long and open stretches of forlorn Western country, you'd be well advised to do so.

Map on page 144

WYOMING AND SOUTHERN MONTANA

Quite simply, the West is not like the rest of the country. The professional sport of choice here is not football or baseball, but rodeo. The sky seems larger here than anywhere else, and you'll see frequent references to "Big Sky" country. This is a land of last stands, last chances, lost dreams; it is also a region of sparsely populated open spaces characterized by a wild natural beauty.

And Wyoming and Montana are the quintessential Western states. They lead all others in statistical extremity – the most bars, drive-ins, gas stations, cars and mobile homes per capita. The myths of the West live on here in the hearts and lives of the people who call this vast country home; theirs is not an easy life, they will tell you, but they would not trade it for anything.

Descending from the Black Hills of South Dakota by way of Spearfish Canyon brings you right to I-90, less than 10 miles (16 km) from the **Wyoming** border. The "Cowboy State," known locally as simply "Wyo," greets you with a sign proving you're in the West: while neighboring South Dakota has chosen somber presidential faces for its license plates, Wyoming has opted for a silhouette of a cowboy riding a bucking bronco. You'll notice this icon everywhere you go in the state.

Wyoming has a small piece of the **Black Hills National Forest**, located not far from the border outside of plain **Sundance** — the town "Where the Kid Got His Name." Indeed, Hardy Longabaugh, better known as the "Sundance Kid," was said to have shot a deputy sheriff near here and subsequently headed for his infamous "**Hole-in-the-Wall**" hideout about 150 miles (240 km) southwest. Once little known outside the West, his memory now lives on – and his name has become a household word – thanks to George Roy Hill and Robert Redford, director and star of the everlastingly popular movie *Butch Cassidy and the Sundance Kid*.

Past Sundance, US 14 loops up toward the Black Hills and **Devils Tower** ⑤, the object of obsession in a very different but equally popular film, *Close Encounters of the Third Kind*. Visible from almost 100 miles (160 km) away, this 860-ft (260-meter) fluted, butte-like rock formation is the tallest of its kind in America. It stands on the other side of the Belle Fourche River, where the Black Hills meet the gullies and grasslands of the plains.

The first white men to explore this region, supposedly misinterpreting a benign name ascribed to it by Native Americans, called it Devils Tower. It held a prominent place in the folklore and legends of the Sioux, and it later served as a landmark for those traveling west, just as it does today.

You can hike around the base of the tower, but beware of rattlesnakes. The majority of visitors simply stare at its almost supernatural shape and size — particularly luminous at sunrise or by the light of the moon. The sight of it so impressed Teddy Roosevelt that he designated it the nation's first national monument in 1906.

South of the monument, the road loops back onto I-90 at **Moorcroft**, an old cow town. The old Texas Trail made its way through here in the 19th century, trampled by cowboys driving cattle all the way to

"There's gold in them thar hills"

—US ARMY SCOUTS, 1874

BELOW: Devils Tower is well known to fans of *Close Encounters of the Third Kind.*

Montana. Farther west, through and beyond drab **Gillette**, the plains are vast and beautiful, marked only by cattle and the occasional river bottom of aspen and cottonwood trees. Even before crossing the Powder River and its tributary, Crazy Woman Creek, you can see the improbable pile of the Crazy Mountains looming, and then the snow-streaked peaks of the **Bighorn Mountains** in the distance: a tremendous relief for the traveler weary of the Great Plains.

Buffalo, Wyoming, is named for the town of Buffalo, New York, not for the hairy bison that roamed the plains and which can still be seen near Yellowstone.

A town called Spotted Horse

If you're taking US 14, you'll go through towns with colorful names such as Spotted Horse and Ucross. Take I-90, though, and you must drive a sparse (if beautiful) 70-mile (113-km) stretch without so much as a town or gas pump to interrupt you, only miles of empty ranch lands. The lone break in this stretch is a forlorn rest area among trees at the crossing of the Powder River.

Traveling westward, the Bighorns gradually become closer. They were named for bighorn sheep, once prevalent here but now infrequently seen. As abrupt as they are majestic, the Bighorns foretell the Rocky Mountain ranges just beyond. These eastern foothills are today traversed by I-90 just as they once were by the Bozeman Trail, a bloody shortcut in the 19th-century push westward through Sioux, Crow and Cheyenne Indian hunting grounds.

Buffalo ㉜, where the interstate highway bends north for Montana, was actually named after the town in New York and not for the formidable animals that once thundered across the plains. It was one of the earliest settlements in this corner of Wyoming, and the main street was formerly an old trail that negotiated Clear Creek. There's little here to see now besides a short main street, but it is a convenient stocking-up point for excursions into the mountains.

BELOW:
rancher's wife
with rancher-to-be.

DETOUR – DENVER

A drive of grand vistas along the base of the Rocky Mountains on I-25 from Buffalo, Wyoming, leads after 82 miles (132 km) to Denver, home of the first ice cream soda and the first bowl of shredded wheat. Celebrating the Gold Rush that built the city is the grand Capitol building, covered in 250 ounces (7 kg) of 28-carat gold leaf. In the mid-1800s, weary, unlucky prospectors flocked to Denver for guns, booze and women; the gambling halls never closed. Throughout the 1880s, money from silver camps bolstered the economy, and the population increased nearly threefold, beginning the city's urbanization. Attractions like the Coors Brewery (free samples), the US Mint (no free samples) and the Denver Art Museum, specializing in Asian, pre-Columbian and Native American art, give the area metropolitan flavor, but for all its culture, the city's natural setting is an easy distraction. Not only do the Rocky Mountains lie less than an hour away, but Denver is in charge of the largest park system in the country. Even its ever-popular concert venue, Red Rocks Amphitheatre, is a natural outdoor wonder, hollowed out of red sandstone on site high above the city. The Denver Visitors Bureau is 303-892-1112 or www.denver.org.

The road from Buffalo to Sheridan passes near the remains – now a state historic site – of **Fort Phil Kearny**. This was the most hated army outpost of all along the Bozeman Trail, and when it was finally abandoned in 1868, it was immediately burned to the ground by local Native Americans.

About 20 miles (32 km) south of the Montana border lies the small historic city of **Sheridan ㊵**, where I-90 and US 14 meet, and county seat in a region once inhabited by Crow Indians but now a major cattle-producing area. The railroad came to town in 1890 following the discovery of coal, and continued to play a major role in the development of the city. There are a number of historic homes, but the real pleasure is strolling Main Street among real-life saloons, cowboys and western-wear stores. Have a drink at the Mint Bar, a most distinctive watering hole, then grab a hat at Dan's Western Wear.

An important inn

Although cattle is of primary importance here, Sheridan is perhaps best known for its annual American Indian Days celebration each July and for its hotel, the **Sheridan Inn**. Across the street from the old railroad station in Sheridan, the inn was built in 1893 by the Burlington Railroad and Sheridan Land Company. A gracious structure with a long, inviting front porch, it fell into disuse and was scheduled for demolition during the mid-1960s. Fortunately, it was saved by a rancher and is once again open for business, not just a way-station for travelers to dine elegantly but also a living museum. After all, William F. "Buffalo Bill" Cody once owned part of this inn and made it his second home; it was customary for Cody to sit on the porch and audition acts for his Wild West Show.

Modeled after a Scottish inn, most of the materials used in its construction

BELOW: bison (buffalo) in the Black Hills. No longer endangered, their numbers are now thought to be over 250,000.

were shipped from back East by rail. In its day, it was considered to be the finest hotel between Chicago and San Francisco; presidents and such celebrities as Ernest Hemingway, General Pershing and Will Rogers all stayed the night here, and this was the first building in the area to feature bathtubs and electric lights. The lights were powered by an abandoned threshing machine and illuminated from dusk until midnight, when a whistle was blown to warn of impending darkness. Later came a telephone, first in the county, with a direct line to the drugstore. But the inn's pride and joy was its bar, constructed in England from oak and mahogany and hauled from Gillette by ox team. Still in use today, it's known as the "Buffalo Bill Bar."

Along I-90 north of Sheridan, as you approach the Montana border, sit two of the most infamous sites of the 1860s "Indian Wars." **Ranchester** is the location of **Connor Battlefield**, where General Patrick E. Connor led a division of more than 300 soldiers in an ambush of an Arapaho encampment. The Arapaho lost 64 of their people and their camp was virtually destroyed. Women and children were brutally massacred here, and as a result Connor lost his command.

Just north of Ranchester is the **Montana** line — also the beginning of the massive, empty-seeming **Crow Indian Reservation**. I-90 passes right through its heart, through the desolate-looking but neatly kept ranch lands of the reserve

The Battle of Little Bighorn, also known as "Custer's Last Stand," took place on June 25, 1876. The battle lasted only one hour, during which time the 7th Cavalry lost over 200 soldiers, the Sioux and Cheyenne fewer than 100 men.

Battle of Little Bighorn

The town of **Garryowen**, named after an Irish drinking song, leads you into the legendary **Little Bighorn Battlefield**. The Battle of Little Bighorn, better known as "Custer's Last Stand," took about as long as it takes for a white man to eat his dinner, according to one observer. But the Sioux and Cheyenne who fought

BELOW: General G.A. Custer, RIP.

Map on page 144

that day were to lose the greater struggle. Two-hundred and sixty white marble stones now sanctify this place along with the words of Oglala Chief Black Elk, in Lakota and English: "Know the Power that is Peace."

Beyond the battle site is **Crow Agency**, headquarters of this 2.5 million-acre (1 million-hectare) reservation — far less than the lands outlined in the original treaty, which designated 38 million acres (15 million hectares) as Crow land. This area, bisected by the Bighorn River and characterized by rolling hills, was described by Crow Chief Rotten Belly in the 1830s as being "exactly in the right place. Everything good is to be found there. There is no country like the Crow Country." To get a glimpse of what modern Indian life is like out here today, pull off the interstate and drop into the gas station or grocery store.

Back on the highway, you'll begin to notice the first of many signs indicating "chain up areas" — turnouts where truckers wrap heavy chains around their tires in foul weather to obtain better traction through the treacherous mountain passes that await further inside Montana.

Make time at the northern edge of the Crow reservation, just south of Hardin, for a stop at the **Big Horn County Historical Museum** (tel: 406-665-1671; www.museumonthebighorn.org). This collection of architectural structures from around the huge, sparse county – which is tops in agricultural production for this state – includes a train station, German church and the original farmhouse and barn that occupied the site. The museum also serves as your first pickup point for Montana information, and its helpful staff can direct you to area attractions such as the superb fishing in **Bighorn Canyon**. Crow guides will take you up the canyon for a price, and if you'd like to stay on the reservation, lodges and motels are thick on the ground in **Fort Smith**.

From Crow Agency to Billings, I-90 skirts the northern boundary of the reservation through towns with names like Big Timber. It doesn't get interesting again until you've reached Livingston and Bozeman. If you wish to see Yellowstone, you can also reach those towns via a scenic — if roundabout — method, by backtracking south a bit to Ranchester, Wyoming.

Towards Yellowstone

Approaching the Bighorn Mountains via I-90 in clear weather, you can sometimes discern a road switch-backing its way up the snow-streaked slopes. Traveling west from Ranchester to Lovell allows you to experience it firsthand. US 14 out of Ranchester ascends Bighorn National Forest past bullet-ridden signposts to **Burgess Junction**. The road is treacherous beyond this point: several runaway truck ramps and brake-cooling turnouts help drivers negotiate the steep grades and sharp turns.

About 20 miles (32 km) beyond Burgess Junction is a 3-mile (5-km) bumpy gravel road leading to the Indian **Medicine Wheel ㊿**. Although well paved, the road is extremely narrow and winding, at one point crossing a narrow ridge. But the views from these highest reaches of the Bighorns are stupendous, and the immediate countryside is sprinkled with wildflowers. Near its end, the road forks and presents you with a clear choice: the 20th-century radar facility to the left or the ancient medicine wheel to the right. Go right. This

BELOW: tall in the saddle.

Buffalo Bill rose to fame through a series of dime novels based on his character. His Wild West show hit the road in 1883 and by the 1890s was performing in Europe in front of royalty.

BELOW: Buffalo Bill Historical Center, Cody, Wyoming.

medicine wheel is the most elaborate of a series of stone circles found east of the Rocky Mountains, its 28 spokes forming an almost perfect circle 74 ft (23 meters) in diameter. It is thought to be about 600 years old, but its creators and its purpose still remain a mystery. According to Crow legend, the wheel was here when they arrived in the 1770s. Today, it serves a ceremonial function for Native Americans. Perhaps a certain amount of visitors, looking over at the radar station, might wonder how *that* structure will be interpreted centuries from now.

Past the Medicine Wheel, US 14A plunges down the mountain into the **Big Horn Basin**. Protected by the mountains, this region enjoys a milder climate than the rest of Wyoming. It is a prime cattle-producing area that saw one of the last great range wars between cattlemen and sheepherders in the early 20th century.

US 14A travels from Lovell to Cody through Shoshone River Valley. **Lovell**, a well-groomed town, was founded by ranchers in the 1870s and remains identified with cattle, though it is also known as the "Rose Town of Wyoming." Past Garland, the Rocky Mountains loom into view for the first time, with square-topped **Heart Mountain** in the foreground. A short drive from here is Cody, a town named after William F. "Buffalo Bill" Cody.

Buffalo Bill's town

You can't pass through **Cody** ❺ without confronting the memory of Buffalo Bill, that one-time Pony Express rider, soldier, buffalo hunter, Army Chief of Scouts, rancher, frontiersman, actor and showman. He has accurately been called a "kaleidoscope of white man's western experience." Through his Wild West Show, his own screen roles and other films that dealt with his character (played by everyone from Roy Rogers to Charlton Heston and Paul Newman), he has, more than any single person, influenced the world view of the West – for better and worse. And he certainly left his mark on Cody.

The place is unquestionably tourist-crazy. When Yellowstone attained national park status, this town jumped in with both feet, billing itself as gateway to the park. (Note, however, that the eastern gate to Yellowstone – the one facing Cody – sometimes closes down for years at a stretch so that crews can repair park roads.) Today, there are enough tour buses, tourist attractions and hoopla in the town that the inclination is to step on the gas. If you can withstand souvenir shops and the phony façade, however, you will discover a bit of the Old West here.

Best is the **Buffalo Bill Historical Center** (tel: 307-587-4771; www.bbhc.org; open daily Apr–Oct, closed Mon Nov–Mar), which is actually five outstanding museums in one. The **Buffalo Bill Museum** is devoted to the man's vast collections of memorabilia. He was known for his flamboyance and excess, and the collection is all the better for it. The **Whitney Gallery of Western Art** spans the period from the 1800s to the present. All the greats are represented – Catlin, Bierstadt, Moran, Remington, Russell; Remington's studio has been re-created here, as well. The **Plains Indian Museum** displays perhaps the world's finest collections of Sioux, Cheyenne, Shoshone, Crow, Arapaho and Blackfoot artifacts. Extremely interesting is a series of precise pictographs executed by Chief Sitting Bull while imprisoned at Fort Randall in 1882. Drawn on Fort Randall stationery, they depict what he considered to be the important events in his life.

Map on page 144

Rodeo capital of the world

Cody is also known for its **Night Rodeo**, a tradition which, along with the annual Fourth of July Cody Stampede, legitimizes the town's claim to be the "Rodeo Capital of the World." **Old Trail Town** (tel: 307-587-5302; open daily mid-May–mid-Sept), which includes the **Museum of the Old West**, is located west at the original town site. The beloved obsession of Bob and Terry Edgar, this is an impressive collection of authentic frontier buildings, horse-drawn vehicles and other artifacts from Wyoming's past. The **"Hole-in-the-Wall Cabin,"** used by Butch Cassidy and the Sundance Kid, is also here, marked by a rock with the oldest inscribed date in northern Wyoming (1811).

Buffalo Bill, claimed by Cody, Wyoming, was actually born in Iowa. The modern artist Jackson Pollock was born in Cody, a fact that is virtually ignored.

A number of legendary frontiersmen have been reburied here at the cemetery, among them John "Jeremiah Liver-eating" Johnson, portrayed by Robert Redford in the film *Jeremiah Johnson*. Johnson died in an old soldiers' home far from the mountains where he lived, and his reburial was marked by a moving ceremony featuring Robert Redford and the Utah Mountain Men, who served as pallbearers. The plaque on his grave simply reads "No More Trails."

US 14 west out of Cody follows the Shoshone River, winding through the formations of **Shoshone Canyon** and past the **Buffalo Bill Dam**, the world's first concrete arch dam. It tunnels through **Rattlesnake Mountain** and continues on through the **Shoshone National Forest** (the nation's first). As you take leave, you'll soon find yourself at the entrance to Yellowstone National Park. ❑

BELOW:
Old Trail Town, Cody, Wyoming.

YELLOWSTONE TO THE OLYMPIC PENINSULA

The Northern Route concludes its coast-to-coast journey by traveling through several of the most glorious national parks in the land to the far northwestern corner of the US

Map on page 144

Seattle

he national parks of the northern Rockies – Yellowstone Grand Teton, and Glacier – are regions of breathtaking natural beauty, vignettes from a more primitive North America. These mountain parks all share an abundance of wildlife, but each possesses a distinct personality. Yellowstone has its geysers; Grand Teton encompasses the incomparable Teton Range, rising above cattle country; and Glacier has its spectacular mountain passes.

The route between Yellowstone and Glacier passes through the westernmost **Great Plains**, the traditional hunting grounds of the Plains Indians. First described by Lewis and Clark in the early part of the 19th century, and later depicted by Charles Russell, the landscape is now dominated by cattle ranches and wide open fields of wheat.

Symbol and sanctuary

Yellowstone National Park 56 (tel: 307-344-7381; www.nps.gov/yell; open daily) is both symbol and sanctuary. Located in the northwest corner of Wyoming, it was the world's first national park – and for many people still the most magnificent despite the damage done by widespread wildfires in 1988. This primitive landscape, forged by fire and water, has been called the "greatest concentration of wonders on the face of the earth," its shapes and colors "beyond the reach of human art." It is a hotbed of geothermal activity, with more than 10,000 thermal features, as well as being one of the last remaining habitats of the grizzly bear in the continental United States. All this, and enough canyons, cliffs and cataracts to please the most jaded eye.

LEFT: Old Faithful, Yellowstone National Park. **BELOW:** skiing near Yellowstone's Mammoth Hot Springs.

Though Native Americans hunted here for centuries, credit for the region's discovery goes to John Colter, the first white man to set foot in what is now Wyoming. Later in the 19th century, trappers and prospectors passed through, among them Jim Bridger, a celebrated mountain man and teller of tall tales. Impressed by the petrified trees of **Specimen Ridge**, he embellished his description a bit, raving of "petrified trees full of petrified birds singing petrified songs." In 1870, Henry Washburn, the Surveyor General of Montana Territory, headed up a more illustrious expedition endeavoring to set the record straight. They returned awe struck and committed to the creation of a "nation's park" – a dream realized in 1872.

Yellowstone encompasses an area of more than 2 million acres (800,000 hectares). Those who prefer being at one with nature can rest assured that 95 percent of this area is backcountry. For the less intrepid,

Cowboy country around Yellowstone is also bison, elk and grizzly bear country.

BELOW:
road through Grand Teton National Park.

there are nearly 300 miles (480 km) of roads. The **Grand Loop Road** provides access to most of the major attractions, from **Yellowstone Lake** and the **Grand Canyon of Yellowstone** to **Mammoth Hot Springs** and **Old Faithful**. They are simply magnificent.

Many visitors view Old Faithful's performance with a sense of obligation. Although not as faithful as it once was, the geyser pleases the crowd regularly – 21 to 23 times daily. This is also a prime location for people-watching; a chance to glimpse a real slice of American life frozen in anticipation.

Don't pet the bears

Some come here primarily to view wildlife, and few depart disappointed. Stopped cars along the road generally indicate that some large mammal is grazing nearby. Unfortunately for both man and beast, visitors tend to forget their natural fear of and respect for these truly wild creatures. A park ranger relates that people who would ordinarily be reluctant to pet a neighbor's dog have no qualms about posing for a snapshot with a wild animal twice their size. Bison gorings are quite common and can be serious. Of ever greater concern to park officials are the bears – both black bears and grizzlies, but the latter are more dangerous and more endangered.

One way to avoid bears is to visit the park in winter, a time of hibernation and a season that comes early to Yellowstone. Snowmobiles and snowcoaches provide limited access, but probably the best way to explore this quintessential winter wonderland is on skis. Kick and glide your way to the thermal areas, good places to spot wildlife warming their hooves and paws.

With the coming of winter, the Yellowstone elk population leaves the high country and heads for the National Elk Refuge outside of Jackson, Wyoming.

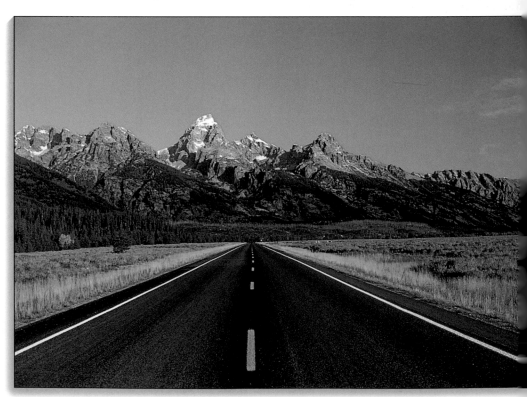

Though not exactly following in their hoofprints, US 89 south nevertheless takes you from the southern boundary of Yellowstone Park, through magestic **Grand Teton National Park** (tel: 307-739-3300; www.nps.gov/grte; open daily) and Jackson Hole, alongside the refuge, to Jackson, the perennial boomtown.

If the Rockies are the crown, then the **Teton Range** is its jewel. Exquisitely beautiful, amethyst-tinged, jagged, snowcapped and hypnotic, they loom above the horizon west of the highway. The **Snake River**, running true to its name, intervenes. The Tetons and **Gros Ventre** ranges encircle the **Jackson Hole** valley. Trappers worked this territory in the early 19th century and it was named for David E. Jackson, a prominent member of the trade. Settlers came in the 1880s as outlaws, homesteaders and ranchers. This is a gorgeous landscape, never more visually stunning than in the classic 1953 western movie *Shane*, filmed on location here.

It is still cattle country, but tourism has become the economic mainstay now. People flock from all over the country to ski here, especially the well-to-do. Nearby **Rendezvous Mountain**'s claim to fame is its vertical drop – the greatest of any US ski resort, which can be appreciated even in summer by taking a ride on the aerial tram with a sheer ascent of nearly 1 mile (1.6 km). The view from the summit is stupendous – to Grand Teton and far beyond.

Map on page 144

Million-dollar cowboy bar

The Old West and the New West have converged in **Jackson**, land of condos and cowboys. This is a big-name resort with its share of local color; you just have to look for it. Look beyond the boutiques, the ski chalets, the nightly "shoot-outs" and the stagecoach rides. Bars are generally the best place for this sort of quest, so pull up a saddle (mounted on a bar stool) at the **Million Dollar Cowboy Bar** and hoist a few beers with the locals.

North of Jackson is the **National Elk Refuge**, established in 1912 and now the winter habitat of a herd some 5,000 strong. Once victims of starvation and disease, these elk are now protected by law. Regularly scheduled sleigh rides transport visitors briefly into the company of these graceful creatures. In spring, the elk shed their antlers, which are expediously retrieved by area Boy Scouts and later auctioned off at a considerable profit.

Gardiner, Montana, sits along US 89 just north of Yellowstone on the southern fringe of **Gallatin National Forest**. Out of Yellowstone, the road passes through barren plains, irrigated farms and a land of many hot springs – mineral bath resorts are thick on the ground here – before reaching the forest, rich in minerals. The road plays hide-and-seek with the Yellowstone River awhile longer before intersecting with US 191 at Livingston.

Livingston ㊼ was put on the map by both the Northern Pacific Railroad and its proximity to Yellowstone, just 56 miles (90 km) to the south. Retaining some of its pure-West authenticity, it has also been the popular haunt of Western authors and painters such as Russell Chatham and Jim Harrison – not to mention modern movie stars and media types such as Andie MacDowell, Ted Turner and Jane Fonda, among others. The town consists of a small grid of

BELOW: around 5,000 elk spend the winter near Jackson, Wyoming.

TIP

Finger pickers should check out Bozeman, Montana. Highly desirable Gibson guitars are made at a factory just outside of town. For tour information, call 406-587-4117.

BELOW: friends on that lonesome road.

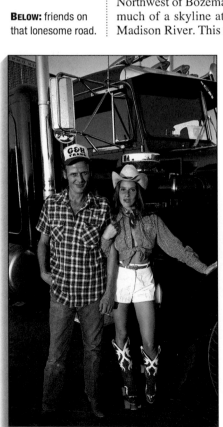

streets with bars and cafés; its proximity to Bozeman has also brought an increasing number of university students and professors.

A little west along I-90 sits **Bozeman** ⑤, nestled in the Gallatin Valley beneath 9,000-foot (2,700-meter) peaks that seem close enough to touch in the gin-clear air. This was known as the "Valley of Flowers" by the Blackfeet, Crow, Cheyenne and Snakes who hunted here. William Clark passed through the area with their blessing in 1806 on the return trip of his path-finding expedition. John Bozeman and Jim Bridger later guided wagon trains through in direct violation of treaty, at considerable risk. The trail became Bonanza Trail, the Bridger Cut-Off and the Bloody Bozeman – a treacherous shortcut for impatient pioneers.

Like so many other Western cities, Bozeman has a historic main street. But it also has a state university – which has brought outdoor gear shops, health food stores and the like – and is becoming another popular Montana spot for movie stars to buy ranch houses. The Gibson Guitar company manufactures quality guitars at a plant just outside town. You might also care to make a visit to the **Museum of the Rockies** (tel: 406-994-2251; open daily), an institution devoted to the physical and cultural heritage of the northern Rockies. Bozeman's own "boot hill" is **Sunset Hills Cemetery**, final resting place of journalist Chet Huntley, pioneer John Bozeman and Nevada miner Henry T. P. Comstock.

Lewis and Clark

Northwest of Bozeman, along Montana 2, sits Manhattan – which doesn't have much of a skyline at all – followed by the town of **Three Forks** across the Madison River. This town was named for the Missouri Headwaters – the Gallatin, Madison and Jefferson rivers – all named by Lewis and Clark. Meriwether Lewis and William Clark led their historic expedition through here in July 1805, having accepted the challenge of exploring the recently acquired Louisiana Purchase by tracing the Missouri River and its tributaries to (they hoped) the Northwest Passage. By the time they reached the Three Forks area, however, they realized that the Missouri drainage system did not in fact lead to the Pacific. Nevertheless, the success of their expedition remains undisputed. They opened up the West for a generation and for all time; a deluge of exploration – and exploitation – soon followed.

Gone today is the abundant wildlife Lewis and Clark found at the headwaters, although a state park has been developed to commemorate and interpret its historical significance. Here, you can have a picnic at the very spot where the expedition stopped to have breakfast on July 27, 1805, and then climb up to "**Lewis Rock**," where Lewis sketched a map of the countryside. At the entrance to the park are the remains of a ghost town, **Second Gallatin City**.

The town moved here from across the headwaters so as to sit astride a main stagecoach route, having by that time been abandoned by the steamboat. But its existence was unfortunately short-lived, bypassed by the next wave of transportation – the "iron horse" itself, the mighty railroad.

A few miles west of Three Forks on I-90, the color suddenly changes to the gold of wheat, and US 287 enters, going north toward Helena. Past **Townsend**, **Canyon Ferry Lake** appears to the east of the road like an oasis on the prairie. Behind it stand the **Big Belt Mountains**. US 287 continues north and merges with I-15, skirting **Helena ⑤⑨**, Montana's seat of government.

Map on page 144

Last Chance Gulch

In Helena, they continue to make Lewis and Clark bourbon, and you still hear talk of Last Chance Gulch – though now it's a pedestrian mall. Fans of cowboy-artist Charles Russell will want to stop by the **Montana Historical Society** (tel: 406-444-2694; www.his.state.mt.us; closed Sun), which houses a collection of his work. Acclaim for Russell runs high in Montana, and one of his master-pieces graces the chambers of the House of Representatives: an enormous, col-orful mural with a name to match, "Lewis and Clark Meeting the Flathead Indians at Ross' Hole."

From Helena, US 12 runs up and over 6,300-foot (1,920-meter) MacDonald pass – don't try this if winter is approaching – and the **Continental Divide**. Spill a drop of water now, and it will (eventually) run into the Pacific instead of the Atlantic. To the west of the Divide, at Garrison, you must get back onto I-90 for another stretch of rugged mountains; you are solidly within the Rockies now, with minor ranges such as the Garnet Range to either side of the road. A rest area on the interstate provides a good chance for you (and your vehicle) to rest from all the mountain-climbing while gazing at the surrounding peaks.

Then it's down to **Missoula ⑥⓪**, the state's most liberal-leaning town thanks to the influence of the University of Montana. You'll note a giant "M" carved in the hills outside town, and that marks the university. The trail actually runs on campus property and makes for a popular hike. The town boasts the usual rough-and-tumble Western bars, certainly, but also good health food shops, bookstores and music – not a bad place to spend the night.

From Missoula, take US 93 due north and begin climbing again, at least for a bit, as you begin to enter the **Flathead Indian Reservation**. Roadside stands and restaurants sell bison burgers and huckleberry shakes, the local twist on fast food. This area was once all Flathead Indian territory by decree of treaty, but the tribal lands were gradually settled by mis-sionaries and sold piecemeal to speculators. Today, a mixture of residents manage to co-exist amid lovely, wild scenery.

At the junction of Montana 200, turn west a short ways to tour the **National Bison Range ⑥①** (tel: 406-644-2211), where some 350 to 500 of these magnifent animals – as well as many other species of wildlife – roam over more than 19,000 acres (7,700 hectares) of beautiful grassland and park-like patches of tim-ber. Again, however, remember not to get too close – technically, you are not even supposed to get out of your car while driving through.

A few miles north again on US 93, **St Ignatius** beckons as a turn-off beneath the splendid Mission Mountain range. The town's chief draw today is

BELOW: Helena is Montana's seat of government.

actually its impressive mission (tel: 406-745-2768; open daily), built in 1854 and possessing some interesting fresco work within. The surrounding mountains are still occupied by Flatheads, and you need tribal permits to fish, hunt or visit. It's a beautiful and rugged country; bears and mountain lions are frequently seen.

North again, US 93 becomes ramrod-straight – one of the most accident-prone stretches of highway in the land, so look sharp. It continues north alongside the mountains to the folksy town of **Polson**, where huge **Flathead Lake** drains through a gorge; then the road bends to circle the lake's western shore. A giant Flathead-owned casino has somewhat marred what was once pristine scenery here, but the lake is still marvelous to contemplate as you climb around it to **Kalispell**, population center of the area and a base for excursions into Glacier National Park. Fittingly, its name means "prairie above the lake."

US 2 turns east to pass through Columbia Falls and then **Hungry Horse**, named for some freight horses that once escaped and nearly starved to death before being discovered and nursed back to health. The highway crosses the middle fork of the Flathead and meanders through the pristine, cathedral-like wilderness of **Flathead National Forest** before finally reaching the natural wonders of the park.

Glacier National Park

BELOW: tour boat on Lake Josephine in beautiful Glacier National Park.

Glacier National Park ② (tel: 406-888-7800; www.nps.gov/glac; open daily) is more remote and less crowded than Rocky Mountain Park or Yellowstone, yet traffic can still be heavy. Traveling here is therefore most satisfying at off-peak times – at sunrise or sunset or during early summer and autumn. It is generally plowed and fit for driving from mid-June to mid-October, when the Park Service closes it down for the winter.

Near the park's western edge is **McDonald Creek**, a final resting place for kokanee salmon who travel here in late autumn from Flathead Lake to spawn. This event attracts hundreds of bald eagles, which in turn attracts an increasing number of bird-watchers, who silently peer through binoculars to watch as nature takes its course.

The Continental Divide forms Glacier's backbone, crossed by spectacular **Going-to-the-Sun Road** at Logan Pass. Opened in 1933, this is the only road that crosses the park, bisecting it into two nearly equivalent sections. It has been called "the most beautiful stretch of road in the world," its twisting 50 miles (80 km) of two-lane pavement climbing from the settlement of West Glacier to the shore of Lake McDonald, to Garden Wall and finally crossing Logan Pass and descending to St Mary.

Along the road, stop for spectacular vistas of the **Hanging Garden Trail**, which leads to vast alpine meadows. Columbian ground squirrels greet hikers at the trail head, which proceeds past deformed trees known as *Krummholz* (the German word for "elfin timber" or "crooked wood") and across the meadow. There is an ever-changing repertoire of glacier lilies, Indian paintbrush, red monkey flowers and mountain heath. Mountain goats can sometimes be sighted from here, as well as grizzly bears, who feed on the meadow's plentiful bulbs and roots. **The Highline Trail**, across the road from the Hanging Garden, is a more challenging and potentially dangerous trail – not recommended for the faint-hearted. Opportunities for backcountry hiking abound inside the park. Its approximately 50 glaciers, 200 lakes, alpine meadows and forests are a haven for fishermen, hikers and wildlife alike. And two rustic stone chalets (called **Granite Park** and **Sperry**), reached only by foot or horseback, offer overnight accommodations; both were built around 1914 by the Great Northern Railroad.

At the eastern edge of the park – and Going-to-the-Sun Road – sits the small town of **St Mary**, which separates Lower St Mary Lake from St Mary Lake proper, and is best known for being at the eastern end of the spectacular road. It's a friendly town, attentive to the needs of visitors on their way in or out of the giant park.

Even the drive out of the park along US 89 is dramatically beautiful, descending rapidly from St Mary to Kiowa and winding sharply as it goes, then turning due east out of the mountains. From there, the enticing road goes to **Browning,** headquarters of the **Blackfeet Reservation** and also the home of the truly interesting **Museum of the Plains Indian** (tel: 406-338-2230; open daily in summer, closed weekends Oct–May), which houses the most comprehensive collection of Blackfeet artifacts in existence.

Of particular note are the Assiniboine drums, some of which have been painted with wonderful visionary designs reminiscent of hallucinatory images; it is thought the hallucinations were caused by prolonged fasting. Browning's biggest event of the year occurs each July, when the town hosts the festival **North American Indian Days,** one of the largest gatherings of its kind.

Map on page 144

A Plains Indian Assiniboine drum.

BELOW:
Going-to-the-Sun Road, Montana, has been called "the most beautiful stretch of road in the world."

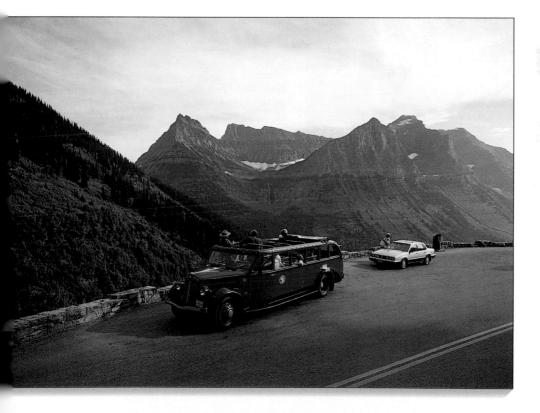

*In the summer of
2000, forest fires
raged throughout the
West, the worst in 50
years. The Bitterroot
Valley, southwest of
Libby near the Idaho
border, was the worst
affected. Check
locally if you're
thinking of visiting
these areas, as the
fires have burned
thousands of acres
of forest.*

BEYOND THE GREAT DIVIDE

As waters flow west of the **Continental Divide** toward the Pacific, so too do paths of civilization. The Nez Percé, the Kootenai, the Pend d'Oreille, the Flathead and other mountain tribes lived and hunted here in peace. Later, the Blackfeet came from the plains across the Divide on horse-stealing raids, a journey many have since followed for different reasons.

The first white people to arrive were trappers and traders in the early part of the 19th century, followed by prospectors in search of gold and silver. Homesteaders heading west conquered the Rockies and moved on, some settling in eastern Washington. With the coming of the railroad, the lumber industry found a permanent home in the forests west of the Divide.

Fire! Fire!

From Browning, take US 2 west over **Marias Pass** and skirt the southern edge of Glacier Park, passing through Hungry Horse and Kalispell once more. West of Kalispell, the **Kootenai National Forest** takes over where the Flathead leaves off. Along the highway toward **Libby**, evidence of the lumber industry's presence in this area becomes progressively more apparent. Timber has been big business here since 1892, when the Great Northern Railroad arrived. But as with all national forests, the Kootenai is a mixed-use area and within its boundaries (an area nearly three times the size of Rhode Island) lie many acres of wilderness: the habitat of elk, moose, deer and Rocky Mountain bighorn sheep. There is one unique way for outsiders to grasp the beauty of this place – and the **Canoe Gulch Ranger Station** (tel: 406-293-7773; open weekdays) holds the key. A system of observation towers, manned around the clock, were once the

BELOW: Mormon reenactment near Salt Lake City.

SALT LAKE CITY

A long but beautiful 793-mile (1,276-km) journey from Coeur d'Alene, Idaho, on US 95 goes through five national forests on the way to the capital of the Mormon church: Salt Lake City, Utah. Founded in 1847 by Brigham Young, who led Mormons from the persecution in the East to the promised lands of the Utah basin, about 70 per cent of Salt Lake's current population belong to the church. The Mormon temple (one of over 100 in the world) is the town's focal point, and is a sacred place for members the faith reserves the temple for its most special occasions so it is not open to visitors. However, the immaculate grounds and visitor's center do allow a glimpse into this close and well-ordered religion. The Mormons live by a stric code shunning alcohol, tobacco and even hot drinks like tea and coffee. Smoking is banned in most places in Salt Lake and much of the state is dry, meaning the purchase o alcohol can be difficult. Like many cities in the Southwest Salt Lake is blessed with a breath-taking setting: mountains in the background offset the desert in the foreground and the strikingly distinctive architecture of this rare religious capital The Salt Lake Convention and Visitors Bureau can b reached at 801-521-2822 or www.visitsaltlake.com.

Map on page 144

primary method of forest fire surveillance. As fire detection methods became more sophisticated, these structures were gradually vacated. The Canoe Gulch Ranger Station has opened its lookout atop **Big Creek Baldy Mountain** to the public, which is available on a reserve-ahead and pay-ahead basis. That being arranged, you drive into Libby and pick up directions and the key. State Highway 37 out of Libby leads to forestry service access roads, the last of which winds its way up to the foot of Big Creek Baldy Lookout. The last mile or so is extremely rough and steeply graded. However, the thrill of making it to the top, mingled with awe upon viewing the panorama that awaits, will take anyone's breath away. A tame mule deer has been known to greet visitors as they disembark. And it gets even better after climbing the steps of the 41-ft (12-meter) tower.

The 225-sq-ft (21-sq-meter) space with unobstructed windows and an observation deck on all sides contains items essential to survival and comfort and nothing more – save a fire-sighting device smack in the middle of the floor. Below, the tranquil beauty of the forest stretches for many miles in all directions; the wind becomes much more than a whistle, no longer muffled by the trees. This is a solitary, spiritual, romantic place to spend the night.

From Libby, where the **Cabinet Mountains** can be seen from downtown, it is a short drive west along US 2 to the Idaho border along the Kootenai River, passing near lovely and dramatic **Kootenai Falls** and through **Troy**, home of the largest silver mine in the United States. You are leaving a land of cowboy hats and rejoining a land of loggers and miners.

INTO IDAHO

The road enters Boundary County – aptly named, as it borders not just Montana but also British Columbia and Washington – joining US 95 just north of **Bonners Ferry**. At **Sandpoint**, on the shores of the huge **Lake Pend d'Oreille**, US 2 splits off to the west, while US 95 bridges the lake on its way southwest toward Coeur d'Alene. From 1890 to 1910, three transcontinental railroad lines forged their way through this part of Idaho, creating a string of towns that dot the highway.

Before reaching **Coeur d'Alene ❻**, US 95 greets the interstate. It is worth back-tracking east along Interstate 90 a little here, not only because the road hugs the banks of **Coeur d'Alene lake** for some 11 miles (18 km), but primarily because it leads to two vestiges of 19th-century Idaho, both unique in their way and completely dissimilar: the Old Mission and the Enaville Resort.

The **Coeur d'Alene Mission of the Sacred Heart** (also known as the Old Mission; tel: 208-682-3814; open daily) stands atop a hill overlooking the main road (I-90), as it has done since 1853. It is the oldest standing building in Idaho. Constructed of timber, mud and wooden pegs by Father Anthony Ravalli and the Coeur d'Alene Indians, it is said to have risen "like a miracle in an almost total wilderness where even log houses were rare."

The Jesuits, Ravalli among them, came to this part of Idaho knowing they would be welcomed by the Coeur d'Alene Indians, who had been told by neigh-

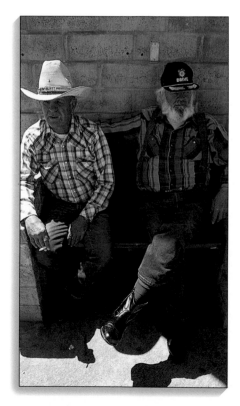

BELOW: buddies on a bench.

boring tribes of the great powers of the "Black Robes." Truly a Renaissance man, Ravalli's European training was reflected in the mission's design, perhaps best described as Native American-Italianate. The spacious, cathedral-like interior is decorated with chandeliers made from tin cans, whitewashed newspaper painted with floral motifs, carved pine crosses, a wooden altar painted to resemble marble and many other precious artifacts.

In 1877, the Coeur d'Alene were forced to abandon their beloved mission for a reservation to the south, but they still consider it their mission today and return each August 15th to celebrate the Feast of the Assumption. Due to its location, the mission also became a rendezvous point for mountain men, fur traders and "all sorts of riff-raff," in the words of the cavalrymen who were often called in to maintain peace and order. July brings an annual Historic Skills Fair – a modern-day rendezvous of crafts, mountain men, Coeur d'Alene and tourists – back to the area.

The Old Mission had no confessional until the late 1800s when one was established, presumably to serve white settlers, some of whom may have sinned at an establishment now called the **Enaville Resort**, located in **Kingston**, east of the mission along I-90 and then north on Coeur d'Alene River Road. The resort was built in 1880 as an overnight stop *en route* to gold and silver country, gaining several nicknames over the years – the Snakepit, Josie's, the Clark Hotel. Located strategically across from a lumberyard, a rail crossroads and a fork of the Coeur d'Alene River, it has served in its time as boomtown bar, hotel and house of ill repute.

BELOW: riding horseback in Washington state.

Today, the Enaville is merely a relaxing place to stop for a drink, eat a bite and meet the locals. Furnishings have piled up over the years and include many pieces hand-wrought by a mysterious man from Finland known only as Mr Egil. His materials were pine burls, antlers, horns and animal hides; his only recompense was a room, board and free beer.

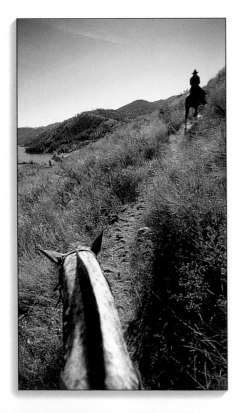

WASHINGTON STATE

A short drive west on I-90 takes you out of Idaho and into eastern **Washington**, a land of deserts, canyons, coulees, wheat fields and irrigated farmland – a sharp contrast to the densely forested terrain of northern Idaho. Historically, this region was home to numerous Native American peoples, most of whom lived along the banks of the Columbia River. Their descendants, members of the Colville Confederated Tribes, live today on a reservation bordered on two sides by the Columbia River. This was uninviting territory for early white explorers. The Grand Coulee itself presented a major obstacle, with few openings through which to pass. In the 1880s, the first white settlers in the region faced enormous hardships. Their numbers remained relatively few until the completion of the Grand Coulee Dam. Built during the height of the Great Depression, the dam and the Columbia Basin irrigation and electrification project changed the face of this region for all time.

Outside **Spokane** ❻, US 2 travels through golden wheat fields toward the dam. Road signs become a little confusing as the road approaches not only th

Map
on page
144

Grand Coulee Dam, but the towns of Electric City, Grand Coulee, Grand Coulee Dam and Coulee City. At Wilbur, State 174 goes north to the town of Grand Coulee, where State 155 continues on to the dam. As they say, "You can't miss it." The impact of the **Grand Coulee Dam** 65 cannot be overestimated – economically or visually. Its aims, achievements and sheer size are all on a grand scale. Although it is over 50 years old, the design of the dam, is of such stylistic integrity that it still looks modern today.

The drive along State 155, from the dam to **Coulee City** and US 2, is surprisingly scenic. The road skirts the lake on one side and the algae-clad coulee walls on the other. West of Coulee City along US 2, gently sloping fields of wheat, dotted with the occasional farmhouse, give the appearance of a vast desert. Layers of blue mountains appear in the distance like a mirage – the first of the coastal chains.

At **Orondo**, the highway meets, follows and crosses the **Columbia River** and then branches off, tracing its tributary the Wenatchee into foothills of the **Cascade Range**. This is orchard country: green patches of fertile land jut into the river and contrast with the golden hills; some of the local stands put out ripe apricots for sale.

Now US 2 climbs and enters a realm of tall timber, passing through the town of **Leavenworth** 66 – a self-styled, pseudo-Bavarian ski resort and gateway to the **Wenatchee National Forest**. Over the rushing south fork of the Skykomish River, and through the **Snoqualmie National Forest**, past several small towns with no-nonsense names like Gold Bar and Startup, US 2 continues west, bringing you just to the northeast of **Seattle** 67 *(see page 172)*, where you catch the expressway and (hopefully) breeze into one of America's most interesting and attractive cities.

The Washington State Ferry system, the largest in the US, runs ferries to the Olympic Peninsula from Seattle.

BELOW: Sol Duc Falls, Olympic Peninsula.

THE OLYMPIC PENINSULA

Before you dig in your heels in Seattle, however, another nearby destination beckons. Washington's **Olympic Peninsula** is the northwesternmost corner of the contiguous 48 states – a remote, exotic and wildly beautiful region within easy reach of both Seattle and Victoria, British Columbia. It is set apart from these places not merely by Puget (pronounced *pyew-jet*) Sound and the Strait of Juan de Fuca, but by its climate, its geology, the mystery of its peaks and forests and by the natural rhythms that guide the pace of life.

From **Edmonds**, due north of Seattle, a ferry crosses the short, scenic distance across the sound to **Kingston** 68 on the peninsula. From here, it is a lovely drive west and north to the peninsula's northeastern tip at the entrance to Puget Sound.

At the heart of the peninsula are the magestic **Olympic Mountains**, snow-streaked even in summer. Long a subject of myth, these mountains remained unexplored until the 1890s, when an expedition from Seattle set off in search of man-eating savages. Even the peninsula's Native Americans avoided venturing into the interior, fearing the wrath of mighty Thunderbird, who was believed to reside atop Mount Olympus. Today, the mountains are preserved and protected in a near-wilderness state as part of Olympic National

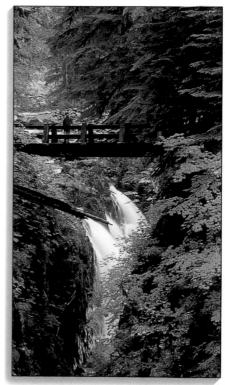

Park, which comprises 923,000 acres (374,000 hectares) of the peninsula, most of it inland but also including a 50-mile (80-km) strip of Pacific Ocean coastline. Only a few roads venture into the park, and these only peripherally. In fact, the park proper is surrounded by the **Olympic National Forest**, which makes it difficult to reach. Because the peninsula is largely under some form of Federal jurisdiction, there is considerable conflict with the lumber industry.

The Olympic Peninsula sustains the rainforests of the Hoh, Quinault and Queets river valleys; the glacial peaks of the Olympics; and the rugged Pacific coastline as well as lumber towns, fishing villages and nine American Indian reservations. Roosevelt elk, cougars and bald eagles all reside here in greater concentrations than anywhere else in the land.

Charming **Port Gamble**, the first town along the route, calls itself "a permanent forest community," and so it is – an authentic lumber town reflecting a bygone era. Just beyond it, a bridge crosses the Hood Canal – the work of glaciers rather than men. At the town of **Discovery Bay** (a good place to buy fresh oysters, clams and herring), State 20 veers off and up to Port Townsend.

Victorian town

Port Townsend 69, first settled in 1851, is the peninsula's oldest town and an attractive base. Sea captains and storekeepers from back East made their homes here, and it was quick to become a boomtown, built in anticipation of being linked with the Union Pacific Railroad and consequently becoming the major seaport of the Northwest. All this came to pass – for Seattle, not Port Townsend. After the bust, settlers tore up the train tracks, closed down the banks and departed for more prosperous parts.

Left behind is the best example of a Victorian seacoast town north of San Francisco. Declared a National Historic District, Port Townsend has become a haven for artists and is also the headquarters of the **Northwest School of Wooden Boatbuilding** (tel: 360-385-4948; www.nwboatschool.org), where a dying art has been revived. Free tours are offered to the public on weekdays throughout the year.

US 101 loops around the peninsula like a misshapen horseshoe, open at the bottom. In the north, it passes through Olympic National Forest and on to the lumber towns of the "West End." The region between Discovery Bay and Port Angeles has been called the "banana belt," sitting as it does in the rain shadow of the Olympics. Farmers here see an average rainfall of only 17 inches (43 cm) compared with upwards of 140 inches (356 cm) on the other side of the mountains. Irrigated farms are a common sight along this part of US 101, as are madrona trees, twisted and terracotta in color.

Small and distinctive

The towns along the way are small and distinctive. **Blyn** is gone before you can say "Little Brown Church of Blyn," its one and only landmark. **Sequim** (pronounced *skwim*) is a bigger town with a sense of humor about its name. Just north of here, on the Strait of Juan de Fuca – explorer De Fuca thought this was the Northwest Passage – is **Dungeness**, where the Dungeness crabs are landed.

Port Angeles, next settlement to the west, is called the "big town." The plants of several major lumber companies are located here, and the smell of wood permeates the air; it's also here that you catch big cruise boats to Victoria, British Columbia, on gorgeous Vancouver Island. From Port Angeles, the road traces Elwha Creek, enters the National Forest and winds down to crystalline Lake Crescent within the National Park. The highway is lined with towering evergreens, the roadside carpeted with ferns, as you continue west toward the ocean and the rainfall amounts suddenly begin rising again.

Map on page 144

West End

Logging is a way of life in the peninsula's "West End." US 101 passes through the towns of **Sappho** and **Forks**, the latter calling itself "logging capital of the world," and evidence of this dubious activity is everywhere: clearcut hillsides denuded of all trees, logging trucks barreling down the roads, brawny lumberjacks and cafés that request all patrons to remove their spiky, tree-climbing boots before entering the premises. Most of the big timber is long since gone now, and what remains is usually though not always – off-limits to these lumber companies.

The temperate rainforests west of the mountains are the most beautiful of all the sights in **Olympic National Park** ⓻ (tel: 360-565-3130; www.nps.gov/olym; open daily). They are the only ones in North America and contain some of the tallest timber in the world. Most accessible of these awe-inspiring forests is the **Hoh River Valley**, located south of Forks and inland on Hoh River Road: the embodiment of the "forest primeval" immortalized by Henry Wadsworth

The peninsula's town of Dungeness is the place to find the famous crabs.

BELOW:
Second Beach at sunset, Olympic National Park.

Map on page 144

Longfellow. Most awesome are the ancient evergreens – western redcedar, Sitka spruce, Douglas fir and western hemlock – shrouded with club moss, filtered by light, surrounded by ferns and the sound of the river. It is an eerie, overgrown, magical place, barely touched by the presence of man – with one exception.

John "The Iron Man of Hoh" Huelsdonk came to the Hoh Valley from Iowa in 1891. Discouraged by all who met him, he nevertheless poled his canoe up the wild river and made his home in this forest. What he could not carry by canoe, such as his cast iron stove, he strapped to his back. Hence the nickname – and the birth of a legend. The Iron Man died and is buried in the forest he so loved, as is his wife.

The village of **La Push**, on the **Quilayute Indian Reservation**, is reached by way of La Push Road (Route 110) from Forks. Those who live here fish for a living, and those who visit here visit for the fishing. If La Push were not so unpretentious, it would surely proclaim itself driftwood capital of the world: its beach is beautiful at night, a string of warming campfires and sea-stacks visible through the perpetual mist.

Land's end

BELOW AND RIGHT:
Henry Wadsworth
Longfellow called
woods like the
Olympic Peninsula's
Hoh Rainforest the
"forest primeval."

You can't get any farther northwest in the continental United States than isolated **Neah Bay**. Forking off the loop of US 101 at Sappho, State 113 and then State 112 winds its way to the ocean along the strait. Vancouver Island is now visible in the distance. Neah Bay is the ancestral and current home of the fine **Makah Indian Nation**, whose presence here for at least 3,000 years has been confirmed by archeologists. Once renowned whale hunters who took to the sea in cedar canoes, they still live off the ocean, though the catch today is more likely to be salmon. Entering town, a sign proclaims: "Makah Nation – a treaty tribe since 1855." The Makah do not underestimate the importance of this treaty, which guarantees their territorial and fishing rights, which to them means survival.

Neah Bay is also a gateway to one of America's most splendid stretches of wilderness coastline. A network of gravel and dirt roads goes part of the distance, but to reach land's end it is necessary to go on foot. If you want some adventure, drive as far as you dare and then hike the precipitous trail down to pretty **Shi-Shi Beach** and simply gaze out to sea. Be aware of time – and tide-tables– as the water rushes in quickly around here.

The trail to **Cape Flattery** is shorter and less dangerous. It descends an intricate stairway of tree roots through the forest, a clearing and a stand of huckleberry bushes before reaching the cliff's edge. Look out over Cape Flattery, knowing you stand as far northwest as possible in the lower 48 states of the USA – and that you have reached the end of a journey that began, thousands of miles ago, beside a different ocean in busy Boston Harbor.

Then retrace your steps back to Seattle, or follow US 101 around the rest of the peninsula and down to the town of Aberdeen, where you can, if you wish, drive all the way to Mexico on US 101 and Highway 1 *(see the Pacific Route, page 382).* ◻

A SHORT STAY IN SEATTLE

Seattle is youthful and friendly, business-minded, busy and beautiful: a city of the 21st century. Here's a list of the not-to-be-missed attractions:

◆ The Space Needle is only one aspect of the huge and impressive Seattle Center; other things to see and do in the center complex include several theaters, a children's museum, a sci-fi museum, a fun fair and the excellent Pacific Science Center.

◆ The Seattle Aquarium features 200 varieties of fish native to Puget Sound, plus environments simulating rocky reefs, sandy seafloors, eelgrass beds and tide pools. It's one part of the vibrant Waterfront area, which also has ships, piers, stores and restaurants.

◆ Filled with shops and food, food, food, Seattle's International District shows off the city's unique mixture of Asian cultures. Beyond Chinatown lies the Curry Triangle, filled with Thai, Laotian and Cambodian shops and restaurants.

◆ Experience Music Project (EMP) is a rock music museum conceived by Paul Allen of Microsoft fame, featuring artifacts like Eric Clapton's guitar, state-of-the-art technology, interactive exhibits and architecture by Frank Gehry.

◆ Beautiful bodies bounding on sandy beaches alongside cyclists, joggers and volleyball players make Alki Beach Seattle's answer to Southern California. Alki Point Lighthouse looks postcard-perfect in front of Puget Sound.

◆ "The mountain" (as it is known by locals) is in Mount Rainier National Park, just outside of the city. A single road loops through miles of parkland and timbered canyons. South of Seattle is Mount St Helens; its crater (caused by a far-reaching 1980 eruption) can be accessed via roads with views of Spirit Lake.

For visitors interested in staying longer in the big city, pick up a copy of *Insight Guide: Seattle*. This is a companion to the present volume, and is packed with insightful text and stunning pictures.

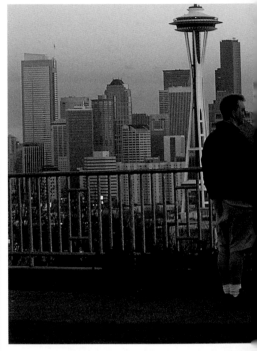

△ SPACE NEEDLE SKYLINE
Built for the 1962 World's Fair, the Space Needle offers the best views of the city and surrounding hills. Relax in the revolving restaurant at the top.

▽ SEATTLE ART MUSEUM
Designed by Robert Venturi, the recently expanded museum holds a highly regarded collection of Northwest Indian art, and paintings by modern artists.

▷ PIKE PLACE MARKET
Started in 1907 as a farmers' market, Pike Place still sells local produce and the freshest of fish, but they have now been joined by crafts people, street muscians, restaurants, cafés and coffee-houses.

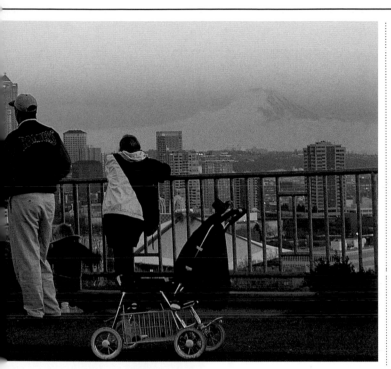

THE EMERALD CITY

Seattle is constantly rated as one of the most livable cities in the US. With a diverse population, rich cultural life and wealthy industries (Boeing and Microsoft), all situated amid awesome scenery, who wouldn't want to live here? Named for Native American chief Sealth, the laid-back lifestyle associated with the city has long been in place; tribes like the Salish and the Duwamish had been living peacefully in the hills for years. As do its residents now, surrounded by water and mountain peaks, working hard, playing easy and drinking gallons of strong coffee. If the future of America is anywhere, it is probably right here.

△ PIONEER SQUARE
The oldest part of the city, Pioneer Square's 19th-century buildings are now showcases for shops and bars.

> WATERFRONT
A vintage streetcar serves the Seattle Waterfront, transporting tourists and locals alike.

Important Information

Population:
573,000.
Dialing code:
206
Website:
www.visitseattle.org

Tourist information:
One Convention Place, 701 Pike Street, Suite 800, 98101 (no drop in)
Tel: 206-461-5840

▽ Red arrows on the map indicate routes from the city detailed in this book

Seattle Throughways

THE CENTRAL ROUTE

*A detailed guide to the Central US, with principal sites
clearly cross-referenced by number to the maps*

It is perhaps fitting to begin a journey across America from the nation's capital of Washington, DC; the many museums and famous landmarks that give a glimpse into the country's past do much to set the scene for the rest of your trip west. In fact, there are a few routes you could choose to head west from here, but for our purposes we've chosen a "south-central" course that combines enough history and beauty to sate any traveler's appetite.

The history lesson begins as soon as you leave Washington, heading first west and then sharply south along the beautiful Skyline Drive and the Blue Ridge Parkway through the Appalachian Mountains of Virginia. This was Stonewall Jackson territory; the route is sprinkled with Civil War sites as well as a myriad of caverns. Interstate 40, which we'll be following for much of the trip west, continues into North Carolina and through the Great Smoky Mountains, taking you past the charming old homes of Knoxville, Tennessee, and Andrew Jackson's home, The Hermitage, before heading into Nashville, capital not only of Tennessee but of country music.

From there, it's truly into small-town America as you hit Arkansas, stopping for a time in Little Rock, with its impressive state capitol building and Historic District and Hot Springs. Then roll on into Oklahoma, where we pick up legendary Route 66 – which originates in Chicago – a highway that crosses eight states and three time zones *(see also "Route 66" essay, page 35)*. Some know Route 66 from legend, others from childhood, when every mile with its weathered telegraph poles and zany-shaped motels were milestones on an exciting journey into a wonderland whose roadside attractions included snake pits, live buffaloes and Indian dancers.

Oklahoma's piece of Route 66 passes through many interesting small towns, but also some bigger ones, such as Tulsa, with its Art Deco downtown, and Oklahoma City. You'll cut across the Texas Panhandle before heading into New Mexico, visiting the attractive cities of Santa Fe and Albuquerque. The state has a wealth of ancient pueblos, homes of early inhabitants that are well worth visiting. As you cross into Arizona, you enter the Navaho Nation; the route passes by the Petrified Forest National Park before reaching Flagstaff, the largest city in the northern part of the state and the jumping-off point for the incomparable Grand Canyon. You'll cross some pretty desolate countryside in western Arizona, and again in eastern California's Mojave Desert, before you start seeing signs of "civilization" as you head into the urban sprawl of Los Angeles. With some 2,900 miles (4,700 km) now behind you, the Pacific Ocean beckons. ❑

PRECEDING PAGES: Route 66 memorabilia in Seligman, Arizona; McLean, Texas.
LEFT: heading straight for Monument Valley in the colorful Southwest.

A SHORT STAY IN WASHINGTON, DC

Planned as a city of monuments and memorials, the nation's capital is also one of its most beautiful. Here's a list of the not-to-be-missed attractions:

◆ The Capitol Building is the home of America's national legislature, and stands as a symbol of Washington, DC.

◆ Whether you wish to retrace the path of Martin Luther King Jr, whose "I Have a Dream" speech came from these steps, or simply take a look at the huge statue of Abraham Lincoln, the Lincoln Memorial celebrates the liberty that the founding fathers hoped the US would provide.

◆ In keeping with the classical motif of the city, the domed Jefferson Memorial honors the third US president and chief author of the Declaration of Independence.

◆ The Vietnam Veterans Memorial lists the names of all known American soldiers killed in the 1960s conflict. It is also a personal monument, as families travel from across the US to find the names of relatives who never returned.

◆ At first a strategic stronghold in the Civil War, the Arlington National Cemetery contained 16,000 headstones by the end of the struggle. The eternal flame at the grave of John F. Kennedy honors the fallen president, and the Tomb of the Unknowns commemorates the nameless soldiers felled in battles over the last 100 years.

◆ Housing the most impressive collection of air and space artifacts in the world, the National Air and Space Museum combines these with hands-on experiments and audio-visual exhibits.

◆ The Library of Congress, founded by Jefferson, is now the largest library in the world. Assistants are sometimes able to give tours to visitors.

▷ **THE WHITE HOUSE**
The President's home dates from 1792 and was designed by Irish architect James Hoban.

▽ **WASHINGTON MONUMENT**
The Washington Monument towers 555 feet (170 meters) above the city. In 70 seconds you can be at the top.

Visitors staying longer in the big city should pick up a copy of *Insight Guide: Washington DC*. This is a companion to the present volume, and is packed with insightful text and stunning pictures.

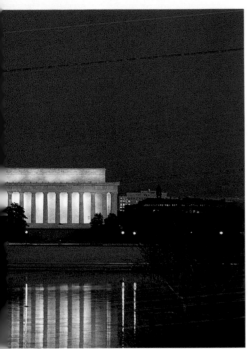

◁ NIGHTTIME REFLECTIONS
At dusk, Washington changes from a political town into a monumental city of beauty. From left to right: the Capitol, the Washington Monument and the Lincoln Memorial.

△ SMITHSONIAN INSTITUTE
Sometimes called "America's attic," the Smithsonian is actually several buildings, and traces developments in diverse fields, particularly science.

THE NATION'S CAPITAL CITY

A visit to Washington, DC, is nothing less than a lesson in history, literally a living history, since the President of the US lives here. The city also has a unique beauty, the credit for which should go to George Washington. The new president insisted on creating a new city as the nation's capital, a place as grand as Paris or London. With this in mind, he hired French architect Pierre Charles L'Enfant to create a "city of magnificent distances." L'Enfant's plan was only partially realized, but Washington *is* magnificent and the distances between monuments deceptively large; bring a good pair of walking shoes.

NATIONAL GALLERY OF ART
M. Pei designed the east wing *(shown)*, which houses collection of 20th-century art. The neo-classical est wing includes works by Da Vinci and Raphael.

mportant Information

opulation:	Tourist information:
51,000	901 7th Street NW
ialing code:	Fourth Floor
02	Washington DC,
Vebsite:	20001
ww.washington.org	Tel: 800-422-8644

▽ Red arrows on the map indicate routes from the city detailed in this book

Washington, DC Throughways

0 ——— 5 miles
0 ——— 5 km

Map on page 184

WASHINGTON, DC TO ARKANSAS

From Asheville, North Carolina, to Nashville, Tennessee, and beyond, this route takes in Virginia, Memphis and the scented highways of Arkansas to Little Rock

Our route begins in **Washington, DC ❶** *(see page 180)*, the first leg of which runs to Winston-Salem, North Carolina, along Interstate 66, and then I-81 south. The interstate will take you to the town of Front Royal and then the Skyline Drive, which runs south along the eastern rampart of the Blue Ridge Mountains, mountains so pine-scented and peaceful we always recommend this drive as the preferred route into North Carolina. On the way to Front Royal, you may want to cruise past the town of **Fairfax**, where, a few miles west is the **Virginia Visitors' Center**, with hundreds of brochures covering every facet of Virginia tourism. Stop in for schedules of current events and festivals throughout the "Old Dominion."

At some point, if you have time, you can change from I-66 to Virginia 55, which runs parallel, as both roads head for the mountains. The pace of life begins to slow almost immediately as you drive along increasingly serpentine roads with vistas opening to reveal the majestic Blue Ridge Mountains looming in the distance. Cumulous clouds hover over the dark peaks to the west. Small waterfalls slide down rock faces along the road. Beautiful pink and purple crown vetch, dandelions and goldenrod grow wild on the hillsides.

LEFT: Grand Ole Opry, Nashville.
BELOW: flying the flag on a bus.

Moving site for Southerners

The fast track on Interstate 66 weaves through a tangle of ever-growing suburbs around Washington, DC, practically obscuring a moving site for Southerners. A detour from I-66 onto the smaller SR 234 leads to **Manassas National Battlefield Park ❷** (tel: 703-361-1339; open daily until dusk), the spot of two great Confederate victories during the Civil War – the First and Second Battles of Manassas (or locally, Bull Run). Ten hours of deadly fighting on July 21, 1861, resulted in a Union defeat, and it was at this battle that General Thomas J. Jackson earned the nickname "Stonewall." The second battle, one year later, proved the genius of Confederate General Robert E. Lee. Driving and walking tours are available, and the visitor center has a museum and slide program. Be warned, however, that even though the site is well signposted, finding the correct turn-off can be maddingly confusing – drive slowly and be alert.

The Civil War looms large in these parts, as Virginia was the site for more than half of its major battles (as an example, the Shenandoah Valley town of Winchester changed hands 74 times). At Front Royal, you can take orientation tours of several Civil War sites, and at **Strasburg**, famous since 1761 for its

Washington, DC to Oklahoma City

Washington ❶
Fairfax
Front Royal
Strasburg
Skyline Drive
New Market
Shenandoah Caverns
Woodrow Wilson
Presidential Library
❻ Roanoke

Washington, DC
Virginia
Manassas National
Battlefield Park ❷
Skyline Caverns ❸
Shenandoah
National Park
Rockfish Gap
Staunton ❹
Lexington ❺
Junc 144   Blacksburg

Virginia
North Carolina
Reynolda House

Junc 80
Mount Airy ❼
Winston-Salem ❽
Hickory
Asheville ❾   Chimney Rock Park

North Carolina
Tennessee
Norris Dam
Cherokee
Gatlinburg   Great Smoky Mountains
Junc 440   National Park ❿
Dandridge
Knoxville ⓫
Oak Ridge
Cookeville

Columbia   The Hermitage   Nashville ⓬
Junc 208
Jackson

Tennessee
Arkansas
Memphis ⓭
Junc 279
Hazen   Plantation Agriculture
Lonoke   Museum State Park
Toltec Mounds State Park
⓮ Little Rock   Junc 153B ⑦ Hot Springs ⓯

Arkansas
Missouri
Kansas
Oklahoma
Oologah
Junc 12
Fort Smith
Joplin ⓰
Junc 313
Miami ⓱
Junc 289
Vinita
Foyil
Claremore
Tulsa ⓲
Sapulpa
Kellyville
Davenport
Arcadia
Oklahoma City ⓳

pottery, there's the **Stonewall Jackson Museum** (tel: 540-465-5884; open daily). Memorabilia of the famous Confederate general includes a bullet-pierced coat worn during his brilliantly flexible 1862 campaign defending the strategic, highly valuable north–south Shenandoah Valley (an "avenue of invasion") against Federal army troops.

"There are two things never to be lost sight of by a military commander," General Thomas J. "Stonewall" Jackson declared. "Always mystify, mislead, and surprise the enemy if possible... Such tactics will win every time." The historic **Museum of American Presidents** (tel: 540-465-5999; open daily), eight of whom were Virginians, is also in Strasburg.

From the earth to the sky

Nestled in the foothills of Virginia's Blue Ridge Mountains – amid farms and woodlands, battlefields, riverbeds, streams and tiny hamlets – are the **Crystal Caverns** (tel: 540-465-5884; open daily), one of a series of cave complexes carved out of the limestone cliffs at each side of the valley. The caverns are near the Stonewall Jackson Museum, also on the battlefield of Hupp's Hill. The **Skyline Caverns** (tel: 800-296-4545) are 1 mile south of Front Royal; the **Endless Caverns** (tel: 800-544-2283), **Luray Caverns** (tel: 540-743-6551) and **Shenandoah Caverns** (tel: 540-477-3115) are all open daily and are near **New Market**, whose other attractions include a State Historical Park and museum on the site where Confederate troops routed a superior Union force in 1864, using teenage cadets from the Virginia Military Institute in Lexington.

Front Royal is a fairly ugly little town full of chain stores and fast-food restaurants crammed into a few town blocks. Luckily, you are not far away from the north entrance of **Shenandoah National Park ❸**, where the 105-mile (169-km) **Skyline Drive** begins. Established in 1926 by an act of Congress, the park was an experiment in land reclamation. At the time, the region was overpopulated and the land was eroding. President Franklin Roosevelt ordered the Civilian Conse

Map on page 184

vation Corps to build recreation facilities and complete construction of the Skyline Drive in 1939. During the decades since, the forests have revived and are once again densely overgrown with oak, hickory, pine and locust trees.

The **Dickey Ridge Visitor Center**, open from April to October, is 4½ miles (7 km) down the road. Here, you can pick up maps of the park, guides to local vegetation and wildlife and information about camping and lodging. If the pioneer spirit of "roughing it" doesn't strike your fancy, there are still informative hikes and talks on the natural life of the park led by rangers; you will undoubtedly be tempted to get off the road awhile and hike some of the beautiful forest trails. Even if you don't, at least pack a meal to eat *al fresco* at one of the seven picnic locations.

Although the earliest access to the Skyline Drive through the park is at Front Royal, the road may be closed in winter, necessitating a drive further south as far as Swift Run Gap, east of **Elkton**, where US 33 crosses southbound US 340.

Oh Shenandoah

Immediately upon entering Shenandoah National Park, the speed limit slows to 35 miles an hour (56 kph), and the lumbering pace of your fellow cars sets the mood for a leisurely drive. Initially, it's a two-lane, winding road covered with dense trees on both sides. As the road ascends, however, you begin to get magnificent glimpses of the **Shenandoah Valley** and **Shenandoah River** to the west. Stop at one of the many overlooks, get out of the car and take in the majesty of the sight. Almost as noticable as the view is the silence; stop frequently, turn off the engine and make the most of it. As you continue south, you'll see **Massanutten Mountain** between the north and south forks of the

The speed limit in the park is a leisurely 35 miles an hour – the perfect pace to enjoy the silence, the view and the deer.

BELOW: Luray, Virginia, in the Shenandoah Valley.

Shenandoah River and then, after about 10 miles (16 km) more, the road switches angles to give you an eastern view of Piedmont country.

At Mile 50.7 (Km 82), stop for a short round-trip hike to **Dark Hollow Falls**, the closest waterfall to the drive. Water tumbles 70 feet (21 meters) over its greenstone face. Nearby Big Meadows is – along with Dickey Ridge – one of the two main visitor centers in the park. For those wishing to stay overnight, the **Big Meadows Lodge and Campgrounds** are a convenient stop.

Hundreds of miles of hiking trails lead off the drive into a wilderness dotted with hickory, white pine, red spruce and chestnut trees, some of which was earlier cleared and planted by the original settlers. After extending their farms onto the hillsides from the fertile Shenandoah Valley, the settlers bragged of being "the breadbasket of the Confederacy."

Natural state

Thousands of tons of grain, leather and iron were left here to support the Southern forces in the Civil War, nourished by the meat from hogs and cattle and equipped with uniforms from the wool of thousands of sheep. Memories of the Civil War are everywhere, and 400 Confederate soldiers are buried at **Mt Jackson**, a town near the Shenandoah Caverns.

BELOW:
Roanoke, Virginia, is known as the Capital of the Blue Ridge.

In a novel experiment, almost a century after the conflict, President Franklin D. Roosevelt allowed the over-used foothills to return to their natural state. Pastures and croplands gradually became overgrown with shrubs and trees, creating a wilderness to which hundreds of species of birds, deer, bear, bobcat and other creatures returned (although few of these can be seen). The Skyline Drive ends at **Rockfish Gap**, where US 64 leads to **Staunton ❹**, a pleasant former

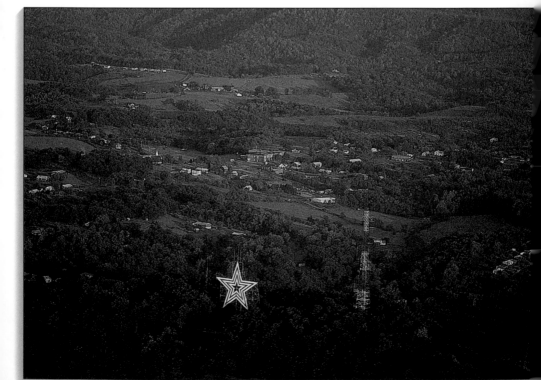

mining town with buildings dating to the 18th century, some of which are B&Bs. Yet another president, also known for his pursuit of peace, is remembered at Staunton, where the **Woodrow Wilson Presidential Library** (tel: 540-885-0897; www.woodrowwilson.org; open daily) illustrates local living conditions in the mid-19th century and portrays the 28th president's political career and eight-year (1913–21) White House stint.

West of I-81 is the attractive town of **Lexington ❺**, where ol' Stonewall was teaching cadets at the state-supported Virginia Military Institute (VMI) shortly after its founding in 1831. You can see the **Stonewall Jackson House** (tel: 540-463-2552; open daily). Jackson's Confederate colleague General Robert E. Lee also lived in Lexington and taught at the college founded by George Washington, known ever since as Washington & Lee University. Both universities welcome visitors. The latter has a chapel containing Lee's office and artifacts, while VMI's museums include one devoted to George C. Marshall, the politician and diplomat who won a Nobel Peace Prize at the end of World War II.

Blue Ridge Mountains

Virginia's alluring landscape is a welcome diversion from the trials of the highway. The air is suddenly refreshingly clear, and the famous blue haze shrouding the Blue Ridge Mountains hoves into view. **Roanoke ❻** (pop. 97,000), known as the "Capital of the Blue Ridge" for its proximity to the Blue Ridge Parkway – the connecting link between Shenandoah and Tennessee's Great Smoky Mountains – is a pleasantly relaxed city famous for a **Farmers Market** that has been operating for 125 years. Adjoining the market is a multi-cultural complex known as **Center in the Square** (tel: 540-342-5700), a vibrant collection

Map on page 184

 TIP

Leave yourself plenty of time to enjoy the walking and hiking excursions offered along the Blue Ridge Parkway; even a tiny walk to a beautiful waterfall can relieve the tedium of driving.

BELOW: the Blue Ridge Parkway was built along the top of the mountains.

of shops, restaurants, art galleries and a planetarium. There are also history and science museums, as well as the **Harrison Museum of African American Culture** (most are closed Mon). Mill Mountain, topped by the huge, illuminated **Roanoke Star**, overlooks the city and is the site of the **Mill Mountain Zoo** (tel: 540-343-3241; www.mmzoo.org; open daily), whose main attraction is a Siberian tiger called Ruby. **Virginia's Explore Park** (tel: 800-842-9163; www.explorepark.org; open Apr–Nov), just off the Blue Ridge Parkway (its junction is with State Road 116), is an environmental and historical site containing a re-created 17th-century village and exhibits dating back to 1000 AD.

Interstate 81 continues south, flanked by the vast Jefferson National Forest offering access at **Blacksburg** to the **Cascades National Recreation Trail**, a picturesque gorge that ends in a waterfall (a 4-mile/6-km hike, round trip). There's another access point farther along I-81 at Wytheville, where US 77 heads north to a campground in the park. But our route turns south just before that on US 52, which crosses the North Carolina border and takes us through the small town of **Mount Airy** ❼ *(see page 69)*, home of the homespun 1960s TV situation comedy *Mayberry RFD*.

Museum of living history

Continue south on US 52 to **Winston-Salem** ❽ (pop. 186,000), founded by Moravian immigrants in 1766. The area where it all began, **Old Salem,** is now a museum of living history. "After traveling through the woods for many days … the first view of the town is romantic, just as it breaks upon you through the woods; it is pleasantly seated on a rising ground and is surrounded by beautiful meadows, well-cultivated fields, and shady woods," wrote William Loughton Smith in his journal of May 1791.

BELOW:
pickin' session
at Mount Airy,
North Carolina.

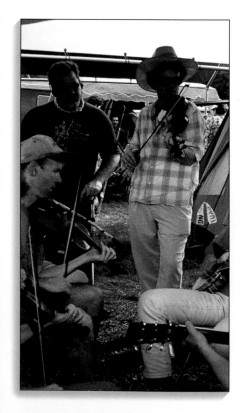

Arriving in Winston-Salem definitely gives one a sense of having "landed" in North Carolina, and the miles of highway driving start to pay dividends. Old Salem is possibly one of the most authentic and inviting living history towns in the US. Its old tavern is an upscale restaurant, and the simple timber homes contain their original furnishings. The printing shop of John Christian Blum, founding publisher in 1811 of *The Farmers' and Planters' Almanac*, is now a souvenir shop selling quill pens as well as cider and cookies. There is a **Children's Museum** (closed Sun morning) with hands-on exhibits. A remarkable timber bridge stands next to the **Frank L. Horton Museum Center**, containing paintings, textiles, ceramics, silver and other 19th-century creative works. And what of the giant-size metal coffee pot standing on the village green? Built by the sons of Salem's founders, Samuel and Julius Mickey, it was used to advertise their tinsmith's shop.

Costumed guides roam another restored Moravian village, **Historic Bethabara Park** (tel: 336-924-8191; www.bethabarapark.org; open Tues–Sun Apr–Nov), in a pleasant green setting off University Parkway.

The city's **Visitor Center** at 6th and Cherry streets (tel: 336-728-4200) distributes a free map of a downtown walking tour that includes the **City Market** – where a farmers market is held on summer Tuesdays and Thursdays – and such interesting structures as the Georgian Revival *Winston-Salem Journal* building (a replica of Philadelphia's Independence Hall), the Renaissance Revival Our Lady of Fatima Chapel and the Art Deco R.J. Reynolds Building (whose New York architects Shreve and Lamb used it as a prototype for their subsequent Empire State Building.) Numerous old brick buildings in nearby streets are being transformed into galleries and artist studios.

Reynolda House, the former 1917 home of Katharine Smith and Richard Joshua Reynolds (founder of the giant R. J. Reynolds Tobacco Company) – along with its gardens and adjoining Reynolds Village, in which the former buildings have been converted into shops, offices and restaurants – is open to visitors (tel: 336-758-5150; www.reynoldahouse.org; closed Mon). *The New Yorker*'s Brendan Gill praised the modesty of the mansion, adding "the intention here is plainly not to show off but to be happy among friends…"

From Winston-Salem, we join I-40, which remains our route for most of the journey. About 73 miles (117 km) along the route is the town of **Hickory**, which is famous for its furniture: 100 such stores are gathered together in one center, and there is even a **Furniture Museum** (tel: 800-462-6278; open daily).

Map on page 184

Coffee break: this gigantic pot sits on the village green in Old Salem.

ASHEVILLE TO NASHVILLE

The Blue Ridge Parkway sweeps across I-40 just before Asheville, home to a popular winery. "More scenery, more music, more country on Country 92 FM," sings the jingle on the car radio, and indeed, when you begin to get a sense of being enveloped by mountains, you've probably arrived. There are vistas around almost every street corner, and the mighty Mount Pisgah to the west signals the beginning of the Great Smokies.

BELOW: Biltmore is the largest private residence in the US.

Exuding a certain amount of small-town charm, **Asheville ❾** is architecturally diverse. Besides Queen Anne, Romanesque and Revival styles, the town also has one of the largest collections of Art Deco architecture in the Southeast, outside of Miami Beach. You'll find the winery, along with shops and restaurants, in the immense landscaped gardens of the 250-room **Biltmore Estate** (tel: 800-624-1575; open daily), America's largest privately owned home. George Vanderbilt's 250-room vision took root in 1887, when he visited Asheville on vacation and became enchanted by the mountain scenery. Vanderbilt set out to create a mansion modeled after the French Loire Valley chateaux, and equipped it with many state-of-the-art luxuries. Today, visitors can enjoy the estate virtually as it was. The estate was a backdrop for *Being There*, one of several movies shot locally, along with *Thunder Road* and *28 Days*.

The natural beauty of Asheville, the largest city near the Blue Ridge Parkway, is emphasized in its botanical gardens, an arboretum with miles of walking trails, a nature center interpreting the area's plant and wildlife, the park-like Riverside Cemetery and the river itself – perfect for white-water activities. Entry to all of these is free (or inexpensive), as is the delightfully named **North Carolina Homespun Museum** (tel: 828-253-7651), which offers weaving demonstrations, and the **Folk Art Center** (tel: 828-298-7928).

Muse of the mountain

Asheville's beauty has attracted its fair share of literary giants, including F. Scott Fitzgerald and the influential author Thomas Wolfe. Wolfe spent his childhood in his mother's sprawling Queen Anne-style boarding house on Market Street, which is now the **Thomas Wolfe Memorial** (tel: 828-253-8304; www.wolfememorial. com; open Tues–Sun Apr–Dec, Tues–Sat Jan–Mar). A fire set by an arsonist caused much damage in 1998, but the house has since been restored. Despite being banned from the town's public library for seven years, Wolfe's *Look Homeward Angel* has never been out of print since it was first published in 1929. Before he died, aged 37, in 1938 he wrote about his old home: "And again, again, in the old house, I feel beneath my tread the creak of the old stair, the worn rail, the whitewashed walls, the feel of darkness and the house asleep, and think, 'I was a child here; here the stairs, here was darkness; this was I, and here is Time.'"

The town of Gatlinburg, Tennessee, is a popular place to get married; over 10,000 couples tie the knot here each year.

Southeast of Asheville, near the intersection of US 64 and 74A, is privately owned **Chimney Rock Park**, a 1,000-acre (405-hectare) Natural Heritage Site including Chimney Rock itself, and the bottomless pools and waterfalls of magestic **Hickory Nut Falls**, a backdrop for the climactic scenes in the movie *The Last of the Mohicans*. Visitors can take an elevator 26 stories up inside a mountain to emerge on its flat rocky top, 1,200 feet (366 meters) above the river, to enjoy spectacular views stretching for up to 75 miles (121 km).

THE GREAT SMOKIES

Great Smoky Mountains National Park ❿, 16 of whose peaks exceed 6,000 feet (1,800 meters), sprawls majestically over the North Carolina and Tennessee borders. Access, on the North Carolina side, is gained from the Blue Ridge Mountain Parkway town of **Cherokee**, reached by taking US 74 east from Asheville and then branching off onto US 19 (also eastbound). The highest point in Tennessee, 6,642-foot (2,025-meter) **Clingmans Dome** (access closed in winter) is on the ridge-clinging Appalachian Trail midway between Cherokee and **Gatlinburg**, the Smoky Mountains gateway town on the Tennessee side of the park.

BELOW:
Pee-Wee League cheerleaders dressed in the colors of the University of Tennessee.

Abundant rainfall keeps the park rich in wildflowers and other plant life; bears and white-tailed deer can sometimes be spotted. An **aerial tramway** (tel: 865-436-5423; open daily) runs from downtown Gatlinburg to Ober Gatlinburg, a ski resort and amusement complex offering fun-but-dumb games and stupendous views. Gatlinburg has become a popular marriage venue, with over 10,000 couples taking their wedding vows here each year.

The more direct route from Asheville into Tennessee is simply to take Interstate 40 north, and then follow it as it turns west toward Knoxville. Just after this turn, on the shore of Douglas Lake, is **Dandridge** (named after George Washington's wife Martha Dandridge), with plenty of boat docks and campgrounds. A scenic route into the Smokies leads from here to Sevierville and Gatlinburg along State Route 92 and then US 411.

Just before Knoxville, the **Armstrong-Lockett House** (tel: 865-637-3163; closed Mon), with its collection of 18th-century furniture and ancient English silver, presides over the former Crescent Bend plantation. There are also many interesting old homes in the former state capital, **Knoxville** ⓫ – among them the **Blount Mansion** (tel: 865-525-2375; www.blountmansion.org; closed Mon) built in 1792 by the governor of the Southwest Territory; the 1797 **Ramsey House** (tel: 865-546-0745; www.ramseyhouse.org; closed Mon); and the 1858 **Mabry-Hazen House** (tel: 865-522-8661; open Wed–Sat), which served as headquarters on different occasions for both sides in the Civil War. **James White's Fort** (tel: 865-525-6514; guided tours Mon–Sat) is a re-creation of the region's first pioneer structure.

Celebrating his roots

Victorian art and architecture are plentiful in the serene and rural **Old Gray Cemetery** on North Broadway, named for the English poet, Thomas Gray, author of *Elegy Written in a Country Churchyard*. Tennesseean and Pulitzer Prize-winning Alex Haley, best known for *Roots* and *The Autobiography of Malcolm X*, is celebrated with a larger-than-life bronze statue in Morningside Park. Among the many museums, worth noting is the **Women's Basketball Hall of Fame** (tel: 865-633-9000; www.wbhof.com; open daily), where you can watch videos of past moments of glory, as well as shoot some hoops.

North of the city on I-75, the **Norris Dam** was the first to be built by the vast Tennessee Valley Authority, which brought electric power to this region in the 1930s. **Norris Lake**, acclaimed as one of the cleanest in North America, hosts several marinas and supports houseboats, fishing and jet skiing. There are trails and campgrounds in the surrounding woods, and a Rice Grist Mill as well as several other museums. The **Museum of Appalachia** (tel: 865-494-

Map on page 184

BELOW: Clingmans Dome straddles both Tennessee and North Carolina.

Nashville's Greek Revival-style state capitol building was used as a fortress during the Civil War.

7680; www.museumofappalachia.com; open daily) calls itself "a living mountain village" and does a superlative job of interpreting rural Tennessee, with a pioneer school, a dirt-floor cabin (used in the *Daniel Boone* TV series) and spinning and weaving among its many exhibits.

West of Knoxville, on State Route 162, **Oak Ridge**, the "secret city" built in 1942 to work on production of the first atomic bomb, today invites visitors to explore historic sites such as the **Graphite Reactor** that formed part of what was known as the Manhattan Project. Somewhat ironic icons are the **International Friendship Bell and Pavilion** intended to serve "as an expression of hope for everlasting peace," and the **New Bethel Church**, which was the wartime meeting place for scientists and engineers planning the Big Bang. At **Cookeville,** which is farther west of Knoxville along State 62, the **Depot Museum** (tel: 931-528-8570; open Tues–Sat) occupies a station built by the Tennessee Central RR in 1909. Fun, faded and aged cabooses are on display in the grounds.

Continue west on US 70N, but consider stopping just before you get into Nashville for a visit to President Andrew Jackson's gracious and beautiful mansion, **The Hermitage** (tel: 615-889-2941; open daily), extensively furnished and on whose grounds still stand some of the cabins in which Jackson lived before becoming America's seventh president. He died there in 1845.

Nashville

BELOW: git-tars in the country music capital of the world.

After the peace and tranquility of Virginia and North Carolina, it's into Tennessee and the "country music capital of the world." **Nashville ⑫** isn't too much of a shock to the senses, however, being a compact and pleasant town to walk around, and it's certainly a good stop for a decent cup of coffee after days on the "filter trail." By this stage in the drive, *all* roads, it appears, lead to Nashville – where Interstates 40, 24 and 65 intersect at what likes to term itself "the Athens of the South."

This moniker is supported by the **Parthenon** (tel: 615-862-8431; closed Mon), a same-size replica built for the Tennessee Centennial Exposition in 1897. Originally constructed of wood, it was rebuilt in the 1920s of more sturdy concrete and is used for art exhibitions and other events in the popular Centennial Park. Fifty years before the Centennial, architect William Strickland had anticipated the style with his Greek Revival **State Capitol**, sturdy enough to be used as a fortress during the Civil War. Also worth seeing is the **Athenaeum Rectory** (tel: 931-381-4822; closed Sun–Mon), which began as a home for President James K. Polk's nephews but later became a school for the affluent offspring of planters and bankers. Polk's own ancestral home is at **Columbia** on I-31, southwest of Nashville.

Follow the green line

A City Walk wends through the downtown area marked by a painted green line on the sidewalk. It includes the **Beaux Arts Hermitage Hotel**, where suffragist groups and their opponents gathered to lobby the state legislature in 1920 – their target being the 19th Amendment to the US Constitution. This gave women the right to vote and was duly ratified by Tennessee's vote. Also on the route is **Printers Alley**, the pre-World War II center of Nashville nightlife, with venues that later featured Waylon Jennings, Chet Atkins, Hank Williams and others. There's a life-size bronze statue of a guitar player outside the Bank of America at 5th and Union streets.

Nashville-born Red Grooms, the whimsical artist and sculptor who made his name in New York, created the city's most popular artwork – a working carousel on the waterfront whose painted figures all depict well-known local characters. They include the late sportscaster Grantland Rice; frontiersman Davy Crockett; musician Chet Atkins; Belle Kinney and her husband Leopold Scholz, who worked on the city's Parthenon; and millionaire socialite Adelicia Acklen.

Tennessee State Museum

Centerpiece of the **Tennessee State Museum** (tel: 800-407-4324; www. tnmuseum.org; closed Mon) is an illustrated history of the Civil War – which killed 600,000 Americans – accenting the role that Tennessee, a Confederate state, played in it. Occupying an entire floor are interactive exhibits with sound effects, film, battle flags, a Confederate cannon, Davy Crockett's powder horn and an old Conestoga wagon in which some long-forgotten family from Virginia migrated to the state in about 1800.

Most of the Civil War battles in Tennessee took place along what is now known as the **Antebellum Trail**. A free leaflet listing battlefields (as well as a score of different old mansions) within a 90-mile (145-km) roundtrip loop,

Map on page 184

BELOW:
Tootsies Orchid
Lounge, Nashville.

south of Nashville to the Natchez Trace Parkway, is available from the Tennessee Tourism Department (tel: 800-836-6200).

Across the street from the State Museum in the 18-story state building is the **Military Museum**, exhibiting pictures and artifacts from America's subsequent wars. The **Tennessee Historical Commission** operates out of an outstanding 1850s mansion (open weekdays). The **Carl Van Vechten Gallery** (tel: 615-329-8720; closed Mon), one of three university art galleries housing the Alfred Stieglitz collection of modern art, has a notable collection of photographs and paintings by major figures.

Nashville's Scarlett O'Hara

Once a famous stud farm and thoroughbred nursery (from which came Iroquois, the 1881 winner of England's Derby), **Belle Meade Plantation** (tel: 615-356-0501; www.bellemeadeplantation.com; open daily) still displays the opulent lifestyles of a century-and-a-half ago, with tour guides in period costume. The 1853 Greek Revival mansion, elegantly restored, presides over what was once a 5,400-acre (2,187-hectare) plantation whose grassy acres now house Nashville's most impressive homes in a multitude of "neo-anything" styles. At one end of the park, **Cheekwood** (tel: 615-356-8000; www.cheekwood.org; closed Mon), the immense home of the founder of Maxwell House Coffee, has botanical gardens, a restaurant and an art gallery. Outdoor concerts take place in summer.

Sometimes regarded as the model for Scarlett O'Hara, Nashville's Adelicia Acklen (1817–89) built the Italian-style **Belmont Mansion** (tel: 615-460-5459; www.belmontmansion.com; open daily), now on Belmont University campus, whose grand salon always incites awe and admiration.

BELOW: Nashville's numerous honky tonk bars were where musicians headed for straight after a gig.

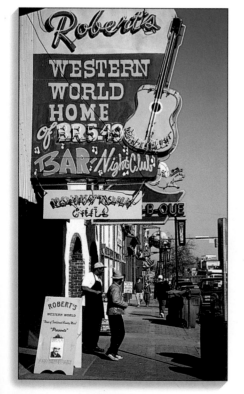

Grand Ole Opry

Almost one-third of the 400-plus record companies in the US are situated in Nashville, so it's no surprise the city has a self-proclaimed **Music Valley**, the area lying between Briley Parkway and the Cumberland River. The "valley" contains at least 100 shops, restaurants, hotels and other attractions, including the famous **Grand Ole Opry** (tel: 615-889-6611; www.opry.com) and its adjoining museum.

Until recently, the Grand Ole Opry – the country's longest-running live radio program, which began in 1925 – was broadcast from Ryman Auditorium ("the Carnegie Hall of the South"), which, since it opened in 1892, has played host to everybody from Enrico Caruso, Rudolf Valentino and Mae West to Bruce Springsteen and the Vienna Choirboys. There's a self-guided tour between 8:30am and 4pm any day of the week. Behind Ryman Hall were (and still are) a row of honky-tonk bars where the country and western stars would throw back a few beers after a foot-stomping gig.

The **Country Music Hall of Fame** (tel: 800-852-6437; www.countrymusichalloffame.com; open daily) moved from historic premises on tree-lined 16th Avenue (which also housed Studio B, where Elvis Presley cut a platter) to huge, state-of-the-art premises Downtown that span an entire city block. Around three hours is recommended to tour the various galleries, which could begin or end in the 214-seat acoustically excellent Ford Theater. The theater shows a film exploring the variety of country music around the world. In the museum itself, an entire showcase is devoted to Hank Williams who, along with fellow musician Ernest Tubb, is credited with inventing the honky-tonk style developed in roadside taverns and dancehalls prior to World War II.

Other exhibits include Elvis Presley's gold Cadillac and his grand piano; George Strait's hat and jacket; scores of guitars from famous owners; and the 1962 Pontiac – with pistols for door handles and steer horns mounted on the front bumper – owned by Webb Pearce. An enormous two-story wall displays every gold and platinum record to make the country charts (you can buy less precious editions of these in the shop). Live entertainment is staged most days.

Interstate 40, the road that connects Nashville with Memphis, is known as "Music Highway."

Southern cookin'

Bronze likenesses of the Hall of Famers themselves – which include promoters and broadcasters as well as performers – are showcased in a huge rotunda "bathed in the natural light admitted by a circle of clerstory windows," proof of how far C&W has come since the humble *Stand By Your Man*. The museum's restaurant serves contemporary Southern cuisine.

If, after this, you're ready to hit the road to visit another famous city of the south, head east out of Nashville on I-40. Some 128 miles (206 km) farther on, you'll come to **Jackson**, and just beyond that is a great family stop at **Casey Jones Village** (tel: 800-748-9588; www.caseyjones.com; open daily), with country stores, lavish buffets, an old-fashioned ice cream parlor, train rides and a caboose to sleep in. But if that doesn't suit your fancy, keep headin' on down the highway straight on into **Memphis ⓮** *(see page 196)*.

BELOW: the Country Music Hall of Fame was in this building for 33 years before relocating to state-of-the-art premises Downtown.

MEMPHIS: MUSIC CITY USA

The gateway to the Mississippi Delta is the home of blues, Beale Street and the site of two kings: Elvis and Martin Luther

The guest list at Memphis's ornate and venerable Peabody Hotel (pronounce it *ho-tel*) has included US presidents as well as the Confederate hero Robert E. Lee, but infinitely more popular today are the Peabody ducks, who live on the roof. Every day at 11am, they take a ride in the elevator to the lobby, walk across a red carpet and, to the strains of John Philip Sousa, climb into the fountain, where they remain until 4pm when the performance is repeated in reverse.

Memphis is best known, of course, for Graceland (tel: 800-238-2000; open daily; mansion tour closed Tues Dec–Feb), about 10 miles (16 km) south along Elvis Presley Boulevard, where there are long lines to view the late singer's home and grave.

Sun Studio (tel: 800-441-6249; open daily) was where "the King" recorded, but BB King, Ike Turner and many other artists preceded him here. In recent years, Bono, U2 and Paul Simon have been Sun clients. Hourly tours are given, and for an extra few dollars you can record a tape of your own.

The Stax Museum of American Soul Music (tel: 901-942-7685; open daily) celebrates the musicians who lived, worked or are buried in the area of Memphis called Soulsville, like Aretha Franklin and Otis Redding, while the Memphis Rock 'n Soul Museum, above the Gibson Guitar Factory near Beale Street, has six galleries that examine the history of Memphis music.

There are plenty of other music venues, among them the Center for Southern Folklore (tel: 901-525-3655; open Mon–Sat) and B.B. King's Blues Club (tel: 901-524-5464; open daily).

Beale Street is where it all began, and this is where W.C. Handy (1873–1958) set to music the songs of the cotton pickers and "inscribed for ever in the heart of the nation his immortal songs," as the inscription reads on his statue here. The street's bars, nightclubs and restaurants are all worthwhile. Schwab's, a store that's been around since 1876, sells hardware, 99¢ neckties, voodoo powders and tools.

Six blocks south is the National Civil Rights Museum (tel: 901-521-9699; closed Tues), incorporating the Lorraine Motel where Martin Luther King, Jr was assassinated on April 4, 1968. Even today, the sight of the rumpled bed, breakfast tray, and a few objects in Room 306 – the last things Dr King saw before stepping onto the balcony – bring a tear to the eye. Other rooms focus on the Civil Rights movement. ❑

LEFT: Beale Street, where W.C. Handy wrote "St Louis Blues;" Music City, USA.
ABOVE: Elvis drove here; Elvis recorded here.

ARKANSAS

After the excitement of Nashville and Memphis, the next part of the journey takes us straight back to small-town America, where Interstate 40 crosses the **Mississippi River** and cuts into the middle of Arkansas. Roadsides in Arkansas are often gloriously colorful, testament to the state's extensive wildflower program, which has lined more than 1,000 miles (1,600 km) of highway with colorful banks of purple larkspur, black-eyed Susan, Indian Paintbrush, goldenrod, pink primrose and bright red cardinal flowers – a native perennial that attracts hummingbirds. The Arkansas highway department claims that almost a quarter million acres of its highways have been graced with 600 species of flowers.

Paralleling the interstate between Memphis and Little Rock is US 70, where along the way you will find **Hazen**, with its wildlife preserve, and **Lonoke**, which houses one of the country's largest fish hatcheries. Southwest of Lonoke, just off US 165, are the **Plantation Agriculture Museum** (tel: 501-961-1409; closed Mon), which tells the story of cotton production in the South, and the **Toltec Mounds State Park**, a sprawling prehistoric site.

US 70 turns southwest at Little Rock, heading through **Benton** with its bauxite deposits. This earthy substance from which aluminum is made is responsible for much of the area's wealth – justification enough for the world's only bauxite building to be constructed here.

The Arkansas River carves a gateway between the Ouachita and Ozark mountains to the delta at **Little Rock ⑭**. The city is, therefore, first and foremost a river city; an amalgamation of the Old South and the Southwest. The downtown area of Little Rock extends south from the Arkansas River. Beside it, under the Union Pacific Railroad Bridge, is the "Little Rock" that lent the city its name,

Map on page 184

BELOW:
steaming down the Mississippi River.

and it's also the first visible rock outcrop to hove into view when traveling up from the Gulf of Mexico. **Riverfront Park**, with its pleasure boat wharf and extravagant fountain, is the site of an amphitheater and an outdoor film festival.

An extensive area called the **River Market**, flanked at the western end by the Convention Center, comprises businesses, shops, bars and cafés, two hotels, the library and a Farmers' Market (closed Sun, Mon). There's parking at the eastern end, near the **William J. Clinton Presidential Library** (tel: 501-374-4242; www.clintonlibrary.gov; open daily), and there's also a transit trolley making life even easier for out-of-towners. Heading back inland, the **Convention & Visitors Bureau** at the corner of Markham and Broadway streets (tel: 501-376-4781) is a good starting point to acquire information.

The greyhound has been the symbol of US bus travel for many decades.

Cast-iron hotel

Across the street is the restored historical **Capital Hotel** where President Ulysses S. Grant stayed in 1877, four years after it opened. The interior and exterior are equally interesting. Note its four-story cast-iron front and an elegant 1908 interior by Little Rock architect George R. Mann. At Second and Center streets is the 10-story Southern Trust Building (now called **Pyramid Place**), the city's first skyscraper when it was built in 1907. Times have changed, and today's Downtown is dominated by the TCBY Tower, that TV and yogurt fans will recognize as being the headquarters of "The Country's Best Yogurt."

Located on President Clinton Avenue, the **Museum of Discovery** (tel: 501-396-7050; ww.amod.org; open daily) entices kids and adults with Kewpie collections, live animal programs and more. A number of venerable old buildings located in downtown streets include the Romanesque Revival **Pulaski**

BELOW: parades are an American institution.

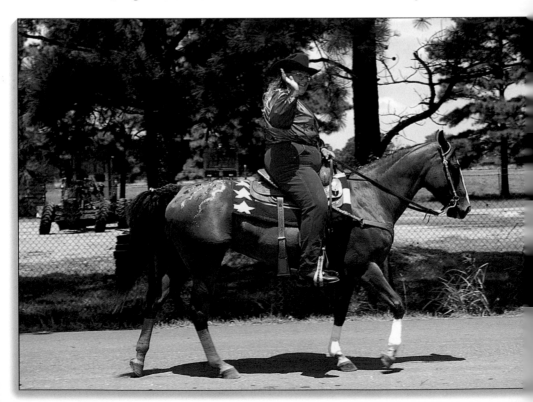

County Courthouse (Markham and Spring streets) with its Classical Revival domed annex, and the **Historic Arkansas Museum** (tel: 501-324-9351; open daily). Inside is the **Hinderliter Tavern**, the city's oldest building.

The impressive **State Capitol** (tel: 501-682-5080; guided tours Mon–Fri) in which Bill Clinton served five terms as governor and where he gave his election-night victory speeches, lies at the western end of Capitol Avenue. Its design details include six brass doors purchased from Tiffany's in New York. Flying atop the building is the state flag, which has a diamond in the center to mark the fact that Arkansas is the only state with a diamond mine (at Murfreesboro).

Grand old dames

Little Rock is understandably proud of its plethora of wonderful old houses – most of them funded and built by successful bankers, cotton brokers or other successful merchants in the 19th century. These interesting mansions are listed in several free books and pamphlets, which offer mapped routes through the various historical districts. A few of the homes have been converted into striking bed-and-breakfasts. Opening times vary and few of the houses are actually open to the public, so if you do have time for a lengthy tour be sure to collect some of this literature from the visitor's bureau before setting out.

A drive around the quiet, tree-lined streets might begin in the **Governor's Mansion Historic District** at the mansion itself (18th and Center streets) and concentrate on the streets between 18th and 15th streets bordered by Louisiana and Gaines. In this area alone, 35 buildings are listed in the Bureau's Tour Number Three. The Queen Anne or Colonial Revival styles, and sometimes a combination of both, predominate in this district and though varying considerably

BELOW: beauty contests are a Southern institution.

in appearance, many of the buildings were designed by the same architect, Charles L. Thompson, who practiced in Little Rock from 1885 for more than 50 years. The sumptuous **Governor's Mansion**, where the Clintons lived for 12 years, has a dramatic curving, walnut staircase and is stylishly furnished with Hepplewhite and Chippendale antique furnishings. A bust of Bill sits by the gate. Down the street are the **Cathedral Park Apartments** at 15th and Center, converted from a one-time Episcopal church, and four blocks west on Arch Street is the English Revival-style **Cornish House**, with its magnificent third-floor ballroom in which Ed Cornish, a prominent banker, and his wife staged lavish parties.

More than bed and breakfast

At 2120 Louisiana Street, the **Hornibrook House** was built by successful saloon owner James Hornibrook who, after a social snub, was determined to build something to make the neighbors gasp. The result is a house known as the "Empress of Little Rock," a Queen Anne-style home with concave front doors, a stained glass skylight, turrets, gables and a wrap-around porch. Inside is a series of luxuriously furnished parlors replete with lace cloths, tasseled lampshades, a dollhouse, antique chairs and divans. The house now serves as an attractive B&B, with eight octagonal rooms named after some of the state's historical characters – such as John Edward Murray, the youngest general in the Confederate army.

Another B&B worth staying the night for is **Hotze House**, at 1619 Louisiana Street. This one was the monumental home of a cotton broker and has a Colonial Revival exterior with 20-ft (6-meter) high pillars. Beneath the stenciled ceilings are walls covered with tapestry and green damask shot with gold thread.

There are equally impressive homes to be found in the **MacArthur Park** district. The 1881 Italianate **Villa Marre** at 1321 Scott Street was named for another successful saloon keeper, Angelo Marre, about whom one of the local guidebooks writes: "Initially known for his quick temper and shady past, Marre eventually became a respectable member of the City Council." The distinctive **Hanger House** at number 1010 on the same block, which looks like a vision from a fairy tale, owes its earthy shade to Frances Hanger, who remodeled the house herself after researching decorating books. She remarked in a letter to a friend that red seemed to be "about as popular as ever for painting houses."

Next to a refurbished 1957 Mobil gas station (with its pumps frozen at 22.5 cents per gallon) at 2125 Daisy Bates Drive is the **Little Rock Central High School National Historic Site** (tel: 501-374-1957; open daily) opposite the (still operating) school that provoked the dramatic desegregation confrontation of 1957.

Photos and other visuals depict the scene when Governor Orval Faubus called out the National Guard to bar admittance to nine black students. Three weeks later President Eisenhower called out the US Army to escort the students into the school. The legal case remained in the courts for an entire year, during which

BELOW:
Capitol building, Little Rock, where former US president Bill Clinton served five times as governor.

Map on page 184

time Little Rock high schools remained closed. At the time, the Mobil station, with the only pay telephone in the area, was the scene of some unseemly competition among the visiting press.

Hot Springs

About 50 miles (80 km) west of Little Rock, in the Diamond Lakes Region off SR 7, is the resort of **Hot Springs ⓕ**, which has been a recreational area for hundreds of years. The springs have played a large part in Arkansas politics – not least for being the boyhood home of Bill Clinton. A lakeside resort city surrounded by low-lying mountains, it offers historic buildings, an alligator farm and petting zoo, spas, ranches, an aquarium, a wax museum and all of the additional resort amenities. There are hundreds of accommodations ranging from hotels and lakeside cottages to campgrounds and houseboat rentals. (Information from 888-SPA-CITY.) One of the resort hotels claims that although Arkansas is famous for its unspoiled beauty, "we're famous…for our spoiled guests." From Little Rock, I-40 heads northwest and crosses the Oklahoma border at the rather unattractive **Fort Smith**. While the old Fort Town might be worth a quick visit on the way through, much of the new town of Fort Smith is memorable only for its used car lots and heavy traffic.

Although I-40 will carry you all the way through the state of Oklahoma and on westward, if you're interested in a more colorful journey, we suggest heading north just before Fort Smith on I-540, which becomes US 71 as it crosses into the southwest corner of Missouri and leads you to the city of **Joplin ⓖ**, where you can pick up America's "Mother Road" – Route 66 – which will cut across the southeast corner of Kansas before heading into Oklahoma. ❑

TIP

You may want to roll down your windows when traveling through Arkanas: a highway department program has resulted in the planting of 600 kinds of wildflowers, some of which attract hummingbirds.

BELOW:
Mother Nature statue in Hot Springs, Arkansas.

OKLAHOMA TO NEW MEXICO

Map on page 184

Take "a stroll on wheels" along Route 66 through Oklahoma and the Texas Panhandle, then cruise through Santa Fe and Albuquerque. The highway anthem begins here

O klahoma was the site of one of the most dramatic land rushes in the country. The new towns of Oklahoma City and Guthrie became home to more than 10,000 residents in the space of a day. The state is where we finally get to know the 2,448-mile (3,940-km) long Route 66 *(see essay on page 35)*. If your plan is to follow the "Mother Road" for most or all of the way, a word of advice: time is of the essence. Staying on the road is not as easy as it sounds, and having just enough – or even worse, *not* enough time – as opposed to having ample time could be the difference between a thoroughly enjoyable road trip and a disappointingly frustrating one. Advocates of the famous route claim that half the fun of Route 66 lies in the adventure of finding it, so plan ahead if it is to be a focal point of your drive. On the plus side, dipping in and out of it is relatively easy because of its proximity to the interstate, so even those with less time on their hands should see something of it.

LEFT: the best way to travel down Route 66. **BELOW:** historic road fans stay here.

Exile on Main Street

Route 66 is a serious business – "business" being the operative word. Real fanatics will arm themselves with maps and guide books, motel directories and red-hot tips gleaned avidly from their *Route 66 Magazine* subscription. Some might even drink coffee from their "Main Street, USA" mug while wearing an "I drove the Mother Road" T-shirt.

Fanatic or not, getting lost is inevitable, as you will come across stretches of the route that are maddeningly difficult to find. In some cases, the not-so-trusty brown "Historic US 66" signs vanish, with little or no indication as to where it has gone, or whether it has been subsumed by the nearby interstate. In many places, it runs parallel with the major highway for mile after mile, sometimes marked and sometimes not. Even experienced map-readers will have their competence sorely tested by some of the numerous maps claiming to trace the entire route. Time, patience and – at the occasional unmarked crossroad – a little bit of guesswork are the keywords to a successful trip.

Paul Taylor, publisher of the aforementioned and intriguing *Route 66 Magazine*, maintains that with sufficient time to explore, driving the route presents only minor setbacks. Owners of some of the Route 66 landmark attractions and memorabilia stores along the way say that one of the reasons travelers lose their way is because too many people steal the signs. "They are popular souvenirs." So, however tempting – leave that sign alone!

Oklahoma City
to Los Angeles

66
Oklahoma City ⑲
Yukon
El Reno
Fort Reno ⑳   Fort Sill
40
Hydro   281
Weatherford
⑳ Oklahoma Route   Foss
66 Museum   Elk City
Sayre
Erick
Oklahoma   Texola
Texas   66   Shamrock
McLean ㉒
Groom
40   Conway   87 217
㉓ Amarillo   Stanley Marsh's   Palo Duro
Cadillac Ranch   Canyon State Park
66   Vega
Adrian ㉔
Texas   Glenrio
New Mexico
40   Tucumcari ㉕

Santa Rosa
Junc 256
84
84   Las Vegas
Santa Fe ㉖   40
285   Junc 218
Clines Corners
Sandia Park   Junc 175
165 14
40   Albuquerque ㉗

Laguna
Paguate Cubero
Durango, CO   Junc 98   53 El Morro National Monument
Grants   Bandera Volcano & Ice Cave
371   Milan   Zuni
Window
Rock   40   Gallup ㉘   Four Corners
New Mexico   264   666
Arizona
Painted Desert   Petrified Forest
National Park ㉙
㉚ Holbrook
40   Joseph City
Homolovi   Winslow ㉛   Meteor
Ruins State   Crater
Park   Junc 233

Walnut Canyon National
Winona   Monument
Monument Valley ㉜ Flagstaff   Oak Creek Canyon
89   Parks   ★ 89A
㉟ Grand Canyon   40   Sedona ㉝
Williams ㉞
64   Ash Fork   89   Jerome
Junc 139   Seligman ㊱
★ Grand Canyon Caverns
66   Peach Springs
Las Vegas   Truxton
Kingman ㊲
93   ★ Goldroad
Oatman ㊳
Arizona   Junc 1   Topock
California   Needles
Goffs
Essex
40   Amboy
Ludlow

40   Newberry Springs
Calico
Ghost Town ★ Barstow ㊴
66   Helendale
15   Victorville
215   San Bernardino ㊵
66   Rancho Cucamonga
La Verne
San Dimas
210   Glendora
Azusa
Monrovia
Arcadia
Los Angeles ㊶

Wondering how long it will take to drive all, or most of the route? This depends on many factors, not least whether you are what author Tom Snyder defines as: "Late starter, get loster, honky tonker, sensitive browser, coffee hound, museum freak, or postcard looker." A reasonably fast trip, he estimates, would be at least eight days – from its origin in Illinois to the final mile in California.

Route 66 enters Oklahoma at **Quapaw** in the northeast corner, traversing 400 miles (644 km) of the state, for much of the way running parallel to (or being replaced by) I-44.

Oklahoma's origins

The creation of the Oklahoma Territory, following the Land Rush 50 years later, shrank Indian territory by half, forcing Native Americans to abandon communal ownership in favor of small individual plots. Nevertheless, more than 30 Native American tribes are still represented in the state, and one of the first more major towns you'll come to after entering the state, **Miami** ⑰, is named after one of these communities.

One of the earliest sections of the highway is found in the vicinity; you'll also find some Route 66 exhibits in the restored **Coleman Theatre** (tel: 918-540-2425; www.colemantheatre.org) in the town.

Just after Miami is one of those places where Route 66 sort of "disappears" – so don't feel you've cheated here by jumping on I-44 for a short stretch. This section of the interstate (up to Tulsa) is also known as the Will Rogers Turnpike (Woody Guthrie wrote a song about it), in memory of the famous homespun comic and No. 1 box office star. You can pick up Route 66 again a little farther on at **Vinita**, which gets its name from Vinnie Ream, who sculpted Washington, DC's Abraham Lincoln statue. The town stages a Will Rogers Memorial Rodeo every August and also lays claim to one of the world's largest (29,135 square ft/ 2,707 square meters) McDonald's.

Farther southwest, in Galloway Park near **Foyil**, is the world's largest totem pole, at 90 feet (27 meters) tall. Foyil's main street is named after Andy Payne, $25,000 winner of the 84-day "Bunion Derby" in 1928, whose contestants hiked 2,400 miles (3,862 km) from New York to Los Angeles, mostly along Route 66. Less than half of the route had been surfaced by then: it was not until 1938 that the entire route was finally paved. "In those days," Tom Snyder writes, "even Lindbergh's solo flight over the Atlantic was easier than a cross-country trek by automobile in the same year."

A few miles farther on is **Claremore**, with a memorial to Will Rogers; his 1879 birthplace is memorialized at **Oologah**, just to the north. After Foyil, Route 66 continues to head southwest to Tulsa – with the route again joining up with I-44 just as you reach the outskirts of the city.

Tulsa ⑱ (pop. 393,000), with its downtown Art Deco buildings and a wonderful 1950s-style diner on East 11th Street, was once known as the "Oil capital of the world." Here, Cyrus Avery was a co-founder and booster of the fledgling Highway 66 Association. Of the hundreds of drive-in movie houses along Route 66, only a handful remain – and one is right here in Tulsa.

Continue to follow I-44 out of the city; you can return to Route 66 by getting off at exit 220. The Mother Road again runs parallel to the main highway between Tulsa and Oklahoma City; the interstate on this stretch is also known as the Turner Turnpike. You'll pass through a string of small towns: **Sapulpa**, where aspiring Western star Gene Autry once sang in the local ice cream parlor, and which has an interesting historical museum; **Kellyville** (look for the Cotton Gin Diner); **Stroud** (order buffalo burgers at the 70-year-old Rock Café); **Davenport**, known for Dan's Bar-B-Q, run by a former trucker; and – as you approach Oklahoma City – **Arcadia**, with its distinctive Old Round Barn.

Crystal bridge

Oklahoma City ⑲ blossomed overnight on April 22, 1889, when the Land Rush opened up the adjoining territory to settlement – attracting 50,000 hopeful prospects. The appeal of today's Oklahoma City owes much to the planning talents of architect I.M. Pei, whose development scheme produced an elegant mix of lakes, parks, landscaped hills and stylish buildings. The centerpiece is **Myriad Botanical Gardens** (tel: 105-297-3995; open daily), a 17-acre (7-hectare) oasis in the heart of Downtown, its seventh-floor Crystal Bridge housing a plant- and tree-filled tropical conservatory and waterfall.

Oil derricks near the State Capitol are a reminder that the city's wealth stemmed from a major gusher 75 years ago. A score of major producing oilfields still operate in the state. Cotton was once king here, but it's cattle ranching that predominates today, and this great heritage is celebrated at **Stockyards City**, where ranchers and real cowboys have been coming since its inception in the early 1900s for apparel, equipment, supplies and a good meal. A "gaslight district" features a variety of western-oriented shops, galleries and restaurants, but the place is still all about cattle: cattle auctions are held Mon–Wed each week, with tours available on Mondays from 8 am throughout the day at the Oklahoma National Stockyards Company.

Maps on page 184 & 204

Throughout the Southwest, be sure to book rooms way ahead during the summer months.

BELOW:
Red Earth festival, Oklahoma City.

More sobering is the site of the April 1995 bombing of the Federal Building at which 168 people were killed. The site has now become a poignant memorial, with 168 empty chairs – reminding visitors of those who died – arranged on a grassy slope under a canopy of trees, facing a shallow reflecting pool.

Cowboys on parade

One of Oklahoma's major attractions is the **National Cowboy & Western Heritage Museum** (tel: 405-478-2250; open daily), just north of I-44 as you come into Oklahoma City (exit 129), whose wide, marble-tiled corridors are flanked with giant landscape paintings and photographs depicting cowboy life. This excellent museum has broad appeal, and even those with no interest in the Wild West might find themselves pleasantly surprised. Movie posters of Gene Autry, Tom Mix and John Wayne decorate the theater, close to a larger-than-life statue of Ronald Reagan and a huge statue titled *The End of the Trail*, by James Earle Fraser. It is matched by his wife Laura's bas-relief of the Land Rush.

Visitors can stroll through the streets of an old Western town with church, dry goods store and blacksmith's shop, while children can don chaps, boots and spurs in the Cowboy Corral, before dismounting and hiding away in a range tent.

Among the hundreds of unique action photographs shot with a converted 1880 Graflex camera by rodeo's first professional photographer, Ralph Russell Doubleday (1881–1958), is one of movie cowboy Hopalong Cassidy leading a small-town parade. Postcards of pictures by "Dub," often created in the bathroom of whatever hotel in which he was staying, sold by the millions.

BELOW: the *Welcome Sundown* statue at the National Cowboy & Western Heritage Museum.

You can continue to head west either on Route 66 or on I-40 (the two become one some 40 miles/64 km out of the city anyway). The Chisholm Trail ran along what is now Ninth Street in tiny **Yukon** – just outside the Oklahoma City limits on Route 66 and hometown of country star Garth Brooks. Both Sid's Diner in this town and Johnnie's Grill in neighboring **El Reno** claim to be the home of that distinctive Oklahoma treat – the onion-fried hamburger. Dustin Hoffman and Tom Cruise shot a scene of *Rain Man* in the Big 8 Motel (now renamed DeLuxe Inn) here. More famous, though, is the El Reno Hotel (now a historical museum), built in 1892 when rooms cost all of 50¢ a night.

Chisholm Trail

Fort Reno ❷ (tel: 405-262-3987; open daily) displays exhibits from the days when it served as a cavalry post in the Indian wars. El Reno is now the headquarters for the Cheyenne-Arapaho tribe.

If you take exit 108 off I-40, a short detour north on US 281 leads to **Geary**, bypassed by Route 66 in 193? despite the locals' work in grading and graveling the road in the hope of enticing the route, and its dollars, through their town. Not far away is **Left Hand Spring Camp**, where Jesse Chisholm, who gave his name to the famous Chisholm Trail, is buried. The trail, which stretched 250 miles (400 km) from San Antonio to Abilene, was first laid in 1860 when buffalo still roamed nearby. Twenty years later, when the trail was more or less abandoned, it had seen the passage of more than 10 million cattle. If you head south on US 281, about 78 miles (126 km) later, you'll come to **Fort Sill**, where the Apache chief Geronimo died in captivity in 1909.

Map on page 204

Driving backwards

Just near where I-40 intersects with US 281 is the 4,000-ft (1,220-meter) long "pony bridge" crossing the South Canadian River, a multiple simple-span bridge typical of the type used in the construction of Route 66. In addition to offering superb vistas of the river, the bridge starred in a scene in John Ford's 1940 movie version of *The Grapes of Wrath*.

The hill leading up to the bridge is so steep that Model T Fords – their engines generating more power in reverse – had to climb it backward. Continuing west on I-40, just north of exit 89 is Lucille's gas station and store at **Hydro** – marked by the plaster animals out front. It is a favorite with Route 66 regulars, some of whom have been buying gas and groceries here since 1941. Other local landmarks include a building with Greek columns (formerly a bank, now a dress shop) and, a little farther along, the century old Cotter's Blacksmith Shop at **Weatherford**, where the **General Thomas P. Stafford Air and Space Museum** (tel: 580-772-5871; open daily), with space suit and moon rocks, commemorates Oklahoma's premier astronaut.

One really begins to get a feel of traversing the old road at **Clinton** (pop. 8,400), where the state-sponsored **Oklahoma Route 66 Museum** ㉑ (tel: 580-323-7866; www.route66.org; open daily) is the most comprehensive – and memorable – of many similar places found along the famous highway. Each era is presented in its individual room, with photographs of the road's construction

BELOW: Clinton, Oklahoma, has one of the best 66 museums along the historic route.

The sounds commonly associated with a trip on Route 66 usually came from wonderful jukeboxes like this one.

BELOW: some of the buildings in Texola, straddling the Oklahoma/Texas border, have seen better days.

in the 1920s. Oklahoma was still "dry" in the 1930s, and the rise of the bootlegger prompted a corresponding increase in the number of law enforcement officers who are pictured in their intimidating uniforms.

Mother Road memories

A typical garage from the same era – with its glass-topped Red Crown gasoline pump – flanks pictures of a few of the three million migrants in their battered trucks bearing "California or Bust" signs. The photos of trucks, crammed with furniture, bedding, pots and pans and crated chickens typify the Dust Bowl years, when parched farmlands induced the westward-flight of almost one-fifth of the state's population. "66 is the path of people in flight, refugees from dust and shrinking land," wrote John Steinbeck in the book that produced the 1940 Academy Award-winning *The Grapes of Wrath*.

"We'll go on forever, Pa, cuz we're the people," declared the movie's Ma Joad. A World War II jeep, a Greyhound bus and a VW bus evoking the hippies-on-the-road era are among the vehicles on show, the "bug" illuminated by fluorescent lighting in a room whose walls display '60s album covers from Sinatra and Dina Shore to Hank Williams and Chuck Berry. A poster promoting a one-time rattlesnake show, a map made by a retired postmaster with franking stamps from every post office along the route, a glass case of souvenirs from long-vanished gift shops, and a video running quaint family movies on an endless loop are also part of the museum tour, which climaxes with an absorbing movie depicting the route's history.

"We heard many years ago in New Zealand Nat King Cole singing 'Get Your Kicks on Route 66'," writes one visitor. "So we came to see it."

Diner lingo

In the museum's replica of a 1950s diner, complete with a 1951 Ford parked out front and interior cozy booths, a jukebox playing Elvis Presley and plastic donuts and coffee displayed on the Formica counter, is a translation of "diner lingo" – the shorthand used by waitresses when shouting orders to the kitchen. Some examples: "Drown one, hold the hail" (Coke no ice); "Boiled leaves" (hot tea); "Rubber in a bun" (steak sandwich).

Until 1999, Clinton's historic Pop Hicks Restaurant was the oldest continuously operating restaurant along the entire route, but in that year it burned down and owner Howard Nichols has no plans to rebuild. Instead, check out Jiggs Smokehouse, just west on I-40, for delicious barbecue food.

West of Clinton, Route 66 parallels I-40, which is only a stone's throw away, and the advantage of traveling along the almost empty Mother Highway is summed up by a Burma Shave aphorism painted on the wall of a local café: *The Guy Who Drives/So Close Behind/Is He Lonesome/Or Just Blind? (see page 38)*

The ghost town of **Foss**; the Cotton Boll at **Canute** (now a private home but sign still extant); and the complex at **Elk City** of relocated old buildings, plus another Route 66 museum, might draw you off the road after leaving Clinton. When the US Highway 6

Map on page 204

Association held its convention in Elk City's Casa Grande Hotel in 1931, more than 20,000 enthusiasts attended. The hotel is now the **Anadarko Basin Museum of Natural History** (tel: 580-243-0437; tours by appointment). Songwriter Jimmy Webb ("Up, Up and Away") was born here.

Sayre, a little bit farther on, is also alarmingly empty these days, but shows traces of having once been a prominent feature along the route. Its Owl Drugstore has a gleaming '50s soda fountain where you can have a root-beer float or a chocolate malt, and the town also has a rather grandiloquent courthouse, which featured fleetingly in the movie *The Grapes of Wrath*. The small, fairly ordinary towns of **Erick** and **Texola** have each – at different times by different surveys – been declared to be sitting on the 100th meridian, the longitudinal arcs running through both the North and the South poles that are used as geographical definitions.

Heading through Erick, Route 66 is renamed Roger Miller Boulevard – a tribute to its songwriting ("King of the Road") native son. Route 66 historian Tom Snyder says that Erick was once one of the nation's worst speed traps, but now behaves itself because its severity caused tourist traffic to dry up.

THE TEXAS PANHANDLE

As you progress west through the high plains of Oklahoma, which merge into the Texas Panhandle, the grass becomes shorter and the hills begin to turn into small buttes and mesas. There's an overwhelming sense of insignificance in the face of the wide, open space stretching as far as the horizon. As might be expected in Texas, there is also a palpable feeling of having arrived in the real West, reflected in the confident pride of most residents. "Character traits, like an independent spirit, found expression in the West," explains the University of Oklahoma's Peter Hassrick. "By going West you escape the social restraints of the East. That same independent spirit could be seen in the mountain man and later the Forty-niners and finally the American cowboy."

Along this route, you'll perhaps get your first glimpse of the impressive mile-long freight trains snaking their way along the Santa Fe tracks, usually paralleling the road but sometimes causing lengthy delays at road crossings. *Slow Down, Pa/Sakes Alive/Ma Missed Signs/Four and Five,* the Burma Shave signs used to admonish.

At **Shamrock**, Texas – where travelers are invited to experience 4 miles (6 km) of historic 66 – is the **Pioneer West Museum** (tel: 806-256-3941; open daily). Don't miss the abandoned lime-green and sand-colored Art Deco masterpiece, the U Drop Inn Café and adjoining gas station with matching tower. The pump's gasoline sign is frozen at a nostalgic 79¢ per gallon.

Early gas stations had to fight hard for customers in a highly competitive market and the filling pump station took many forms. One, on the site of Albuquerque, New Mexico's present-day Lobo movie theater, was shaped like a giant chunk of ice. Companies made a big deal of cleanliness. Texaco, for example, established its White Patrol in 1938 – a team of

BELOW: Art Deco U Drop Inn Café, Shamrock, Texas.

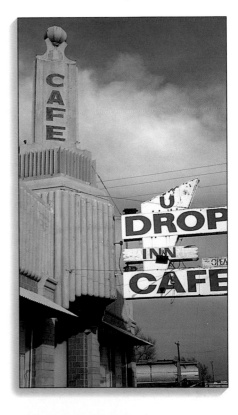

Gas stations were highly competitive during the heyday of Route 66. In 1939, Phillips 66 hired registered nurses to inspect the cleanliness of the restrooms. These "Highway Hostesses" also carried ice water, and were told to be of assistance to motorists in trouble.

inspectors in white coupés who toured the highways inspecting the company's rest rooms. The following year, Phillips followed suit, hiring registered nurses and sending them out on a similar mission as Highway Hostesses who were mandated to carry ice water and render assistance to motorists in trouble. The Union Oil Company countered with its Sparkle Corps.

At picturesque, sleepy **McLean** ㉒ (pop. 790), which describes itself as "the heart of old Route 66," an old Phillips 66 gas station has been restored by volunteers, one of a surprisingly small number along the route (there are none at all in Arizona). The Phillips Petroleum Company records some of the many erroneous explanations people have offered for the "66" in the company's name, for example: there are 66 books in the Bible; the company's founders were down to their last $66 when they drilled their first successful oil well; or that founder Frank Phillips was 66 years old when he founded the company (he was actually 44).

The Devil's Rope

The **Devil's Rope Museum**, formerly a brassiere factory, is here (tel: 806-779-2225; www.barbwiremuseum.com; open Tues–Sat) – the "rope" in question being barbed wire, a large rusty ball of which sits outside. Although the museum has a relatively small selection, there are as many as 8,000 different types of barbed wire in existence. Oklahoma's National Cowboy & Western Heritage Museum *(see page 206)* has the largest collection, including the popular "Dodge Spur" with its single line. In the mid-19th century, there were hundreds of competing designs, but it was Joseph F. Glidden's patent for fencing material, consisting of barbs wrapped around a single strand of wire, that eventually predominated.

BELOW: heartfelt wall mural, Texas.

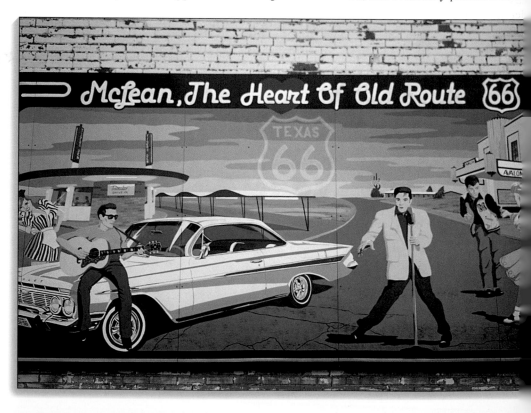

Towards Amarillo

As you drive out of McLean, look for the large wall mural depicting Elvis performing next to a yellow Cadillac, on whose hood sits a guitar player. The unpaved section of Route 66 between Alanreed and **Groom** has always been a problem for unwary drivers. Bob Moore and Patrick Grauwels, the acknowledged experts on the road, write that the section, once known as Jericho Gap, "was notorious for bogging down cars and trucks in a black, gumbo mud every time it rained." Their *Illustrated Guidebook to the Mother Road,* with pictures by Yannis Argyropoulos, is indisputably the most comprehensive of the many guides available: a spiral-bound, mile-by-mile summation, it has sold more than 50,000 copies. Moore points out that despite their years of research errors do occur "because Route 66 is still a living entity, and as such, changes are constantly taking place."

The route, which mostly parallels I-40 in this part of Texas, and sometimes merges with it, is hard to follow between here and Amarillo. At the entrance to many towns, it's safer, when in doubt, to take the off-ramp road labeled *Business I-40,* which usually follows the old Route 66 through town. This is the case at **Conway**, recognizable by its huge grain elevators and decrepit, old motels. Located on the route as you head toward Amarillo is the 24-hour Cattleman's Club & Café, with a large steer on its sign. An interesting breakfast stop, this place is about as Western as you'll find, with half the customers of both sexes wearing Stetsons, rows of slot machines to keep them occupied and gigantic rubbery omelets big enough to feed a ravenous cowpoke.

Palo Duro Canyon

Just before Amarillo (where local rancher J.F. Glidden invented his barbed wire), you could turn south on US 87 to visit the vast **Palo Duro Canyon**, closely associated with the legendary Charles Goodnight. Goodnight – inventor of the chuckwagon and once owner of the largest ranch in Texas – was the first rancher to move into the Panhandle in the 1870s. A musical named simply *Texas* takes place at the Canyon nightly in summer (tel: 806-655-2181) against a steep cliff-side backdrop. Chuckwagon tours beginning or ending with "cowboy" breakfast or dinner are offered on the rim of the canyon, where part of an Indiana Jones movie was filmed (tel: 800-658-2613).

Amarillo ㉓ itself, always a major shipping point for cattle, stages regular rodeos (for information tel: 806-374-1497) and is the home of the **Big Texan Steak Ranch** (tel: 800-657-7177), a world-renowned restaurant offering 72-ounce steaks free to anybody who can eat one within an hour. A unique natural resource found locally is helium, a monument to which sits on Streit Drive near the Botanical Gardens.

The city's one-way traffic system can be confusing, but you'll be back on Route 66 proper if you follow 6th Street, which leads into "**antique row**," where plenty of Route 66 shops and modern cafés entice visitors with their colorful signage, such as Smoky Joe's, Cup A Java and Amigo's Café. It's worth parking the car to take a closer look at some of the

Map on page 204

BELOW:
stop for a cup of java in Amarillo's "antique row."

brightly-colored wall murals harking back to the good ol' days. There are three churches on one block, which ends with the San Jacinto Apartments, San Jacinto Heights being the old name for this particular suburb.

South of I-40 just outside town is **Cadillac Ranch**, the much-photographed and often repainted line of ten Cadillacs, their rear ends sticking out of the earth to make some kind of sculptural statement by art financier Stanley Marsh. The Cadillacs are literally in the middle of a field. To get closer, look for a frontage road parallel to the interstate, where you can park for free and walk through a gate to take your snapshots of the cars.

Death by highway

There's not much to see at the ghost town of **Vega**, except the vintage Vega Motel. By 1928, motels were breeding fast along the fledgling Route 66, but in 1956 the creation of the Interstate Highway System sounded the death knell for scores of businesses, which suddenly found themselves bypassed by the traffic that for more than a quarter of a century had brought them prosperity. "As the world changes," says Joe Kisicki of Oklahoma's Route 66 Association, "so do things along the Mother Road. It mirrors life both modern and nostalgic, tacky and clever, restless and changeless."

Tiny and, in parts, dilapidated **Adrian** ❷ declares itself to be at the exact center of Route 66, with a sign announcing that it is 1,139 miles (1,833 km) to Chicago and 1,139 miles to Los Angeles. There are other, more curiously philosophical signs dotted around its handful of streets – *You Will Never Be the Same* and *If A Man Could Have Half His Wishes He Would Double His Troubles.* Adrian has been the site of Route 66 gatherings and jamborees.

Abandoned buildings such as the "First in Texas/Last in Texas Motel" dot **Glenrio**, the last Texas town you'll come to on this route and another virtual ghost town, although the four-lane Route 66 highway sits invitingly (albeit starting to disintegrate) at the edge of town.

NEW MEXICO

However well prepared you think you might be for New Mexico, no amount of reading can dull the initial, and rather pleasant, shock of finding the aesthetic beauty of Spanish South America dropped right in the middle of this vast, though sometimes bland, scenescape. It feels oddly surreal. In some parts of the state you won't see a gaudy neon sign, motel chain or pair of golden arches for miles. Make the most of it while you can.

Route 66 is well promoted throughout New Mexico, where it extends more than 300 miles (483 km) across the state. The State Fairgrounds in Albuquerque were selected as the site of the 2001 75th anniversary celebration of Route 66 – with exhibits like a photographic display of historic buildings (many in Albuquerque itself) and a vintage car show.

An excursion along the route was once made by members of a European travel club in 30 vintage American cars that were shipped from Europe. Ric Williams, president of the state's Route 66 Association, says the road "still vibrates" and embodies "a kind of mythology, the best of American culture. And everybody wants to experience that – the authentic American spirit that really created this country."

A sign outside the drive-in tourist information and rest area just across the border in New Mexico informs drivers that the surrounding terrain, the Llano Estacado (Staked Plain) – a high plateau covering 33,000 square miles (85,430 square kilometers) – is one of the flattest areas of the continental United States. Spanish explorer Francisco Vasquez de Coronado unsuccessfully combed the region for the fabled Seven Cities of Cibola back in 1540, expecting to uncover unimaginable hoards of gold and silver. Instead, he discovered innumerable Indian pueblos, where the glitter came from beautiful jewelry shaped by native craftsmen. Nineteen of the pueblos still exist and can be visited today (phone ahead, tel: 800-747-0181 or 505-552-6654).

Route 66 crosses and re-crosses I-40 before running through **Tucumcari** ㉕ ("two miles long and two blocks wide") where the Tee Pee Curio Store (*circa* 1944) is one of the oldest souvenir shops along the route. Every conceivable type of souvenir item turns up here, and in dozens of independently-run shops in one small town after another along the route: pop-up art of paper buildings, old postcards, caps, jackets, scarves, traffic signs, sheriff's badges, playing cards, mugs, glasses, paperweights, ashtrays, earrings, belt buckles, money clips and even baby bibs bearing the 66 logo. Almost everywhere can be found either original or reproduced Burma Shave signs: *Be a Modern/Paul Revere/Spread the News/From Ear to Ear/Burma Shave*.

Tucumcari once advertised it had 2,000 motel rooms and watched a nonstop stream of traffic pass by. Not the case today, but keep an eye out for such veterans of the highway as the historic Blue Swallow Motel, its characterful rooms replete with flowered pillows, and the Safari Motel with its neon sign of a man on a camel. Among Route 66's achievements was the molding of the bus and trucking industries, both able to supply essential transportation in an era of wartime gasoline rationing. A museum in Oklahoma City is devoted to Lee Way, one of the more famous freight companies along the route. Parking meters also began to make an unwelcome appearance in the main streets here and in other towns along the route.

It's worth turning off Tucumcari's main highway to sip a malted milkshake at the long-standing Big Dipper Café, situated near the Spanish Revival railroad station, and there's a wide variety of fascinating old artifacts and Route 66 memorabilia worth looking at in the **Historical Museum** (tel: 505-461-4201; open Mon–Sat in summer, weekdays in winter).

Santa Fe

Farther along the route, just past **Santa Rosa** at exit 256, you can swing north on US 84, crossing the Pecos River to Las Vegas (not to be confused with the Nevada city of the same name), and then follow the highway as it turns sharply west to **Santa Fe** ㉖, one of the oldest and best-known Western cities by virtue of the Santa Fe Trail. The trail ran from here almost 800 miles (1,290 km) to Kansas City and was

Map on page 204

Cow's Skull: Red, White and Blue *by Georgia O'Keeffe; visit a museum devoted to the artist in Santa Fe, NM.*

BELOW: smiles near Santa Fe.

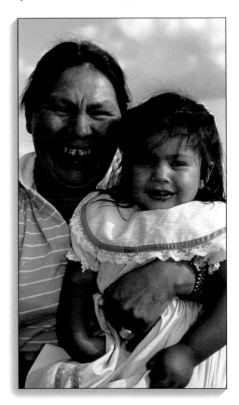

the major western trade route in the 18th and 19th centuries. Less a road than a beaten track for freight wagons across the Plains, it segued into El Camino Real, which led into central Mexico. The capital of New Mexico was on the original Route 66 until 1938 when a straighter route superceded it and cut 126 miles (200 km) off the journey.

Today's Santa Fe, its central buildings in matching adobe shades (coated with stucco instead of the traditional, yet fragile, mud plaster), is chic, tasteful and expensive, with sleek hotels filled with affluent boutique shoppers. There are exceptions, though – such as the charming El Rey Inn (tel: 505-982-1931; www.elreyinnsantafe.com) with its 1940s ambience and more moderate rates, and there are numerous cheaper but very pleasant and quite homey B&Bs sprinkled among the more expensive hotels.

Whoever designed the streets of Santa Fe must have been drunk and riding backwards on a mule.

— WILL ROGERS

Archbishops and artists

Santa Fe's impressive historic center and plaza is designed for relaxed strolling, but if you are intending to conduct a more thorough walking tour, it might be a good idea to arm yourself with one of the free local maps. Will Rogers once said: "Whoever designed the streets of Santa Fe must have been drunk and riding backwards on a mule." An alternative is to take one of the organized walking tours or take the narrated Open Air Tram City Tour. This covers a 10-mile (16-km) loop through historic and residential areas.

A landmark is **St Francis Cathedral**, whose archbishop, Jean Baptiste Lamy, buried below the altar, was the model for Willa Cather's novel, *Death Comes to the Archbishop*. The **Museum of New Mexico** (tel: 505-827-6463; open daily) is actually several museums, including the **Museum of Indian**

BELOW: Southwest style, Santa Fe.

Arts & Culture. Fans of Georgia O'Keeffe will find plenty of the artist's work in the **Georgia O'Keeffe Museum**, a few blocks from the plaza (tel: 505-995-0785; closed Wed in winter) and designed by Richard Gluckman, the man who was responsible for Pittsburgh's interesting Andy Warhol Museum.

Artists have always loved Santa Fe, and many of them live in historic adobes along **Canyon Road**, off Paseo de Peralta south of the river, once a burro track but now a chic area of art galleries, restaurants and shops. Look for **El Zaguan** and the **Rafael Borrego House**, both charming haciendas; the **Cristo Rey Church**, filled with Hispanic religious art; and the boutiques of **Gypsy Alley**. The **Old Santa Fe Trail** (now US 285) was, in 1821, the channel of communication between the Spanish Rio Grande and America. It crosses the Paseo, and on the trail are historic sites like the San Miguel Mission, the **Loretto Chapel** with its "Miraculous Staircase" and the **State Capitol**.

Gene Autry made his film debut in 1935 with *In Old Santa Fe* and the city has since decorated many titles – *Santa Fe Stampede* (with John Wayne), *Santa Fe Passage* (Slim Pickens), *Santa Fe Trail* (Ronald Reagan and Errol Flynn) – in addition to providing the setting for Hollywood movies as wide-ranging as the 1958 *The Left-Handed Gun* (Paul Newman) and the more recent 1988 *Twins* (Danny De Vito and California governor Arnold Schwarzenegger).

Towards Albuquerque

You can take US 285 south to connect up with the main route west again, and just before the intersection with I-40, you'll come to **Cline's Corner**, which founder Roy Cline subsequently described as "the coldest, the meanest, the windiest place on Highway 66." The town features in many of the tales told by Howard Subtle in his *Behind the Wheel on Route 66*. Subtle spent 28 years as a Greyhound bus driver heading back and forth along the highway, and his book is a ragbag of reminiscences about mislaid children, garrulous passengers and the occasional stowaway hiding behind the rear seats. On one occasion, he spotted an elephant tied to a tree; it turned out the beast had not been abandoned, but had been left with food and water after the truck that was transporting it broke down.

At Tijeras, east of Albuquerque, is the turn-off through Cedar Crest to the 10,700-ft-high (3,260-meter) **Sandia Mountains**, which offer fabulous panoramic views and one of the world's longest (2¾ miles/4 km) aerial tramways (tel: 505-856-7325; open daily). The Sandia Ranger Station is open daily (tel: 505-281-3304).

In **Albuquerque ⓱**, the old Route 66 runs along what is now Central Avenue, where the Civic Center, the tourist office and a handful of vintage buildings lie across the Atchison, Topeka and Santa Fe railroad tracks just past Second Street. Local Route 66 revitalization projects are very much in evidence along this stretch of the route, where shops and businesses seem to be doing a roaring trade. Note the elaborate Rococo KiMo Theater; the Avalon Restaurant with its arresting cowboy sign; and the 1880 railroad symbol carved into the metal fretwork street lamps.

Map on page 204

BELOW:
Christmas Eve
in Albuquerque's
Old Town.

Albuquerque's Old Town

Two miles (3 km) further west, on the other side of the Rio Grande, the **Old Town** with its attractive shops and restaurants is one block to the right of Central Avenue, its ancient plaza grandly dominated by the adobe **San Felipe Church** (1706). Five flags have flown over this plaza: Spanish, Mexican, Confederate, the Stars and Stripes and that of New Mexico. Allow at least an hour to wander around Old Town and try to time it with lunch or an early dinner to take advantage of one of the many cafés.

The **Albuquerque Biological Park** (tel: 505-764-6200; open daily) with its aquarium, zoo and botanical garden, is at 2601 Central Avenue, and nearby are the **Explora** center (tel: 505-224-8300; www.explora.mus.nm.us; open daily), the **Albuquerque Museum of Art & History** (tel: 505-243-7255; closed Mon), the **New Mexico Museum of Natural History & Science** (tel: 505 841-2800; open daily) and the shuddery **Rattlesnake Museum** (tel: 505-242-6569; www. rattlesnakes.com; open daily). One block north, on 12th Street, the **Indian Pueblo Cultural Center** (tel: 505-843-7270; open daily) has galleries, a museum, gift shop, restaurant and free traditional dance performances on weekends.

Albuquerque, like so many places in the state, has been popular with moviemakers. Mary Pickford was there in 1912 to appear in an early silent movie, *The Old Actor*. Leaving town along Central Avenue, look out for the venerable DeAnza Motel, relic of the 1950s when there were almost 100 motels in Albuquerque. There are now half as many, and old neon motel signs have become collectors' items as valuable Art Deco artifacts.

Eric Szeman, co-owner of the Route 66 Malt Shop in Albuquerque, made the cross-country trip with his parents over 50 years ago. "America became

BELOW:
Southwestern cities often have breathtaking settings.

Map on page 204

more mobile than it ever had been," he recalls. "The mass migration westward was pretty much handled by Route 66."

Westward, Route 66, running side by side and sometimes absorbed by Interstate 40, passes through **Laguna** with its early 18th-century church, **Paguate Cubero** (near which novelist Ernest Hemingway settled in to write *The Old Man and the Sea*), and past the gas station and casino below **Acoma Sky City** which, perched on a mesa 367 feet (112 meters) overhead, is the oldest continuously occupied village in the country. **Grants** (named after three brothers) actually *looks* like a street from the mid-20th century with its Zia and Franciscan motels, Grants Café, El Jardin and Monte Carol Restaurant – all of which date from that era.

Volcanos and ice caves

Interesting side trips can be made to the dormant **Bandera Volcano** and nearby **Ice Cave** (tel: 888-ICE-CAVE, www.icecaves.com; open daily), 25 miles (40 km) south on Highway 53; and to **El Morro**, or Inscription Rock, 28 miles (45 km) farther along. The sandstone pillar is a written history of those who have passed by, from Native Americans, Spanish explorers and the US Army Camel Corps to pioneers heading west in the mid-19th century.

For most of the way between Grants and Gallup, Route 66 and the interstate are only a few yards apart, with **Milan**'s funky Crossroads Motel (*circa* 1948) the first landmark and – 15 miles (24 km) farther west – the Continental Divide marked by a roadside café of the same name. The **Prewitt Trading Post**, once called the Zuni Mountain Trading Post, dates back to 1946. An unbroken chain of steep, red rock mesas flank the highway to the north.

Route 66 gas stations were made as pretty as possible in a competitive marketplace.

BELOW: picking up groceries.

Map
on page
204

Gallup's movie-star hangout

One of the high spots of the entire route is surely the **El Rancho Hotel and Motel** (tel: 800-543-6351) at **Gallup ㉘,** built in 1937 by Raymond E. Griffith, who passed himself off as the brother of movie pioneer D. W. Griffith. This town is worth an overnight stay as Gallup is very appealing as a genuine New Mexico town. At first glance, it's not nearly as pretty to look at as picture-perfect Santa Fe or Albuquerque, but it has lots of character and plenty of lingering remnants of the Route 66 era. There's definitely a sense here of a place that gets on with everyday life, rather than one which is filled with admiring tourists, or one that is now deserted following the route's demise. The hotel was a favorite with movie stars from the beginning; by the 1960s, at least 15 movies had been shot using the hotel as headquarters, among them *Sundown*, *Streets of Laredo* and *The Hallelujah Trail*.

El Rancho is enormous and resembles everybody's dream of a huge ranch house with its Navajo rugs, solid Western furniture, wagon wheels and mounted moose heads. Its wooden staircase is distinctive enough to bear a designer credit and leads to a balcony decked out with signed photographs from Ronald Reagan, Rosalind Russell, Paulette Goddard, Humphrey Bogart, Jack Benny and a host of others. Off the immense lobby is a charming restaurant and bar, and burgers and sandwiches are named after the likes of Doris Day, Errol Flynn and Burt Lancaster. The "Mae West" sandwich is cheerfully defined as "stacked beef or ham."

Gallup tags itself "where the Indian southwest begins" and remains, as it has always been, a major trading post for the native peoples – these days as many as 200,000 of them – who live on the 17½-million-acre (7,088,000-hectare) **Navajo Nation**. This sprawls across the distinctive **Four Corners** region to the north where the states of New Mexico, Arizona, Colorado and Utah meet. The percentage of Native-American owned land is second only to Arizona.

BELOW: on the road in the desert.
RIGHT: scaling a Southwest slot canyon.

Indian territory

The Navajo capital of **Window Rock** is 25 miles (40 km) from Gallup (and *just* across the border in Arizona) on State Route 264. The largest pueblo in the state, that of **Zuni** (tel: 505-782-7000) with its Our Lady of Guadeloupe Mission (1629) is 40 miles (64 km) south on Highway 53. Zuni artisans are famous for their intricate silver jewelry skillfully inlaid with turquoise and coral. If you shop around, Zuni pieces can look surprisingly contemporary.

Indian artifacts such as rugs, jewelry and other crafts can be bought at many stores along Route 66, which happens to be Gallup's main street, the center of town being located in a 12-block area around Hill Avenue and Fourth Street.

The century-old **Rex Hotel** is now a museum, and a new cultural center staging ceremonial dances nightly in summer occupies the historic railroad station. **Red Rock Museum** (tel: 505-863-1337), with its Indian handicrafts, is 20 minutes' drive to the east in the park of the same name. There is a balloon rally in Red Rock Park every December. ❑

ARIZONA TO LOS ANGELES

Wigwam motels, gorgeous gas stations, soda fountains that work –
the cruise along Route 66 continues, taking in ghosts
and the Grand Canyon along the way

Map
on page
204

Los Angeles

The Mother Road becomes difficult to follow just over the border from New Mexico into Arizona, so if cruising the length of Route 66 is not a priority, you can remain on Interstate 40 through Holbrook, Arizona. About 25 miles (40 km) inside the state, exit 330 from I-40 leads into **Petrified Forest National Park ㉙**, whose 220,000 acres (89,000 hectares) are littered with giant petrified logs. More than 200 million years ago, the region was a swampy, tropical zone whose mineral-rich soil helped to preserve the fossilized bones of prehistoric animals. In the northern section of the park is the **Painted Desert Inn National Historic Landmark** (tel: 928-524-6228), now a museum.

Dinosaur statues line the road on the way to **Holbrook ㉚**, whose outstanding attraction is the roadside **Wigwam Motel**, a long-standing favorite (particularly with kids) on Route 66 (tel: 928-524-3048). A collection of 15 cozy rooms, each one is inside its own tall, stone teepee built by owner John Lewis' father in the 1940s from plans by architect Frank Redford. He allowed seven similar motels around the country to be built from his plans, stipulating only that each be equipped with a radio that played 30 minutes for 10¢.

Parked outside the teepees is the family collection of '50s Fords and Buicks, while inside the main building a small museum exhibits chunks of petrified trees, Indian artifacts and rifles and powder horns from the frontier days. A Visitor Center and historical museum can be found in the **Old Navajo Courthouse** (*circa* 1898) on Navajo Boulevard (Route 66), which runs through the center of town.

Pony Express

Holbrook's evocatively named Butterfield Stage Co., a contemporary of the Pony Express, is a good spot to stop for barbecue food. The spirit of the short-lived but legendary Pony Express, whose demise was induced by the telegraph system some 150 years ago, is kept alive in the town by the Navajo County Sheriff's posse, who carry mail to Scottsdale (near Phoenix) in late January every year.

Under a contract with the US Postal Service, the 40-strong "Hashknife Posse" (www.hashknifpony express.com) carries out a tradition begun in 1954, when a similar posse carried to the state governor an invitation to attend a stampede. An estimated 15,000 letters (sent in by admirers throughout the world) are hand-stamped with the official ride logo and franked with a Pony Express postmark before being sent off in mail bags relayed by the riders every few miles in the course of the 200-mile (320-km) journey.

The posse's name is derived from The Hash Knife Outfit, a branch of the third-largest cattle company in the country, which began shipping out thousands of

LEFT: the
Wigwam Motel,
Holbrook, Arizona.
BELOW: "It's
a rough life,
but somebody's
gotta do it."

BELOW: the Museum Club is the Southwest's largest log cabin.

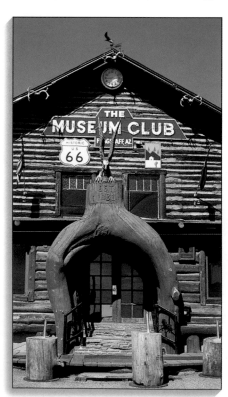

cattle after 1881 when the life-changing railroad began to go through here.

Holbrook's preserved **Blevins House** across from the Santa Fe depot was the scene of a spectacular shoot-out on September 4, 1857, when the county sheriff went to arrest a horse thief and survived after being shot at by several members of the thief's family. Nearby are the notorious Bucket of Blood Saloon, the 1910 J&J Trading Post and the one-time Campbell's Coffee House (now a Rexall's drug store), which became famous for its "Son of a Bitch stew."

Anasazi ruins

Five miles (8 km) off I-40 near **Joseph City** ("Joseph Small Town" would be more appropriate) is the Jackrabbit Trading Post, with its original crouching rabbit sign, while 16 miles (26 km) farther on, a turn north on State Route 87 – just before you get to Winslow – will take you to the extensive 14th-century Anasazi site of **Homolovi Ruins State Park** (tel: 928-289-4106).

Winslow ㉛ achieved fame from its inclusion in the pop song "Take It Easy" by Jackson Browne. The Eagles' hit single refers to "Standin' on a corner in Winslow, Arizona," and visitors pour into town to do just that at Standin' on the Corner Park (Kinsley and Second streets), where there is a 6-foot (2-meter) high bronze statue of a man with a guitar. The lyric goes: *Well, I'm standing on a corner in Winslow, Arizona/Such a fine sight to see/It's a girl, my Lord/In a flatbed Ford/Slowing down to take a look at me.*

Until the 1960s, Winslow, born with the arrival of the railroad in 1880, was the largest town in northern Arizona, but business began to fade when it was bypassed by the interstate. Its rebirth began with the renovation of Downtown, and, most notably, **La Posada** (tel: 928-289-4366), the 1930 Fred Harvey railroad hotel *(see pages 225 and 230)*. Three eating places associated with the highway (around Second and Third streets) have evocative names: the Whole Enchilada, Miss Zip's and the Falcon Restaurant.

South of Winslow off SR 99, Anasazi petroglyphs can be admired in **Chevelon Canyon**, west of town, to which tours are conducted from Rock Art Canyon Ranch. Anglers know the area well for its rainbow and – more enticingly – brown trout that live in the lake and creek here.

About 20 miles (32 km) west on I-40, Exit 233 leads south to **Meteor Crater**, a 600-foot (183-meter) deep hole almost a mile across created by the impact of a meteorite nearly 50 centuries ago. Astronauts were trained here before the moon visit, and the Astronaut Park has an Apollo Space Capsule. The new museum has exhibitions documenting the history of meteorites impacting the earth and a theater recreating those impacts as if you were at ground zero (tel: 928-289-2362; www.meteorcrater.com; daily tours). Back on the main road heading west, the ghost town of **Two Guns** sits on an abandoned portion of Route 66.

Although **Winona** features in Bobby Troup's "Route 66" song, it's actually a dead-end, and what Route 66 historian Tom Snyder calls "a one-blink town." Near Winona, 7 miles (11 km) before Flagstaff, is the **Walnut Canyon National Monument** (tel: 928-526-3367), where a short hike down a paved trail reveals ancient cliff dwellings that fell into disuse hundreds of years ago.

Flagstaff

The only large town in northern Arizona, **Flagstaff** ㉜ (pop. 57,400) is a staging point for trips to the Grand Canyon, 80 miles (129 km) to the north. The trip up US 89 and then along State Route 64 is longer, but more scenic, than the shorter route from Williams farther along the highway. Two of Flagstaff's museum attractions, the **Pioneer Museum** (tel: 928-774-6272; closed Sun) and the **Museum of Northern Arizona** (tel: 928-774-5213; open daily), are not far apart on Fort Valley Road, or from US 180, which also leads to the canyon. Flagstaff's other attractions are either in or near the historic and attractive downtown railroad district, through which Route 66 runs. The city stages a Route 66 Celebration each June with live music, a parade of classic cars and displays of arts and crafts.

On the way into Flagstaff from the direction of the east, be sure to stop by the **Museum Club**, a 1931 roadhouse which in Prohibition days began as a "zoo" filled with stuffed animals. This is now supplemented with more bizarre exhibits and, more importantly, the memories of dozens of country-music legends that have performed in the Southwest's largest log cabin. Nearer to Downtown are the **Lowell Observatory** (tel: 928-774-2096; open daily) and the richly furnished 40-room **Riordan Mansion** (tel: 928-779-4395; open daily), set in an attractive park.

Leroux Street is opposite the train station, and is where you'll find the remarkable **Weatherford Hotel** (tel: 928-774-2731, www.weatherfordhotel.com), which opened its doors on the first day of 1899. That day, it welcomed among its scores of distinguished guests the publisher William Randolph Hearst, President

Map on page 204

BELOW: the Hotel Weatherford played host to presidents, publishers and Wyatt Earp.

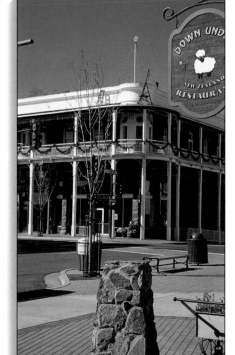

MONUMENT VALLEY

A 182-mile (293-km) journey from Flagstaff, Arizona, leads to one of the most famous sights in the Southwest. Monument Valley is easily recognized from far away *(see picture on page 178)* thanks to scenes from countless Westerns, especially those by director John Ford, who often used the valley as the backdrop for his movies. With its serene rock formations dominating the surrounding barren desert plains, the valley's mesas were not just attractive to Hollywood, but also served as significant religious monuments for local Native Americans. Medicine men once climbed the Rain God Mesa – home to a sacred burial ground – to pray for rain. The Totem Pole formation served as a center for mythical incidents in folklore, while the Yei-Bi-Chei resembles holy Navajo figures performing a traditional dance. Like the Grand Canyon or Sedona, the timeless mystery of these rocks are humbling in their presence. What seems an impossible creation is the result of ageless erosion of the sandstone and shale, which leaves the harder stone intact. Monument Valley lies entirely within the Navajo Nation reservation, and the tribe conducts tours through its desolate beauty. Telephone 435-727-5874 for more information.

Native American sign near Williams, Arizona.

Theodore Roosevelt and lawman Wyatt Earp. The bar boasts an antique counter that came from Tombstone, and the ballroom is named for Western author Zane Grey, who stayed here while writing *Call of the Canyon*.

A young reader of Zane Grey's books was one Cecil B. De Mille, who concluded that Flagstaff sounded like a good place to launch his movie career. When he arrived in the town from the East, however, it was snowing, and De Mille decided to continue on the train to Los Angeles, thus altering the course of movie history forever.

An attractive side trip from Flagstaff is along State Highway 89a through the red rocks of spectacular **Oak Creek Canyon** to the artist community of **Sedona ❸**, 28 miles (45 km) south. A daily shuttle service (tel: 928-282-2066) connects the two communities. Further south is another artist's haven, **Jerome**, a former ghost town named after a defunct copper mine.

Back on Route 66

Between Flagstaff and Williams, Route 66 is mostly unsurfaced and not very well maintained, but has the distinction of containing the highest point of the route at 7,300 ft (2,225 meters) above sea level, about a mile or two before **Parks**. The Parks in the Pines general store has been in business for more than 80 years. Nearby are the remains of the **Beale Wagon Road Historic Trail**, a sturdy 120-ft (37-meter) wide track constructed in 1857 on which pioneers could safely travel as far as the Colorado River.

BELOW: Navajo women on their Arizona reservation.

Back on I-40, the next town, **Williams ❸**, with its main street on Route 66 and nearby mountain were all named after Bill Williams (1787–1849), an early fur trapper whose statue stands at the west end of town. The excellent *Route 66*

Map on page 204

Magazine was once published here, the last town on Route 66 to be bypassed by I-40 and the main departure point for the Grand Canyon. The Grand Canyon Railway (tel: 800-THE-TRAIN) departs here for the canyon every morning. The five-hour round-trip – by vintage steam locomotives in summer, diesel locomotives the rest of the year – allows for three hours' sightseeing at the canyon, but is a worthwhile trip in itself (particularly for families), complete with strolling cowboy musicians and, on the return trip, a "train robbery."

The Grand Canyon

The South Rim of the **Grand Canyon** ㉟ (which can also be reached by traveling about 40 miles/64 km north on US 180 from Williams) is open around the clock every day of the year, although the Visitor Center and most park facilities operate only from 8am to 5pm. Free canyon shuttle buses operate between mid-March and mid-October, allowing visitors access to different points so that they can hike along the rim of the canyon. (To reserve accommodation at one of the Grand Canyon lodges, tel: 303-297-2757. Be sure to book early, as rooms are highly prized.)

Near the Williams railroad depot (which also houses an interesting museum) is the restored **Fray Marcos Hotel** (now the Grand Canyon Railway Hotel; tel: 928-635-4010), originally a unit of the once-ubiquitous Harvey House chain, which an English immigrant, Fred Harvey, established in the 1880s along the route of the Santa Fe line, revolutionizing the then-abysmal standards of railway food. One of Harvey's basic rules was that the coffee – served by smiling "Harvey Girls" in black dresses and spotless white aprons and bows – was re-made every two hours, even if the urn was still full. For 75¢,

The Grand Canyon is more than 270 miles (435 km) long and averages 10 miles (16 km) in width. It passes through five of the seven temperate zones at which different species flourish.

BELOW:
the Grand Canyon is open around the clock, every day of the year.

customers could choose from seven entrees and take second helpings, too.

A tan-colored 1953 Cadillac and life-size cutouts of James Dean and Marilyn Monroe sit outside **Twisters**, a self-proclaimed "back-to-the '50s diner" that displays hundreds of snapshots of families taken along the route, along with an old glass-topped Sky Chief gasoline pump that has been converted into a holder for typical road souvenirs.

Sit here for 20 minutes or so and immerse yourself in pure, unadulterated kitsch. A menu offers a dozen different shakes, malts, floats and cherry phosphates. For those seeking more conventional fare, the best-known restaurant in town, **Rod's Steak House**, has been serving customers along Route 66 for more than half a century.

Beyond Williams

From Williams, 19 miles (31 km) west along Interstate 40, it's worth getting off the busy road to visit somnolent **Ash Fork**, which was a stage coach depot until the arrival of the railroad in 1882. This was also a regular stop along Route 66 until the town was bypassed by the bigger thoroughfare; a Confederate flag flies over the Route 66 Grill. One of the adorable Harvey Girls *(see page 230)* lived nearby until her death, and she donated several artifacts from the defunct Harvey House chain to a fledgling museum located in a vast, empty warehouse beside the tourist office.

A former railroad dispatcher, Dan Ayres, who has a print shop in town, is the author of a series of "railway novels," which are highly regarded locally. Half a dozen sandstone companies, whose flagstone wares are piled high around the station, mine the surrounding mountains for an earth-colored stone that is shipped nationwide.

BELOW:
Seligman Suzy Q.
RIGHT:
buy malts and
soda pop here.

Toward the California border

Returning briefly to the interstate, it's advisable to leave it again at the Crookton Road exit for the longest and most nostalgic section on the entire Historic 66 Highway. It's quite simple to remain on it all the way to the California border at Topock, a distance of about 180 miles (290 km).

Map on page 204

You won't miss **Seligman** ㊱, whose main thoroughfare resembles a permanent state of Christmas. The solitary main road and Route 66 are lined with strangely compelling gift shops devoted to the highway's history. One of these is run by Myrna Delgadillo, whose father, Angel, is a hero to fans of the road. The walls of his barber shop (which doubles as a Visitor Center), are covered with business cards from all over the world, and a day rarely passes without a stranger seeking him or the shop out. It was Angel who got the state's Historic Route 66 Association off the ground and who revived attention in a dying Seligman after the town was bypassed.

Sumachs and gas tanks fueled here.

BELOW:
Juan Delgadillo in his Snow Cap Drive-In; brother Angel fought for Route 66 recognition.

Born and raised in the town, Angel is apt to reminisce about the early days, recalling that when migrants came through he could guess their relative wealth by how many mattresses sagged over the sides of their overloaded trucks. Angel's brother Juan operates the Snow Cap Drive-In next door, at the rear of which lies a "garden" of oddities, including two old-fashioned wooden outhouses equipped with modern plumbing. Seligman's gift shops carry every conceivable type of souvenir, from US 66 highway signs, Mother Road license tags and oil company signs, to old Coca Cola posters and bottles – as well as the now-familiar inscribed mugs, glasses and T-shirts. There's a vast range of books about the road, some esoteric like the *Gas Pump Collectors' Guide* and, of course, Frank Rowsome's *The Verse by the Side of the Road*.

TIP

Travelers might care to visit Oatman *outside* the summer months, when temperatures are hot enough to hold an annual Sidewalk Egg Fry at high noon, right in the middle of Route 66.

BELOW:
Clark Gable and Carole Lombard were married in Kingman, Arizona.

Small as it is, Seligman includes enough sites to offer a 20-minute walking tour, for which a free leaflet is available at Angel Delgadillo's barbershop. Visitors might note the 1932 Deluxe Motel on the main street, the Cat Bar (1936) at the western end of town, and the boarded-up, pseudo-Tudor Harvey House beside the rail track. Twenty-five miles (40 km) west of Seligman is the deep **Grand Canyon Caverns** (tel: 928-422-3223; open daily), into which early visitors paid 25¢ to be lowered 150 feet (46 meters) by rope. Today, there's an elevator and illuminated paths on which to walk.

The oldest operating garage on the route, together with some abandoned motels and the Hualapai Tribal headquarters, are in **Peach Springs**, and good cooking can be found at the Frontier Café at **Truxton**. At **Hackberry**, the owners of the general store (which doubles as a Visitor Center) have established a Bobby Troup Memorial Oasis. These are the main points of interest along 66 until **Kingman** ➌, where the tubby, gruff-voiced movie star Andy Devine was born. The main street is named after him, and on this and the adjoining Beale Street are the oldest buildings, including the old Beale Hotel where Clark Gable and Carole Lombard were married in March, 1939.

Kingman's **Route 66 Museum** (open daily) is located in a converted powerhouse, and one of its exhibits is a re-creation of a small-town Main Street, complete with 1950s yellow Studebaker car. The **Mojave Museum of History and Arts** (tel: 928-753-3195; closed Sun) displays attractive turquoise jewelry and a re-created Hualapai dwelling, among other historical artifacts.

Heading west, the highway takes on a desolate, rocky wilderness appearance – an indicator of what's to come; be sure you have good brakes. Before long, the road is climbing between jagged peaks in a series of seemingly endless switchbacks and scary, blind curves to the 3,500-ft (1,067-meter) high summit at **Sitgreaves Pass** (named, like the Beale Wagon Trail, for a mid-19th-century Army surveyor), before beginning an equally twisting and turning segment down into the tiny town of Oatman.

Haunted hotel

On the way down into Oatman, you'll pass **Goldroad**, the site of a mine that produced $2-billion-worth of gold in its early years, but closed down in the '90s when gold prices dropped. The mine is open every day to tour groups from Oatman (tel: 928-768-1600; www.goldroadmine.com; open daily), with transportation provided.

Hundreds of wild burros turned loose by early miners roam the mountains, occasionally straying across the highway and wandering into **Oatman** ➌, proving irresistible camera fodder for photographers. Oatman looks exactly the way you'd imagine an ancient Western town to look, with sagging wooden shacks lining the solitary unpaved street on which amusing mock gunfights are conducted daily.

Across the street from Fast Fanny's (selling clothes, sunglasses and postcards), a bed on wheels promotes the annual Great Oatman Bed Races, which are held every January. Summer temperatures can reach 118°F (48°C), prompting the annual Sidewalk Egg Fry. The 1926 Mission Inn, located next to a sidewalk display

HISTORIC ROUTE 66

WELCOME TO KINGMAN

HEART OF HISTORIC ROUTE 66

of life-size wooden bears, is a popular local place to eat; it serves substantial tasty, cholesterol-laden breakfasts of the sort that fat-obsessed and health-conscious Californians can only dream – or have nightmares – about.

The worn and characterful 1902 **Oatman Hotel** (tel: 928-768-4408), its walls plastered with photographs, newspapers and movie posters, makes no concession to such modern comforts as television, or even running water in the rooms, but is nonetheless an irresistible place to stay. History rules here, not luxury, and the hotel even has its own ghost called Oatie, supposedly the spirit of a lonely and homesick drunken Irishman who lay undiscovered at the hotel for three days before being kicked into a shallow grave.

Honeymoon hideaway

A very much alive Clark Gable and Carole Lombard spent their honeymoon night in Room 15, after being married in Kingman, and the simple room is preserved as a sort of shrine to the glamorous Hollywood couple with pictures of the pair on the walls and a pink nightdress draped over a chair.

The "honeymoon suite" and Oatie the ghost's room cost an extra few dollars to stay in, in addition to the suggested (inexpensive) donations for the other rooms. There's a cozy, fairly "local" bar downstairs where the talk is good, but no food after 6pm when (for much of the year) restaurants and shops close up tight as soon as the tourists have left.

Twenty miles (32 km) of desert scrub land lies between Oatman and **Topock**, where the Colorado River marks the California border. Route 66 comes to a dead-end at Moabi Regional Park with its lake and boat rentals – a refreshing stop after the long drive in the hot sun.

Map on page 204

BELOW: Viva Las Vegas!

DETOUR – LAS VEGAS

A desert drive of 101 miles (163 km) from Kingman, Arizona, on US 93 leads straight to Sin City. Each year, 12 million visitors empty their pockets of $4.2 billion in a time-honored homage to frivolity, greed and gluttony – not to mention plain old fun. For a long time after gambling was legalized in 1931, Las Vegas remained a sleepy desert town. It took visionary underworld hit man Bugsy Siegel to free this seething neon dragon. In 1946, Siegel opened the Flamingo Hotel, sparing no expense in mob finances for its plush interior, which sported a flashing pink neon facade and set a new standard in sheer swank. From a high-roller's point of view, Las Vegas is divided into two parts. First is the Strip, where modern hoteliers vie with each other to offer the latest in accommodation extravaganzas, replicating Venice, Paris, Rome, ocean liners and Egyptian pyramids. Then there's Downtown – the original Vegas – also known as Glitter Gulch. As for gambling, either way you lose, but Downtown casinos are said to afford better odds. The best advice is simply enjoy it: win, lose or draw, there's nothing quite like the Strip at night, ablaze with electric light and self-indulgence. The Las Vegas Convention and Visitors Authority is at 702-892-0711; www.visitlasvegas.com.

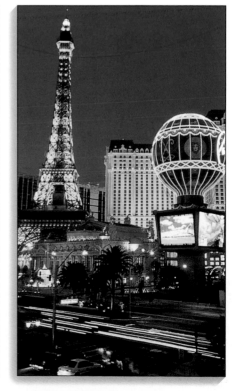

CALIFORNIA

As the car heads ever closer toward the setting sunset, spare a though for the former migrants, for whom crossing the border into the "promised land" was not always a pleasant experience in the early days of Route 66. Swamped by a tide of refugees from the Dust Bowl states, Californians were worried what might happen to property prices or already low-paid jobs. It's a story that is still familiar today, albeit at a different border.

Don't Take A Curve At 60 Per We Hate to Lose A Customer.
– BURMA SHAVE

Sadly, once in California, much of the old Route 66, apart from a few parched stretches through the Mojave Desert, has been largely supplanted and is submerged beneath a welter of busy freeways to re-emerge only in occasional short stretches or as the main routes through towns such as Barstow, Victorville and Rancho Cucamonga. In the first town you'll come to in California, **Needles**, Route 66 passes through the business section and along Broadway where, across from an old covered wagon at the junction of Front Street, the vintage 1930s Palms Motel is now a bed and breakfast renamed the Old Trails Inn.

Needles and grins

There are more historic motels past the Amtrak terminal, where the defunct 1906 Fred Harvey House, known as El Garces and regarded as the crown jewel of the chain, is now just a part of the station. Harvey Girls lived in the upper floors. Trained in neatness and courtesy, the girls signed a contract of employment agreeing not to marry for a year, and lived on the upper floors of the hotel.

BELOW:
motel signs
from the Mother
Road are now Art
Deco collectibles.

The **Needles Regional Museum** (tel: 760-326-5678; closed Sun) has a fanciful collection of stuff guaranteed to raise a grin: vintage clothes, old jars and bottles, obsolete currency, pictures curling with sepia, cartridge shells and Indian artifacts. The **Mojave Tribal Center** with its **Indian Village** sits near the Needles Bridge, and there's a marina park and golf course near the river.

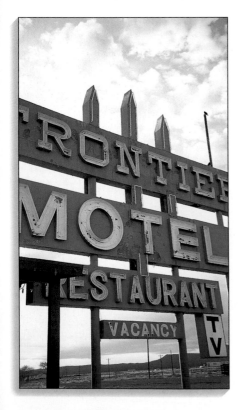

In World War II, General George Patton established an army training center in the Mojave, realizing that a familiarity with its harsh terrain would prepare the troops for the forthcoming Africa campaign, and indeed, conditions are similar. The US Army National Training Center is still headquartered at Barstow, 145 miles (233 km) due west of Needles.

The route from Needles to Barstow can be traveled swiftly on I-40, but the old Route 66 runs north of the interstate and heads through **Goffs** before diverting south through the barely existing communities of Essex, Amboy and Baghdad (famous for its landmark café and, earlier, another Harvey House). Bob Moore recalls in his guidebook that **Essex** (pop. 90) appeared on NBC's *Tonight Show* in 1977, claiming to be the only town in America without television. A Pennsylvania company promptly donated the necessary equipment. About a mile from **Amboy** (now a ghost town owned by preservationist Albert Okura and featuring a closed-down café and gas station, once a favorite with filmmakers) is an extinct volcano known as the **Amboy Crater**.

Ludlow, where Route 66 links up once more with the interstate, was once a boom town served not only by the Santa Fe railroad, but also by two others (local lines bearing ore from Death Valley), and in fact was named for a Central Pacific repairman. The 1940s Ludlow Cafe building is derelict, as is the abandoned Ludlow Mercantile Building (1908) down by the railroad tracks, but the newer Ludlow Coffee Shop is usually bustling with activity. Water, always scarce in these parts, was at one time brought in to fill the steam trains by tank cars from **Newberry Springs**, 40 miles (64 km) to the west (site of the cult movie *Bagdad Café*). There really are springs here, and they supplement the water supply from the region's numerous artesian wells.

The State Agricultural Inspection Station, which tended to hassle visitors in the early days, more often than not these days just waves cars through. Just before Barstow is **Daggett**, whose landmark **Stone Hotel** (beside an old alignment of the route) was popular with Tom Mix and other movie cowboys. On show in the fledgling museum (tel: 760-254 2629; open weekends) is a scale model of the California Edison Company's Solar One thermal plant out in the desert. Giant mirrors focused the sun's energy on tanks of nitrate salt intended to convert water into the steam required to power a turbine generator.

Barstow

The Mojave Desert was a forbidding, yet paradoxically inviting place in the 1870s when gold, silver and borax were among the valuable metals and minerals that drew prospectors and miners from all over the country. The arrival of the Santa Fe railroad in 1883 connected up – and in many cases created – isolated small towns, and the Mediterranean-style Santa Fe Depot at **Barstow** ㊟ and renovated 1911 Casa del Desierto, a former Harvey House and now a route 66 Museum, give some idea of the forgotten splendor of the times. Gift shops and a McDonald's, at which customers eat in converted railroad cars, are among the station's attractions.

Remember This If You'd Be Spared Trains Don't Whistle Because They're Scared.
    – BURMA SHAVE

BELOW:
"As the world changes, so do things along the Mother Road. It mirrors life both modern and nostalgic..."

With the arrival of the pre-World War II National Old Trails Highway, the predecessor to Route 66, Barstow's importance as a transportation center was quite literally cemented. Sitting at the major junction of I-15 and I-40, it has shown little sign of decline. Midway between Los Angeles and Las Vegas, it is a convenient rest stop for drivers on their way to and from the resort city. The older Route 66 motels are to the west end of town. Watch for the splendid El Rancho, built with railroad tiles, and whose 100-ft (30-meter) high neon sign has been a landmark since the early days of the highway.

Barstow's Route 66 Mother Road Museum has a special exhibit devoted to the large number of Hispanic people who traveled along Route 66 when migrating west from New Mexico.

The **Mojave River Valley Museum** (tel: 760-256-5452; www.mojaverivervalleymuseum.org; open daily) and the **Desert Discovery Center** (tel: 760-252-6060; open Tues–Sat) will together answer all your questions about the desert – past and present.

Side trips from Barstow

One worthwhile side trip from Barstow is to the **Rainbow Basin** (for information, tel: 760-252-6000) where a 4-mile (6-km) loop road circles an area filled with fossilized animal remains and fringed by multi-colored cliffs; another is to **Calico Ghost Town** (tel: 800-TO CALICO; open daily), 11 miles (18 km) to the east, whose prosperity between 1881–96 came from mining a $12-million seam of silver, a boom that was supplemented by the discovery of borax nearby.

When both "cash crops" gave out, the town's 22 saloons closed one after another as the population drifted to other areas to seek their fortunes, but many of the old buildings have been rehabilitated, and such tourist attractions as wagon rides, mock gunfights and gold panning were introduced. A few miles to the east at the town of **Calico**, the **Early Man Site** (open Wed–Sun) displays relics from the Pleistocene era, which was approximately 50,000 years ago.

BELOW: you can take all sorts of desert rides at Calico Ghost Town.

Apart from one small diversion, it's an uneventful 40-mile (64-km) drive on a good road (which parallels I-15) to Victorville, where Route 66 is merely another city street. In the town of **Helendale**, the **Exotic World Burlesque Museum** (currently closed for renovations; www.exoticworldusa.com) houses a collection of burlesque souvenirs assembled by curator Dixie Evans, a one-time performer and Marilyn Monroe impersonator. A bawdy comedy show of the late 19th and early 20th centuries, the striptease eventually became one of burlesque's main elements.

The incomparable *Route 66 Magazine* ran a story about Dixie's collection of costumes, fans, photographs and performance bills. "People went to the theater to have a good time," she told writer Dan Harlow, "and burlesque gave them that. It's as American as apple pie."

Hula Ville

Victorville (pop. 64,000) began as a mining camp in the 19th century and became a magnet during Hollywood's golden age for movie-makers attracted by its "Western" feel. For a while, it also attracted the Roy Rogers-Dale Evans Museum, where the galleries glittered with the huband-and-wife cowboy stars' sequined costumes, before the museum moved to the country-music town of Branson, Missouri.

The **California Route 66 Museum** (tel: 760-951-0436; www.califrt66 museum.org; open Thur–Mon) offers a final chance for westbound travelers who haven't yet had their fill of ephemera from the Mother Road to dose-up; the museum building itself was once a road house called the Red Rooster Cafe. Its premier exhibit is Hula Ville, an example of the folksy roadside attractions once found all along Route 66. In the mid-1950s, a man named Miles Mahan decided to drive nails into fence posts and hang from them all the bottles left behind by transients. Later, he rescued a huge metal sign of a dancing hula girl and arranged for her to tower over the fences, practically stopping traffic along the route. Locals began to donate other items to Mahan's "Cactus Garden," and in time Hula Ville became a Route 66 high desert legend.

Among the free tabloids available in Victorville is a *Desert Survival Guide*, but don't take it seriously, as it's merely an advertising give-away containing no specific information whatsoever about survival in the desert.

San Bernardino

South of Victorville, I-15 heads over the 4,300-foot (1,310-meter) Cajon Summit, which, after taking the Oak Hill exit, brings you to Mariposa Road and the **Summit Inn**, a longtime Route 66 landmark that has been serving diners since 1952. Apart from a brief stretch, I-15 has subsumed much of the old route, but you're on it if you follow Cajon Boulevard into **San Bernardino ㊵**, a Mormon town in the 1850s, and once a major citrus center. It's the gateway to the mountainous **San Bernardino National Forest**, more than 600,000 acres (243,000 hectares) of wilderness dominated by 11,500-ft (3,505-meter) high Mt San Gorgonio, the highest in Southern California. Deep in the forest are the

Map on page 204

Black beetle on white sand.

BELOW: the Mojave Desert was a forbidding place when gold was discovered in the 1870s.

Map on page 204

well-known resorts of **Big Bear** and **Lake Arrowhead**, long hideaways for Hollywood stars. State Route 18, romantically known as the Rim of the World Drive, is the lofty 40-mile (64-km) highway that leads to these destinations.

Rim of the World Drive

With panoramic views, switchback turns and lots of overlooks, **Rim of the World Drive** is particularly exhilarating to do on a motorcyle. The best stretch is the 25-mile (40-km) run from Redlands up the hill towards **Big Bear Lake**.

Back down on the ground in San Bernardino itself, the classy old (1928) **California Theater**, on West Fourth Street, is worth noting. Head out of town on Mt Vernon Avenue past some aged motels and a hard-to-miss Santa Fe railroad smokestack, and eventually you'll pass another Wigwam Motel (1950) – which recently underwent extensive renovations – along Foothill Boulevard. This leads into **Rancho Cucamonga** and begins with a series of large and anonymous shopping malls, but at the corner of Vineyard Avenue there's a glimpse of earlier times, with an old-fashioned Mobil station from the 1920s sitting on the opposite corner to the Thomas Winery. A radio museum is located nearby.

Further down is the historic **Sycamore Inn**, a huge, rustic log palace and steak house on the site of an 1848 trailside inn that catered to the Gold Rush adventurers. In 1858, it became a stop along the route of the Butterfield Stage.

Past **Claremont**, where the old route suddenly moves upscale with a grassy median and eucalyptus trees, are a few eating places that old-timers might remember. There's Wilson's restaurant (now La Paloma) at **La Verne**; the Pinnacle Peak Steak House, where they cut off customers' ties, at **San Dimas**; and the Golden Spur Restaurant (which began as a hamburger stand over 80 years ago) in **Glendora**.

There are many old motels and eateries along this part of Route 66, including the Derby Restaurant and Rod's Grill in **Arcadia**, and in **Monrovia**, the distinctive one-story Aztec Hotel (tel: 626-358-3231). This hotel dates from 1925, when it was built by architect Robert Stacy-Judd in a pseudo-Mayan style to catch the attention of motorists along the route.

The end of the road

Just before **Los Angeles ㊶** proper *(see page 236)*, Route 66 becomes what is now the Pasadena Freeway, but which started life in the closing days of 1940 as the Arroyo Seco Parkway, the first freeway in a bold, new experiment that was eventually to cover the entire state of California with a network of similarly fast motorways. Continue driving and take the Sunset Boulevard exit, then head west along Sunset until it joins Santa Monica Boulevard, which runs all the way to the Pacific Ocean.

Nobody can recall ever seeing a Burma Shave sign in Santa Monica itself, where Route 66 ends, but if the company had ever put one there it would probably have been the one that read *If You/Don't Know/Whose Signs/These Are/You Can't Have/ Driven Very Far!* ❑

BELOW: diamondback rattlesnake in strike pose.
RIGHT: Calico Ghost Town, near Barstow.

A SHORT STAY IN LOS ANGELES

The city of fantasy and film, LA has endless sun, an easy ambiance and, of course, Hollywood. Here's a list of the not-to-be-missed attractions:

◆ The Hollywood Museum is the place to pay homage to the achievements of the silver screen. Included are displays on history, personalities and Max Factor innovations.

◆ Part amusement park, part working film studio, Universal Studios is one of the most visited sites in LA. Sensational stunts and special effects are just some of the attractions; simulations of earthquakes, shark attacks and infernos are others.

◆ Lined with jewelers, designer studios, upmarket fashion and accessories boutiques, Rodeo Drive in Beverly Hills is one of the most exclusive temples to commerce in the world.

◆ Backdrop to a million holiday snapshots, the Hollywood sign is now a protected monument. Behind it, Griffith Park extends for miles and has (smog permitting) wonderful, far-reaching views over LA and the San Fernando Valley.

◆ With a church-like entrance hall crowned by an impressive dome, and a floor in shades of marble, City Hall was constructed in 1928.

◆ Art lovers should not miss the Los Angeles County Museum of Art. Costumes and pottery, gold and silverware are displayed, as well as paintings and sculpture from all eras.

◆ The Hollywood Bowl, a natural amphitheater for outdoor concerts, plays host to some of the best acts in the world.

◆ Historic and modern-day injustices of racism and prejudice are the focus of the thoughtful Museum of Tolerance on West Pico Boulevard.

 For visitors interested in staying longer in the big city, pick up a copy of *Insight Guide: Los Angeles*. A companion to the present volume, it is packed with insightful information and stunning pictures.

△ **A TOUCH OF CHINESE**
Sidney Grauman, who "invented" the movie premiere, designed Grauman's Chinese Theatre in the 1920s. Its big attraction is the forecourt, with stars' hand- and foot-prints.

▷ **GETTY CENTER**
Architect Richard Meier's fabulous building on top of a hill with stunning views almost distracts from the collection of treasures inside.

CITY OF ANGELS

In 1781, Father Junípero Serra named a dry, dusty settlement after St Francis of Assisi's first church, St Mary of the Angels. No one could have conceived that hot, arid place would turn into glittering Los Angeles, the capital of moviedom and a world-famous synonym for glamor and fun. Residents of most big cities pretend to be blasé in the presence of celebrities, but Angelenos really are: movie stars are the stock-in-trade here, as common as scarlet-suited guardsmen in London or yellow cabs in New York. LA is also a city of adventure and innovation: Disneyland, rollerblading, beach culture, rap music – it all started here first.

∇ DISNEYLAND
The first Magic Kingdom opened in 1954. Disney's California Adventure opened nearly 50 years later.

△ UNIVERSAL STUDIOS
The theme park's spoof of attractions like the Hollywood sign and early star Betty Boop keep the crowds coming.

∇ Red arrows on the map indicate routes from the city detailed in this book

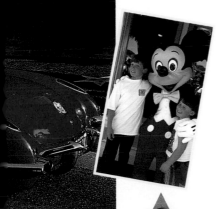

> STARS AT THEIR FEET
The Walk of Fame on Hollywood Boulevard commemorates stars from James Dean to Tom Cruise.

Important Information

Population:
3.8 million

Dialing codes:
213, 310, 323, 562, 626, 714, 818

Website: www.lacvb.com

Tourist Information:
LA Visitor Info Center
685 Figueroa Street
CA 90017
Tel: 213-689-8822
Fax: 213-624-1992

Los Angeles Throughways

0   10 miles
0   10 km

THE SOUTHERN ROUTE

*A guide to the South and the Southwest, with principal sites
clearly cross-referenced by number to the maps*

Sit back, relax and enjoy the ride if you've chosen the Southern route across the continent: this is a laid-back land that just cries out to be explored, absorbed and not rushed through. Even if you're not ready to, you'll probably adapt to the pace soon enough as you meander down a Georgia street lined with trees draped in Spanish moss, tour a gracious antebellum mansion, sit down to a plateful of down-home cookin', relax on a Texas beach or kick up your cowboy boots in a turn-of-the-century saloon in Tombstone, Arizona.

Our nearly 2,500-mile (3,900-km) journey through America's South kicks off in Atlanta, unofficial capital of the "New South," dynamic home to some well-known global corporations but still blessed with enough of the equally well-known "Southern hospitality" to make it a pleasant and very liveable city. After a detour in Macon – to get a taste of the "Old South" – your trip west begins, moseying through Alabama and its true southern cities of Montgomery and Mobile and on into Mississippi for just a spell before hitting Louisiana and its belle of a city: New Orleans, full of fabulous food, unforgettable music and unique architecture – despite the destruction and spiritual defeat left behind by Hurricane Katrina.

Our route then takes you through the boggy bayous of Louisiana and across America's largest swamp (watch out for those 'gators) before dipping into Texas – so that *you* can dip your toes into the warm Gulf of Mexico in between catching some rays on one of Galveston's gorgeous beaches. Then we jog north to Houston – known for its space connections but with much, much more to please the visitor – before continuing west to Austin, the Texas capital, and charming San Antonio, with its history (remember the Alamo) and delightful Paseo del Rio (River Walk).

It's a long haul, then, to the next major city – El Paso – but we keep things more interesting by avoiding the interstate and instead following the winding Rio Grande at the Mexican border. There's a worthy detour on the way to beautiful Big Bend National Park before you hit El Paso and its infinitely more interesting Mexican "sister city," Ciudad Juárez, across the border.

New Mexico's next, with its high-tech weaponry and missile sites, but also home to the natural beauty of White Sands National Monument and some ancient cliff dwelling sites. You'll cross the Continental Divide before entering Arizona, where the "Old West" really comes to life in places like Tombstone and Bisbee. The state's "big cities" of Tucson and Phoenix also have much to keep you busy before continuing on west into California to your ultimate destination: sunny San Diego. ❑

PRECEDING PAGES: the best American cars – ever; everybody's somebody in the Texas town of Luckenbach.
LEFT: sax appeal on a soft Southern night.

A SHORT STAY IN ATLANTA

Atlanta is bold, brash and self-confident, a cosmopolitan island surrounded by rural Georgia. Here's a list of the not-to-be-missed attractions:

◆ In its expanded location beside the Georgia Aquarium, the new World of Coca-Cola *(shown right)* houses everything you ever wanted to know about this fizzy drink. You'll explore the largest collection of Coke memorabilia and be able to taste over 70 different products.

◆ Underground Atlanta is the shopping, eating and entertainment center of Downtown. Filled with shops and watering holes, the complex stretches six blocks above and below ground.

◆ Sometimes called the "Beverly Hills of the South," Buckhead contains more than beautiful homes. It also serves as the dining room of Atlanta and the shopping center of the Southeast, not to mention being good for nightspots.

◆ Consisting of many acres of gardens, trails and woodlands, the Atlanta History Center makes for a wonderful day hike, taking in the Tullie Smith farmhouse and the Swan House mansion.

◆ If eclecticism interests you, don't miss Little Five Points. This area's shops specialize in everything from New Age crystals and vintage clothes, to music and books. It's good for art, too.

◆ Architecture, sculpture and art come together at the High Museum of Art. The building, designed by Richard Meier, has a sculpture by Rodin outside, while inside, works by Picasso, Matisse and that all-American favorite, Norman Rockwell, line the museum walls.

◆ Centennial Olympic Park is one of the last remaining features of the 1996 athletic games. In the middle of this small park is the Fountain of Rings, utilizing the Olympic symbol of five interconnecting rings.

◆ A highlight of a visit to Midtown is the Fox Theatre at 660 Peachtree Street. The Moorish-style movie palace was built in 1929, and is best seen on a tour by the Atlanta Preservation Center.

▷ **SKYSCRAPER CITY**
Atlanta's skyline is filled with gleaming, state-of-the art skycrapers, many designed by local boy John Portman, the architect of modern landmarks in many countries.

▽ **MARTIN LUTHER KING, JR**
Retrace the life of the Civil Rights leader in the Freedom Walk, a four-block area that includes King's birth home *(shown)*, his gravesite and the church in which he preached.

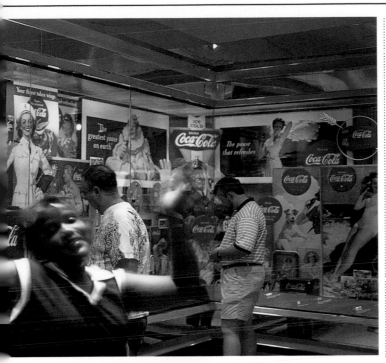

CAPITAL OF THE NEW SOUTH

Atlanta has always been a city alert to opportunity. Many think this determination to succeed is a consequence of being burned down during the Civil War – but, in fact, Atlanta has always been this way. It's an urban phenomenon, a new city in microcosm, with the air of a prosperous, self-confident and self-absorbed town inventing itself every day. Winning the bid for the 1996 Olympics was just the beginning; now Atlanta wants to take on the world. It's not the easiest of towns for visitors – streets are confusing, signs non-existent – but the longer you stay, the better it gets.

∇ Red arrows on the map indicate routes from the city detailed in this book

HERE'S THE NEWS
50-minute studio tour allows you to watch the professionals t work; the weather map is nmissable.

GONE WITH THE WIND
uthor Margaret Mitchell me from Atlanta, and her me and other locations e now museums.

Important Information

Population:
471,000
Dialing codes:
404, 770
Website:
www.atlanta.net

Tourist information:
Atlanta C & V Bureau,
233 Peachtree Street,
Suite 100, GA 30303
Tel: 404-222-6688
Fax: 404-577-3293

ATLANTA TO NEW ORLEANS

Map on page 248

The mournful whistle of freight trains, small towns on hot summer nights and grand, glorious antebellum towns highlight this trip through Georgia and Alabama

A mong all the states of the "Deep South," **Georgia** has been the most successful in keeping pace with, and even outstripping, its rivals in the North and West. For more than a century after its cataclysmic encounter with historical destiny – as the focus of the Confederacy during the American Civil War (1861–65) – the South continued to set itself apart from its conquerors (the Federal Government, or Union), stubbornly maintaining its identity with the antebellum days on the Cotton Belt. Finally, however – and in part unwillingly, as a result of the changes forced upon it by the civil rights campaigns of the 1950s and 1960s – a "New South" has begun to emerge. While there's still truth in the popular image of the region as a poor, undeveloped and un-educated rural backwater, many of its urban communities have recast themselves beyond recognition, as high-tech high-achievers to match any in the nation.

Georgia on my mind

Nowhere is that more true than in the cities of Georgia, and above all in its dynamic capital **Atlanta ❶** *(see page 244)*, on the broad Piedmont Plateau of its north-central region. Home to global corporations from Coca-Cola to CNN, Atlanta can justly claim to be the heart of the "New South." Nonetheless, it has managed to retain the more appealing aspects of its past, such as the South's traditional mannered gentility and famed flair for hospitality. Macon, too, on the "fall line" that runs from Augusta to Columbus to separate northern Georgia from the Coastal Plain, has prospered without losing sight of its heritage, while Savannah, on the Savannah River close to the Atlantic Ocean, surrounds its stunning, antebellum city center with modern industry and shipping activity *(see "Atlantic Route," page 78)*.

Banking, manufacturing, media, military installations and tourism may have come to dominate its cities, but much of the rest of Georgia remains rural. Agricultural produce such as the state's trademark peaches and sweet Vidalia onions, together with lumber, cattle and poultry, continue to figure prominently in the economy.

Throughout Georgia, you can expect hot days and pleasant nights from May through September, temperate comfort in April and October and cool to cold temperatures November through March. Georgia blooms most beautifully in the spring, which is ideal visiting season. Southern Georgia, on the Coastal Plain, is balmiest, often sweltering in summer.

If finding parking in downtown Atlanta leaves you crying for escape, take a trip 7 miles (11 km) east of 285 on US 78 to **Stone Mountain Park** (tel: 770-498-5690), a recreation complex including an ice rink,

LEFT: Stone Mountain Park, outside Atlanta. **BELOW:** dressed with finesse.

Atlanta to San Antonio

golf course, campground, waterslides, boating, fishing, tennis, wildlife trail, "Scenic Railroad" ride and reconstructed plantation. Stone Mountain's plantation showcases buildings imported from points throughout the state.

The park sprawls around the central figure which gives the area its name: **Stone Mountain**. The exposed portion of this granite giant occupies a volume of 7.5 trillion cubic ft (213 million cubic meters) and is thought to be almost 3 million years old. Its gestation period was long, as igneous rock struggled to push through the surface. Stone Mountain's thrust to the sky is a fine metaphor for the concrete explosion of modern Atlanta after its razing by the Union army.

The mountain itself, smooth but for light pocks in the surface, is spectacle enough. However, its focus has become the **Stone Mountain carving**, over 50 years in production, depicting the Confederate leaders Jefferson Davis, Robert E. Lee and "Stonewall" Jackson. The sculpture, which spreads 147 ft (45 meters) across and towers 400 ft (122 meters) above the ground, was completed in 1972.

Macon

Heading southeast out of Atlanta on I-75 – one of the major north–south arteries in the United States – you'll begin to encounter what the Federal Writers' Project called "the rolling character of the land [which] makes for undulations in the roadways, the fields and the pine forests that border them. The clay hills are deeply gullied by erosion and their red color against the dark pines of the wooded regions creates a perpetually vivid landscape." Some 80 miles (129 km) after leaving the "big city," I-75 takes a sharp turn to the south and straight into the heart of **Macon** ❷ (pronounced to rhyme with "bacon"); you can venture into the city from either I-75 or I-16, which continues southeast to Savannah. Don't expect any classic skyline views: downtown Macon has long since ceased to be the commercial center, and those few skyscrapers it does hold, such as the **Liberty Federal** and **Hilton Hotel** buildings, are if any thing eyesores rather than symbols of prosperity. First impressions can be misleading, however, and while Downtown may not be exactly bustling, Macon itself has experienced something of an economic boom in recent years.

The effect of industry – together with any number of huge shopping malls – taking over green-field sites all around the periphery of the city has been to spare Downtown from large-scale "development," while generating the capital to restore the treasures of the past. Macon's marvelous antebellum mansions and civic buildings were spared destruction during the Civil War by a simple ruse. When in 1864 General Sherman and his troops launched shots into the city across the Ocmulgee River, they were met with return fire suggesting a substantial resistance force. However, the troops that turned Sherman and his all-too-tragic torch down in the direction of Savannah were not Confederate regulars, but old men and young children.

The Old South

The architecture that has been preserved and restored is incredibly diverse, yet thoroughly Southern. As one resident puts it: "When people from outside the South come to find the "Old South," it's not in Atlanta, which is too new, nor is it in Savannah, which by virtue of its settlers and design is closer to a European city. The Old South is right here in Macon."

During the "cotton boom" of the early 19th century, cotton kings built lavish homes in the early Federal style with classical touches. These were followed by structures in the Greek Temple style adapted to the climate. Over the years, waves of commercial expansion inspired forays into new styles for mansions and civic and commercial buildings. Italianate Revival Roman Revival and

Georgia's best-loved local hero

BELOW: Macon is the epitome of the Old South.

Academic Revival experiments carried through to the 1920s. Among fine examples open daily to visitors are the huge **Hay House** (tel: 478-742-8155) on Georgia Avenue, and the **Cannonball House** (tel: 478-745-5982) on Mulberry Street, scarred by a shot from Sherman's artillery and now appropriately housing a **Confederate Museum**.

All can be enjoyed at their best in March each year, when the Cherry Blossom Festival celebrates the simultaneous flowering of Macon's pride and joy, the incredible 150,000 Japanese cherry trees that have been planted along the downtown streets.

Macon's visitor center, on Cherry Street, can provide detailed walking tours to aid explorations of the city's architectural heritage. Next door, the **Georgia Music Hall of Fame** (tel: 478-751-3334; www.gamusichall.com; open daily) pays tribute to the state's many musical heroes, from Johnny Mercer to Little Richard and James Brown.

If you wish to step farther into the past than 1800, take the short trip to **Ocmulgee National Monument**, crossing the Ocmulgee River from Downtown by means of a drab concrete bridge named in honor of Macon-born soul-music legend Otis Redding. The monument conserves traces of the civilizations that populated the plateau from 8000 BC.

The greater part of the exhibits in the Visitor Center and out on the trails reconstruct the life of the Mississippian Indians in the 10th to 13th centuries. At Ocmulgee, they painstakingly erected huge mounds of sand and clay; many were used for ceremonial purposes, as evidenced by the altar-like structure inside the largest mound. Regrettably little is known about the mounds, but their very presence is fascinating.

BELOW:
The Whistle Stop Cafe in Juliette, Georgia, was built for the movie *Fried Green Tomatoes*. The food is filling and not to be missed.

Backwoods whistle-stop

Taking US 23, which winds northward from Macon along the approximate line of the Ocmulgee River, enables you to get an appealing taste of rural Georgia. Tiny **Juliette**, 20 miles (32 km) along, was reinvigorated in the early 1990s, when its air of picturesque deep-woods dereliction made it the perfect location for the movie *Fried Green Tomatoes at the Whistle Stop Cafe*. A **Whistle Stop Cafe**, built for the film beside a still-used country railroad station and across from an ivy-covered abandoned mill, does indeed dish up copious platefuls of fried green tomatoes. Another traditional Southern delicacy is available on the outskirts of the peaceful county town of **Jackson**, 15 miles (24 km) farther on, where the roadside **Fresh Air Barbecue** serves succulent barbecued pork; ask to peek into the giant ovens, bursting with whole, slow-roasting hogs.

US 23 rejoins I-75 10 miles (16 km) north of Jackson, but the lull of simple highway cruising is cruelly shattered 7 miles (11 km) south of Atlanta as you reach I-285, the **Atlanta ByPass**, which rings the sprawling Atlanta metropolitan area, appearing deceptively on the map as the quiet fringe outside the bustling city. But the eye of a hurricane is calmest, while its perimeter spins fastest.

The Atlanta ByPass is this city's answer to the Indianapolis 500. It's an almost mythical, lawless road-rally in which Southern gentlemen and ladies vent their frustrations on the way to and from their suburban homes. In the words of one southern Georgina, "If you do 55 in Atlanta the way they do up North, you'll get blown off the highway." Average speed on I-285 can reach 75 mph (121 kph); top speed goes up from there. Fortunately, to continue your journey west, you only have to endure the ByPass for a short stretch before turning off on I-85 southwest to Alabama.

ATLANTA TO SOUTHWEST ALABAMA

Alabama and much of the land to its west passed through several hands before it was taken over by the United States in the late 18th century. Labyrinthine Colonial struggles involving the Indian "Five Nations" (Cherokee, Seminole, Muscogee, Chickasaw and Choctaw) mark Alabama's early history, and its coat-of-arms displays the emblems of the five non-native nations that successively held sovereignty over it: France, Great Britain, the United States, the Confederacy and again the United States.

The last two of these regimes, of course, have left the clearest stamp on Alabama, named for the Alabama River, itself named after an Indian tribe. Alabama rose to its economic apex during the cotton boom of the 19th century, and has been markedly reluctant to let go of the memory of its Confederate heyday. Only following bitter campaigns in the 1990s did the state capitol building in Montgomery finally cease to fly the Confederate flag. The state has seen better days, economically and socially, but its natural resources, hardworking citizenry, and enduring pride refuse to admit decline.

From downtown Atlanta, I-85 cuts a sure path southwest to the heart of Alabama. It's a slightly hair-raising drive at first, as airplanes pass alarmingly

Map on page 248

TIP

A memorable experience is to attend a Southern church service. Locals can be wary of "foreigners," however, so be prompt, well-dressed and respectful.

BELOW: Sunday morning in a small Southern town.

close overhead as they descend into the airport, but the interstate soon becomes an attractive parkway through the rolling Piedmont highlands, with woods to either side and a grassy central median erupting with wildflowers. "Alabama the Beautiful" is barely an hour's drive away, but there's potential for a last dip into rural Georgia. Leaving I-85 to join US 29 at **Grantville ❸**, 50 miles (80 km) out, offers an undulating ride through characterful little towns such as **LaGrange**, and also takes you along a brief stretch of the 525-mile (845-km) shoreline of **West Point Lake**. Engineered under the Flood Control Act of 1962, this enormous power source features 43 recreational areas for fishing, swimming, boating, hunting and general relaxation.

State line

Sign of the South: This climbing vine, known as kudzu, was brought from Asia and used by the government to stop soil erosion. It is now virtually unstoppable, smothering thousands of acres of land.

BELOW:
Tuskegee, Alabama.

Although in principal the **Chattahoochee River** delineates the boundaries of Georgia and Alabama, in fact at this point you cross the Alabama state line a short way west of the river. Even then, you don't join the rest of Alabama on Central Time – one hour earlier – until you're beyond the Lanett Valley here. The vigorous promotion of the state by the Alabama Welcome Center, just across the state line on I-85, stands in sharp contrast to Georgia's *laissez-faire* attitude. This distinction is certainly attributable to Alabama's image as a backwater state with little to offer either the traveler or the prospective settler.

After rolling through a forested area along I-85 westbound, you can turn off at exit 38 to **Tuskegee ❹** via State 81 south and State 126 west. Tuskegee is the site of Booker T. Washington's **Tuskegee Normal and Industrial Institute**, which is one of the few institutions of higher learning for American blacks that existed during the 19th century.

In the words of the leading black intellectual, W. E. B. DuBois, Washington was "the greatest man the South produced since the Civil War." Politically deft and enormously inspired, Washington believed in cooperation with the ruling whites and in practical education to serve the needs of the black masses concentrated in the South. Washington's policy of avoiding confrontation made enemies among other educated blacks and "liberal whites," but he kept Tuskegee alive.

While the institute remains very much active, much of its historic campus has been preserved with the aid of the National Park Service. Its centerpiece is the **Carver Museum** (tel: 334-727-6390; open daily), named after the black agricultural chemist George Washington Carver, who worked and taught on campus from 1896 until his retirement to **The Oaks** in Tuskegee, where he died in 1943.

He had abandoned artistic aspirations to forge the pioneer science of industrial agriculture, and his discoveries literally saved the Southern economy from collapse after the boll weevil infestation of 1919 destroyed the cotton industry. Many of his "bulletins" (pamphlets) are displayed in the museum; through such works as *How To Grow The Peanut and 105 Ways of Preparing It for Human Consumption*, a black man saved a region whose elite had oppressed and would continue to oppress his race. The museum also shows a well-made documentary film entitled *Up from Slavery*, which details the history of the institution and of Washington's struggle without shying away from the controversies that surround them.

Map on page 248

Old Acres and Pecan Grove

Back on I-85 south, travel 41 miles (66 km) from Tuskegee to the boundary of **Montgomery ❺**. Montgomery consists of a small, quiet downtown area surrounded by wide outlying neighborhoods whose names smack of agricultural gentility: Old Acres, Pinedale, Pecan Grove, Open Acres, Spring Valley and Park Manor. While the prairie muds are still rich, Montgomery bases its livelihood on government services, construction and manufacturing. Montgomery also benefits from the patronage of the US Air Force, whose elite members are frequently assigned to **Maxwell Air Force Base** on the site of famed aviators Wilbur and Orville Wright's flight school.

Although Montgomery is not exactly unattractive, little about it is glamorous. By and large, no one in the city seems all that excited about selling its image to outsiders – except those who enthusiastically maintain and promote the city's "rich heritage." They are not exaggerating when they use this term to describe the marble-columned **State Capitol** on Goat Hill and the surrounding historic sites. Two grand structures stand across Washington Street from the Capitol: the quiet **First White House of the Confederacy** (tel: 334-242-1861) and the imposing **Alabama Archives and History** building (tel: 334-242-4435; open Tues–Sat). The White House, moved next to the Archives from its original site at Bibb and Catoma streets, was the home of Confederate president Jefferson Davis during Montgomery's stint as first capital of the Confederate States of America. This rebel nation was comprised of the 13 states and territories that seceded from the United States in 1860 and 1861 over the issue of states' rights – among them the right to maintain slavery. Davis has been eclipsed in history by Confederate General Robert E. Lee, but in the South he is still revered as an emblem of distinction and self-determination, as evidenced by the frequently-seen bumper sticker "Don't Blame Me – I Voted For Jefferson Davis."

BELOW:
Montgomery,
Alabama.

Civil rights sites

The neo-classical Archives Building is a rich storehouse of Native American arts, Confederate history and state development. From relics of the "first Alabamians," the Shell Mound Indians of the 10th century, to the Hank Williams Collection of the great Alabamian country singer's clothing, the Archives pieces together the multi-textured story of "Dixie."

Barely a hundred yards down from the Capitol is the **Dexter Avenue King Memorial Baptist Church**, whose 26-year-old pastor, Rev. Martin Luther King, Jr, was thrust somewhat unwillingly into the limelight in December 1955 when he was invited to spearhead the civil rights campaign known as the Montgomery Bus Boycott. A mural inside the church, "Montgomery to Memphis, 1955–1968," commemorates the long struggle for dignity and equality. Outside the Southern Poverty Law Center nearby, the moving

Civil Rights Memorial, designed by Maya Lin (who was also responsible for the celebrated Vietnam Veterans Memorial in Washington, DC), honors King and 40 other martyrs of the movement. The most significant cultural event in Montgomery is **Jubilee CityFest**, a springtime community celebration held on the third weekend of May. During the rest of the year, the zoo, historic districts, riverboat ride and fine arts museum do nicely.

Another Alabama

I-85 into Montgomery dovetails into I-65 and continues south into the rural glades of southwestern Alabama. Along the way, the radio bands are striped with black contemporary music, pop, country, gospel, sermons and jazz.

Skid marks that swerve off to the shoulder suggest high-speed highway adventure. The soil deepens again to red where it had been sandy and gray in the "Black Belt" through the midsection of the state. Deeper exploration of rural Alabama is definitely recommended, and US 31 is a good place to start. Branching away from the interstate near the cute little town of **Evergreen**, US 31 arcs through Escambia and Baldwin counties, grazing the northwesternmost edge of Florida near Atmore and Perdido. The land surrounding towns such as Castleberry – "Home of the Alabama Strawberry" – is dotted with small green ponds and spread with groves of pine and oak. Cattle graze on the muddy soil, and farmhouses call forth images of peaceful backwaters.

BELOW:
the right side of the tracks, Evergreen, Alabama.

Before reaching **Atmore**, you pass through **Canoe** ➏, Alabama, where you might see a horse and buggy along one side of the road as a 100-car-long freight train whistles by on the other. Atmore is weary-palmed, open-fielded and railroad-tied, with churches signposted in all directions off the highway. If you

Map on page 248

head back up to the interstate on State 21, close to the intersection, you'll come to the invitingly named Good and Plenty Restaurant, Bakery and Gift Shop run by Mennonites transplanted from Pennsylvania. Religious books, cookies, breads and buffet lunch and dinner are served.

Continue on I-65 along a 13-mile (21-km) stretch before the next exit (exit 45) to **Perdido ❼**. Just south of the highway, the fruit of Jim and Marianne Eddins' gumption and perseverance continues to thrive: **Perdido Vineyards**.

'Bama wine

Winemaking in Alabama, once a great domestic industry, was effectively killed by Prohibition. Even afterward, Baptist leaders maintained that drinking – let alone manufacturing – alcohol was next to ungodliness. The Eddins family dared the opposition and began their muscadine vineyard in 1971, marketing the grapes to a Florida winemaker. When that arrangement fell through, the Perdido Vineyard began producing its own wine in 1979.

The muscadine varieties grown at Perdido – scuppernongs, higgins, nobles and magnolias – are from a tough vine indigenous to the southeastern United States. Perdido's table wines, which may be sampled at the vineyard, are mostly sweet wines with a few drier varieties, including an extra-dry white which is reminiscent of some California wines.

The Perdido venture met with initial hostility from the community, but its success and the subsequent attention it brought to Baldwin County considerably warmed their reception. But as one disgruntled entrepreneur put it: "Sometimes you gotta get down on your hands and knees and pray for deliverance from the Christian businessmen."

Baldwin County is subject to a "pressure-cooker" climate, hot and prone to extremes of humidity. Nature has been hard on American farmers for centuries, but the environment was very attractive to a settlement of Greeks who came to the shores of Mobile Bay before World War II. Under the leadership of a Greek Orthodox priest named Malbis, the community established the lushest plantation in the county. When Malbis died in Nazi hands after he returned to Greece, the community carried out his plan to build an Orthodox Church in what is now the town of **Malbis**, between US 31 and 10, 4 miles (6 km) east of Mobile Bay. The church was constructed from materials imported from Greece and includes stunning tile work and stained glass.

MOBILE TO NEW ORLEANS

The coastline of the Gulf of Mexico, arcing from northwest Florida to southeast Texas, can well lay claim to the title of "the American Riviera" – though less reverently, it's also known as "the Redneck Riviera." Not so much a Cote d'Azur as a Cote de Blanc, the Gulf Coast spreads its white sands beside warm waters stocked with fine shrimp, oysters and other delicacies. While never quite ranking as an international destination, the superb beaches of Gulf-coast Alabama, Mississippi and Texas have attracted vacationers from the South and Midwest since the mid-19th century. Tourism, gambling and fishing are

The Gulf of Mexico arcs from northwest Florida to southeast Texas. One of its many names is "the Redneck Riviera," a derogatory title that locals find funny but gets "correct" Yankees writing hotly to newspapers.

BELOW: the beaches of the Gulf coast have attracted visitors since the mid-19th century.

Crest of the Historic Development Commission in Mobile, Alabama.

BELOW: Mobile's visitor center is housed in this replica of the town's Fort Condé.

the economic mainstays of the region, but they have been impinged upon by hurricanes and the growth of the oil industry, which often drills and explores within sight of the sunbathers. Whatever the ecological effects of oil retrieval may be, the petrochemical industry has been crucial to the survival of cities such as Mobile, Alabama.

Former French capital

Interstates 10 and 65 and US 90 (which pick up from US 31) all straddle the mouth of the Mobile River as they cross westward from Baldwin County into the port of **Mobile ❽** (pronounced *Mo-beel*). Mobile's locale on river and gulf has made it the most contested area in all of Alabama's twisted power struggles, and to this day it feels resolutely atypical of a state that outsiders regard as the most insular in the South. That sense of cosmopolitan diversity is hardly surprising; after all, Mobile began life in 1706 as the capital of the French colony of Louisiana, which covered a far larger, if not all that precisely defined, area than the modern state of the same name.

Mobile is the most attractive destination for visitors in what might otherwise be dismissed as a "pass-through" state. Its Colonial past remains evident everywhere, while parallels with Louisiana in general, and New Orleans in particular, range from the intricate iron grill-work that adorns the city's balconies to the oysters and gumbo sold in its restaurants. Most striking of all is Mobile's Mardi Gras, which – say locals – pre-dates its more famous counterpart in New Orleans. Arrive in the week before Lent, and you'll be dazzled by the parades and costumes, but throughout the year tell-tale strings of colored Mardi Gras beads festoon the live oaks and telephone wires Downtown.

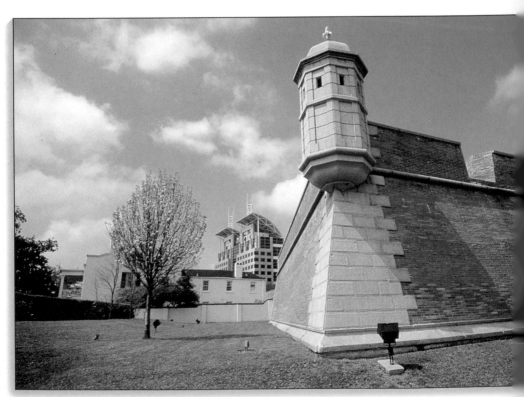

A stroll along downtown avenues such as lower **Government**, **Church** and **Dauphin streets** is much the best way to get a flavor of Mobile. Start at the south end of Royal Street, where the city's visitor center is housed in a faithful replica of **French Fort Condé**. The original was built from 1724 onwards; this version, on the same site, was constructed to mark the Bicentennial in 1976. Its cannons now point forlornly across a concrete underpass, but the chambers below serve as a good museum of local history, and feature a fine photo gallery of recent carnival queens, the vast majority of whom appear to be called "Tammy." From there, a short walk will take you through stately historic districts that flourish with magnolia, azalea and oak, all of which thrive in the semi-tropical climate. Yet again, serious commerce has fled to the outlying malls, so the old department stores have closed down, but cafés, clubs and restaurants are present in abundance.

Map on page 248

Semi-tropical jungle

Government Street becomes US 90 as it pulls away from Mobile Bay and widens into the usual mall-motel-and-fast-food sprawl. On reaching the town of **Theodore**, you'll spot a huge billboard directing you south on State 59 to **Bellingrath Gardens and Home** ❾ (tel: 251-973-2217; open daily), "The Garden For all Seasons." All the hype – "Incomparable," "One of the World's Most Beautiful Year-Round Gardens" – turns out to be pretty much true. Originally a semi-tropical jungle on the Isle-aux-Dies River, the land was purchased by Walter Bellingrath, who made his fortune as the first bottler of Coca-Cola in Alabama. Mr and Mrs Bellingrath landscaped 65 acres (26 hectares) of the 905-acre (367-hectare) plot, sculpting an evolving, living work of art to surround their magnificent riverfront home. Azaleas, roses, hibiscus,

BELOW: the Japanese section of Bellingrath Gardens.

chenille, chrysanthemums, poinsettias, lilies, violets and dogwood are all part of the "rapturous floral beauty." The Oriental-American Garden, honking geese, flamingos and teeming bayou will charm where the gift shop and restaurant depress; renting a taped tour is an unnecessary distraction. The mapped walk is well-designed, but its much more fun to let yourself wander aimlessly, dream by the ponds and waterfalls, and lounge languidly in the gazebos.

Town life in the Deep South

US 90 is the "old highway" along the Gulf Coast from Florida to Louisiana, and it's recommended over the bald interstate. The going is generally slower, and traffic lights are more frequent in places. Nevertheless, US 90 offers a glimpse of town life in the deepest South.

Out of Mobile and Theodore, US 90 passes in a dispiriting blur through dreary **St Elmo**, where the only relief from the endless succession of trailer parks are a couple of large dragway stadiums. Five miles (8 km) westward, you arrive in **Grand Bay**, "home of the world's largest watermelon festival." At Grand Bay, State 188 swoops south into State 16 to **Bayou La Batre**, an oil, shipbuilding and shrimping town where the Blessing of the Shrimp Fleet in early May and the Seafood Festival in late July are two of Mobile County's big attractions. About 5 miles (8 km) outside Grand Bay, US 90 crosses with remarkably little ceremony into the state of Mississippi. The highway crawls through the towns of Pecan, Orange Grove and Kreole before skirting **Pascagoula**, one of the three major Mississippian anchors on the Gulf Coast (the two that follow are Biloxi and Gulfport). Although the "old highway" is immediately announced as the "Scenic Beach Route to New Orleans," it takes

BELOW: born again in the eyes of the Lord.

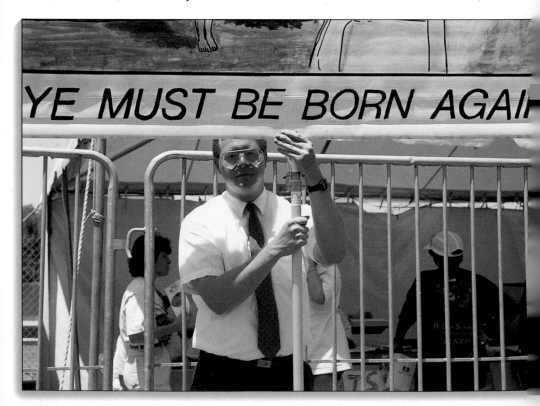

about 27 miles (43 km) of unattractive inland commercial districts and malls to get from state line to scenery. A billboard puns that Jackson County is a "shipshape community" before you climb onto the drawbridge over the ship-dotted **Pascagoula River**. The land from Gautier to Biloxi is swampy, and the gray-blue skies are crystal clear. Another drawbridge delivers you into Harrison County, and straight into the resort city of **Biloxi** ❿ (pronounced locally: *Bluxi*).

Mississippi resort

Biloxi was the second base of operations for the French government of the Louisiana Territory, following Mobile. Founded in 1699 across the Biloxi Bay from its present location, the city sits on a peninsula cut by two bays and the Gulf of Mexico, providing a brilliant and popular beach. The somewhat forlorn slogan with which it celebrated the tercentenary of its "discovery" in 1999 – "Rediscover Biloxi" – owes much to the extent to which Biloxi has transformed itself since the legalization of casino gambling in Mississippi. Several huge new casinos – superficially eye-catching, but far from architecturally distinctive – now dominate the Biloxi shoreline.

Mailbox with tiny Confederate flag in the deep South.

The 19th-century stately homes on which Biloxi's reputation as a posh winter resort had rested have largely disappeared. Most of the credit for that rests with a succession of severe storms that have swept in from the Gulf. Severe damage was wrought by the vicious onslaught of Hurricane Camille in 1969, a head-on hit from Hurricane Georges in 1998 also caused widespread destruction, but Hurricane Katrina, in August 2005, surely wreaked the most havoc, shredding homes and businesses, including the new Hard Rock Hotel and Casino – which had been only days from opening prior to the storm and plans to reopen in summer of 2007.

BELOW: fat crabs from the warm waters of the Gulf.

Map on page 248

The extent to which gambling can be credited with turning around the economy of Mississippi as a whole is debatable, but there's no disputing its impact on Biloxi. That said, it's so hedged around with arcane restrictions as to make Biloxi a peculiar hybrid. First of all, casinos can only be built on existing commercial property, so long swathes of pristine beach still survive, and in the quest for room to build, some of the largest casinos have located themselves facing inland on the previously sleepy Back Bay.

Secondly, state laws only allow for gambling on boats, not on land, so the huge structures you see from the road are in fact just the hotel and restaurant segments of the operation, while the actual gaming takes place on "barges" situated behind. Once inside, however, you can't tell where building ends and barge begins. As with much of the Gulf, the appeal of Biloxi remains more for weekenders from adjoining states than international travelers; the casinos may be glitzy but they have none of the flair of their Las Vegas equivalents, and the fact that you can see beautiful expanses of ocean through their floor-to-ceiling windows merely serves – except to die-hard gamblers – to make them feel all the more claustrophobic.

BELOW: gambling has transformed the Mississippi resort of Biloxi. **RIGHT:** the Lake Pontchartrain Causeway, gateway to New Orleans.

Gulfport and Long Beach

Biloxi does at least hold one genuine historical attraction – though it, too, suffered enormous damage during Hurricane Katrina. The white-columned oceanfront mansion of **Beauvoir**, the last home of Confederate president Jefferson Davis, served until recently as a showcase for his possessions, and also as a wide-ranging Confederate museum. Davis's continuing appeal for diehard Southerners was demonstrated by an addition to the no-expense-spared **Jefferson Davis Presidential Library**. The house and library, though indefinitely closed, are presently undergoing restoration, with plans to reopen in the future.

If it's beach fun you're after, continue along the coast on US 90, where the golden strands of **Gulfport** and **Long Beach** ⑪ are lined with kiosks that rent out jet-skis, beach tractors with inflatable wheels or simply multi-colored beach parasols. One final community, the intriguingly named **Pass Christian**, harks back to more gracious days in Mississippi, with an avenue of live oaks whose branches intertwine above the highway to create a cool green tunnel, but by the same token its lack of commercial development means that it offers little incentive for drivers to get out of their cars.

US 90 then curves sharply away from the coast and crosses the Bay of St Louis, where a bridge terminates in lovely **Bay St Louis**, "Gateway to the Gulf Coast." With little warning, the road forks: State 609 takes the northwestern way toward I-10 and a National Aeronautics and Space Administration (NASA) test site; US 90 slides southwestward. Both bring you shortly to Louisiana. Eight miles (13 km) of bridges form Interstate 10 from shore to shore – from St Tammany "Parish" (as counties are called in Louisiana) into Orleans Parish. As the car crosses on **Lake Pontchartrain Causeway** *(see page 265)*, you feel you're dipping and climbing through the water itself. Suddenly, wistful **New Orleans** ⑫ *(see page 262)* rises from the opposite shore of **Lake Pontchartrain** ⑬, a crescent of skyscrapers amid a green lake of oak.

NEW ORLEANS: THE BIG EASY

Anchor of the Gulf Coast, cradle of jazz, home of exotic food – this is without doubt the most fascinating city in the South

Curling sinuously and luxuriantly around a mighty bend in the Mississippi, New Orleans is known as the "Crescent City" – the home of jazz, blues and great food. It is also synonymous with Mardi Gras. Since 1857, Carnival has been the unbridled expression of New Orleans' spirit: at the private balls, in the wild parades, behind masks and under the glitter of costume jewelry, locals and visitors join together to celebrate. With the advent of Lent, it's back to business as usual, which, at least in the rowdier parts of Bourbon Street, is simply a muted version of the same.

Although Hurricane Katrina devastated New Orleans in late 2005, flooding homes,

taking lives and dampening the city's spirits, tourists continue to flock to this unique place. The first stop for most visitors is the Vieux Carré ("Old Square"), otherwise known as the French Quarter. Occupying the site, and still following the gridded street pattern of the original walled French settlement, the Vieux Carré rests beside the Mississippi River between what are now Canal Street and Esplanade Avenue. Due to a series of disastrous fires in the early days, only one building survives from the city's first, French, incarnation – the Ursuline Convent (1750) at 1114 Chartres Street (tel: 504-529-3040; closed Mon) – but in its exquisite harmony and display, the entire ensemble of buildings works wonderfully in this haunting locale.

The heart of the French Quarter is Jackson Square, the true "old square" fronted by St Louis Cathedral (1794). The flagstones immediately outside the cathedral are the domain of street musicians, portrait artists and transparently fraudulent but flamboyant fortune tellers – not to mention the "Lucky Dog" hot-dog sellers, their carts shaped like garish giant sausages, immortalized in John Kennedy Toole's comic masterpiece *A Confederacy of Dunces*. To either side, the red-brick Pontalba Buildings (1849), with their fine cast-iron balconies, are considered the oldest apartment buildings in the US. Two excellent museums flank the cathedral itself, housed in cupola-topped Colonial structures known as the Cabildo and the Presbytere.

The main drag (in every sense) of the French Quarter is high-spirited Bourbon Street, a pedestrian circus at all hours and in every season. In contrast to Bourbon, one block toward the river, parallel Royal Street plays host to an array of classy galleries and antique shops, interspersed with formal restaurants such as Brennan's – legendary for its breakfasts – and the Court of Two Sisters, whose spacious, well-shaded courtyard makes it the ideal spot for a leisurely "jazz brunch."

The architecture along Decatur Street, the main riverfront thoroughfare, is less fascinating. Tourists continue to descend upon the old French Market, and the Jackson Brewery a block away, but both have recently lost so much of their original identity in the process of "restoration" that they amount to little more than shopping centers. The

Mississippi itself lies on the far side of a high levee. For an appealing half-mile or so, the aptly-named "Big Muddy" is lined first by a wooden boardwalk known as the "Moonwalk," then by grassy parks, one of which contains the well-stocked Aquarium of the Americas (tel: 800-774-7394; closed Mon). Free ferries cross to the quiet suburb of Algiers on the far side, while replica sternwheelers offer longer sight-seeing cruises.

Well-meaning but misguided regulations have ensured that while no developer can tamper with the gorgeous facades of the French Quarter, almost any degree of re-building is permitted inside. However, Lafitte's Blacksmith Shop at 941 Bourbon Street, the tumbledown brick smithy where the pirate Lafitte plotted many a high-seas escapade, is an atmospheric if almost impenetrably gloomy bar that makes an appropriate starting point for nightly walking tours of "Haunted New Orleans," while the stately Napoleon House at 500 Chartres Street, allegedly the focus of a scheme to rescue the exiled emperor from St Helena and bring him to the United States, is another ravishingly Stygian bar with its own courtyard café.

Traditional jazz can be heard in nightspots such as Preservation Hall (tel: 504-522-2841), a dilapidated wood and concrete structure on St Peter Street, or the more upmarket Storyville development on Bourbon Street, a complex of bars and restaurants that aims to recall the spirit of New Orleans' early 20th-century Red Light district. A more youthful form of brass-band music, often incorporating soul, reggae and rap, is played in clubs such as Donna's on Rampart Street, while truly excellent house bands entertain diners at countless cafés and restaurants.

Best with Creole food is a cold draught of Abita beer, Louisiana's own brew. The definitive local liquor drinks are Sazerac and Ramos Gin Fizz; a rum-based Hurricane at Pat O'Brien's; or a cooling Pimm's Cup at the Napoleon House. New Orleans is also famous for its chicory coffee. The home of

the rich *cafe au lait*, the sidewalk Café du Monde in the French Market, also serves the sweet local specialty, *beignets* – doughnut-like pastries heaped with powdered sugar.

Away from the Vieux Carré, the Continental influence decreases, as New Orleans merges the Old South with the New. Take a scenic drive through the Central Business District, the home of the Louisiana Superdome, and into the lush and wealthy Garden District, where you can find antebellum houses standing amid the azalea and dog-wood, and baroque oak trees shading marvelous structures built in Greek Revival, Renaissance and Victorian styles. ❏

LEFT: fabulous food found here; Jazz Fest in the spring is the best time to hear the best music.
RIGHT: tomb of a voodoo queen; elegance in wrought-iron; St Louis Cathedral, Jackson Square.

NEW ORLEANS TO SAN ANTONIO

Map on page 248

Cruising across what claims to be "the longest bridge in the world," take an alligator-enhanced trip through Cajun Country and end up in cowboy country

This route from New Orleans to the Texas border takes in, first, Cajun country and then the state's capital. Leaving the city and driving north, Lake Pontchartrain is spanned by **Lake Pontchartrain Causeway**, "the world's longest bridge." The causeway is a 24-mile (39-km) double stripe of highway propped above the surface of the lake. For miles, nothing can be seen on the horizon, and the camelback plunge into the void is akin to crossing the barren yet subtle plains of Texas *(see picture on page 261)*.

On the trip north over the causeway to **Mandeville**, land initially appears as a thin blue sliver on the horizon, an airy gray-blue strip melting off the murky waters into the sky. Gradually, the land becomes more distinct, broader and deeper in color until it becomes the interface of two great azure bodies: sea and sky. If you choose to cross the Lake Pontchartrain Causeway, it might be best to do so on your way out of the city.

A round-trip across the lake may be a little overwhelming, and concentration sometimes tends to falter on the second stretch. When the Causeway touches land in Mandeville, it becomes US 190. Four miles (6 km) north of the lakeshore, it interchanges with I-12, which runs 61 miles (98 km) west to the capital of Louisiana, Baton Rouge.

LEFT: Cajun music in Breaux Bridge.
BELOW: Vermilionville museum, Lafayette.

Acadian bayous

Alternatively, if you follow the efficient I-10 out of New Orleans, you cut through the boggy, baroque bayou country on the southwest bank of Lake Pontchartrain in St Charles and St John the Baptist parishes. The highway is stilted out of grass-fringed still water where the thin trunks that disappear into the mire mimic the somber poles that support the parallel powerlines.

Bayous – narrow, sluggish rivers usually surrounded by wetlands – run in veins throughout southern Louisiana, otherwise known as Acadiana. This expansive region is named after the Acadians, Catholic French refugees driven out of Nova Scotia by the British in the late 18th century. Settling the Louisiana lowlands, mostly Spanish dominions, they were joined by Frenchmen fleeing the Revolution, and created a culture known as "Cajun" (a corruption of "Acadian").

Acadiana, stretching along the Gulf Coast to Texas and west from the Mississippi River up to Avoyelles Parish, has been described as "South of the South," although in many ways it's more conspicuously akin to the societies of the French and Spanish West Indies than to the traditional American South.

The land of the Kingfish

I-10 meets the Mississippi River at the city of **Baton Rouge** ⑭, capital of Louisiana and the state's major port. That name, in French, means "red stick." It's generally agreed that the "stick" was a tree, red either from the blood of animals hung there by Indians or from the stripping of its bark. In the latter case, the tree may have been used to mark the boundary of Houma and Bayou Goula Indian land. Although Baton Rouge abuts Acadiana, it has little to do with it, except for governing it and shipping its oil. The ambience is definitely "Southern," and you'll notice, in comparison to New Orleans, a deepening of accent and of provincial ways. The rather quiet, laid-back tempo of the streets belies the intense industry and politicking at the city's heart.

The principal sights of Baton Rouge are the old and new trappings of government. The **Old Capitol** building (tel: 225-342-0500; open daily), a Gothic folly constructed beside the Mississippi in 1849, attracted the full force of Mark Twain's considerable scorn. Blaming the "debilitating influence" of Sir Walter Scott for the antebellum South's obsession with notions of "chivalry," he charged "It is pathetic enough that a whitewashed castle, with turrets and things, should ever have been built in this otherwise honorable place; but it is much more pathetic to see this architectural falsehood undergoing restoration and perpetuation in our day, when it would have been so easy to let dynamite finish what a charitable fire began."

In contrast, the skyscraping Art-Deco **New Capitol** commands an eminence at the north end of town. Resembling a scaled-down Empire State Building, it was built in 1932 during the regime of legendary governor Huey Long, the so-called "Kingfish" who reigned supreme over Louisiana through the Great Depression. By all accounts a distasteful and corrupt man, Long was nevertheless an enlightened despot who brooked no opposition to his semi-socialistic rule for the "common man." Highways, schools and hospitals were built; the unemployed put to work; the privileged heavily taxed. He was gunned down in the capitol in 1935 – a case of memorabilia on the exact spot admits that he may have been killed by his own bodyguards as they panicked in the face of a supposed assassin who never fired a shot – and is now buried in the adjacent garden, alongside a larger-than-life statue. Despite the lessons of Long's death, security in the Capitol is refreshingly minimal; tourists are free to ride the elevator to its topmost tower for wonderful views, or to join Louisiana's political elite for lunch in the basement canteen.

To the outsider, Baton Rouge is largely impenetrable and culturally poor, but it's worth a stop to savor the Mississippi River breeze that cuts the unusually balmy air. The twin foundations of the city's wealth are best appreciated as you leave. From the huge **Baton Rouge Bridge**, on which I-10 crosses the river, you can see belching petrochemical refineries stretching away into the distance they help make so hazy. Down below stands Baton Rouge's port, the fourth most active in the nation thanks to being the farthest inland of all deep-water ports serving the Gulf of Mexico. That status was not achieved by chance; one

BELOW:
Baton Rouge's Old Capitol was constructed along the Mississippi in 1849, causing great scorn.

of Long's most brilliant ploys to boost his own state was to build this very bridge too low for ocean-going vessels to continue any farther upstream.

West of the Mississippi, you re-enter Acadiana in West Baton Rouge Parish, and soon pass beyond into Iberville Parish. For the first time in this trip – but not for the last, as you head toward the open spaces of the West – you're treated to spectacular scenery without having to leave the interstate. Here, it becomes the **Atchafalaya Swamp Freeway**, crossing America's largest swamp, dividing into two separate highways, supported on precarious concrete stilts and separated by an expanse of soupy open water that holds lozenge-shaped islets.

Map on page 248

Drowned forests

To either side, the landscape is a magical melding of water and drowned forest, punctuated by clumps of trees, telegraph poles and strangely-shaped cypress "knobs" (those parts of the root systems of cypress trees that poke out of the morass). Locals fish sedately, or even race speedboats, just below the highway, and every unidentified piece of flotsam may potentially be an alligator. Not a place to run out of gas, let alone to take your eyes off the road and go over the edge. On the far side of the 20-mile (32-km) wide swamp, you find yourself safely back on terra firma. Louisiana natives draw a distinction between the Prairie Cajuns, who farm the soil of south-central Louisiana, and the Bayou Cajuns, the "half-man, half-gator" shrimp-fishing river dwellers of the marshlands closer to the Gulf. In terms of what the rest of the world thinks of as being Cajun culture, like the accordion- and fiddle-based Cajun music, or the spicy food, the two are not far apart.

Lafayette ⑮, 50 miles (80 km) west of Baton Rouge, is the largest city in

Now crossing alligator land, Atchafalaya Swamp, Louisiana.

BELOW: 'gator in a glade, Atchafalaya.

Acadiana, and standing close to the hypothetical line that divides the prairies from the bayous, makes an ideal hub for exploring the region. It's a sprawling and far from prepossessing city, but in addition to some excellent restaurant-cum-music-clubs, such as **Prejean's** and **Randol's**, it also holds a couple of entertainingly informative "living museums."

Land of the Cajuns

The best, **Vermilionville** (tel: 337-233-4077; closed Mon), consists of an idealized village of restored and transplanted 19th-century buildings where experts demonstrate traditional Cajun crafts. Quilter Nell Barron, for example, painstakingly stitches together authentic century-old patterns, dismissing visitors' awe at the sheer work entailed: "This isn't work; to me work is what you don't like to do. I don't count the hours; it's not a nine-to-five job."

If you're pressed for time and decide to stick to the interstate, the Texas border is barely 100 miles (160 km) west of Lafayette. The temptation to explore Cajun country in more depth, however, is liable to prove irresistible. A short excursion north, for example, leads to the welcoming real-life prairie town of **Eunice**, and to **Opelousas**, home of Cajun music's blacker, bluesier counterpart, zydeco. More ambitious travelers can add half a day or so to the long haul westward by taking the longer detour south to parallel the more interesting coast along the **Jean Lafitte Scenic Byway**. Start by backtracking slightly from Lafayette on I-10, leaving at exit 109 to little **Breaux Bridge**, where **Mulates Restaurant** justly claims to be the "most authentic Cajun restaurant in Louisiana." State 31, briefly renamed Main Street as it passes through Breaux Bridge, follows Bayou Teche another 11 miles (18 km) south to St Martinville.

Acadiana is named after the Acadians, Catholic French refugees driven out of Nova Scotia in the late 18th century. Joined by a few French fleeing the Revolution, they created a culture known as "Cajun," a corruption of "Acadian."

BELOW: eat catfish *etouffée* at Mulates in Breaux Bridge.

Paris to the paddy-fields

St Martinville **⑯** is one of the most unspoiled towns you will find in your travels in America. A former indigo plantation and Spanish holding, it was populated by Acadians and Frenchmen in the late 18th and 19th centuries, an era when its culture was so rich that its inhabitants nicknamed it "Petit Paris." After its transformation to a minor port on the bayou, St Martinville settled into its current form of small agrarian center, with visible Cajun and French roots.

Locals are glad to recite half-remembered and half-invented histories in small cafés, which might serve Coca-Cola and catfish *etouffée*. The town is thoroughly infused with the legend of Evangeline (subject of a well-known Henry Wadsworth Longfellow poem), who allegedly walked from Nova Scotia to St Martinville in search of her lover.

The venerable **Evangeline Oak** beside the **St Martin de Tours** church (1765), where she arrived only to hear that her faithless sweetheart had married another, is now a riverside beauty spot where Cajun couples hold their wedding services, while the **Longfellow-Evangeline State Commemorative Area** preserves Acadian history in the interesting Acadian House Museum.

South of St Martinville, State 675 and then State 14 will take you west into Vermilion Parish and the attractive parish seat, **Abbeville ⑰**. Home to the Giant Omelette Celebration (www.giantomelette.org) in November, Abbeville consists of three interlocking and very sleepy squares, as well as a couple of oyster restaurants. Picking up State 82 west here, you're swiftly carried down toward the Gulf, as the distinction between land and water grows increasingly blurred.

Grazing cattle indicate solid ground, but the next field along may be a waterlogged rice paddy through which cranes and herons meticulously pick their

Map on page 248

BELOW:
the musicians
at Mulates play
authentic Cajun
sounds.

Spanish moss is found draped over live oak trees. It is not really Spanish nor is it really moss; it is an air plant and a member of the pineapple family.

BELOW: paddling a *pirogue* (canoe) at Vermilionville.

long-legged way. Locals fish patiently in the channels that run alongside the roadway, or wade through with shrimping nets.

The farther you go, the fewer signs of human life there are along this bleak and windswept drive, but the birds are a constant source of delight. The trees are bent at ever more acute angles as you approach the Gulf, and in places it feels as though you're having to force yourself through the thick tangles of Spanish moss that hang from overhead. This wispy, gray, romantic shroud is not a parasite but an epiphyte, which means it draws no sustenance from its host, and is therefore equally at home dangling from telephone wires. Turn on the radio for company, and you'll find French- and English-language stations in equal measure, together with Spanish baseball commentaries from Houston as you come within earshot of that city.

Marsh trail

Seventy-two miles (116 km) from Abbeville, highway signs announce that you're arriving in **Grand Chenier**, but apart from a few trailer parks, or a Catholic church surrounded by praying statues, no recognizable town ever appears. Another 30 miles (48 km) on, beyond a straggle of run-down motels and rudimentary restaurants catering to workers in the occasionally-glimpsed oil refineries, the highway is interrupted by an on-demand platform ferry that shuttles a dozen vehicles at a time across the outlet of **Lake Calcasieu**. On the far side, the open ocean lies barely 50 yards (46 meters) off to your right, and mighty drilling rigs are visible far out to sea. It's said that early Spanish explorers would beach their vessels here to caulk their hulls with the mysterious black substance found oozing on the beaches; a boon for Louisiana, perhaps, but no

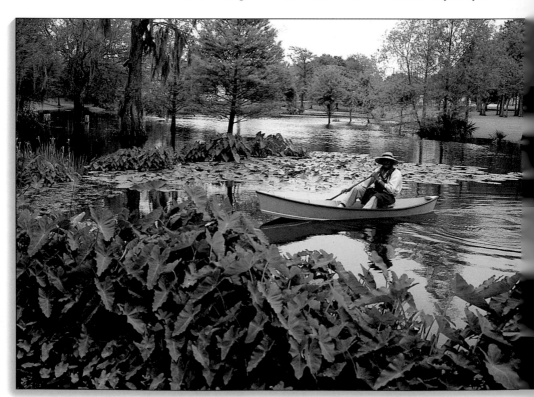

Map on page 248

incentive for a quick dip at **Holly Beach**. In any case, it's time to turn your wheel back inland. The coastal road ahead has been closed by one Gulf storm too many, and to reach Texas you'll have to head 35 miles (56 km) north to rejoin the interstate. One final highlight remains, however, in the shape of the **Sabine National Wildlife Refuge** ⓲, 9 miles (15 km) up State 27. As you walk the short, paved Marsh Trail here, which starts beside the **Intracoastal Waterway** – a mind-boggling canal that spans almost the entire length of the state – close-up sightings of alligators are all but guaranteed.

EAST TEXAS TO SAN ANTONIO

Few people who haven't been to, say, Idaho have a clear image of that state. But everyone has at least one picture of Texas. Tumbleweeds and cacti, oilfields, cowboy millionaires, humming border towns, cattle ranches: popular culture has disseminated a rugged, romantic vision of the largest of the "lower 48" states. Such familiar cultural snapshots, however, both over and underestimate the sprawling diversity and vitality of Texas. This *is* where the West begins, but it is a West with no coherent definition. At the risk of over-simplifying, one can think of a passage through Texas as a micro-cosmic passage from East to West, with the point of transition coming at San Antonio, the westernmost of the state's major cities.

Within the compact urban triangle of Houston, Dallas-Fort Worth and San Antonio is centered Texas' vast wealth and power. From Galveston through Houston to Austin, the Southern tour arcs through the heart of East Texas – its resort, its port and the state capital. Wherever you go, note the change in the triangular yellow signs that elsewhere in the South advise motorists to "Drive Safely." Here, they read: "Drive Friendly." The name "Texas," after all, is derived from "Tejas," meaning "friendly" – the name given by the Spanish to the Native Americans whom they encountered.

Port Bolivar ferry

From the moment you enter Texas on I-10 from Louisiana, highway signs start to count down the mileage to New Mexico. The magnitude of what lies ahead is clear; shortly after the state line, exit 877 branches off to the town of Orange, and the first sign you'll see for El Paso shows it as an incomprehensible 857 miles (1,379 km) distant. The chances are, however, that you'll feel ready to leave this nondescript stretch of highway long before the first city of any size – Houston, 110 miles (177 km) in. The best, and most obvious alternative, is to return to the Gulf coast as soon as possible, and head for the resort community of **Galveston** ⓳.

Halfway to Houston, as you approach exit 829, look out for the billboard that lets drivers know whether the Port Bolivar ferry is in operation. Assuming that it is, pick up State 124 at Winnie, which runs due south to the ocean. En route, as you cross first Spindletop Bayou and then Elm Bayou, little about this marshy landscape suggests that you've left Louisiana. Rice and even crawfish farms stand on either side of the highway, while indefati-

BELOW: the "drowned forests" of Louisiana's swamplands.

gable little oil pumps diligently bob away, atop mounds of scrubby vegetation. About 20 miles (32 km) down from the interstate, a steep humpback bridge crosses the Intracoastal Waterway at **High Island**, a dismal little town where the only sign of life is a junkyard advertising "Kahla's Fresh Junk." State 87 runs the full 27-mile (43-km) length of the slender spit of land known as the **Bolivar Peninsula**.

For much of the way, all that separates State 87 from the ocean is a low sandbank held together by bedraggled wind-battered telegraph poles; through the occasional gaps that permit beach access, you'll catch glimpses of the churning muddy waves beyond. Little by little, the closer you get to Galveston, beachfront structures grow grander and more numerous. Flimsy trailer parks give way to ambitious real estate developments with names like "Copacabana By The Sea." The only genuine town is **Crystal Beach**, near the western end, which celebrates the Texas Crab Festival in mid-May. A couple of miles beyond that, State 87 ends at the terminal of the **Port Bolivar Ferry**, a free 24-hour shuttle service provided by two or three large vessels that take 20 minutes to traverse the busy mouth of Galveston Bay.

Pirate on the beach

Galveston initially impresses with an air of Southern California as you roll down Ferry Road (Second Street) to Seawall Boulevard. The spacious streets, salmon colored buildings and regal palms have a West Coast feel that extends up Broadway (Avenue J) past Avenues O 1/2 and N 1/2. Farther Downtown, however, the Victorian/neo-Classical aspect brings you back to the South, while along Seawall Boulevard, the feel is more Gulf Coast than Long Beach.

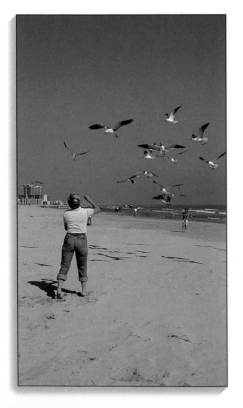

BELOW: seagulls on the beach along Seawall Boulevard, Galveston, Texas.

Galveston first came to prominence during the early 19th century as a seaport that served as headquarters for the pirate Jean Lafitte, whose name may also be familiar from his activities in New Orleans. In the local economic boom that followed the Civil War, it flowered into a fully-fledged city, becoming Texas' leading manufacturing center and, by 1899, the largest cotton port in the world. Galveston had the first telephone system in Texas, the first newspaper, electric lights, golf course, brewery and Ford dealership, while the Strand, thanks to its profusion of great commercial houses, was renowned as "The Wall Street of the Southwest."

Galveston remains an active shipping center, but Houston's port has entirely over-shadowed the island's, and these days it's more involved with the vacation industry. Of its 32 miles (51 km) of beach, the most popular stretch lies on the Gulf side of the island, along **Seawall Boulevard**. This broad thoroughfare is lined on its inland side by sprawling motels and fast-food restaurants, while the beach itself is interrupted by a succession of privately-owned piers that jut out into the ocean and offer competing attractions and diversions. The waters are not as temperate as the southern Gulf Coast beaches, but the grayish sands might as well be gold to vacationing Houstonians. Remarks one Galvestonian, "You'd think they'd never seen a beach before."

Old wealth

Galveston's acclaimed **East End Historical District**, bounded roughly by Broadway, Mechanic Street, 19th Street and 11th Street, is where the Victorian homes stand, intermixed with buildings that betray neo-Classical, Renaissance and Italianate influences. Bungalows rest in the shade cast by oleanders, oaks, maples and palms, and are slightly raised from the ground out of respect for the gulf. A walk in this district, especially down Post Office and Church streets, gives a glimpse of how the first rich Texans displayed their wealth. Downtown, **The Strand** has undergone the familiar renovation-into-tourist-attraction, arguably losing its soul in the process of gaining a money-spinning assortment of galleries, cute shops and Art-Deco restaurants.

Renovation projects have managed to preserve a few marvelous structures, like the beautiful Italianate **Ashton Villa** (1859; tel: 409-762-3933; open daily), Broadway at Tremont, but a truer Galveston rises in the form of the eyesore **American National Insurance Company** at 19th Street between Mechanic and Market. This shamelessly ugly monstrosity is the legacy of William Lewis Moody, Jr, the founder of that company, as well as Galveston's City National Bank and many other enterprises in the early 20th century.

From a glance at the map, Galveston appears to lie a full 50 miles (80 km) south of Houston. In fact, however, the build-up to the megalopolis begins as soon as you cross back to the mainland on the I-45 Causeway, to be confronted by massed ranks of smoke-belching oil refineries.

From there on in, strip malls and garish billboards line the interstate for the full 27 miles (43 km) up to the Sam Houston Tollway, which circles the entire city at a distance of around 20 miles (32 km). As you pass beneath its stacked

Map on page 248

"Galveston" is an anglicized version of "Galvez," the original Spanish name for the island settlement. It was named for Bernardo de Galvez, the Spanish Governor of Louisiana.

BELOW: dining room of Galveston's Ashton Villa, built in 1859.

HOUSTON: SPACE AGE CITY

Once an oil town, Houston now houses a wide range of high-tech industries and quintessentially Texan self-confidence

Houston boasts that the first word uttered by the first man on the moon was – you guessed it – "Houston." Mission Control Center, receiver of the greeting, is the city's prime tourist attraction, called "Space Center Houston." Officially the Lyndon B. Johnson Space Center (tel: 281-244-2100), it's located on NASA Road 1 off I-45, about 25 miles (40 km) south of Houston. Displays commemorate milestones in the US space program, and a tour takes visitors through a campus of structures containing moon rocks and astronauts, into the Mission Control Center and full-scale replicas of the Space Shuttle used for training. Follow I-45 straight into downtown Houston

for Tranquility Park. Named for the July, 1969, *Apollo* moonshot, the park at Bagby and Walker streets is a landscaped monument to the space race. Craters encircle the focal point of the park: five golden phalluses cascading water in the image of a takeoff.

More deserving of the name "Tranquility" than the park is the hushed, tranquil Rothko Chapel located in the Museum District at the southwestern corner of the city. American abstract-impressionist Mark Rothko created this chapel for non-denominational worship and meditation. Inside, it houses 14 large Rothko canvases. Outside rises Barnett Newman's disturbingly moving *Broken Obelisk*, dedicated to Martin Luther King, Jr. The worthy Museum District houses many collections, all interesting in their ways, as is the Victorian Romanesque campus of Rice University,

The galleries of Houston show how "black gold" has enriched the state through the purchase of works of art. On Sul Ross Street, the Menil Collection houses arts and artifacts of mankind from the earliest days in the Near East to contemporary abstract pieces. The Matisse bronzes that turn their backs to you at the Museum of Fine Arts Houston (tel: 713-639-7300; closed Mon) at Main and Bissonet streets, make their case about Houston's attitude toward the norm. The collection is particularly strong in American paintings. Across the street is the Contemporary Arts Museum Houston (tel: 713-284-8250; closed Mon), dedicated to current works. At Hermann Park is the Museum of Natural Science (tel: 713-639-4629; open daily), with a walk-through greenhouse aflutter with butterflies.

An emblem of Houston's appreciation for huge size is the unbelievable Astrodomain, comprised of the Astrodome stadium (Eighth Wonder of the World); Astroworld (a 100-ride amusement park); and Astrohall (the world's largest one-level convention facility). ❏

LEFT: Museum of Health and Medical Science exhibit; Johnson Space Center on NASA Parkway.
ABOVE: the Astrodome; Rice University.

and spiraling freeways and connecting concrete loops, **Houston**'s ⑳ *(see page 274)* futuristic downtown skyline finally rises on the northern horizon.

Map on page 248

If you see Texas as a microcosm of the whole country, then it's as you head west of Houston that you leave the South behind and enter the Great Plains. The state capital, **Austin** ㉑, is approximately 150 miles (240 km) west, but as I-10 runs directly to San Antonio instead, along a slightly more southerly route, reaching Austin entails at least 40 miles (64 km) of driving off the interstate. Whichever route you choose will be much the same, a mildly attractive but far from enthralling cruise through the lush plains and gently rolling hills of the "ranch country" that lies within the Houston–Dallas–San Antonio triangle. Probably the most bucolic option is to leave I-10 at exit 696, near little Columbus, and join State 71 as it meanders back and forth across the equally sinuous Colorado River – not the one in Colorado – all the way up to Austin.

Well-sheltered Austin

Austin itself nestles amid verdant woodland in the middle of an agricultural paradise that's unique among the many Texan climates and terrains. Sheltered from the humid heat that sweeps in waves over Houston, this locale makes a pleasant ideal for ranching and recreation. Unlike Houston, and despite having experienced similarly phenomenal growth, Austin is fairly well contained. Exit between Martin Luther King, Jr, Boulevard and Eighth–Third streets from I-35, and you'll be in the middle of a walkable Downtown. For most visitors, the experience of the city is confined to the area from First Street and the Colorado River up to 24th Street and the heart of the **University of Texas** (UT) at Austin along Guadalupe Avenue.

BELOW: the tower of the University of Texas at Austin glows orange (the school color) after sports victories.

High tech and outlaws

Austin manages the difficult double act of being not only Texas' political capital, but also its true cultural capital. Having attained that distinction during the 1960s, when it was a hippy mecca, it went on to spearhead the "outlaw country" movement of the 1970s, when musicians such as Willie Nelson and Waylon Jennings first came to prominence. Its reputation as a center for live music and the arts no doubt contributed to its 1980s growth as "the Silicon Valley of Texas," when more and more high-tech and financial firms relocated here. That process, of course, brought with it an influx of young urban professionals, and one need look no farther than **Sixth Street** to see the impact of aggressive consumerism on the culture. Experiencing the same gentrification as San Francisco's Haight Street, formerly gay-dominated Sixth Street is still a good place to bar-hop, but not nearly so much of a community as it used to be.

Despite its changing face, Austin retains much of its spirit. At the University of Texas – with over 50,000 students, the largest university campus in the state – the counter-cultural element will always have its place. At heart, it's still got long hair and a beard, though it might also have a Mercedes and a kid, and its image as a hotbed of new ideas sits uncomfortably with its dubious claim to fame as the place where the determinedly dumbed-down "slacker" student ethos of the 1990s first emerged.

Austin also continues to rock. Nightclubs abound, offering a nightly wide-ranging choice between hard-edged country, "new music," ska, classical, blues, R&B or jazz. Theater and literary events are numerous, while good bookstores, record stores, cafés and tiffany-glass restaurants intermix with low-down funkier spots. Above all, local legends have persisted despite the changes – for

BELOW: Austin's Sixth Street is for entertainment and shopping trips.

DETOUR – DALLAS

A 195-mile (314-km) drive along Interstate 35 from Austin leads to the glittering town of Dallas. With just over a million residents, Dallas attracts visitors with its sky-high architecture, quality art collections and high class shopping malls. The city began with the cabin of trapper John Neely Bryan beside the Trinity River, which Bryan believed to be navigable for trade all the way to the Gulf of Mexico. It wasn't, but the Houston and Texas Railroad brought people and commerce soon enough. The most extravagant of local institutions is Neiman Marcus department store, whose Christmas catalog once contained a page entitled "how to spend a million dollars." Fortunately, the penchant for extravagance extends to wonderful art collections bought with the revenues of black gold. Darker history also plagues Dallas: the most visited site is the former Texas School Book Depository, where Lee Harvey Oswald shot President John F. Kennedy in 1963. The Sixth Floor Museum overlooks Dealey Plaza, through which the president was riding when he was assassinated. The Conspiracy Museum records developments, while across the road stands a memorial to the fallen president. The Dallas Convention and Visitors Bureau, tel: 214-571-1000 or www.dallascvb.com.

example, **Scholz Garden**. "The most historic restaurant and beer garden in Texas," Scholz Garden was founded in 1866, 16 years before work began on the capitol building. Through various ownerships, additions, retractions, rowdies of all ages and storms of legislative dispute, Scholz has kept its original front room and unspoiled diversity. You can find good food here with unpretentious charm and heartfelt – if stumbling – music; you may even care to dance on occasion. Try the chicken-fried steak, a Texas favorite.

Map on page 248

Lone star capitol

Scholz Garden is a few blocks from the **State Capitol** (tel: 512-463-0063; open daily for tours) and the lower edges of UT, two major sources of business. The capitol itself is unmistakable, a red-granite version of the nation's capitol in Washington, DC. Its white, classical interior focuses on the great rotunda, commemorating the six governments that reigned supreme over Texas (Spain, France, Mexico, the Confederate States, the United States and, most proudly, the Republic of Texas). Above, at the apex of the dome, is the lone star that is the state's emblem: independence, self-determination and singularity.

Portraits of the state's governors ring the rotunda and, to all sides, wings lead to the offices of state legislators. *The Surrender of Santa Anna*, a painting at ground level, captures the dramatic moment when Mexico's "Napoleon of the West" surrendered to Sam Houston, "Liberator of Texas" and commander-in-chief of its forces during the Texas Revolution against Mexico. Among the monuments to Texas' glory in that war and in the War Between the States (Civil War) is the quiet sculpture by Bill Bond, *150 Years of Texas*, which honored the state's sesquicentennial in 1986.

You know you're in Texas when… the State Capitol is the largest of all the state capitols in the US. On completion, it was thought to have been the seventh biggest building in the world.

BELOW: Austin has more than its share of young urban professionals.

Exhibit from the LBJ Library, Austin. This part of Texas is full of tributes to the locally born 36th President of the US.

Hill Country

Historic San Antonio is barely an hour's drive southwest of Austin on I-35, but there's a diverting half-day's sightseeing to be had if you make your way between the two along the **Texas Hill Country Trail** to the west instead. At first, leaving Austin, the "trail" – in reality, US 290 – crosses a somewhat dreary Western landscape of thin grassland.

Beyond **Dripping Springs**, however, which calls itself the "Gateway to the Hill Country" but has nothing more to offer than an ugly stone-clad high school, the road starts to climb through a rich rolling terrain of open meadows, scattered with a delightful profusion of wildflowers. When it reaches **Johnson City ㉒**, 50 miles (80 km) west of Austin, it's undulating through pastoral countryside. Johnson City acquired its name long before local boy Lyndon Baines Johnson became the 36th President of the United States, following the assassination of John F. Kennedy in 1963. However, the downtown birthplace of "LBJ," who shared his initials with his wife Lady Bird Johnson, and the nearby LBJ Ranch, to which they retired after the Vietnam War put an end to his political career, are now major tourist attractions in the area.

This very middle-European region must have seemed almost heavenly to early European immigrants, and it's hardly surprising that it attracted hundreds of German settlers during the 19th century. The Main Street of the town of **Fredericksburg**, another 32 miles (51 km) west, for example, is labeled "Haupstrasse" and lined with pseudo-Teutonic beer gardens and bakeries, while numerous German-named farms along the intervening highway, like "Der peach garten," sell German-style wines and liquors.

BELOW: restaurant in Johnson City.

To get a real feel for the best of the Hill Country, take the lesser State 1376

Map on page 248

down to San Antonio. Cutting away south from US 290 just south of the Pedernales River, 4 miles (6 km) east of Fredericksburg, this route passes within a few feet of the tiny village of **Luckenbach ㉓**, another 4 miles (6 km) on. Unless you know where to look, however, you'll miss it altogether; the unmarked turning comes immediately before South Grape Creek. A much-loved ghost town – more of a joke town, really – Luckenbach was bought in its entirety by humorist Hondo Crouch in 1970, and made famous by a No. 1 Country & Western hit, recorded in 1976 by Willie Nelson and Waylon Jennings, that featured the refrain "Let's Go To Luckenbach Texas."

Country music town

Hundreds of country fans now do just that, to while away an afternoon in the diminutive post office as the postmaster cracks corny jokes and sings songs, and perhaps buy a souvenir such as a stuffed armadillo drinking a bottle of Luckenbach beer. Willie Nelson hosts a picnic here on July 4th each year, while most summer weekends there's some sort of large-scale concert in the dancehall. From Luckenbach, State 1376 continues south toward San Antonio by way of some beautiful hills, where you're liable to startle wild deer grazing beside the highway. Ten miles (16 km) northeast of the city limits, it meets I-10/US87 at Boerne.

San Antonio ㉔ at first seems deceptively pastoral; not far from the interstate, luxurious Italianate villas perch on isolated rocky knobs that look like Tuscan hill towns. Soon enough, however, you're forced to run the gauntlet of manic freeways entailed in reaching every large American city; just before it finally spits you out into Downtown, the interstate for no reason splits alarmingly into two separate highways, one stacked on top of the other. ❑

BELOW: Luckenbach was put on the map by a Willie Nelson/ Waylon Jennings C&W song.

SAN ANTONIO TO SOUTHERN NEW MEXICO

*Davy Crockett and Billy the Kid are only two of
the people who left their mark on the lands
that border Mexico and the Rio Grande*

Map
on page
282

San Diego

O f all the major cities in Texas, El Paso and San Antonio are the oldest. El
Paso began as the first Spanish mission in the future state, while it was in
San Antonio that American Texas was born and nearly slaughtered by the
Mexicans at the Alamo. Stretching between the two is the vast expanse of
Trans-Peco Texas, a largely barren yet subtly beautiful mountainous desert.
There is a timeless quality to the landscape that stands in most marked contrast to the booming spectacle of the metropolitan east.

In the anchor cities, Hispanic culture has consistently revitalized itself,
much more effectively than in Galveston, Houston or Austin. El Paso and
sister city Juárez are bound as a Mexican/American metropolis, the gateway
to the American Southwest.

Cradle of Texas liberty

San Antonio ㉔, the "Cradle of Texas Liberty," was the capital of Texas before
Mexico won its independence from Spain in 1821 and opened the territory to
settlement by anyone who would develop the land. After Stephen Austin led the
first wave of pioneers into the new land, the flood-
gates were open. Just before Austin's pilgrimage, there
were 2,500 persons of European descent in Texas. By
1836, 30,000 Anglos, 5,000 blacks and 4,000 Mexicans populated the area.

When Spaniards first came in the late 1680s to the
San Antonio River Valley, which cradles modern San
Antonio, they found it occupied by the Payaya Indians, hunters who supplemented their catches with the
fruits of the pecan and mesquite trees and the prickly
pear cactus. The Payaya cooperated readily with the
Europeans, but the Apache, who controlled the plains
to the north, took more convincing, and the nomadic
Comanche were always a threat.

Intent on securing their claims in the area and on
taming the godless heathens, the Spanish established
a mission on the west bank of the San Antonio River
in 1718. Mission San Antonio de Valero, later known
as **The Alamo** (tel: 210-225-1391; open daily), was
relocated to the east bank and then closed down in
1793. Mexican troops were transferred there to protect
the pueblo that had grown around the riverbanks.
Renamed *El Alamo* (the Cottonwood), it became a
crucial fortification.

The dubious glory of the converted mission arises
from an ill-conceived standoff with the forces of Mexican president General Antonio Lopez de Santa Ana,
the self-styled "Napoleon of the West," on March 6,

LEFT: mountain
lions are fairly
common in the
wild Southwest.
BELOW: Texas is the
gateway to Mexico.

San Antonio to San Diego

San Antonio 24 — Texas
90 — Castroville 25
Hondo
Knippa
Uvalde
90
International Amistad Reservoir — Del Rio 26 — Ciudad Acuña
277 377
27 Langtry
90
Marathon 28
385
Big Bend National Park 29 — The Chisos Basin
170 — Lajitas 30
Ojinaga
Presidio 67
67
Marfa 31
90
Junc 138 — Van Horn 32
10
Texas
New Mexico
54 — El Paso 33 — Ciudad Juárez
54
Mescalero Apache Indian Reservation — Lincoln N.F. — Orogrande
244 82
54
Ruidoso — Cloudcroft — Alamogordo 34
Ski Apache Resort, Trinity Site — 70
70
35 White Sands National Monument — San Augustine Pass 5719
Las Cruces
Rio Grande — La Mesilla 36
10 — Deming 37
38 Gila Cliff Dwellings National Monument
180
15 — Silver City
Western New Mexico University — 90
New Mexico
Arizona — 10 — Lordsburg — Shakespeare Ghost Town
Fort Bowie National Historic Site — Junc 362
186 — Chiricahua National Monument 39
181 — Gleeson — 90
191
80 — Tombstone 40 — Bisbee
Saguaro National Park — Benson
Mission San Xavier del Bac
41 Tucson
Tumacácori National Historical Park
79 — Biosphere 2
77 — 10
42 Theodore Roosevelt Dam, Tonto National Monument, Tortilla Flat — 88 — Apache Junction
60 — Picacho Peak State Park
Phoenix 43
Junc 112
85 — Junc 119 — Gila Bend
10 — Dateland 44
8
Arizona — Quartzsite — 95 — Yuma 45
California
Winterhaven
Imperial Sand Dunes Recreation Area 46
El Centro
8 — Ocotillo — Jacumba
Live Oak Springs — 94
El Cajon 47
48 San Diego

1836. Mexico's 5,000 troops were met by 187 (or 186, depending on who you ask) "Texian" martyrs-to-be. In the words of memorializer Frank J. Davis, "All dead within one sanguinary hour; yet the heroes of the Alamo are deathless."

Remember the Alamo

"Remember the Alamo!" was adopted as the Texan battle cry, and revenge came swiftly. Seven weeks later, Santa Ana was defeated within a mere 18 minutes at the Battle of San Jacinto, whereupon the Texas Revolution culminated with the declaration of the newly independent Republic of Texas.

Riddled though it is with as many contradictions as bullet holes, the Alamo today is an essential pilgrimage destination for tourists. Its defenders during the battle were, after all, recent arrivals from foreign countries that included England, Ireland, Scotland and even Denmark – as well as the United States – while their 26-year-old commander, William B. Travis from South Carolina, wrote three days before he died that "the citizens of this municipality are all our enemies."

Davy Crockett

His associates included opportunists such as Jim Bowie, remembered for his namesake knife (though the museum here can only rustle up one of his less celebrated spoons), and the legendary Davy Crockett, a three-term Congressman from Kentucky who sought his fortune in the West after the evaporation of his presidential ambitions. The independent Texas for which they fought and died survived just nine years before being subsumed by the United States.

A plaque on the front door of the grafitti-etched **Alamo Shrine**, originally the mission's chapel, requests "Be quiet friend here heroes died to blaze a trail for other men." The request is roundly ignored.

Because the taking of photographs in the shrine is prohibited, most visitors raise their brief squall, then retire first to the lovely garden, shaded by everything from myrtles to a mescal bean tree, and then on to the very busy gift shop. On sale are such reverent mementos as Alamo mugs, belts, patches, playing cards, pencils, plaques, postcards, dishware, license-plate frames, keychains, banners, bells, pins, coasters, caps, tote-bags and erasers.

Map
on page
282

A river runs through it

That San Antonio ranks second only to New Orleans as the loveliest city on the Southern Route is largely due to its delightful and distinctive **Paseo del Rio**, otherwise known as the **River Walk**. This highly original and elegantly simple concept, instigated in 1939 as part of Franklin Roosevelt's New Deal, consists of confining the San Antonio River into a tight and very narrow little channel as it loops through the city center, paving and landscaping both banks, and garnishing them liberally with restaurants, patio cafés, stores and gardens.

Though San Antonio is in truth a large, sweltering city, you'd never know it as you amble along the shaded, lively and completely pedestrianized River Walk, which stands roughly 10 ft (3 meters) lower than the busy Downtown streets. Flat-bottomed cruise boats ply gently along the river itself, and at night, in particular, the effect is quite magical. There's even an open-air theater, the ingenious **Arneson River Theatre**, where the stage is arranged on one side of the river while the audience watches from a stucco Spanish-style amphitheater of benches on the opposite bank.

If you can bear to tear yourself away from the pleasures of the River Walk, downtown San Antonio holds several other worthwile attractions. The beautifully restored **Spanish Governor's Palace** (tel: 210-224-0601; open daily), a tranquil little gem, is located near to the original site of Spain's Presidio de Bexar (1722), the **Plaza de Armas**, where a sign notes that in the Republic of

*Mural along the
River Walk in
San Antonio.*

BELOW: the Alamo,
symbol of the
Republic of Texas.

TIP

Once past San Antonio, this route skirts the Mexican border all the way to California. Roadblocks and checkpoints by the US Border Patrol are commonplace, so foreign travelers should always keep their papers handy. Passports or green cards are required if you cross into any Mexican border town.

BELOW: San Antonio's River Walk at nighttime.

Texas era, running from 1836 to 1845, the grounds had already become a busy market teeming with "noisy vendors of vegetables, fresh eggs, chili peppers, and live chickens. Strolling guitarists, tourists, and girls selling songbirds mingled with pickpockets…"

Hemisfair Park, not far southeast of the Alamo, is dominated by the slender, Space Needle-like **Tower of the Americas**, but trips to its 75th floor observation deck are rewarded only with fairly dull views of monotonous plains. Even the Hill Country amounts to little more than a few vague bumps on the horizon. Nearby, however, the **Institute of Texan Cultures** (tel: 210-458-2300; closed Mon) takes an entertaining look at the many different peoples, from Comanches to Czechs, who have contributed to the cosmopolitan blend of modern Texas. Perhaps the least-known group are the Wends, 600 of whom arrived from Prussia in 1854; their descendants have maintained their identity ever since. There's also a glorious evocation of the cowboy past; one early African-American *vaquero* is quoted as saying "we loved to work cattle so much we'd just be sittin' around cryin' for daylight to come."

Miles, mesas and mountains

You're going to have to devote at least a day of your life to driving the 500-mile (800-km) distance between San Antonio and El Paso, so it makes sense to make the most of what this largely desolate expanse has to offer. Rather than stick to I-10, which plots a northerly course across the barren plains, head due west on US 90 to meet up with the legendary Rio Grande at Del Rio. Following the Mexican frontier from there enables you to relish the magnificence of Big Bend National Park, among the most remote yet stunning national parks in the US.

Almost as soon as you leave San Antonio on US 90, there's a parched quality about the roadside grasslands even in springtime that presages the dessication ahead. At first, however, agriculture maintains a foothold. **Castroville** ㉕, 40 miles (64 km) out, proclaims itself to be "A Touch of Alsace France," and has several Alsatian restaurants (catering to humans, not dogs), while **Hondo** just beyond has the feel of the Great Plains, with huge fields of corn and wheat.

Next come **Knippa** – "Go Ahead and Blink, Knippa is Bigger than You Think" – which is devoted to stone quarrying, and **Uvalde**, where unless you need to rent a tractor, there's no imaginable reason to stop. This region seems to be the spiritual home of the Drive-Thru Beverage Barn, where locals can stock up on hard liquor without having to peel themselves off the leatherette seats of their pick-up trucks.

The Rio Grande

By now, you'll almost certainly have logged your first sighting of the agents and vehicles of the US Border Patrol, who are going to remain an ever-vigilant presence for the rest of your trip. Across most of Texas, the desert makes a far more effective barrier against illegal entrants from Mexico than does the Rio Grande. Rather than monitor every inch of the river, therefore, the Border Patrol simply erects roadblocks along the few highways that lead away from it; be sure to have your papers in hand at all times.

Once past Uvalde, US 90 dwindles to a single lane in either direction. The only distraction in the 72-mile (116-km) stretch to Del Rio is Bracketville, where the set used by John Wayne to film *The Alamo* will no doubt confuse future archeologists. **Del Rio** ㉖ itself comes as an anti-climax; it's home to the large Laughlin Air Force base, and any number of shopping malls catering to daytrippers from the adjacent Mexican town of **Ciudad Acuna**, but apart from a couple of 19th-century buildings, there's not much to divert tourists.

A further 12 miles (19 km) northwest, **Amistad Reservoir** carefully claims to be the "third largest international man-made lake in the world." It was created by the completion of the Amistad Dam, a huge curving wall of concrete jointly dedicated by the presidents of the US and Mexico in 1969. Above this point, the Rio Grande is officially designated in the finest American tradition as a "Wild and Scenic River," but the dam firmly puts paid to any remaining wildness. At the monument in the middle, you can stand astride, with a foot in either country, watching anglers and even scuba-divers as they sport in the waters below.

Another 30 miles (48 km) northwest, the highest highway bridge in Texas crosses the deep gorge of the Pecos River, just before its confluence with the Rio Grande. The stern "No Diving From Bridge" signs seem somewhat superfluous, but it's worth stopping to admire this first of the many Western canyons to come, and envy the eagles and falcons that soar so majestically above it.

Beyond the Pecos, there's no longer any doubt that you've reached true desert, while confirmation that

Map on page 282

BELOW: welcome to cowboy country.

British actress Lily Langtry, for whom the eccentric Judge Roy Bean named the tiny Texas town of Langtry.

you're in the Wild West soon comes with your arrival in **Langtry** ㉗. This tiny hamlet is celebrated as the home of Judge Roy Bean, the "Law West of the Pecos." Judge Bean was a storekeeper who was appointed as a Justice of the Peace in 1882, despite an ignorance of all legal matters that he never attempted to rectify. His saloon-cum-courtroom, a hundred yards shy of the dry-as-bones canyon of the **Rio Grande**, is now a museum and information center.

Until you come to **Marathon** ㉘, 120 empty miles (193 km) west of Langtry, you've added no extra mileage to your trip by taking US 90 rather than I-10. This is where you'll have to decide whether to detour down to Big Bend, however – a decision best contemplated in the luxury of the restored **Gage Hotel**. (Most of the towns *en route* have had a handful of rundown motels, but this is the first really appealing accommodation since San Antonio.)

Bears and mountain lions

It would be hard to recommend **Big Bend National Park** ㉙ too highly. Even the 40 mile (64 km) drive south to the park entrance on US 385 is a delight, as you head straight toward a mysteriously misty wall of mountains, centering on one giant pyramidal peak, only to shimmy around them at the last minute to find yourself confronted by another equally alluring range on the horizon. Once inside the park, 30 more miles (48 km) brings you to the main visitor center, but the prime destination, the **Chisos Basin**, lies another 12 miles (19 km) beyond that. A truly glorious dead-end road – too narrow for large RVs – climbs steeply into the park's central cluster of mountains. It feels for all the world as though you're entering another kingdom. Tall yucca plants stand like sentries to either side as the road picks its way through a labyrinth of towering rocks, where

BELOW: Big Bend National Park.

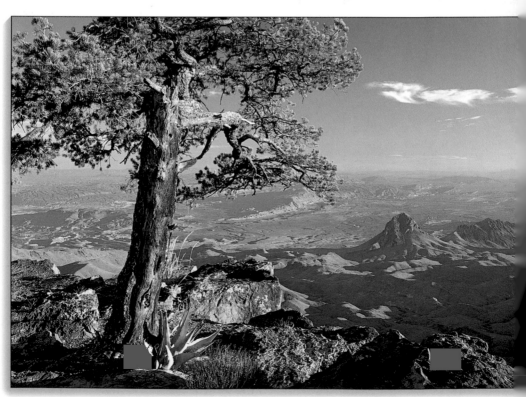

wonderful pink-blossomed cacti and other desert succulents look down from the high scree slopes. Finally, you drop down a succession of tight hairpin bends into the basin itself, a grassy bowl ringed by mountains that holds the park's lodge, campsite and other visitor facilities. This is bear and mountain lion country, so you may prefer to stay close to your motel-style room, but even in these there's a risk you'll find a rattlesnake coiled on your doorstep. Marked hiking trails enable the more intrepid to explore the wilderness; the best trail winds 3 miles (5 km) down to the **Window**, a natural gap in the circle of mountains that looks westward across an eerie desert landscape of buttes and mesas.

Map on page 282

River-rafting trips

State 170 west of the park, also known as the **River Road**, is one of Texas' most attractive highways, providing a rare opportunity to drive along the Rio Grande in all its glory. It reaches the river 41 miles (66 km) west of the Chisos Basin at the small resort town of **Lajitas ㉚**, which specializes in offering river-rafting trips through high-walled Santa Elena Canyon into the park. Until recently, Lajitas was noteworthy for having a goat as its mayor – and not just any goat at that, but Clay Henry, the Beer-Drinking Goat. Sadly, however, Clay has come to prefer beer to politics; stripped of his civic responsibilities, he's now a sorry specimen. For 50 miles (80 km) from Lajitas, the River Road sticks close to the river, sometimes scrambling over high sandstone outcrops, at others meandering through well-watered fields. Cattle can often be seen grazing in Chihuahua, Mexico, and in several places the river is shallow enough for them to wade across. If you're tempted, there's another chance to cross into Mexico at **Presidio**, where **Ojinaga** on the far side holds a couple of seafood restaurants – you'd have to wonder how fresh their supplies can be – plus cut-rate opticians and pharmacies.

BELOW: Marfa is known for its mysterious lights; some people think they are UFOs.

From Presidio, a 61-mile (98-km) drive north on US 67 enables you to rejoin US 90 at **Marfa ㉛**, known for its highly-regarded contemporary art musuem – a legacy of the New York-born artist Donald Judd – as well as its mysterious lights illuminated in the sky, which most people think are UFOs, and as the place where the 1956 movie *Giant* was filmed. For almost all the 74-mile (119 km) drive northwest to I-10, the road is paralleled on one side by an endless procession of telegraph poles, and on the other by a railroad along which colossal freight trains – larger than any of the settlements *en route* – drag themselves toward California. Little "dust devils," created by local air disturbances, swirl in the fields in the distance, while frail tinder-box tumbleweeds blow in from the desert when you least expect them. It may seem Texan through and through, but the tumbleweed is in reality the Siberian thistle operating under a homely alias, and as such is an unwanted foreign pest.

Van Horn ㉜, 120 miles (193 km) east of El Paso on I-10, is a typical interstate pit-stop whose fast-food restaurants, motels and gas stations nonetheless make it seem like a land of plenty after the austerity of the desert crossing. Even the long radio silence comes to a sudden end, with four different stations devoted to the weather alone; the one snag is that there's no weather to speak of. As you continue westward, there's an additional bonus in the form of an extra hour to your day, gained when you enter the Mountain Time Zone close to Allamore. This final stretch into El Paso passes through perhaps the most featureless landscape it's possible to imagine. Its sheer emptiness induces a sort of meditative calm, leaving you free to ponder such eternal questions as, why does everyone seem to be towing gigantic ocean-yachts across this infinite sandscape, when the tide went out for the last time approximately 60 million years ago?

Border town

Where San Antonio has profited from redeveloping historic districts and monuments, the city of **El Paso** ㉝ has failed. Of course, San Antonio has the Alamo; nothing in El Paso is comparable as a marketable emblem. Nevertheless, San Antonio has made exceptional efforts to upgrade and maintain its attractions while injecting romance into its riverfront. El Paso, on the other hand, has left the excitement and romance (well, excitement anyway) to its much larger sister city *across* the riverfront. That city is **Ciudad Juárez** (*see below*), and the river is the Rio Grande, separating the United States and Mexico.

El Paso, which spreads around the base of the Franklin Mountains, lies in the oldest European-settled area of Texas. In the 16th century, Spaniards first crossing the Rio Grande to explore their territories in New Mexico headed along *El Paso del Norte* – the Pass of the North – which sent the river through a break in the mountain ranges. Soon, *El Camino Real* was extended from south of Chihuahua City, Mexico, to what is now Santa Fe, New Mexico, by conquistador Juan de Oñate. When the Spanish colonists were driven out of Santa

BELOW: Eagle Dancer statue outside the Speaking Rock Casino, El Paso.

DETOUR – MEXICO

Ciudad Juárez, across the bridge from El Paso, Texas, is probably the most interesting Mexican border town outside of Tijuana, south of San Diego. But whereas San Diego is sleek and efficient, confirming the US's superior grasp of the modern world, the difference between El Paso and Ciudad Juárez is definitely in Mexico's favor. El Paso is gray, grim and depressing, whereas Juárez, the biggest city in the state of Chihuahua, is vibrant and colorful. Bullfights and bright souvenirs to take home make a strong impression right away. The Juárez Museum of History traces the area's development, with special attention paid to the Mexican Revolution and the Mexican hero (American criminal) Pancho Villa. Our Lady of Guadalupe Mission explores the rich religious tapestry of the country. Juárez's food is wonderful and spicy, but don't drink the water, or eat ice cream or ice cubes (an urban myth recommends a shot of tequila with each meal to kill impurities). It's certainly worth a day trip to experience another country, but don't be fooled by the ease of crossing to Ciudad Juárez; the Border Patrol is much more strict in the other direction, and a passport, green card or other paper work might be required to get back into Texas.

Fe by the Pueblo Indian Revolt of 1680, a dispirited column of refugees regrouped here, around an adobe Franciscan mission they called Ysleta del Sur. It took 12 long years before the Spaniards returned in force to reconquer New Mexico, by which time the towns of Ysleta and El Paso had sprung up around the mission. El Paso gradually absorbed Ysleta, but was itself split in two after the designation of the Rio Grande as the United States–Mexico border. The US city remained El Paso and the Mexican city was dubbed Juárez.

El Paso's strategic location has made it a travelers' stop for centuries. The Gold-Rush '49ers passed through on their way to fortune in California. Refugees, desperados and tourists have all met here. Much of the commemorated history invokes gunfights, with the notorious Marshall Dallas Stoudenmire and John Wesley Hardin on many a winning end before finally biting the dust. There's a lot of dust to bite. El Paso's climate is singularly dry, although rain is not unknown. But the rain just wets down the dust and refuses to be kicked up by the winds which herald it. Watering holes are few in the city proper, which is underdeveloped and unremarkable.

The Rio Grande in El Paso these days is more of a fortified moat than a river. In a sad parody of San Antonio, what water it holds is compressed into the narrowest of cement channels, but here the aim is very decidedly to keep visitors away, and the channel is lined on both sides not by peaceful walkways but by high, barbed-wire fences.

Until 1994, when the Border Patrol instigated "Operation Hold The Line" to halt the perceived flood of illegal immigrants from Mexico and beyond, El Paso had been notorious as one of the weakest links in the "Tortilla Curtain" between the United States and Mexico. Now, it's a sulky, shame-faced kind of city, professing friendship for neighboring Ciudad Juárez while demonizing the mass of its inhabitants as would-be "wetbacks" to be corralled like cattle.

Only a bridge over the Rio Grande separates El Paso, Texas, and Mexico's Ciudad Juárez.

BELOW: down Mexico way.

Back in the USA

Coming back across the bridge from Ciudad Juárez, it's America, alright, but Mexico hasn't ended. In fact, save for the ghost-town feeling, it's really the same city as Juárez. The Mexican population of El Paso is large, and it's focused at the border. But the Latino presence is felt everywhere. It's said that English is spoken as widely as Spanish in Juárez; the statement is equally true in El Paso.

Due to its geographic and commercial situation, El Paso is an inexpensive city, but an unexciting one. Tourism is ultimately channeled to its environs and up to **Ranger Peak** in the Franklin Mountains. The **Tigua Indian Reservation**, a living pueblo of the oldest identifiable Indian tribe in Texas, is on the eastern edge of the city, while the **Ysleta Mission** (converted) is in the Ysleta neighborhood in western El Paso, between Zaragosa and Old Pueblo roads. And that's about it, apart from **Fort Bliss** in the northeast, the site of the largest Air Defense School in the "free world," which is also home to the **National Border Patrol Museum** (tel: 915-759-6060; open Tues–Sat). So, after a brief nod and an *adios* to "old Mexico," it's time to cross over into that bright, shiny state, New Mexico.

NEW MEXICO

New Mexico is among the youngest of the United States (as the 47th to be admitted to the Union), but it has had one of the longest histories. At its northeastern edge, near Folsom, archeologists have dug up spearheads at least 10,000 years old, and by the time the first Spanish conquistadores reached the valley of the Rio Grande, in 1540, the region held as many as 100 separate village communities – "pueblos" – each home to a distinct Native American tribe. The Spaniards named the infant colony New Mexico in the misplaced hope that it might yield similar treasures to the Aztec empire of Mexico.

By the late 16th century, the *Camino Real* (now US 85) extended along the Rio Grande from Mexico to Santa Fe, site of the oldest government building in north America and the oldest US capital. However, although New Mexico covered an area far greater than the modern state, including all of modern Arizona and much of Nevada, California and Utah, until the Yankees arrived in 1846 it remained an impoverished provincial backwater, whose farmers had to battle against, not only the unforgiving desert environment, but also Navajo, Apache and Comanche raiders.

Under American rule, New Mexico has attended to its somewhat mundane motto: *Crescit Eunde* ("It grows as it goes"). Railroading, ranching and mining have all thrived on the state's rocky surface, warm valleys and subterranean waters. A deliberate US policy during World War II of siting defense installations in remote land-locked locations has also brought unexpected dividends. It was in New Mexico that scientists developed and tested the first atomic bombs, and military facilities continue to play a major part in the state's economy. New Mexico is sparsely populated by approximately 1.9 million people, roughly 16 per sq. mile (6 per sq. km). Among its notable residents have been sworn enemies Pat Garrett and Billy the Kid, "king of the innkeepers" Conrad Hilton, novelist D. H. Lawrence, artist Georgia O'Keeffe and firefighting legend Smokey the Bear.

New Mexico promotes itself as "The Land of Enchantment." Its natural beauty and the mysteries of its landscape have captivated all who come here, from prehistoric Indians, via generations of Hispanics, to modern new-age tourists drawn to cities such as Santa Fe, Albuquerque and Taos. Even little green men from outer space seem to love it here; supposedly drawn by the first signs of mankind's nuclear capability, they've been flocking to places such as Roswell ever since.

Exiting El Paso, US 54 east skirts the eastern slopes of the Franklin Mountains. As soon as you leave the city, you find yourself in an absolute wasteland; there are virtually no services in the entire 83-mile (134-km) stretch to Alamogordo and the Tularosa Valley. New Mexico arrives, with the minimum of ceremony, 10 miles (16 km) out of El Paso, at which point US 54 contracts to a two-lane undivided highway. These dusty plains appear totally uninhabited, but they're no stranger to modern man.

As you ride the gorge between the Organ Mountains that lie to the west and the Hueco Mountains that lie to the east, you will soon be passing through

BELOW: Harley-Davidson at the Golden Aspen Motorcycle Rally held in Ruidoso, New Mexico.

the **Fort Bliss Military Reservation**, home of the **McGregor Missile Range**. Beyond that, you nick the edge of the **White Sands Missile Range**. Roadside signs warn of unexploded ammunition lying in the desert, and advise you not to leave the highway.

A store that sells rocks

A barely perceptible wiggle in the road announces **Orogrande**, 46 miles (74 km) from El Paso, where the only distraction apart from two gas stations and a barbecue joint is a store that optimistically attempts to sell rocks. After all that emptiness, **Alamogordo** ❸ itself feels like a major metropolis, though a sojourn of any length soon reveals that there's not actually all that much behind the bonanza of billboards and signs lining the highway. A small but fascinating museum next to the visitor center displays artifacts allegedly made by the pygmy Indians who once inhabited the area. What's more certain is that Alamogordo was explored by ancestors of the Navajo and Apache before the Spanish passed through, naming it for its "fat" (*gordo*) cottonwood trees and eventually settling on the Tularosa River at La Luz.

The locale of the present-day town was left virtually untouched before two enterprising brothers from the East, C. B. and John A. Eddy, founded Alamogordo as a stop on their railroad line. Seduced by the forestland in the valley and its commercial potential as a rich source of lumber, the Eddys sold the railroad and settled down in Alamogordo to reap their riches from the indigenous resources. Alamogordo grew as a trade center, but the development of the White Sands Proving Ground and nearby Holloman Air Force Base radically recast the contours of the city. In the words of one local historian, "No longer was it a

Local boy William H Bonney, otherwise known as Billy the Kid, looms large in these parts. Cattle rustler and killer, the Kid escaped capture several times before being gunned down, at the age of 21, by Sheriff Pat Garrett.

LEFT: Billy the Kid gift shoppe.
RIGHT: the badge says it all.

sleepy, peaceful land of *mañana* [tomorrow], but a hustling, bustling, fast-growing city." Still a trade and manufacturing center, Alamogordo is dominated by the high-tech weaponry community. It also harbors, however, a tribute to the peaceful uses of technology in the exploration of space, in the shape of the **New Mexico Museum of Space History** (tel: 505-437-2840; open daily), standing prominently on the foothills at the edge of the valley.

This well-conceived museum chronicles the international race for the stars, featuring a "Hall of Fame" of pioneers in space exploration, from early dreamers to the moon-walking astronauts of NASA's Apollo missions. After admiring space shuttle models, a lunar TV camera and samples of foods brought aboard *Apollo* and *Skylab* missions (e.g., canned vanilla ice cream and dehydrated peach ambrosia), you can watch a video presentation of highlights from the *Apollo* 11, 12 and 14 moon landings.

Land of many uses

Although attractions in Alamogordo proper are relatively sparse, oases of natural beauty abound in the Sacramento Mountains to the east. In summer, these well-wooded hills provide a welcome cool relief from the heat of the plains, attracting visitors from all over southeastern New Mexico and west Texas. In winter, when top-class skiing is on offer, the appeal is even more compelling. A scenic half-day's driving tour from Alamogordo begins by taking US 82 to **Cloudcroft**, 19 miles (31 km) northeast of Alamogordo. The highway swiftly climbs through scrubby reddish-tinged sandstone hills to reach the tree-covered slopes of the **Lincoln National Forest**.

As highway signs inform you, the US government sees a national forest as a "Land of Many Uses." They're not nearly so protected as national parks, so commercial logging, ranching and even mining is often allowed. None of which mars the beauty of this particular stretch. Cloudcroft is an attractive little faux-Western town filled with rental cabins, snackeries and souvenir stores, and there's good hiking in the hills nearby.

BELOW:
White Sands
Missile Range.

Just north of Cloudcroft is the southern edge of the **Mescalero Apache Indian Reservation**. A 28-mile (45-km) drive northward through the reservation on State 244 takes you through some delightful Alpine scenery, complete with shimmering little lakes and flower-filled meadows, where you're likely to see Apache cowboys riding the range. Any notions you may have of Native American reservations as desolate or depressing places will soon be shattered.

The Mescalero are in fact prosperous entrepreneurs; while parts of the reservation are closed to outsiders, the tribe operates some very successful commercial enterprises on adjoining lands.

These include the region's grand resort hotel, the **Inn of the Mountain Gods**, which shares its lovely lakeside setting with a yet greater money-spinner, the glitzy **Casino Apache**. Even more incongruous is the tribe's luxury winter-sports venue, **Ski Apache** The ski resort is set above the fast-growing mountain town of **Ruidoso**, which is home to the Ruidoso Downs racetrack and a newer year-round attraction the **Hubbard Museum of the American West** (tel: 505-378-4142; open daily). From Ruidoso, US 70 drops back down to the Tularosa Valley by way of the principal reservation community, **Mescalero**, to reach Alamogordo in 46 miles (74 km).

Map on page 282

Blinding white gypsum

Taking the optional detour described above, you'll enjoy long-distance views of the most unique and spectacular feature of the region. Glimpsed at first as a dazzling white line on the western horizon, **White Sands National Monument** ❸ is located 15 miles (24 km) southwest of Alamogordo. This stunning 144,458-acre (58,505-hectare) expanse of gypsum sand dunes is carved out of the otherwise off-limits White Sands Missile Range. The only access road, US 70–82, is regularly closed for up to two hours at a time so the military personnel can drive their strange top-secret cargoes along it in peace; enquire at local visitor centers before you set off. As you approach White Sands, jets no doubt roaring overhead, the glowing dunes rise from the base of the San Andreas Mountains. Upon arrival, stop at the information center for some background on the formation of the dunes and on their stubborn inhabitants.

Gypsum is one of the most common compounds found on earth, but it's rarely seen on the surface because it dissolves readily in water. Surface sand elsewhere is almost always composed of quartz. The Tularosa Basin, however, is all but unique in having a climate dry enough, and winds strong enough, to produce the rare, surreal dunes of powdered gypsum crystal.

White Sands is breathtaking at any time of day, but especially so toward sunset. In the middle of the day, the sands are a beautiful, blinding, pure white,

Would-be cowboys should visit the Hubbard Museum of the American West in Ruidoso.

BELOW: White Sands National Monument.

reflecting so strongly they sting the naked eye. As you clamber over the dunes, occasionally marked by the pawprints of nocturnal wanderers, you should periodically remove your sunglasses to appreciate the hallucinatory expanse fully. As the afternoon cedes to evening, the sands begin to refract the light, breaking it down into a rainbow. The park is open until 10pm, and with care you might observe some of the 500 different animals that populate the dunes, from coyotes and roadrunners to owls and skunks. There is also a sparse scattering of beautiful plant life, including the hedgehog cactus with its brilliant red flowers.

A paved driveway, equipped with spacious parking and picnicking areas, loops through the dunes. The deeper it penetrates into the heart of White Sands, however, the more liable the road surface is to be obscured by drifts of gypsum sand. The effect is both disorienting and remarkable.

Concealed amid the roadless wastes to the north, the **Trinity Site** is the awesome crater that was created in July 1945, when the United States detonated the first atomic bomb. Public access to this sobering site is only permitted on the first Saturdays in April and October, when convoys of vehicles set off from an inconspicuous gateway north of Alamogordo. Check with the town's visitor center for details.

The Wild West

US 70–82 slowly but surely rises out of the Tularosa Valley as you continue west toward Las Cruces. For almost 30 miles (48 km), as you drive in a dead straight line towards the sheer wall of the San Andreas Range, it seems impossible that there could be any way through these mottled peaks. Eventually, the highway jinks to the right and climbs to reach its apex at the **San Augustine Pass**, 5,720 feet (1,740 meters) high and overlooking the valley that holds Organ and, beyond it, Las Cruces. After taking the pass, you plunge down an exhilarating 3-mile (5-km) slope to find yourself back in the beautiful low valley of the Rio Grande, where greens and browns evolve through shades and mixtures below the pearly blue peaks in the distance.

The route briefly engages **Las Cruces** before hooking into I-10 to Deming. Las Cruces is unremarkable; in fact, it's downright ugly. Nevertheless, a degree of historic significance lies buried beneath the unrelenting mallscape; human occupation of the Mesilla Valley has been shown to date back to the 4th century. Under Spanish rule, the valley was forever liable to the depredations of Apache raiders. Las Cruces – "the crosses" – acquired its name in 1830, after a caravan of travelers coming from Taos were ambushed and slaughtered, and white crosses were erected to mark their graves.

The town of **La Mesilla** 36, a short drive from downtown Las Cruces on State 28 and State 292 (Motel Boulevard), has made greater efforts at historical preservation. Its restored **Plaza**, dominated by its old gazebo, offers a real taste of the Wild West. This was where the Gadsden Purchase was sealed in 1854, establishing the current boundaries of Mexico and the United States, while a gift store in one corner was originally the courthouse where the notorious out law Billy the Kid was tried and sentenced to hang for murder in 1881. The Kid managed to escape before his hanging, but subsequently met his maker at the hands of Pat Garrett, who was in turn murdered near Las Cruces in 1908. Crafts and curios merchants have now taken over most of the plaza, selling rugs and wind chimes, Indian jewelery and ceramic ornaments, though the "Emerald Isle" Irish shop strikes a discordant note. At least there's still room for the historic **Double Eagle Restaurant**, which is not only attractive but has tasty food.

Across the Great Divide

A short distance out of Las Cruces on I-10 west, a double ribbon of landscaped orchards lines the narrow Rio Grande, which flows here from its source in Colorado by way of Santa Fe and Albuquerque. Beyond the shallow sandy ridge on the far side, the highway levels out to cross the windblown chapparal of Luna County, where more and more specimens of the ostrich-like state plant, the yucca, scrutinize travelers as they make their way westward. From here to the Arizona state line, freeway exits are commonly marked with frontier-style outlets for supposedly characteristic goods. Behind false façades spring a trading post, Wild West town or teepee where moccasins, cactus jelly and plant candy are available to tourists.

Fifty-six miles (90 km) out of Las Cruces is **Deming ❸⓿**, which is enriched by four short mountain ranges: the **Florida Mountains** to the southeast, the **Little Floridas** to the east, the **Tres Hermanas** to the south and **Cooks Range** to the north. Cooks Range is the largest of these, and its highest point – Cooks Peak, about 8,400 feet (2,560 meters) in elevation – commands an impressive vista. The Cooks Range was once in the heart of Apache lands and served as an

Billy the Kid's tombstone in Fort Sumner, New Mexico.

BELOW: the historic Double Eagle Restaurant in La Mesilla, NM.

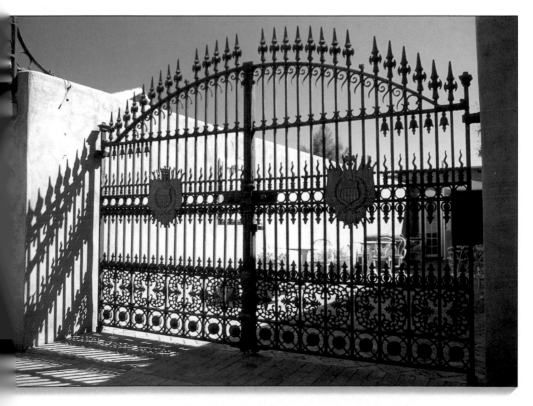

ideal lookout. Before there was Deming, there was New Chicago, an "end of the track" railroad town with a supply of water – crucial to locomotives – in the subterranean **Mimbres River**. Relocated 10 miles (16 km) west of its present site, Deming was of great strategic importance to railroad magnate Charles Crocker, who joined his Southern Pacific line to the Santa Fe Railroad at the site. Early settlers included soldiers, professionals, merchants and a large population of gunmen who dominated local affairs until the town was "cleaned up" in 1883. There's a fine museum of local history and Mimbres crafts located in central Deming in the former **National Guard Armory** (1916). One exhibit re-creates frontier life, which, in the words of one guide, was "as you can see just by looking around, not easy here. This wasn't a luxury place." Today, Deming is an easy-going, temperate city of about 15,000 where everybody seems to know everyone else, folks drive and walk slowly, and shade trees throw up their defenses against the sun.

Deming has become popular as a retirement settlement because of its dry climate, 98 percent sunshine and relatively mild temperatures. Agriculture, however, remains a real struggle. As you look out across the valley, it's not unusual to see up to a dozen separate "dust devils"– swirling little clouds of desert detritus – spinning across the barren fields.

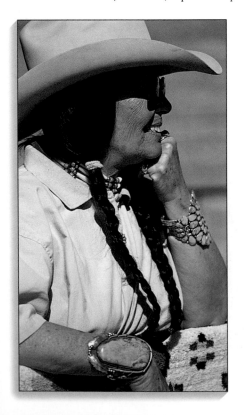

BELOW:
Silver City has historically been the base for Indian turquoise miners and Hispanic silver miners.

Relics of the Mimbres

Rather than stay on dreary I-10 for the 60 miles (97 km) west to Lordsburg, it makes sense to veer northward on US 180 towards the Gila Mountains. Between the 10th and 12th centuries, this region was roamed by the Mimbres Indians, a peaceful people noted for their exquisite ceramics. Author J.W. Fewkes has claimed that "no Southwestern pottery, ancient or modern, surpasses that of the Mimbres; and its naturalistic figures are unexcelled in any pottery from prehistoric America."

The Mimbres take their name from the Mimbres river, which at lower elevations remains a bone-dry sandy wash for much of the year. US 180 crosses it repeatedly *en route* to **Silver City**, 53 miles (85 km) out of Deming. This rough-and-tumble Wild West settlement has successively been the base for Indian turquoise miners, Hispanic silver miners and modern copper conglomerates. Billy the Kid lived here as a child, but most of the town he knew was wiped out by a cataclysmic flood in 1895.

The **Western New Mexico University Museum** (tel: 505-538-6386; www.wnmu.edu; open daily), 12th and Alabama streets, holds the world's finest collection of Mimbres pottery, decorated with elegant animal designs and abstract patterns. They're considered priceless by collectors, not least because perfect specimens are all but unknown. Each pot is thought to have belonged to a single individual, and to have been buried with its owner, having first had a symbolic "kill hole" punched through its base.

With half a day to spare, it's well worth taking a laborious 88-mile (142-km) round-trip drive up into the Gila Mountains. The exhilarating scenery *en route* culminates at the **Gila Cliff Dwellings National**

Monument ㊳ (tel: 505-536-9461; open daily), where intact adobe dwellings used by the Mimbres people or their immediate successors still nestle in caves above the Gila River. Many centuries later, around 1829, this beautiful and remote spot was also the birthplace of legendary Apache leader Geronimo.

State 90 runs 44 miles (71 km) southwest from Silver City to rejoin I-10 at **Lordsburg**. Along the way, it surmounts the Continental Divide, then descends slowly and gloriously to the vast sagebrush sea in which Lordsburg seems to float alone. The largest settlement in Hidalgo County, Lordsburg sprawls languidly beside the interstate and the Southern Pacific railroad tracks at the northern edge of the Pyramid Mountains. The train tracks themselves tell the story of modern Lordsburg, which eventually eclipsed neighboring **Shakespeare**. Shakespeare had been a stop on the great Butterfield Stagecoach Line run by the post office from St Louis, Missouri, to San Francisco, California, at the time Charles Crocker laid his railroad tracks.

Map on page 282

This town's got ghosts

Today, Shakespeare is a ghost town, privately preserved in its current state of decay after being abandoned for more profitable pastures. (Aside from the glaring Motel Drive, you might think Lordsburg is the ghost town.) Shakespeare, a short drive south on Main Street from Lordsburg, is the genuine item, although it *is* inhabited. As a rule, residents and owners Rita and Janaloo Hill open up the town for two weekends each month, conducting anecdote-peppered tours at 10am and 2pm on Saturday and Sunday. Several notable characters are known to have graced the dining room of its **Stratford Hotel**, including an escapee from Silver City jail: Billy the Kid. ❑

Near the town of Shakespeare is a cemetery that claims to be the oldest of its kind in the Southwest. According to a handpainted sign, one of its "residents" is the outlaw Sandy King, convicted of being a "damned nuisance" and hung by committee.

BELOW: Gila Cliff Dwellings National Monument, NM.

SOUTHERN ARIZONA TO SAN DIEGO

Map on page 282

From its ponderosa pine forests and saguaro-studded deserts to modern cities and ancient reservations, this part of the Southwest has made the most of its gifts

To most English speakers, the word "Arizona" suggests one image: aridity. Yes, water is indeed precious here – "Arizona's most precious resource, next to its people" – but the name has nothing to do with lack of water. It is in fact derived from a far less familiar tongue – either from the Pima Indian word for "little spring place," or from the Basque *arritza onac*, meaning "valuable rocky places." The latter perhaps rings truer, as Arizona's first industry was silver mining.

But there *are* "little spring places" in Arizona, as well as just about every climatic, topographic and ecological variant known to America. From its ponderosa pine forests and saguaro-studded deserts to modern cities and reservations unchanged since ancient times, exquisite Arizona has made the most of its natural gifts.

Arizona would not be what it is today, however, without irrigation and air conditioning. Technology has tamed the desert, although a great deal of arid land remains untouched. Though beautiful, the desert can be unbearable in the summer. Winter is "the season" in most parts of Arizona, particularly in the south and west, although prices tend to rise, also.

LEFT: Yaqui deer dancer; Yaquis live in the Phoenix and Tucson areas. **BELOW:** chilis are local staples.

Stone spirits

Leaving Lordsburg, New Mexico, on Interstate 10, there's one final 20-mile (32-km) stretch of desiccated grassland to cross before you reach the Arizona state line. The serried ranks of mountains that then confront you on the western horizon were in the 19th century the stronghold of the Chiricahua Apache, whose chief, Cochise, memorably declared "When I was young I walked all over this country, east and west, and saw no other people than the Apaches."

Two sites indelibly associated with the tragic confrontation between the Apache and the US Army stand just inside the border: Fort Bowie and Chiricahua National Monument. Both can be reached by taking exit 366 from I-10 at the run-down little pitstop of Bowie, then heading south on Apache Pass Road. For its first 3 miles (5 km), this skirts some meticulously groomed pistachio orchards, but it then climbs through much scrubbier ranching country, to become an unpaved but well-maintained gravel road 12 miles (19 km) out of Bowie.

Soon after that, a small parking lot marks the start of the wonderful hiking trail up to **Fort Bowie** (tel: 520-847-2500; open daily). Built in 1886 following two bloody clashes between the Route Army and the Chiricahua, the fort was the headquarters for the next

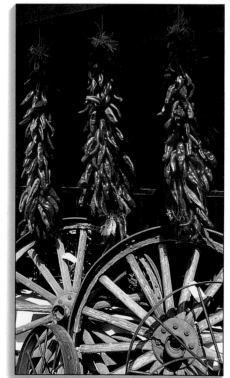

25 years of a campaign that eventually drove the Apache from this region altogether. As you walk the 3 miles (5 km) up to its evocative ruined adobe walls, you seem at first to be in a dry, bowl-shaped depression entirely ringed by mountains. Eventually, however, you come to tranquil, well-wooded Apache Spring, teeming with wildlife, which made this spot so precious to the Apache, and then to the fort, commanding wonderful views out across the valley below.

Stacks of rocks

Another 8 miles (13 km) of easy driving beyond the parking lot, the unpaved road reaches State 186. Head west from here to I-10 if you're in a hurry to reach Tombstone, by way of Willcox and Benson, but **Chiricahua National Monument ㊿** (tel: 520-824-3560; open daily) lies a mere 14 miles (23 km) east. Chiricahua may be a little off the beaten track, but it's a magnificent spot, ideal for hiking, camping and scenic drives. From the informative visitor center close to the park entrance, Bonita Canyon Drive climbs to an elevation of 6,870 feet (2,090 meters). All the way up, alarmingly balanced stacks of rock loom precariously above the road, while the viewpoint at the top surveys a panorama of bizarrely shaped stone towers and columns. This unique landscape has taken shape over a period of 27 million years, as deposits of ash left by volcanic eruptions have been eroded by water, wind and ice. Benefitting from twice the rainfall received by the yellowed, dusty plains and gorges below, the Chiricahua highlands provide a rich environment for juniper, fir, piñon, yucca, oak, cypress and sycamore, and harbor many rare species of birds and animals. This petrified maelstrom can be explored along several well-marked hiking trails; an easy half-hour stroll along **Echo Canyon Trail**, for example, will take you through a forest of weird formations.

BELOW: real-life victims of the OK Corral shootout are buried in Tombstone's Boothill Graveyard.

The most direct route between Chiricahua and Tombstone is to thread your way steadily westwards on State 181, which has the advantage of passing the rattlesnake craft shops, saloons and crumbling buildings on the main drag of an old copper-mining town called **Gleeson**. Just outside of town on the opposite side of a curvy hillside, the town of **Tombstone ㊵** can be seen shining in the distance.

Tales from Tombstone

Tombstone was whimsically named by founder Edward Schieffelin after he was advised that the only thing he would find on his mad hunt for silver would be exactly that, his own tombstone. The most famous of "Wild West" mining towns, Tombstone did indeed sit in the heart of lands rich in silver. Its dizzying growth and wealth in the early 1880s attracted more than its share of troublemakers, but Tombstone's decline was every bit as precipitous. Its main silver mine was flooded in 1886, and the town has barely changed since then. Today, it's a tacky but undeniably endearing tourist trap, happy to provide visitors with a sanitized and glamorized taste of the lawless days of the Wild West.

Tombstone might well be forgotten now had it not played host to the quintessential frontier "showdown" at the **OK Corral** (tel: 520--457-3456; www.ok-corral.com; open daily), which pitted Wyatt

Earp, his brothers and the consumptive dentist Doc Holliday against the Clanton and McLaury brothers. The latter were at the forefront of a "cowboy" gang that allegedly engineered a series of stagecoach robberies, while the Earps – themselves no angels – represented "establishment" Tombstone. Political and personal clashes culminated in the legendary, bloody "Shootout at the OK Corral" on October 26, 1881, which left three men dead.

Map on page 282

The OK Corral

The OK Corral still stands on Allen Street, preserved as it looked on the fateful day. Mannequins of the various participants pose in its yard, guns in hand, despite the general agreement of historians that the shootout in fact took place on neighboring Fremont Street. Alongside, the former studio of Wild West photographer Camillus Fly showcases some of his finest work, including shots of Apache warrior Geronimo. In season, as many as three rival groups of gunfighters roam the streets of Tombstone looking for customers for their staged gunfights; so far, however, there's been no showdown to thin their ranks. Stagecoaches clatter evocatively past landmarks like the Bird Cage Theatre and Tombstone Courthouse, as well as some very ritzy galleries of Western art. The real-life victims of the shootout rest in **Boothill Cemetery** at the edge of town, on a dusty hillside where the peace of their slumbers is disturbed by loudspeakers concealed amid the boulders that play mournful country music.

Another 24 miles (39 km) south of Tombstone on State 80, the more sedate but equally attractive former mining town of **Bisbee** squeezes into a cleft in the Dragoon Mountains. Those of its Victorian mansions that don't house comfortable hotels and B&Bs are instead home to intriguing little crafts and antique

Wyatt Earp, one of his brothers and Doc Holliday were the "good guys" in the OK Corral saga.

BELOW: a saloon in the Southwest.

stores. The one drawback is having to negotiate all the steep stairways that connect streets at widely varying elevations.

From Bisbee, you can either retrace your steps along State 80 (through Tombstone) or take State 90 (which initially heads west and then takes a jog north in Sierra Vista) to meet up with I-10 at **Benson**. Whichever way you choose, a worthy stop before you head off down the highway is a unique Arizona attraction: **Kartchner Caverns State Park**, just 9 miles (14 km) south of I-10 off of State 90. Hailed by many to be the best of Arizona's state parks, its focal point is the recently discovered (1974) "living" cavern – its formations inside are still growing – with its miles of surveyed passages.

Tours are given daily, but numbers are limited so as to protect the cave's environment, so it is necessary to book ahead (tel: 520-586-2283). In addition to the cave, there is a world-class Discovery Center, 5 miles (8 km) of hiking trails, a picnic area and campground and a hummingbird garden.

Tucson

From Benson, there are another 43 miles (69 km) to go before you reach the city of **Tucson ㊶** (pronounced *too-sawn*) to the west. Tucson is a classic sprawling "boom" city, which has had so much room to expand in the prosperous years since World War II that it has been able to do so without destroying the evidence of its 18th-century Hispanic origins. Having been founded in 1776, it's exactly the same age as the United States, though it only passed into American hands with the Gadsden Purchase of 1854.

BELOW: vivid video shop, Tucson.

Downtown Tucson still centers on the narrow area that was originally contained within the adobe walls of the Spanish *presidio*. This delightfully spacious area is now dotted with artisans' shops, cafés, several good shade trees and some extremely interesting architecture, anchored by **St Augustine Cathedral,** built in 1897. An attraction for tourists here is the **Tucson Museum of Art** (tel: 520-624-2333; www.tucsonarts.com; closed Mon), whose collection concentrates especially on pre- and post-Colonial Mexican artifacts.

Map on page 282

Emblem of the West

As a whole, however, Tucson is a somewhat formless city, far too large to explore on foot, whose appeal lies less in its modern buildings than in the fantastic scenery that surrounds it. **Saguaro National Park** occupies two separate tracts of land to either side of the city proper. As its name suggests, it was established to protect dramatic expanses of multi-armed saguaro (pronounced sah-WA-row) cacti. Although it's often considered emblematic of the Wild West, the saguaro – which can live for 200 years, and grow to the height of 50 ft (15 meters) – is in fact a native of the Sonoran Desert, only a small portion of which extends into Arizona from Mexico. Tucson is thus one of the few places in the US where you can see this fascinating cactus. The western segment of the park, the **Tucson Mountain District**, holds an extraordinary "forest" of towering saguaros, which take on an other-worldly magnificence at sunset.

Car advertising a cowboy museum, Arizona.

Nearby, the **Arizona-Sonora Desert Museum** (tel: 520-883-2702; open daily) holds showpiece gardens of cacti and desert plants of all kinds, as well as desert mammals from prairie dogs to mountain lions. Its real highlights, however, are its walk-through aviaries alive with darting, iridescent hummingbirds.

The Mexican border at Nogales, 100 miles (160 km) south of Tucson, is perhaps too much of a diversion for travelers heading west, but no one should visit

BELOW: reflection of St Augustine Cathedral, Tucson.

TIP

May is the month for the Tucson Folk Festival, a melange of dance, music and good food.

Tucson without venturing at least a short distance down the **Mission Trail** that served as the city's original lifeline. Just 9 miles (14 km) out of Downtown, the **Mission San Xavier del Bac** (tel: 520-294-2624; open daily) is renowned as the most beautiful of all the Spanish missions in North America. It was established at the end of the 17th century near the village of Bac ("where the water emerges"), inhabited by a people the Spanish called the Pima – who are now known by the name they call themselves, Tohono O'odham. Its showpiece, the ornate whitewashed mission church, dates from around 1783. Both its resplendent façade and its imposing baroque interior have recently been restored to their full glory by the Tohono O'odham, working with experts from the Vatican; its soubriquet of "Sistine Chapel of the Southwest" has never seemed appropriate. Especially on Sunday mornings, the windswept, cactus-studded plaza in front throngs with tourists and Indians intently studying each other. As one O'odham writer put it, "sometimes just 'hanging out' in front of the mission and looking at the tourists is a good way to pass the time."

Missions and missiles

There's another wonderful mission church, this time abandoned in ruins, at **Tumacácori National Historical Park** (tel: 520-398-2341; open daily), 53 miles (85 km) south. Much closer at hand, however, is a relic from more recent times. The **Titan Missile Museum** (tel: 520-625-7736; open daily), near Green Valley 16 miles (26 km) south of San Xavier, preserves the only one of the 27 US Titan Missile II sites not to have been dismantled at the end of the Cold War. In the 20 years between going into operation in July, 1963, and being decommissioned in November, 1982, it held two missiles, capable of being fired over

BELOW:
Mission San Xavier del Bac is called the "Sistine Chapel of the Southwest."

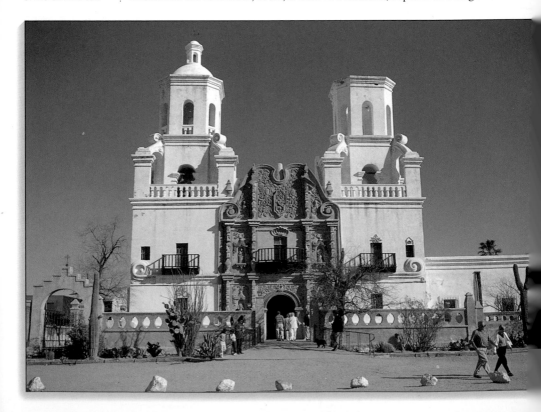

5,000 miles (8,000 km) in less than 20 minutes. Gung-ho guides lead equally gung-ho tour parties down into the underground silo and through subterranean passages to reach its control room, which was designed to remain functional even in the event of a direct nuclear hit on the surface above. What they can't tell you, however, is where the missiles were aimed; each was trained on a specific, unchanged target for all its active life, but that information remains Top Secret. The whole installation is eerie and unsettling, and nowhere more so than its restrooms, which feature prominent "watch for rattlesnakes" signs.

Map on page 282

Onward to Mars

For lovers of the truly bizarre, the Tucson area has one final, unmissable curiosity to offer: **Biosphere 2** (tel: 520-838-6200; www.bio2.com; open daily), just outside **Oracle**, 32 miles (51 km) north of the city on State 77. Completed in 1991, Biosphere 2 was designed as an hermetically sealed replica of Biosphere 1 – the planet Earth – albeit cunningly disguised as a giant greenhouse. Its aim was nothing less than to pave the way for the colonization of Mars. To that end, a group of ex-actors and scientists were locked into it for two full years, to see whether they could survive in a closed and self-sufficient environment. Detractors were quick to point out the obvious flaws in the experiment, such as the fact that it had an external power source, and gleefully noted such ironies as the chopping down of the "rainforest" inside the capsule to grow more crops.

To counter those criticisms, Biosphere 2 has scaled down its ambitions; now operated by Columbia University, it holds no permanent residents, and is used for more closely controlled scientific programs. All the publicity, however, has turned it into a major tourist attraction. Tours are inevitably less exciting now

BELOW:
Biosphere 2, a hermetically sealed environment, was home to ex-actors and scientists for two years.

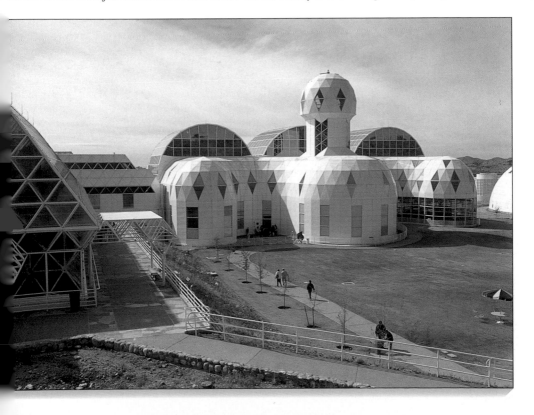

that there are no "Biospherians" to be glimpsed through the windows, but by way of compensation you can at least go inside the huge and oddly beautiful structure, including its luxurious living quarters.

The Apache Trail

Dutch prospector Jacob Walz allegedly struck a lode of gold in the Superstition Mountains, but no one from his mining expedition was ever seen again; the Lost Dutchman Mine remains hidden to this day.

The most direct route between Tucson and Phoenix is I-10, on which the long, flat 100-mile (160-km) drive takes well under two hours. The main visual distraction along the way, **Picacho Peak**, looks like a double-pronged molar tooth as it looms up 30 miles (48 km) out of Tucson, but then resolves into two separate sharp fangs. At its foot, the **Rooster Cogburn Ostrich Farm** just off the highway provides an unexpected photo opportunity, selling bags of seed that you can feed to the aggressive and ungainly birds, as well as feather dusters and colossal eggs.

Alternatively, State 79 sets off from close to Biosphere 2 to follow a parallel and similar course that ends up by approaching Phoenix from the east rather than the south. Known as the **Pinal Pioneer Parkway**, it's lush with native vegetation, from the prickly pear and saguaro cactus to the catclaw and mesquite tree.

It eventually brings you to **Apache Junction**, due east of central Phoenix, which is the start of the **Apache Trail**. This modern road was constructed in 1905 to provide access to **Theodore Roosevelt Dam** ⓮, the first of the great dams of the West, built to quench the ever-growing thirst of nearby Phoenix. Named the Apache Trail in the hope of encouraging tourism, it was hailed by President Teddy Roosevelt, when he dedicated the dam in 1911, as combining "the grandeur of the Alps, the glory of the Rockies, and the magnificence of the Grand Canyon." Although the president made a wide-sweeping overstatement, it is indeed a ravishing drive.

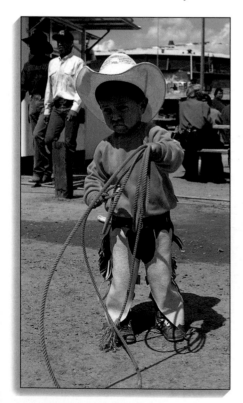

BELOW: learning the ropes at an Arizona pow wow.

Shortly after leaving Apache Junction, the Apache Trail passes the enjoyably (albeit touristy) ramshackle **Goldfield Ghost Town**, where you can take horse or jeep rides amid the abandoned mine machinery and falsefront stores, or simply pick up a snack at the bakery. Beyond that comes your first clear sighting of the **Superstition Mountains**. The Spanish called these peaks the "Mountains of Foam" because of their effusive volcanic ridges, but they're best known for the legends that surround the Dutch prospector Jacob Walz. He seems to have struck a huge lode of gold in the Superstitions in the late 19th century, but no one who followed him on his expeditions was ever seen again, and the "Lost Dutchman Mine" remains hidden to this day. The Superstition Mountains have taken the life of many an overly curious fortune-seeker.

The Apache Trail cuts into **Tonto National Forest** where vistas and foot trails skirt the highway. The fun really begins as it winds its narrow way into the high lands. Drivers beware: you'll have to keep your eye more on the road than the alpine rises, glorious vistas and lush canyons. Saguaros and mesquite, dry riverbeds and wave upon wave of mountain ridges follow a scenic overlook of the **Canyon River**. When you descend into the valley, pull up and strip down because the blue waters are irresistible.

The trail is well-paved for the 18 miles (29 km) u

to **Tortilla Flat**, a required stop for lovers of desert lore and witty western character. The essence of Tortilla Flat is sold in two forms: a postcard reading *Tortilla Flat/Pop. 6/30 Miles from Water/2 Feet from Hell!*; and the hokey cans of Jack Rabbit Milk, "a balanced diet for unbalanced people." One of the six residents remarks: "Oh, it works wonders. Especially that vitamin P."

Best chili in the West

A hotel, post office, café/restaurant, gift shop, riding stable, curio shop, a legend and a marvelous view – Tortilla Flat is a great place to stop for "the best chili in the West" and a "Howdy" from "the friendliest town in America." Admire the hundreds of dollar-bills tacked under business cards on the ceiling and walls of the café before you exit back to the sun-drenched desert. Roosevelt Dam lies another 30 miles (48 km) up the precipitous but passable dirt road beyond Tortilla Flat. Above and behind it spreads **Roosevelt Lake**, the reservoir it created. The best views are from a steep hiking trail in **Tonto National Monument** (tel: 928-467-2241; open daily), just west of the dam on State 88.

That short but grueling hike culminates in a "cliff-dwelling" once occupied by the Salado Indians, who disappeared from this area before the Apache arrived. Retrack State 88 back into the valley. You'll pass through two unique suburbs, as State 88 becomes Main Street in Mesa, then Apache Boulevard in Tempe. **Mesa** contains Arizona's largest Mormon community and you'll pass by the beautiful **Latter Day Saint Temple**. Things change as you pass into **Tempe**, home of Arizona State University, and its young student population (over 40,000). Turning left on University, you'll come to I-10, which quickly whisks you into the heart of **Phoenix ⓭** *(see page 308)*.

Map on page 282

BELOW: Wishing Shrine, El Tiradito.

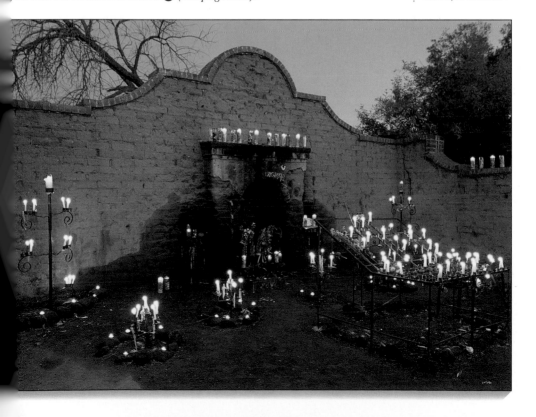

PHOENIX: VALLEY OF THE SUN

Business is booming in Phoenix, with plenty of industry, tourism and golf courses. Just be sure to come in winter

Phoenix may not have had any real *ashes* to rise from, but its founders were inspired by the knowledge that the merciless heat of the Salt River Valley had been overcome before. Between approximately 1100 and 1450, the Hohokam people successfully irrigated this region by means of over 300 miles (480 km) of canals, while Jack Swilling, in 1867, established modern Phoenix by simply re-digging the waterways.

In World War II, the military, utilizing the desert for aviation training, revolutionized Phoenician life further with air-conditioning. Suddenly, life in the great hot desert became a year-round possibility, and the great migra-

tion was on. Now, Phoenix, a city of nearly 3 million people, is booming.

It's hard not to be impressed by the city's setting. To the east soar the massive Four Peaks and Superstition Mountains, while the Sierra Estrella rides the southeast horizon. Hemming in the city north and south are lower mountain ranges, framing Camelback Mountain. All of these make for excellent day-hikes, and provide the visitor with an opportunity to witness the beauty (and silence) of the Sonoran desert.

But beware: the average high temperature June through August is 103°F (39°C); May and September aren't much better. Peak tourist season is the winter, when daily maximum temperatures hover around 70°F (21°C) and the valley's resorts and 190 golf courses fill up with tourists.

Phoenix is easily divided into urban districts. Downtown holds the skyscrapers, and the modern Arizona Center mall, home to the city's main visitor center. Once lacking a strong downtown character, Phoenix invested considerable energy in locating museums and cultural venues in the city center.

Heritage Square (tel: 602-262-5029; open Tues–Sun), just east of the Civic Plaza, remains from the city's Victorian days and forms part of Downtown's Heritage and Science Park. Rosson House, a striking red Victorian home built in 1895, stands out from the square's 11 buildings.

The Phoenix Museum of History (tel: 602-253-2734; www.pmoh.org; closed Sun–Mon), with interactive exhibits of the city's development, and the Arizona Science Center (tel: 602-716-2000; open daily), a $50-million hands-on funhouse of science, embellished with a planetarium, attract the scientific and the simply curious to Heritage Square.

The beautifully designed and organized Heard Museum (tel: 602-252-8848; www.heard.org; open daily) is near Downtown at 2301 North Central Avenue. The Heard focuses on Native American arts and crafts, both ancient and modern. Extensive galleries cover the long-vanished Anasazi, Hohokam and Mogollon groups as well as the still-thriving Navajo and Apache tribes. Former Republican senator Barry Goldwater gathered and donated the exquisite and fascinating collection of Hopi *kachina* dolls. The museum complex is worth visiting in its own right, with its older structures arrayed around a quiet courtyard planted with orange trees which manage to blend seamlessly in with the newer state-of-the-art facilities.

If you see nothing else, visit the Arizona Biltmore Resort (tel: 602-955-6600; www.arizonabiltmore.com) at 24th Street and Missouri, 5 miles (8 km) northeast of Heritage Park. Phoenix owes the arrival of the renowned American architect Frank Lloyd Wright to this hotel. Built in 1929, Albert Chase McArthur, a former student of Wright, originally designed the building, but found himself in trouble and summoned the master for help.

Wright probably gave more help than required, for the hotel is a delightful masterpiece from Wright's middle period. Gutted by fire in 1973, refurbished furniture and textile designs from all periods of Wright's career now decorate the interior.

Wright stayed on in Phoenix to found his architectural school and residence, Taliesin West (tel: 480-860-2700; open daily), hidden in the desert beyond the upscale suburb of Scottsdale, in the northeast.

Wright intended the buildings and facilities to be an ongoing, hands-on educational exercise for architectural and design students. A variety of different tours give visitors an insight into Wright's visionary architectural style, as well as the facility's interesting "apprentice" program.

Scottsdale is known for its abundance of luxury resorts, such as the ravishing Phoenician at the foot of Camelback Mountain, which caters to travelers visiting Arizona for sun and sport rather than pure scenery. Scottsdale also spawned some swish shopping malls, like Fashion Square, while its "Hometown USA" central streets are, in fact, filled with expensive galleries of so-called Western Art.

At the southern end of Scottsdale lies the Phoenix Zoo (tel: 602-273-1341) as well as the compelling Desert Botanical Gardens (tel:

480-941-1225; open daily). The arid gardens, located in Papago Park, display plants from the world's deserts, including half the known species of cactus. The excellent landscaping, and the exotic power of these acres cannot fail to impress.

South of the zoo and gardens lies Tempe. Home of Arizona State University and an artificial lake under a picturesque, old (but still in use) railroad bridge, Tempe is perhaps the most attractive of all of Phoenix's areas, and definitely the most self-contained. The city's active nightlife centers on Mill Avenue, which is within easy walking distance of both the hotels and the lake. ❑

LEFT: Frank Lloyd Wright fell in love with the desert and moved here in 1937; a view of the skyscrapers in downtown Phoenix.
RIGHT: Hopi doll from the Heard Museum; Frank Lloyd Wright's home and studio, Taliesin West; the pool area of the architect's Biltmore Resort.

PHOENIX TO SAN DIEGO

The 150 miles (240 km) between Phoenix and the Colorado River, which marks the border with California, include some of the bleakest desert terrain in the entire Southwest. Taking the southern route to San Diego, you have a choice between sticking with I-10 as far as Quartzsite and then changing to US 95 south, or dropping south much earlier, to meet I-8 at Gila Bend. Either way, your final destination in Arizona will be the state's third largest city, Yuma, which is even hotter than Phoenix and Tucson.

Quartzsite is only really worth visiting if you're passing through in January or February, when up to 750,000 sun-seeking, northern "snowbirds" (most in RVs) descend on the town for a sort of mineralists' convention – a huge, open-air "flea market" for seekers and sellers of precious, semi-precious and not-under-any-circumstances-even-slightly-precious stones and gems of various shapes and sizes. In a miracle on a par with the loaves and the fishes, Quartzsite's three motels and half-dozen restaurants somehow cope with this rock-hungry throng of oldsters.

Otherwise, you'd do better to turn off I-10 25 miles (40 km) west from Phoenix, and take State 85 down to the I-8 truckstop of **Gila Bend**. (For that matter, if you're in a hurry to get to the beach from Tucson, I-8 enables you to bypass Phoenix altogether.) Named, logically enough, for its location on a big bend in the Gila River, Gila Bend holds a predictable array of fast-food restaurants and motels, plus one outstanding exception. The **Best Western Space Age Lodge** is a marvelous 1950s-style folly, kitted out with kitsch Sputnik-shaped neon signs. Its **Outer Limits Restaurant**, which features a dazzling lunar-exploration mural, is well worth a stop for a bite to eat. The visitor center nearby, which doubles as a museum of local history, will confirm your suspicions that not a lot happens in Gila Bend.

Signs on the interstate near Gila Bend warn that this is a "Blowing Dust Area," while bridges repeatedly cross "rivers" that are in truth little more than scrubby strips of sand. Somehow, however, **Dateland** ⑭, 50 miles (80 km) west of Gila Bend, manages to grow a bumper annual crop of dates. If you're desperate for a diversion, stop for a date shake or whatever other date-related product may strike your fancy in Dateland's solitary diner.

The Devil's road

Surprisingly soon after you leave Dateland, you begin to be aware that you're approaching **Yuma** ⑮. The city avenues are numbered a mile apart, corresponding to the signs on the interstate that count the mileage down to California, and thus you pass an Avenue 51B that's a full 50 miles (80 km) east of downtown Yuma. In reality, Yuma is large, but it's not *that* large. There's still a long way to go, including the final climb over the ridge of the Gila Mountains and descent into the Colorado River Valley, before there's any sign of life. That is, apart from the low-flying jets that screech overhead. Southwest Arizona is another proving ground for the US military, and the latest top-secret warplanes are constantly being tested

BELOW: tarantula: a creature of the desert.

above the barren desert that lies between I-8 and the Mexican border. It has to be admitted that even most Arizonans roar with laughter at the very notion of anyone choosing to go to Yuma. Combine its somewhat shame-faced claim to be the hottest place on earth with its long-standing reputation as one of the worst hell-holes in the Wild West, and it makes an unlikely tourist destination. When Padre Eusebio Kino, the most tireless of all Spanish missionaries to the American Southwest, opened a trail in 1699 from Sonoita, Mexico, to what is now Yuma, he called the trail *El Camino del Diablo* – the Devil's Road. It seemingly led straight into the inferno. Yuma smolders to this day, but it's been tamed by the air conditioner into a city fit for human beings.

Starry-eyed gold diggers

Set just below the confluence of the Gila and Colorado rivers, Yuma has been known for centuries as the site of the only natural ford on the southern trail to the Pacific. As such, it was a crucial way-station on the road to California even before the Gold Rush of 1849. Originally, local Quechan Indians kept a monopoly on the lucrative river crossing, but as ever greater numbers of starry-eyed miners demanded to be ferried across into gold country, control was wrested away in some astonishingly bloodthirsty conflicts. When gold was discovered to the *east* of Yuma as well, in 1858, the city duly blossomed as a port, where ore was transported by steamboat down the Colorado River and into the Gulf of California.

Space cowboys should take a break from the road at the Outer Limits Restaurant, part of the Best Western Space Age Lodge, Gila Bend.

After the mines dried up and the river was dammed, Yuma converted itself into an agricultural center, with help from irrigation technology. But it's still a crossroads, where Interstate 8 from San Diego meets US 95, replete with an

BELOW:
watermelon-eating contest; no spitting allowed.

The slow road to Yuma – camels have been in the Wild West since the 1850s.

BELOW: camels were brought to the West by the US Army, to test whether they fared better than horses in the harsh terrain.

international airport. During the winter, it's heavily trafficked by sun-seekers.

Thanks to diminished water flow, the Gila and Colorado now meet 5 miles (8 km) upstream from downtown Yuma. The bluff that once overlooked their intersection remains occupied by the surprisingly interesting **Yuma Territorial Prison State Historic Park**. This museum (tel: 928-783-4771; open daily) preserves the remaining structures of the infamous prison of the Arizona Territory, which closed in 1909 three years before Arizona achieved statehood. These include its guard house, courtyards, cell block and notorious "Dark Cell" for solitary confinement.

Rogues gallery

All the lawlessness of Arizona a hundred years ago is on show in the rogues' gallery of former inmates that decorates the central building. Larcenists, adulterers, manslaughterers, outright murderers, rapists and criminals "against nature" all found a home here by the Colorado. You can rest assured the cells weren't air-conditioned, so Yuma Prison must have been a fate so dreaded that at least a few desperadoes thought twice before pulling the trigger.

The gray railroad bridge that spans the Colorado close to the prison was completed in 1915 as the "Ocean to Ocean" bridge that finally spared travelers the ferry ride across the river. The point from which the ferries once set off, down below on the fringes of Downtown, is now occupied by **Yuma Crossing State Historical Park**. Assorted overworked wagons, carriages and even locomotives have been put out to pasture in this pleasant but not wildly exciting open-air park, which is perhaps more interesting simply for providing a spot where you can walk along the riverbanks.

At the core of downtown Yuma, "**Old Yuma**" consists of a few blocks of sleepy but atmospheric Victorian-era buildings. Lutes Casino, on South Main Street, resembles a featureless barn on the outside, but you'll find the interior is positively busting with memorabilia and bric-a-brac, as well as dispensing drinks and snacks. The rest of the city sprawls for several miles south and east from Downtown, though it seems to hold almost nothing apart from motels, fast-food outlets and a giant Air Force base.

Map on page 282

Miniature pyramid

Yuma does manage one surprise, though. Camels. Camels have apparently been a feature of the Western landscape since the late 1850s, when the US Army imported a batch of the beasts to see whether they were any better equipped than horses and mules to negotiate Arizona's rough terrain. Though the camels produced amazingly high scores on their "endurance tests," they were prone to stampede, and smelled atrocious. After the Civil War put them out of a job, they were set free, and became a nuisance until camel hunting became a brief but effective fad.

Their Syrian driver, incidentally, Haiji Ali, is buried beneath a miniature pyramid in Quartzsite under the name of "Hi Jolly." For several years, Yuma's Saihati Camel Farm maintained the tradition by breeding a herd of drooling, slobbering, one-humped dromedaries. Despite being a popular tourist attraction in an area woefully lacking in interesting sites – and teaching skills such as how to survive in the desert for a week without water and how to close your nostrils against the gritty desert wind – the future of the camel farm looks uncertain, so ask around locally before heading south of the airport to visit.

BELOW: Apache girl at Arizona rodeo.

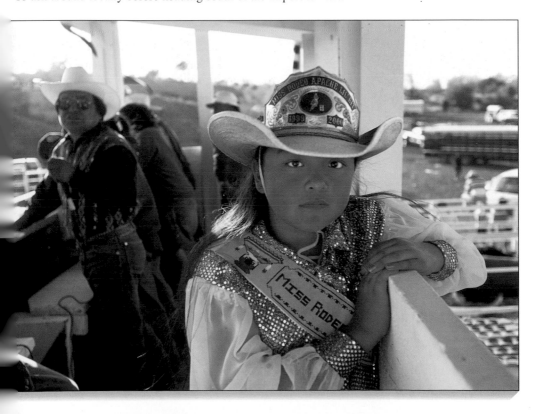

EUREKA! CALIFORNIA

Over the Colorado River, the down-at-heel community of **Winterhaven** provides a deceptively low-key introduction to California, the third largest and most populous state in the nation. Northwest of here, the **Imperial Valley** – thanks to extensive damming and irrigation – is one of the most agriculturally productive regions on earth. As you follow I-8 to the coast, however, where the Pacific laps on the forever-sunny beaches, it takes a while before the myth of California begins to be fulfilled. First, there is the desert to deal with.

A grand garden, the like of which in sheer pattern does not exist, I think, in the world.

– FRANK LLOYD WRIGHT
ABOUT THE DESERT

The **Algodones Dunes**, immediately west of the Colorado, were every bit as much of an obstacle to early travelers as the river itself. This strip of deep, shifting sands stretches 40 miles (64 km) north to south. It's only around 6 miles (10 km) wide at this point, but for the first motorists to attempt to cross, this might as well have been the Sahara Desert. In 1915, a "**Plank Road**" of railroad ties was laid down to enable automobiles to rumble their way over. By 1925, when as many as 30 cars were using the road each day, it had deteriorated alarmingly. A two-lane paved highway, California State Route 80, finally opened in August 1926, and has long since been superceded in turn by I-8.

A small segment of the original plank road can still be seen by leaving the interstate 20 miles (32 km) west of Yuma on Grays Well Road, to enter the **Imperial Sand Dunes Recreation Area** ⑳ immediately south. Roughly 4 miles (6 km) along, parallel to the interstate and also to the very long **All American Canal**, the dried-out old planks descend a short slope. These arid dunes are now a raucous playground for the Californian youths who race their dune buggies and other off-road vehicles over the razor-edged inclines, while older "snowbirds" tan themselves sleepily beside their RVs. Incongruously, however, they're also closely monitored by the US Border Patrol, who – besides digging out hapless tourists who attempt to drive their rental vehicles over the sand – reckon on arresting around 300 illegal immigrants per day. As one officer remarked, they're not hard to spot as they plod the 5 miles (8 km) from the Mexican border across the white sands, and "they pretty much know what to expect."

BELOW: purple prickly pear cactus.

Islands of irrigated green, dotted with palms, spell "oasis" at the end of the 58-mile (93-km) tumble from Yuma to **El Centro**. Supposedly the largest city below sea level in the Western hemisphere, and definitely the birthplace of the entertainer Cher, El Centro prospers quietly as a supply center for the Imperial Valley, but has little to detain the average tourist.

To the west, high winds howl across the valley, kicking up a dusty haze around the straggling palms. Beyond the reach of the canals, the vegetation all but disappears, and you enter the bare **Yuma Desert**. Scattered with only the occasional 14-foot (4-meter) orange-blossomed ocotillo cactus, the desert floor appears to have undergone an unsuccessful hair transplant. The appropriately named **Ocotillo**, 28 miles (45 km) west of El Centro, is no more than a fly-blown little hamlet.

The mountain ranges that sweep down from the northwest just past Ocotillo are at first obscured by the dust, but soon you find yourself embarking on the very steep climb up their rocky flanks. The east- and westbound lanes of the interstate divide at this point, each plotting its own course across a terrain that consists of no more than piles of rust-colored boulders. Every few hundred yards stand roadside barrels filled with "Radiator Water," as the risk of over-heating is so high. Atop a minor eminence at an elevation of 3,000 ft (914 meters), 5 miles (8 km) out of Ocotillo, the **Desert View Tower** commands a stunning view back across Imperial Valley. Constructed in 1922 using blocks of hewn granite, it holds an enjoyable jumble of exhibits on local history. Enter-ing San Diego County at Mountain Spring, I-8 pulls south to skirt the Mexican border; a minor turn-off leads to the border town of **Jacumba**.

Map
on page
282

San Diego revealed

Near **Live Oak Springs**, 27 miles (43 km) west of Ocotillo, the winds die down and the rises level off. Interstate 8 soon swoops to green valleys and into the **Cleveland National Forest**, winding through Pine Valley and Alpine. As you drop toward Alpine, you should get your first glimpse of the Pacific Ocean, glinting on the horizon ahead. **El Cajon** ㊼, 43 miles (69 km) beyond Live Oak Springs, is a nicely landscaped city that marks the first major outpost of the San Diego metropolitan area. **La Mesa** follows, set picturesquely amid the hills that rise on El Cajon's western outskirts.

Past La Mesa, traffic on I-8 becomes increasingly congested; the overpass of I-15 is the portal to San Diego. As the interstate pushes out to the Pacific beaches, its shoulders open up onto shopping malls and skyscraper hotels. To the south, buildings arched by trees glimmer on the slopes. Behind them lies the sunny city of **San Diego** ㊽ *(see page 322).* ❑

El Centro is an oasis surrounded by the California desert. The singer Cher is from El Centro.

BELOW: the long arm of the desert.

THE PACIFIC ROUTE

*A guide to the Pacific Coast, with principal sites
cross-referenced by number to the maps*

America's historic US 101, which stretched from San Diego all the way up the coast through Oregon and Washington to the Canadian border, and eventually became in part today's California Highway 1, has a history that is comparable with its more famous companion, Route 66. It began with joint financing from the state of California, San Diego and the city of Oceanside, which from 1909 to 1918 financed the concrete and macadam road. Up until then, it had been a narrow, bumpy, dirt-surfaced track on which horse-drawn wagons and primitive autos competed for space.

The spiffy new road stimulated the rise of a new phenomenon known as "car culture," epitomized in sunny California, and which spawned all the enterprises that subsequently came to be associated with travel along the road, such as gas stations, garages, automobile dealers, hotels, motels, cafés and even auto laundries.

The highway led visitors from all parts of the Pacific Coast to San Diego's Balboa Park for the 1915–16 Panama-California Exposition, enticed movie stars and others from Hollywood and elsewhere to its pristine beaches, and lured those in search of a good time during Prohibition to Mexico's Tijuana, where, as one historian put it, "booze flowed freely, horses raced continuously and one could gamble and dance the night away."

In 1925, the new road officially became US 101 and served the military in World War II, when it became a major conduit for the country's largest Marine Corps base at Camp Pendleton. Increased traffic spelled its doom, however, and by the end of the war a new four-lane highway, eventually to become Interstate 5, bypassed the old route. Today, the Pacific Coast Highway, often abbreviated to "PCH," and also known as the El Cabrillo Trail, is a sometimes-scrappy, often sea-scented mixture of the old US 101, California Highway 1 and roaring, ever-busy Interstate 5. We have followed it here as faithfully as possible, stopping off at breathtaking sites like California's San Juan Capistrano Mission, Big Sur and Hearst Castle, and the Oregon Sand Dunes Recreation Area, and only diverting inland and away from its old-fashioned charms to visit not-to-be-missed places like Portland and Seattle.

The Pacific Coast Highway's villages and towns – as well as much of its old structure – is still here, and for those travelers who have time, gasoline and a romantic desire to reclaim an earlier America, following Highway 1 and historic 101 along the Pacific Coast to Seattle can lead to unimaginable pleasures. ❏

PRECEDING PAGES: rustic living in beautiful Big Sur; Huntington pier at sunset, Southern California.
LEFT: the California dream, on wheels.

A SHORT STAY IN SAN DIEGO

San Diego is a busy, elegant harbor town with a history unsurpassed in the state of California. Here's a list of the not-to-be-missed attractions:

◆ The Mission San Diego (1769) offers a peaceful sanctuary with fragrant gardens. A museum and a walking tour tell the story of the mission, while Mass is still celebrated in the church.

◆ Old Town is where Spanish soldiers and their families lived until the 1800s; Old Town State Historic Park preserves much of the original settlement and, through its structures, adobes and shops, offers a glimpse of California as it was in the Mexican and early-American periods.

◆ Board at Broadway Pier for a harbor excusion: choose between a one-hour cruise or a two-hour cruise, or take a dinner-dance excusion in the evening. Whale-watching cruises in season, too.

◆ From Dixieland jazz to haute cuisine, the old, restored Gaslamp Quarter offers some of the city's best entertainment and nightlife, as well as interesting Victorian architecture. Shopaholics should make a beeline for nearby Horton Plaza, which has around 150 upmarket shops.

◆ Situated in the heart of San Diego is Balboa Park: over a thousand acres with 15 museums, theaters, flora and fauna, art galleries and more. A pass at the park's Visitors Center allows admission to up to 13 of the museums, some of which are housed in old buildings. Have lunch at the rose garden, visit the Spanish Village Art Center and afterward, soak up some culture at the Starlight Bowl or Old Globe Theatre.

◆ Tijuana is just a hop, skip and a jump from San Diego, the perfect distance for a day trip. Shop for leather and silver, then lunch on spicy-hot tortillas washed down by tequila.

△ **SAN DIEGO HARBOR**
Much of the harbor is centered around Seaport Village, which has an antique carousel, shops and cafés.

▽ **HOTEL DEL CORONADO**
A dozen presidents have stayed in this Victorian resort; it also featured prominently in the movie *Some Like It Hot.*

△ **TROLLEY TOURS**
There's a real trolley that ends at the Mexico border, and there are trolley tours by bus where you can get on or off at any stop along the way.

▷ **SAN DIEGO ZOO**
This highly regarded zoo is home to over 800 species of animals, including cute panda bears. The walk-through Owens Rain Forest Aviary simulates a Southeast Asian jungle environment.

 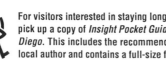
For visitors interested in staying longer in the city, pick up a copy of *Insight Pocket Guide: San Diego*. This includes the recommendations of the local author and contains a full-size fold-out map.

POLAR BEAR PLUN
WORLD-FAMOUS SAN DIEGO

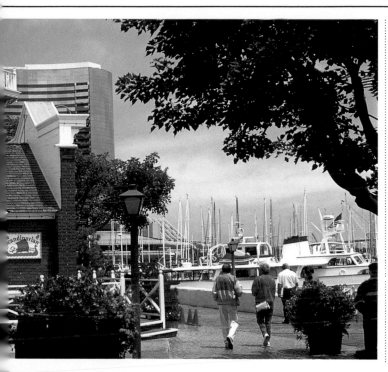

THE BIRTHPLACE OF CALIFORNIA

California began at San Diego's Presidio Hill on July 16, 1769, when Father Junípero Serra conducted a mass dedicating the newly created Mission San Diego de Alcalá; the mission was moved to its present site in Mission Valley only five years later. History and luxury can be found in many parts of this harbor city, which has more than its fair share of upscale shops, plus at least 80 golf courses. Although San Diego's harborfront, the Embarcadero, can be tacky and touristy, there are enough historic sites, shady walks, harbor cruises and sandy beaches to appeal to the most discerning of visitors.

△ SEAWORLD SAN DIEGO
Killer whales *(shown)* have always been popular; now there's adventure rides, a 3D movie and special effects.

◁ NATIVE AMERICAN ART
Buy local arts and crafts, and then learn about the craftsmens' ancestors in Balboa Park's Museum of Man.

mportant Information

Population:
.23 million
ialing codes:
19, 760, 858
Jebsite:
ww.sandiego.org

Tourist information:
San Diego C&VB, 1040
1/3 West Broadway,
San Diego, CA 92101
Tel: 619-236-1212
Fax: 619-230-7084

▽ Red arrows on the map indicate routes from the city detailed in this book

San Diego Throughways

0 _____ 5 miles
0 _____ 5 km

SAN DIEGO TO LOS ANGELES

Beach towns, beach facilities and beaches themselves –
more than 20 of them – line this short stretch of coastline.
Is it any wonder the bikini first became famous here?

Map
on page
326

Seattle
San Diego

The journey from seaside **San Diego ①** *(see page 322)* to glittering Los Angeles is only around 125 miles (200 km), but following the ragged coastal roads can take much longer than that short distance implies. It's also much more rewarding, as the coastal route meanders past Southern California's best beaches, prettiest towns and most exclusive residential areas. For navigational purposes, the road signs along the way go by a variety of names – Highway 1, US 101, Interstate 5 – but to most Californians, this mix of roads paralleling the ocean is known simply as the Pacific Coast Highway.

LA JOLLA TO OCEANSIDE

The first stop out of San Diego is **La Jolla ②** (pronounced *la-hoy-ya*), a seaside community that once boasted "the richest zipcode in America." This college community and upscale town can be reached in a few minutes by heading north up Interstate 5, but a more scenic way is to start the drive to Los Angeles as you intend to proceed – using water as your navigator. From SeaWorld, take the road called SeaWorld Drive to West Mission Bay Drive, routes that curl along the bottom of **Mission Bay** itself. The road turns north (changing into Mission Boulevard) to parallel Mission Beach, then the livelier Pacific Beach, before rolling into La Jolla. La Jolla has beautiful homes and a downtown area – which calls itself "the village" – filled with expensive shops, as well as a contemporary art museum. Described by writer Raymond Chandler as "a nice place for old people and their parents," La Jolla featured in Tom Wolfe's 1960s surfer novel *The Pump House Gang*. On the campus of the University of California is the La Jolla Playhouse, whose forerunner was founded by the late actor Gregory Peck. The caves carved into its coastal bluffs have long been a paradise for both deep-sea divers and cliff divers, and nearby **Black's Beach** was once legally – and is now illegally – a nudist beach.

Architecturely awesome

At the north end of town above Point La Jolla is the renowned **Scripps Institution of Oceanography**, whose well-stocked **Birch Aquarium** (tel: 858-534-3474; www.aquarium.ucsd.edu; open daily) offers whale-watching cruises in season. Among the 33 sea-filled tanks is a two-story tank that replicates a kelp bed with all its familiar and unfamiliar creatures. Farther north and also by the sea is the **Salk Institute**, designed by the late Louis I. Kahn, perhaps one of America's most admired contemporary architects. The institute is named after its famous resident scientist, Jonas Salk, who devised the polio vaccine.

La Jolla Shores Drive parallels Torrey Pines Road,

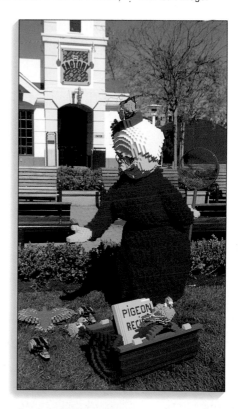

LEFT: romance under the sun.
BELOW: Legoland, Carlsbad, California, near San Diego.

PIGEON
RE

San Diego to San Francisco

San Diego ❶
California
La Jolla ❷
Torrey Pines State Beach & Reserve
Del Mar
Solana Beach
Legoland
★
Carlsbad ❸
Oceanside ❹

San Antonio de Pala Mission 76
5

San Clemente ❺
Dana Point
Mission 5
San Juan Capistrano ❻
1
Laguna Beach ❼
Newport Beach
Huntington Beach ❽
Bolsa Chica Ecological Reserve
Sunset Beach
Seal Beach
Long Beach ❾
Los Angeles ❿
Redondo Beach
Manhattan Beach
1 Venice ⓫
Santa Monica ⓬
Palisades Park
Malibu ⓭
Leo Carrillo State Park
101
Ventura ⓮
Ojai 101
33 San Buenaventura Mission

Santa Barbara ⓯
101
Gaviota State Park

1 Lompoc

1

Guadalupe
1

Pismo State Beach
101
San Luis Obispo ⓰
Paso Robles 1 Morro Bay
Cayucos
46
Hearst Castle ⓱
San Simeon
State Historical Monument
San Simeon
Big Sur ⓲
1 Los Padres National Forest
Big Sur Village ⓳

Point Lobos State Reserve
Carmel ⓴
Salinas Monterey ㉑
68 1

1

1
Capitola
Santa Cruz ㉒

Davenport
1
Pigeon Point Light Station ㉓
State Historic Park
Half Moon Bay ㉔
1 San Francisco ㉕
California

a winding hill out of La Jolla through the affluent suburb of the same name where the trees are environmentally protected. The road gives access to **Torrey Pines Scenic Drive**, off which is a windswept hillside used by flying enthusiasts for launching gliders over the ocean since the 1930s. The **Torrey Pines Gliderport** (tel: 858-452-9858) offers introductory lessons in paragliding and hang-gliding; spectators are welcome. There's also a restaurant and flight sport shop at the site. The **Torrey Pines State Reserve** and **Torrey Pines State Beach** are two places perfect for picnics.

Del Mar and Solana Beach

A series of small coastal roads, which together make up US 101, parallel I-5 as far as the town of Oceanside, where the mighty interstate takes over until it reaches Dana Point. From then on, the Pacific Coast Highway becomes Highway 1, and more or less stays Highway 1 until San Francisco.

Both the coast road and the interstate lead to the community of **Del Mar**, which has an Amtrak Station and has attracted crowds since the 1930s with its famous racetrack, which was rescued from collapse by actor Pat O'Brien and singer Bing Crosby. The entertainers turned the track into one of America's most popular racing circuit venues. The season begins in July, a week after Del Mar's big fair ends, and runs until mid-September.

The track's sandy-colored main building, in a sort of California-meets-Mediterranean style, can be seen from the interstate, but much of the town itself lies farther down the hill beside the coast road. Along the roads, storekeepers favor a pseudo-Tudor style, with the upper part of the buildings displaying a brown-and-white timbered look.

The communities of **Solana Beach** – with its futuristic-looking railroad station – Cardiff-by-the-Sea, Encinitas and Leucadia run into each other along this stretch of coast, and a profusion of stop signs and red lights can slow progress. Otherwise, it is a pleasant stretch to drive with plenty of roadside trees, the beach and the railroad track both near the road, and here and there a "Historic US 101" sign. Watch for the 101 Cafe (built in 1928) as you drive through Oceanside. The sweet-smelling **Quail Botanical Gardens** (tel: 760-436-3036; www.qbgardens.org; open daily) at **Encinitas** may be worth a stop to admire the waterfall and extensive collection of exotic plants. The **San Dieguito Heritage Museum** (tel: 760-632-9711; open Wed–Fri) specializes in the history of the area – from the Diegueno Indians of 10,000 years ago to the present day – and includes a fine collection of more than 8,000 photographs. The beach is a few blocks away; the railroad parallels the road to the east. At the north end of the community are the golden domes of the Self Realization Fellowship temple.

Making music

At **Carlsbad** ❸, the road runs along the beach and heads past an ugly pink power plant with a tall stack, and then through a town where the European-looking buildings reflect the heritage of its spa-town namesake in the Czech Republic. The region is known for flowers, its bulbs being sold widely throughout the country, and almost 50 hillside acres are resplendent with bright colors. (To visit the Flower Fields, call 760-431-0352.) The **Museum of Making Music** spans a century of music-making in America. Exhibits include vintage instruments, samples of music from each era and photographs and paintings.

Carlsbad's 128-acre (52-hectare) **Legoland California** (tel: 760-918-5346; www.legoland.com; hours vary) was the first of these theme parks in the US. It used 120 million of its signature toy plastic bricks to depict such scaled-down landmarks as New York City and Washington, DC – as well as Castle Hill with an "enchanted walk" where children can search for hidden treasure.

Map on page 326

TIP

San Diego's Scripps Institution of Oceanography offers whale-watching cruises December to March through its highly regarded aquarium. Tel: 858-534-3474 for more information.

BELOW: these waters form part of the migratory path for whales.

Let's go surfing now

With almost 4 miles (6 km) of white, sandy beaches and "world-class surf," **Oceanside ❹** is an appropriate place to find – on the main street opposite the Longboarder Café – the **California Surf Museum** (tel: 760-721-6876; www.surfmuseum.org; open daily), which displays the evolution of surfboards from 16-footers weighing 200 pounds (90 kg) to fiber-glass creations known as potato-chip boards. There's a huge market among surfing dudes for memorabilia and thus much of the museum's collection is priceless. Surfing veterans such as Olympic-medal swimmer Duke Kahanamoka are honored here.

Other interesting museums include that of the **Historical Society** (tel: 760-722-4786; open Thur–Sat); **Oceanside Museum of Art** (tel: 760-721-2787; closed Mon) and **Buena Vista Audubon** (tel: 760-439-2473; closed Mon) beside a lazy lagoon on the highway south of town. Four miles (6 km) inland from the beach is the lovely **Mission San Luis Rey de Francia**, near which is **Heritage Park** (tel: 760-433-8297; park open daily, buildings open Sun) whose old buildings include the cottage that was once Oceanside's post office.

Oceanside has cafés and shops located in a pleasant man-made harbor, with a lighthouse that serves as a marina for several hundred boats at the north end. From here, boats run across to **Santa Catalina Island** (for information, contact the Catalina Island Chamber of Commerce and Visitors Bureau, tel: 310-510-1520; www.catalina.com). Oceanside's pier, just north of Mission Avenue, is the longest recreational wooden pier on the West Coast. Hundreds of Downtown walkways are marked with the mysterious O.U. MIRACLE, the name of contractor Orville Ullman Miracle, whose construction company submitted the winning bid in the 1920s to improve the community's streets.

BELOW: granddads make waves, Southern California.

OCEANSIDE TO LOS ANGELES

An interesting diversion from Oceanside is to drive inland along State Route 76 for a few miles to **San Antonio de Pala Mission**, on the Pala Indian Reservation. This is the only Californian mission still serving Native Americans. San Antonio has celebrated its Corpus Christi Festival, with an open-air mass, dances and games, on the first Sunday of every June since 1816.

Map on page 326

The United States Marine Corps occupies the coastal area north of Oceanside, where the coast road is incorporated into I-5 and the sea is half a mile away. Just north of the controversial San Onofre Nuclear Power Plant is **San Clemente ⑤**, where former US president Richard Nixon, an Orange County native, set up a western White House on his 25-acre (10-hectare) estate, and where he lived until moving to the East Coast in 1980. This attractive town, with its Spanish-looking tiled roofs and white stucco walls, prompted the *Los Angeles Times* to write in 1927: "If the charms of this place could be shown to the poor, snow-bound, wind-beaten people back East, there would be an exodus so great the hills above San Clemente would be covered like mushrooms."

It was the resort of Oceanside, along with San Diego and the state of California, that financed historic US 101 in the early 1900s. The improved road allowed visitors from up the coast to spend time in the sunny south.

The **Heritage of San Clemente Visitor Center** (tel: 949-369-1299; open Mon–Sat) has exhibits from Nixon's western White House and also has some surfing history. The town's founder, a former mayor of Seattle named Ole Hanson, is memorialized in **Casa Romantica**, his old home near the Parque Del Mar, as well as the Ole Hanson Beach Club and Ole's Tavern. In 1925, Hanson purchased and designed a 2,000-acre (810-hectare) community on what was then empty space. His instincts were sound then and even sounder now; San Clemente's population is expected to double over the next 20 years.

Writing in the *San Clemente Journal*, Ann Batty claimed that it was San Clemente designers who first popularized the bikini on local beaches, of which there are many (bikinis *and* beaches). San Clemente and Doheny beaches allow camping for a small fee, and Doheny, Dana Point, Laguna Niguel, Irvine Coast and Newport Beach all have marine life preserves (patrolled by state fish and game wardens) that are open to the public.

BELOW: lapping up the sunshine.

Festival of Whales

Capistrano Beach and Doheny State Beach lie astride the San Juan Creek just before **Dana Point**, where most of the buildings in the harbor complex are a lot younger than they look – although the overall effect is quite attractive. There are dozens of places to shop and eat, and whale-watching excursions depart from here in season (December–March). Dana Point's annual Festival of Whales is a well-attended, amusing event with its imaginative whale costumes, and a parade of clowns, jugglers and antique cars, as well as a lively street fair.

The **Ocean** (tel: 949-496-2274; www.ocean-institute.org; open daily) at the northern end of the harbor commemorates Richard Henry Dana, whose seafaring exploits from here resulted in the novel *Two Years Before the Mast,* which became a 1946 movie starring Alan Ladd. **Santa Catalina Island** can be reached from here, too, in daily trips that take 90 minutes each way (tel: 877-447-5263).

Sometimes it's pigeons, rather than swallows, that arrive at Capistrano.

BELOW:
Capistrano's bells are among the mission's most valued treasures.

San Juan Capistrano

Interstate 5 now veers away from the coast and heads inland to the town of San Juan Capistrano. Following it into town, Del Obispo Street leads to Camino Capistrano, on which sits the famous **San Juan Capistrano Mission ❻** (tel: 949-234-1330; open daily), seventh in the chain of 21 established by Franciscan padres late in the 18th century. There's a statue of Father Junípero Serra, who founded this and eight other California missions.

The Serra chapel behind the church is the oldest building still in use within the state of California. Pick up a free map that identifies and dates the chapel's treasures, including the bells to the left of the church, and also tells where the swallows' nests can be found during their residence between their scheduled arrival on St Joseph's Day (March 19) and their departure for the warmer climate of Argentina on October 23. By some mysterious alchemy, the swallows have almost always been on time; their arrival here is marked by a week-long festival with mariachi bands leading a parade. Nevertheless, disappointed tourists sometimes arrive to find only pigeons.

Highway 1

Back on the coast, the Pacific Coast Highway now officially becomes Highway 1. It's been a while since the long-gone Serpentarium at **Laguna Beach ❼** used to advertise that *rattlesnake à la Maryland* would be on the reptile zoo's menu, but this community still has more attractions than you would expect in a beach city. Laguna was always a favorite of Hollywood's movie colony, and Mary Pickford, Bette Davis, Judy Garland and Rudolph Valentino were just a few of the movie stars who maintained homes here.

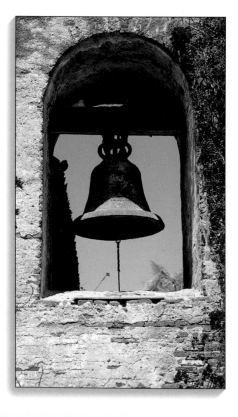

The resort has established a worldwide reputation with its annual **Pageant of the Masters** each summer, at which well-rehearsed volunteers take up their roles in living reproductions of famous paintings.

On specific evenings of each month, the popular **Laguna Art Museum** (tel: 949-494-8971; open daily) organizes the Art Walk, which includes visits to 40 local galleries. The Visitors Bureau located at 252 Broadway (tel: 949-497-9229; open Mon–Sat) offers guidance on numerous other "heritage tours," which might include the **Murphy-Smith Historical Bungalow** (tel: 949-497-4525; open Fri–Sun), one of the few houses in downtown Laguna Beach remaining from the 1920s.

For lovers of the outdoor life, there are many choices in addition to the annual whale-watching safaris. These include the **Laguna Caost Wilderness Park** (tel: 949-923-2235), a native plant and wildlife refuge on Lugina Canyon Road; the worthwhile **Pacific Marine Mammal Center** for sick and injured seals (tel: 949-494-3050; open daily); plus the excursions to inspect tide pools (tel: 949-874-6620; transportation from all hotels) and the **Glenn E. Vedder Ecological Reserve** at the north section of the main beach, where marine life can be explored by divers.

There are thousands of acres of wilderness parks surrounding Laguna Beach, and maps are available at the Visitors Bureau.

Balboa peninsula

The upscale **Balboa peninsula**, with its 6 miles (10 km) of sandy shore, encloses a harbor that is usually filled with yachts, with a large paddle-wheeler moored beside the highway bridge. Given pride of place on Main Street, it's hard to miss the **Balboa Pavilion**, built in 1905 as a railroad terminal, with its distinctive but totally unnecessary steeple. Behind it, if you get here early enough, you'll find fishing boats unloading their daily catch. Almost as old is the ferry that makes the 3-minute trip from the end of Palm Street to **Balboa Island**, with its million-dollar homes and classy shops and cafés. The hour-long walk around the island on the sidewalk hugging the water's edge is enjoyable, particularly just before twilight, not only for the fiery sunset, but for the evening lights reflected across the water from the Balboa Pavilion.

On your way back across the narrow channel, someone will surely point out, on nearby islands, the former homes of John Wayne and cowboy hero Roy Rogers. From **Balboa Pier**, you can admire the kite-flyers, frisbee-throwers and bodysurfers. Check out the restaurant at the end of the pier before finishing up at the Balboa Fun Zone with its rides and video arcades.

Depending on the month, if you stay a couple of weekday nights in pretty **Newport Beach**, the tourist office (tel: 800-942 6278) will give you round-trip tickets on the *Catalina Flyer*, yet another way to reach Santa Catalina. Waves cascade over the breakwater here, so it's not a great place for swimming; expert bodysurfers are the only people to truly excel in the water. The town does have other things to offer visitors, though, including a **Nautical Museum**; the well-stocked **Orange County Museum of Art** (tel: 949-759-1122; open Wed–Sun) or the shopping paradise of **Fashion Island Newport Center**, which the Irvine Company built when there was barely the population to support it. The shopping center sits on the right-hand side of the road, past Avocado Drive, as you leave town. In **Corona del Mar**, just to the south, the gardens of the Sherman Library and Roger's Gardens are pleasant places to pause.

Beaches and birdwatching

Many of the communities around here are in dispute about which most deserves the desirable Southern California title "Surf City," but **Huntington Beach ❽** claims to have the best case; in 1994, the town inaugurated a sidewalk **Surfers Walk of Fame** in the presence of its surf fanatical congressman, Dana Rohrabacher.

The highway heads along the coast past the state's longest municipal pier, rebuilt in concrete after the original was destroyed by a fierce storm. Three blocks up Main Street and directly opposite the pier is Plaza Almeria, with an attractive collection of shops, restaurants and homes. Farther uptown, another old mall, the Huntington Beach Center, is an entertainment and shopping complex. Rail tycoon Henry Huntington first brought the railroad here late in the 19th century, and a subsequent oil boom introduced prosperity to a town that ironically is now best known for its environmental awareness. Its 350-acre (140-hectare) Central Park, 50 percent of which is devoted to wildlife

Map on page 326

BELOW: San Juan Capistrano, 7th in the chain of 21 missions founded by Father Serra, is the most famous in California.

and greenery, is nothing but a taster compared with the sprawling **Bolsa Chica Ecological Reserve,** a vast coastal salt marsh that serves as a resting place for birds migrating between North and South America.

The best spot for birdwatchers is on the inland side of the highway between Golden West Street and Warner Avenue, opposite the entrance to the state beach. There are walking trails and plenty of parking. The **Interpretive Center** (tel: 714-846-1114; open Tues–Sun), which offers bird checklists, is at Warner Avenue. Not far away, between Warner and Heil avenues, is the **Monarch Butterfly Habitat**, where rare butterflies gather in the eucalyptus trees between November and March. Passing through the small, waterside community of **Sunset Beach**, you cannot help but notice a huge wooden water tower beside the highway that became a residence some years ago. Although the tower is private, it is a local landmark for miles around.

Life's a beach

At the Los Angeles County line, **Seal Beach**, an unspoiled enclave with an 80-year-old inn and a lengthy pier uncluttered with modern diversions, is the last place at which the ocean can be seen from the highway for many miles. To the right of the highway at **Belmont Shore**, you can make a diversion along Second Street, which skirts the beach of Alamitos Bay. Gondola Getaway on East Ocean Beach Boulevard operates hour-long tours in real gondolas along canals that pass the elegant homes of neighboring **Naples**. Operating from 10am–midnight daily, the gondolas carry from two to six people.

Highway 1 goes inland here, bypassing Long Beach, San Pedro and the Palo Verdes Peninsula to hit the coast again just south of Redondo Beach.

BELOW:
each beach in Southern California has its own fans and habitués.

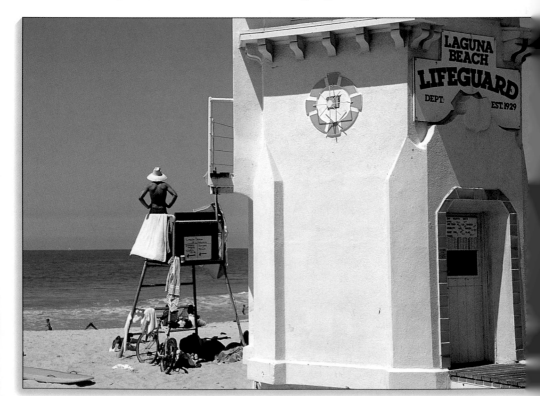

Long live the *Queen*

Although the Pacific Coast Highway bypasses **Long Beach ❾**, it's worth passing through town to see some of its attractions, which includes the world's largest mural, a panorama of marine life that covers the entire surface of the Long Beach Arena on Ocean Boulevard. Other sights include the magnificent **Aquarium of the Pacific** (tel: 562-590-3100; open daily) and the venerable ship the *Queen Mary* (tel: 800-437-2934 or 562-435-3511; www.queenmary.com; open daily) – which made 1,000 trans-Atlantic crossings and was a hero of World War II before ending its journey here – moored in the harbor. The ship's history is a starry one, having been the carrier of choice for both celebrities and royalty; visitors can pretend to be the same by staying overnight in a cabin, or dine in the elegantly restored Art Deco restaurant.

Long Beach has positioned itself as a sleek, modern city in recent years, and it certainly has a number of architecturally chic new structures. But it's also anxious to promote its historic downtown buildings from the early part of the 20th century. A walking tour map of more than 40 of these landmarks is available from the Visitors Bureau (tel: 800-452-7829). Anyone traveling with kids might like to know that State Highway 22 east from Long Beach hooks up with I-5 and leads to Anaheim, where the attractions include **Disneyland**, Knotts Berry Farm, Adventure City and Medieval Times.

Harbor tours

Headquarters of Southern California's fishing fleet, **San Pedro** once carried the distinction of being a genuine fishing port. The old town is now long gone, replaced by an imaginatively-designed pseudo-19th-century construction called Ports O'Call Village. Several blocks of saltbox-type weathered-looking shops – 75 in all, plus numerous restaurants – are a pleasure to walk around. Harbor tours and fishing trips leave from here (as well as the *Catalina Express* and a beautiful classic sailing ship), and there's masses of free parking space. Green and white trolleys run along the waterfront, stopping at the World Cruise center, the maritime museum, Ports O'Call Village and the Frank Gehry-designed Cabrillo Marine Aquarium.

San Pedro's **Cabrillo Beach** has earned a reputation as one of the best places in the area to go windsurfing, and beginners especially favor the sheltered waters inside the harbor breakwater. Between March and September – twice a month, like clockwork – milky-white grunion fish ride in by the thousand on the tide to deposit their eggs in the sand.

On the **Palos Verdes** peninsula are multi-million dollar Italianate villas and French chateaux overlooking the ocean. Abalone Cove, the beach west of Narcissa Drive, is an ecological preserve at the end of a steep path, perfect for divers and tide-poolers. Just past the Golden Shores mall is a lighthouse beside which, at the **Point Vicente Interpretive Center** (open daily), are long-lens telescopes for sighting passing whales (December to April), and an exhibit in which visitors can don earphones to hear the mournful voices of these loveable mammals.

The famous Art Deco ocean liner, the Queen Mary, is now a restaurant and hotel in Long Beach.

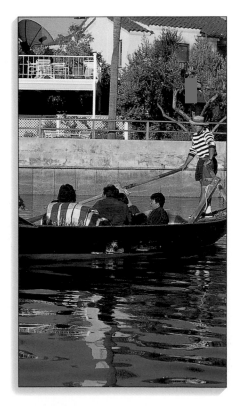

BELOW: gondolier in Naples.

About a mile farther on is the wood-and-glass **Wayfarers Chapel,** designed by Frank Lloyd Wright's son, whose inspiration is said to have been Northern California's majestic redwood trees. The chapel was built in 1951 as a memorial to the 18th-century Swedish theologian Emmanuel Swedenborg. Walking around the peaceful gardens to the sound of songbirds, a fountain and the gurgling stream is a very tranquilizing experience. There are services in the chapel at 11am every Sunday.

Walking on water

By now we are well and truly in **Los Angeles ❿** *(see page 236),* although most of this sprawling city's inland tourist attractions lie quite a ways farther north. LA's southern beaches are varied and linked by a combination of Highway 1 and minor roads. After its chances of becoming a major port were wrecked by its vulnerability to severe storms, **Redondo Beach** turned its attention to tourism. A Pacific Electric Railway developer hired a Hawaiian teenager to demonstrate surfing, and before long visitors were flocking to watch "the man who can walk on water."

In the 1930s, even bigger crowds were lured by the gambling ships moored offshore – the most famous being the *Rex* – which could accommodate 1,500 customers, who took 25¢ rides out to the boat from the town pier. Offshore gaming was outlawed by Congress in 1946, but a pier remains at the center of the town's colorful boardwalk. The current pier is horseshoe-shaped, after several predecessors were destroyed by storms, while Redondo Beach itself is a big draw for bodybuilders.

BELOW: boardwalk.

Following Catalina Avenue from Redondo Pier leads to **Hermosa Beach,** an

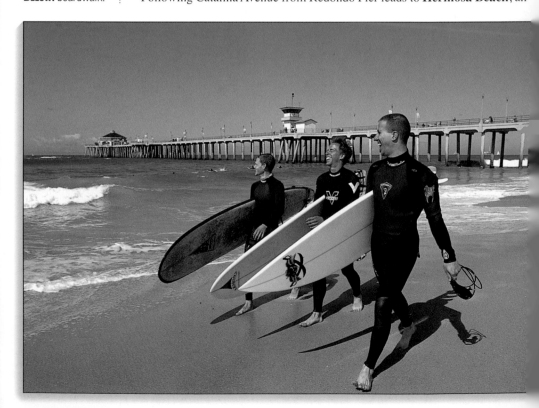

inland road leading past Kings Harbor Marina, opposite which an enormous ocean mural is painted on the wall of the power plant. Hermosa Avenue continues for quite a way one block from the beach. The beach itself stretches for 8 sandy miles (13 km) between Kings Harbor and **Marina Del Rey**, the longest uninterrupted stretch in Los Angeles County. There are pedestrian-only streets leading from Hermosa Avenue to the beach at every block.

At 22nd Street, a good neighborhood place to sit outside and watch the locals while drinking a cup of coffee is Martha's Corner. Hermosa is known for its nightclubs, Marina Del Rey for its child-friendly beaches.

In between the two is **Manhattan Beach**, whose name came about because of a homesick New Yorker, who was living in the area in 1902 when just a dozen families made up the community. Its population grew dramatically during World War II when aircraft plants sprang up along Avalon Boulevard. In recent years, the Disney company has erected a dozen huge sound stages in what is still largely a commuter community of LA.

But in the last few years, this part of Orange County has become second only to Hollywood as a venue for moviemakers, with its coastal piers especially attractive to the makers of television commercials. The scene down by the water resembles an old episode of *Baywatch*, with plenty of bronzed and beautiful joggers, rollerbladers and volleyball players.

Venice

Just north of Marina Del Rey, the long pedestrian and bicycle path linking **Venice ⓫** (and **Venice Beach**) with Santa Monica is a lively hub of activity, especially in Venice itself, where you'll encounter skimpily-attired rollerbladers

Map on page 326

Manhattan Beach was named by a homesick New Yorker in 1902. Hermosa Beach stretches for 8 miles (13km) between Kings Harbor and Marina Del Rey, making it the longest in LA County.

BELOW: roller-dancers, Venice Beach.

Near Muscle Beach.

BELOW: castles
in the sand,
Santa Monica.

of both sexes, rainbow-haired punks, magicians, fortune tellers, itinerant musicians and pumped-up bodybuilders flexing their biceps at **Muscle Beach**. You can rent rollerblades on Windward Avenue or a bicycle on Washington Street (opposite the abandoned pier) or just sit at one of the sidewalk cafés and admire the passing parade. The most interesting place to grab a snack in Venice is probably the art- and artist-filled Rose Café on Rose Avenue. If you feel like getting away from the noise and the rentlentless body-beautiful activities, this is also a good spot from which to begin exploring Venice proper, which is surpringly different from the image normally associated with the place.

Canals near the coast

The lesser-visited town of Venice is much more charming than the beach. Take a stroll through the residential area around the inland canals, where a proliferation of bright flowers tumbles over sagging fences and ducks nestle under upturned boats on tiny jetties. Visitors can pick their way along rutted paths, over gentle hump-backed bridges and past lovingly tended gardens, admiring the variegated architecture, numerous birds and floral displays.

More than 70 years after the death of Abbott Kinney, who acquired and reclaimed what was worthless marshland in anticipation of creating an "Italy in California," some of his vision still remains in what is probably the most pleasant walk in urban Los Angeles. The original circulation system for the canals – which envisaged seawater pulsing through 30-inch (76-cm) pipes with every fresh tide – proved unworkable, and the canals themselves became sand-clogged and stagnant. In 1993, a $6 million overhaul dredged and refilled the canals, repaired the adjoining paths and rebuilt some of the bridges.

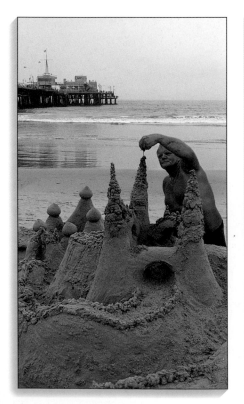

LA's AUTO MUSEUM

Lovers of automobiles and travel will want to make a sidetrip into Los Angeles to visit the Petersen Automotive Museum, one of the world's largest museums devoted exclusively to the history and cultural impact of the car. For when it comes to vehicles, no city knows them like Los Angeles, and no one can know Los Angeles without a vehicle. This city, unlike few others, was designed for the car and its endless miles of freeway tie together the way rivers tie together London or Paris. With a board of advisors comprising high-profile enthusiasts like actor Paul Newman and racing ace Parnelli Jones, the four floors of this $40 million museum detail everything you ever wanted to know about four wheels, and the culture that rides above them. The second floor houses racing and classic cars, hot rods, movie-star cars and vintage motorcycles. But the Petersen is not just about transportation; it's also about style. Although the museum has yet to do an exhibition on why balding old men buy flashy red sports cars, it does have rotating cultural exhibitions covering such novelties as low riding cars, and the history of that quintessential American icon: the pick-up truck. The Petersen Museum is at 606 Wilshire Boulevard, tel: 323-930-2277.

Movie-star coast

Santa Monica is a seaside resort where Los Angeles's West Side meets the ocean. In the streets behind and the canyons above lie the most famous of LA's attractions: Hollywood, Beverly Hills, Rodeo Drive. But down near the waterside, the "Bay City" of Raymond Chandler's novels is a pleasant place to be. The boulevards and side streets are attractive places to stroll and shop; a wide pedestrian mall at Third Street leads down to the sparkling Frank Gehry-designed **Santa Monica Place**, which is flanked by department stores. The trendy **Third Street** pedestrian mall, lined with restaurants, stores and movie theaters, is usually filled with street performers, while the waterside, century-old **Santa Monica Pier** offers a predictable assortment of amusement arcades, souvenir stands, snack bars and sedentary fishermen. There's also a wonderful carousel with 44 hand-carved horses which featured in the 1973 film *The Sting*.

Good places to spend a couple of quiet hours in Santa Monica are the library, where there's an extensive collection of current magazines and a well-lit reading area, and the clifftop **Palisades Park**, a eucalyptus-fringed grassy stretch along Ocean Avenue that offers views of boats and sunsets. In recent years, the park has proved to be a popular venue for the homeless – though their presence should not deter you from visiting. To one side is an information cabin for brochures and useful tips on where to catch local buses.

The mansions along the seashore at the northern end of Santa Monica were mostly built by moviedom's former elite. The grandest, at 415 Pacific Coast Highway, was the 118-room compound designed for William Randolph Hearst and his paramour, Marion Davies. The house was sold to the owner of the Hotel Bel Air, who turned it into a beach hotel and club. ❑

Map on page 326

BELOW: the 100-year-old Santa Monica Pier is lined with shops and cafés.

LOS ANGELES TO SAN FRANCISCO

Map on page 326

This legendary stretch of Highway 1 takes in the California coast's most famous attractions: extravagant Hearst Castle and fog-shrouded Big Sur

The distance from Los Angeles to San Francisco is 380 miles (611 km). Taking Interstate 5 all the way means a city-to-city trip can be accomplished in around six hours, but that would be a pity. Highway 1 hugs the coast almost the entire way, presenting heart-stopping curves, breath-taking scenery, pretty inns, scenic sites and two of California's best attractions – Hearst Castle and Big Sur. With all of this to savor, allowing two days rather than six hours makes far more sense.

LOS ANGELES TO SANTA BARBARA

The Pacific Coast Highway out of Los Angeles cruises along **Malibu** ⑬ with the ease that community's name implies. Despite its worldwide reputation for hi-jinks and hedonism, the area is largely a private residential community where much of the beach has been cordoned off (at the junction with Webb Way) into the exclusive Malibu Colony. The must-see place in Malibu is **Adamson House** (tel: 310-456-8432), built in 1929 for May Ridge, the widow of the man who bought most of what now comprises Malibu back in 1897. The richly decorated house, replete with tiles from the Ridge's short-lived Malibu Pottery, is a fascinating repository of history about the early Hollywood crowd, who were perfectly content with ocean-front shacks.

North of Malibu, the beaches are more accessible and there's a string of them – **Point Dume**, **Zuma** and **Leo Carrillo** – until the highway turns inland toward Ventura. Highway 1 is submerged into US 101 here, and you must leave it to visit **Ventura** ⑭ itself, which has a huge city hall perched on the hillside and a heavily restored "Olde Towne." The 1782 **San Buenaventura Mission** (tel: 805-643-4318; open daily) is pretty and worth a visit, and Ventura's harbor area has lots of seafood restaurants. Most of the town's sites are connected by trolley.

Inland along State Route 150, hidden away on the edge of the Los Padres National Forest, is **Ojai** (pronounced *O-hi*), a sleepy artists' and writers' colony near which the 1926 movie *Lost Horizon* was filmed. The town is centered around a main street on which a graceful tower offsets a row of unpretentious shops built under a covered veranda. Artifacts in the Historical Society Museum include those from Chumash Indian times through the ranching period to the days when heavyweight champion Jack Dempsey cleared rocks from what became "Pop" Soper's training ranch. Dozens of boxers trained here, including hero Dempsey himself, while preparing for his fight against

LEFT: Santa Barbara's Spanish-style architecture.
BELOW: hitting the highway *à deux*.

Gene Tunney in 1926. On the outskirts of Santa Barbara, the **Montecito Inn** (tel: 805-969-7854) has been popular with discerning refugees from Hollywood since the 1920s, when one of its original owners was Charlie Chaplin and guests included Fatty Arbuckle, Fred Astaire and Will Rogers. More than 1,000 two-reeler movies were shot in the Santa Barbara area, most of them between 1913 and 1918; Chicago producer Samuel S. Hutchinson's Flying A Studios alone brought in such silent-screen film celebrities as Mary Pickford and D. W. Griffith. Because of its lower costs and proximity to Los Angeles, many movies and television shows continue to be shot in the region today.

Montecito's legendary **San Ysidro Ranch** (tel: 805-969-5046; www.san ysidroranch.com), in a canyon lined with sycamore and eucalyptus trees, was where John F. Kennedy honeymooned with his wife Jackie; where Lauren Bacall says she fell in love with Humphrey Bogart; and where Laurence Olivier and Vivien Leigh had a midnight wedding in 1940.

Santa Barbara

The most striking aspect of **Santa Barbara** ⑮ is its distinctive Mediterranean architecture: the ubiquitous white-washed adobe, tiled roofing and iron grill-work permeate a city in which, as one local writer noted, "its architects were able to create a myth of a tradition, which turned out to be far more believable than the realities of factual history." There are miles of enticing wide beaches; the coast's "queen of the missions," arguably the most beautiful in the state – the **Santa Barbara Mission** (tel: 805-682-4149; open daily); and historic **Stearns Wharf**, the oldest pier on the California coast. The pier contains an aquarium, wine-tasting rooms, fishing facilities and seafood stands. A waterfront shuttle tram operates between the wharf, Downtown and the zoo, connecting the beaches which line the shore with volleyball courts on both sides of the pier, and with the expensive hotels at the eastern end.

Two blocks from the Greyhound bus station in the town's center is the handsome 1929 Spanish-Moorish **Court House** (open daily). Its lobby is lined with mosaics and murals, and there's a lovely view from the top of gently sloping roofs and the multi-level lawn below. Turn up State Street to reach the area where the city began around the old **Presidio**. Inspect 18th-century adobes, and have lunch in the charming cobbled street called **El Paseo**, where the local theater once featured a dancer named Rita Cansino, later to become better known as Rita Hayworth.

Channel Islands

Between Christmas and late March, there are daily excursions into the offshore Santa Barbara Channel for whale watching. Year-round trips are also made to Santa Barbara Island, whose desolate 640 acres (260 hectares) are a haven for birds, sea lions 10,000 breeding seals and other marine life. None of the **Channel Islands**, run by the National Park Service, is inhabited, but overnight camping is allowed and island rangers conduct tours. For more information, go to www.nps.gov/chis/.

BELOW:
Santa Barbara's architects "were able to create a myth of a tradition."

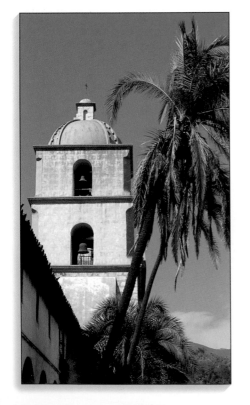

SANTA BARBARA TO BIG SUR

After meandering through **Gaviota State Park**, Highways 1 and 101 split apart, but both turn inland. It's most fun to continue driving on Highway 1, the road nearest the coast, which heads through sleepy **Lompoc**, ennobled by the presence of the **La Purisima Concepcion** (tel: 805-733-3713; open daily), the state's 11th mission. North of town, the road passes through an immense area of agri-business-dominated land, irrigated fields used for growing broccoli, cauliflower and strawberries as well as extensive fields of flowers, which in season offer an extraordinary display of magentas, pinks, golds and purples. These supply most of the floral seeds that color the fields of the entire USA.

Vast fields continue past **Guadalupe,** a quiet, old-fashioned town with an Amtrak station and one-story buildings dating to the turn of the 20th century. Eighteen miles (29 km) north, an enormous oil refinery dominates the landscape. **Pismo State Beach**, once famous for its huge clams (still celebrated with a Clam Festival every October) has fabulous sandy shores stretching all around the bay and leads directly into San Luis Obispo, which is more or less the midway point between Los Angeles and San Francisco. Pismo is one of the few beaches where driving is allowed, so look out for dune buggies. Just before San Luis Obispo, keep an eye open for the extraordinary **Madonna Inn** (tel: 805-543-3000; www.madonnainn.com), each of whose 109 rooms are individually decorated in memorably kitsch fashion. The "old English" suite is large enough for two families to move into for the night.

The attractive, low-key college town of **San Luis Obispo** ⓰ (SLO) also has an 18th-century mission (tel: 805-781-8220; open daily), with a downtown community located around its plaza. There's an Art Center (tel: 805-

Map on page 326

The Santa Lucia mountain range is a successful wine producing region.

BELOW: Firestone Vineyard near Santa Barbara.

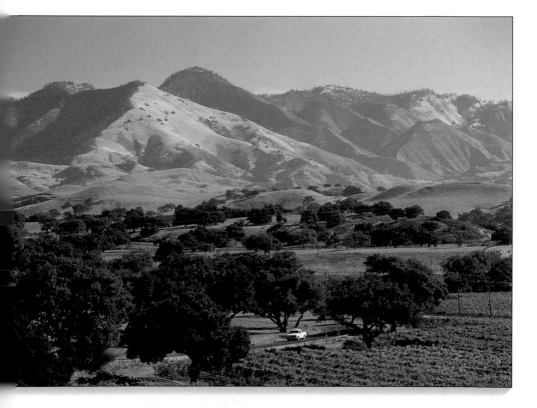

543-8562; closed Tues), the adjoining County Historical Museum (open Wed–Sun) and the Apple Farm Mill House on Monterey Street – an authentic working gristmill set in scenic gardens with waterfalls. Every Thursday night, part of Higuera Street is closed to traffic to facilitate a farmers market and street fair along with bands and entertainment.

Morro Bay

Morro Bay is dominated by its 576-ft (176-meter) high rock, whose aeries now shelter the endangered peregrine falcon, the 175-mph (282-kph) dive-bomber that feeds on live game. There's an excellent beach, and the restaurant-fringed harbor is an attractive place to walk around – but be aware that the harbor drive dead-ends in both directions and parking can be difficult. The beach is busy long before the tourists arrive, however – ubiquitous are the coastal snowy plover, "those little cupcake-sized birds that run along the beach looking for something to eat." Alas, the snowy plover is a threatened species. The **Museum of Natural History** (tel: 805-772-2694; open daily) contains exhibits that deal with coastal animal, marine and plant life, including the Monarch butterfly. This short-lived beauty, with its amber and black wings, can be seen near Pacific Grove (up by Monterey) during the winter months.

At the pretty town of **Cayucos**, you'll say good-bye to the ocean, which remains out of sight almost to **Cambria**, a pleasant little place just off the highway. In between the two towns, State Highway 46 winds east through the barren but beautiful hills of the Santa Lucia mountain range, linking up to US 101 and **Paso Robles**. This is a charming, small, wine-producing region where most of the wineries offer free daily tastings. A map of local wineries is available from

BELOW: Roman pool, Hearst Castle.

the Visitor and Conference Bureau (tel: 805-238-0506) in Paso Robles, not far from the **Paso Robles Pioneer Museum** (tel: 805-239-4556; open Thur–Sun afternoons), which provides a little lesson in local history.

Map on page 326

Hearst Castle

Back on the coast, the hamlet of **San Simeon** is the nearest community to the house of San Simeon, more famously known as **Hearst Castle ⑰** (open daily). For many years, Hearst Castle was the largest private residence in the US; now it vies with Disneyland for the title of "the state's most popular attraction." Perched over the sea on a hill so high the house is often wreathed in fog, its construction began in 1919, financed by newspaper and movie tycoon William Randolph Hearst. Craftsmen labored for 28 years to create the twin-towered home on *La Cuesta Encantada*, "the Enchanted Hill," which Hearst then filled with carvings, furnishings and works of art from European castles and cathedrals. (During his lifetime, Hearst accumulated one of the largest collections of private art in the world, with a value measured in the hundreds of millions of dollars.) All materials for the house had to be brought up the coast by steamer, then hauled up that impossible hill. San Simeon's grounds were stocked with animals from all over the world, and Hollywood's elite, like Jean Harlow and Clark Gable, were invited to stroll through the beautiful gardens or enjoy the magnificent indoor and outdoor swimming pools.

Reservations for Hearst Castle (tel: 800-444-4445) are virtually mandatory to secure a place on one of the five daily tours, some of which include the home movies of Hearst, whose lonely, lavish lifestyle was the subject of Orson Welles' most celebrated movie, *Citizen Kane*. Tour 1 is probably the best for first-time

She was very nice and I liked her. She didn't have an awful lot to say... all the men used to flock around her. She was very attractive in an evening dress because she never wore anything under it.

– MARION DAVIES ON JEAN HARLOW

BELOW: the Assembly Room decorated for Christmas, Hearst Castle.

visitors, as it gives the best overview of the castle and main rooms. Although Hearst Castle is extremely busy, especially during the summer months, the estate is efficiently run, and timed entry means you can go away and have a picnic on the beach below if the wait proves to be a long one. Unmissable.

Big Sur

The 94-mile (151-km) stretch of coastline between San Simeon and the Monterey Peninsula is known as **Big Sur** ⑱, a legendary wilderness of holistic healing retreats and remote homesteads inhabited by third-generation pioneers. The area was barely accessible to traffic until 1937, and even now the sheer cliffs of the Santa Lucia Mountains hugged by the highway occasionally slide into the sea, leaving residents in complete isolation until the road is rebuilt. There have been numerous occasions in recent years when Highway 1 has been closed for months at a time due to landslides, and as there are no roads inland between Cambria and Monterey, it is wise to check the situation at a gas station before proceeding.

The dark, thicketed mountains rise steeply to the right; the foamy sea to the left constantly changes shape and color. Only the two-lane road separates the two, which means the curling ribbon of road has its own distinct weather pattern. For this read: fog. Although the sun may be shining brightly on the other side of the mountain, and can often be seen slatted through the trees, Highway 1 can be distinctly chilly, and the fog comes on quickly, obliterating the world for unexpected moments. Infrequent guard rails, looking suspiciously flimsy, are small comfort in the face of the menacing rocks below. Driving along Big Sur is not for the faint-hearted *(see photograph on page 42),* but for those with a

BELOW: the best way to experience Big Sur is in a convertible or on a Harley. Be sure to wrap up, as the fog is chilly, even in the summertime.

sense of adventure and time on their side, this stretch of the California coastline is one of the most exhilarating routes in the US. For added excitement, try it in a convertible or – better yet – on a motorcycle, preferably a Harley-Davidson (which can be rented in either Los Angeles or San Francisco). Traveling non-stop with good weather, you could arrive in Carmel in about 3 hours, but the best way is to pause, then pause again, then stay at least for lunch or dinner. This is especially important for the person doing the driving, as the view is so fabulous, but the road so hazardous, it can be frustrating for the person at the wheel if frequent stops are not taken. Overlooks are numerous.

Coming from San Simeon, the hills begin gently enough, and the road fairly easy to navigate. The first sight on the right is **Los Padres National Forest**, the southern tip of the coastal redwood belt, which contains several almost preternaturally beautiful state parks. **Julia Pfeiffer Burns State Park** and **Pfeiffer Big Sur State Park** have wonderful trails that lead up into the mountains or down toward the sea, the former park with a waterfall near McWay Cove that rewards the completion of a (non-demanding) hike.

The long and winding road

As the road twists and turns northward, anybody on a motorcycle will wish they had worn a heavy sweater. Arriving at **Big Sur Village** 🟚 confirms it is really little more than a huddle of shops and a post office. Places to stay are few and far between; if you're planning to be in Big Sur overnight during the summer months or on *any* weekend, be sure to book well in advance. The range of accommodation embraces the private campgrounds of Fernwood (tel: 831-667-2422) and Big Sur (tel: 831-667-2322) to the extravagant **Post Ranch Inn**

Map on page 326

Highway 1 runs almost the entire length of California. The Big Sur stretch is not for the faint-hearted.

BELOW: Post Ranch Inn, Big Sur.

TIP

Despite the carefree, wind-in-hair, bugs-in-teeth image portrayed in countless movies, the state of California requires that all motorcylists wear a helmet while traveling on the road.

BELOW:
sea lions and birds, a common sight on this part of the Pacific Coast.

(tel: 831-667-2200), an architectural gem set high on a hill, or the four-star, hot-tub haven of **Ventana** (tel: 831-667-2331) with its award-winning restaurant. A handful of motels and inns complete the picture.

Big Sur has always attracted unusual people. Until 1945, it was mainly populated by ranchers, lodgers and miners, but soon after literary people turned up to stay. The **Henry Miller Memorial Library** near **Nepenthe restaurant**, where everybody goes for sunset, has works by and about this local literary hero, who called the area "the face of the earth as the creator intended it to look." In the 1960s, New Agers began communing at the hot spring called Esalen, named after the Native Americans who discovered it. Now the spring is owned by the **Esalen Institute**, where New Agers still congregate. North of the village is the area's crowning man-made achievement, the **Bixby Bridge**. Spanning the steep walls of Bixby Canyon and often obscured by fog, the bridge was called an engineering marvel when it was constructed in 1932.

BIG SUR TO SAN FRANCISCO

Leaving the lush lands of Big Sur for the cities on the Monterey Peninsula can be a shock to the system. A way to ease this uncomfortable transition is to visit one last natural wonder on the way, the undramatic but still lovely **Point Lobos State Reserve** (tel: 831-624-4909; open daily). Miles of trails with glimpses of deer, rabbits, sea lions and sea otters are gentle features that children will love. So did Robert Louis Stevenson, who is said to have been inspired to write *Treasure Island* while at Point Lobos. Several short footpaths traverse the rock-strewn headland, on which is one of two existing groves of ghostly Monterey Cypress trees.

Carmel and Monterey

Carmel ❷⓪ ("Gateway to the Monterey Peninsula") has gained a reputation as being something of an artists' and writers' haven, but – due to the cost of local real estate – is really more a place for selling creative works than making them. Carmel is a classically beautiful little town that has outlawed high-rises, neon signs, traffic lights, parking meters – anything possessing the foul taint of city life, including artificial house plants. Although Carmel is undeniably attractive, the town's postcard-prettiness can be cloying, its prices inflated, and the snooty attitude of some of its residents (which include Hollywood's Clint Eastwood and Doris Day), does not inspire one to linger. **Carmel Mission** and **Carmel Beach** are very appealing, though; and just to the north is justly famous **Pebble Beach**, home to the challenging golf course of the same name.

Be warned: motorcyclists are not allowed on the peninsula's **17-Mile Drive**, which even charges an entrance fee to drive around admiring its luxurious private homes. These look, in fact, much like any other affluent American neighborhood, and given the proximity to the exquisite Big Sur coast, the shoreline along this private road is pretty expendable.

Cannery Row in **Monterey** ❷① at the north end of the peninsula basks in the glow of John Steinbeck's brilliant novel of the same name. What Steinbeck celebrated, however, were "weedy lots and junk heaps, sardine canneries of corrugated iron, honky tonks, restaurants and whore houses," not a tacky tourist trap. Steinbeck's world withered with the mysterious disappearance of the sardines in the mid-1940s, about the time the movie version of Steinbeck's *Sweet Thursday* was filmed here. A visit is redeemed, however, by a few hours spent at the excellent **Monterey Bay Aquarium** (tel: 831-648-4800; open daily),

Map on page 326

BELOW:
statue of Father
Serra in front of
Carmel Mission.

Map on page 326

California's finest and one of the best in the world, which explores to admirable effect the marine life found in a Grand Canyon-sized trench just offshore. Wall-length tanks house solitary sharks, regal salmon and schools of tiny fish amid beds of kelp that writhe with the simulated tides. Keepers in glass tanks talk to spectators through underwater microphones during feeding times. Definitely a place to visit. In **Salinas**, Steinbeck's life is celebrated at the **National Steinbeck Center** (tel: 831-796-3833; www.steinbeck.org; open daily), whose films and exhibits are devoted to the author's life.

Half-moons and lighthouses

Traffic on this stretch of coast towards San Francisco is usually horrendous, with a virtually permanent traffic jam both sides of and within the resort of Santa Cruz, which sits at the head of Monterey Bay. The road is a divided highway, four lanes bordered by flat agricultural fields. Although the beach town of **Capitola** is cute in a noisy sort of way, the main things to alleviate the disappointment about this stretch is the sunshine, welcome after the chilly fog of Big Sur, and the freshest of produce sold along the roadside: California's finest artichokes, cherries and strawberries. Santa Cruz is a mile from the highway, and driving there is such a chore that you might want to continue up the coast through fields of artichokes to the attractive wide beach at **Scott Creek**, north of **Davenport**. On State Highway 156 to **Castroville**, the "Artichoke Capital of the World," is the Giant Artichoke Restaurant, which serves delicious deep-fried leaves. If you do choose to stop off in **Santa Cruz ㉒**, you can console yourself with a visit to the surfing museum or the **Boardwalk Amusement Park** (with scary roller coaster), or dine on yummy Dungeness crab in one of the restaurants on the pier, watching the pelicans play with swimmers in the sea.

BELOW: Monterey's Fisherman's Wharf.
RIGHT: Bixby Bridge, Big Sur, was called an engineering marvel in 1932.

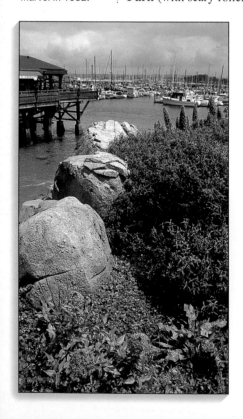

Tan, black and white cows graze together in fields high up on the cliffs before Highway 1 swoops down to **Waddell Creek** and the driftwood-lined beaches (such as Bean Hollow State Beach) all the way up to the Santa Cruz county line. Thin slivers of fog can sometimes obscure the view, but when it shifts (which it does every few minutes), drivers are rewarded by views of **Pigeon Point Lighthouse ㉓**, which can be seen from the highway in both directions. Weekend tours are available; enquire locally.

Heading toward San Francisco, wide, flat fields lie between the highway and the coast. For a change of pace, horses can be rented at the coastal Seaview Riding Stable Ranch. Attractive **Half Moon Bay ㉔** is only half an hour's drive from the city, but is famous – not only for its pumpkins – but for the huge waves that pound its shores. Surfers from all around come to tackle the big ones – up to 40 feet (12 meters) high – and the talk in the bars is all of "mavericks" and "tubes." Sunday lunchtimes at Half Moon often include jazz or rock concerts.

With the suburbs of the city on the horizon, the coastline becomes rocky and untrafficked again. **Gray Whale Cove State Beach** or **Big Basin Park** are peaceful places for a final walk or picnic before hitting the big time – **San Francisco ㉕** *(see page 350)*. ❑

SAN FRANCISCO: CITY BY THE BAY

Fisherman's Wharf, Chinatown, the Golden Gate Bridge – this city wins hearts straightaway and effortlessly

Each visitor takes a different memory away from San Francisco: the steep street that drops off toward the bay, the fog drifting through the Golden Gate Bridge, the dishes expertly blended making the perfect meal or the simple fun of a cable-car ride, admiring Victorian houses along the way.

Begin at Union Square, where a winged statue commemorates Admiral George Dewey's naval victory over the Spanish in 1898. Chinatown Gate appears just to the northeast. While it is no secret to tourists, crowds of Chinese residents vying for space on the sidewalk show the area still caters to locals. Tiny herb shops in mysterious alleys

promise everything from rheumatism relief to the restoration of sexual prowess.

Chinatown ends where North Beach begins. While a few seedy clubs still promise lap dances, critically acclaimed restaurants and posh nightclubs entice a different crowd altogether. This old-fashioned Italian neighborhood still attracts writers and artists, however, particularly to the City Lights bookstore.

To the east, Telegraph Hill rises above North Beach, offering spectacular views across San Francisco Bay. Coit Tower (tel: 415-362-0808), with its momentous views and frescoes, crowns the hill and can be climbed. Follow Columbus Avenue to Fisherman's Wharf. The fishing boats put out before dawn; their catch determines the "special of the day" at the numerous restaurants clustered around the wharf. Lined with shops and ready to please tourists, this is a "must" stop for all; even locals eat here, even if they do not shop here.

A mile offshore from San Francisco is windswept Alcatraz (boat tickets – tel: 415-981-7625). Once home to such hardened criminals as Al Capone and the notorious Machine Gun Kelley, officials closed the prison in 1963 when repair costs grew too great. A tour of the prison is surprisingly rewarding; be sure to bring a sweater for the breezy boat ride over.

A ride on the Powell-Hyde cable car begins two blocks inland from Hyde Street Pier, offering a tour of Russian Hill's high-rise apartments and mansions. The cable car passes near the curvy section of Lombard Street often seen in movies and continues on to Nob Hill, called the "hill of palaces," by Robert Louis Stevenson.

At the corner of Washington and Mason streets, the Cable Car Museum (tel: 415-474-1887) exhibits the city's transit history alongside the operating machinery that pulls the glamorous transportation through town.

The Financial District holds three impressive landmarks. The Embarcadero Center, the Bank of America building – so tall its roof sometimes disappears in the fog, and the distinctive Transamerica Pyramid, with 48 floors the tallest building in San Francisco.

"South of Market," or SoMa, is a focal point for art galleries, cafés, nightclubs and local theaters. The San Francisco Museum of Modern Art (tel: 415-357-4000; open daily) spearheads the attractions, which also include the Yerba Buena Gardens, the Center for the Arts, the Cartoon Art Museum, the Museum of the California Historical Society and the Ansel Adams Center for Photography. The Asian Art Museum moved to the nearby Civic Center in 2003. It contains 10,000 artifacts dating back 3,500 years.

Mission Street heads south into the heart of the Mission district, San Francisco's melting pot of Latin American cultures. The thick adobe walls of Mission Dolores, built in 1776, still form the oldest building in San Francisco, which can be visited.

To the west lies the celebrated gay community of Castro. Same-sex couples and rainbow flags fill the streets lined with table-hopping bars. It's a lively, fun and light-hearted area, regardless of your gender.

Farther west is the Haight-Ashbury district. Haight Street was once so gaudy and bizarre that tour buses full of goggle-eyed tourists ran up and down it. Like most such radical departures from the social norm, the hippie experiment fell victim to time and fashion. The neighborhood retains its anti-establishment roots, but today piercing shops and tattoo parlors replace flower power. It's still a fun stretch, however, with great shopping and a wide range of inexpensive restaurants and cafés.

Golden Gate Park (tel: 415-831-2700), 3 miles (5 km) long and almost half a mile wide, consists of tree groves dotted with lakes, meadows, windmills and dells. Despite the thousands of visitors, it's easy to find tranquility here. In addition to peace, the Conservatory of Flowers offers sweet scents and botanical beauty, and the Music Concourse holds Sunday concerts.

The California Academy of Sciences (tel: 415-750-7145; open daily) includes animal dioramas, 16,000 specimens of marine life at the Steinhart Aquarium and a laser light show at the Morrison Planetarium. The Japan-

ese Tea Garden claims to be the birthplace of the fortune cookie.

The beautiful and neo-classical Legion of Honor (tel: 415-863-3330; open Tues–Sun) is unmissable. At the entrance is one of five bronze casts of Rodin's *The Thinker*.

The Golden Gate Bridge extends beyond the wonderful Golden Gate National Recreation Area. A promenade goes through Crissy Field, an airfield-turned-picnic area that belongs to the 1,480-acre (600-hectare) Presidio. In it stands the Plaster Palace, the classic rococo rotunda of the Palace of Fine Arts, housing the hands-on exhibits of the Exploratorium (tel: 415-EXPLORE). ❑

LEFT: a cable car trundles up Nob Hill; the landmark Transamerica Pyramid was ridiculed when it was built in 1972.
RIGHT: follow the seagull signs for the best drive in town; Pacific Heights' Haas-Lilienthal House; the fabulous Golden Gate Bridge.

SHRINE
DRIVE-THRU TREE
5000   HEIGHT 275 FT.
21 FT.   CIR. 64 FT.
YERS FLAT, CALIFORNIA

SAN FRANCISCO TO OREGON

*The Pacific Coast Highway threads its way
past golden beaches, hot-tub hideaways,
good wineries and the tallest living things on earth*

F rom San Francisco to the town of Crescent City, which is itself about half an hour's drive from the Oregon border, is 363 miles (584 km). Coastal beaches, wineries and redwood forests are the attractions of this beautiful journey, with trees so massive you can even drive through a few of them.

A trio of "goldens" marks the contributions of **San Francisco ㉕** to the Pacific Coast Highway, as Highway 1 passes straight through the city's Golden Gate Park, across the Golden Gate Bridge, and flirts with the southeastern edge of the Golden Gate National Recreation Area. The pretty little harbor of **Sausalito ㉖** is located just off the highway, over the fabled golden bridge, with a turn-off to the right. The waterside shops, the warrens of pricey but perfect boutiques and the houses perched behind them on a steep slope draw comparisons to Mediterranean villas of the Riviera. As there is little to do except stroll around or eat and drink, Sausalito might best be visited on a day trip by ferry from San Francisco, leaving you free to cruise westward toward the coast, passing near **Mount Tamalpais**, with its gorgeous views of the city in the far distance, the giant redwoods of 300-acre (120-hectare) **Muir Woods**; and **Stinson Beach**, the city's favorite destination on the few occasions it gets hot enough to swim. The coast road bypasses the town of **Bolinas**, on a thin sliver of a peninsula, which tries so hard not to attract visitors that a hard-core body of locals keeps stealing the highway signs.

The gorgeous **Point Reyes National Seashore** stretches northward for miles along a peninsula off which is the **Point Reyes Lighthouse** (visitor center open on weekends). On the way, the highway passes through tiny Olema; north of here, it's possible to make a short (dead-end) diversion into the peninsula to attractive **Inverness**, which has a couple of pleasant eating places.

Coastal drama

The road then travels lazily through pretty, upscale Marin County ("hot tub capital of the world") and out the northern end. A carved wooden fisherman in a bright yellow waterproof jacket sits outside a shop as the road enters **Bodega**, which has a prominent sushi restaurant in midtown.

It's no coincidence that Alfred Hitchcock filmed his 1963 movie *The Birds* around **Bodega Bay ㉗**, where hundreds of bird species can be found. Brown pelicans are especially abundant.

After **Sonoma Coast State Beach**, another really dramatic portion of the California coast begins, where Rivers End sits overlooking the mouth of the Russian River at **Jenner**. For miles, Highway 1 snakes around the canyon at ascending levels. The top of a subsequent canyon has been plugged with stone, making a

LEFT: bikers love this big tree.
BELOW: Russian chapel, Fort Ross.

bridge on which to site the road. The unfenced parts of the road are genuinely disconcerting; not a drive you'd want to make on a foggy night when – in any case – the fabulous views would be wasted.

The road goes right past the timbered stockade of **Fort Ross** (tel: 707-847-3286; open daily), but for history buffs it's worth exploring the cannon-studded fort with its church and blockhouses – if only to muse on how those early 19th-century Russian otter hunters withstood the rugged winters in flimsy wooden buildings on one of the windiest parts of the coast. So well fortified were they that their Indian and Spanish neighbors left them strictly alone until, in 1842, after 30 years of relentless otter hunting (for furs), they sold the place to rancher John Sutter and left. Between the fort and the sea is the former home of rancher G.W. Call, who farmed the area from 1873, shipping vast cargoes of potatoes, cattle, sheep and wood products to San Francisco in his own coastal boats. The rear garden is a popular picnic spot.

Look but don't swim

Back on the highway, the road descends to a dramatic cove before ascending once more. **Stillwater Cove Ranch** (tel: 707-847-3227) atop the hill is a delight – imaginative architecture and a stylish lobby whose gift shop features Ansel Adams books, paintings of blue cranes and stuffed-wool racoons (whose real-life counterparts live in the hotel grounds). A number of sensationally situated inns, lodges and ranches can be found around here, among them **Timber Cove Inn** (tel: 707-847-3231), "a place to be in love," according to the owners. They could be right, if its giant stone fireplace in a high-ceilinged lounge facing a beautiful bay is any indication.

At **Salt Point State Park**, the trees march down to the water's edge. Off the highway, other beaches abound – such as Stump Beach and Fisk Mill Cove, the former being closer to the road, though suitably remote. Much of the time, you'll find yourself a solitary visitor, as swimming is unsafe because of rip tides and what the coast guards call "sleeper waves." **Stewarts Point** was once a "doghole" for schooners, so-called because of its anchorages, so tiny "only a dog could fit into them." This region was once part of the 5,000-acre (2,025-hectare) Rancho de Herman sheep farm, and sheep still graze south of **The Sea Ranch**, which – apart from being an irresistibly luxurious resort – is also a self-contained community with its own post office where locals come to pick up their mail. It's a popular place for weddings and other celebrations, for which there is a separate function space beside the ocean.

The Annapolis Winery announces itself with a sign at the beginning of a road of the same name, after which come Pebble Beach, Stengel Beach and 8 more miles (13 km) of a winding two-lane road. Signs warn of deer crossing, and a bridge across the Gualala River marks the end of Sonoma County.

Mendonoma

Mendonoma, a name derived from the adjoining counties of Sonoma and Mendocino, identifies the coastal region between the Russian River at Jenner and the Navarro River, north of Point Arena. They'd like to share one telephone area code, but sadly the split was recently defined here at the Gualala River.

A heterogeneous mix of Russians, Germans and Spaniards settled **Gualala** (pronounced *wah-**lah**-lah*) in the 1800s, which by the middle of the last century had four sawmills and four bars. Wells Fargo and Western Union had offices in the Gualala Hotel, built by the town's founder in 1903 when rooms with bath and ocean view cost $5. The writer Jack London stayed here a century ago, and things don't appear to have altered much. Since the last mill closed, upscale tourism has filled the gap.

Map on page 354

Russian Orthodox priest at Fort Ross.

BELOW:
Bodega Bay
at dawn.

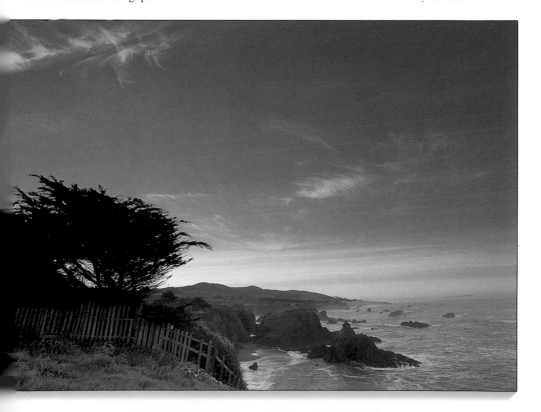

On the first Saturday of each month, people come from far and wide to attend the rummage sale in the **Gualala Arts Center**, where they sometimes find pleasant surprises. A recent visitor ran across a small wooden owl collage her mother had made years before and which, as part of her vast collection of owl pictures, figurines, greeting cards and jigsaw puzzles, had been sold for charity at her death. "I picked it up out of habit thinking fondly of Mom and how this was something she would really have liked," she told the *Coast Observer*. "Words cannot describe the feeling that came over me when I turned it over and found, in Mom's unmistakable handwriting, *Put together by me, 12/15/77*."

A distinctive wooden Olde West structure with a tower marks **Anchor Bay**. Farther along, a carved blue-striped white wooden horse sits in a field, after which the coast-hugging, sometimes lonely road seems mostly deserted. Fifteen miles (24 km) of winding two-lane highway allow ample time to contemplate that state law decreeing that slow-moving vehicles must use a turn-off if five or more vehicles back up behind them.

One of the truly great coastal experiences is **Point Arena Lighthouse** ㉘, the tip of which can be spotted at the beginning of the 2-mile (3-km) diversion. A classically beautiful 111-foot (34-meter) high white tower with 145 steps, it replaced an earlier lighthouse damaged by the 1906 San Francisco earthquake. Its 2-ton (1,800-kg) French-made Fresnel lens (floating on a tub of mercury) was itself replaced in the 1970s with an aircraft-type beacon. It is maintained by a non-profit group of local citizens and takes 5 minutes to climb to the top.

BELOW: shave and a haircut, Mendocino.

Miles of open pasture dotted with ramshackle barns and grazing cows follow Point Arena. Then the road dips, turns, climbs and dives, punctuated by fancy hostelries with such names as the Inn at Schoolyard Creek and Little River Inn. These types of bed-and-breakfast inns, plus restaurants serving high-level "California cuisine," are also features of tiny **Elk** and **Albion**, pretty roadside communities on either side of the Nararro River, with sloping tracks down to the beach. Soon after crossing the river, the highway twists and turns around high cliffs before descending to a leafy stretch past **Van Damme State Park** (which contains a "pygmy forest" of pines and cypresses), offering occasional glimpses of the sea. Keep an eye out for the colorful steel sculptures on the lawn of the Stevenswood restaurant to the right.

Mendocino

The lovely old town of **Mendocino** ㉙, which lacks motels, supermarkets and fast-food joints, is one of the most admired places on the coast and thus is usually filled with tourists, most of whom are just passing through. If you choose to stay the night after they have gone, you'll be rewarded with great restaurants (some with health-obsessed menus) and numerous small bed-and-breakfast inns, as well as art galleries and a Fetzer Vineyards tasting room adjoining the Mendocino Hotel. The entire village, established by New England whalers, is on the National Register of Historic Places. Among several Victorian homes, the 1854 **Ford House** and the 1861 **Kelley House** (both open daily in summer) each contain small museums. Be warned: parking spaces in Mendocino are as rare as gold dust.

North of Caspar, the delightful **Mendocino Coast Botanical Gardens** (tel: 707-964-4352; open daily) are worth a stop if only to walk through the aromatic pine forest to the sea, enjoying the interplay between light and shade. Plants can be bought here, too. Next comes Noyo Harbor, once the biggest lumber port between Eureka and San Francisco and now a marina for sports fishing boats along with a "fisherman's village" and plenty of restaurants.

Shipwrecks and microbreweries

An 1820 shipwreck led to the founding of **Fort Bragg ㉚**, when treasure seekers came to loot the wreckage and discovered the redwoods. A fort was built and the Bureau of Indian Affairs established a reservation for the Pomo Indians. Lumber mills sprang up, along with a railroad to transport their product. When the 1906 earthquake devastated so much of San Francisco, it was Fort Bragg's mills that provided the wood for rebuilding. The famous old "**Skunk Train**" (tel: 800-960-8099) that once carried timber across the mountains to the sawmill at Willits has been a tourist favorite for years, and it still follows the same picturesque route along the Noyo River and through redwood groves.

What remains of the original fort, along with surviving Victorian buildings, can be seen one block east of Main Street (Highway 1) near the Skunk Train depot at Laurel and Franklin. Both the Guest House Museum (local history) and the North Coast Brewing Company (free tours, tel: 707-964-2739), one of America's best microbreweries, are on Main Street. The town also blossoms with nurseries, one of which grows millions of trees for reforestation projects.

Map on page 354

The "Skunk Train" at Fort Bragg once carried timber; now it transports tourists through enormous redwood groves.

BELOW: Mendocino.

TIP

If you don't feel like
making the fairly
arduous 4–5-hour
round-trip drive to see
the hidden attractions
of the Lost Coast, you
can hire a guide in
Ferndale; inquire
locally for details.

Fort Bragg is an unpretentious working town refreshingly free of the leisure chic that pervades the surrounding areas. After Fort Bragg, 22 miles (35 km) of incessantly twisting and winding tree-shaded, narrow road (30 mph/48 kph is the most you'll manage) are interspersed with sections of freeway. Gift shops selling carved wooden figures (Big Foot is a favorite) and gimmicky attractions such as the circular house carved from a single redwood log and **Confusion Hill** (tel: 707-925-6456) vie for attention. The latter really is pretty weird: water runs uphill here; there's also a wooden shack in which a golf ball climbs a slope and a chair prevents you from getting up without using your arms.

The guy who bought Confusion Hill discovered these apparent paradoxes when he first tried to build his home on the hillside, and although some of the effects are obviously optical illusions, the owner says there are things he still hasn't figured out. There's also a funicular ride up the mountain.

The Lost Coast

A few miles north of **Westport**, Highway 1 takes a final look at the sea before heading 25 miles (40 km) inland. Here, it merges with US 101 at Leggett and – apart from a brief stretch near Eureka – disappears forever. The relatively inaccessible (and often unpaved) coastal road leads up through the evocatively named Sinkyone Wilderness and beyond, onto the justly celebrated **Lost Coast**, which has gloriously and almost uniquely escaped development. It's an area of "black sand beaches and old-growth forests on a wall of windswept peaks," as one writer noted. There are 80 miles (129 km) of trails and six campgrounds under the aegis of the Bureau of Land Management (tel: 707-822-7648).

Once projected for an extension of Highway 1, the coast can be visited via a

BELOW: rustic
residents of the
Lost Coast.

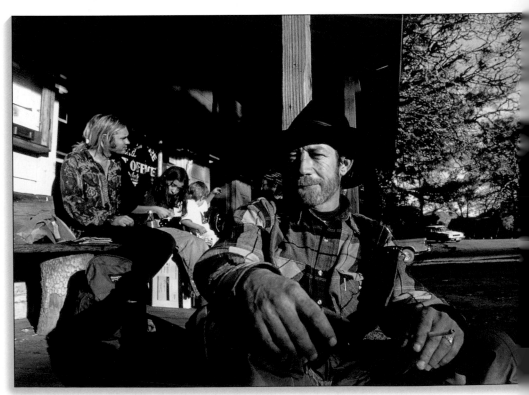

loop road picked up at the town of Weott, north of Leggett. The narrow side road crosses the Mattole River at Honeydew, heads through Petrolia, the site of the state's first but disappointingly unproductive oil strike, and follows the coast north to Ferndale, where it veers inland again to rejoin US 101 (*see page 361 for more about the Lost Coast*).

Avenue of the Giants

South again, Highway 1 merges into US 101 at **Leggett** ("a fern-carpeted setting," claims one local resident), followed by **Garberville**, a pleasant little town known for its good manners and even better marijuana. Containing several restaurants and motels, Garberville is an ideal place to break your journey before heading into redwood country proper. Farther north, at **Phillipsville**, the 31-mile (50-km) **Avenue of the Giants ㉛** offers an irresistible alternative to US 101, to which it runs parallel, allowing occasional on-off access. There are trees here more than 300 feet (91 meters) high and up to 20 feet (6 meters) in diameter. "From them come silence," wrote John Steinbeck.

A handful of buildings are all that remain of two small towns that once straddled the route until they were washed away by floods in 1964. Otherwise, the route in this stupendously awesome 50,000-acre (20,250-hectare) forest is untrammeled by human life. A series of small groves are dedicated to various groups and individuals that have fought to preserve this magnificent enclave. They are places for contemplation. "We do not see nature with our eyes," wrote William Hazlitt, "but with our understandings and our hearts." Many of the trees on the east side were planted in the 1980s under reforestation projects. Near the town of **Myers Flat** is the **Drive-Thru Tree**, a favorite with children and

BELOW: the Avenue of the Giants is a scenic drive of many miles.

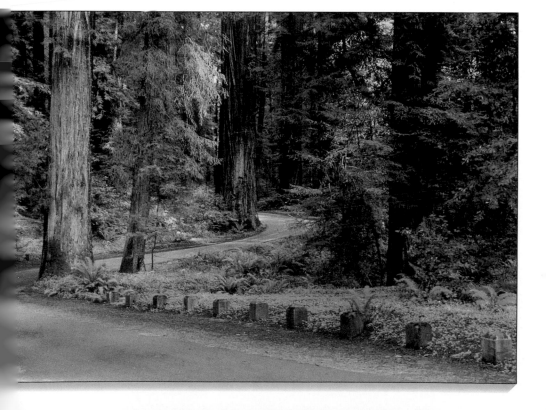

tourists. Before Weott, the **Humboldt Redwoods State Park Visitor Center** (tel: 707-946-2263) is filled with explanatory exhibits about the magnificent redwoods, which attract tree fans from around the world.

All about trees

I never saw a discontented tree. They grip the ground as though they liked it, and though fast rooted they travel about as far as we do.
— JOHN MUIR

Redwood has long been prized for its density and deep color, and despite slumps in the building industry and competition from more common trees such as cedar, it remains in demand. The logging industry, born in tandem with the Gold Rush, made hardly a dent in the redwood belt until the advent of power saws in the 1940s, which made it possible to clear acres in a single day. It takes 40 years to raise a stand of redwoods for such uses as pulp and press board, and 500 years to develop the fine grain and blood-red tint that have made the wood so popular: virgin forest remains at a premium. Conservationists estimate that trees are logged at two and a half times the rate of regeneration.

The company town of **Scotia**, built by the Pacific Lumber Company in 1869 entirely of ancient redwood, has a logging museum and fisheries exhibit and offers a self-guided sawmill tour (tel: 707-764-2222; closed weekends). This nature trail through a "Preservation Forest" is a skillful public relations ploy intended to ease visitors gently into the conception of this magnificent forest as a well-managed renewable resource. John Muir was not a friend to lumbermen. "Any fool can destroy trees," he commented. "They cannot defend themselves or run away... It took more than 3,000 years to make some of the oldest of the sequoias, trees that are still standing in perfect strength and beauty, waving and singing in the mighty forests of the Sierra."

BELOW: haunting Humboldt County.

The redwoods inspire not only passing tourists, but also the entire livelihood of the Humboldt community. Sculptors carve timbers into life-sized grizzly bears for sale at the roadside. Others, for a pretty hefty admission fee, show off the stout trunks growing in their backyards. Huge logging trucks carrying both raw timber and finished boards along the highway are a constant reminder that the trees in this area are an economic necessity as well as a natural wonder.

Fortuna's **Depot Museum** features local logging and railroading history. Located on a back road between Fortuna and Eureka is minuscule **Loleta**, celebrated for cheese and ice cream production. Its factory, which starred in the 1982 movie *Hallowe'en III: the Season of the Witch,* makes supermarket ice cream in loads of varieties for 11 different companies.

Fascinating Ferndale

The fascination of **Ferndale** ❸, on the Eel River west of US 101 (reached by turning west off the highway just north of Fortuna), stems from its large numbers of garishly hued Victorian stores and houses, many of which have been converted into enticing bed-and-breakfasts. (The Creekside Inn advertises "Bed and No Breakfast" but does serve afternoon tea). The whole town, designated a State Historical Landmark, naturally attracts tourists by the thousand. The elaborately turreted and gabled **Gingerbread Mansion Inn** on Berding Street is outstanding, and the town's old-

Map
on page
354

est building, the 18-room **Shaw House Inn**, is fashioned after Nathaniel Hawthorne's *House of the Seven Gables*. The year-round mild climate encourages productive gardening, and one is apt to see tamed cypresses shaped like giant gumdrops, or other evidence of extensive topiary work. At the head of Main Street, the 110-year-old **Victorian Inn** (tel: 888-589-1808) accurately boasts of its "luxurious comfort and exquisite craftsmanship;" also notable is the **Ferndale Emporium**, farther down the street, which serves genteel afternoon teas from Thursday to Saturday.

A top-hatted driver offers rides around town in a horse and carriage, while there's a genuine soda fountain on Main Street. Understandably, Ferndale attracts moviemakers, who use its setting for movie and TV dramas. Check out the **Kinetic Sculpture Race Museum** (tel: 707-786-9259; open daily) with its people-powered models used in the annual three-day race from Arcata.

Wildcat Road

The drive south along the Lost Coast from Ferndale follows the old stagecoach route that's known locally as Wildcat Road, climbs high into the hills and then, after 30 miles (48 km) of twists and turns, descends to cross the Bear River and arrives at the defunct community of Capetown. Off the deserted black sand beach is the immense Sugarloaf Rock and nearby Steamboat Rock, which resembles a big tanker stranded at sea.

The **Cape Mendocino Lighthouse** – replaced in 1951 with an automatic beacon – had at least nine ships wrecked off this rugged shore during its 65-year history. But it's not necessary to drive the 4- to 5-hour round trip to the Lost Coast if you hire the knowledgeable local guide and historian who has been trans-

BELOW:
Gingerbread
Mansion Inn,
Ferndale.

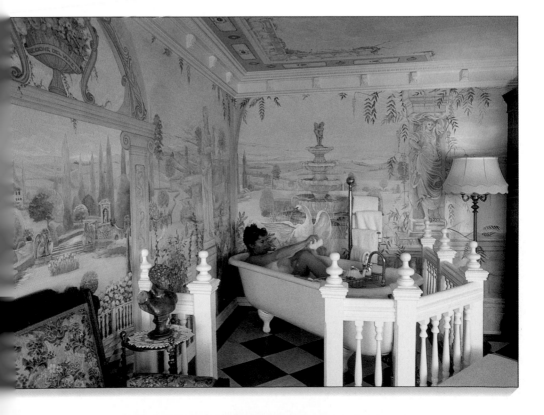

porting tourist groups around the region in his minibus for many years; it's worth checking while you're in Ferndale to see if he's available.

The biggest coastal city on the California coast north of San Francisco, **Eureka** ㉝ (pop. 26,000) and its **Old Town** area on the waterfront has often stood in for the Bay Area city in movies. It has been anchored since 1922 by the **Eureka Inn** (tel: 877-275-7814), a massive Tudor Revival mansion whose early guests included Laurel and Hardy, Shirley Temple, John Barrymore and Britain's Winston Churchill, who stopped by Eureka to visit an old friend who was editing the local paper. The town's distinctive 1886 **Carson Mansion** – built by a lumber baron with a yen for gables, towers and turrets – is generally regarded as the handsomest Victorian building in the state, if not in the entire West. It is now a private club.

At the **Blue Ox Millworks** (tel: 707-444-3437; closed Sun), a working Victorian sawmill, visitors can watch craftsmen at work and see how much of the characteristic "gingerbread" ornamentation for such houses was crafted. The old Carnegie Library, with its wonderful balconies and redwood pillars, has been converted into an art museum; other attractions include the **Humboldt Bay Maritime Museum** with its lighthouse memorabilia, and the **Clarke Memorial Museum** with its collection of weapons, Native American crafts and Victoriana.

Across the bay on a peninsula is the famous **Samoa Cookhouse** (tel: 707-442-1659; open daily), which is the last remaining example of the 1890s lumber camp cookhouses, whose rules included eating as much as you could for a fixed price and helping yourself to anything within reach as long as one foot remained on the ground. Today, huge meals are served family style at long tables – and the same rules apply.

BELOW: Eureka's Carson Mansion is one of the finest Victorian houses in California.

EUREKA TO OREGON

Just north of Eureka, with a reputation for being "the Galapagos of North America," **Arcata** is famous for its birdwatching opportunities. Its variety of bird life is greater than anywhere else in the state, and Marbled Godwit, White-tailed Kite and Cinnamon Teal are frequently observed. The Chamber of Commerce on G. Street, two blocks north of the plaza, publishes a free leaflet detailing all the different bird types and where to find them, as well as a self-guided walking map of old Victorian homes. Such establishments as Rookery Books and a coffee company advertising "our coffee is for the birds," are an indication of the level of interest in our feathered friends.

Birdwatchers from all over the country converge on the town for the annual Godwit Days in April to go on field trips and attend workshops with such intriguing titles as "Advanced Identification," and "Intermediate Owls." Adjoining the filtration plant on Arcata Bay (which produces more than half of California's oyster crop) is the main center of birding activity, the **Marsh and Wildlife Sanctuary**. Aleutian geese, once down to less than 1,000 in number, are now abundant after years of protection under the Endangered Species Act.

The town of Arcata, founded by a group of miners from the Trinity River region in 1849, grew up around the **Jacoby Building** on the plaza. It was erected in 1857 of masonry, when wood usually sufficed, by a far-sighted merchant whose pack trains serviced the gold-mines upriver. Elegantly restored and refitted, it now houses stylish shops, a rail-road museum and two of the town's best restaurants. On the ground floor is a store selling the stylish (and expensive) glassware made by Fire and Light, owned by a local group who conceived the company to take advantage of the huge amounts of recycled glass available. Their small factory offers demonstrations of the glass-making process.

Humboldt State University's **Natural History Museum** exhibits everything from butterflies to dinosaur tails. **McKinleyville**, the fastest growing town in Humboldt County, is also the nearest one to the misnamed Eureka-Arcata airport. It claims to have the world's tallest single-tree totem pole (at the shopping center). Its 30-acre (12-hectare) **Azalea Reserve**, which blooms in spring, can be reached via a trail off North Bank Road (Central Avenue exit from US 101; for information, tel: 707-488-2041).

Map on page 354

A fine place to meet good swimmers.

Moonshine Beach and Wedding Rock

At **Moonshine Beach**, just north of the airport, Highway 1 detaches itself from US 101, under which it has been submerged for the past 100 miles (161 km). For a delightful stretch of 20 miles (32 km) or so, it runs along the coast through the lovely clifftop village of **Trinidad ㉞** (pop. 500), named by a Spanish explorer in 1775 and the site of a small museum. It is also the last gas station for 30 miles (48 km). Farther north is the entrance of **Patrick's Point State Park**, named for an Indian scout who settled here in 1851. Seals can be admired basking on the rocks off Rocky Point, and at low tide there are tide pools to explore.

BELOW: gathering seaweed is a good test for would-be mermaids.

The lands within one mile of the Klamath River comprise the Yurok Reservation. Near Wedding Rock is the site of an old Yurok village, preserved with its sweat lodge, ceremonial dance pit and simple plank houses with circular doorways, through which women were obliged to enter backwards.

BELOW: pretty as a picture of a picnic.

Farther north, **Wedding Rock** is a popular site for marriages conducted to the accompaniment of crashing waves below. The rock got its name from the park's first caretaker, Vieggo Andersen, whose marriage there to his housekeeper in 1933 began a popular custom. Scenes from Steven Spielberg's *Lost World* were filmed in the parking lot. Nearer to the highway, by the site of the old Yurok village, is an old canoe hollowed out by fire from a tree trunk, which sits near a native garden of indigenous plants. Camping is allowed and *yurts* (highly comfortable, wooden-floor tents) can be rented by the night.

About 25 miles (40 km) north of Patrick's Point on the highway before Orick, the **Redwood Information Center** (tel: 707-464-6101) distributes free maps depicting the various trails and camping sites of the redwood forests that extend northward from Crescent City. Seldom-seen black bears roam through the parks – as well as Roosevelt elk, which occasionally emerge onto the highway (don't get too close!) – but for the most part it's trees, trees, trees – the tallest living things on earth, which can reach heights of more than 360 feet (110 meters). Fossil records indicate that millions of years ago they blanketed the northern hemisphere when the climate was warmer and wetter. Today, only isolated patches of redwoods remain – mainly in California and China.

Judging by the stalls along the road, the main industry of **Orick**, once a major logging center, appears to be the sale of "burl slabs," which are grotesquely shaped redwood roots. Check out the venerable Palm Café and Motel (tel: 707-488-3381). When driving along, take the signposted Newton B. Drury Scenic Parkway through **Prairie Creek Redwoods Park**, a long avenue of incredibly tall trees. Somewhere along the way, you'll probably see the resident herd of Roosevelt elk, which has a tendency to graze beside the highway. These animals should be treated with respect because they can be unpredictably dangerous. A worthwhile sidetrip is to drive down the narrow, pot-holed Coastal Trail along **Golden Bluffs Beach** through dense woodland to **Fern Canyon**; a ravine bordered on either side by sheer, fern-carpeted cliffs.

Trees of Mystery

For a few miles before **Klamath ㉟**, US 101 runs alongside the broad **Klamath River**, crossed by a bridge marked at each end by life-size statues of golden bears. For a spectacular view of where the river meets the ocean, take the Requa Road on your left to an overlook 600 feet (183 meters) above the water. (This side road dead-ends after a few miles.) Gold mines farther up the Klamath River were once served via Klamath from steamers that brought supplies up the coast from San Francisco. Today, the river is popular for jetboat tours from Klamath to see such wildlife as elk and bears. Huge "cartoon" figures herald the **Trees of Mystery** (tel: 800-638-3389; open daily). A trail leads past some unusual groupings: nine trees growing from one root structure to form the so-called **Cathedral Tree**; a dozen others growing from a single Sitka Spruce trunk. Admission is charged to each trail, but the absorbing museum, with its large collection of Indian costumes and crafts, is free.

US 101 hugs the coast around many attractive bays

before beginning a lengthy climb where traffic along the narrow road is controlled by solar-powered lights. Tall trees flank most of the final 10 miles (16 km) into Crescent City, until the sea comes into view once again just before town.

Tallest living things on earth

Crescent City ❻, named for the shape of the bay on which it sits, sprawls somewhat unattractively behind an interesting harbor replete with restaurants, a seafood market and a **Marine Mammal Center** where distressed seals and sea lions are rehabilitated. West of the harbor, the **Battery Point Lighthouse** (tel: 707-464-3089; open Wed–Sun) can be visited at low tide and contains a museum with photographs of some of the shipwrecks off this treacherous coast. When John Muir visited Crescent City in 1896, he went out on a logging train to see "the work of ruin going on." Some of the trees, he observed, were up to 200 ft (61 meters) high and 20 ft (6 meters) in diameter and yet two men could chop them down in a single day. His experiences doubtless led him to fight for the redwoods' preservation. Crescent City has named a shopping center after Jedediah Smith, the fur trapper who first explored the region in the 1820s, and after whom the vast **Jedediah Smith Redwoods State Park** to the east is named. The spectacular and turbulent Smith River, which runs through 300 miles (483 km) of wild scenery, offers white-water rafting between soaring canyon walls. At **Gasquet**, on US 199, which runs through the **Smith River National Recreation Area**, a Forest Service office (tel: 707-457-3131) provides maps, general information and the opportunity to book a night in a remote fire-lookout cabin atop Bear Basin Butte. Whether you head north from Crescent City or Gasquet, in less than 25 miles (40 km), you'll be in **Oregon**. ❑

This huge tribute to lumberjack Paul Bunyan signals the entrance to the Trees of Mystery.

BELOW: parade at Klamath's Yurok Salmon Festival.

OREGON TO WASHINGTON

Oregon's rugged coastline stretches for 400 miles, offering wilderness glimpses of deer, elk and bald eagles, before heading into the state of Washington for more of the same

Trusty US 101 trundles all the way up the Oregon coast and into the state of Washington, serving the same function that Highway 1 served in California – offering some of the best coastal scenery in the United States. Rural and more rugged than much of its southern neighbor, Oregon's section of US 101, signposted as the Pacific Coast Scenic Highway, offers tantalizing views of elk and bald eagles.

BROOKINGS-HARBOR TO WALDPORT

The southern part of the Oregon Coast – the **Siskiyou Coast** – begins calmly enough; a drive taking the car through relatively peaceful farmland after the turbulence of the Smith River near the state border. Ships pop up on dry land, first a huge one beached beside the appropriately named Ship Ashore Motel, and then an old tugboat beached and converted into a souvenir store just south of **Brookings-Harbor ③**. This is the town (although technically "towns": Brookings is the larger of the two side-by-side communities) where the sports fishing fleet anchors, and it also contains the local Visitor Information Bureau (tel: 800-535-9469).

At the mouth of the Chetco River, Brookings is a popular retirement spot because of its reputation as being in the "banana belt," with winter temperatures often reaching 65°F (18°C). The technical explanation for its moderate climate is that the town's southeast to northwest geographical layout combines with constant low-pressure thermal troughs that pull down the highly compressed air following a storm system. One consequence is that the region produces most of the country's Easter lilies, and visitors swarm in to see **Azalea Park** (tel: 541-469-1100) in the springtime when the flowers are in bloom. There's an Azalea Festival on Memorial Day weekend. Some of the most spectacular scenery is to be found in coastal Samuel H. **Boardman State Park** just south of town. March brings daffodils, May the wild azaleas and July the snow lilies, while every month of the year brings eager photographers.

Anyone for gas?

As Oregon's coastline stretches for 400 miles (644 km), you won't be in the state for long before discovering that state law prohibits customers pumping their own gas, ostensibly to "boost the economy" by providing more jobs, but also because it is supposedly unsafe. This particular part of the Oregon Statute unpopular with locals), cites 20 potential hazards, including the fact that customers are not trained in the safe handling of flammable liquids and that exposure o toxic fumes is a health hazard.

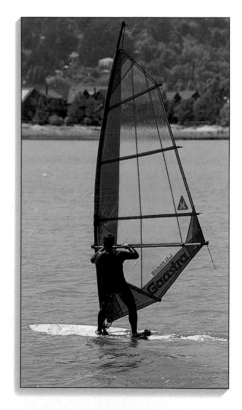

LEFT: Yaquina Head Lighthouse, Oregon. **BELOW:** windsuring is popular with Washingtonians.

North of town past the large, green barns of the South Coast Lumber Company, and near the **Harris Beach State Park**, are numerous parking bays beside the highway from which to gaze at the ocean. Harris is one of 30 places on the Oregon coast designated as a whale-watching site, and is attended by trained volunteers on winter mornings to assist visitors.

Kissing Rock dates its name from 1850, when prospectors discovered that the sands surrounding the rock were sprinkled with gold dust.

Around 100 gray whales spend the summer feeding off the Siskiyou coast; the smaller mammals often nursing a calf. Larger gray whales can reach 45 feet (14 meters) in length – bigger than a Greyhound bus – and weigh up to 45 tons (45,720 kg). Their annual migration between the Bering Sea and Mexico is a gruelling 10,000-mile (16,000-km) round trip at a speed of around 5 mph (8 kph) heading southbound.

Kissing Rock

US 101 soon crosses the **Thomas Creek Bridge**, the state's highest at 345 feet (105 meters), then a string of beaches begins just before Pistol River. The best of these are around the rather eye-catching **Kissing Rock**, popular with windsurfers, between Meyers Creek and Gold Beach. The latter's name dates from the 1850s, when prospectors discovered that the sands around the mouth of the Rogue River were salted with gold dust.

BELOW:
woman casting her nets wide and contributing to the local economy.

Today, several companies offer excursions in powerful hydro jetboats up the river, whose upper reaches encompass dramatic canyons hundreds of feet deep. Sport fishing for salmon and steelhead trout can be arranged, as well as ocean fishing, and horses can be rented for riding on the beach. Stop for an espresso at **Gold Beach**, where you'll see the large mural on the side of the Soakery Coffee House, and make time to visit the Curry County Historical Museum

Map on page 354

(tel: 541-247-6396; open Tues–Sat afternoons in summer). There are more farms and more cows north of town and there's even a pastoral community farther north called Denmark where, appropriately enough, cows appear to be the only visible inhabitants.

Seven miles (11 km) north of the Rogue River at **Nesika Beach**, the highway levels with the shoreline. Low-lying, tree-covered hills flank the right-hand side and marshland sits between road and sea. Massive moss and lichen-covered rocks stick out of the water, and around **Humbug Mountain** the scenery is particularly stunning. Towering mountains taper down to the road, which flanks a series of bays enlivened by crashing white surf. "The mountains are fountains of men as well as of rivers, of glaciers, of fertile soil," wrote John Muir. "The great poets, philosophers, prophets, able men whose thoughts and deeds have moved the world, have come down from the mountains – mountain dwellers have grown strong there with the forest trees in Nature's workshop."

Westernmost city

Keep an eye out on the right for the painted dinosaur outside the **Prehistoric Gardens** in the rainforest. **Port Orford ❸❽** ("a jewel like coastal village perched on scenic bluffs," wrote one observer) is the westernmost city in the contiguous United States, and was a major lumber shipping port more than a century ago. Just offshore, past the battered shack that houses the Crazy Norwegians Café, is a wooded island called **Battle Rock**. In 1851, the island's original party of settlers was besieged by local Indians who resented their claim to the land. A month later, a larger white group arrived and took possession.

Take a lingering look at Port Orford's lovely bay, because it will be your last

BELOW: logging pond full of rich timber destined for a large lumber mill.

uninterrupted view of the ocean for nearly 100 miles (161 km), although frequent "Coastal Access" signs dot the highway. Northeast of town on Elk River Road is the **Elk River Fish Hatchery**, where salmon smelts are raised.

Lighthouses and lazy countryside

A 6-mile (10-km) side trip can be made to the cliffs of **Cape Blanco** to inspect the 1870 lighthouse (tel: 541-756-0100; open Thur–Mon in summer), which sits 245 feet (75 meters) above the sea and is operated by the Bureau of Land Management. Next comes **Langlois**, with its half a dozen antique shops located in serene countryside filled with cows and sheep. In the surrounding hills are many lonely sheep ranches. Miles of bright yellow gorse line the approach to **Bandon ㊴**, twice destroyed by fire in the last century; a brick chimney on the site of the old bakery stands as a memorial just off the highway. Artists' homes and studios along with craft shops cluster around Bandon's **Old Town** area. The historical society's museum includes an exhibit about cranberry cultivation. This has been taking place in nearby bogs for more than a century, ever since the early settlers learned the technique from the Indians. The town celebrates with a Cranberry Festival every fall, and cranberry farms can be toured by appointment. Near Bandon is another lighthouse, the **Coquille River Lighthouse**.

Coos Bay is a major lumber shipping port, and the town itself, with warehouses and stacked timber lining the road, is not very attractive. Back in 1850, Asa Simpson established a sawmill and shipyard here, which built about 50 vessels before the end of the century. Tours can be made of the giant Weyerhauser Lumber Mill (where trees are stripped, sliced and shaped) and also of the **Oregon Connection** factory, where myrtlewood logs are fashioned into bowls, goblets and other products. To the east is **Golden and Silver Falls State Park** with its 100-ft (30-meter) waterfalls, and on the coast, south of the fishing village of **Charleston**, is **Shore Acres State Park**, once the gardens of the spacious house of lumber baron Louis J. Simpson, son of the legendary Captain Asa M. Simpson. New Englander Simpson founded an Oregon lumbering and shipbuilding empire.

Dune walk

Across the long bridge spanning the Hayes Inlet is Coos Bay's neighbor, **North Bend**, where the useful Visitors Information Bureau (tel: 541-756-4613) sits opposite the ancient steam locomotive outside the Coos County Historical Museum (tel: 541-756-6320; open Tues–Sat).

The **Oregon Dunes National Recreation Area ㊵** begins at North Bend, a huge expanse of sand that blocks easy access to the sea for 40 miles (64 km) of coast. There are 11 different places offering beach access, at least one of which, **Spineel** (watch for the highway sign) offers a chance to rent dune buggies (tel: 541-750-7000) and cavort in the sandy wilderness. These dunes reach heights of several hundred feet, giving refuge to many types of flora and fauna, and are constantly sculpted into different shapes by wind and water. In addition to campgrounds and hiking trails, they are rife with wildlife and birds, as well

BELOW:
eat it now and
catch it later in
Bandon.

as red and yellow salmon berries, thimble berries (similar to raspberries), wild strawberries and, in the fall, huckleberries.

Lower **Umpqua Bay** is said to be the most fertile place for big soft-shell clams, some weighing around half a pound (220 grams). The delicious Dungeness crab is found in the Winchester Bay area, where the Umpqua River meets the ocean. Shops sell crabbing equipment and bait.

At the Umpqua Dunes Trailhead (watch for the highway sign), you can park the car and climb the dunes. Camp facilities here include *yurts*: structurally supported domed tents with plywood floors, lockable doors, comfortable beds and light and heating. Designed to withstand high winds and retain heat in winter, they are 126 ft (38 meters) in diameter with very high ceilings. Altogether, the state of Oregon has 155 of them spread over 19 different parks, (tel: 800-551-6949 for information). In summer you might care to take a 5-mile (8-km) side trip to visit the **Umpqua Lighthouse** (open Wed–Sat afternoons), an 1894 replacement for the first one that had been built on the Oregon coast 37 years previously.

Rusty frogs and bald eagles

Just before **Salmon Harbor** (unsurprisingly the largest salmon fishing port on the Oregon coast), watch for the Rusty Frog Gallery to your right and then cross the bridge into **Reedsport**, where an interpretive facility called the **Umpqua Discovery Center** (tel: 541-271-4816; open daily) explains the dunes and much else besides. An additional source is the **Dunes Visitor Center** on US 101, which publicizes preservation efforts, issues bird checklists (there are five different types of seagull alone) and books campground sites (tel: 541-271-3611). A mile

Map on page 354

ATVs (all terrain vehicles) are the perfect way to play on the dunes; you can rent them in the town of North Bend.

BELOW: the Oregon Dunes National Recreation Area.

Many people not born near the sea confuse sea lions with seals. Sea lions have external ears, and can rotate their hind flippers to walk on land. Seals live exclusively on the edge of – or in – the water.

or two to the east, visitors can admire herds of Roosevelt elk at the pleasant **Dean Creek Elk Viewing Area**, which is also a haven for bald eagles, osprey and blue herons. Occasional signs warn that elk may stray into the road.

Continuing north, with water on both sides of the highway, the enormous plant of the International Paper Company stretches beside the Sound for half a mile. The road soon narrows to two lanes. "The law requires slow-moving vehicles to use turn-outs" is a sign frequently seen around these parts. A sensible law, indeed, you'll think when caught behind one of those huge family RVs ambling along at 30 mph (48 kph). There are numerous campgrounds in the flanking forest, and about a mile before the bridge into Florence is the **Siuslaw Pioneer Museum** (closed Mon), displaying old photographs and household items.

Check the conditions

Florence has a picturesque harbor back-dropped by some ancient buildings, but it is not a place to detain the visitor for long except when the rhododendrons display their vivid pink blossoms in late spring. When landslides block US 101 to the north (as happened for months early in 2000), it's the last chance to turn inland before Waldport. If traffic conditions have been bad, check with the Oregon Department of Transportation (tel: 888-275-6368), because even when the road is "closed," it's sometimes open for an hour or two each day, usually early morning and early evening.

BELOW:
watching boats,
collecting driftwood
and studying tide
pools are popular
pastimes along this
low-key coast.

Eleven miles (18 km) north of Florence is the **Heceta Head Lighthouse**, which has been beaming its warning to mariners since 1894. Also, not far from Florence are the interesting **Sea Lion Caves** (tel: 541-547-3111; open daily) at the bottom of cliffs accessed by an elevator. Harbor seals (which have spotted coats) and elephant seals are the types most commonly found on this coast; neither has external ears – as opposed to sea lions. The latter can also rotate their hind flippers and thus walk on land.

The curiously named **Yachats** ❹, a tourist resort nestled between the mountains and the sea, has beach trails, rewarding tide pools and good fishing. Yachats is the only town between Florence and Waldport, and visitors come to watch smelts (a silvery sardine-like fish) when they gather to spawn in summertime. The tiny community celebrates rather ungratefully with an annual Smelt Fry every July, which is very well-attended, not least by classically trained musicians from San Francisco.

Cape Perpetua is the highest point (803 feet/245 meters above sea level) on the coast, and has a helpful **Visitor Center** that provides maps and advice for hikers bound for explorations along the trails of Siuslaw National Forest. From its overlook, the highway looks like a thin sliver of silver ribbon threading along the coast.

Waldport ❷ lies at the mouth of the Alsea River, which arrives at the ocean from its origin in Siuslaw National Forest, whose northern section is traversed by US 101, just before Neskowin. Waldport (pop. 1,600) is mainly known for its fishing, crabbing and clamming. It's also a particularly good base for anyone interested in hiking.

Map on page 354

WALDPORT TO SEASIDE

Look to the right while crossing Yaquina Bay into the town of **Newport ㊸**. The section below the bridge is Newport's **Historic Bayfront**, whose attractions include old taverns, a harbor filled with fishing boats and a trio of commercial attractions. There's the obligatory Ripley's Believe It Or Not Museum, and the Undersea Gardens (a below-the-surface aquarium where divers cavort behind glass). Across the bay, **South Beach** has the larger **Oregon Coast Aquarium** (tel: 541-867-FISH; open daily), whose famous former resident, Keiko the Orca whale, starred in the film *Free Willy*.

To reach the Bayfront, turn off the main street at the traffic light (opposite the Mazatlan Mexican Restaurant in a gray, wooden building) and head down Hurburt Street. Farther on through town, several streets lead west to the seaport with its pedestrian promenade. Down Olive Street, just before the ocean, the Eager Beaver Secondhand Store sports an attractive mural on its sea side. One block farther, Third Street leads to **Nye Beach**, at one time the Oregon Coast's major draw. The Visual Arts Center (tel: 541-265-6540; closed Mon) is also here, while a boarding house from the 1890s forms part of the Lincoln County Historical Society Museum.

Just outside Newport is the much loved and much photographed **Yaquina Head Lighthouse ㊹**, built in 1873. Composer Earnest Block spent the last decades of his life at his home near here, and a memorial to him has been constructed. An interpretive center opened a few years ago.

About 5 miles (8 km) farther north of Newport, don't miss the signs for the **Devil's Punchbowl**, a couple of hundred yards off the highway. This is where a huge stone basin fills dramatically – and noisily – as the tide crashes in. Waves are higher in the Pacific than the Atlantic because the wind blows uninterruptedly over a larger distance, and the study of waves – whose height is measured as the distance between the highest point (crest) and lowest point (trough) – is understandably one of great interest to coastal communities. Tide tables are listed around here in local phone directories. A tide could be regarded as a very slow wave, with high tide representing the crest, and low tide the trough.

Festival of glass

The coastal views from these cliffs and capes are spectacular, and sometimes whales can be spotted on their 12,000-mile (19,300-km) round trip between Alaska and Baja California. The awesome cliffs and headlands are basalt, formed by molten lava hitting the ocean aeons ago and hardening instantly. Sometimes, this instant cooling creates oddly shaped rock structures known as pillow basalt, which can be seen offshore near Cape Foulweather and at **Depoe Bay**, a pretty place that claims to be the world's smallest navigable harbor. At high tide, seawater shoots skyward through two rock formations known locally as the **Spouting Horns**. Visitors get a close-up look at the wave action just by walking along the sea wall, which runs the full length of the town. When a storm is about to hit, everyone heads to a Depoe Bay restaurant for a full-frontal view, complete with sound effects.

BELOW:
Heceta Head Lighthouse has been beaming its warning to mariners since 1894.

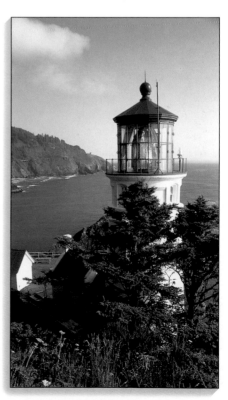

Cape Foulweather was named in 1778 by the British navigator Captain James Cook. It was his first sighting of the American mainland following his return from discovering Hawaii. The winds here, 500 ft (152 meters) above the ocean, can reach 100 mph (161 kph), but don't seem to ruffle the friendly ginger cat that wanders around the cape's observation platform. Its home is the small gift shop with its collection of carved driftwood figures, kitschy souvenirs, and the much-prized green glass bubbles that have drifted here from fishermen's nets all the way from Japan. Lincoln City, also renowned for its kite flying, recently launched 2,000 floats of its own as part of a Festival of Glass.

Pink starfish

Trawling for glass floats, collecting driftwood and studying tide pools are all popular pastimes along this stretch of low-key coast. Tide pools could be regarded as miniature ocean habitats, where some creatures wait in anticipation for the waves to wash in their lunch. Orange and pink starfish, urchins and sea anemones can usually be seen among the tiny fish that dart about the shallows, while rocky residents such as long-tapered mussels and white barnacles cluster on the rocks.

BELOW: the cheese factory at Tillamook offers free tours and samples; this is the place to learn "udderly amazing" facts about cows.

Lincoln City ⊕, which has 7 miles (11 km) of beaches beginning with a half-mile-deep strand when the tide is out at Siletz Bay, also has 20 antique stores and several second-hand bookstores. There is the Chinook Winds Casino for night-time action and a **factory outlet** for daytime shopping, which, depending on the enthusiasm of the competition, is usually regarded as the largest in Oregon. Bus tours and tourists come in droves for great bargains from around 70 stores. The tiny D River links nearby **Devil's Lake** with the ocean, providing both freshwater and oceanside fun.

North of town, **Cascade Head** is the home of such raptors as falcons, hawks and bald eagles – predators that deploy keen eyesight, outstanding hearing and amazing speed to hunt and eat other mammals with their large clawed feet and hooked bills. Bird-watching is a popular local pastime and Lincoln City's Backyard Bird Shop is well stocked with books, tools and birdhouses.

Cows versus people

The highway skirts residential **Neskowin** and then heads inland, passing meadows of grazing cows (which outnumber people in this very pastural county owned by the 180 working farms that provide the milk for the delectable Tillamook cheese. After colorful **Cloverdale**, with its big blue barn and bright yellow church, the highway traverses wonderful, fresh-scented **Siuslaw National Forest**, its highest peak Mount Hebo, ascending to 3,000 ft (914 meters).

Sturdy wooden barns and springtime daffodil catch the eye before the towns of Hebo and Beaver appear. **Hebo** itself has houses that are set back beside the creek, and an airplane atop a pole that announces the **Blimp Hangar Air Museum** (tel 503-842-1130; open daily), which is housed in an enormous hangar containing World War II vintage planes and a welcome 1940s-style café.

Cheesy town

Tillamook ㊻ is justly famous for its huge, pristine cheese factory, which offers a free tour to inspect the manufacturing process and admire a life-size, painted plaster cow, beribboned with a computer chip that has replaced the old cow bell. A wall chart lists such "udderly amazing" facts as the fact that 2,600 pints of blood pass through the udder to produce one pint of milk and that a cow yields 10,000 gallons of milk in her lifetime. Help yourself to the free cheese samples, because it's a sure bet that you're bound to buy something in the tempting Aladdin's Cave that calls itself a gift shop. Not to be outdone, the **Blue Heron French Cheese** factory offers wine with its cheese tastings. Needless to say, the Dairy Parade is a major event each June.

West of Tillamook a sidetrip could be made along the 20-mile (32-km) **Three Capes Scenic Drive** to view the "Octopus Tree" – a Sitka spruce with multiple trunks – and the **Cape Meares Lighthouse**, built in 1890 with a lens imported from Paris. An early lighthouse keeper wrote of the harrowing all-night horse-and-buggy trip required to reach a doctor in Tillamook, a trip that today takes about 16 minutes.

Two miles (3 km) out to sea is the **Tillamook Lighthouse**, situated on a solitary rock amid crashing waves that in 1934 roared into a maelstrom, climbing more than 100 feet (30 meters) high to engulf the entire building. "Terrible Tilly" was how lighthouse keepers used to describe the building. Life on the rock was too hazardous to allow families to accompany staff to their jobs, who were routed every three weeks and allowed 96 days leave each year to recover. It was decommissioned in 1980.

For a taste of big city life, take a detour from Tillamook along State Route 6

Map on page 354

Net gain. Some of the "bubble floats" from fishermen's nets have floated to Oregon all the way from Japan.

BELOW: competitors for the day's catch.

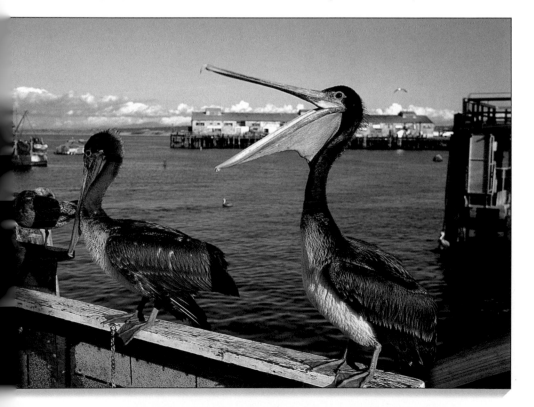

PORTLAND: CITY OF ROSES

A ride-for-free transit system, stunning scenery and microbreweries everywhere – no wonder Portland smells like roses

Portland, voted one of America's best walking towns, has always prided itself on its pedestrian friendliness and trees-and-parks image. Its Forest Park is the largest urban wilderness in the US, and in the metro area alone there are 37,000 acres (15,000 hectares) of parks and gardens.

The Metropolitan Art Commission (tel: 503-823-5111) and Art Media (tel: 503-223-3724) have brochures locating museums and art galleries; the Portland Development Commission (tel: 503-823-3200) has a map showing interesting historical and architectural sites, and private guided walking tours are also available (tel: 503-684-1978).

Downtown Portland is focused around Pioneer Courthouse Square, where the Weather Machine, an earth-shaped sphere by local artist Terence O'Donnell on a 25-foot (8-meter) column comes to life with a musical fanfare at noon each day. Portland's efficient transit system is centered around a 300-block "Fareless Square" Downtown, the area where passengers ride free on buses or the light rail system. Washington Park subway is within easy access of many major attractions. These include the Oregon Zoo, the World Forestry Center, the Hoyt Arboretum and the Children's Museum.

A streetcar system links the downtown area with the Pearl District (an area colonized by local artists) and the Nob Hill neighborhood with its fine Victorian and Georgian mansions. In the historic Skidmore District, there's a large weekend open-air market with live entertainment. Portland also has more microbreweries and brew pubs than any other city in the nation.

The state's history comes to life in the Oregon History Center and in the Pittock Mansion (tel: 503-823-3624), the 1914 home of the founder of Portland's well-regarded daily newspaper, *The Oregonian*. Various tour boats operate along the river, some venturing up the Columbia River as far as the Bonneville Lock and Dam, 40 miles (64 km) to the east. At the Oregon Museum of Science and Industry (tel: 503-797-6674; open daily; closed Mon in winter) you can experience a simulated earthquake or board a jetboat for a worthwhile river excursion.

Two attractions are unique: the Church of Elvis (open 24 hours), a coin-operated shrine offering marriage counseling and more; and the American Advertising Museum (tel: 503-232-0433; weekends only), whose 200,000 artifacts include a complete set of Burma Shave signs (*see page 38*). ❏

LEFT: sweetly-scented namesake; Mount Hood, the city and gardens.
ABOVE: buy local; Pioneer Courthouse Square.

east to the "City of Roses," otherwise known as **Portland** ❹ *(see page 376).* Past Tillamook, the highway hugs the 13-square-mile (34-sq-km) shallow bay, which is rarely deeper than 6 feet (2 meters). Estuaries such as this, where fresh water mingles with that of the ocean, are especially inviting to plant and marine life. Eelgrass provides shelter and nourishment to crabs as well as young salmon and other small fish; mudflats harbor gourmet treats for the stately great blue heron, which can often been seen rummaging. The Arago Cape is the home of the elephant seal, a deep-diving mammal that has been known to reach depths of 4,000 feet (1,200 meters).

Map on page 354

Garibaldi and ghosts

Next on the Pacific Coast Scenic Highway, preceded by a giant, abandoned smokestack, comes **Garibaldi** (named for the 19th-century Italian liberator), which has a battered Ghost Hotel Tavern, a Lumberman's Memorial Park and Museum (tel: 503-322-0301) and the annual Crab Races, which presumably take place sideways.

At **Rockaway Beach**, a red caboose beside the highway is the tourist office (tel: 503-355-8108; open weekdays, albeit sporadically), run by volunteers. Freight trains loaded with lumber can occasionally be seen running on the roadside track, which follows the course of the Nehalem River. Tiny **Wheeler** has an art gallery that sponsors wine tasting, presumably from the winery at nearby **Manzanita**, a community that welcomes visitors with a brightly colored mural of a blazing sun and wave-lashed rocks.

After the long climb from Manzanita, there are spectacular views from an overlook above the sea where the **Oswald West State Park** begins. Down to the

BELOW: four-footed firmness required for this trip to the seashore.

Haystack Rock at Cannon Beach.

trestle bridge over the canyon, Tillamook County (which bills itself as "the land of cheese, trees, and gentle breeze") comes to an end just before the tunnel. A bridge over Arch Creek abuts a residential seaside community.

An unmistakable landmark at **Cannon Beach** ⓭ is 235-ft (72-meter) high **Haystack Rock**, offshore. The very active community, an artists' haven with over 40 visual arts studios and galleries, is named after a cannon washed ashore after an 1846 shipwreck. It is another kite-flying paradise, where professionals turn up in April to perform at the annual Puffin Kite Festival.

The town also sponsors an annual Sandcastle Day in June and a dog show on the beach in October with contests for best bark, Frisbee catch and owner/dog look-alike. There's even a Stormy Weather Festival (indoors) in November; the town publishes a chart of coastal tide tables with predictions for the entire year. If you can manage all this activity, telephone 503-436-2623 to request *Cannon Beach Magazine*.

Seaside

Twenty-eight miles (45 km) north of Tillamook, US 101 descends into the town of **Seaside** ⓮ (pop. 6,000), the largest resort on the Oregon Coast, and bisected by the Necanicum River, with its historic downtown area on the western side of Broadway. A wide sandy beach is flanked by a pedestrian promenade, along which is the **Aquarium** (open daily). Three blocks farther north is Seaside's **Historical Society Museum** (open daily). Note the attractive, blue, make-believe lighthouse of the Sundowner Inn on Oceanway, which is in the downtown area. Seaside's free *Visitors Guide* also includes annual tide tables (tel: 888-306-2326) for a copy, which also includes events.

BELOW: hitchhiking across America.

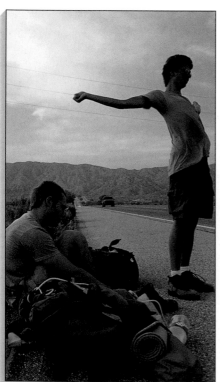

It was at Seaside that members of the Lewis and Clark exploration party set up a camp to make salt by boiling seawater. For that first cold, wet winter of 1805 the expedition established – southeast of what is now **Warrenton – Fort Clatsop**, naming it for a local tribe of Indians who brought whale meat to trade (Clark cooked and ate some, describing it as "very palatable and tender").

A replica of the fort (tel: 503-861-2471; open daily) – a 50-sq-foot (5-sq-meter) stockade with a parade ground and two rows of small cabins – helps visitors to visualize the conditions. There's also a summer program in which buckskin-clad rangers offer demonstrations. Nearby **Fort Stevens** in the state park was built to defend the mouth of the Columbia River in the Civil War.

ASTORIA TO ABERDEEN

Astoria ⓯ – 22 miles (35 km) north of Seaside – was once known as the "the salmon canning capital of the world," and in an 1872 book, Frances Fuller Victor was able to write: "The immense numbers of all kinds of salmon, which ascend the Columbia annually, is something wonderful. They seem to be seeking quiet and safe places to deposit their spawn, and thousands of them never stop until they can reach the great falls of the Snake River, more than 600 miles (966 km) from the sea." As late as 1915, fishermen were taking

21,000 tons of salmon from the river. But then came the giant dams. The protest by the Cayuse Indians that it would abrogate their rights by eliminating most of the salmon sadly turned out to be true. Some salmon runs have declined 85 percent from what they once were, despite the production of 170 million fish each year by artificial hatcheries. In this place alone, at its mouth, is the Columbia River unchanged.

Map on page 354

The mighty Columbia

Here, at its most powerful, the river thrusts 150 billion gallons (682 billion litres) of water a day through the sandbars into the Pacific Ocean, a torrent that has capsized 2,000 boats in the 185 years since John Jacob Astor's Pacific Fur Company created the first American settlement on shore. In recent years, the Federal government has dredged a 40-ft (12-meter) channel and placed long jetties at each side to narrow the channel, but despite constant dredging and other attempts to tame the river at its mouth, it remains one of the most dangerous in the world. The weather so consistently stirs up stormy seas that the Coast Guard set up its National Motor Lifeboat School at the tip of Cape Dis appointment; at times the waves reach as high as 30 ft (9 meters). Nevertheless, cruise boats regularly call at Astoria, depositing hundreds of passengers at the 17th Street Dock, used regularly by Coast Guard cutters.

The **Columbia River Maritime Museum** (tel: 503-325 2323; open daily) is all about shipwrecks, lighthouses, fishing, navigation and naval history. Much of Astoria's history is reflected in its handsome old houses, which fall into particular styles: Italianate, whose overhanging eaves have decorative brackets and tall or paired windows and doors, or Queen Anne (multiple roof lines, tow-

BELOW: full moon over the gorgeous gorge of the Columbia River.

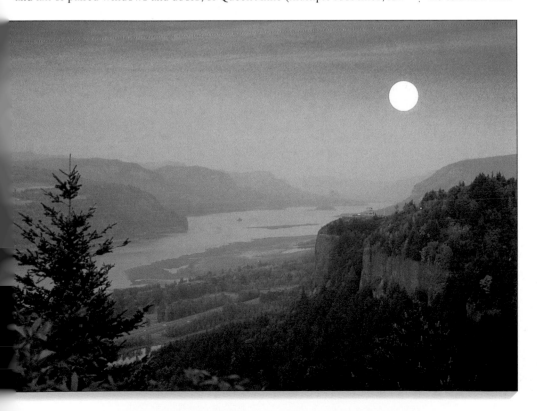

ers and turrets, paneled doors and stained glass). An interesting example of the latter is the **Captain George Flavel House**, dating from the 1880s, on Eighth Street (tel: 503-325-2203; open daily).

It's a steep, winding drive past old Victorian houses up the hill on which sits the **Astoria Column**, with its 164 winding steps, each one individually sponsored. The Great Northern Railroad and Vincent Astor, great-grandson of fur-trading tycoon and town founder Jacob Astor, were responsible for the 125-foot (38-meter) high tower that was completed in 1926. The views, of course, are stupendous, but once back on the ground you'll be glad to warm up in the hut as you buy a postcard.

WASHINGTON STATE'S DISCOVERY COAST

It was three weeks before the Lewis and Clark exploration party managed to cross the wide Columbia River, setting up another camp near today's **Chinook** on Washington state's west coast (publicized as the Discovery Coast). Here, US 101 continues past a bird-filled wildlife refuge to the pretty, unspoiled town of **Ilwaco** with its murals, carved wooden statues and **Heritage Museum** (tel: 360-642-3446; closed Sun in winter). The expedition stayed for three lonely months in this isolated area.

The 4-mile (6-km) long bridge that crosses from Oregon into Washington state is unusual in that it climbs steeply. Overhead seagulls swoop with keening cries and the wind is almost gale force. Be careful when driving.

BELOW: piano player at a party in a log cabin along the Pacific Coast.

Ilwaco sits at the bottom of the Long Beach peninsula – 28 miles (45 km) of uninterrupted sandy beach – which gets nicer the farther north you go. In the southwest corner, **Fort Candy** guarded the mouth of the Columbia for almost

Map on page 354

a century before becoming a state park in 1957. It houses a very interesting **Lewis and Clark Interpretive Center** (open daily) where you can study biographies of members of the original party and entries from the actual journals they kept. **Cape Disappointment Lighthouse**, built in 1856, is less than a mile away at the southwestern-most tip, but such was the continuing toll of wrecked ships that it had to be supplemented before the century was out by another lighthouse at nearby **North Head**. This can be toured in summer (tel: 360-642-3078 for times).

Long Beach itself is a rather déclassé resort – its main street lined with tatty souvenir stores, a Ripley-style "museum," uninteresting restaurants and numerous inexpensive motels. But it does have a pleasant boardwalk, as well as a 2-mile (3-km) Dune Trail. The peninsula's beaches are popular for clamming. **Nahcotta** and **Oysterville** at the northern end became prosperous from oyster gathering before the crop was over-harvested, but some fine Victorian homes remain from those days, and the **Willapa Bay Interpretive Center** (open weekends) at Nahcotta explains the history of it all. Leadbetter Park, at the northern tip, is also a wildlife refuge where birds stop over on their way south

Pacific Ocean fish and oysters find a ready market in the watering holes of Seattle and Portland.

Oyster capital

Back on "the mainland," US 101 crosses the Naselle River and a number of sloughs (inlets) before arriving at **South Bend 🛈**, which sits on a bay at the mouth of the Willapa River. Signs announcing oysters for sale in what calls itself the "oyster capital of the world" are a reminder that a century ago tons of these succulent bivalves were harvested by Native Americans, which all now find a ready and willing market in the gourmet restaurants of Seattle, Portland

BELOW: homesteaders at home.

Map on page 354

and San Francisco. Also in search of the same is the black oystercatcher, a bird whose long red bill helps it open the shellfish once it has found them.

Two ancient wooden warehouses contain a shipwright and an iron works in South Bend, which stages its annual Oyster Stampede every May. South Bend's near neighbor **Raymond** is an unspoiled, un-touristy sort of place with a library built in the style of a timbered English cottage – its art-glass panes depicting fairy tale characters.

Reckless extravagance

Architecturally, Raymond's pride and joy is the old courthouse, with its spiral staircase and stained glass dome. "A gilded palace of reckless extravagance" was how the local paper described it when the courthouse first went up in 1910. Life-size metal silhouettes of sculptured animals and local figures line the grassy verges around town. Four miles (6 km) east of Raymond on State Route 6 is the (marked) grave of Willie Kiel, a 19-year-old who died of malaria just before the family wagon train left Missouri in 1855. Preserved in whisky in a lead casket by his doctor father, the body came along for the trip and was buried atop a grassy knoll, now crowned with towering cedars.

Access to west coast beaches is via State Route 105, which runs past the Shoalwater Indian Reservation and the cranberry bogs between North Cove and Grayland. Cranberries blossom in late June, and **Grayland** holds its annual cranberry festival in October, following the harvest.

Between Raymond and Aberdeen, US 101 bends and twists through a glorious forest of mist-shrouded pines and other trees before emerging beside the smoke-belching, century-old Weyerhaeuser lumber plant, a mile or two south of town. It is from Weyerhauser that the Federal government is buying a 274-acre (111-hectare) grove of cedars in a difficult-to-reach part of the peninsula. When the bridge over the broad Chehalis River is raised, vehicles must wait to continue their journey.

Aberdeen ㊿, a major lumber port for more than a century, is, like its Scottish namesake, at the meeting of two rivers. It is known for **Grays Harbor**, the seaport around which the town grew after Robert Gray sailed in on the *Lady Washington* in 1788 to help arrange fur trading between the Pacific Northwest and China. A replica of the 170-ton ship is used for educational trips, but is usually on show in the harbor, and more about the town's early days can be explored in the **Aberdeen History Museum**. By the time the first mill was built in 1852, the government was making treaties with the Indians of the region and Aberdeen was developing into a rowdy, honky-tonk shipping town.

San Diego to Seattle

US 101 reaches the end of the journey that began all the way south in sunny San Diego with a flourishy loop around the magnificent Olympic Peninsula *(see the Northern Route, page 167)*, ending up not far from Seattle. Alternatively, head straight for **Seattle ㊿** *(see page 172)* from Aberdeen by taking US 12 to **Olympia**, then Interstate 5. ❑

BELOW: and then there were three.
RIGHT: dreaming of fish.

CONTENTS

Getting Acquainted

The continental US spans four time zones. These are divided as follows:
•**Eastern** (Greenwich Mean Time minus five hours)
•**Central** (Greenwich Mean Time minus six hours)
•**Mountain** (Greenwich Mean Time minus seven hours)
•**Pacific** (Greenwich Mean Time minus eight hours)

DAYLIGHT SAVING TIME

This begins each year at 2am on a Sunday in March when clocks are advanced one hour, and ends on the first Sunday in October. Arizona and Indiana do not observe Daylight Saving Time.

Electricity

Standard electricity in North America is 110–115 volts, 60 cycles AC. An adapter is necessary for most appliances from overseas, with the exception of Japan.

Weights & Measures

The US operates on the imperial system of weights and measures. Metric is rarely used. Below is a conversion chart:
1 inch = 2.54 centimeters
1 foot = 30.48 centimeters
1 mile = 1.609 kilometers
1 quart = 1.136 liters
1 ounce = 28.40 grams
1 pound = 0.453 kilograms
1 yard = 0.9144 meters

Public Holidays

As with other countries, the US has gradually shifted most of its public holidays to the Monday closest to the actual dates, thus creating a number of three-day weekends throughout the year.
Keep in mind that during public holidays, post offices, banks, government offices and many private businesses are closed. Holidays celebrated no matter on what day they fall in the year are:

•**January 1** New Year's Day
•**July 4** Independence Day
•**November 11** Veteran's Day
•**December 25** Christmas Day
Other holidays are:
•**Third Monday in January**
Martin Luther King Jr Day
•**Third Monday in February**
Presidents' Day
•**March/April**
Good Friday, Easter Monday
•**Last Monday in May**
Memorial Day
•**First Monday in September**
Labor Day
•**Second Monday in October**
Columbus Day
•**Fourth Thursday in November**
Thanksgiving.

Business Hours

Banks 9am–5pm, weekdays. Some stay open until 6 and Saturdays.
Post Offices 8am–4 or 5.30pm, weekdays, Saturday closing earlier and opening later.
Shops 10am–9pm generally.
All-hours services Most cities have 24-hour restaurants, convenience stores and supermarkets.

Planning the Trip

Visas & Passports

A machine-readable passport, a passport-sized photograph, a visitor's visa, proof of intent to leave the US after your visit and (depending upon your country of origin) an international vaccination certificate, are required of most foreign nationals for entry into the US. Visitors from the UK staying less than 90 days no longer need a visa. Vaccination certificate requirements vary, but proof of immunization against smallpox or cholera may be necessary.
US citizens traveling by air between the US, Canada, Mexico, the Caribbean and Bermuda must present a current passport; a birth certificate and photo ID are no longer valid proof.
Information Up-to-date details on entry requirements and machine-readable passports may be found on the US State Department's website: www.travel.state.gov/visa_services.html.

Extension of stay

Non-US citizens should contact US Immigration and Naturalization Service at 425 I Street, Washington, DC 20536
Tel: 202-501-4444
US Freephone: 888-407-4747

Customs

For a breakdown of customs allowances write to:
United States Customs Service
P.O. Box 7407,
Washington, DC 20044
Meat or meat products, illegal drugs, firearms, seeds, plants and fruits are among the prohibited goods. Also do not bring in any duty-free

Tipping

Although rarely obligatory, many service personnel in the US rely on tips for a large part of their income. Going rates are:
- **waiters and bartenders**
  15–30 percent
- **taxi drivers**
  15 percent
- **airport/hotel baggage handlers**
  around $1 per bag
- **chambermaids**
  for overnight stays, it is not necessary to tip, for longer stays a minimum of $1–2 per day
- **doormen**
  50¢–$1 for helping unload a car or other services
- **hairdressers, manicurists and masseurs**
  15 percent

goods which are worth more than $400 (returning Americans) or $100 (foreign travelers). Visitors over 21 may bring in 200 cigarettes, 3 lbs (1.3 kg) of tobacco or 50 cigars and 34 fl. oz (1 liter) of alcohol.

Airport Security

In light of events on September 11, 2001, air travel in the US has changed drastically. Be at the airport early, expect searches and questions to be asked, and do not attempt to carry any sharp objects in your hand luggage. This includes scissors, nailclippers, pen-knives, nailfiles and other seemingly innocuous items.

Health & Insurance

Medical services are extremely expensive. Always arrange full and comprehensive travel insurance to cover any emergencies. Check the small print – most policies exclude treatment for water, winter or mountain sports accidents unless excess cover has been included. If you need medical assistance, consult the Yellow Pages for the physician or pharmacist nearest to you. In large cities, there is usually

a physician referral service number listed. If you need immediate attention, go directly to a hospital emergency room (most are open 24 hours a day). You may be asked to produce proof of insurance cover before being treated.

Care should be taken to avoid dehydration and overexposure to the sun. In the desert, or at high altitude, this can happen rapidly even on cloudy days. A high-factor sun lotion, hat and water bottle are essential accessories.

Money Matters

American visitors
Credit cards are accepted almost everywhere, although not all cards at all places. Most hotels, restaurants and shops take the major ones such as American Express, Diners Club, MasterCard, Visa and En Route. Along with out-of-state or overseas bank cards, they can also be used to withdraw money at ATMs.
Travelers' checks are widely accepted, although you may have to provide proof of identification when cashing them at banks (this is not required at most stores).

Overseas visitors
Travelers' checks in US dollars are much more widely accepted than those in other currencies. The best rates of exchange for them are in banks. Take along your passport.

Tax

Most states levy a sales tax. The amount varies from state to state, (up to around 8 percent in some) and is invariably excluded from the marked price. You may also have to pay a local sales tax on top of this.

When looking at prices, beware of other costs that may or may not be included in the stated price such as lodging or "bed tax" and taxes on restaurant meals, drinks and car rental. These are especially hefty in tourist towns like Miami. If in doubt – ask.

Practical Tips

Postal Services

POST OFFICES

Even the most remote towns are served by the US Postal Service. Smaller post offices are limited to business hours (Monday to Friday 9am–5pm), although central, big-city branches may have extended opening times. Stamps are sold at all post offices, plus at some convenience stores, filling stations, hotels and transportation terminals, usually from vending machines.

EXPRESS MAIL

For reasonably quick delivery at a modest price, ask for priority mail. For overnight deliveries, try US Express Mail or one of several domestic and international courier services, including:
Fedex, tel: 800-463-3339
DHL, tel: 800-225-5345
United Parcel Service, tel: 800-742-5877

POSTE RESTANTE

Visitors can receive mail at post offices if it is addressed to them, care of "General Delivery," followed by the city name and (very important) the zip code. You must pick up this mail in person within a week or two of its arrival and show some personal identification.

Telecommunications

TELEPHONE

Coin-operated telephones are ubiquitous: they are to be found in hotels, restaurants, shopping centers, gas stations and often in lighted booths on street corners. To call long-distance, dial 1+area code +local number. Have plenty of change with you to deposit on the operator's prompting.

Toll-free calls

When in the US, make use of toll-free (no-charge) numbers. They start with 800, 1-800, 888 or 877.

Cheaper rates

Long-distance rates are cheaper after 5pm on weekdays and throughout weekends.

TELEGRAMS & FAXES

Western Union (tel: 800-325-6000) takes telegram and telex messages, plus orders to wire money over the phone. Faxes can be found in most hotels and copy centers.

EMAIL & INTERNET

Many public libraries, copy centers and hotels offer email and Internet access. Or visit a cyber café. Service providers such as Earthlink (www.i.e.w.com) and Hotmail (www.hotmail.com) offer web mail accounts that will enable access while traveling.

Useful Numbers

•**Emergencies** 911 (the operator will put you through to the police, ambulance or fire services)
•**Operator** 0 (dial if you are having any problems with a line from any phone)
•**Telephone information**
Local: 411
Long-distance: 1+area code +555-1212
Toll-free directory: 800-555-1212

Phone Codes

More than perhaps any other country, the United States has embraced the telephone. But now, with the proliferation of fax lines, modems and cellular phones, the system is seriously overloaded. To cope with these demands, the country has been forced to divide, then sub-divide its existing telephone exchanges, in some cases every six months. Although every effort has been made to keep the telephone prefixes listed here up to date, it's always a good idea to check with the operator if you're in any doubt about a number.

Embassies

Australia: 1601 Massachusetts Ave NW, Washington, DC 20036
Tel: 202-797-3000
Canada: 501 Pennsylvania Ave NW, Washington, DC 20001
Tel: 202-682-1740
Denmark: 3200 Whitehaven St NW, Washington, DC 20008
Tel: 202-234-4300
France: 4101 Reservoir Road NW, Washington, DC 20007
Tel: 202-944-6000
Germany: 4645 Reservoir Road NW, Washington, DC 20007
Tel: 202-298-4000
Great Britain: 3100 Massachusetts Ave NW, Washington, DC 20008
Tel: 202-462-1340
Ireland: 2234 Massachusetts Ave NW Washington, DC 20008
Tel: 202-462-3939
Israel: 3514 International Drive NW, Washington, DC 20008
Tel: 202-364-5500
Italy: 3000 Whitehaven St NW, Washington, DC 20008
Tel: 202-612-4000
Japan: 2520 Massachusetts Ave NW, Washington, DC 20008
Tel: 202-238-6700
Mexico: 1911 Pennsylvania Ave NW, Washington, DC 20006
Tel: 202-728-1600
New Zealand: 37 Observatory Circle NW, Washington, DC 20008
Tel: 202-328-4800

Singapore: 3501 International Place NW, Washington, DC 20008
Tel: 202-537-3100
Spain: 2375 Pennsylvania Ave NW, Washington, DC 20037
Tel: 202-452-0100

Security & Crime

ON THE ROAD

If you are driving, never pick up anyone you don't know. Always be wary of who is around you. If you have trouble on the road, stay in the car and lock the doors, turn on your hazard lights and/or leave the hood up to increase your visibility and alert passing police. It's well worth carrying a sign requesting help. Do not accept a rental car that is obviously labeled as such. Company decals and special license plates may attract thieves on the look-out for tourist valuables.

Hitchhiking

Hitchhiking is illegal in many places and ill-advised everywhere. It's an inefficient and dangerous method of travel. Don't do it!

IN THE CITY

Most big cities have their share of crime. Common sense is your most effective weapon. Try to avoid walking alone at night – at the very least stick to livelier, more brightly lit thoroughfares and move about as if you know where you are going.

Keep an eye on your belongings. Never leave your car unlocked, or small children by themselves. Hotels usually warn that they do not guarantee the safety of belongings left in their rooms. If you have any valuables, you may want to lock them in the hotel safe. Take particular care when using bank ATMs at night. If you are in doubt about which areas are safe, seek advice from hotel staff or police.

Clothes Sizes Guide

This table gives a comparison of American, Continental and British clothing sizes. It is always best to try on any article before buying it, as sizes may vary.

Women's Dresses/Suits

American	Continental	British
8	40/36N	10/32
10	42/38N	12/34
12	44/40N	14/36
14	46/42N	16/38
16	48/44N	18/40

Women's Shoes

American	Continental	British
5½	37	4
6½	38	5
7½	39	6
8½	40	7
9½	41	8

Men's Suits

American	Continental	British
34	44	34
-	46	36
38	48	38
-	50	40
42	52	42
-	54	44
46	56	46

Men's Shirts

American	Continental	British
14	36	14
14½	37	14½
15	38	15
15½	39	15½
16	40	16
16½	41	16½
17	42	17

Men's Shoes

American	Continental	British
6½	-	6
7½	40	7
8½	41	8
9½	42	9
10½	43	10
11½	44	11

Smoking

Smoking is banned on public transportation, domestic flights and in most cinemas and public buildings. Always check the policy in hotels and restaurants. Many have designated smoking areas; others – even bars and all of NYC – forbid it altogether.

Getting Around

Airports

If it is too impractical because of long distances to drive to the destinations listed here, an easy alternative is to fly. Airlines that serve the airports in the major hub cities include American, Delta, Continental, Northwest, Southwest, TWA, United and US Airways.

California: Los Angeles International; San Diego International
Florida: Miami International Airport
Georgia: Hartsfield International Airport (Atlanta)
Massachusetts: Logan International (Boston)
New York: John F Kennedy (JFK) International (New York City); La Guardia (New York City).
Washington State: Seattle-Tacoma International
Washington, DC: Reagan National, Dulles, Downtown Airport Terminal

By Train

Although passenger services were greatly curtailed in the latter part of the 20th century, it is still possible to travel the length and breadth of the continent by rail. Amtrak is the major rail passenger carrier in the US. Its network links many cities, but sadly bypasses many more. However, there are still some excellent transcontinental routes that glide through breathtaking scenery. Not the fastest or cheapest way of getting around America, but riding the rails can be a leisurely and highly enjoyable experience if you have the time.

Train passes

Passes for unlimited travel on Amtrak over a fixed period of time are available only from a travel agent in a foreign country. Proof of non-US residency is required. Be sure to ask about two- or three-stopover discounts, senior citizens and children's discounts, and also Amtrak's package tours.
Information: Details about Amtrak's train service may be obtained by calling 1-800-872-7245 or by visiting their website: www.amtrak.com.

By Bus

The national bus line, Greyhound, as well as a number of smaller charter companies, provide an impressive network of ground travel throughout the country, offering daily service to major towns and cities. Routes and schedules are subject to change; it is a good idea to check all arrangements with local stations in advance.

Most cities also have municipal bus systems. As both Greyhound and municipal stations are often situated in somewhat squalid areas, try to stay alert and do not wander too far, particularly after dark. Plan your journey for daylight arrival if possible. On the whole, the buses themselves are safe and reasonably comfortable; choosing a seat near to the driver may discourage unwanted attention from any fellow passengers.
Information: reservations and local bus station details are available on tel: 1-800-229-9424, or their website at: www.greyhound.com.

Bus passes

An Ameripass offers unlimited travel to 2,600 destinations within 68 consecutive days. The pass may be purchased only outside the US. Details are available from the Greyhound bus company and most foreign travel agents.

By Car

Car rental agencies are located at all airports and in cities and large towns. In most places you must be at least 21 years old (25 at some locations) to rent a car and you must have a valid driver's license and at least one major credit card. Be sure to check insurance provisions before signing anything. Cover is usually $15–25 per day. You may already be covered by your own auto insurance or credit card company, however, so check with them first.

CAR RENTAL COMPANIES

Alamo, tel: (US) 800-462-5266; www.goalamo.com
Avis, tel: (US) 800-230-4898; www.avis.com
Budget, tel: (US) 800-527-0700; www.budget.com
Dollar, tel: (US) 800-800-4000; www.dollar.com
Enterprise, tel: (US) 800-736-8222; www.enterprise.com
Hertz, tel: (US) 800-654-3131; www.hertz.com
National, tel: (US) 800-227-7368; www.nationalcar.com
Thrifty, tel: (US) 800-847-4389 www.thrifty.com

RV RENTALS

No special license is necessary to operate a motor home (or recreational vehicle – RV for short), but they aren't cheap. When you add up the cost of rental fees, insurance, gas and campsites, you may find that renting a car and staying in motels or camping is less expensive. Keep in mind, too, that RVs are large and slow and may be difficult to handle on narrow mountain roads. If parking space is tight, driving an RV may be extremely inconvenient. Access to some roads may be limited. For additional information about RV rentals, call the **Recreational Vehicle Rental Association,** tel 800-336-0355

AAA Membership

The Automobile Association of America (AAA) can help members with personalized itineraries. Benefits of AAA membership include a 24-hour emergency breakdown service, great road maps and travel literature. Insurance is also available through the association, which has a reciprocal arrangement with some of the automobile associations in other countries. Tel: 1-800-874-7532 or visit their website: www.aaa.com.

DESERT & MOUNTAIN DRIVING

A word of caution for desert travelers: the single most important precaution you can take is to tell someone your destination, route and expected time of arrival. Check tires carefully before long stretches of desert driving. Heat builds pressure, so have them at slightly below normal air pressure. The desert's arid climate makes carrying extra water – both for passengers and vehicles – essential. Carry at least one gallon per person. Keep an eye on the gas gauge. It's a good idea to have more than you think you need. Remember, if you should have car trouble or become lost, do not strike out on foot. A car, visible from the air and presumably on a road, is easier to spot than a person, and it affords shelter from the weather. Wait to be found. Mountain drivers are advised to be equally vigilant. Winter storms in the Sierras occasionally close major roads, and at times chains are required on tires. Phone ahead for road conditions before you depart.

Traveling with Children

Two words of advice about traveling with children: first, be prepared and, second, don't expect to cover too much ground.

Take everything you need: Western towns may be small and remote with supplies limited. If you need baby formula, special foods, diapers or medication, carry them with you along with a general first-aid kit. Games, books and crayons help kids pass time in the car. Carrying snacks and drinks in a day pack will come in handy when kids (or adults) get hungry on the road. Give yourself plenty of time, as kids do not travel at the same pace as adults. They're a lot less interested in traveling from point A to point B than in exploring their immediate surroundings. What you find fascinating, they may find boring. And what they think is "really cool" (the game room at the hotel), you may find totally uninteresting.

Be sure wilderness areas, and other back-country places are suitable for children. Are there abandoned mine shafts, steep stairways, cliffs or other hazards? Is a lot of walking necessary? Are food, water, shelter, bathrooms and other essentials available at the site? Avoid dehydration by having children drink plenty of water before and during outdoor activities. Don't push children beyond their limits. Rest often and allow for extra napping.

Disabled Travelers

For general information on travel for the handicapped, contact **Moss Rehabilitation Hospital Travel Information Service,** 1200 West Tabor Road, Philadelphia, PA 19141 Tel: 215-456-9600 TDD 215-456-9602, or **The Information Center for Individuals with Disabilities,** PO Box 750119 Arlington Heights, MA 62475 Fax: 781-860-0673.

Where to Stay

Hotels & Motels

Chain hotels and motels are reliable and convenient but tend to lack unique character. You can, however, usually depend on a clean, comfortable room for a reasonable price. In general, prices range from $50 to $150 depending on the location, the season and additional amenities. When making reservations, ask specifically about special weekend or corporate rates and "package deals." Reservations staff in America are notorious for quoting only the most expensive rates, but many hotels offer a variety of discounts and promotions.

Book your room by credit card and secure a guaranteed late arrival, in the foreseeable circumstance that your flight is interminably stacked up over the airport or your 40-minute limo ride from the airport turns into a two-hour nightmare of traffic jams. The telephone numbers listed below are the main numbers that should be dialed in order to make reservations once in the US.

CHAIN HOTELS

Best Western, tel: 1-800-780-7234
Choice Hotels, tel: 1-877-424-6423
Hilton, tel: 1-800-774-1500
Holiday Inn, tel: 1-800-465-4329
Hyatt, tel: 1-800-633-7313
La Quinta, tel: 1-866-725-1661
Marriott, tel: 1-888-236-2427
Radisson, tel: 1-888-201-1718
Ramada, tel: 1-800-272-6232
Starwood, tel: 1-888-625-5144

MOTELS

Budget Host Inns,
Tel: 1-800-283-4678
Comfort Inn,
Tel: 1-800-228-5150
Days Inns of America,
Tel: 1-800-544-8313
Econolodge,
Tel: 1-800-553-2666
Hampton Inns,
Tel: 1-800-426-7866
Motel 6,
Tel: 1-800-466-8356
Red Roof Inns,
Tel: 1-800-843-7663

Hostels

**Hostelling International/
American Youth Hostels**
8401 Colesville Road
Suite 600
Silver Spring, MD 20910
Tel: 301-495-1240
www.hiayh.org.
YMCA
YMCA of the USA, Association
Advancement, 101 North Wacker
Drive, Chicago, IL 60606
Tel: 312-977-0031
www.ymca.com
YWCA
1015 18th Street NW
Suite 1100
Washington DC 20036
Tel: 202-467-0801
www.ywca.com
Dude Ranchers Association
PO Box 2307, Cody, WY, 82414
Tel: 307-587-2339
www.duderanch.org

Bed & Breakfasts

B&Bs tend to be more personal than hotels. In some cases, you're a guest at a person's home where the accommodations are fairly simple; in others the rooms are in (large) historic homes or inns decorated with antiques, quilts, art and other period furnishings. Many do not allow smoking, so ask first. Before booking, also ask whether rooms have telephones or televisions and whether

Campgrounds

Most state and natural parks are serviced by campgrounds offering primitive facilities: a place to park, rest rooms and outdoor cooking. Fees are around $5 per site. Private campgrounds are usually a little more expensive and offer additional facilities such as hook-ups, coin laundries, pools and restaurants. Most are busy from mid-June to September and are allotted on a first-come-first-served basis. Camping space in popular national parks, like Yosemite and Yellowstone, should be booked up to a year in advance. For information on camping grounds call or write to individual parks and recreation departments or contact:
American Park Network
Columbus Circle Station
PO Box 20113
New York, NY 10023
Tel: 212-581-3380
www.americanparknetwork.com
Kampgrounds of America (KOA)
Tel: 406-248-7444
www.koa.com
National Park Service
Department of the Interior
18th and C Streets NW
Washington, DC 20240
Tel: 202-208-6843
www.nps.gov
US Forest Service
Tel: 202-205-1706
US Freephone: 800-280-2267
www.reserveusa.com
Bureau of Land Management
Tel: 202-452-5125

bathrooms are private. Inquire about breakfast, too. The morning meal is included in the price but may be anything from a couple of muffins to a multicourse feast. For more information contact:
B&B Central Information
PO Box 829, Madison, TN 37116;
tel: 615-868-1946;
www.bbonline.com
American Historic Inns
www.bnbinns.com

Atlantic Route

Useful Addresses

New York City tourist information
New York Convention and Visitors Bureau, 810 Seventh Avenue, NY 10019
Tel: 212-484-1222
www.nycvisit.com
New York State tourist information
Empire State Development, Empire State Plaza, Concourse Level, Room 110, Albany, NY 12223
Tel: 800-225-5697
www.iloveny.com
New Jersey tourist information
Lafayette and Barrack streets, Trenton, Mercer County
Tel: 1-800-VISIT NJ
www.state.nj.us/travel
Pennsylvania tourist information
Chamber of Business and Industry, 417 Walnut Street, Harrisburg, PA 17120
Tel: 717-255-3252
US Freephone: 800-847-4872
www.experiencepa.com
Maryland tourist information
Office of Tourism, 217 E Redwood Street, Baltimore, MD 21202
US Freephone: 800-634-7386
www.mdisfun.org
Virginia tourist information
Division of Tourism, 901 East Byrd Street, Richmond, VA 23219
Tel: 800-847-4882
www.virginia.org
North Carolina tourist information
North Carolina Division of Tourism, 301 North Wilmington Street, Raleigh, NC 27601
Tel: 800-847-4862
www.visitnc.com
South Carolina tourist information
Department of Tourism, 1205 Pendleton Street, Room 505, Columbia, SC 29201

Tel: 803-734-1700
www.travelsc.com
Georgia tourist information
285 Peachtree Center Avenue, Suite 1000, Atlanta, GA 30303
US Freephone: 800-847-4842
www.georgia.org
Florida tourist information
Visit Florida, PO Box 1100, Tallahassee, FL 32302
Tel: 850-488-5607
www.flausa.com
Miami tourist information
Miami Visitor's Bureau, 701 Bricknell Avenue, Suite 2700, FL, 33131
Tel: 305-539-3063
www.miamiandbeaches.com

Hub City: NEW YORK CITY

GETTING AROUND

Public transportation
From the airport: East of Manhattan on Long Island, New York's two major airports, John F. Kennedy International and LaGuardia, are respectively 15 and 8 miles (24 km and 13 km) from the city, with driving time from Kennedy estimated at just under one hour. In practice, heavy traffic can sometimes double this. Most charters and domestic flights and some international flights use LaGuardia. New York's third airport, Newark, is actually in New Jersey and, although further away from Manhattan than JFK and LaGuardia, can be easier to reach. New York Airport Service operates buses from both JFK and LaGuardia airports to Manhattan drop-off points, including Grand Central Terminal. New Jersey Transit and Olympia Trails Coach Service operate regular express buses between Newark airport and Manhattan, the former to the somewhat sleazy Port Authority Bus Terminal at Eighth Ave and 41st St, the latter to Penn Station and Grand Central Terminal.

Rapid transit and buses Subways and buses run 24 hours, less frequently after midnight, with the fare payable by token or (buses

only) exact change, as well as by MetroCard pass (available at subway ticket booths), which allows free transfers within two hours of use. Unlimited-ride passes are good for seven days or 30 day-passes are also available, as is a day pass sold at newsstands, hotels and electronic kiosks in some subway stations. For general bus and subway information and for other details about the MetroCard pass call: 718-330-1234. Greyhound buses run from the Port Authority bus terminal, 41st and Eighth Avenue (tel: 800-229-9424).
Trains: PATH (Port Authority Trans Hudson) trains run under the Hudson from six stations in Manhattan to New Jersey, including Hoboken and Newark. The fare is $1; tel: 1-800-234-7284. National rail trains arrive and depart from Manhattan's two railroad terminals: Grand Central Terminal at Park Ave and 42nd St, and Pennsylvania Station at Seventh Ave and 33rd St. City buses stop outside each terminal and each sits atop a subway station. Amtrak information, tel: 1-800-872-7245.

Private transportation
Driving around Manhattan is not much fun although, should the need arise, there is a wide range of firms available at airports from which cars can be rented. Check the *Yellow Pages* for a list of local firms.
Car Rental Companies
Avis, tel: 1-800-230-4898
Budget, tel: 1-800-527-0700
Hertz, tel: 1-800-654-3131
Taxis, all metered, cruise the streets randomly and must be hailed, although there are official taxi stands at places like Grand Central Terminal. Be sure to hail an official yellow cab, not an unlicensed "gypsy" cab. One fare covers all passengers up to four (five in a few of the larger cabs). After 8pm there is a 50¢ surcharge on all taxi rides. Telephone 212-302-8294 for lost property or to make a complaint.

WHERE TO STAY

La Quinta Manhattan
17 West 32nd Street
Tel: 736-1600
www.applecorehotels.com
Like others in the Apple Core Hotels group (Quality Hotel East Side, etc.), rates at this 176-room hotel, a short walk from Macy's and Madison Square Garden, are extremely reasonable, especially considering that the comfortable rooms come with such conveniences as data ports and voice mail. There's also a lobby café with entertainment, a restaurant with room service, and an open-air rooftop bar where music and snacks can be enjoyed in summer, along with views of the Empire State Building. **$**

Hotel Prices

Categories based on average cost of a double room for one night.
$ = under $65
$$ = up to $100
$$$ = up to $150
$$$$ = over $150

The Carlyle
35 East 76th Street
Tel: 744-1600
Fax: 717-4682
www.thecarlyle.com
Posh, reserved and serene in its elegance, The Carlyle remains one of the city's most highly acclaimed luxury hotels. Home of Café Carlyle and Bemelmans Bar, two of the city's most enduring and upscale evening spots. The Carlyle is a favorite with visiting royalty. **$$$$**

The Chelsea Hotel
204 West 23rd Street
Tel: 929-9353
Fax: 741-6309
A red-brick, Victorian landmark of bohemian decadence, home to beatnik poets, then Warhol drag queens, then Sid Vicious, and now... some of all of the above. Accommodations vary from a few inexpensive "student rooms" to suites. **$$–$$$**

New York International Youth Hostel
891 Amsterdam Ave
(at W 103rd St)
Tel: 932-2300
Fax: 932-2574
Accommodations in dormitory-style rooms range from $25–28 per person per night; $3 less for IYH members. **$**

The Paramount
235 West 46th St (at Eighth Ave)
Tel: 764-5500
Fax: 354-5237
A New York fashion statement in the heart of Times Square (and one of former Studio 54 king – now hotel king – Ian Schrager's ever-growing roster of hotels). The Paramount's rooms and public spaces, designed by Philippe Starck, dazzle and amaze: amenities include beds with headboards made of reproductions of famous paintings, a fitness club, a supervised playroom for children, and The Whiskey, a trendsetting small bar. Rooms are also small, but well-equipped. **$$–$$$**

Washington Square Hotel
103 Waverly Place
Tel: 777-9515
US Freephone: 800-222-0418
Fax: 979-8373
www.wshotel.com
An almost century-old hotel that offers the perfect Village locale. The rooms are small but nicely appointed. In a former incarnation, this was the seedy Hotel Earle, where Papa John wrote the 1960s rock classic *California Dreaming*. **$**

WHERE TO EAT

There are literally thousands of restaurants in New York, of all sizes, specialties and qualities. The following does not even begin to hint at an "exhaustive" list. We cite here several of the best, those we recommend with few or even no qualms at all. Reservations are often necessary and almost always recommended.

Carnegie Deli
854 Seventh Ave at 55th Street
Tel: 757-2245

Restaurant Prices

Categories based on average cost of dinner and a glass of wine, before tip.
$ = under $15
$$ = up to $30
$$$ = over $30

A pilgrimage site in the heart of Midtown, this is one of New York's most famous Jewish delicatessens, where the corned beef sandwich is a must. No credit cards. **$$**

Excellent Dumpling House
111 Lafayette
(just below Canal St)
Tel: 219 0212
Unpretentious, unadorned and on the outskirts of Chinatown proper; always packed with locals and devoted visitors who love its no-nonsense atmosphere, reasonable prices, and stellar dumplings (especially the vegetable dumplings, steamed or fried). No reservations, but there's sometimes a short wait; best for mid-afternoon lunch. No credit cards. **$$**

Oyster Bar
Lower level, Grand Central Terminal
Tel: 490-6650
A New York institution and a must for seafood lovers. The best fresh oysters and clam chowder in town, and you can sit at a counter, dining room or salon. **$$–$$$**

San Domenico
240 Central Park South
Tel: 265-5959
One of the most highly rated Italian restaurants in the city, this Central Park South establishment offers unusual Bolognese fare, with a wide variety of Northern Italian pastas and an extremely large wine list. A fine place to take a big party, but not necessarily for an intimate romantic meal. Reservations required. **$$$$**

Totonno's Napolitano Pizzeria
1524 Neptune Avenue, Brooklyn
Tel: 718-372-8606
Totonno's freshly baked brick-oven pizzas may well be the finest in the five boroughs. **$**

Union Square Café
21 East 16th Street
Tel: 243-4020
Possibly the friendliest service in New York and some of the best new-American cuisine anywhere. Reservations are difficult as this very popular restaurant's innovative menu attracts a hip, crowd. Definitely call ahead. **$$$–$$$$**

SHOPPING

Shopping is a major pastime in New York: there isn't much to be found anywhere that can't be found here, and usually more of it. **Art**, of course, is a good bet; apart from the major auctioneers, **Sotheby's** and **Christies**, where record prices are set for world-famous works, there are hundreds of art galleries in which to browse (if not to buy).

Antiques can be found in Greenwich Village along Bleecker St and on side streets off University Place; along Upper Madison Ave, on 60th St near Third Ave.

The city's famous **department stores** offer something for almost everyone but differ somewhat in their clientele: the most famous are the bustling **Bloomingdale's** (1000 Third Ave at 59th St) and **Macy's** (151 West 34th St), which sell everything from housewares to furniture and clothing. **Lord & Taylor** (424 Fifth Ave at 39th St); and **Saks Fifth Avenue** (611 Fifth Ave) concentrate on clothes, with the latter offering the most upscale fashions.

Electronic and photographic suppliers can be found almost everywhere, including Times Square and on Lexington Avenue near Grand Central Terminal. A few outlets are less than scrupulous, so it's best to do some comparison shopping before actually buying. A better bet might be in the downtown City Hall district or on Fifth Avenue between 37th and 40th streets.

The real bargains are often downtown: along Orchard St on the Lower East Side; in Chinatown; on Canal St between Sixth and Third avenues, and in the East Village, particularly the cross streets between First and Second avenues. Savvy New York shoppers also flock to Manhattan's **flea markets**, including the eclectic weekend **Chelsea antiques market** on Sixth Ave between 25th and 27th streets and the **Sunday flea market** at Columbus Ave and 77th St on the Upper West Side.

There are some excellent antiquarian and second-hand bookstores around town, especially the **Strand Book Store**, 828 Broadway at 12th St, tel: 473-1452, which claims to have two million volumes in stock and is a wonderful place to browse.

Hotel Prices

Categories based on average cost of a double room for one night.
$ = under $65
$$ = up to $100
$$$ = up to $150
$$$$ = over $150

NEW JERSEY

WHERE TO STAY

LAMBERTVILLE
Apple Inn
31 York Street, NJ 08530
Tel: 973-764-3735
Well-kept Victorian-style bed and full breakfast in the heart of Lambertville. Five nice rooms with private baths. **$$$**
Chimney Hill Farm Estate
207 Goat Hill Road,
NJ 08530
Tel: 609-397-1516
Fax: 609-397-9353
www.chimneyhillinn.com
An impressive gabled fieldstone house located in the hills 5 miles (8 km) from Lambertville. Candlelit country breakfasts and many other nice touches. **$$$$**

MORRISTOWN
The Madison Hotel
1 Convent Road, NJ 07960
Tel: 973-285-1800
US Freephone: 800-526-0729
Fax: 973-540-8566
www.themadisonhotel.com
Central, luxury accommodation with indoor heated swimming pool, Jacuzzi and sauna. Disabled access. **$$$$**
The Westin
2 Whippany Road, NY 07960
Tel: 973-539-7300
Fax: 973-984-1036
www.westin.com
Large, recently renovated hotel in the heart of Morristown. Facilities include 200 attractive guest rooms, two restaurants and two lounges. **$$**

TRENTON
Best Western Bordentown Inn
1068 Rt 206 Dunsmill,
NJ 08505
Tel: 609-298-8000
Fax: 609-291-9757
www.bestwesternnewjersey.com
This inn features attractive, spacious rooms with movies, cable TV, HBO and refrigerators. Other amenities include an attractive indoor pool, exercise room, sauna, bar, free parking and fishing. **$$$**
Laurel Notch Motor Lodge
US 206, Bordentown,
NJ 08505
Tel: 609-298-6500
Simple but very clean rooms. Close to local attractions. **$**

WHERE TO EAT

TRENTON
Mastoris Diner-Restaurant
144 Hwy 130, Bordentown
Tel: 609-298-4650
Excellent prime rib and an impressive 77 varieties of sandwiches. For dessert choose from the many pies baked on the premises. **$**
Sal De Forte's Ristorante
200 Fulton Street
Tel: 609-396-6856
Romantic Italian – a little bit

northern, a little bit southern – located in a century-old building with a Victorian floral style dining room and wood-paneled bar. **$$**

PENNSYLVANIA

WHERE TO STAY

LANCASTER
Strasburg Village Inn
1 W. Main St, Strasburg, PA 17579
Tel: 717-687-0900
US Freephone: 800-541-1055
Fully renovated 18th-century bed-and-breakfast inn with Colonial decor in the center of town. Amenities include: private bath, some rooms with Jacuzzi, complimentary full breakfast, air conditioning, TV, free parking. **$–$$**

PHILADELPHIA
Best Western
11580 Roosevelt Blvd, PA 19116
Tel: 215-464-9500
Fax: 215-464-8511
www.bestwesternphiladelphia.com
Good, clean, motel lodging at a decent price, about 25–30 minutes north of city center by car. Amenities: restaurant, lounge, fitness center, outdoor pool, game room and free parking. **$–$$**
Omni Hotel at Independence Park
401 Chestnut St, PA 19106
Tel: 215-925-0000
Fax: 215-925-1263
www.omnihotels.com
Plush hotel located in Old City adjacent to Independence National Park. Featuring Azalea, a gourmet restaurant and lounge; indoor pool, health club and sauna. **$$$$**
Thomas Bond House
129 S. 2nd St, PA 19106
Tel: 215-923-8523
US Freephone: 800-845-2663
www.winston-salem-inn.com/philadelphia
A handsome, Federal-style B&B maintained by the National Park Service with 10 rooms and two suites in the heart of the historic district. Amenities: private and shared bath, some rooms with fireplace, whirlpool, sofa bed, free continental breakfast. **$$–$$$**

Omni Hotel at Independence Park
401 Chestnut Street.
Tel: 215-925-0000;
US Freephone: 1-800-THE-OMNI.
Plush, sleek, hotel located in Old City adjacent to Independence National Park. Amenities: Azalea, a gourmet restaurant, lounge; indoor pool, health club, sauna, concierge, air-conditioning, TV. **$$$**

WHERE TO EAT

LANCASTER
Olde Greenfield Inn
595 Greenfield Road
Tel: 717-393-0668
www.theoldegreenfieldinn.com
Interesting, carefully prepared international seafood, poultry, steak and pasta in a historic farmhouse just outside of town. **$$**

PHILADELPHIA
Le Bec-Fin
1523 Walnut St
Tel: 215-567-1000
Regarded as one of the finest restaurants in the country, this very expensive French favorite near Rittenhouse Square garners rave reviews from critics and clients alike. Reservations required. A la carte menu served at the downstairs bistro. **$$$$**
La Famiglia
8 S. Front St
Tel: 215-922-2803
An Old City favorite for high-class Italian food in a lovely formal setting. **$$$–$$$$**
Jim's Steaks
400 South St
Tel: 215-928-1911
Many cheese-steak connoisseurs consider this funky little place the tastiest in town. **$**

Restaurant Prices

Categories based on average cost of dinner and a glass of wine, before tip.
$ = under $15
$$ = up to $30
$$$ = over $30

Joe's Peking Duck House
925 Race St
Tel: 215-922-3277
Many think this Chinatown standard, with non-existent decor and crowded ambiance serves the best Chinese food in town. **$$**

SHOPPING

PHILADELPHIA
Numerous *haute couture* boutiques line the streets around Liberty Place and Rittenhouse Square. The largest shopping district in the city is on Market Street east of Broad Street. Here you'll find **Lord & Taylor**, formerly John Wanamaker, (13th and Market), the grandad of Philadelphia department stores housed in a landmark building across from City Hall.

Farther east on **Market Street**, past discount shops, sporting goods, electronics, shoes and clothing stores, is **The Gallery**, a modern shopping mall which occupies three square blocks and four levels between 11th and 8th streets. There are over 200 shops and restaurants around the airy, sky-lit atrium including three department stores (**Kmart, J.C. Penney** and **Strawbridges**) and a surprisingly interesting food court that's convenient for quick and inexpensive meals or snacks.

Market Place East is next to **The Gallery** at 8th and Market streets. Housed in a magnificent cast-iron structure once occupied by **Lit Brothers Department Store**, this block-long mixed-use complex is now divided between offices and about 25 stores and restaurants.

For more adventurous tastes, **South Street** is the place to go. The shops and eateries on or near South Street from 9th to Front streets include everything from punk shops and art galleries to rock bars and fine restaurants. This is the hip, edgy part of town, popular with, but certainly not limited to, young people. It tends to be a bit of a carnival on Friday and Saturday nights, but it's almost always interesting. At one time, South Street ran through a large Jewish neighborhood. A remnant of those days can still be found on **Fabric Row**, which runs along 4th Street south of South Street. Mammoth **King of Prussia Mall** is beaten in size only by Minnesota's Mall of America.

MARYLAND

WHERE TO STAY

ANNAPOLIS
Maryland Inn
16 Church Circle, MD 21401
Tel: 410-263-2641
Fax: 410-268-3613
US Freephone: 800-847-8882
www.annapolisinns.com
A pub and tavern with splendid rooms, many dating to the revolutionary era. The wooden porches,and marble tiled lobby are Victorian. **$$$$**

Hotel Prices

Categories based on average cost of a double room for one night.
$ = under $65
$$ = up to $100
$$$ = up to $150
$$$$ = over $150

BALTIMORE
Admiral Fell Inn
888 South Broadway, MD 21231
Tel: 410-522-7377
Fax: 410-522-0707
www.admiralfell.com
Pleasing proportions and custom-crafted Federal-style furnishings characterize this well-preserved Fells Point inn. The Admiral Fell has received many accolades for its New American cuisine and award-winning wine cellar. Guests are offered free parking and transportation to local attractions. **$$$$**
Celie's Waterfront B&B
1714 Thames Street, MD 21231
Tel: 410-522-2323
Fax: 410-522-2324
US Freephone: 800-432-0184

www.celieswaterfront.com
Seven gorgeous rooms with private balconies commanding superb harbor views. **$$$**
Inn at the Colonnade
4 West University Parkway
Tel: 410-235-5400
US Freephone: 800-222-TREE
Fax: 410-366-6734
www.colonnadebaltimore.com
Just across from Johns Hopkins University, this is a businessman's haunt in a land of students. **$$$$**
Mount Vernon Hotel
24 W Franklin Street, 21001
Tel: 410-727-2000
Located in Baltimore's mid-town areas, you are very near the Peabody Conservatory and other attractions. **$$$**

WHERE TO EAT

ANNAPOLIS
Carrol's Creek Restaurant
410 Severn Avenue
Tel: 410-263-8102
Critically acclaimed waterfront restaurant with fabulous views. **$$$**

BALTIMORE
Obrycki's Crab House
1727 East Pratt Street
Tel: 410-732-6399
Rich, well-flavored seafood dishes. Super-fresh Chesapeake Bay crab is often the star of the show. **$$**
Woman's Industrial Exchange
333 North Charles Street
Tel: 410-685-4388
Well-prepared American home-style cooking. Wonderful egg and bacon breakfasts accompanied by fat clouds of "scratch" biscuits. For lunch try the well-seasoned crab cakes or an old fashioned chicken salad. Welcoming atmosphere. **$$**
4 West
4 West University Parkway, Doubletree Inn at the Colonnade
Tel: 410-235-8200
A favourite with the business travellers looking for dependable fine dining. A raw bar offers a fresh selection of seafood. **$$**

Ixia
518 N Charles Street
Tel: 410-727-1800
Baltimore's fresh seafood gets dressed up with a contemporary Asian flare. **$$$**

SHOPPING

BALTIMORE
Harborplace & The Gallery
200 East Pratt Street
Over 100 shops, restaurants and cafes in a sensational atrium mall.

VIRGINIA

WHERE TO STAY

BLACKSBURG
Best Western Red Lion Inn
900 Plantation Road, VA 24060
Tel: 540-552-7770
Fax: 540-552-6346
Close to Virginia Tech and Smithfield Plantation. Cable TV, lounge, pool, playground and restaurant. **$$**

CHARLOTTESVILLE
Cavalier Inn
1613 Emmett Street, VA 22905
Tel: 434-296-8111
Standard motel rooms in the university district. Complimentary breakfast, courtesy shuttle, seasonal outdoor pool, and restaurant. **$**
Clifton – The Country Inn
1296 Clifton Inn Drive, VA 22911
Tel: 434-971-1800
Fax: 434-971-7098
US Freephone: 888-971-1800
www.cliftoninn.com
Elegant Federal and colonial revival-style historic manor house surrounded by 40 wooded acres (17 hectares). Guest rooms are furnished with antiques and a wood-burning fireplace. Facilities include clay tennis courts, pool, whirlpool and award-winning cuisine. **$$$$**
Silver Thatch Inn
3001 Hollymead Drive, VA 22911
Tel: 434-978-4686
Fax: 434-978-6156
US Freephone: 800-261-0720
www.silverthatch.com
This delightful clapboard home is one of the oldest buildings in

central Virginia. Accommodations comprise seven guest rooms all with private baths and several with canopy beds and fireplaces. The uniquely appointed rooms are named after early Virginian-born presidents. There are three dining rooms and a bar. **$$$–$$$$**

LEXINGTON
Historic Country Inns
11 North Main St, VA 24450
Tel: 877-283-9680
Fax: 540-463-7262
www.lexingtonhistoricinns.com
This firm runs three inns in the area: two in the Lexington Historic District – the Alexander Withrow House and McCampbell Inn – and Maple Hall 6 miles (9 km) to the north on 56 acres (22 hectares). All inns feature fireplaces, fine dining, trails and pool. **$$$–$$$$**
B&B at Llewellyn Lodge
603 Main Street, VA 24450
Tel/Fax: 540-463-3235
US Freephone: 800-882-1145
www.llodge.com
Six comfortable, individually decorated rooms in an attractive gray brick colonial building. This inn is known for its tempting breakfast menu featuring the innkeeper's award-winning omelets. A health-conscious menu is also available. Other features include four poster beds, ceiling fans and a porch swing. Situated close to Downtown, this is the ideal base for visiting Lexington's attractions. **$$$**

RICHMOND
West-Bocock House
1107 Grove Avenue, VA 23220
Tel: 804-358-6174
This elegant 19th-century historic house is well-placed for visiting the city's attractions. Guest rooms have private baths, fresh flowers and French linen. **$$**

WHERE TO EAT

CHARLOTTESVILLE
Blue Bird Café
625 West Main Street
Tel: 434-295-1166

Appetizing lunches featuring steaks, fried chicken and crab cakes. **$$**
C&O Restaurant
515 East Water Street
Tel: 434-971-7044
Imaginative dishes with a French influence served in an attractively converted rail workers' layover. Try the sliced, marinated and seared flank steak. Elegant but casual atmosphere. **$$**
Millers
109 West Main Street
Tel: 434-971-8511
An old-style and pleasantly smoky atmosphere bar. Formerly a drugstore specializing in "Miller's Tonic" in the early 1900s. The current Millers' dispenses great cheeseburgers and a nice grilled chicken salad. Sit on the outdoor patio with bubbling fountain and listen to live jazz. **$**

FREDERICKSBURG
Kenmore Inn
1200 Princess Anne Street
Tel: 540-371-7622
Good steak and seafood restaurant with live entertainment. **$$**

LEXINGTON
Virginia House
722 South Main Street, VA 24450
Tel: 540-463-3643
Mouth-watering southern cooking. **$**

RICHMOND
Bill's Barbecue
3100 N Boulevard
Tel: 804-358-8634
Bill's is justly popular for lavish portions of succulent barbecue and excellent breakfasts. **$**
Millie's Diner
2603 East Main
Tel: 804-643-5512
Excellent New Southern cooking in a remodeled traditional diner. **$$**

Restaurant Prices

Categories based on average cost of dinner and a glass of wine, before tip.
$ = under $15
$$ = up to $30
$$$ = over $30

The Tobacco Company
1201 East Cary Street
Tel: 804-782-9555
www.thetobaccocompany.com
This restaurant features creative New American cuisine in a converted tobacco warehouse. **$$**

ROANOKE
Awful Arthur's
2229 Colonial Avenue SW
Tel: 540-777-0007
Much-loved seafood restaurant in an attractive historic location. Entrees include steamed crab, oysters, clams and fresh fish. **$**
Roanoker
2522 Colonial Avenue
Tel: 540-344-7746
Short on atmosphere but long on portions of delicious, southern cooking. A wide array of well-prepared vegetable side dishes, rich gravies, and other good trimmings. **$**

NORTH CAROLINA

WHERE TO STAY

CHAPEL HILL
Carolina Inn
211 Pittsboro Street, NC 27516
Tel: 919-933-2001
US Freephone: 800-962-8519
Fax: 919-962-3400
www.carolinainn.com
This elegantly furnished historic inn provides a good base for exploring downtown Chapel Hill and the shops and restaurants of Franklin Street. Extras include complimentary breakfast and newspaper. The inn's Crossroads restaurant has been awarded a four diamond rating by the AAA. **$$$$**

DURHAM
Carolina Duke Motor Inn
2517 Guess Road, NC 27705
Tel/Fax: 919-286-0771
US Freephone: 800-438-1158
Very reasonable rooms and suites. Amenities include pool and area transportation. **$**

GREENSBORO
Microtel Inn
4304 Big Tree Way, NC 27409
Tel: 336-547-7007

Hotel Prices

Categories based on average cost of a double room for one night.
$ = under $65
$$ = up to $100
$$$ = up to $150
$$$$ = over $150

Clean, comfortable, good-value motor inn. **$**

MANTEO
Tranquil House Inn
405 Queen Elizabeth St, NC 27954
Tel: 252-473-1404
US Freephone: 800-458-7069
A pleasant waterfront inn with suites, rooms and a deck. Extras include a complimentary breakfast and wine & cheese evening. A good place to relax and renew. **$$–$$$**

MT AIRY
Mayberry Motor Inn
1001US Hwy 52N, NC 27030
Tel: 336-786-4109
www.mayberrymotorinn.com
Well-kept, comfortable rooms. Very good value. Continental breakfast. Nearby jogging and nature trail. **$**

NAGS HEAD
Carolinian Hotel
2313 Virginia Dare Trail, NC 27959
Tel: 252-441-7171
Fax: 252-441-9514
A rustic waterfront hotel with 86 rooms, cooking facilities. Amenities include exercise and game rooms, lounge, restaurant and pool. **$$$**
First Colony Inn
6720 S Virginia Dare Trail, NC 27959
Tel: 252-441-2343
Fax: 252-441-9234
US Freephone: 800-368-9390
www.firstcolonyinn.com
Handsome older inn, carefully restored and furnished with antiques. Babysitting services, two Jacuzzis, pool. **$$**

OCRACOKE
The Island Inn and Dining Room
PO Box 9, NC 27960
Tel: 252-928-4351

US Freephone: 877-456-3466
Fax: 252-928-4352
www.ocracokeislandinn.com
The characterful older section (c.1901) offers rooms with antiques, private baths and a heated outdoor pool. The newer motel-style section also has a pool and welcomes families. Villa "full efficiencies" with cooking facilities are also available. The inn's dining room is known for its fresh, well-cooked seafood and hush puppies. Guests may use the inn's canoes, boats and rafts. **$$$**

WILMINGTON
Carolinian Inn
2916 Market Street, NC 28403
Tel: 910-763-4653
US Freephone: 800-528-1234
Between Downtown and the Atlantic beaches. Recently remodeled incorporating de luxe amenities, and lovely mature gardens. Free continental breakfast. **$$**
The Inn on Orange B&B
410 Orange Street, NC 28401
Tel: 910-815-0035
US Freephone: 800-381-4666
Fax: 910-762-2279
www.innonorange.com
An historic Italianate Victorian home located within walking distance of the riverside and close to Downtown. The inn features ceiling fans, fireplaces and TVs on request. Full breakfast is served on the weekends; continental breakfast is available on weekdays. There is a two-night minimum stay on the weekend. **$$–$$$**

WINSTON-SALEM
Tanglewood Manor House B&B
Hwy 158W, 4061 Clemmons, NC 27012
Tel: 336-778-6370
Fax: 336-778-6379
www.tanglewoodpark.org
Located in a country park with fishing pier, horseback riding, jogging and nature trail nearby. Canoes, boats and rafts are available for use by guests. Restaurant, playground and some rooms with fireplaces. **$$**
Best Western Salem Inn
127 South Cherry St, NC 27101
US Freephone: 800-533-8760

Fax: 336-725-2318
www.saleminn.com
Well-maintained budget inn with exercise room, lounge, pool, jogging and nature trail. Continental breakfast provided. **$**

WHERE TO EAT

CHAPEL HILL
Spanky's
101 East Franklin Street
Tel: 919-967-2678
Buzzing restaurant serving sandwiches, seafood and pasta. Spanky's club sandwich is a favorite with both locals and visitors. **$**

MOUNT AIRY
Snappy Lunch
125 North Main Street
Tel: 336-786-4931
The Snappy Lunch is known for its hefty pork chop sandwich — a cornucopia of juicy meat, condiments and trimmings. Plenty of atmosphere too. **$**

WILMINGTON
Elijah's Restaurant
2 Ann Street
Tel: 910-343-1448
Award-winning seafood chowder and other delectable, equally praiseworthy dishes. The adjoining oyster bar with outdoor covered patio faces onto Cape Fear. **$$**

WINSTON-SALEM
Village Tavern
221 Reynolda Village
Tel: 336-748-0221
Popular family restaurant offering pub-style food and lively atmosphere. **$$**

SOUTH CAROLINA

WHERE TO STAY

BEAUFORT
Rhett House
1009 Craven Street, SC 29902
Tel: 843-524-9030
Fax: 843-524-1310
US Freephone: 888-480-9530
www.rhetthouseinn.com
Plantation house bordering the

Intercoastal waterway. Built in 1820 and restored following the Civil War, the inn features stately white columns, broad verandahs, rocking chairs and period decor. Many rooms have fireplaces, private balconies and whirlpool baths. Afternoon tea. **$$$$**

CHARLESTON
Governer's House Inn
117 Broad Street, SC 29401
Tel: 843-720-2070
US Freephone: 800-720-9812
www.governorshouse.com
Attention to detail, elegant decor and exceptional service are hallmarks of this historic inn. Originally the residence of Governor Edward Rutledge, the youngest signer of the Declaration of Independence, the house still retains an air of tradition with its broad verandah, chandeliers, numerous fireplaces and spacious rooms. In the center of the historic district and close to many land-marks and restaurants. **$$$$**
Two Meeting Street Inn
Two Meeting Street, SC 29401
Tel: 843-723-7322
www.twomeetingstreet.com
The distinguished sister of the Governor's House. Built in 1844, the inn originally housed a saloon and restaurant. Having fallen into disrepair after Hurricane Hugo it has been lovingly restored. **$$-$$$**

GEORGETOWN
Carolinian Clarion
706 Church Street, SC 29440
Tel: 803-546-5191
Pleasant affordable rooms. Pool. **$**
Harbor House Bed and Breakfast
15 Cannon Street, SC 29440
Tel: 843-546-6532
US Freephone: 877-511-0101
www.harborhouse.com
Large waterfront inn with distinctive red roof. Built in 1740 as a shipping warehouse. Lovely, spacious rooms. **$$$**

MYRTLE BEACH
Coral Beach Resort
1105 South Ocean Blvd, SC 29577

Tel: 843-448-8412
US Freephone: 800-843-2684
Fax: 843-626-0156
www.coral-beach.com
Full service oceanfront resort with nicely furnished guest rooms and public areas. Facilities include indoor and outdoor pools, saunas, whirlpool, restaurant and lounge. Disabled access. **$$$**
Compass Cove
2311 S Ocean Blvd, SC 29577
Tel: 843-448-8373
US Freephone: 800-331-0934
www.compasscove.com
Large family-friendly resort situated 2½ miles (4 km) from the Pavilion with ocean-front rooms. The complex has pools, Jacuzzis, restaurant and lounge. **$$**

WHERE TO EAT

CHARLESTON
Cru Café
18 Pinckney Street
Tel: 843-534-2434
An imaginative menu featuring fresh, well-cooked seafood combined with a pleasant terrace, relaxed atmosphere, fragrant coffees and irresistible desserts justify its popularity. **$**

GEORGETOWN
Pink Magnolia
719 Front Street
Tel: 843-527-6506
Fresh seafood salads, creole and crab cakes served at your table right on the harbor walk or indoors. The non-seafood specialty is a fried chicken salad. **$$**

JACKSONBORO
Edisto Motel Cafe
US Hwy 17
Tel: 843-893-2270

Restaurant Prices

Categories based on average cost of dinner and a glass of wine, before tip.
$ = under $15
$$ = up to $30
$$$ = over $30

Luscious fried seafood in a casual setting. **$$**

MYRTLE BEACH
Omega Pancake and Omelet House
2800 North Kings Hwy
Tel: 843-626-9949
Favorite breakfast spot for tourists and locals alike. **$**

GEORGIA

WHERE TO STAY

BRUNSWICK
Hostel in the Forest
P.O. Box 1496, GA 31521
Tel: 912-264-9738
www.foresthostel.com
This hostel offers beds in tree houses or geodesic dome. Amenities include tranquility and natural beauty. **$**

ST SIMONS ISLAND
The Lodge on Little Simons Island
PO Box 21078, GA 31522 0578
Tel: 912-638-7472
US Freephone: 888-733-5774
Fax: 912-634-1811
www.littlestsimonsisland.com
This unique lodge, set on an un-spoiled barrier hosts only 30 over-night guests. The only way there is by boat. Price includes three southern meals and on-island activities. Idyllic. **$$$$**

SAVANNAH
The Gastonian
220 East Gaston Street, GA 31401
Tel: 912-232-2869
US Freephone: 800-322-6603
Fax: 912-232-0710
www.gastonian.com
This 16-unit historic B&B consists of restored, connected late-1800s houses. Six rooms with whirlpool bath. No pets allowed. **$$$$**
East Bay Inn
225 East Bay Street, GA 31401
Tel: 912-238-1225
US Freephone: 800-500-1225
Fax: 912-232-2709
www.eastbayinn.com
An historic bed-and-breakfast, this 28-unit restored 1853 warehouse features large, Georgian-style rooms. **$$$-$$$$**

Magnolia Place Inn
503 Whitaker Street, GA 31401
Tel: 912-236-7674
US Freephone: 800-238-7674
Fax: 912-236-1145
www.magnoliaplaceinn.com
A 12-unit restored Victorian
mansion, this historic B&B has a
hot tub in the courtyard and
whirlpools and fireplaces in some
rooms. No pets. **$$$$**

Olde Harbour Inn
508 East Factors Walk, GA 31401
Tel: 912-234-4100
US Freephone: 800-553-6533
Fax: 912-233-5979
www.oldharborinn.com
A 24-unit historic bed-and-breakfast
in the historic riverfront district.
River-view suites with fully equipped
kitchens. **$$$–$$$$**

WHERE TO EAT

BRUNSWICK
GA Pig
Exit 29 off I-95
Tel: 912-264-6664
Expertly prepared barbecue dished
up in pleasant surroundings. A
mighty fine pit stop. **$**

MIDWAY
**Ida Mae & Joe's North Midway
Restaurant**
US Hwy 17
Tel: 912-884-3388
Very fresh, expertly fried fish. **$**

ST SIMONS ISLAND
Dressner's Village Cafe
223 Mallory Street
Tel: 912-634-1217
A good choice for breakfast. **$**

SAVANNAH
The Chart House
202 West Bay Street
Tel: 912-234-6686

Restaurant Prices

Categories based on average
cost of dinner and a glass of
wine, before tip.
$ = under $15
$$ = up to $30
$$$ = over $30

Reserve a table and order the
prime rib in this three-story
nautical-themed restored
warehouse. **$$**

Mrs. Wilkes' Boarding House
107 West Jones Street
Tel: 912-232-5997
Southern-style communal dining,
the old boarding house way. Pass
the biscuits and fried chicken, and
get there early. Lunch only. **$**

The Pirates' House
20 East Broad and Bay streets
Tel: 912-233-5757
Seafood galore at this Savannah
landmark. **$$$**

Downtown Cafe at Main
1 West Broughton Street
Tel: 912-233-9666
A touch of seafood enhances this
mostly Italian menu. Good location
and a wine list straight from the
Sonoma Valley. **$$$**

SHOPPING

SAVANNAH
Oglethorpe Mall
7804 Abercorn Street
Savannah Festival Factory Stores
11 Gateway Boulevard, South
Savannah Mall
Rio Road and Abercorn Ext

FLORIDA

WHERE TO STAY

*BAHIA HONDA STATE
RECREATION AREA*
For information about the park,
Tel: 305-872-2353.
Big Pine Key Fishing Lodge
33000 Overseas Hwy,
Summerland Key, FL 33048
Tel: 305-872-2351
Spick and span lodge rooms and
five canal-side motel rooms with
cooking facilities. **$$**
Deer Run Bed & Breakfast
Long Beach Road, FL 33043
Tel: 305-872-2015
Spacious guest rooms with
ocean views located in two
houses near the bay. Deer roam
the surrounding native wooded
land (also a good bird-watching
area). Amenities include a Jacuzzi

on the beach, porches and private
balconies. **$$**

BRADENTON
Silver Surf Motel and Efficiencies
1301 Gulf Drive North, FL 34217
Tel: 941-778-6626
US Freephone: 800-441-7873
Fax: 941-778-4308
www.silverresorts.com
A de luxe waterfront hotel featuring
panoramic Gulf views, pool and
private sandy beach. **$$**

CLEARWATER BEACH
Belleview Biltmore
25 Belleview Boulevard, FL 33756
Tel: 727-442-6171
US Freephone: 800-237-8947
www.belleviewbiltmore.com
This grand old four season resort
has been welcoming guests since
1897. Recreational facilities include
red clay tennis courts, an excellent
golf course, a de luxe spa and
fitness center. **$$–$$$$**

**Hostelling International –
Clearwater Beach**
606 Bay Esplanade, FL 33767
Tel/Fax: 727-443-1211
www.clearwaterbeachhotel.com
Close to shops with pool,
landscaped courtyard, barbecue
and picnic area, kitchen, laundry
lockers and on-site parking. **$**

EVERGLADES NATIONAL PARK
For information about the park,
Tel: 239-242-7700.
40001 State Road 9336
Homestead, FL 33034
**Flamingo Lodge and Marina and
Outpost Resort**
1 Flamingo Lodge Highway, 33034
Tel: 239-695-3101
US Freephone: 800-600-3811
Fax: 239-695-3921
www.flamingolodge.com
Simple rooms and decent food in
this remote Everglades outpost. **$$**

FORT MYERS
Mantanzas Inn
414 Crescent Street, FL 33931
Tel: 239-463-9258
US Freephone: 800-462-9258
Fax: 239-765-9258
www.mantanzasinn.com
Nicely decorated rooms and close

to the beach. Facilities include pool and restaurant. **$$**

HOMESTEAD
Everglades Motel
605 South Krome Ave, FL 33030
Tel: 305-247-4117
Tidy rooms with pool and laundry facilities. **$–$$**

ISLAMORADA
Lime Tree Bay Resort Motel
PO Box 839, Limekey 33001
Tel: 305-664-4740
Delightful cottages, apartments and de luxe motel rooms. Amenities include a private sandy area with beach chairs, hot tub, pool, small watersports rental concession and snorkeling. **$$–$$$**

KEY LARGO
Jule's Undersea Lodge
From 51 Shoreland Drive, off MM 103.2, FL 33037
Tel: 305-451-2353
www.jul.com
A unique two-bedroomed lodge 22 ft (7 meters) beneath the sea. Originally a research facility, accommodations are basic, but comfortable. Each of the two bedrooms has a 42-inch (107-cm) round window looking into the sea, hot and cold shower, and TV/VCR. The only way to get there is by scuba diving. The price includes all gear and unlimited diving. Reserve well in advance. **$$$$**
Kona Kai Bayfront Resort
97802 Overseas Hwy, FL 33037
Tel: 305-852-7200
US Freephone: 800-365-7829
www.konakairesort.com
Waterfront resort with full kitchen facilities. **$$$**

KEY WEST
Hostelling International – Key West
718 South Street, FL 33040
Tel: 305-296-5719
Fax: 305-296-0672
www.keywesthostel.com
Located two blocks from the beach, this hostel offers scuba diving lessons, and snorkeling. There is an outdoor courtyard, barbecue pit, pool table, and laundry facilities **$**

The Marquesa Hotel
600 Fleming Street, FL 33040
Tel: 305-292-1919
US Freephone: 800-869-4631
Fax: 305-294-2121
www.marquesa.com
This late 19th-century landmark has been lovingly restored to its original splendor. Tucked in the heart of Key West's Historic District, four handsome buildings encircle two swimming pools and luxurious tropical gardens. Amenities include marble baths and fine dining in the adjoining Café Marquesa. **$$$$**
Southernmost Motel in the USA
1319 Duval Street, FL 33040
Tel: 305-296-6577
US Freephone: 800-354-4455
Fax: 305-294-8272
127 guest rooms in a beautiful old home. Two large pools and poolside bars, Jacuzzi, public beach access, bicycle moped rental and warm, friendly service. **$$$–$$$$**

KISSIMMEE
Sevilla Inn
4640 West Irlo Bronson Hwy, FL 34746
Tel: 407-396-4135
A well-maintained motor inn with pool. **$**

MELBOURNE BEACH
Hostelling International – Melbourne Beach
1135 North A1A, FL 32903
Tel: 407-951-0004
Email: emccan@aol
Situated on the beach and convenient for area attractions. Amenities include kitchen, lockers, laundry and volleyball. Ocean kayaks and surfboards are available for guests' use. **$**

MICANOPY
Scottish Inns
17110 SE CR 234, FL 32667
Tel: 352-466-3163
Squeaky clean budget rooms and a restaurant. **$**

NAPLES
Vanderbilt Inn on the Gulf
11000 Gulf Shore Dr N, FL 34108
Tel: 239-597-3151

Hotel Prices
Categories based on average cost of a double room for one night.
$ = under $65
$$ = up to $100
$$$ = up to $150
$$$$ = over $150

US Freephone: 800-648-8654
Fax: 239-597-3099
www.vanderbiltinn.com
With a Caribbean flavor, this full-service Gulf resort features 300 ft (100 meters) of fine sandy beach, restau-rant, lounge and beachside bar. Very comfortable rooms, with balcony or patio. **$$$$**

OCALA
Travelodge
1626 SW Pine Ave, FL 34474
Tel: 352-622-4121
Well-fitted rooms some with microwaves and refrigerators. Pool and free continental breakfast. **$**

ORLANDO
Embassy Suites – Lake Buena Vista
8100 Lake Avenue, FL 32836
Tel: 407-239-1144
Fax: 407-238-0230
www.embassy-suites.com
Spacious suites with in-room movies, fitness center, whirlpool, steam room and family fun center. Free breakfast and transportation to Walt Disney World. **$$$$**
Extended Stay
8750 Universal Blvd, FL 32819
Tel: 407-903-1500
Fax: 407-903-1555
www.sierra-orlando.com
Good-sized, family friendly suites. Conveniently located for all area attractions. Heated pool, exercise room and spa. Very good value. **$$**
Hostelling International – Orlando/Kissimmee
4840 West Irlo Bronson, FL 34746
Tel: 407-396-8282
A stone's throw from Walt Disney World and close to other attractions. Facilities include air-conditioning, lake, en-suite bath-rooms. Wheelchair accessible. **$**

Hotel Prices

Categories based on average cost of a double room for one night.
$ = under $65
$$ = up to $100
$$$ = up to $150
$$$$ = over $150

Walt Disney World All-Star Resorts
The cheapest rooms within Walt Disney World.
All Star Movie Resort
Tel: 407-939-7000. $$$
All Star Music Resort
Tel: 407-939-6000. $$
All Star Sports Resort
Tel: 407-939-5000. $$

ST AUGUSTINE
Kenwood Inn
38 Marine Street, FL 32084
Tel: 904-824-2116
US Freephone: 800-824-8151
Fax: 904-824-1689
www.thekenwoodinn.com
This time-honored Victorian hotel is close to the seafront and other attractions. $$–$$$

ST PETERSBURG
Coral Reef Beach Resort
5800 Gulf Boulevard, FL 33714
Tel: 727-360-0821
Fax: 727-367-3718
A first-class resort with de luxe suites and nicely appointed rooms. The pool is enormous. Beach bar and restaurant. $$–$$$

SANIBEL ISLAND
South Seas Plantation
PO Box 194, 5400 South Seas Plantation Road, FL 33924
Tel: 941-472-5111
US Freephone: 800-237-3102
www.southseas.com
Sprawling resort occupying most of the island and Sanibel's first. Guests can choose from condominium style and well-fitted standard guest rooms. $$$$

TAMPA
East Lake Inn
6529 E Hillborough Ave, FL 33610
Tel: 813-622-8339

Clean and comfortable rooms, some with refrigerators. $
Radisson Bay Harbor Inn
7700 Courtney Campbell Causeway, FL 33607
Tel: 813-876-4648
Handsomely appointed rooms with balconies. The inn also has a restaurant and lounge, pool, private beach with watersports and exercise room. Close to local attractions. $$$
Quality Suites – University of South Florida/Busch Gardens
3001 University Center Drive, FL 33612
Tel: 813-971-8930
Nice rooms and lots of extras including complimentary beverages and snacks, a buffet breakfast. Pool and Jacuzzi. $$$

TARPON SPRINGS
Tarpon Shores Inn
40346 US Hwy 19N, FL 34689
Tel: 727-938-2483
Fax: 727-738-2486
Good-value rooms, some with microwaves and refrigerators. Facilities include pool, Jacuzzi and laundry facilities. $

WHERE TO EAT

BRADENTON
Crab Trap and Crab Trap II
4815 Memphis Road, Ellenton
Tel: 941-729-7777
Hwy 19 at Terra Ceia
Tel: 941-722-6255
A local favorite for fine fresh-catch and game dishes. $$
Sandbar Restaurant
100 Spring Avenue, Anna Maria
Tel: 941-778-0444
Good food and excellent views. $

CLEARWATER BEACH
Kaiko Japanese Restaurant
2475 McMullen Booth Road
Tel: 727-791-6640
First-rate sashimi, sushi and teriyaki. $$

FORT MYERS
The Veranda
2122 Second Street
Tel: 941-332-2065

Continental cuisine served in a mellow old mansion with pleasant courtyard. Try the rack of lamb. Mellow atmosphere and steep prices. $$$

GAINESVILLE
Sovereign
12 Southeast Second Avenue
Tel: 352-378-6307
Fine dining in a posh 19th-century carriage house. $$$

ISLAMADORA
Manny & Isa's Restaurant
US Hwy 1 Mile Marker 81.6
Tel: 305-664-5019
Manny and Isa's is justly famous for mouthwatering key lime pie – possibly the best, certainly the freshest – to be had anywhere. The limes come from Manny's orchard. The spicy and savory dishes are seriously tempting as well. $

JACKSONVILLE
Matthews at St Marco's
2107 Hendricks Avenue
Tel: 904-396-9922
Spare and chic interior – innovative menu. The five-course tasting menu is a good intro-duction to this innovative and varied menu. $$$

KEY LARGO
Crack'd Conch
105045 Overseas Highway
Tel: 305-451-0732
A sublimely relaxed venue for soaking up a few beers with the local atmosphere and tucking into a heaped plateful of fried conch. $

KEY WEST
Blue Heaven
729 Thomas Street
Tel: 305-296-8666
Relaxed, time-worn and popular cafe serving West Indian-style breakfasts, lunches and dinners. $
Pepe's Cafe
806 Caroline Street
Tel: 305-294-7192
Excellent grilled steak, succulent oysters and fragrant, fresh-baked breads, indoor and outdoor dining and a very popular bar. $$

Louie's Backyard
700 Waddell Avenue
Tel: 305-294-1061
Fine American and Caribbean
cooking in a romantic, seaside
setting with old Key West ambience.
One of Florida's finest. **$**
Camille's
1202 Simonton Street
Tel: 305-296-4811
With a menu that changes daily,
Camille's is one of the Keys'
best buget eateries for Breakfast,
lunch or dinner. Specialties
include pecan waffles, stone
crab cakes, smoked salmon and
garlic pork. **$$**

MARATHON
Herbie's
Mile Marker 50.5
Tel: 305-743-6373
Great seafood and chowders. **$$**

OCALA
Petite Jardin
2209 East Silver Springs Boulevard
Tel: 352-351-4140.
Authentically French bistro dishes
including *escargots*. **$$**

ORLANDO
Harvey's Bistro
6400 Time Square Avenue
Tel: 407-313-2020
A Downtown eatery with a loyal
following. Good soups, casseroles
and pizzas. **$$**
Fulton's Crab House
Aboard three-deck riverboat at
Downtown Disney (priority seating)
Seafood specialties with fresh fish
flown in daily. Raw seafood bar.
$$$
Hard Rock Cafe
Universal Citywalk
Tel: (407) 351-7625
Burgers and sandwiches, fries
and shakes, in an over-the-top
shrine to rock's biggest stars. **$$**
Wild Jacks
7634 International Drive
Tel: (407) 352-4407
A Western-style eatery with
mounted buffalo heads on the
walls and an open-pit barbecue
(tangy grilled shrimp, big steaks,
Texas rice and sweet molasses
bread). **$**

Restaurant Prices

Categories based on average
cost of dinner and a glass of
wine, before tip.
$ = under $15
$$ = up to $30
$$$ = over $30

ST AUGUSTINE
Fiddler's Green Oceanside Bar
2750 Anahma Drive
Tel: 904-824-8897
www.thefiddlersgreen.com
Fine views and good food. **$$**
Raintree
102 San Marco Avenue
Tel: 904-829-5953
www.raintreerestaurant.com
Very good seafood with freshly
baked breads and pastries served
in a restored older home. **$$**

TAMPA
Silver Ring Cafe
7419 US 301
Tel: 813-677-1487
Heaped platters of authentic Cuban
dishes. **$**

VENICE
Saltwater Café
1071 Tamiami Trail South
Tel: 941-488-3775
Well-liked seafood restaurant. **$$**

SHOPPING

If you are into kitsch – plastic
flamingo ashtrays, canned
sunshine, orange perfume – you
will find Florida a veritable
treasure house. From roadside
shacks to massive, futuristic
malls, stores carry plenty of
traditional souvenirs. (Don't be
surprised if your souvenir plate
has a sticker on the bottom that
says "Made in Taiwan.") And then,
of course, there are the
homegrown souvenirs like
oranges, tangerines, limes,
kumquats and grapefruits that can
be shipped home for a small fee.
But if you look a little harder,
Florida also has an array of quality
goods to take home from a trip.

There are shops worth seeking out
that sell designer clothing at
factory prices, primitive Haitian
art, Art Deco and old Florida
antiques, Native Indian crafts, and
shells that forever smell of the
sea. For more humdrum shopping
there is the usual array of
convenience stores, drugstores,
department stores and
supermarkets. Many Floridians do
their shopping in shopping malls,
which contain the usual mix of
department stores, boutiques,
chain stores and one-of-a-kind
shops. The **Gold Coast** has the
biggest choice of malls,
particularly Miami, Fort
Lauderdale and Boca Raton. Just
ask the staff in your hotel for
details of the best malls in your
area. Hours vary, but most
shopping centers are open seven
days a week. The following list
highlights just a few of Florida's
most famous shopping spots.

Everglades National Park
Miccosukee Indian Village, west of
the Shark Valley entrance, sells
Native American crafts.

Fort Lauderdale
Fashion Mall at Plantation's
University Drive north of Broward
Boulevard contains over 100
specialty shops and several
nationwide outlets. The food court
is a cut above the ordinary.

Key West
Gingerbread Square Gallery at
1207 Duval Street sells works by
local artists.

Hub City:
MIAMI

GETTING AROUND

Public transportation
From the airport: Miami
International Airport is 7 miles
(12 km) from Downtown. Super
Shuttle (tel: 305-871-2000)
operates between the airport
and major hotels. Metrobus
service departs from Level 1
next to Concourse E.

Rapid transit: Metrorail is an elevated rapid transit system connecting Downtown with Dadeland and Hialeah. The Metromover monorail system circles the Downtown area. Metro-Dade Transit runs both (tel: 375-5675). Single fares under $2.
City buses: Metro-Dade Transit also runs the Metrobus fleet from stops indicated by distinctive blue and green signs. Single fares under $2.
Intercity buses: The main Greyhound terminal is at Bayside Station, 700 Biscayne Boulevard (tel: 800-229-9424).
Commuter rail: The Tri-Rail (tel: 800-874-7245) service links Miami-Dade with Palm Beach and Broward.
Trains: Amtrak trains run from the Miami Terminal (tel: 800-872-7245).

Private transportation

Miami is not a difficult city to negotiate by car but try to avoid weekday rush-hour snarls. Parking in the Miami Beach area can be scarce and restrictions are stringently imposed by a fleet of super-efficient tow-trucks. Fortunately, Miami Beach is a delightful place to explore by foot. Most of the car rental companies have offices at Miami International airport or Downtown. Check the *Yellow Pages* for a full list of firms.
Ports: Florida has several major cruise ship ports, with Miami and Port Everglades leading with the most sailings. Others include Port Canaveral, Palm Beach, St Petersburg, Tampa, Port Manatee (in Tampa Bay), and Madeira Beach and Treasure Island (just north of St Pete Beach). The Port of Miami is the largest cruise port in the world. Seven cruise lines carry more than 1.5 million passengers a year into the port, which represents over two-thirds of all cruise passengers worldwide. The port is just a five-minute ride from downtown and Miami Beach. Tel: 305 371-7678.
Taxis: Taxis are relatively plentiful in South Beach with fares under $3 per mile (1.6 km). They can also be found at airports, train stations bus

terminals and the major hotels, or ordered by telephone. Call Yellow Cab Co (tel: 305-633-1111); Metro Taxi (tel: 305-888-8888); or Flamingo Taxi (tel: 305-759-8100).
Car rental companies
Avis, tel: 800-462-5266
Hertz, tel: 305-654-3131

WHERE TO STAY

Astor
956 Washington Ave,
Miami Beach
Tel: 305-672-7217
Understated stylishness is the hallmark of this trendy deco hotel. Bedrooms – mostly suites – and their wall-to-wall marble bathrooms come in muted creams and beiges. The pool is striking, and Astor Place is one of South Beach's top restaurants. **$$$**
Brigham Gardens Guesthouse
1411 Collins Avenue,
Miami Beach
Tel: 305-531-1331
Charming owner-run and homely little complex of 1930s buildings. Bedrooms are jolly and arty, and vary considerably in size according to price. The best feature is the large tropical garden, with its exotic caged birds. **$$**
Cardozo
1300 Ocean Drive,
Miami Beach
Tel: 305-535-6500
US Freephone: 800-782-6500
Owned by Gloria Estefan, a Streamline Moderne Art Deco masterpiece that is bathed in purple neon at night. A lively bar, seductive dining terrace, and eye-catching bedrooms with hardwood floors, iron beds and zebra-striped furniture. **$$$**

Hotel Prices

Categories based on average cost of a double room for one night.
$ = under $65
$$ = up to $100
$$$ = up to $150
$$$$ = over $150

**Hostelling International –
Miami Beach**
1438 Washington Ave, FL 33139
Tel: 305-534-2988
US Freephone: 800-379-2529
Fax: 305-673-0346
www.clayhotel.com
Great location in the heart of the Old Miami Beach Art Deco District. Amenities include kitchen, laundry facilities, lockers/baggage storage and restaurant. **$**
Marlin
1200 Collins Avenue,
Miami Beach
Tel: 305-531 8800
US Freephone: 800-688-7678
This much-photographed lilac-colored Art Deco building houses a very hip all-suite hotel and recording studios (U2 and Aerosmith have made albums here). Rooms are high tech and have outlandish "Afro-urban" decor (exotic furniture and stainless-steel kitchens). The Opium Den bar often has live music in the evenings. **$$$$**
The Tides
1220 Ocean Drive,
Miami Beach
Tel: 305-531-8800
US Freephone: 800-688-7678
This sleek white oceanfront block contains a small luxury hotel of immaculate taste. The giant, minimalist bedrooms are really special. As well as a CD player, cordless phone and mischievous postcards with the message "Let's make love at The Tides," each has uninterrupted views of the ocean and the beach, with telescopes to spy on sunbathers. Also a good-sized swimming pool. **$$$$**

WHERE TO EAT

Casa Juancho
2436 Southwest Eighth Street
Tel: 305-642-2452
Authentic Cuban/Spanish fare. **$**
Joe's Stone Crab Restaurant
11 Washington
Tel: 305-673-0365
Regional specialties featuring the prized and delectably sweet stone crab. A Miami institution. **$$$**

Categories based on average
cost of dinner and a glass of
wine, before tip.
$ = under $15
$$ = up to $30
$$$ = over $30

News Cafe
3300 Rice Street
Tel: 305-774-1662
Very fashionable oyster bar with
outdoor dining. **$$**
Bubba Gump Shrimp Company
907 Biscayne Boulevard,
Downtown-Miami
Tel: 305-379-8866
American food, shrimp and other
specialties. **$$**
Pacific Time
915 Lincoln Road, South Beach
Tel: 305-534-5979
A rotating menu that includes
Pacific/Asian dishes such as
grouper in ginger sauce and
tempura sweet potatoes. **$$$**
Scotty's Landing
33381 Pan American Drive,
Coconut Grove
Tel: 305-854-2626
A salty shack with million dollar
views. Grilled dolphin sandwiches. **$**
Versailles
3555 SW 8th Street, Little Havana
Tel: 305-444-0240
Delicious Cuban cooking in a
wonderfully gaudy atmosphere. **$**

SHOPPING

Aventura Mall
19501 Biscayne Blvd, Aventura.
One of Miami's newest malls. Over
200 shops with a half dozen of the
major nationals including **Macy's**
Bloomingdale's, and **Lord &**
Taylor.
Kafka's
1464 Washington Ave, North
Beach
Wonderful new and second-hand
bookshop with cafe.
A&J Unique Deco
2000 Biscayne Boulevard
Exquisite, authentic Art Deco
furnishings.

Northern Route

Useful Addresses

Massachusetts tourist information
Boston
Greater Boston Convention and
Visitors Bureau, 2 Copley Place,
Suite 105, MA 02116
Tel: 800-SEEBOSTON
www.bostonusa.com
State:
Massachusetts Office of Travel and
Tourism, 10 Park Plaza, Suite
4510, Boston, MA 022116
Tel: 800-227-6277
www.mass-vacation.com
New Hampshire tourist
information
Division of Travel and Tourism
Development, PO Box 1856,
Concord, NH 03302-1856
Tel: 1-800-386-4664
www.visitnh.gov
Connecticut tourist information
The Connecticut Tourism
Department, 505 Hudson Street,
Hartford, CT 06106
Tel: 860-270-8081
US Freephone: 800-282-6863
www.tourism.state.ct.us
Maine tourist information
Maine Office of Tourism, 59 State
House Section, Augusta ME
04333-0059
Tel: 207-287-5711
US Freephone: 888-624-6345
www.visitmaine.com
Vermont tourist information
Vermont Tourist Information
Office, 6 Baldwin Street,
Montpelier, VT 05633
Tel: 800-VERMONT
www.travel-vermont.com
Ohio tourist information
Office of Travel and Tourism, PO
Box 1001, Columbus, OH 43266
Tel: 800-282-5393
www.ohiotoursim.com

Indiana tourist information
Indiana Division of Tourism, 1 North
Capitol, Suite 700, Indianapolis,
IN 46204
Fax: 317-233-6887
US Freephone: 888-ENJOYIN
www.enjoyindiana.com
Michigan tourist information
Michigan Travel Bureau, PO Box
3393, Livonia, MI 48151
US Freephone: 888-784-7328
www.michigan.org
Illinois tourist board
Illinois Department of Commerce
and Community Affairs, 620 East
Adams Street, Springfield, IL 62701
US Freephone: 800-2-CONNECT
www.enjoyillinois.com
Wisconsin tourist information
Wisconsin Department of Tourism,
201 W Washington Avenue, PO Box
7976, Madison, WI 53707
US Freephone: 800-432-8747
www.tourism.state.wi.us
Minnesota tourist information
The State Office of Tourism, 100
Metro Square, 121 7th Place E,
St Paul, MN 55101
Tel: 651-296-5029
US Freephone: 888-TOURISM
www.exploreminnesota.com
South Dakota tourist information
Dept of Tourism, Capitol Lake Plaza,
711 E Wells Avenue, c/o 500 E
Capitol Avenue, Pierre, SD 5701
Tel:605-773-3301
US Freephone: 800-732-5682
www.travelsd.com
Wyoming tourist information
Wyoming Business Council, Tourism
Division I-25 at College Drive,
Cheyenne, WY 82002
Tel: 307-777-2883
US Freephone: 800-225-5996
www.wyomingtourism.org
Montana tourist information
Travel Montana, 1424 Ninth
Avenue, PO Box 200533 Helena,
MT 59620-0533
Tel: 406-444-2654
US Freephone: 800-847-4868
www.visitmt.com
Idaho tourist information
The Idaho Travel Council,
Department of Commerce, 700 W
State Street, Boise, ID 83720
Tel: 208-334-2470
Fax: 208-334-2631
www.visitid.org

Seattle tourist information
The Seattle-King County Visitor's Bureau, One Convention Place, 701 Pike Street, Suite 800, Seattle WA 98101
Tel: 206-461-5840
www.seeseattle.org
Washington tourist information
Washington State Tourism Division PO Box 42500, Olympia, WA 98504-2500
Tel: 1-800-544-1800 ext. 101
www.tourism.wa.gov
State Parks and Recreation Commission, 7150 Clearwater Ln, Olympia, WA 98504
US Freephones:
800-452-5687 (reservations)
800-233-0321 (information)

Hub City: BOSTON

GETTING AROUND

Public Transportation
From the airport: Logan International Airport, just 3 miles (5 km) from downtown Boston, is closer to town than any other major airport in the nation: this refers to distance and not to time. Traffic can back up at the tunnels under the harbor connecting the airport and city. The MBTA Blue Line from Airport Station is the fastest way to downtown (about 10 minutes) and to many other places as well. Free shuttle buses run between all the airport terminals and the subway station. Cabs can be found outside each terminal. Fares to downtown should average about $20, including tip, providing there are no major traffic jams. Airways Transportation buses leave all terminals every half hour for downtown and Back Bay hotels, and several major bus companies, including Bonanza, Concord Trailways, Peter Pan and Vermont Transit, serve many outlying suburbs and distant destinations.
Rapid transit: Boston is the only New England city with a subway system (the MBTA, or "T" for short); the cost is relatively low. The Boston Passport, offering one, three or seven days of unlimited

rides, can be purchased at the Boston Common Visitor Information Center at 147 Tremont Street, Tel: 617-426-3115.
City buses: The majority of the MBTA's 160-plus bus routes operate feeder services linking subway stations to neighborhoods not directly served by the rapid transit system. Some crosstown routes connect stations on different subway lines without going into downtown. Only a few MBTA buses actually enter downtown Boston, and most of these are express buses from outlying areas. The basic MBTA bus fare is under $1.
Intercity buses: Several intercity bus companies serve Boston. The two largest, Greyhound (US Freephone: 800-229-9424) and Peter Pan (US Freephone: 800-237-8747), have frequent daily services from New York City and Albany, NY, as well as services from points within New England.
Commuter rail: The MBTA Commuter Rail extends from downtown Boston to as far as 60 miles (100 km) away and serves such tourist destinations as Concord, Lowell, Salem, Ipswich, Gloucester and Rockport. Trains to the north and northwest of Boston depart from North Station, while trains to points south and west of the city leave from South Station. All south side commuter trains, except the Fairmount Line, also stop at the Back Bay Station. For information on trains from any of these stations, telephone 617-222-3200.
National rail: Amtrak Passenger trains arrive at South Station (Atlantic Avenue and Summer Street, US Freephone: 800-872-7245; TDD: 800-523-6590) from New York, Washington, DC, and Philadelphia with connections from all points in the nationwide Amtrak system. They also stop at Back Bay Station (145 Dartmouth Street).

Private Transportation
Boston, it is justly claimed, is a walker's city – a good thing, for it is certainly not a driver's city. The city planners, as Emerson noted, were the cows, and it has been

suggested that the Puritan belief in predestination extended even to urban design. Streets appeared where Providence chose to lay them – along cow paths, Native American trails and colonial wagon tracks – and are linked by crooked little alleys. City planners, however, did come into their own in the middle of the 19th century, and the Back Bay, South Boston to a lesser extent, and the South End have impeccable grid systems. If you attempt to drive in the city, and feel frustrated and inadequate, be consoled that many Bostonians feel the same way. Being faced by cars coming the wrong way on a one-way street, being stuck in a traffic jam, getting lost and then being unable to find a parking space is about par for the course. It's said that indicating a turn is considered "giving information to the enemy." Most car rental agencies have offices at the airport and/or Downtown. Check the *Yellow Pages* for a full list of local firms.
Car rental companies:
Avis, tel: 800-230-4898
Budget, tel: 800-527-0700
Hertz, tel: 800-654-3131
Conveniently located public parking facilities are found at Government Center; Post Office Square; the Public Garden; the Prudential Center; on Clarendon Street near the John Hancock Tower; and elsewhere. Private lots are scattered here and there.
Taxis: Taxi stands are common at popular tourist sites. Companies to call include:
Bay State Taxi, tel: 617-566-5000
Boston Cab, tel: 617-536-2600
Checker Taxi, tel: 617-536-7000
Metro Cab, tel: 617-242-8000
Red Cab, tel: 617-734-5000

Hotel Prices

Categories based on average cost of a double room for one night.
$ = under $65
$$ = up to $ 100
$$$ = up to $150
$$$$ = over $150

WHERE TO STAY

Boston Harbor Hotel
70 Rowes Wharf, MA 02110
Tel: 617-439-7000
US Freephone: 800-752-7077
Fax: 617-330-9450
www.bhh.com
Board the airport water shuttle at
Logan and, seven minutes later,
step into the luxury of the city's
foremost waterside hotel.
Bedrooms all have either harbor or
skyline views. Eighteen rooms are
specially designed for the physically
handicapped. A museum-quality art
collection decorates the public
areas. Across the road is the
Financial District, while minutes
away (on foot) is the Aquarium and
Quincy Market **$$$$**

Boston International Youth Hostel
12 Hemenway St, Fenway, 02115
Tel: 617-536-9455
Fax: 617-424-6558
www.bostonhostel.org
Well located at the western fringe of
the Back Bay. Very close to public
transportation with 220 beds in
4–6 bed dormitories: bring or rent
sheets. **$**

Lenox Hotel
61 Exeter Street at Boylston, Back
Bay, 02116
Tel: 617-536-5300
US Freephone: 800-225-7676
Fax: 617-267-1237
www.lenoxhotel.com
Modest and moderate traditional
family hotel built in 1900.
Bedrooms, some with functional
fireplaces, have been redecorated
in French Provincial, Oriental or
colonial decor. Just a few steps
from the Prudential Center and the
Public Library, and a block from the
subway. **$$**

Omni Parker House
60 School Street, MA 02018
Tel: 617-227-8600
US Freephone: 800-THEOMNI
Fax: 617-742-5729
www.omnihotels.com
Reportedly the oldest continuously
operating hotel in America (since
1854); yet, the frequently renovated
present building dates only from
1927. Some rooms have showers
only. Malcolm X and (allegedly) Ho

Restaurant Prices

Categories based on average
cost of dinner and a glass of
wine, before tip.
$ = under $15
$$ = up to $30
$$$ = over $30

Chi Minh both worked here, they
claim. A favorite with politicians,
and one of the most centrally
located hotels in the city. **$$$**

WHERE TO EAT

Many claim that Boston has the
best seafood in the nation, and it is
certainly a great town in which to
indulge in all sorts of fish. Boston
specialties include clam chowder
(made with cream, not tomatoes),
scrod (not a separate species of
fish but the name given to small
tender haddock or cod) and
steamers (clams served with broth
and melted butter). Baked beans,
once synonymous with Boston, and
Boston brown bread are not
especially popular and may be
difficult to find.
    The Back Bay, especially
Newbury and Boylston streets,
has many sidewalk cafés and
restaurants, pleasant for people-
watching. A recent hotbed of haute
cuisine, mainly contemporary
American, is the South End. Other
high concentrations of restaurants
include Faneuil Hall Marketplace,
Chinatown and the North End.
Also, excellent international
dining can be enjoyed in nearly
all major hotels. The following
are just a few of the many places
worth seeking out:

Sasso
116 Huntington Avenue
Tel: 617-247-2400
Serving a variety of contemporary
Italian dishes, with an assortment
of fine wine. **$$$$**

Durgin Park
30 North Market Street (Faneuil
Hall Marketplace)
Tel: 617-227-2877/2038
Yankee cooking attracts flocks of

tourists to this legendary old dining
hall, where they are seated with
others at long, picnic-cloth covered
tables and insulted by the waiters.
Try Brontosaurus-sized prime ribs.
No reservations; long waits. **$$**

Imperial Seafood
70 Beach Street
Tel: 617-426-8439
Large, busy Cantonese restaurant.
Main attraction: *dim sum.* **$–$$**

Legal Sea Foods
26 Park Plaza
Tel: 617-426-4444
Copley Place, 100 Huntington
Avenue
Tel: 617-266-7775
255 State Street
Tel: 617-742-5300
800 Boylston Street
Tel: 617-266-6800
What started as a small Cambridge
fish store now has a justly deserved
international reputation. Enormous
variety. No reservations and waits
can seem interminable. **$$–$$$**

Parker's
Omni Parker House
60 School Street
Tel: 617-227-8600
A New England tradition since
1854. Home of Parker rolls and
Boston Cream Pie, with formal and
attentive service. **$$$–$$$$**

SHOPPING

Downtown Crossing, a pedestrian-
only zone, is Boston's largest
shopping area, complete with
outdoor kiosks and street-vendors.
The popular **Faneuil Hall
Marketplace** has many small
shops and foodstands. Boston's
version of Fifth Avenue is **Newbury
Street**, an 8-block stretch of
expensive clothing stores, salons,
and art galleries. Boston's **Copley
Place** on Copley Square has almost
100 upscale stores and
restaurants. Boston's historic
Haymarket, selling inexpensive
fruit and vegetables, meat and
seafood, is open every Friday and
Saturday near Faneuil Hall
Marketplace. Boston and
Cambridge are havens for buyers
and browsers of new and used

books. Check out **Wordsworth**'s **three stores in Harvard Square, Cambridge. For travel, nothing beats** Globe Corner Bookstore, 500 Boylston Street, Boston and 49 Palmer Street, Harvard Square, Cambridge. As for used bookstores, **Avenue Victor Hugo**, 339 Newbury Street and **Trident Booksellers and Cafe,** Newbury Street are both great. Two mammoth retailers worth checking out on Washington Street, Boston are **Filene's** and **Macy's.** For bargain hunters the floor below Filene's is the place to head for, a unique way of reducing prices. Boston's **Charles Street** has a number of antique dealers, including the **Boston Antique Co-op** on Charles Street.

Hotel Prices

Categories based on average cost of a double room for one night.
$ = under $65
$$ = up to $100
$$$ = up to $150
$$$$ = over $150

MASSACHUSETTS

WHERE TO STAY

CAMBRIDGE
The Charles Hotel
1 Bennett Street, MA 02138
Tel: 617-864-1200
US Freephone: 800-882-1818
Fax: 617-864-5715
www.charleshotel.com
A modern hotel with 296 rooms in Harvard Square, with airy, neo-traditional rooms, some overlooking the river. Home to the popular Regatta jazz club which draws nationally known jazz artists. **$$$$**
The Harvard Square Hotel
110 Mount Auburn St, MA 02138
Tel: 617-864-5200
Fax: 617-864-2409
A six-floor motel in the heart of Harvard Square. All rooms with picture windows; a complimentary continental breakfast. **$**

Mary Prentiss Inn
6 Prentiss Street, MA 02140
Tel: 617-661-2929
Fax: 617-661-5989
Tastefully appointed Greek Revival B&B with a spacious deck. Some of the 18 rooms have antique armoires and four-poster beds. Situated on a residential street between Harvard and Porter Squares. **$$–$$$**

CONCORD
Best Western Bass Rocks Ocean Inn
107 Atlantic Road, MA 01930
Tel: 978-283-7600
A 48-room motel looking straight out to sea. **$$**
Colonial Inn
48 Monument Square, 01742
Tel: 978-369-9200
US Freephone: 800-370-9200
Fax: 978-369-1533
www.concordscolonialinn.com
A 1716 inn on Concord's town common with 53 rooms. **$$**
Harborview Inn
71 Western Avenue, MA 01930
Tel: 978-283-2277
US Freephone: 800-299-6696
Fax: 978-287-4949
A comfortable house-turned-B&B near the Fishermen Memorial statue. Some of the nine rooms have an ocean view. **$–$$**
Hawthorne Inn
462 Lexington Road, 01742
Tel: 978-369-5610
B&B with seven rooms in the historic district, opposite Hawthorne's Wayside. **$$**
Longfellow's Wayside Inn
72 Wayside Inn Rd, S Sudbury, 01776
Tel: 978-443-1776
Fax: 978-443-8041
A mid-18th-century tavern with 10 rooms, near Concord. **$**

GREENFIELD
Brandt House
29 Highland Avenue, 01301
Tel: 413-774-3329
US Freephone: 800-235-3329.
Fax: 413-772-2908
www.brandthouse.com
Eight comfortable, simply decorated rooms, huge porches and a tennis court. **$$–$$$**

DEERFIELD
Deerfield Inn
81 Old Main Street, 01342
Tel: 413-774-5587
US Freephone: 800-926-3865
www.deerfieldinn.com.
A traditional inn surrounded by historic houses; 23 large rooms furnished with antiques and period reproductions. **$$$–$$$$**

WHERE TO EAT

CAMBRIDGE
East Coast Grill
1271 Cambridge Street (Inman Square)
Tel: 617-491-6568
www.concordscolonialinn.com
A stylish, wildly popular spot for innovative grilled seafood (often topped with exotic spice rubs or fruit salsas), creative salads, barbecue and fiery "pasta from hell." Margaritas help ease the often long waits for a table. **$$$**
Rialto
Charles Hotel, I Bennett Street
Tel: 617-661-5050
Restaurateur Michela Larson and chef Jody Adams have earned international accolades for flavorful Mediterranean cuisine in a coolly elegant dining room. **$$$–$$$$**

CONCORD
Colonial Inn
48 Monument Square
Tel: 978-369-2373
A 1716 inn serving traditional New England fare as well as afternoon tea. **$$–$$$**
Walden Grille
24 Walden Street
Tel: 978-371-2233
Contemporary cuisine in an old brick firehouse. **$$–$$$**

GLOUCESTER
Rudder Restaurant
73 Rocky Neck Avenue
Tel: 978-283-7967
A rollicking tavern in the Rocky Neck artists' colony. **$$**
Franklin Cafe Cape Inn
118 Main Street
Tel: 978-283-7888

Upscale bistro with a popular wine bar, blending fresh fish and local produce into intriguing French creations. **$$$**

White Rainbow
64 Main Street
Tel: 978-281-0017
Rich, evolved Continental in a dramatic granite-walled hideaway. **$$$**

GREENFIELD
Pete's Seafood Restaurant
54 School Street
Tel: 413-772-2153
Local favorite for fish and chips. **$$**

IPSWICH
The Clam Box
246 High Street
Tel: 978-356-9707
One of the best places in the region for fried clams. You can't miss the place – it's housed in a building shaped like a clam box. **$$**

LEXINGTON
La Boniche
143 Merrimack Street
Tel: 978-458-9473
An intimate restaurant in a landmark Art Nouveau building with creative French fare. **$$–$$$**

Dabin
10 Muzzey Street #1 (off Mass Avenue)
Tel: 781-860-0171
Traditional Japanese and Korean fare in a peaceful shelter from the bustle of Lexington Center. A small patio for outdoor dining. **$$**

The Olympia
453 Market Street
Tel: 978-452-8092
A friendly, family-run Greek restaurant. **$–$$**

WILLIAMSTOWN
The Orchards
222 Adams Road
Tel: 413-458-9611
www.orchardshotel.com
Accomplished New American cuisine in elegant setting. **$$$**

SHOPPING

CAMBRIDGE
The area in and around Harvard Square is chock-a-block with stores, most of which, not unexpectedly, have a youthful appeal. Some stores are gathered in mini-malls. Four such covered complexes are **The Garage** and the **Galleria**, both on John F. Kennedy St, **Atrium Arcade** on Church St and **The Shops at Charles Pl** on Bennett St.

Those who want to show that they have been to Harvard – even if only as a tourist – will delight in the Harvard Shop, crammed with Harvard insignia merchandise.

It is claimed that here is the greatest concentration of bookshops in the nation. Most are in and around the Square, and some open until midnight. **Grolier** carries the largest selection of poetry books in the country; go to **Robin Bledsoe** for out-of-print books on art, architecture and design, and a large selection on women artists. The **Globe Corner Bookstore**, specializes in travel. For foreign books, used as well as new, visit **Schoenhof's Foreign Books**, more an institution than a bookstore.

NEW HAMPSHIRE

WHERE TO STAY

CLAREMONT
Claremont Motor Lodge
On Beauregard Street, NH 03743
Tel: 603-542-2540
Refrigerators in some rooms and free continental breakfast. **$**

PORTSMOUTH
Inn at Strawbery Bank
314 Court Street, NH 03801
Tel: 603-436-7242
An elegant older house with well-proportioned rooms. Great breakfasts. **$$**

WOLFEBORO
Wolfeboro Inn
90 North Main, P O Box 1270, NH 03894
Tel: 603-569-3016
US Freephone: 800451-2389

Restaurant Prices

Categories based on average cost of dinner and a glass of wine, before tip.
$ = under $15
$$ = up to $30
$$$ = over $30

Fax: 603-569-5375
www.wolfeboroinn.com
Picturesque 17th-century waterfront inn with an inviting tavern. **$$$**

WHERE TO EAT

MEREDITH
George's Diner
10 Plymouth Street
Tel: 603-279-8723
www.gaslightco.com
No-nonsense New England grub featuring such staples as corn chowder and red-flannel hash. **$**

PORTSMOUTH
Portsmouth Gas Light Company
64 Market Street
Tel: 603-430-9122
In an attractive landmark building, this is a local favorite for its attractive surroundings and delicious brick-oven pizza. **$**

WOLFEBORO
The Front Porch
19 Orchards Road
Tel: 603-569-3662
Serving American-style food for over 60 years. The menu ranges from swordfish and prime ribs to peanut butter and jelly sandwiches. They freeze their own ice cream. **$$**

MAINE

WHERE TO STAY

CAPE ELIZABETH
Inn by the Sea
40 Bowery Beach Rd, ME 04074
Tel: 207-799-3134
US Freephone: 800-888-4287
Fax: 207-799-4779
www.innbythesea.com

Large, rambling coastal resort with 43 luxury suites all with porch or deck with ocean view. **$$$–$$$$**

CORNISH
Cornish Inn
Maine Street, Box 266, 04020
Tel: 207-625-8501
www.cornishinn.com
Lovely colonial house at the base of the White Mountains. *(see page 107)* **$$–$$$**

KENNEBUNKPORT
1802 House
15 Locke St (PO Box 646-A), ME 04046
Tel: 207-967-5632
US Freephone: 800-932-5632
Fax: 207-967-0780
www.1802inn.com
Warm, intimate guest rooms with wood-burning fireplaces, antiques and original artwork. The private tiled bathrooms feature double whirlpool baths. Secluded hideaway minutes from Dock Square. **$$$**
Maine Stay Inn and Cottages
34 Maine St (PO Box 500A), ME 04046
Tel: 207-967-2117
US Freephone: 800-950-2117
Fax: 207-967-8757
www.mainestayinn.com
A graceful and distinctive mid-Victorian house featuring wrap-around porch, suspended staircase and prominent cupola. Several of the rooms have fireplaces. Accommodation includes full breakfast and afternoon tea. **$$$**

OGUNQUIT BEACH
The Beachmere Inn
62 Beachmere Place, ME 03907-2340
Tel: 207-646-2021
US Freephone: 800-336-3983
Fax: 207-646-2231
www.beachmereinn.com
Intimate and stylish Victorian inn with wonderful coastal views and a small private beach. Many rooms have private balconies or decks and several also have wood-burning fireplaces. **$$$**

The Dunes
260 US Rt 1, Dunes Road, (PO Box 917), ME 03097
Tel: 207-883-5829
Established in 1936, The Dunes features 17 well-kept guest rooms and 19 traditional New England cottages set in trim open grounds overlooking the tidal river. **$$$**

PORTLAND
Inn on Carleton
46 Carleton Street, ME 04102
Tel: 207-775-1910
US Freephone: 800-639-1779
Fax: 207-761-0956
www.innoncarleton.com
A beautifully restored Victorian home in the center of Portland's historical district. **$$$–$$$$**
Pomegranate Inn
49 Neal Street, ME 04102
Tel: 207-772-1006
US Freephone: 800-356-0408
Fax: 207-773-4426
www.pomegranateinn.com
A tranquil hideaway set in the Western Promenade Historical District. Downstairs guest room with private terrace and a secluded upstairs carriage house. **$$$**

YORK
Dockside Guest Quarters
Harris Island Road, PO Box 205, ME 03909
Tel: 207-363-2868
US Freephone: 888-860-7428
Fax: 207-363-1977
www.docksidegq.com
Situated on a private peninsula surrounded by sweeping views of Maine's scenic beauty. **$$–$$$**

WHERE TO EAT

KENNEBUNKPORT
The Clam Shack
2 Western AvenueDock Square
Tel: 207-967-2560
Superlative fried clams and lobster rolls dispensed to appreciative locals from a simple hut. **$**

OGUNQUIT BEACH
Ogunquit Lobster Pound Restaurant and Lounge
504 Main Street

Tel: 207-646-2516
Grilled seafood and steak with well-prepared pasta dishes. **$$$**

Restaurant Prices

Categories based on average cost of dinner and a glass of wine, before tip.
$ = under $15
$$ = up to $30
$$$ = over $30

PORTLAND
Back Bay Grill
65 Portland Street
Tel: 207-772-8833
www.backbaygrill.com
In an attractive century-old building with high pressed-tin ceilings. Imaginative regional and New American dishes are prepared fresh daily in the open kitchen. The wine list is extensive and the desserts are exquisite. **$$**
Becky's
390 Commercial Street
Tel: 207-773-7070
www.beckys.com
Downtown diner with all-day breakfasts and hearty homestyle platters of fried seafood, turkey, meatloaf, and lobster rolls. Small, friendly and very popular. **$–$$**

WELLS
Barnacle Bill's
Perkins Cove
Tel: 207-646-4711
Two restaurants side-by-side – one specializing in lobster – the other in steamed clams, mussels, and other fresh local catch. **$$**

SHOPPING

FREEPORT
Home of the famous outdoor sportwear manufacturer **L L Bean**, established in the early 1900s, now a 24-hour megastore. Numerous other factory outlets and swanky fashion shops have sprung up along Hwy 1 and in converted homes.

VERMONT

WHERE TO STAY

ARLINGTON
Arlington Inn
Route 7A, VT 05250
Tel: 802-375-6532
US Freephone: 800-443-9442
Fax: 802-375-6534
www.arlingtoninn.com
An elegant Greek Revival mansion with comfortable Victorian-style interior furnishings in the 19 guest rooms. Located between Bennington and Manchester. **$–$$$**
Arlington's West Mountain Inn
River Rd (off Route 313), VT 05250
Tel: 802-375-6516
Fax: 802-375-6553
www.westmountainn.com
A family-friendly 1840s farmhouse turned 18-room inn with mountain views on 150 country acres. Trails for hiking or cross-country skiing, game room and the resident llama ranch amuse all ages. **$$$–$$$$**

BRIDGEWATER CORNERS
October Country Inn
Upper Road, PO Box 66, VT 05035
Tel: 802-672-3412
US Freephone: 800-648-8421
Fax: 802-672-1163
www.octobercountryinn.com
A cozy farmhouse with 10 rooms on a back road, about 5 miles (8 km) from the Killington ski area. **$$**

DORSET
Barrows House
Route 30, VT 05251
Tel: 802-867-4455
US Freephone: 800-639-1620
Fax: 802-867-0132
www.barrowshouse.com
An 18th-century Federal-style inn and carriage house with homey touches in the 28 rooms and a well-regarded restaurant. Pool, tennis courts. Located 6 miles (10 km) north of Manchester. **$$$$**
Cornucopia of Dorset
PO Box 307, 3228 Route 30, VT 05251
Tel: 802-867-5751
US Freephone: 800-566-5751
Fax: 802-867-5353
www.cornucopiaofdorset.com

Hotel Prices

Categories based on average cost of a double room for one night.
$ = under $65
$$ = up to $100
$$$ = up to $150
$$$$ = over $150

Five prettily appointed rooms; pampering services include champagne welcome, marvelous breakfasts (served by candlelight), cozy down comforters or quilts, and terry-cloth robes. **$$–$$$$**
Dorset Inn
8 Church St and Main, VT 05251
Tel: 802-867-5500
US Freephone: 877-367-7389
Fax: 802-867-5542
www.dorsetinn.com
One of the state's oldest – and reliably enjoyable – inns, opened in 1796, with 31 rooms. **$$$–$$$$**
Marble West Inn.
Dorset West Road, VT 05251
Tel: 802-867-4155
US Freephone: 800-453-7629
www.marblewestinn.com
An eight-room B&B in a marble-columned 1840s Greek Revival manse, elegantly decorated. **$–$$**

FAIRLEE
Silver Maple Lodge and Cottages
520 US Rt 5 South, VT 05045
Tel: 802-333-4326
US Freephone: 800-666-1946
www.silvermaplelodge.com
A handsome old farmhouse with comfortable lodge rooms and well-fitted rustic, knotty-pine cabins. **$$**

KILLINGTON
Cortina Inn
Route 4, VT 05751
Tel: 802-773-3333
Fax: 802-775-6948
Ninety-seven surprisingly lush and spacious rooms; indoor pool, tennis courts, health club, ice skating, horseback riding. **$$–$$$$**
Inn of the Six Mountains
2617 Killington Road, VT 05751
Tel: 802-422-4302
US Freephone: 800-228-4676
Fax: 802-422-4898

www.sixmountains.com
A 103-room modern hotel with a Rockies feel; everything, including the central fieldstone hearth, is lavishly overscale. **$–$$$**
Mountain Meadows Lodge
285 Thundering Brook Road, 05751
Tel: 802-775-1010
US Freephone: 800-370-4567
www.mtmeadowslodge.com
A large lakeside farmhouse offering 18 rooms, with extensive cross-country trails. Child care center with a playground and farm animals. **$$**

MANCHESTER
1811 House
PO Box 39Route 7A, VT 05254
Tel: 802-362-1811
US Freephone: 800-432-1811
www.1811house.com
A Federal manse that has been an inn/B&B for most of its history. Fourteen spacious, antiques-filled guest rooms. Located at the north end of Manchester Village. **$$–$$$**
The Equinox
3567 Main Street, VT 05254
Tel: 802-362-4700
US Freephone: 800-362-4747
Fax: 802-362-4861
www.equinoxresort.com
A grand old hotel with 155 rooms, beautifully refurbished. **$$$$**
Village Country Inn
3835 Main Street, 05254
US Freephone: 800-370-0300
Fax: 820-362-7238
www.villagecountryinn.com
A rambling 33-room old inn with romantic country decor. **$$$–$$$$**

MIDDLEBURY
Swift House Inn
25 Stewart Lane, 05753
Tel: 802-388-9925
Fax: 802-388-9927
www.swifthouseinn.com
An elegantly detailed 1815 Federal house with 21 luxurious guest rooms; the Carriage House features spacious suites with whirlpool baths. **$$–$$$**
Middlebury Inn
Court House Square, VT 05753
Tel: 802-388-4961
US Freephone: 800-842-4666
Fax: 802-388-4563
www.middleburyinn.com

An 1825 inn (plus 1827 annex and modern motel extension, offering a total of 80 rooms) overlooking the village green. Dining room serves traditional New England fare. **$–$$$**

NORWICH
Beaver Meadow Bed and Breakfast
Beaver Meadow Rd, VT 05055
Tel: 802-649-1053
Fax: 802-649-1054
www.beavermeadowbb.com
A cozy cottage and four comfortable bedrooms in a mellow farmhouse. Guests are invited to indulge in generous breakfasts and fine evening dining by candlelight. **$$**

QUECHEE
Quechee Inn at Marshland Farm
Main Street, VT 05059
Tel: 802-295-3133
US Freephone: 800-235-3133
Fax: 802-295-6587
www.quecheeinn.com
With Wilderness Trails, cross-country skiing, biking and canoeing, this inn has much to offer those seeking an active holiday. **$$$**

RIPTON
The Chipman Inn
Rt 125, VT 05766
Tel: 802-388-2390
US Freephone: 800-890-2390
www.chipmaninn.com
Small, gracious historic inn with appealing rooms and tranquil atmosphere. **$$**

WATERBURY
Inn at Blush Hill
7841 Blush Hill Road, VT 05676
Tel: 802-244-7529
US Freephone: 800-736-7522
Fax: 802 244-7314
www.blushhill.com
An exemplary B&B high on a hill with sweeping mountain vistas. Five cheerful rooms and gourmet breakfasts in a 1790s room with its original open hearth fireplace. **$–$$**

WINDSOR
Juniper Hill Inn
153 Pembroke Road, VT 05089
US Freephone: 800-359-2541
Fax: 802-674-2041
www.juniperhillinn.com

A 100-year-old Greek Revival mansion Bed and Breakfast set on a broad lawn. Sixteen elegantly appointed rooms furnished with Queen Anne and Edwardian pieces. Near Ascutney Mountain. **$$–$$$**

WOODSTOCK
Kedron Valley Inn
Route 106, South, VT 05071
US Freephone: 800-836-1193
Fax: 802-457-4469
www.kedronvalleyinn.com
Heirloom quilts line the walls and dress up the 27 prettily decorated rooms of this Bed and Breakfast. The restaurant is exceptional. The ski lodge-style building behind the main inn attracts families, who also enjoy the swimming pond. **$$–$$$$**
Three Church Street
3 Church Street, VT 05091
Tel: 802-457-1925
Eleven-room B&B in a gracious early 19th-century house near the common, with tennis court and pool; Well-priced elegance. **$**
Woodstock Inn & Resort
14 The Green (Route 4), VT 05091
Tel: 802-457-1100
US Freephone: 800-448-7900
Fax: 802-457-6699
www.woodstockinn.com
The Rockefellers' homage to country inns past, full of Americana. The decor is corporate/country with modern furniture and patchwork quilts. Facilities include 144 bedrooms, indoor and outdoor pools, tennis courts, golf, health club, racquet ball and squash courts. **$$$–$$$$**

Restaurant Prices

Categories based on average cost of dinner and a glass of wine, before tip.
$ = under $15
$$ = up to $30
$$$ = over $30

WHERE TO EAT

ARLINGTON
Arlington Inn
Route 7A
Tel: 802-375-6532

Fairly formal candlelit restaurant creating French Continental dishes – rack of lamb, roast duck – prepared with local meats and produce. **$$$**
West Mountain Inn
144 W Mountain Inn Road
Tel: 802-375-6516
New American fare in a low-beamed paneled dining room at a romantic and family-friendly inn. **$$$–$$$$**

DORSET
Barrows House
23156 Route 30
Tel: 802-867-4455
www.barrowshouse.com
New American cuisine in an intimate setting; the tavern serves lighter fare. **$$$**
Chantecleer
Route 7A, East Dorset
Tel: 802-362-1616
Swiss and French provincial cuisine in a former dairy barn. **$$$**
Dorset Inn
8 Church Street On The Green
Tel: 802-867-5500
www.dorsetinn.com
Honest American cooking: a choice of formal dining or tavern feasting in a 1796 hostelry. **$$$**

FAIRLEE
Fairlee Diner
Route 5, Bradford
Tel: 802-333-3569
Neat little diner with a nicely balanced menu blending classic and current fare. **$**

KILLINGTON
Cortina Inn
Route 4
Tel: 802-773-3333
Chefs from the New England Culinary Institute ensure deft and innovative fare. **$$$**
Hemingway's
4988 Route 4
Tel: 802-422-3886
Inspired regional cuisine, consistently hailed as one of the nation's best. **$$$$**

MANCHESTER
The Equinox
3567 Main Street
Tel: 802-362-4700

Spectacular regional cuisine in a formal barrel-vaulted dining room looking out on Mount Equinox. **$$$**

Bistro Henry
Route 11/30
Tel: 802-362-4982
A spacious dining room on the edge of town preparing authentic Mediterranean cuisine. Extensive wine list. **$$$**

Mother Myrick's Confectionery and Ice Cream Parlor
Route 7A
Tel: 802-362-1560
www.mothermyricks.com
The place to indulge your sweet tooth with a slice of freshly baked pie, homemade fudge, or an ice cream treat. **$**

Up for Breakfast
4935 Main Street
Tel: 802-362-4204
Fabulous pancakes, omelets and baked goods. Jammed on the weekends but worth the wait. **$**

MIDDLEBURY
Swift House Inn
25 Stewart Lane
Tel: 802-388-9925
Elegant regional cuisine in a formal, paneled Federal dining room. **$$$**

Tully & Marie's
7 Bakery Lane
Tel: 802-388-4182
Unfussy Regional American cuisine with congenial crowd. Looking out on Otter Creek. **$$$**

QUECHEE
Parker House Inn
1792 Main Street
Tel: 802-295-6077
Tasteful continental cuisine in a brick Victorian mansion with grand views. **$$$**

Quechee Inn at Marshland Farm
1119 Main Street
Tel: 802-295-3133
www.quecheeinn.com
Seasonal specialties in a tastefully restored tavern. **$$$**

Simon Pearce Restaurant
The Mill, Main Street
Tel: 802-295-1470
Fine country cuisine, with Irish touches set in an old riverside mill. Extensive wine list.
(see page 109) **$$$**

Hotel Prices

Categories based on average cost of a double room for one night.
$ = under $65
$$ = up to $100
$$$ = up to $150
$$$$ = over $150

WOODSTOCK
White Cottage Snack Bar
462 Route 4W
Tel: 802-457-3455
(see page 111) **$**

NEW YORK STATE

WHERE TO STAY

BUFFALO
Hostelling International – Buffalo
667 Main Street, NY 14203
Tel: 716-852-5222
www.hostelbuffalo.com
Convenient central location in the historic Downtown Theater District with rapid access to shops and restaurants via the Metrorail Transit Line. Amenities include kitchen, bicycle/luggage storage, lockers and free linen. **$**

Lenox Hotel and Suites
140 North Street, NY 14201
US Freephone: 800-82-LENOX
Fax: 716-885-8636
www.lenoxhotelandsuites.com
Historic hotel offering luxury suites and guest rooms.
$$

Lord Amherst
5000 Main Street, NY 14226
Tel: 716-839-2200
US Freephone: 800-544-2200
Fax: 716-389-1538
www.lordamherst.com
Well-maintained motel close to shopping malls. Exercise room and restaurant. **$$**

Victorian Hotel
8261 Main Street
Williamsville, NY 14221
Tel: 716-633-4900
Gracious old-style country inn with warm comfortable rooms. A good base for visiting Niagara Falls. Close to Downtown.
$$$

CAMBRIDGE
Blue Willow Motel
51 South Park Street, NY 12816
Tel: 518-677-3552
Squeaky clean, standard motel rooms. **$$**

CANANDAIGUA
Morgan-Samuels Inn
2920 Smith Road, NY 14424
Tel: 585-394-9232
www.morgansamuelsinn.com
This stately English-style mansion with tree-lined approach invites you to unwind in civilized comfort. The inn stands in extensive wooded grounds and is furnished with oil paintings and antiques. **$$$$**

COOPERSTOWN
The Inn at Cooperstown
16 Chestnut Street, NY 13326
Tel: 607-547-5756
www.inatcooperstown.com
A distinctive Second Empire-style inn designed by Henry J Hardenbergh, known for his New York City projects – the Dakota Apartments and Plaza Hotel. Built in 1874 as an annex to the plush Hotel Fenimore. **$$$**

FREDONIA
The White Inn
52 East Main Street, NY 14063
Tel: 716-672-2103
US Freephone: 888-FREEDONIA
Fax: 716-672-2107
www.whiteinn.com
Dignified older inn tastefully furnished with antiques and reproductions. Restaurant offers excellent American cuisine with top-quality, fresh ingredients. **$$–$$$**

GENEVA
Chanticleer Motor Inn
473 Hamilton Street, NY 14456
Tel: 315-789-7600
US Freephone: 800-441-5227
Comfy and clean with free continental breakfast, pool and wheelchair accessible rooms. **$$**

HAMBURG
Tally Ho-tel
5245 Camp Road, NY 14075
Tel: 716-648-2000
Reliable chain motor inn with pool,

airport transportation, laundry facilities, cable TV. Wheelchair accessible rooms. **$$**

NIAGARA FALLS
Crown Plaza
300 Third Street, NY 14303
Tel: 716-285-3361
Fax: 716-295-3900
www.holidayinn.com
Swanky and central. First-rate facilities include a hair salon, whirlpool and game room. And for those overcome by the romance of the Falls, there is a wedding chapel on the premises. **$$$$**
Hostelling International – Niagara Falls
1101 Ferry Avenue, NY 14301
Tel: 716-282-3700
The hostel occupies a historic Georgian-style home within walking distance of the Falls. Amenities include kitchen, TV room, on-site parking and laundry facilities. **$**

ROME
Quality Inn of Rome
200 South James Street, NY 13440
Tel: 315-336-4300
Comfortable, attractive rooms, with balconies and refrigerators. Restaurant, lounge and pool. Disabled access rooms. **$$**

SARATOGA SPRINGS
Batcheller Mansion Inn
20 Circular Street, NY 12866
Tel: 518-584-7012
US Freephone: 800-616-7012
Fax: 518-581-7746
www.batchellermansioninn.com
A marvelous High Victorian Gothic inn, impeccably preserved. The inn features 9 elegantly appointed rooms and 5 suites. Complimentary breakfast. **$$$$**

SYRACUSE
Hostelling International – Downing
535 Oak Street, NY 13203
Tel: 315-472-5788
Fax: 315-426-0662
Attractive hostel occupies an enormous old house in the center of Syracuse. Amenities include equipment storage, laundry facilities and baggage storage.
$

Restaurant Prices

Categories based on average cost of dinner and a glass of wine, before tip.
$ = under $15
$$ = up to $30
$$$ = over $30

Hotel Syracuse
500 South Warren St, NY 13202
Tel: 315-422-5121
www.hotelsyracuse.com
Very central historic hotel with many modern first-rate amenities. Pool, fitness center, sports bar & grill, restaurant and club. **$$$$**

UTICA
Red Roof Inn
20 Weaver Street
Tel: 315-724-7128
Email: i0203@redroof.com
Spotless, well-fitted rooms and friendly service. Restaurants and shopping close by. Children under 12 stay free. **$–$$**

WATERLOO
Waterloo Motel
989 Waterloo Geneva Road, NY 13165
Tel: 315-539-8042
Plain but comfortable rooms. **$–$$**

WESTFIELD
The William Seward Inn
6645 S Portage Road, NY 14787
Tel: 716-326-4151
Fax: 716-326-4163
www.williamsewardinn.com
Fine old inn furnished with antiques and famed for its fine dining. **$$$$**

WHERE TO EAT

BUFFALO
Anchor Bar
1047 Main Street
Tel: 716-886-8920
(see page 120) **$$**
Hemmingway's
492 Pearl St
Tel: 716-852-1937
This fun and vividly decorated restaurant serves snacks and salads to full entrees. **$**

Lord Chumley's
481 Delaware Avenue
Tel: 716-886-2220
www.lordchumleys.com
Holding the cobblestone-street sidewalk cafe atmosphere alongside quality dishes from premium ingredients. **$$$**

FREDONIA
Barker Brew Company
34 West Main Street
Tel: 716-679-3435
A wide array of microbrews and hefty sandwiches served in attractive surroundings. **$**

LOCKPORT
Garlock's Restaurant
35 South Transit Street
Tel: 716-433-5595
Popular all-round restaurant. **$**

ROME
Teddy's Restaurant
851 Black River Boulevard North
Tel: 315-336-7839
Popular family restaurant. **$$**

SARATOGA SPRINGS
Wheat Fields
440 Broadway
Tel: 518-587-0534
Wholesome, fresh foods and good salads on a pleasant outdoor patio. **$$**

SCHENECTADY
Blue Ribbon Diner
1801 State Street
Tel: 518-393-2600
Much-loved diner. **$**
Brandywine Diner
970 Emmett Street
Tel: 518-372-6030
Italian-American diner fare. **$**

SYRACUSE
Empire Brewing Company
120 Walton Street
Tel: 315-475-2337
www.empirebrewco.com
Housed in an smartly converted old grocery warehouse with much exposed stone and brick, this popular micro brewery has a long list of beers and an eclectic menu with the accent on Cajun.
$$

Hartford Queen Diner
4784 Commercial Drive
Tel: 315-736-0312
Good value, constantly changing daily specials. The perennial favorite is "Chicken 'n' Biscuits," which features every Wednesday. Round it all off on any day with a slice of one of Hartford's many freshly made cream pies.
$

PENNSYLVANIA

WHERE TO STAY

ERIE
Super 8 Motel
8040 Perry Highway, PA 16428
Tel: 814-864-9200
Serviceable budget accommodations. Phone, cable. **$**
Super 8 Motel Downtown
205 West 10th Street, PA 16501
Tel: 814-456-6251
Clean and very central. Pool. **$**

WHERE TO EAT

ERIE
Smuggler's Wharf
3 State Street
Tel: 814-459-4273
Very pleasant waterfront restaurant serving seafood, prime ribs, and creative appetizers. **$$$**
Stonehouse Inn
4753 West Lake Road
Tel: 814-838-9296
Upmarket and romantic. The Continental menu changes daily, and the wine list is one of the longest in the area. **$$$**

OHIO

WHERE TO STAY

ASHTABULA
Cedars Motel
2015 West Prospect Rd, OH 44004
Tel: 440-992-45406
Good rooms with phone & cable. **$**

CLEVELAND
Glidden House
1901 Ford Drive, OH 44106
Tel: 216-231-8900

US Freephone: 800-759-9358
Fax: 216-231-2130
www.gliddenhouse.com
Attractive historic hotel on the Case Western Reserve campus and close to the city's museums. Amenities include pool, lounge, restaurant and children's playground. Wheelchair-accessible rooms. **$$$**
Hostelling International – Stanford House
6093 Stanford Road, OH 44264
Tel: 330-467-8711
Fax: 330-467-8711
Email: hi-stanfordhostel@juno.com
Housed in a Greek revival farmhouse, this hostel has kitchen and laundry facilities, parking, covered bicycle and motorcycle parking, piano and picnic table.
$
Wyndham Cleveland Hotel at Playhouse Square
1260 Euclid Avenue, OH 44115
Tel: 216-615-7500
Fax: 216-615-7500
Adjacent to the theater district and convenient for local attractions. Nicely decorated rooms, restaurant, lounge, pool and fitness center. Wheelchair-accessible rooms. **$$$$**

SANDUSKY
Greentree Inn
1935 Cleveland Road, OH 44870
Tel/Fax: 419-626-6761
Attractive, well-fitted guest rooms. Exercise room, pool, whirlpool, lounge, restaurant.
$$

TOLEDO
Cross Country Inn
1704 Tollgate Dr, Maumee,
OH 43537
Tel: 419-891-0880
With 120 standard rooms with outdoor heated pool. **$**
Wyndham Hotel
2 Sea Gate/Summit Street,
Perrysburg, OH 43604
Tel: 419-241-1412
Fax: 419-241-8161
Plush riverview hotel in downtown Toledo. Exercise room, restaurant, grill and lounge. Wheelchair-accessible rooms. **$$$**

Hotel Prices

Categories based on average cost of a double room for one night.
$ = under $65
$$ = up to $ 100
$$$ = up to $150
$$$$ = over $150

WHERE TO EAT

CLEVELAND
Flat Iron Cafe
1114 Center Street
Tel: 216-696-6968
www.flatironcafe.com
Established in 1910 as a fisherman's cafe. Now folks come from miles around to indulge in the local delicacy – fried freshwater yellow perch. Also popular are the half pound hamburgers. Other menu items include pastas, salads and hot sandwiches.
$$
Hornblower's Barge and Grill
1151 N Marginal Road
Tel: 216-363-1151
Take to the barge for brunch on this cosmopolitan floating restaurant with lake and city views. **$$**
Ruthie and Moe's Diner
4002 Prospect Avenue
Tel: 216-431-8063
Fine traditional diner fare with the emphasis on soups, stews and casseroles. **$**

SANDUSKY
Cedar Villa Restaurant
1918 Cleveland Road
Tel: 419-625-8487
Italian-American food. Pastas, steaks, pizzas and seafood.
$

TOLEDO
Tony Packo's Cafe
1902 Front Street
Tel: 419-691-6054
www.tonypackos.com
Packo's hot dogs are a Toledo insti-tution – don't leave uninitiated.
$

INDIANA

WHERE TO STAY

ANGOLA
Inn at Amish Acres
1234 West Market St, IN 46550
Tel: 574-773-2011
US Freephone: 800-800-4942
www.amishacres.com
A chance to enjoy some of life's quiet pleasures: porch rockers, checker boards, hot tub and twining flowers. Disabled-access rooms. **$$**

Potawatomi Inn
Pokagon State Park, 6 Lane, 100A
Lake James, IN 46703
Tel: 219-833-1077
US Freephone: 877-768-2928
Set in Pokagon State Park, overlooking Lake James, this inn features a tranquil landscaped courtyard adjoining the pool and cafe. Other amenities include fitness room, recreation room, library, and gift shop. **$$**

Restaurant Prices

Categories based on average cost of dinner and a glass of wine, before tip.
$ = under $15
$$ = up to $30
$$$ = over $30

SOUTH BEND
The Oliver Inn
630 West Washington St, IN 46601
Tel: 219-232-4545
US Freephone: 888-697-4466
Fax: 219-288-9788
www.lodging-south-bend.com
Very pretty early 20th-century house with corner porches, bay windows and trim gardens. The wood-burning fireplace and piano music add to the flavor of the common areas. **$$$**

VALPARAISO
The Inn at Aberdeen
3158 SR 2, IN 46385
Tel: 219-465-3753
Fax: 219-465-9227
Comfortable guest rooms, some with hot tubs. Pool, full gourmet

breakfast, evening dessert, unlimited beverages and snacks. Disabled access. **$$**

WHERE TO EAT

SOUTH BEND
Miller's Home Cafe
110 East Michigan St, New Carlisle
Tel: 574-654-3431
Home-style cooking featuring a popular all-you-can-eat buffet. **$**

VALPARAISO
Strongbow Inn
2405 Hwy 30
Tel: 219-462-5121
In business for over half a century. Good home-style steaks and seafood dishes and specializing in turkey. Imaginative vegetarian options are also available. **$$**

MICHIGAN

WHERE TO STAY

DEARBORN
Mercury Motor Inn
22361 Michigan Avenue, MI 48124
Tel: 313-274-1900
Comfortable downtown motor inn. Kitchenette rooms available. **$**

WHERE TO EAT

DEARBORN
Antonio's Cucina Italiana
26356 Ford Road
Tel: 313-278-6000
Traditional Italian *trattoria*. **$$**

Talal's Restaurant
22041 Michigan Avenue
Tel: 313-565-5500
Popular Lebanese restaurant serving well-flavored kebabs with a good selection of side dishes. **$$**

ILLINOIS

WHERE TO STAY

CHICAGO
Cass Hotel
640 N. Wabash, 60611
Tel: 312-787-4030

US Freephone: 800-227-7850
Not special, but great location. **$$**

The Drake Hotel
140 E. Walton Place, 60611
Tel: 312-787-2200
Fax: 312-787-1431
Lavish lobby, worth a visit even if you're not staying. Shopping arcade and three restaurants including the Cape Cod Room. **$$$$**

Whitehall
105 E. Delaware Place, 60611
Tel: 312-944-6300
US Freephone: 800-323-7500
Fax: 312-573-6250
A 1920s hotel refurbished in the mid-1990s. **$$$–$$$$**

WHERE TO EAT

CHICAGO
Everest Room
440 S. LaSalle Street
Tel: 312-663-8920
One of the top restaurants (and views) in the country, **$$$$**

Pizzeria Uno
29 E. Ohio Street
Tel: 312-321-1000
Where Chicago pizza was born. **$$**

The Pump Room
1301 N. State Parkway
Tel: 312-266-0360
A Chicago institution and the place to celebrate that special occasion. Known since the 1930s for its "Booth One," which is reserved for celebrities. **$$$$$**

Twin Anchors Restaurant and Tavern
1655 N. Sedgwick Street
Tel: 312-266-1616
Among the best ribs in Chicago. Great burgers too. Pleasant neighborhood watering hole. **$$$**

SHOPPING

Chicago has a number of vertical shopping malls, in particular along N. Michigan Avenue. It also has several of America's best department stores and a myriad of boutiques, fashion shops and discount houses. There's no shortage of manufacturers' outlets in the suburbs. Most stores and shops open at 9 or 10am and stay open until at least 6pm; many often remain open until 8 or 9pm. Here's a taster. State Street has two major department stores: **Carson Pirie Scott**, at State and Madison streets and **Marshall Field's**, at 111 N. State Street. **The Magnificent Mile** (Michigan Avenue from Chicago River to Oak Street) is *the* glamorous shopping area including **Tiffany**, **Cartier**, **Saks Fifth Avenue**, and **Bloomingdale's**. **Chicago Place Mall** (700 N. Michigan Avenue) houses fifty specialty shops including **Saks Fifth Avenue** and **Williams-Sonoma**. The eighth-floor food court is in a tropical garden, and there's a European gourmet supermarket. **Oak Street**'s outstanding specialty shops emphasize diversity and quality. A fun place to window shop. The antique district is on the North Side in Lakeview and there are a number of stores and malls on **W. Kinzie** as well:

Chicago Antique Center
3036 N. Lincoln Avenue
Wrigleyville Antique Mall
3336 N. Clark Street

Bookstores include:
Barbara's Bookstore
Navy Pier and
1350 Wells Street
Unabridged Books
3251 Broadway

WISCONSIN
WHERE TO STAY

DODGEVILLE
Don Q Inn
RR1 Box, 53533
Tel: 608-935-2321
US Freephone: 800-666-7848
Fax: 608-935-2416
(see page 133) **$$–$$$**
**Hostelling International –
Folklore Village Farm**
3210 County Hwy BB, WI 53533
Tel: 608-924-4000/608-924-2107
Best known for its folk music and dance program. Also has basic accommodations with kitchen and on-site parking. **$**

House on the Rock
3591 Hwy 23, WI 53533
Tel: 608-935-3711
US Freephone: 888-935-3960
Fax: 608-935-1691
www.houseontherockinn.com
A modern inn situated a few miles south of the unique House on the Rock, echoing some of its features. An attractive lounge opens onto a deck overlooking the pool. **$$**

MADISON
**Hostelling International –
Madison Summer Hostel**
141 South Butler Street
Tel: 608-441-0144
Close to University of Wisconsin and the State Street pedestrian mall. Facilities include kitchen, lounge and TV. Disabled access. **$**
Madison Concourse Hotel
1 West Dayton Street, WI 53703
Tel: 608-257 6000
US Freephone: 800-356-8293
A smart, downtown hotel with indoor pool, fitness center, game room, bar and restaurant. **$$**
Mansion Hill Inn & Governor's Club
424 North Pinckney St, WI 53703
Tel: 608-255-3999
Fax: 608-255-2217
US Freephone: 800-798-9070
www.mansionhillinn.com
A mid 19th-century Romanesque Revival mansion situated in the historic district. Tastefully furnished with fine antiques. Expect a warm welcome and attentive service. **$$$**

RICHLAND CENTER
Park View Inn
511 West 6th, WI 53581
Tel: 608-647-6354
Fifteen well-maintained units some with kitchenettes. Playground. **$**
Prairie House Motel
East 4884, Hwy 14, WI 53588
Tel: 608-588-2088
Spacious rooms, fitness center, whirlpool, sauna and lounge area. **$$**

WHERE TO EAT

MADISON
Dotty Dumpling's Dowry
317 N Frances Street
Tel: 608-255-3175

Hotel Prices
Categories based on average cost of a double room for one night.
$ = under $65
$$ = up to $100
$$$ = up to $150
$$$$ = over $150

www.dottydumplingsdowry.com
Excellent burgers, fun decor and cheerful atmosphere. **$**
Essen Haus
514 East Wilson Street
Tel: 608-255-4674
Excellent German food and a long list of beers, Rollicking good fun. **$$**
Sunporch
2701 University Avenue
Tel: 608-231-1111
Interesting and well-flavored vegetarian food. **$**

MINNESOTA
WHERE TO STAY

BLOOMINGTON
Hotel Sofitel
5601 West 78 Street, MN 55439
Tel: 952-835-1900
Luxury accommodation close to the Mall of America, with several French restaurants. **$$$**

LE SUEUR
Le Sueur Downtown Motel
510 North Main Street, MN 56058
Tel: 507-665-6246
Clean, central and cheap. Wheelchair-accessible rooms. **$**

MANKATO
Riverfront Inn
1727 N Riverfront Dr, MN 56001
Tel: 507-388-1638
Small, recently remodeled hotel. **$**

MINNEAPOLIS
Courtyard
225 Third Avenue, MN 55404
Tel: 612-375-1700
Fax: 612-375-1300
www.marriott.com
Well-maintained, comfortable rooms near city center. A Downtown shuttle service is provided. **$$**

Econ Lodge
2500 University Avenue South East,
MN 55414
Tel: 612-331-6000
Clean, affordable rooms in central
Minneapolis. Swimming pool and
coffee shop. **$**
Evolo's B&B
2301 Bryant Ave S, MN 55405
Tel: 612-374-9656
Pleasant bed and breakfast in
Victorian house. **$$**
The Marquette Hotel
710 Marquette Avenue, MN 55402
Tel: 612-333-4545
Fax: 612-376-7419
De luxe boutique-style hotel. Pricey,
but lower weekend rates are
available. **$$$$**
Nicollet Island Inn
95 Merriam Street, MN 55401
Tel: 612-331-1800
Fax: 612-331-6528
Prime riverside location. Individually
appointed rooms and top-notch
restaurant featuring local cuisine.
Valet service. **$$$**

NEW PRAGUE
Schumacher's Hotel & Restaurant
212 West Main Street, MN 56071
Tel: 952-758-2133
US Freephone: 800-283-2049
www.schumachershotel.com
A central European-style hotel
with 16 uniquely themed rooms.
Warm and cozy atmosphere
with folk-painted furniture, billowing
eiderdowns and pampering service.
The inn is renowned for John
Schumacher's award-winning
central European cuisine. **$$$$**

PIPESTONE
Historic Calumet Hotel
104 West Main Street, MN 56164
Tel: 507-825-5871
US Freephone: 800-535-7610
Fax: 507-825-4578
www.calumetinn.com
(see page 137) **$$**

RED WING
Parkway Motel
3425 Hwy 61W, MN 55066
Tel: 651-388-8231
US Freephone: 800-762-0934
With twenty-seven simple,
comfortable units. **$**

Restaurant Prices

Categories based on average
cost of dinner and a glass of
wine, before tip.
$ = under $15
$$ = up to $30
$$$ = over $30

ST PAUL
The St Paul Hotel
350 Market Street, MN 55102
Tel: 651-292-9292
Fax: 651-228-9506
Historic hotel located in city center,
overlooking Rice Park. **$$$$**

WHERE TO EAT

MANKATO
Applewood
11 Telemark Dr
Tel: 507-625-4105
Pleasant restaurant featuring
excellent Sunday Brunch. **$**

MINNEAPOLIS
Buca di Beppo
1204 Harmon Place
Tel: 612-288-0138
Generous portions of Italian fare.
Friendly service; amusing decor. **$$**
Kramarczuk's East European Deli
215 East Hennepin Avenue
Tel: 612-379-3018
Eastern European deli specializing
in cheese and cabbage rolls,
varenyky and sausages. The
combination plate gives you a taste
of everything. **$**
Modern Café
337 13th Avenue, North East
Tel: 612-378-9882
Hip crowd and huge servings of
tasty grub. **$**
Nye's Polynesian Room
112 E Hennepin Avenue
Tel: 612-379-2021
Hearty Polish fare and live music in
plush surroundings. **$$**

ST PAUL
Café Latte
850 Grand Avenue
Tel: 651-224-5687
www.cafelatte.com
Soups, salads, stews and fragrant

hearth-baked breads, as well as full
afternoon tea and award-winning
desserts. Pizzas available in the
attached wine bar. **$**
Mickey's Dining Car
36 Seventh Street
Tel: 651-222-5633
Vintage diner in the heart of town
serving up the usual fried and
griddled fare. **$**
St Paul Grill
350 Market Street
Tel: 651-224-7455
Fine dining with great view of Rice
Park. **$$$**

SHOPPING

BLOOMINGTON
Mall of America
Hwys 494 and 77
The largest shopping and
entertainment center in the US.
There are no fewer than 500 shops,
an amusement park, a throng of
restaurants and cafés. Wheelchairs
and strollers are provided.

MINNEAPOLIS
Gaviidae Common
60 South 6th Street
Downtown shopping center featuring
50 shops and several restaurants.
Ingebretsen's
1601 East Lake Street
Scandinavian foods and crafts
situated in a quaint marketplace.
Nicollet Mall
Downtown pedestrian avenue lined
with boutiques, department stores
and malls – links to further shops
by means of the city skyway
system.

ST PAUL
World Trade Center
30 East Seventh Street
Specialty shops and restaurants.

SOUTH DAKOTA

WHERE TO STAY

BADLANDS NATIONAL PARK
Cedar Pass Lodge
SD, 57750
Tel: 605-433-5460
Open mid-March to October. **$–$$**

DEADWOOD

The Bullock Hotel
633 Main Street, SD 57732
Tel: 605-578-1745
Fax: 605-578-1382
Well-decorated older hotel in
historic town with 24-hour gaming,
theater and gift shop. **$$**

Franklin Hotel
700 Main St, Deadwood, SD 57732
Tel: 605-578-2241
US Freephone: 800-668-1876
www.deadwood.com/franklin
Located on Deadwood's historic
Main Street, this lovely old hotel
was built in 1903 and is now
thoroughly restored. Amenities: air
conditioning, television, parking,
restaurant, bars, casino. **$$**

**Hostelling International –
Black Hills at the Penny Motel**
818 Upper Main Street, SD 57732
Tel/fax: 605 578-1842
Email: pennymot@mato.com
Minutes from historic downtown.
Amenities include kitchen, bicycle
rental, parking, patio, laundry
facilities, luggage storage. **$**

INTERIOR

Badlands Inn
PO Box 103, SD 57750
Tel: 605-433-5401
Very comfortable rooms with
Badlands views. Pool, restaurant. **$**

MITCHELL

Anthony Motel
1518 W Havens Street, SD 57501
Tel: 605-996-7518
Fax: 605-996-7251
Well-kept motel with pool, miniature
golf, free movies, and laundry. **$**

PIERRE

River Place Inn Bed and Breakfast
109 Riverplace Drive
Tel: 605-224-8589
Fax: 605-945-2216
Email: upland@cybernex.net
An attractive three-level home
commanding magnificent views of
the Missouri River. Full breakfast
and evening snacks. **$$–$$$**

RAPID CITY

Alex Johnson Hotel
523 Sixth Street, SD 57701
Tel: 605-342-1210

US Freephone: 800-888-2539
www.alexjohnson.com
Commissioned by rail tycoon, Alex
Johnson, said to be a great
admirer of Native American
culture. An intriguing blend of
German and Plains Indian
influences. Don't miss the
chandeliers fashioned from war
lances or the portrait of Johnson
in Sioux Indian apparel. **$$$**

Stardust Motel
520 E North Street, SD 57701
Tel: 605-343-8844
A newly remodeled motel with
spacious rooms, queen-sized
beds, outdoor heated pool and
free continental breakfast.
$

SCENIC

Homestead Bed and Breakfast
24880 Sage Creek Rd, SD 57780
Tel: 605-993-6201
The owners of this third-
generation, 5,500-acre (2,226-
hectare) working ranch invite you
to enjoy a peaceful retreat on the
edge of the Badlands. Ranch or
continental-style breakfasts are
offered and evening meals on
request. **$$**

SIOUX FALLS

Brimark Inn
3200 W Russell Street, SD 57101
Tel/Fax: 605-332-2000
Good motor inn with Jacuzzi, pool
and coin laundry. **$**

SPEARFISH

Spearfish Creek Inn
403 West Kansas, SD 57783
Tel: 605-642-9941
Email: kapust@trib.com
Peaceful and secluded creekside
inn in the center of Spearfish.
Heated pool. **$**

Hotel Prices

Categories based on average
cost of a double room for one
night.
$ = under $65
$$ = up to $100
$$$ = up to $150
$$$$ = over $150

WALL

Wall Motel
604 Glenn Street, SD 57790
Tel: 605-279-2624
Clean and comfortable rooms
fitted with cable TV/Showtime.
Tub/shower combos, microwaves,
refrigerators and coffeemakers.
Restaurants and lounges nearby.
$

WHERE TO EAT

DEADWOOD

Jake's Atop the Midnight Star
677 Main Street
Tel: 605-578-1555
www.midnightstar.com
Casual dining on the top floor of
Kevin Costner's casino. Lounge.
$$

INTERIOR

Wooden Knife Drive Inn
101 6th Avenue
Tel: 605-433-5463
Clean, friendly family restaurant. **$$**

LEAD

Cheyenne Crossing Store & Cafe
21415 US Hwy 14A
Tel: 605-584-3510
Scenic spot for tucking into a rib-
sticking breakfast any time of day. **$**

MITCHELL

Chef Louie's
601 East Havens Street
Tel: 605-996-7565
Varied menu, mainly steaks. **$$**

PIERRE

Chikadily's Restaurant
808 West Sioux Avenue
Tel: 605-224-7183
Popular homestyle restaurant. **$**

RAPID CITY

Firehouse Brewing Company
610 Main Street
Tel: 605-348-1915
Microbrewery serving "pub-grub." **$**

SCENIC

Kristina's Café and Bakery
334 S Phillips Avenue
Tel: 605-331-4860
Excellent baked goods. **$**

Hotel Prices

Categories based on average cost of a double room for one night.
$ = under $65
$$ = up to $100
$$$ = up to $150
$$$$ = over $150

SIOUX FALLS
Minerva's
301 S Phillips Avenue
Tel: 605-334-0386
Prime-cut steaks, fish, pasta. **$$**

SPEARFISH
Bay Leaf Cafe
126 West Hudson
Tel: 605-642-5462
Friendly and informal cafe in historic building serving a variety of well-prepared dishes from piping hot soup to rib-tickling and plate filling buffalo steaks. **$$**

WYOMING

WHERE TO STAY

BIG HORN
Bozeman Trail Bed and Breakfast
304 Hwy 335 (PO Box 416), WY 82833
Tel: 307-672-2381
Spend some time in an old west homestead fitted out with modern comforts. Sweeping mountain views, hot tub and chuckwagon breakfast. Families welcome. **$$–$$$**

CODY
Irma Hotel
1192 Sheridan Ave, WY 82414
Tel: 307-587-4221
www.irmahotel.com
Built in 1902 by Buffalo Bill Cody for his daughter, Irma, the hotel still retains the flavor of the Old West. Amenities: air conditioning, television, restaurant. **$–$$**

GRAND TETON NATIONAL PARK
Park information:
PO Box 170 Moose, WY 83012
Tel: 307-739-3300
Lodgings within the park include cabins at Signal Mountain Lodge (**$$**) and the more luxurious **Jackson Lake Lodge. $$$–$$$$** Both are managed by:
Grand Teton Lodge Co.
PO Box 240, Moran, WY 83013
Tel: 307-543-2811

GILLETTE
Deer Park Bed and Breakfast
305 Cottonwood Lane
Tel: 307-682-9832
Two nice rooms with private baths in an attractive historic home. **$$**
Heartspear Hideaway
425 Bowers Road, WY 82716
Tel: 307-682-0812
Fax: 307-685-6383
Expect stunning views from this guesthouse, which is located on a working cattle and horse ranch. Full or continental breakfast available. Guests may use the pool situated at the ranch house. **$$$–$$$$**

GREYBULL
Yellowstone Motel
247 Greybull Avenue, WY 82426
Tel: 307-765-4456
Warm, comfortable rooms. Putting green, heated pool and restaurant directly opposite. **$**

JACKSON
Buckrail Lodge
110 E Karns Avenue, WY 83001
Tel: 307-733-2079
Fax: 307-734-1663
Large, comfortable cedar-log room with cathedral ceilings and western decor. Set in spacious grounds in quiet residential neighborhood. Good views. Jacuzzi, cable TV. **$–$$**
Teton Inn
165 W Gill WY 83001
Tel: 307-733-3883
Fax: 307-739-9351
Modest rooms and rates. Free local calls and newspaper. **$**
Wagon Wheel Village
435 N Cache Street, WY 83001
Tel: 307-733-2357
Fax: 307-733-0568
Log cabins in peaceful park setting near a quiet elk refuge but also convenient to Town Square. Restaurant, saloon, gift shop, coin laundry. **$$**

LOVELL
TX Ranch
PO Box 501, WY 82431
Tel: 406-484-6415
Guests help out with duties on this working cattle ranch situated at the foot of Pryor Mountain. Tents, horses, gear and food provided. **$$**

SHERIDAN
Sheridan Inn
Guest House Motel
612 North Main, WY 82801
Tel: 307-674-7421
Clean, good-sized, rooms. Amenities include free coin laundry, refrigerators in some rooms. **$**

SUNDANCE
Sundance Mountain Inn
26 Hwy 585
Tel: 307-283-3737
This is a modest but pleasant inn. Amenities include free movies, breakfast, local phone calls and indoor pool. **$**

YELLOWSTONE NATIONAL PARK
Park information:
WY 82190
Tel: 307-344-7901
www.travelyellowstone.com
Amfac Parks and Resorts manages all lodgings within the park. Contact them well in advance as facilities are frequently fully booked up to a year in advance.
Old Faithful Inn and Lodge
Magnificent log inn built in 1903. Terrace Bar overlooks Old Faithful Geyser. Accommodation for most budgets, but early booking is essential. **$–$$$$**
Old Faithful Snow Lodge
This heavy timber lodge features a stone fireplace and hand-wrought iron details. The cabins are tastefully fitted with specially designed furnishings. **$$$**
Roosevelt Lodge Cabins
Very basic, inexpensive. In wooden shelter. No bedding provided. **$**

WHERE TO EAT

CODY
The Noon Break
927 12th Street
Tel: 307-587-9720
Cheerful breakfast and lunch spot
serving Western, Mexican and Tex-
Mex dishes. Beware of the chili. **$**
Proud Cut Saloon
1227 Sheridan Avenue
Tel: 307-527-6905
Local favorite for sandwiches,
burgers and steak. **$–$$**

GILLETTE
Humphrey's Bar and Grill
408 West Juniper Lane
Tel: 307-682-0100
Lively sports bar with an excellent
salad bar. **$**

JACKSON
Blue Lion
160 North Millward Street
Tel: 307-733-3912
www.bluelionrestaurant.com
Long-established local favorite in
an older, renovated building.
Excellent regional and continental
dishes including elk, chicken and
vegetarian options. Dine indoors
or al fresco. **$$$**
Cadillac Grill
55 North Cache Street
Tel: 703-733-3279
Lively atmosphere and decor with
fashionable cuisine featuring
seafood, game and pasta. **$$**
Snake River Grill
84 East Broadway
Tel: 307-733-0557
American seafood and steak grill
with an Asian influence. The menu
varies with the season. **$$$**

SUNDANCE
ARO Family Restaurant
205 East Cleveland Street

Restaurant Prices

Categories based on average
cost of dinner and a glass of
wine, before tip.
$ = under $15
$$ = up to $30
$$$ = over $30

Tel: 307-283-2000
Well-prepared food served in
warm, atmosphere. Excellent
value. **$**

MONTANA

WHERE TO STAY

BOZEMAN
Gallatin Gateway Inn
Hwy 191, Gallatin Gtwy,
MT 59730
Tel: 406-763-4672
US Freephone: 800-676-3522
www.gallatingatewayinn.com
Attractively decorated, light and
spacious rooms in a beautifully
restored historic railroad hotel.
American cuisine fine dining by
reservation. **$$$**
Mountain Sky Guest Ranch
Box 1128, MT 59715
Tel: 406-587-1244
US Freephone: 800-548-3392
The ranch overlooks the lovely
Paradise Valley about 30 miles
(48 km) from Yellowstone National
Park in southwestern Montana.
Amenities: horseback riding
and instruction, children's
counselors, fishing, tennis, pool,
hot tub. **$$$**

COLUMBIA FALLS
Meadow Lake Resort
100 St Andrews Dr,
MT 59912
Tel: 406-892-8700
Fax: 406-892-0330
www.meadowlake.com
Luxurious resort comprising
vacation homes, combos and inn
rooms. Amenities include golf
course, tennis and fitness center,
Amtrak and ski shuttles, indoor
and outdoor pools, restaurant and
lounge. **$$$–$$$$**

CORAM
A Wild Rose
10280 Hwy 2 East,
MT 59913
Tel: 406-387-4900
www.cyberport.net/wildrose
Cradled in stunning mountain
scenery bordering Glacier National
Park, this inn provides tranquility
and pampering services with

therapeutic spa and massage,
whirlpool suites and gourmet
breakfasts. **$$$**

ESSEX
Paola Creek
HC 36 Box 4C, MT 59916
Tel: 406-888-5061
www.wtp.net/go/paola
A rustic, handcrafted larch-log home
featuring an impressive river rock
fireplace and magnificent views of
Mount St Nicholas. Sumptuous full
breakfasts, sack lunches and
dinners by reservation. **$$$**

GLACIER NATIONAL PARK
Park information:
Glacier National Park
West Glacier, MT 59936
Tel: 406-888 7800
www.nps.gov/glac/index.htm
Lodgings within the park are
managed by:
Glacier Park Inc.
May–September: East Glacier Park,
MT 59434.
October–April: Station 1210,
Greyhound, Phoenix, AZ 85077
Glacier Park Lodge
PO Box 127, MT 59936
Tel: 406-755-6303
A chalet-style lodge constructed
from hand-hewn logs and
fronted by a broad verandah
with dramatic views of Glacier
National Park. Set in 240 private
acres (97 hectares), and offering
many civilized comforts, this is a
fine wilderness retreat. Open May
to September. **$$$**

HELENA
Appleton Inn B&B
1999 Euclid Avenue, MT 59601
Tel: 406-449-7492
Fax: 406-449-1261
Century-old house listed on the
National Historic Register. It's now
a comfortable bed-and-breakfast
inn. **$$**
Elkhorn Mountain Inn
1 Jackson Creek, Clancy,
MT 59634
Tel: 406-442-6625
Fax: 406-449-8797
Attractively furnished and
affordable. Coffee makers, free
local calls and newspaper. **$**

HUNGRY HORSE
Mini Golden Inns Motel
8955 Hwy 2E, MT 59919
Tel: 406-387-4313
Modern rooms with mountain views.
Amenities include breakfast, coin
laundry and free local calls. **$**

KALISPELL
Kalispell Grand Hotel
100 Main Street, MT 59901
Tel: 406-755-8100
US Freephone: 800-858-7422
Fax: 406-752-8012
www.kalispellgrand.com
Fine old historic hotel. **$$**

LIVINGSTON
63 Ranch
Box 979, MT 59047
Tel: 406-222-0570
Fax: 406-222-6363
www.63ranch.com
Founded in 1929, this working
ranch is set on 2,000 acres
(810 hectares) in the Absaroka
Mountains about 50 miles
(81 km) north of Yellowstone
National Park and is listed on
the National Register of Historic
Places. Amenities: horseback
riding and instruc-tion, fishing,
overnight trips. **$**
The Murray Hotel
201 West Park Street,
MT 59047
Tel: 406-222-1350
www.murrayhotel.com
Numerous celebrity guests have
stayed in this gracious old hotel –
from Peter Bogdonovich to the
Queen of Denmark. Elegantly
furnished rooms, a rooftop hot tub,
workout room and a good cafe.
$$–$$$

MISSOULA
DoubleTree Hotel
100 Madison Street,
MT 59802
Tel: 406-728-3100
Fax: 406-728-2530
Comfort service. Dining room.
$$$
Downtown Motel
502 E Broadway,
MT 59802
Tel: 406-549-5191
Comfortable rooms in town center.

Reasonable rates. Coffee makers,
free movies. **$**
Goldsmith's Bed and Breakfast Inn
809 East Front, MT 59802
Tel: 406-721-6732
Fax: 406-543-0045
A quiet riverside B&B in an older
house, just a pleasant stroll away
from Downtown. **$$$**

POLSON
Best Western KwaTaqNuk Resort
303 Hwy 93, MT 59860
Tel: 406-883-3636
US Freephone: 800-882-6363
Fax: 406-833-5392
This bayfront resort has many
first rate facilities including two
pools, whirlpool, marina, fine
dining restaurant and gift shop.
$$$

ST IGNATIUS
Sunset Motel
32670 Hwy 93, MT 59865
Tel: 406-745-3900
Well-placed small hotel newly
decorated in "mountain theme."
Cable TV and refrigerators. **$**

WHITEFISH
Duck Inn Lodge
1305 Colombia Avenue,
MT 59937
Tel: 406-862-3825
Fax: 1-800-344-2377
www.duckinn.com
This is a pretty lodge by the river.
Fireplaces, patios, Jacuzzi, deep
soak tubs, breakfast. Courtesy
Amtrak van. **$$**

WHERE TO EAT

BOZEMAN
John Bozeman's Bistro
125 West Main Street
Tel: 406-587-4100
Eclectic menu featuring Thai and
Italian dishes. Relaxed, informal
atmosphere. **$$**

HELENA
Frontier Pies Restaurant & Bakery
1600 Prospect Avenue
Tel: 406-442-7437
Good food and freshly baked pies
worth traveling for. Western decor **$**

Windbag Saloon
19 S Last Chance Gulch Street
Tel: 406-443-9669
Sample the lively atmosphere and
range of microbrewery beers in
this popular, local spot. Good
burgers and great pasta. **$–$$**

KALISPELL
Moose's Saloon
173 North Main Street
Tel: 406-755-2337
The genuine article. Good pizzas **$**

LIVINGSTON
Peterson's Spirits & Eatery
201 West Park
Tel: 406-222-5193
This popular local meeting place
adjoining the Murray Hotel
serves fresh well-prepared
fish, meat and pasta dishes.
Convivial atmosphere –
occasionally rowdy. **$$**
The Sport Restaurant
114 South Main
Tel: 406-222-8221
Juicy burgers with a wide
choice of toppings and great
slabs of toothsome, fresh pies
to follow. **$**

MISSOULA
Edgewater Steak & Seafood
100 Madison Street
Tel: 406-728-3100
Excellent seafood, steaks,
pasta. **$$$**
Food for Thought
540 Daly Avenue
Tel: 406-721-6033
Great breakfasts, lunches and
freshly prepared salads. **$**

POLSON
Watusi
318 Main Street
Tel: 406-883-6200
Delicious healthy lunches. **$**

WHITEFISH
Dos Amigos
6592 US Highway 93 S
Tel: 406-862-9994
Good choice of dishes. Mainly
Mexican but with several Cajun and
American dishes on offer. **$$**

SHOPPING

BOZEMAN
Country Book Shelf
28 West Main Street
Comprehensive collection of
regional titles.
Country Mall Antiques
8350 Huffine Lane
Around two dozen stalls selling
antiques and collectables.

HELENA
Reeder's Alley
100 South Park Avenue
Specialty shops in a district that
developed during the Gold Rush.

MISSOULA
Freddy's Feed and Read
1221 Helen Avenue
Do exactly what it says on the sign.
A pleasant bookstore with an
in-house deli.
Southgate Mall
Highway 93 and South Avenue
105 shops.
Grizzly Boot Company
814 S. Higgins Ave

IDAHO

WHERE TO STAY

BONNERS FERRY
**Best Western Kootenai River Inn
and Casino**
Rt 4, Box 4740, ID 83805
Tel: 208-267-8511
US Freephone: 800-346-5668
Fax: 208-267-3744
Excellent facilities and beautiful
view. Very reasonable. Pool, hot
tub, waterfront access, exercise
room. **$$**

COEUR D'ALENE
The Coeur d'Alene Resort
On Lake Coeur d'Alene, 83814
Tel: 208-765-4000

US Freephone: 800-688-5253
Fax: 208-667-2707
www.cdaresort.com
Luxury resort on scenic Lake
Coeur d'Alene. The many first-rate
amenities include a floating
moveable golf green. Close to
fishing, skiing and other area
attractions. **$$$**

NAPLES
Hostelling International – Naples
Hwy 2, ID 83847
Tel: 208-267-2947
Fax: 208-267-4118
Circa 1950s dance hall now a
comfortable hostel. Amenities
include kitchen, laundry facilities,
baggage storage, on-site parking,
basketball court and piano. **$**

SANDPOINT
Coit House Bed & Breakfast
502 N Fourth Avenue, ID 83864
Tel: 208-265-4035
Fax: 208-265-4035
www.keokee.com/bdgecenresv
Comfortable B&B at reasonable
rates. Breakfast. **$$**
Selkirk Lodge
Schweitzer Mountain Resort,
10000 Schweitzer Mt Rd, ID 83864
Tel: 208-265-0257
US Freephone: 800-831-8810
www.schweitzer.com
Cozy European-style ski lodge with
sweeping views of Lake Pend Oreille
and the surrounding mountains. Hot
tub, pool, mini-mart, cable TV.
Breakfast included. **$$$**

Hotel Prices

Categories based on average
cost of a double room for one
night.
$ = under $65
$$ = up to $100
$$$ = up to $150
$$$$ = over $150

WHERE TO EAT

BONNERS FERRY
Alberto's
6536 South Main Street
Tel: 208-267-7493
Authentic, first-rate Mexican fare in

gaily decorated surroundings. **$$**

COEUR D'ALENE
Cedars Floating Restaurant
1 Marine Drive
Tel: 208-664-2922
Warm and welcoming restaurant
moored on Lake Coeur d'Lane
affording panoramic views.
Extensive, nicely balanced menu
featuring very fresh, expertly
prepared fish. **$$**

SANDPOINT
Hydra
115 South Lake Street
Tel: 208-263-7123
Steak and seafood restaurant with
cocktail bar. Sunday brunch. **$$**

WASHINGTON

WHERE TO STAY

EDMUNDS
Andy's Motel
22201 Hwy 99, WA 98026
Tel: 425-776-6080
Simple and comfortable.
Wheelchair accessible. **$**

FORKS
Miller Tree Inn
654 East Division St, WA 98331
Tel: 360-374-6806
Nice and quiet. **$**

INDEX
Bush Country House Inn
300 Fifth Street, WA 98256
Tel: 360-793-2312
Handsome century-old house. Good
rooms and restaurant. **$**

LA PUSH
La Push Ocean Park Resort
PO Box 67, WA 98350
Tel: 360-374-5267
Recently remodeled resort complex
with very nice cabins and guest
rooms, some with fireplaces. **$$**

LEAVENWORTH
Alpenrose Inn
500 Alpine Place, WA 98826
Tel: 509-548-3000
US Freephone: 800-582-2474
www.alpenroseinn.com
Intimate Bavarian-style B&B inn in
scenic alpine setting. **$$**

Haus Rohrbach Pension
12882 Ranger Road, WA 98826
Tel: 509-548-7024
US Freephone: 800-548-4477
Fax: 508-548-5038
www.hausrohrbach.com
Cozy and convivial European-style pension. High on a hill with views across the valley. **$$–$$$**

NEAH BAY
Silver Salmon Resort
PO Box 156, WA 98357
Tel: 360-645-2388
US Freephone: 888-713-6477
www.silversalmonresort.com
Adjacent to the marina with 11 small rooms. Close to store, restaurants and gift shop. **$**

PORT ANGELES
DoubleTree Hotel
221 N Lincoln Street, WA 98362
Tel: 360-452-9215
Fax: 360-452-4734
Waterfront location with harbor view. Some rooms have balconies. Facilities include dining room, valet service and laundry. **$$$**
Uptown Inn
101 E Second Street, WA 98362
Tel: 360-457-9434
Individually appointed rooms. Whirlpool, free movies. **$$**

PORT TOWNSEND
Hostelling International – Olympic
272 Battery Way, WA 98368
Tel: 360-385-0655
www.washingtonhostels.org.
Located in Fort Worden State Park. Sleeping bags allowed. **$**
Palace Hotel
1004 Water Street,
WA 98368
Tel: 360-385-0773
Fax: 360-385-0780
Nicely restored historic Downtown edifice. Decorated in original Victorian style. Restaurant. **$$$**
The Tides Inn
1807 Water Street,
WA 98368
Tel: 360-385-0595
US Freephone: 800-822-8696
On the waterfront; some rooms have kitchenettes, Jacuzzis. **$**

SEQUIM
Ridpath Hotel
West 515 Sprague Ave, WA 99204
Tel: 509-838-2711
Fax: 509-747-6970
Elegant older hotel in a convenient central location. Tastefully decorated, well-equipped rooms. **$$**
Suntree 8 Inn
123 South Post Street, WA 99201
Tel: 509-838-8504
Downtown chain motel. **$**

Restaurant Prices

Categories based on average cost of dinner and a glass of wine, before tip.
$ = under $15
$$ = up to $30
$$$ = over $30

WHERE TO EAT

FORKS
Rain Drop Cafe
111 South Forks Avenue
Tel: 360-374-6612
Good breakfasts. The international lunch and dinner menu features tacos, gourmet burgers, fish and chips and very nice salads. **$**

LEAVENWORTH
Café Christa
801 Front Street
Tel: 509-548-5074
A pleasant café right on the city square. **$$**

PORT ANGELES
Destiny Seafood and Grill
1213 Marine Drive
Tel: 360-452-4665
Mediterranean and Middle Eastern cuisine. Nice baked goods. **$**
First Street Haven
107 E First Street
Tel: 360-457-0352
Sweet-smelling cakes, muffins and scones baked in-house. Breakfast served all day on Sundays. **$**

PORT TOWNSEND
Salal Cafe
634 Water Street
Tel: 360-385-6532
Wholesome meals served in

pleasant surroundings. **$**
The Silverwater Café
237 Taylor Street
Tel: 360-385-6448
Well-prepared, fresh local seafood and produce. Easy ambiance. **$**

SEQUIM
Three Crabs Restaurant
11 Three Crabs Road
Tel: 360-683-4264
Fine view of the harbor and freshest Dungeness crabs around. **$**

SPOKANE
Fugazzi Bakery and Cafe
117 N. Howard Street
Tel: 509-340-2253
Nice sandwiches and pastries. **$**
Niko's
725 West Riverside Avenue
Tel: 509-624-7444
Excellent Greek food. **$$**
Patsy Clark's
2208 West Second Avenue
Tel: 509-838-8300
Acclaimed fine dining in a fabulous old mansion with super fresh salmon entrees and the sublime President Steak. **$$$**

Hub City: SEATTLE

GETTING AROUND

Public transportation
From the airport: Seattle-Tacoma Airport, known as Sea-Tac (tel: 206-431-4444, 800-544-1965) is 13 miles (20 km) south of Seattle. Access to Sea-Tac is via I-5 (exit 154 from south I-5 or exit 152 from north I-5), or via Highway 99/509 and 518. Stop-and-go traffic on I-5 is not uncommon, especially during rush hours, so the alternate route on the highway is often quicker. Buses provide the least costly method of transportation. The 194 is the most direct, bringing passengers downtown in about 30 minutes. The 174 makes local stops on its way downtown. Bus or van companies that link the airport with metropolitan Seattle or Bellevue include:
The Grayline Airport Express
(tel: 206-624-5077)

Shuttle Express (tel: 206-622-1424) Metro Transit (tel: 206-553-3000) Quick Shuttle (tel: 206-684-9373, 800-665-2122) STITA (tel: 206-246-9999) provides a taxi service to and from the airport. From the airport to downtown (or vice versa) costs about $30.

National buses: The Greyhound terminal is located at 811 Stewart Street (tel: 800-229-9424).

National trains: The Amtrak station is at Third Avenue and S. Jackson Street (tel: 1-800-872-7245)

Commuter trains: Metro Transit (tel: 206-553-3000) provides a "Ride Free Area" in the downtown core bordered by the I-5 to the east, the waterfront to the west, Jackson Street to the south and Battery Street to the north.

Streetcar: Metro also operates a waterfront streetcar, a 1927 vintage trolley which runs 1½ miles (3 km) along the waterfront every 20–30 minutes from Myrtle, and from Edwards Park to the Pioneer Square district. The ticket requires exact change.

Monorail: The Monorail, which was built for the 1962 World Fair, runs every 15 minutes between Seattle Center and Fourth and Pine streets to Westlake Center. The ride is just under 1 mile (2 km) and takes only 90 seconds. It's clean and spacious with large windows.

Ferries: The Washington State Ferry system (tel: 206-464-6400, 800-843-3779), the largest in the country, covers the Puget Sound area, linking Seattle (at Pier 52) with the Olympic Peninsula via Bremerton and Bainbridge Island. State ferries also depart from West Seattle to Vashon Island and Southworth and from Edmonds, 7 miles (11 km) north of Seattle, to Kingston on Kitsap Peninsula. They also go from Anacortes, 90 miles (145 km) northwest of Seattle, through the San Juan Islands to Victoria, on Canada's Vancouver Island. Passengers to Canada need a passport. The Black Ball Ferry (tel: 206-622-2222) departs from Port Angeles on the Olympic Peninsula to

Victoria, BC, four times a day in summer and twice daily the rest of the year. Ferries carry cars.

Private transportation

When the weather is fine, Seattle is a very pleasant city to walk about in – it is hilly, but many of the sights may be toured comfortably on foot. Heavy traffic congestion and scarce, expensive parking make driving in the center a less attractive option. Many of the major car rental agencies have offices at Seattle-Tacoma Airport or in the downtown area. Consult the Yellow Pages phone book for a full listing of rental firms.

Car rental companies
Avis, tel: 800 831-2847
Budget, tel: 800-922-2899
Hertz, tel: 800 654-3131

WHERE TO STAY

The Edgewater Inn
Pier 67, 2411 Alaskan Way, WA 98101
Tel: 206-728-7000, 800-624-0670
Seattle's only downtown waterfront hotel. Atrium lobby, stone fireplaces and mountain lodge decor. Restaurant features northwestern cuisine. Rates vary depending on water- or city-view rooms. $$$

Ben Carol Motel
14110 Pacific Hwy S, WA 98168
Tel: 206-244-6464
The best of several cheap motels halfway to the airport, adjacent to a family-type restaurant and a huge 24-hour supermarket. Pool. $

Challenger Bunk and Breakfast
1001 Fairview Ave N, WA 98101
Tel: 206-340-1201
Unusual tugboat-turned-B&B on Lake Union with rooms decorated with nautical charts and brass ornaments. The views alone are worth the stay. $$$

Hostelling International – Seattle
84 Union Street, WA 98101
Tel: 206-622-5443
Lounge, library and self-service kitchen, laundry available. $

Inn At The Market
Pike Place Market, 86 Pine Street, WA 98101

Hotel Prices

Categories based on average cost of a double room for one night.
$ = under $65
$$ = up to $100
$$$ = up to $150
$$$$ = over $150

Tel: 206-443-3600
www.innatthemarket.com
In Pike Place Market with splendid views of Elliott Bay. Surrounded by trendy shops, spa and restaurant. Free downtown shuttle. $$$$

Shafer-Baillie Mansion
907 14th Avenue East, WA 98112
Tel: 206 322-4654
Antique-furnished B&B in spacious grounds. Gourmet breakfast included. $$$

University Plaza Hotel
400 North East 45th St, WA 98105
Tel: 206-634-0100
In the heart of the University District, with 135 rooms. Pool, fitness center, beauty salon, laundry service, restaurant, lounge with entertainment. $

WHERE TO EAT

Campagne
86 Pine Street.
Tel: 206-728-2800
In Pike Place Market, serving southern French cuisine with a rustic ambiance. Daily specials from seafood caught that day along with fresh local produce. $$$

The Gravity Bar
Broadway Market, Capitol Hill
Tel: 206-325-7186.
Imaginative vegetarian dishes, wheatgrass juice and espresso. A great place to people-watch. $

Macrina Bakery & Café
2408 1st Avenue
Tel: 206-448-4032
Pleasant coffee house with plenty of good eats. $

Le Pichet
1933 1st Avenue
Tel: 206-256-1499
This cute French cafe is regularly acclaimed by locals as one of the

best French restaurants in town. The fare is simple and delicious, as are the espresso and pastries. **$$**
Ray's Boathouse
6049 Seaview Avenue NW
Tel: 206-789-3770
Truly a local establishment from the wonderful view of Puget Sound to elegant preparation of local ingredients in this upscale eatery. **$$**
Salty's on Alki
1936 Harbor Avenue South West
Tel: 206-937-1600
Alder-smoked salmon stuffed with Dungeness crab, but it's the view at night that steals the show. **$$**
Shanghai Garden
524 6th Avenue South
Tel: 206-625-1689
Brightly painted pink restaurant. Anything with the homemade shaven noodles is a good bet. **$$**
The Yankee Diner
5300 24th Avenue NW
Tel: 206-783-1964
The food lives up to the name of this casual cafe serving old-fashioned meat and potatoes type meals with an excellent view. **$**

Central Route

Useful Addresses

Washington DC tourist information
Washington DC Convention and Tourism Corporation, 901 7th Street NW, Fourth Floor, 20001
Tel: 202-789-7000
www.washington.org
Tennessee tourist information
Department of Tourist Development, Fifth Floor, Rachel Jackson Building, 320 Sixth Avenue North, Nashville, TN 37243
Tel: 615-741-9001
www.www.state.tn.us
Arkansas tourist information
Arkansas Department of Parks and Tourism, One Capitol Mall, Little Rock, AR 72201
US Freephone: 800-628-8725
www.arkansas.com
Oklahoma tourist information
Tourism Department, PO Box 52002, Oklahoma City, OK 73152
Tel: 800-652-6552
www.travelok.com
Texas tourist information
Texas State Board of Tourism, PO Box 141009, Austin, TX 78714-1009
Tel: 512-486-5876
US Freephone: 800-452-9292
www.traveltex.com
New Mexico tourist information
New Mexico Department of Tourism PO Box 20002, Santa Fe, NM 87503
US Freephone: 800-733-6396
www.newmexico.org
Arizona tourist information
Arizona Office of Tourism, 1110 West Washington Street, Suite 155, Phoenix, AZ 85007
Tel: 866-275-5816
www.arizonaguide.com

Los Angeles tourist information
Los Angeles Convention and Visitors Burea, 633 W Fifth Street
Tel: 213-689-8822
Fax: 213-624-9746
www.lacvb.com
California tourist information
The California Office of Tourism, 801 K Street, Suite 1600, Sacramento, CA 95814
Tel: 916-322-2881
US Freephone: 800-862-2543
www.gocalif.com

Hub City: WASHINGTON, DC

GETTING AROUND

Public Transportation
From the airport: Transportation between Washington's three airports and downtown hotels is good. National Airport, the airport closest to the center of town, is on the metro system. The metro station is a short walk from the arrivals lounges, but can also be reached by regular shuttle buses. SuperShuttle (tel: 703-416-7873) runs a door-to-door service from between $10–$30. National Airport shuttle buses run to the downtown terminus at 1517 K Street NW. Taxi fares into downtown Washington are reasonably priced. Dulles International has a shuttle bus service to the downtown terminus at 1517 K Street NW, as well as shuttles to West Falls Church metro station, which feeds right into the metro system, and to National Airport. The Washington Flyer is a taxi service operated by the Dulles Airport. Trips into downtown Washington cost just over double the amount from National Airport. BWI Airport runs a shuttle service into the downtown terminus at 15th and K Street NW. Taxis to central Washington are also available. Amtrak runs a service from BWI into Union Station.
Rapid transit: The Metrorail (tel: 202-637-7000) subway service is fast and efficient with stations serving all of the major sights.

City buses: Metrobus (tel: 202-637-7000) operates a comprehensive network of routes covering the city and outlying areas. Single fares are under $1.50.

National buses: Greyhound buses operate out of the station at 1005 First Street NE.

National rail: Amtrak runs from Union Station, 60 Massachusetts Avenue NE.

Private Transportation

Washington DC is compact enough to make it one of the best cities in the country for exploring on foot. Another good way to get around – particularly if you are interested in some of the worthwhile day trips – is to rent a car. You can do this at the airport, your hotel, or any car rental agency, checking the phone book under "Automobile Renting." Cars can often be delivered to you. Car rental companies all charge roughly the same price. Most hotels (but not all) offer free parking for their guests; if staying in the city for any length of time, leave your car in the garage. Parking around DC is difficult on the street and expensive in car parks. Some of the bigger companies are Avis, Budget, Hertz, Alamo and Dollar. All have numerous offices around the city, so consult the phone directory for the one nearest you.

Most rental agencies require you be at least 21 years old and possess a valid driver's license. If you are insured in the US, you should not have to purchase insurance from the agency. If uninsured, read the rental agency's insurance policy carefully before purchasing the car insurance.

Taxis: Long-distance taxi fares are steep, but traveling inside Washington is cheaper than in other American cities and much cheaper than in some European capitals. For planned trips, reserve a taxi at least an hour in advance of departure. Some of the major taxi cab companies are:

Taxi Transportation Service, Tel: 398-0500

Checker Cab Company, Tel: 398-0532

Taxi cabs outside DC are all the same price – a fixed fare to get in the cab, then additional fees for every mile (or part of) thereafter. If you are going a long distance, you can usually negotiate with the cab driver to give you a fixed rate.

Hotel Prices

Categories based on average cost of a double room for one night.
$ = under $65
$$ = up to $100
$$$ = up to $150
$$$$ = over $150

WHERE TO STAY

Allen Lee Hotel
2224 F Street NW, 20037
Tel: 202-331-1224
Simple but clean hotel – some rooms share baths. Great for the young. Amenities: free coffee and cookies in lobby on Sunday mornings, maid service daily. All rooms have TV; some have baths. $$

The Channel Inn
650 Water Street NW, 20024
Tel: 202-554-2400
US Freephone: 800-368-5668
Washington's only waterfront hotel, close to the marina restaurants, with large and simple but comfortable rooms. Amenities: good seafood restaurant, coffee shop, outdoor pool, plus the Arena Stage, golf course, indoor and outdoor tennis courts are close by. $$$$

The Jefferson
1200 16th Street NW, 20036
Tel: 202-347-2200
US Freephone: 800-368-5966
A relatively small hotel, offering discreet and sensitive service in elegant surroundings. Amenities: restaurant, Saturday jazz, high tea, bathrobes, hair dryers, exercise and swimming facilities at University Club opposite, laundry, one-hour pressing, valet parking, pets accepted. $$$$

Washington International Youth Hostel
1009 11th Street NW, 20001
Tel: 202-737-2333
Located one block north of the Convention Center, with common areas for meeting other travelers, information desk, ride board, free tours and movies, tight security, large kitchen available for groups. $

WHERE TO EAT

The benefit of Washington as a magnet to political refugees and other immigrants from around the world is that there is almost no cuisine that is not represented somewhere in the city and its surrounding suburbs. Everything from Ethiopian cooking to Nepalese, from British high tea to the best French cuisine, can be found somewhere. Reservations are strongly recommended:

I Ricchi
1120 19th Street NW
Tel: 202-835-0459
Traditional Tuscan restaurant serving fresh, simple and hearty cook-ing. Bread, meat and fish cooked and grilled in the dining room's wood-burning stove. Wonderful sage and ricotta-stuffed tortellini, flavorful sauces for pastas and risottos, and excellent seafood. $$

La Brasserie
239 Massachusetts Avenue NE
Tel: 202-546-9154
The menu ranges from luxurious lobster to a variety of thick quiches to devilishly rich creme brulee. In warm weather, the terrace makes a nice backdrop to the gastronomic delights. $$$

Market Lunch
225 7th Street SE
Tel: 202-547-8444
It's no surprise there's a fight to get in here for Saturday breakfasts. The crabcakes and homemade bread are superb, and the prices are cheap. You have a better chance of getting a seat for a weekday lunch. Don't expect to pay with plastic. $

Meskerem
2434 18th Street NW
Tel: 202-462-4100
Try for a table on the top floor, with basket tables under a tented ceiling. Best with a large group, so that many dishes can be ordered. For two, try the combination platter to sample an array of items presented on *injera,* the curious gray, spongy sourdough pancake bread that is ripped off and used as the utensil for the food. **$$**

Nora
2132 Florida Avenue NW
Tel: 202-462-5143
Sometimes trying a little too hard to be original, Nora's is nonetheless worth a visit for its audacious balancing of seemingly incompatible ingredients, served in an intimate dining room (and outdoor dining area in clement weather). It declares its produce organic and biodynamic, but those bored by the thought need not expect a diminution of interesting flavors. **$$**

SHOPPING

Shopping ranges from the downtown and Chevy Chase outlets of international fashion names, to small specialty shops located all over town and the glitzy new shopping complexes and malls that have mushroomed both in the center and in the suburbs. One of the most individual of these in design is the renovated **Old Post Office Pavilion** at 1100 Pennsylvania Avenue NW. A glass-enclosed elevator carries visitors to the Observation Tower for a magnificent view over the city. In **Georgetown**, along Wisconsin Avenue and M Street, are smaller specialty fashion and accessory boutiques, like **Hugo Boss**. Top European designers, such as **GianFranco Ferre**, **Giorgio Armani**, **Byblos**, and **Gucci** can be found at the **Watergate complex**, the **Mazza Galerie** mall in Chevy Chase and on **Wisconsin Avenue** at Chevy Chase. Upscale department store **Saks Fifth Avenue** is found at 2051 International Drive, McLean, VA.

Montgomery Mall has undergone a complete overhaul to bring it up to the glitzy standard of the White Flint Mall and Tyson's Corner. A mall that because it has more shopping outlets than there are days in the year also provides hotel accommodation, for those who *do* want to shop until they drop.

Hotel Prices

Categories based on average cost of a double room for one night.
$ = under $65
$$ = up to $100
$$$ = up to $150
$$$$ = over $150

VIRGINIA

WHERE TO STAY

FRONT ROYAL
Relax Inn
1801 N. Shenandoah Avenue, VA 22620
Tel: 540-635-4101
Situated on the Shenandoah River 2 miles (1.6 km) from the entrance to the Shenandoah Parkway, all 20 guest rooms in this well-maintained older motel have double beds, bathtub, shower, refrigerator, microwave. There is a pool and pleasant picnic area. **$**

LURAY
Shenandoah River Inn B&B
201 Stagecoach Lane, VA 22835
Tel: 540-743-1144
US Freephone: 888-666-6760
www.washingtonpost.com/yp/bandbriver
This former stagecoach inn has been welcoming guests since 1812. Located on the river with fine mountain views. Facilities include private baths, king/queen beds, screened porches, and gourmet breakfasts. Cabins available. **$$$**

The Mimslyn
401 West Main Street, VA 22835
Tel: 540-743-5105
A handsome hotel set high on a hill in its own grounds. Sweeping dining room, rooftop solarium and secluded nooks and crannies convey an elegance not reflected in the price. Suites also available. **$$**

NEW MARKET
Blue Ridge Inn
2251 Old Valley Pike, VA 22844
Tel: 540-740-4136
Pleasant with cable TV and refrigerators. **$**

SHENANDOAH NATIONAL PARK
For information about the park,
Tel: 540-999-2243
Lodgings within the park are managed by:
ARAMARK Services
Shenandoah National Park
PO Box 727, Luray, VA 22835
Tel: 540-743-5108
US Freephone: 800-778-2851
www.visitshenandoah.com
Big Meadows Lodge
Tel: 800-778-2851
(Open mid May – late October)
An attractive oak and chestnut structure, built in 1939, adjacent to the grassy "big meadow." Disabled access. **$$–$$$**
Lewis Mountain Cabins
Tel: 800-778-2851
Open May – October. These historical cabins are reasonable and ideal for families. Facilities include sheltered outdoor cooking, recreation area with fireplace and picnic table. Wheelchair accessible. **$–$$**
Skyland Resort
Tel: 800-778-2851
Open March – early December. At 3,680 ft (1,122 meters), this resort is located at the highest point of Skyline Drive. Fabulous views from airy suites and rustic cabins. Disabled access. **$–$$**

STRASBURG
Hotel Strasburg
213 South Holiday St, VA 22657
Tel: 540-465-9191
US Freephone: 800-348-8327
www.hotelstrasburg.com
Massanhutten Mountain forms the backdrop for this former hospital, converted into a lovely hotel in 1915. Featuring creative Southern-style fine dining. **$$**

WHERE TO EAT

FRONT ROYAL
14 Street Bistro
101 West 14th Street
Tel: 540-636-8403
Good food and friendly service. **$$**

NEW MARKET
Southern Kitchen
Hwy 11
Tel: 540-740-3514
Great fried chicken and regional favorites. **$**

NORTH CAROLINA

WHERE TO STAY

ASHEVILLE
Richmond Hill Inn
87 Richmond Hill Drive,
NC 28806
Tel: 828-252-7313
US Freephone: 888-742-4550
Fax: 828-252-8726
www.richmondhillinn.com
This romantic 19th-century mansion commands fine panoramic views from atop a wooded hill. Quiet, individual cottages and Garden Pavilion rooms with a library, croquet court, porch rockers and fine dining featuring an extensive wine list. A peaceful haven. **$$$$**

CHEROKEE
Best Western Great Smokies Inn
441 North and Acquoni,
NC 28719
Tel: 828-497-2020
US Freephone: 800-528-1234
Fax: 828-497-3903
Well-fitted guest rooms and suites. Pool, laundry, restaurant and movies. Near area attractions. **$$**

WHERE TO EAT

ASHEVILLE
Blue Moon Bakery and Cafe
60 Biltmore Avenue
Tel: 828-252-6063
A popular all-rounder. Above-average sandwiches, pizzas, desserts and breakfasts. **$**

TENNESSEE

WHERE TO STAY

DANDRIDGE
Barrington Inn
1174 McGuire Road, TN 37820
Tel: 423-397-3368
US Freephone: 888-205-8482
Set on 24 wooded acres (10 hectares). The inn comprises seven guest rooms with private baths and several with wood-burning fireplaces. Full breakfast. **$$**
Mountain Harbor Inn
1199 Hwy 139, TN 37725
Tel: 865-484-1050
Fax: 865-397-0264
Nicely decorated rooms, all with breathtaking mountain and lake views. Extras include fluffy quilts, antiques and good food. **$$**

KNOXVILLE
Hostelling International – Knoxville Hostel
404 East Fourth Avenue, TN 37917
Tel: 865-546-8090
In historic Fourth and Grille neighborhood. Facilities include kitchen, laundry, car park and internet. **$**
Maplehurst Inn Bed and Breakfast
800 West Hill Avenue, TN 37902
Tel: 865-523-7773
Elegant rooms, and a secluded penthouse with private balcony, fireplace and Jacuzzi. Marble tubs, full breakfast. **$$–$$$**
Clubhouse Inn and Suites
208 Market Place Lane, TN 37922
Tel: 865-531-1900
Fax: 865-531-8807
www.clubhouseinn.com
A full service hotel featuring spacious guest rooms, cable TV, an exercise room, three whirlpool rooms and a restaurant. Complimentary breakfast is offered on weekends. **$$**

MEMPHIS
The Bridgewater House B&B
7015 Raleigh La Grange Road,
Cordova, 38018
Tel: 901-384-0080/800-466-1001
Email: mistilis@bellsouth.net
This intimate B&B is housed in a

Restaurant Prices

Categories based on average cost of dinner and a glass of wine, before tip.
$ = under $15
$$ = up to $30
$$$ = over $30

century-old former schoolhouse shaded by 2 wooded acres (1 hectare) of mature oaks. Many pampering extras including bathrobes, down comforters, and a full gourmet breakfast. Ceiling fans, antiques and hardwood floors. **$$**
Heartbreak Hotel
3677 Elvis Presley Blvd, TN 38116
Tel: 901-332-1000
www.heartbreakhotel.net
Opened in 1999, adjacent to Graceland, owned and operated by Elvis Presley Enterprises, Inc. Features in-room Elvis movies. Packages include Graceland tours. **$$–$$$**
The Peabody
149 Union Avenue, TN 38103
Tel: 901-529-4000
www.peabodymemphis.com
(see page 196) **$$$**

NASHVILLE
Fiddlers Inn
2410 Music Valley Drive, TN 37214
Tel: 615-885-1440
One of the district's more affordable options. Clean rooms, cable TV and pool. **$$**
The Hancock House
2144 Nashville Park, TN 37066
Tel: 615-452-8431
A Colonial Revival c. 1851, furnished with period antiques, private baths and fireplaces. The inn also has a well-fitted cabin and Jacuzzi suite. Full breakfasts include french toast and freshly baked biscuits. Fine dining by reservation. **$$$**
The Beaux Arts Hermitage Hotel
Corner of 6 and UNN, TN 37201
Tel: 615-244-3121
(see page 193) **$$–$$$**
Opryland Hotel
2800 Opryland Dr, TN 37214-1297
Tel: 615-889-1000
A Music City extravaganza with Vegas-Disney overtones. Showy and very pricey. **$$$$**

OAK RIDGE
Garden Plaza Hotel
215 South Illinois Ave,
TN 37830
Tel: 865-481-2468
Fax: 865-481-2474
Spacious, attractive rooms with
coffee makers and refrigerators.
The hotels facilities include an
exercise room, indoor/outdoor
pools and whirl-pools, restaurant
and lounge. **$$**

SEVIERVILLE
**Blue Mountain Mist Country Inn
and Cottages**
1811 Pullen Road,
TN 37862
Tel: 865-428-2335
Fax: 865-453-1720
Lovely rooms and cottages
furnished with antiques in beautiful
mountain scenery. **$$–$$$**

Restaurant Prices

Categories based on average
cost of dinner and a glass of
wine, before tip.
$ = under $15
$$ = up to $30
$$$ = over $30

WHERE TO EAT

COOKEVILLE
City Square Cafe
453 East Broad Street
Tel: 931-526-4535
Fine homestyle cooking. Great
breakfasts. **$**
Crawdaddy's
53 West Broad Street
Tel: 931-526-4660
Classic Cajun dishes, live music. **$**

KNOXVILLE
Calhoun's
400 Neyland Drive
Tel: 423-673-3355
Enjoy excellent barbecue ribs and a
fine river view. **$**

MEMPHIS
Buntyn Restaurant
3070 Southern Avenue
Tel: 901-458-8776
Glorious home-style southern food

featuring catfish, fried chicken,
chicken fried steak and savory
vegetables. They pile it high and
serve it hot – you couldn't want for
more – but by all means ask for a
dessert anyway. **$**
Cozy Corner Restaurant
745 North Parkway
Tel: 901-527-9158
Succulent hickory-smoked barbecue
sandwiches, ribs and chicken with
tasty sides. **$**
The Dixie Cafe
4699 Poplar Avenue 38117
Tel: 901-683-7555
A great little place for Americana,
serving old-fashioned food and with
a nostalgic soda fountain. **$**

NASHVILLE
Loveless Cafe
8400 Hwy 100
Tel: 615-646-9700
Authentic southern cooking served
family-style. With a choice of first-
class preserves, grits, ham and red-
eye gravy, breakfast is a real treat.
Generous portions and abundant
atmosphere. **$**
Valentino's Ristorante
1907 West End Avenue
Tel: 615-327-0148
Fine Northern Italian cuisine at
reasonable prices. Consistently
voted one of Nashville's best
Italian restaurants for its good
service and elegant but casual
atmosphere. **$$**
The Wild Boar Restaurant
2014 Broadway
Tel: 615-329-1313
Creative French cuisine and
courteous, helpful service.
Excellent wine list. **$$–$$$**

OAK RIDGE
Village Restaurant
123 Central Avenue
Tel: 865-483-1675
Tasty and affordable home-style
cooking. **$$**

SEVIERVILLE
Applewood Farmhouse Restaurant
240 Apple Valley Road
Tel: 423-428-1222
Very pleasant and reasonable
family restaurant. Apple fritters with
every meal. **$**

ARKANSAS

WHERE TO STAY

HAZEN
Super 8
2809 Highway 63N
Tel: 807-255-2888
Standard budget motel with pool
and laundry facilities. **$**

HOT SPRINGS
**The Arlington Resort Hotel
and Spa**
239 Central Avenue, AR 71902
Tel: 501-623-7771
Fax: 501-623-6191
www.arlingtonhotel.com
This full-service resort has been
pampering visitors since 1873.
Facilities include an on-premises
bath house with thermal water
baths and massages, twin
cascading heated pools, shops,
restaurant and beauty salon. **$$**
Wildwood 1884 B&B Inn
808 Park Avenue, AR 71901
Tel: 501-624-4267
www.bbonline.com/ar/gablesinn
Carefully restored 1884 Queen
Anne mansion with original wood-
work, antiques and stained glass.
Some rooms have porches. **$$**

LITTLE ROCK
Capital Hotel
111 West Markham St,
AR 72201
Tel: 501-374-7474
Handsome Victorian hotel. **$$$**
The Empress of Little Rock
2120 Louisiana Street,
AR 72206
Tel: 501-374-7966
www.TheEmpress.com
Impressive Gothic Queen Anne
house featuring elegant double
stairway and tower with poker
room. Gourmet breakfast. **$$$**
Pinnacle Vista Lodge
7510 Highway 300,
AR 72223
Tel: 501-868-8905
www.pinnaclevista.com
Log house situated at the foot
of Pinnacle Mountain in 23 acres
(9 hectares) of grounds. Country
breakfast served indoors or on
the deck. **$$$**

WHERE TO EAT

HOT SPRINGS
McClard's
505 Albert Pike
Tel: 501-624-9586
Serving savory, well-seasoned barbecue since 1908. **$**
Miller's Chicken and Steak House
4723 Central Avenue
Tel: 501-525-8861
Long-standing favorite for freshly cooked country-style food. **$$**

LITTLE ROCK
Doe's Eat Place
1023 West Markham Street
Tel: 501-376-1195
Choice-cut steaks. Famed locally for its burgers. Funky atmosphere. **$$**
Faded Rose Restaurant
1615 Rebsamen Park Road
Tel: 501-663-9734
Steaks, burgers and Yankee grub. **$**
Franke's
300 South University
Tel: 501-666-1941
Few better places to sample southern cooking cafeteria-style. Savory and satisfying. **$**

Hotel Prices

Categories based on average cost of a double room for one night.
$ = under $65
$$ = up to $100
$$$ = up to $150
$$$$ = over $150

OKLAHOMA

WHERE TO STAY

BRISTOW
Carolyn Inn
HWY 66N at I-44 exit, OK 74010
Tel: 918-367-2299
Simple, clean rooms, some with whirlpool tub. **$**

CHANDLER
Lincoln Court Motel
740 East First Street, OK 74834
Tel: 405-258-0200
A well-maintained vintage Route 66 motor inn. **$**

CLAREMORE
Motel Claremore
812 E Will Rogers Blvd, OK 74017
Tel: 918-341-3254
Small, clean motel with seven two-bedroom units and free movies. **$**

CLINTON
Best Western Elk City
2015 West Third Street, OK 73644
Tel: 580-225-1811
Fax: 580-225-1277
Good-sized rooms with cable TV/HBO. Free continental breakfast, pool and airport transportation. **$$**
Tradewinds Inn
2128 Gary Boulevard, OK 73601
Tel: 580-323-2610
Comfortable and friendly motel with pool, whirlpool, free movies and laundry facilities. Ask to see #215 – the Elvis Room – graced by the King on four occasions. **$**

MIAMI
Best Western Inn of Miami
2225 E Steve Owens Blvd, OK 74354
Tel: 918-542-6681
This inn is set in landscaped grounds with many mature trees. Good-sized rooms with free cable and refrigerators. **$**

OKLAHOMA CITY
Best Western Saddleback Inn
4300 SW Third Street, OK 73108
Tel: 405-947-7000
Fax: 405-948-7636
Pool, hot tub, sauna, fitness center, restaurant. **$$**
Carlyle Motel
3600 NW 39th Exp, OK 73112
Tel: 405-946-3355
Central with pool, TV and free movies. **$**
Hampshire Inn
3501 S Prospect, OK 73129
Tel: 405-672-1193
Clean, comfortable rooms. Pool. **$$**

STROUD
Skyliner Motel
717 West Main Street, OK 74078
Tel: 918-968-9556
Comfortable and well-kept Route 66 establishment dating from 1950. **$**

TULSA
Lexington Hotel Suites
8525 E 41st Street, OK 74145
Tel: 918-627-0300
Fax: 918-627-0587
A very clean and tidy motor lodge; each room with its own kitchen. With 162 rooms, you should always be able to fit in somewhere. **$$$**
McBirney Mansion B&B
1414 S Galveston, OK 74127
Tel: 918-585-3234
An elegant and cozy (only 8 rooms) mansion on lovely landscaped grounds overlooking the Arkansas River. **$$$$**
Ramada Inn Downtown Plaza
3131 East 51st Street
Tel: 918-743-9811
Above-average motor inn. Very comfortable rooms and good facilities. Complimentary breakfast. Pool, exercise room. Close to area attractions. **$$**

VINITA
Park Hills Motel and RV Park
Southwest of Vinita, OK 74301
Tel: 918-256-5511
Modest, clean and serviceable. **$**

WEATHERFORD
Best Western Mark Motor Hotel
525 East Main, OK 73096
Tel: 580-772-3325
Well-fitted guest rooms including free full breakfast, morning paper, and cable TV/HBO, in-room coffee and refrigerator. **$**

WHERE TO EAT

AFTON
Route 66 Cafe
5 Northeast First Avenue
Pull in for decent roadside grub and pleasant atmosphere. **$**

ARCADIA
Hillbillee's Cafe
206 East Hwy 66
Tel: 405-396-8177
Good food and interesting surroundings in this former Route 66 garage. **$**

CATOOSA
Molly's Landing
Hwy 66, OK 74015
Tel: 918-266-7853
Steak and seafood in a log cabin by the river with the Blue Whale landmark. **$**

CHANDLER
Martha's Cafe
600 North Price
Tel: 405-258-2382
Top quality steaks, hamburgers and sandwiches. **$**

CLAREMORE
Hammett House Restaurant
1616 West Will Rogers Boulevard
Tel: 918-341-7333
Tasty, freshly prepared grub. **$**

DEPEW
Spangler's General Store
322 Main Street
Tel: 918-324-5472
Classic Route 66 landmark serving good burgers and sandwiches. **$**

EL RENO
Robert's Grill
300 South Bickford Avenue
Tel: 405-262-1262
Home of the unique Fried Onion Burger and creators of the World's Largest Hamburger – annually on Memorial Day. **$$**

ERICK
Cowboy's
401 I-40 (Exit 7)
Tel: 580-526-8116
Burgers, chicken or steaks anytime for lunch or dinner. **$**

OKLAHOMA CITY
Cattleman's Steakhouse
1309 S Agnew Avenue
Tel: 405-236-0416
Excellent steaks served up a stone's throw from the stockyards. Relaxed atmosphere. **$$**
Classen's Grill
5124 N Classen
Tel: 405-842-0428
Emphasis on southwestern and midwestern fare with a few creative twists. Portions are abundant. **$$**

Sleepy Hollow
1101 Northeast 50th
Tel: 405-424-1614
Superlative home-style fried chicken dinners. A local legend. **$**

SAPULPA
Mission Street Cafe
115 North Mission
Tel: 918-248-7484
Good for a pit-stop near Route 66. **$**

SAYRE
Owl Drug Store
115 Main Street
Tel: 918-485-2722
(see page 209) **$**

TULSA
Ollie's Station Restaurant
41st and Southwest Boulevard
Tel: 918-446-0524
Fun place with good food and a dozen or so model trains chugging merrily around. **$**
Rib Crib
1601 South Harvard Avenue
Tel: 918-742-2742
Southwestern and American grub, specializing in barbecue ribs. **$**
Warren Duck Club
6110 S Yale Avenue
Tel: 918-495-1000
This club is on the dressy side of Tulsa, serving a healthy and well-prepared menu to the heirs of oil barons no doubt, and with wonderful views of the manicured lawns. **$$**

VINITA
Clanton's Cafe
319 East Illinois Street
Tel: 918-256-9053
Classic Route 66 eatery. **$**

YUKON
Johnnie's Grill
442 West Main Street
Tel: 405-354-2030
(see page 206) **$**

TEXAS

WHERE TO STAY

AMARILLO
The Big Texan Motel
7701 I-40E, TX 79120
Tel: 806-372-5000

Old West themed motel with good, clean rooms and continental breakfast. **$**
Sleep Inn Amarillo
2401 I-40 E, TX 79104
Tel: 806-372-6200
Fax: 806-372-6242
Perhaps too literal a choice for some, this clean and typical motor inn will live up to its name and even let you shower en-suite. **$$**
Travelodge West
2035 Paramount Drive, TX 79109
Tel: 806-353-3541
US Freephone: 800-578-7878
Fax: 806-353-0201
Comfortable rooms. Indoor pool and workout facilities. **$**

CONWAY
Budget Host S&S Motor Inn
I-40 and Hwy 207 (Rt 2, Box 58)
Panhandle, TX 79068
Tel: 806-537-5111
Standard motel rooms and restaurant. **$**

Hotel Prices

Categories based on average cost of a double room for one night.
$ = under $65
$$ = up to $100
$$$ = up to $150
$$$$ = over $150

CANYON
Buffalo Inn
300 23rd Street, TX 79015
Tel: 806-655-2124
Run-of-the-mill rooms, free movies and restaurant nearby. **$**

SHAMROCK
Texan Motel
Old Hwy 66, TX 79079
Tel: 806-256-3569
Classic Route 66 motel. **$**

VEGA
Vega Motel
1005 Vega Boulevard, TX 79092
Tel: 806-267-2205
Another good example of a vintage Route 66 motel. Worth a look and maybe an overnight stop. **$**

WHERE TO EAT

ADRIAN
Hickory Inn Cafe
1004 Vega Boulevard
Tel: 806-267-2569
Typical ranch fare. Steak burgers
and homemade pies. **$**

Restaurant Prices

Categories based on average
cost of dinner and a glass of
wine, before tip.
$ = under $15
$$ = up to $30
$$$ = over $30

AMARILLO
**Big Texan Steak Ranch and
Emporium**
7701 I-40E
Tel: 806-372-6000
If you can eat a 72 oz steak,
plus side dishes, in under an
hour you don't pay for it. More
modest portions of beef, buffalo,
rattlesnake, etc. also available.
$$
Calico County
2410 Paramount Boulevard
Tel: 806-358-7664
Famed for its outstanding
customer service, you'll be
treated like a king as the staff
makes all the delicious food from
scratch. **$**
Santa Fe
3533 Coulter Drive
Tel: 806-358-8333
A southwestern oasis for the
health-conscious, providing
wonderful Mexican decor and food
without all the lard. **$**

GROOM
Chalet Inn
I-40 FM 2300, TX 79039
Tel: 806-248-7524
Unexciting, but serviceable enough
if you are in need of a break from
the road. **$**
Mitchell's Restaurant
I-40 and Hwy 83
Tel: 806-256-3424
Generous portions of honest
home-style cooking and an
abundant salad bar. **$**

NEW MEXICO

WHERE TO STAY

ALBUQUERQUE
Hi Way House
3200 Central SE, NM 87106
Tel: 505-268-3971
One of the last in the old Hi Way
House chain seen frequently on
the old Route 66. **$**
Hyatt Regency
330 Tijeras South West,
NM 87102
Tel: 505-842-1234
Elegant and contemporary
downtown hotel. Pool, fitness
room, restaurant, bar. **$$–$$$**
La Puerta Lodge
9710 Central Ave SE,
NM 87123
Tel: 505-229-1770
Adobe-style 1940s; fab sign. **$**
La Posada de Albuquerque
125 2nd Street N. West,
NM 87102
Tel: 505-242-9090
US Freephone: 800-621-7231
Comfortable old-fashioned hotel
with nice architectural touches
dating from the 1930s. Restaurant
and bar. **$$**

GALLUP
El Rancho Hotel and Motel
1000 E. Highway 66,
NM 87301
Tel: 505-863-9311
(see page 218) **$–$$**

GRANTS
Best Western Inns and Suites
1501 E Santa Fe Ave,
NM 87020
Tel: 505-287-7901
Fax: 505-285-5751
Scenic location and excellent
facilities. The restaurant features
south-western food and western
decor, a sports bar, free full
breakfast and newspaper, game
room, fitness center, sauna and
Jacuzzi. **$$**
Leisure Lodge
1204 E Santa Fe Ave,
NM 87020
Tel: 505-287-2991
Time-honored and traditional
Route 66 landmark. **$**

LAS VEGAS
Plaza Hotel
230 Old Town Plaza, NM 87701
Tel: 505-425-3591
US Freephone: 800-328-1882
A fine historical hotel with attractive
restaurant and saloon overlooking
the Old Town Plaza. **$$**

MILAN
Crossroads Motel
1601 Old W Highway 66
Tel: 505-287-9264
(see page 217) **$**

SANTA FE
Alexander's Inn
529 East Palace Ave, NM 87501
Tel: 505-986-1431
US Freephone: 888-321-5123
Fax: 505-982-8572
For a bit of romance off Route 66, try
this quiet, but central B&B in Santa
Fe. The owners have lovingly cared
for this cottage and it shows, with
their attention to detail becoming
your nurturing atmosphere. **$$$**
La Fonda de Santa Fe
100 E San Francisco St, NM 87501
Tel: 505-982-5511
US Freephone: 800-523-5002
Historic Pueblo Revival-style hotel
on the Plaza rebuilt in 1919.
Amenities: air conditioning,
television, parking, pool, restaurant,
bars, nightclub, some rooms with
fireplaces, shops. **$$$–$$$$**
El Rey Inn
1862 Cerrillos Road, NM 87505
Tel: 505-982-1931
US Freephone: 1-800-521-1349
Nice rooms at a reasonable price. **$**
St Francis
210 Don Gaspar Ave, NM 87501
Tel: 505-983-5700
US Freephone: 800-666-5700
Delightful older hotel built in the
1920s, fully restored with period
decor. Restaurant, bar. **$$–$$$**

TUCUMCARI
Blue Swallow Motel
815 E Tucumcari Blvd, NM 88401
Tel: 505-461-9849
(see page 213) **$**
Safari Motel
722 E Tucumcari Blvd, NM 88401
Tel: 505-461-1048
(see page 213) **$**

WHERE TO EAT

ALBUQUERQUE
Avalon Restaurant
(see page 215) **$$**
Assets Grill Brewing Company
6910 Montgomery NE
Tel: 505-889-6400
Mixed ethnic cuisine in a lively
country setting; great selection of
beers and brew made in-house. **$**
M & J Sanitary Tortilla Factory
Tel: 505-242-4890
Authentic and filling Mexican dishes
in a casual diner-like setting. **$**
66 Diner
1405 Central Avenue NE
Tel: 505-247-1421
Spiffy old-time diner on old Route
66 near the university. **$**

GRANTS
Golden 50s/Uranium Cafe
West Santa Fe Avenue
Tel: 505-287-7540
Cafe with good grub. **$**
Grant's Cafe
932 E. Santa Fe Avenue
Tel: 505-285-6474
(see page 217) **$**
El Jardin Restaurant
319 West Santa Fe Avenue
Tel: 505-285-5231
(see page 217) **$$**
Monte Carlo Restaurant
721 West Santa Fe
Tel: 505-287-9250
(see page 217) **$$**

LAS VEGAS
Landmark Grill
230 Old Town Plaza
Tel: 505-425-3591
Very good regional dishes. **$**

SANTA FE
Coyote Cafe
132 West Water Street
Tel: 505-983-1615
American and New Mexican fare
served in an imaginatively
decorated site (a former bus depot);
its popularity is partly due to the
owner's cookbooks. **$$**
Geronimo
724 Canyon Road
Tel: 505-982-1500
1756 adobe with intimate dining
rooms and near the town's art

galleries. Food is diverse and
delicious. **$$–$$$**
Natural Cafe
1494 Cerrillos Road
Tel: 505-983-1411
Healthy and vegetarian menu
served in a cozy, arty setting. **$**
Tomasita's
500 South Guadalupe Street
Tel: 505-983-5721
Spicy New Mexican dishes at
the former Santa Fe Railroad
terminal; popular, lively and
informal. **$**
Villa Fontana
Highway 522
Tel: 505-758-5800
Gourmet northern Italian cuisine
at a lovely country restaurant. **$$**

Restaurant Prices

Categories based on average
cost of dinner and a glass of
wine, before tip.
$ = under $15
$$ = up to $30
$$$ = over $30

SANTA ROSA
Joe's Bar and Grill
865 Will Rogers Drive
Tel 505-472-3361
Regional dishes and good salad
bar. A Route 66 classic. **$**

ARIZONA

WHERE TO STAY

FLAGSTAFF
Hotel Monte Vista
100 N San Francisco, AZ 86001
Tel: 928-779-6971
US Freephone: 800-553-2666
A reasonably priced older hotel.
Pleasant, simple rooms and
dormitory accommodation. Very
central, but affordable. **$**
Jeanette's Bed and Breakfast
3380 E Lockett Rd, AZ 86004
Tel: 928-527-1912
Fax: 928-527-1713
Pouring all their energy into
just four Victorian rooms, the
attention shows from the hand-
made soap to the romantic
fireplaces. **$$$**

The Weatherford Hotel
23 North Leroux Street, AZ 86001
Tel: 928-774-2731
(see page 223) **$$–$$$**

GRAND CANYON
For park information:
PO Box 129, Grand Canyon,
AZ 86023
Tel: 928-638-7888
www.thecanyon.com/nps
All lodgings are managed by:
Xanterra Parks and Resorts
14001 E Iliff, No. 600, Aurora,
CO 80014
Tel: 928-638-2631 (same-day
reservations: South Rim);
928-628-2611 (North Rim).
Tel: 303-297-2757 (advance).
Bright Angel Lodge
W. Rim Drive
Tel: 928-638-2631
Old rustic lodge and bungalows with
simple accommodation. Restaurant
and bar. **$$**
Grand Canyon Lodge
Bright Angel Point
Tel: 303-297-2757
Basic accommodations and cabins
on the North Rim; open seasonally.
With a restaurant and bar. **$$**
El Tovar Hotel
Grand Canyon National Park
Lodges.
Tel: 928-638-2631
This century-old rustic lodge is on
the edge of the South Rim.
Restaurant, bar, some rooms with
balcony. **$$$$**

HOLBROOK
Wigwam Village
811 West Hopi Drive, AZ 86025
Tel: 928-524-3048
Time your journey for an overnight
stop in Holbrook and head for
Wigwam Village. A night in a 1950s
concrete teepee is a quinessential
Route 66 experience. **$**

JEROME
Inn at Jerome
309 North Main Street, AZ 86331
Tel: 928-634-5094
A small, friendly inn occupying
the 1899 Frontier-style Clinksdale
Building. Compact rooms attractively furnished with period
antiques. **$**

Hotel Prices

Categories based on average cost of a double room for one night.
$ = under $65
$$ = up to $100
$$$ = up to $150
$$$$ = over $150

KINGMAN
Hill Top Motel
1901 E Andy Devine Ave, AZ 86401
Tel: 928-753-2198
Pleasant, well-maintained hotel accommodation with pool. $

OATMAN
Oatman Hotel
HWY 66, AZ 86433
Tel: 928 768-4408
Characterful adobe hotel. $$

PEACH SPRINGS
Hualapai Lodge
PO Box 538, AZ 86434
Tel: 928-769-2230
Basic but comfortable accommodation popular with rafters going down the canyon. $

SEDONA
Graham Inn and Adobe Village
150 Canyon Circle Drive, AZ 86351
Tel: 928-284-1425
Fax: 928-284-0767
www.sedonasfinest.com
A stylishly furnished inn commanding spectacular views of the red rocks. In addition to the six de luxe guest rooms, there are four romantic *casitas* (cottages) with waterfall showers, bathroom fireplaces, and breadmakers. Includes early morning coffee, full breakfast, afternoon refreshments and evening snacks. $$$$
Historic Route 66 Motel
500 West Rt 66, AZ 86337
Tel: 928-422-3204
Nice clean rooms with queen-sized beds and coffee makers. $
Quality Inn – King's Ransom
771 Hwy 170, OK 86336
Tel: 928-282-7151
Comfortable and affordable motel with few surprises. $$

WILLIAMS
Fray Marcos Hotel
163 Grand Canyon Blvd, AZ 86046
Tel: 928-635-4010
(see page 225) $$
El Rancho Motel
617 East Rt 66, AZ 86046
Tel: 928-635-2552
Clean rooms with free movies. $

WINSLOW
The La Posada Hotel
303 East Second Street, AZ 86047
Tel: 928-289-4366
(see page 222) $$

WHERE TO EAT

ASH FORK
Route 66 Grill
424 Lewis Avenue
Tel: 928-637-2528
(see page 226) $

FLAGSTAFF
Black Bart's Steak House and Musical Revue
2760 E Buner Avenue
Tel: 928-779-3142
Oh go on, you know you want a big steak and some country music over your gravy and potatoes. Indulge. $$
Cottage Place
126 West Cottage Avenue
Tel: 928-774-8431
Best fine dining. $$
Kathy's
7 North San Francisco Street
Tel: 928-774-1951
Friendly place for breakfast or lunch. Vegetarian dishes. $

HOLBROOK
Joe and Aggie's Cafe
120 West Hopi Drive
Tel: 928-524-6540
Good Mexican dishes. $

JEROME
English Kitchen
119 Jerome Avenue
Tel: 928-634-2132
Since 1899. $–$$

SEDONA
L'Auberge De Sedona Restaurant
301 L'Auberge Lane
Tel: 928-282-7131
So good they named a whole street (well, lane) after it. The French cuisine at this elegant restaurant is still top notch. $$$
Shugrue's Hillside Grill
671 Highway 179
Tel: 928-282-5300
A health-conscious American menu in the ideal Sedona setting, looking onto the mountains. $$

WILLIAMS
Rod's Steak House
301 East Bill Williams Avenue
Tel: 928-635-2671
Much-loved Route 66 dining landmark. $
Twisters
417 East Route 66
Tel: 928-635-0266
(see page 226) $

WINSLOW
Falcon Restaurant
1113 East Third Street
Tel: 928-289-2628
(see page 222) $

SHOPPING

ARIZONA
One of the leading New Age centers in the US, which is reflected in the number of shops scattered throughout the state selling crystals, dreamcatchers and so on.
Arizona Craftwork
Native American arts and crafts, baskets, jewelry, blankets and so on are available at: **Cameron Trading Post**, Highway 89N, approximately 4 miles (7 km) outside Flagstaff. **Navajo Arts and Crafts Enterprises**, off route 264 adjacent to Navajo Nation Inn.

CALIFORNIA

WHERE TO STAY

CLAREMONT
Claremont Inn
555 West Foothills Blvd, CA 91711
Tel: 909-626-2411
Nice rooms, some with refrigerators. Exercise room and whirlpool. $$

MONROVIA
Aztec Hotel
311 W. Foothill Blvd, 91016
Tel: 626-358-3231
(see page 234) **$$**
Best Western Colorado River Inn
2371 Needles Hwy, CA 92363
Tel: 760-326-4552
Fax: 760-326-4562
Spacious rooms and mini suites
with large-screen TVs/HBO,
microwaves and refrigerators. Very
nice indoor pool, sauna and Jacuzzi
area. Restaurant adjacent. **$$**
**Four Points Barcello
Hotel-Sheraton**
700 West Huntington Dr, CA 91016
Tel: 626-357-5211
Comfortable rooms, some
with laundry, refrigerators and
micro-waves. The hotel has a pool,
three spas, whirlpool, exercise
room, a restaurant and a lounge.
$$

SAN BERNARDINO
San Bernardino Hilton
285 East Hospitality Lane,
CA 92408
Tel: 909-889-0133
www.hilton.com
Luxurious rooms. Fine dining, pool
and whirlpool. **$$$**
Wigwam Motel
2728 N. Foothill Blvd 92408
Tel: 909-875-3005
(see page 234) **$$**

VICTORVILLE
Best Western Green Tree Inn
14173 Green Tree Blvd, CA 92392
Tel: 760-245-3461
Bright and cheerful decor. Over-
looks an 18-hole championship
golf course. Some rooms have
refrigerators. Pleasant dining
room. **$$**

WHERE TO EAT

AMBOY
Roy's Café
National Trails Hwy
Tel: 760-733-4263
(see page 230) **$$**
Trails Restaurant
2519 Huntington Drive
Tel: 626-359-2850

Hotel Prices

Categories based on average
cost of a double room for one
night.
$ = under $65
$$ = up to $100
$$$ = up to $150
$$$$ = over $150

Another classic roadhouse on Route
66 journey, *c.*1953. **$**

NEWBERRY SPRINGS
Bagdad Café
46548 National Trails Hwy
Tel: 760-257-3101
Decent cafe rechristened after the
Peter Adlon film of the same name
was shot here. **$**

OAK HILLS
Alfredo's Pizza and Restaurant
251 West Base Line Street
Tel: 909-885-0218
Excellent pizzas. **$–$$**
Magic Lamp Inn
8189 Foothill Boulevard
Tel: 909-981-8659
Another 66 landmark. **$–$$**
Summit Inn
5960 Mariposa Road
Tel: 760-949-8688
(see page 233) **$$**

Hub City:
LOS ANGELES

GETTING AROUND

Public transportation
This major city is notorious for its
lack of public transportation,
although the new Metro Rail
system is slowly nearing
completion. The primary public
transportation available is the
Southern California Metropolitan
Transit Agency bus company,
which everyone calls the MTA. MTA
offers a discount of about 10
percent if you buy booklets of 10
tickets or more. For information
and schedules, tel: 213-626-
4455, or see www.mta.net.
Southern California is still in the
early stages of implementing its
most ambitious public transit

plans for half a century which,
when completed, will link areas as
far apart as Los Angeles port of
Long Beach and Palmdale, 50
miles (80 km) north of the city.
The 400-mile (645 km) system of
light rail, subway and other
transportation facilities will not be
fully in place until 2010, although
Metro's Blue Line between Long
Beach and Pasadena is already in
operation as is part of the Metro
Red Line from downtown heading
towards Hollywood, North
Hollywood and Canoga Park; and
the Metro Green Line to El
Segundo. Passengers for Long
Beach board at Pico and Flower
streets for the one-hour trip, with
the last train from LA at 9pm and
the last train from Long Beach at
7.50pm. Check the phone number
or website above for up-to-date
bus and rail schedules.
From the airport: Public
transportation is found on LAX's
lower level, which is where arriving
passengers claim baggage. At this
level, there are stops for taxis, LAX
shuttles, buses, courtesy trams,
and vans in front of each airline
terminal. Information boards about
ground transport are located in all
the baggage claim areas and they
are very easy to understand.
Shuttles from the airport are
reasonably priced, the fare varies
depending on your destination.
Among the companies operating
24 hours a day are Prime Time
Shuttle, tel: 310-342-7200;
LA Xpress, tel: 310-342-2800;
Best Shuttle, tel: 310-783-4500,
The Super Shuttle, tel: 310-222-
5500 or 800-554-3146. Hopping
in a taxi at LAX should be avoided if
at all possible. Los Angeles' cabs
are very expensive – more so than
most US cities – and are almost
never found driving the streets
looking for customers. Free shuttle
service is now provided to the
Metropolitan Transit Authority –
Metro Green Line Light Rail's
Aviation Station. Pick up is on the
Lower/Arrival level under the LAX
Shuttle sign. Check out the MTA
bus and Metro Rail routes and
schedules at www.mta.net.

Private transportation

Taxis: Taxis are fairly expensive and you will rarely find them cruising the streets. Nevertheless, they can be ordered or found at airports, train stations, bus terminals and at major hotels.
Try: Yellow Cab Co, tel: 213-204-0999 or UITD, tel: 213-385-2227. The LA Checker Cab Co, tel: 213-747-8209 also offers vans with wheelchair lifts. An average fare from the Los Angeles Airport to Downtown Los Angeles would be at least $30.

The most efficient way to get around Los Angeles is to rent a car. Rental agencies may be found at the airport, your hotel, or any car rental agency (check the *Yellow Pages* under "Automobile Renting.") Cars often can be delivered to you. Car rental companies all charge basically the same price.
Avis, tel: 800-230-4898; www.avis.com
Budget, tel: 800-527-0700; www.budget.com
Hertz, tel: 800-654-3131; www.hertz.com

WHERE TO STAY

Argyle
8358 Sunset Boulevard
Tel: 323-654-7100
Fax: 323-654-9287
www.argylehotel.com
Sixty three rooms, mostly suites. Art Deco landmark, formerly the Sunset Tower and one-time home of Harlow, Gable, Monroe and Flynn. Restaurant, butler service, pool, fitness center. **$$$**
Bayside Hotel
2001 Ocean Avenue
Tel: 310-396-6000
1-800-525 4447
Fax: 310-396-1000
www.baysidehotel.com
Cozy rooms, comfy beds, oversized desks and ocean views await guests at this affordable Santa Monica hotel, not far from the beach. **$$**
Comfort Inn
1710 W. 7th Street
Tel: 213-616-3000

1-877-424 6423
Fax: 213-483 6971
www.choicehotels.com
True to its name, this is a comfortable hotel located just west of Downtown. Outdoor heated pool. **$$**
Hotel Oceana
849 Ocean Avenue, Santa Monica,
Tel: 310-393-0486
Fax: 310-458-1182
www.hoteloceana.com
Sixty three suites. Mediterranean-villa like, across from the ocean, a short walk to pier and promenade. Room service by Wolfgang Puck Café. Pool, laundromat, fitness center, car rental. **$$$**
Los Angeles Marriott Downtown
333 S Figueroa Street
Tel: 213-617-1133
US Freephone: 800-228-9290
Fax: 213-613 0291
www.marriott.com.
Luxury hotel with 469 rooms on 4 acres (1.6 hectares) of landscaped grounds, near Music Center and Dodger Stadium. Executive floor, health club, business center, valet parking, airport bus service, restaurants, pool, courtesy coffee, babysitting, foreign currency exchange. **$$$**
Orchid Hotel
819 S Flower Street
Tel: 213-624-5855
US Freephone: 800-874-5855
Fax: 213-624-8740
Sixty-three rooms. Cozy. Transportation to LAX. **$**
Residence Inn Santa Clarita
25320 The Old Road
Tel: 661-290-2800
Fax: 661-290-2802
www.residenceinn.com
Ninety suites, close to Magic Mountain, 20 miles (33 km) to Downtown LA. Free breakfast, room service, pool, exercise room, full kitchens, some fireplaces. **$$**
Venice Beach House
15 Thirtieth Avenue, Venice
Tel: 310-823-1966
Fax: 310-823-1842
Pretty B&B near the beach built in 1911. Nine rooms, full breakfast, some share bathrooms. **$$**

WHERE TO EAT

Southern Californians dine out an average of two or three times a week and variety is one of the main reasons. The most prevalent ethnic food you'll encounter here is Mexican, but the Golden State has also been the birthplace of several culinary trends over the years, including Szechuan, sushi, and of course, California cuisine. The best-known of the celebrity chefs are Wolfgang Puck (Spago, Chinois on Main) and Joachim Splichal (Cafe Pinot), but in a place where achievement equals celebrity there are many others. The following list is a mere sampling of some notable restaurants across the city.
Ciudad
445 S. Figueroa Street
Tel: 213-486-5171
Latin and Southwest cross in a wild way. From Salvadorean *pupusas* (corn meal puffs with cucumber *curtido* and mango *rocoto* sauce) to Colorado lamb steak with sweet-roasted *poblano* chili. Incredible desserts and liqueurs. The new darling of downtown. **$$$**
Grand Central Market
317 S Broadway
Tel: 213-624-2378
Bustling shoppers, neon signs and varied produce – a feast for the eyes. Stalls offer fish tacos and other cheap street food. **$**
Ji Raffe
502 Santa Monica Blvd
Tel: 310-917-6671
Innovative California cuisine at this hip scene. Good wine list. Interesting open architecture. **$$$**
Mandarin Chateau
970 N Broadway
Tel: 213-625-1195

Restaurant Prices

Categories based on average cost of dinner and a glass of wine, before tip.
$ = under $15
$$ = up to $30
$$$ = over $30

Serving a wide assortment of Chinese dishes. **$$**
Musso & Frank's
6667 Hollywood Boulevard
Tel: 323-467-7788
A menu of old faithfuls that's basically unchanged since it began eons ago when Hollywood giants could be seen through the gloom (some still can). **$$**
A Thousand Cranes
120 S Los Angeles Street

Tel: 213-629-1200
The classiest of three restaurants in the New Otani Hotel, this one overlooks the lovely third-floor garden. Refined Japanese cuisine with sushi and tempura bars and tatami rooms. **$$$**

SHOPPING

For intrepid shoppers, southern California can be right up there with the big guns like Paris and Hong Kong. A recent press report released by the tourist bureau claimed that the area is becoming "the unofficial seamstress to the casually clad masses." Much of the high-class fashion, of course, can be found along that glitziest shopping street, Beverly Hills'

renowned **Rodeo Drive**. While Rodeo has now become quite a tourist trap, with more people window shopping than buying, some of the world-class shops along the drive include **Chanel**, **Armani**, **Ungaro**, **Alaia** and **Bottega Veneta**. A trip down **Melrose Avenue** is essential. First there's the **Pacific Design Center** – The Blue Whale – with its 200 designers' showrooms at the corner of San Vicente, and then there are several blocks of raffish shops between **Croft** and **La Brea**. Lively **Chinatown,** rife with the aromas of herbs, dried fish, ginseng, and ginger is the primary source of Asian imports. Try **F. See On Company**, 507 Chungking, for teak furniture and porcelain; **Fongs**, 939 Chungking, for

Route 66

STATE AND NATIONAL ORGANIZATIONS
Ash Fork Tourist Center
Old Route 66, Ash Fork, AZ 86320
California Historic Route 66 Association
2117 Foothill Boulevard #66, LaVerne, CA 91750
Tel: 562-997-9817
Historic Route 66 Association of Arizona
PO Box 66, Kingman, AZ 86402
Oklahoma Route 66 Association
PO Box 21382, Oklahoma City, OK 73156
Tel: 405-258-0008
www.nowka.com/ok66html
Old Route 66 Association of Texas
PO Box 66, McLean, TX 79057
Tel: 806-267-2828
National Historic Route 66 Federation
PO Box 1848, Lake Arrowhead, CA 92352-1848
Tel/Fax: 909-336-6131
www.national66.com
New Mexico Route 66 Association
1415 East Central, Albuquerque, NM 87106
Tel: 505-224-2802

MUSEUMS
California Route 66 Museum/ Victorville
16849 D Street, Route 66, Victorville, CA 92392
Tel: 760-951-0436
National Route 66 Museum
2717 West Third
Elk City, OK 73644
Tel: 580-225-6266
Route 66 Hall of Fame
Dixie Trucker's Home, I-55 and US 136, McLean, IL 61754
Route 66 Museum
2229 Gary Boulevard, Clinton, OK 73601
Tel: 580-323-7866
www.route66.org

RADIO
KBLU 560 AM – Yuma, Arizona (news and golden oldies).
KIXE 940 AM – Douglas, Arizona.
KAVV 97.7 FM – Benson, Arizona (news and Country & Western).
KRCY 105.9 – Arizona (1960s pop).
KNFT 102.9 FM – Deming, New Mexico (Country).
KDAP 96.5 FM
Radio Sonora 101.3 FM
Sonora, Mexico.

PUBLICATIONS
Behind the Wheel on Route 66 by Howard Suttle (Data Plus! 1993)
The Grapes of Wrath by John Steinbeck, (William Heinemann, 1939)
A Guide Book to Highway 66 by Jack D. Rittenhouse (Originally published 1946, now published in facsimile edition by the University of Mexico Press)
Guide to Historic Route 66 in California by Vivian Davies & Darin Kuna (California Historic Route Assn, 1994)
Historic Route 66, a hard-bound, fold-out map (Global Graphics)
Route 66: An Illustrated Guidebook to the Mother Road by Bob Moore & Patrick Grauwels/ Yannis Argyropoulos (Roadbook International, 1998)
Route 66 Magazine quarterly from PO Box 66, Laughlin NV 89028; tel: 702-299-0856
www.route66magazine.com
Route 66 Travelers Guide & Roadside Companion by Tom Snyder (St Martin's Press, 1995)
The Verse by the Side of the Road by Frank Rowsome, Jr. (Penguin Books, 1965, 1990)

Hotel Prices

Categories based on average cost of a double room for one night.
$ = under $65
$$ = up to $100
$$$ = up to $150
$$$$ = over $150

antiques, cloisonne, figurines, handpainted bottles; **Win Sun**, 951 Chungking, for jade and opal jewelry. All three are in the **Chungking Mall**. It mustn't be forgotten that for mall lovers, Southern California is a shopper's Valhalla. One of the Southland's most famous landmarks, the outstanding former Uniroyal tire plant beside the Santa Ana Freeway in the City of Commerce has re-emerged as the **Citadel Outlet Collection**, an enticing shopping plaza whose 42 stores spread around a tree-flanked courtyard.

Further afield, the San Fernando Valley is renowned for its malls, the most famous and biggest of which are the **Glendale Galleria** (270 stores, www.glendalegalleria.com), the **Northridge Fashion Center** (212 stores), and the **Sherman Oaks Fashion Square** (140 stores). A little further afield, in addition to Orange County's **South Coast Plaza**, are the **Del Amo Fashion Square** in Torrance, the 200 specialty shops in a Mediterranean-village type atmosphere of Newport Beach's **Fashion Island**, 1045 Newport Center Drive.

Southern Route

Useful Addresses

Atlanta tourist information
Atlanta Convention and Visitors Bureau Center, 233 Peachtree Street, GA, 30303
Tel: 404-521-6600
www.atlanta.net
Georgia tourist information
(see page 392)
Alabama tourist information
Bureau of Tourism and Travel, 401 Adams Ave, Suite 126, Montgomery, AL 36104
US Freephone: 800-252-2262
www.touralabama.org
Louisiana tourist information
Louisiana Office of Tourism, P.O. Box 94291, Baton Rouge, LA 70804-9291
Tel: 225-342-8100
www.louisianatravel.com
Mississippi tourist information
PO Box 849, Jackson, MS 39205
Tel: 601-359-3297
US Freephone: 866-733-6477
www.visitmississippi.org
Texas tourist information
(see page 426)
New Mexico tourist information
(see page 426)
Arizona tourist information
(see page 426)
California tourist information
(see page 426)

Hub City: ATLANTA

GETTING AROUND

Public transportation
From the airport: Hartsfield International, the second busiest in the country, is located 10 miles (16 km) from Downtown. Many hotels offer courtesy buses from

the airport. Atlanta Airport Shuttle is one of several companies providing service into the city. A single ticket is under $10.

Public transportation in the metropolitan area includes buses and MARTA trains, sublimely safe, swift, reliable and clean.
Rapid transportation/buses: MARTA (Metropolitan Rapid Transit Authority) is a rapid-rail system comprising north–south and east–west lines intersecting at the main Five Points Station in downtown Atlanta. Stations are designated N, S, E, W or P, denoting their compass relationship to Five Points. (P represents the current single-station Proctor Creek Line.) The Hartsfield International Airport Station is designated Airport S7.
National buses: Greyhound operates from the depot at 81 International Boulevard NW, Atlanta, tel: 800-229-9424
National rail: Amtrak trains run from Peachtree Station, 1688 Peachtree Street NW, Tel: 800-872-7245

Private transportation
Atlanta – sprawling, suburban and subject to extremes of weather – is not ideally suited for extensive walking tours. Should you decide to explore by car instead, car rental agencies may be found at the airport, and/or downtown. Check the *Yellow Pages* for a full list of firms.
Avis, tel: 800-462-5266
Budget, tel: 800-527-0700
Hertz, tel: 800-654-3131
Taxis: Taxi and limousine companies are numerous. Ask at a hotel for assistance; hotels are always good places to find a taxi.
Tel: 658-7600 for information regarding taxi companies and fares. These fares are approximate: flag falling, $1.50; each additional ⅛ mile 20 cents; waiting, $12 an hour. Typical fare: airport to Buckhead, $25. Airport to downtown, $15. Fares are subject to 6 percent tax.

WHERE TO STAY

Atlanta Marriott Marquis
265 Peachtree Center Ave,
GA 30303
Tel: 404-521-0000
Fax: 586-6299
This whale of a hotel is another
John Portman beauty: the atrium
lobby has a volume of 9.5 million
cu. ft (269,010 cu. meters), and
visitors feel they've entered the rib
cage of some mythical beast.
Pool, sauna, whirlpool, steam
room, health club – all the perks.
$$$$

Holiday Inn at Lenox
3387 Peachtree Road, GA 30326
Tel: 404-261-5500
Fax: 404-261-6140
Dwarfed by adjacent high rises,
this modest hotel has cool views
of Lenox Square and suburban
greenery, in-room cable and HBO
films on TV, in-room safes and
coffee-makers. **$$–$$$**

Hostelling International – Atlanta
223 Ponce de Leon Ave,
GA 30308
Tel: 404-872-1042
Email: rsvp@mindspring.com
Located in the heart of downtown
Atlanta. Amenities include kitchen,
parking, games and courtyard. **$**

Terrace Garden Inn
3405 Lenox Road NE, GA 30326
Tel: 404-261-9250
Fax: 404-848-7391
Southern hospitality comes to
mind here, especially towards
guests. Some 364 recently
renovated rooms and suites,
a health and racquet center,
three dining venues; Marta and
Lenox Square just across the
street. **$$$–$$$$**

Westin Peachtree Plaza
210 Peachtree Street, GA 30343
Tel: 404-659-1400
Fax: 404-589-7424
With its 1,068 pie-shaped rooms,
this 72-story, circular high rise
is an Atlanta landmark and the
tallest hotel in America to date.
Designed by famed architect
John Portman, the structure is a
must-see for visitors, whether
checking in or not. Small pets
allowed. **$$$$**

WHERE TO EAT

If you were to randomly parachute
into Atlanta, odds are you would
land on a good restaurant. The
following list is nothing if not
extremely limited and idiosyncratic.
You should not leave Atlanta without
stopping in at that Jimmy Dean –
Ford Fairlane dream of a diner on
Ponce de Leon Avenue, the
Majestic. Don't miss that other
paean to junk food, on "Ponce"
as well, the **Krispy Kreme** donut
shop. Other restaurant listings are
glossed in the text, and ethnic
eateries are covered in *Atlanta
Magazine* and *Creative Loafing*
listings. The magazine *Southern
Living* is a great reference.

Restaurant Prices

Categories based on average
cost of dinner and a glass of
wine, before tip.
$ = under $15
$$ = up to $30
$$$ = over $30

Anthony's
3109 Piedmont Road NE
Tel: 404-262-7379
Surely Atlanta's "Belle of the Ball,"
from the first cocktail on the
verandah through "Roasts Carved
From Our Silver Chariot," and on to
a chocolate soufflé. The setting is
antebellum plantation home; the
service is Anglo-Atlantan. (Yes, one
of the owners does have a Sheffield
accent.) Reservations urged. **$$$**

Buckhead Diner
3073 Piedmont Road (at East
Paces Ferry Road)
Tel: 404-262-3336
If Anthony's represents the Old
South, the Buckhead Diner
represents the New. See and be
seen here, and enjoy the glorified
pizza, hamburgers, soft-shell crabs,
onion rings and tarted-up southern
icons such as Banana Cream Pie.
It's all "down home" – if home has
a pair of BMWs parked out back. **$$**

Danté's Down the Hatch.
3380 Peachtree Rd NE, Buckhead,
Tel: 404-266-1600

For around 25 years in Atlanta,
Danté Stephensen's fine
fondue cuisine (using only
Australian beef), 18th-century
sailing-vessel decor, live jazz
(and live crocodiles in the moat)
have been turning heads and
returning patrons such as Jimmy
and Rosalyn Carter, Burt Reynolds
and William S. Buckley. Keep
your strawberry frozen daiquiri
glass as a souvenir. Reservations
urged. **$$**

The Dining Room
Ritz-Carlton Hotel, Buckhead,
3434 Peachtree Road
Tel: 404-237-2700
This five-star, four-course gem is
probably Atlanta's top restaurant.
Fantastic wine list, a once-in-a-
lifetime dining pleasure. **$$$**

Kamogawa Japanese Restaurant
3300 Peachtree Road
Tel: 404-841-0314
This three-peach jewel is said to
be local resident Elton John's
favorite bite in town. Stunningly
authentic Japanese cuisine in
four unique settings: the sushi
bar; white-linen-draped tables
overlooking the Nikko's splendid
Japanese garden; the teppanyaki
grill; private tatami rooms.
Reservations urged. **$$$**

The Varsity
61 North Avenue
Tel: 404-881-1706
One of Atlanta's most famous
restaurants, a drive-in burger-and-
Coke joint. Take antacid tablets
before ordering the chili dogs,
onion rings, fried fruit pies or
fluorescent orange shake. **$**

GEORGIA

WHERE TO STAY

LA GRANGE
Amerihost Inn
107 Hoffman Drive,
GA 30241
Tel: 706-885-9002
Fax: 706-885-1977
www.amerihostinn.com
Pleasant rooms with continental
breakfast and morning newspaper.
Indoor pool, whirlpool suites.
Close to shops and restaurants. **$**

MACON

1842 Inn
353 College Street, GA 31201
Tel: 912-741-1842
Fax: 912-741-1842
A historic bed-and-breakfast.
Features 19th-century ambiance
with 21st-century perks. Some of
the 21 units have fireplaces and
whirlpool baths. **$$$$**

Best Western-Riverside
2400 Riverside Drive, GA 31204
Tel: 912-743-6311
Fax: 912-743-9420
A 125-unit motor inn with pool. **$**

Courtyard by Marriott
3990 Sheraton Drive, GA 31201
Tel: 912-477-8899
Pay movies, heated pool, exercise
room, 108 units. No pets **$$**

WHERE TO EAT

JACKSON
**Buckner Family Restaurant and
Music Hall**
I-75
Tel: 770-775-6150
Enjoy marvelous home-style
suppers with gospel music. **$**

JULIETTE
Whistle Stop Cafe
443 McCrackin Street
Tel: 478-994-3670
(see page 250) **$**

ALABAMA

WHERE TO STAY

ATMORE
Royal Oaks
5415 Hwy 21N, AL 36502
Tel: 251-368-8722
French-style country inn in a lovely
peaceful setting. **$$**

BAYOU LA BATRE
Best Western Bayou La Batre Inn
13155 N Wintzell Ave, AL 36509
Tel: 251-824-2020
Fax: 251-824-1153
Close to the beach with 40
comfortable rooms. Continental
breakfast, pool, microwaves and
refrigerators. Hot tubs in some
rooms. Restaurant adjacent. **$**

EVERGREEN
Evergreen Inn
I-65 and Hwy 83 (Mail: Rt 2 393-B),
AL 36401
Tel: 251-578-5500
Fax: 251-578-5168
Clean and comfortable. **$–$$**

MOBILE
Azalea House
115 Providence Street
Tel: 251-438-9921
This Colonial home was built
in 1904. There is a spacious
porch overlooking the beautiful
grounds. **$$**

Malaga Inn
359 Church Street,
AL 36602
Tel/Fax: 251-438-4701
US Freephone: 800-531-5900
This unique downtown inn is set in
a gas-lit courtyard. The rooms are
nicely decorated and many feature
hardwood floors. **$$**

My Victorian
504 Church Street
Tel: 251-219-9961
In the heart of historic downtown
Mobile, this quaint B&B is just
a short stroll from the waterfront.
$$

MONTGOMERY
Lattice Inn
1414 South Hull Street, AL 36104
Tel: 334-832-9931
US Freephone: 800-525-0652
Fax: 334-264-0075
A thoughtfully restored,
peaceful inn set in the Garden
District. **$$**

Red Bluff Cottage
551 Clay Street, AL 36104
Tel: 334-264-0056
US Freephone: 888-551-2529
Fax: 334-263-3054
A cottage with gazebo and large
porch commanding excellent
views of the Alabama River and
State Capitol. Pretty rooms. **$$**

WHERE TO EAT

MOBILE
Big Time Diner
4936 Cottage Hill Road
Tel: 251-666-2141

This is the place to go if you yearn
for Ma's home cooking. **$**

Dew Drop Inn
1808 Old Shell Road
Tel: 251-473-7885
Classic American chili dogs and
chili cheeseburgers. **$**

MONTGOMERY
Farmers Market Cafe and Pit BBQ
315 North McDonough Street
Tel: 334-262-1970
They come in droves to this vast
and clamorous cafeteria for
excellent southern-style barbecue
and set-you-up breakfasts. **$**

Moses Crawford Catering
2227 E South Boulevard
Tel: 334-281-0053
Satisfying soul food in laid-back
atmosphere. **$**

MISSISSIPPI

WHERE TO STAY

BILOXI
Beau Rivage Resort
875 Beach Boulevard
Tel: 228-386-7111
A resort and casino that has the
feel of the French Riviera. **$$**

Grand Biloxi Hotel
280 Beach Boulevard
US Freephone: 800-949-2949
Located in the heart of the
Mississippi Gulf Coast. **$$**

GAUTIER
The Villas of Hickory Hill
7900 Martin Bluff Road,
MS 39553
Tel: 228-497-5150
US Freephone: 800-568-3155
Fax: 228-497-6427
Wheelchair-accessible rooms,
pool, exercise and game rooms,
lounge. **$$**

Hotel Prices

Categories based on average
cost of a double room for one
night.
$ = under $65
$$ = up to $100
$$$ = up to $150
$$$$ = over $150

GULFPORT

Crystal Inn
9379 Canal Road, MS 39503
Tel: 228-822-9600
Fax: 228-822-0666
Attractive rooms and excellent
facilities including complimentary
hot breakfast, pool, spa. Close to
Gulf beaches and casinos. **$$$**

Hampton Inn
9445 Highway 49
Tel: 228-868-3300
Centrally located and reasonably
priced. **$**

LONG BEACH

**Red Creek Inn Vineyard and
Racing Stable**
7416 Red Creek Road, MS 39560
Tel: 228-452-3080
US Freephone: 800-729-9670
A late 19th-century French cottage
surrounded by 11 wooded acres
(4.5 hectares). The inn is fitted with
antiques, old-fashioned wooden
radios and porch swings. Generous
continental breakfasts. **$$$**

PASS CHRISTIAN

Harbour Oaks Inn
126 West Scenic Drive, MS 39571
Tel: 228-452-9399
US Freephone: 800-452-9399
Fine views of the historic harbor
and beach from this elegant inn's
porch and second-story verandah.
Five rooms with private baths, a
guest kitchen and billiard room.
Southern breakfast included. **$$**

WHERE TO EAT

BILOXI

Port-o-Call
15200 Lemoyne Boulevard
Tel: 228-392-0335
A truly Southern take on seafood.
This is a place to drop your anchor.
$$

GULFPORT

Chappy's Seafood
624 East Beach Boulevard
Tel: 228-865-9755
Popular restaurant with some
interesting regional specialties. Try
the frogs legs with a side order of
fried green tomatoes. **$**

PASCAGOULA

Krystal
2603 Denny Avenue
Tel: 228-762-5204
Friendly atmosphere and offering
hamburgers, big portions and lots
of meat dishes. **$**

LOUISIANA

WHERE TO STAY

ABBEVILLE

Sunbelt Lodge
1903 Veterans Memorial Dr,
LA 70510
Tel: 337-898-1453
Standard rooms with free
continental breakfast, cable TV
and HBO. Near shops and
restaurants. The lodge has a
pool and wheelchair-accessible
rooms. **$**

BATON ROUGE

**Radisson Hotel and Conference
Center**
4728 Constitution Ave,
LA 70808
Tel: 225-925-2244
Fax: 225-930-0140
www.radison.com/batonrougela
Attractive, comfortable rooms.
Amenities include: health club,
laundry, pool, restaurant and free
airport transportation. **$$$**

The General Lafayette
427 Lafayette Street, LA 70802
Tel: 225-387-0421
Basic rooms at reasonable rates. **$**

BREAUX BRIDGE

Bayou Boudin & Cracklin
100 Mills Ave, Hwy 94,
LA 70517
Tel: 337-332-6158
Atmospheric 19th-century Cajun
cabins with porches overlooking
Bayou Teche. **$**

Restaurant Prices

Categories based on average
cost of dinner and a glass of
wine, before tip.
$ = under $15
$$ = up to $30
$$$ = over $30

EUNICE

The Seale Guesthouse
125 Seale Lane, LA 70535
Tel: 337-457-3753
www.angelfire.com/lq2/
guesthouse
Pretty guest house in tranquil
wooded grounds with large front
porch. Six rooms tastefully
decorated with antiques. **$$**

LAFAYETTE

Bois des Chênes
338 North Sterling Drive, LA 70501
Tel: 337-233-7816
Lovingly converted Plantation
carriage house close to the city
center. Breakfast included. **$$**

Lafayette Hilton and Towers
1521 Pinhook Road, LA 70503
Tel: 337-235-6111
Fax: 337-261-0311
Luxurious rooms, some with views
of Vermillion Bayou. Pool, exercise
facilities, spa. **$$$$**

NEW ORLEANS

Bourbon Orleans
717 Orleans Street, LA 70116
Tel: 504-523-2222
Fax: 504-525-8611
www.bourbonorleans.com
Queen Anne furnishings and
marble baths. Phones and mini-
TVs are among the amenities in
this French Quarter hotel built
around an outdoor courtyard
where cabanas encircle the
pool. Rooms with balconies
overlook Bourbon Street, but it is
quieter on the courtyard side.
Restaurant and lounge. **$$$$**

Chateau Hotel
1001 Chartres Street, LA 70130
Tel: 504-524-9636
Fax: 504-524-9636
A small, tastefully furnished
motel with a charming courtyard,
located in the residential Lower
Quarter – a good choice for
budget travelers. **$**

**Hostelling International –
Marquette**
2253 Carondelet Street,
LA 70130
Tel: 504-523-3014
The nation's fourth-largest
youth hostel is set in a complex
of century-old buildings one

Hotel Prices

Categories based on average cost of a double room for one night.

$ = under $65
$$ = up to $100
$$$ = up to $150
$$$$ = over $150

block from St Charles Avenue. There are dormitory rooms with bunk beds, private rooms and apartments. **$**

Lafayette Hotel
600 St Charles Avenue, LA 70130
Tel: 504-539-9000
www.thelafayettehotel.com
A small gem, the very Gallic Lafayette's beautiful rooms have minibars, ottomans, easy chairs and bookshelves. Many have four-posters, and some on St Charles Avenue open on to balconies – great during Carnival season. **$$$**

Le Richelieu
1234 Chartres Street, LA 70116
Tel: 504-529-2492
Fax: 504-524-8179
This lovely 88-room hotel, consid-ered by many the best bargain in town, is in a restored macaroni fac-tory and 19th-century row of houses in the Lower Quarter. Large rooms are individually decorated, with balconies, brass ceiling fans and fridges. Paul McCartney stayed in one of the suites while cutting an album. **$$**

OPELOUSAS
Best Western of Opelousas
5791 I-49 Service Road,
LA 70570
Tel: 337-942-5540
Comfortable modern inn offering free continental breakfast, coffee and morning newspaper. Pool, cable TV. Disabled access. **$$**

ST MARTINVILLE
The Old Castillo Hotel
220 Evangeline Blvd,
LA 70582
Tel: 337-394-4010
Fax: 337-394-7983

Email: phulin@worldnet.att.net
Beautiful historic inn with excellent restaurant on Bayou Teche. **$$**

WHERE TO EAT

ABBEVILLE
Black's Oyster Bar
319 Pere Merget Street
Tel: 337-893-4266
Plump, fresh oysters – on the half shell, fried or po' boy style (tucked into crusty white bread). **$**

Dupuy's Oyster Shop
108 South Main Street
Tel: 337-893-2336
Highly acclaimed oyster and seafood restaurant. Since 1869. **$**

BATON ROUGE
Drusilla Seafood Restaurant
3482 Drusilla Lane
Tel: 225-923-0896
Local favorite for seafood, steaks, Cajun food. Good atmosphere. **$**

BREAUX BRIDGE
Mulate's Restaurant
325 Mills Avenue
Tel: 337-332-4648
Email: mulates@1stnet.com
Wildly popular Cajun food and music spot. **$$**

EUNICE
Ruby's Cafe
221 West Walnut Avenue
Tel: 337-457-2583
Generous portions of well-flavored Cajun food for next to nothing. **$**

LAFAYETTE
Dean O's
305 Bertrand Drive
Tel: 318-233-5446
Superb pizzas. **$**

Old Tyme Grocery
218 West St Mary Boulevard
Tel: 318-235-8165
Sample the famed po' boy sandwich. Crusty white bread and an array of meat fillings. **$**

Prejeans
3480 I-49 North
Tel: 337-896-3247

Famous for its live Cajun music and award-winning gumbos, but look out for tour groups. **$**

NEW ORLEANS
New Orleans' extraordinary range of food includes everything from haute cuisine and Bananas Foster to blackened catfish and Creole soul. Unless it is otherwise noted in the description with words like "casual" or "informal", men are requested to wear a jacket and tie in the restaurants listed.

Antoine's
713 St Louis Street,
French Quarter
Tel: 504-581-4422
Fax: 504-581-3003
This well-known French Creole restaurant has been run by the same family since 1840. Famous dishes such as Oysters Rockefeller originated at Antoine's. Many dishes are sensational, especially the Baked Alaska. **$$$**

Café Maspero
601 Decatur Street
Tel: 504-523-6250
A great French Quarter restaurant when you want to give your wallet a rest. **$**

Felix's Uptown
4938 Prytania Street
Tel: 504-895-1330
Serving an assortment of reasonably priced creole and cajun food. **$**

OPELOUSAS
Palace Cafe
167 West Landry Avenue
Tel: 337-942-2142
A long-established Opelousas favorite excelling in gumbo and other Louisiana seafood staples. **$**

ST MARTINVILLE
Clambeaugh's Restaurant
111 North Main
Tel: 337-394-3949
Creole cuisine in the historic district bordering St Martin de Tours. **$**

Josephine's Creole Restaurant
830 South Main Street
Tel: 337-394-8030
Bona fide Creole and Cajun cooking using time-honored family recipes. Informal atmosphere. **$$**

Restaurant Prices

Categories based on average cost of dinner and a glass of wine, before tip.
$ = under $15
$$ = up to $30
$$$ = over $30

SHOPPING

Baton Rouge
Mall of Louisiana
6401 Bluebonnet Boulevard

Lafayette
Cajun Country Store
401 East Cypress Street

New Orleans
Royal Street is the place for antiques, although the entire town is great for shopping. Buy candy, Carnival souvenirs or spices.

TEXAS

WHERE TO STAY

ALPINE
Sunday House Motor Inn
E Hwy 90 (PO Box 578),
TX 799831
Tel: 915-837-3363
US Freephone: 800-510-3363
Clean rooms, 24-hour restaurant, club and pool. Rail station, bus and airport shuttle available. $

AUSTIN
Austin Motel
1220 S. Congress,
TX 78704
Tel: 512-441-1157
Fax: 512-444-1157
Very central and a few blocks south of Town Lake. Restaurant, Laundromat, pool, spa, video rental and library. $
Driskill Hotel
604 Brazos, TX 78701
Tel: 512-474-5911
US Freephone:
800-252-9367
Fax: 512-474-2214
Historic downtown landmark. Includes workout facilities, suites and a bar. $$$

BANDERA
Silver Spur Guest Ranch
PO Box 1657, TX 78003
Tel: 830-796-3037
The ranch offers stone cottages in the Hill Country outside San Antonio. Amenities: horseback riding and instruction, hayrides, cookouts, pool, entertainment. $

BIG BEND NATIONAL PARK
For park information,
tel: 915-477-2251
Lodgings within the Park are managed by: National Park Concessions, Inc.
Casa Grande
Modern units with private balconies overlooking the ruggedly beautiful surrounding mountains. $$
Chisos Mountain Lodge
Tel: 915-477-2291
The lodge comprises four types of accommodations:
Lodge Units
Situated on a wooded hillside in the Chisos Basin. The lodge rooms are equipped with private baths, ceiling fans and electric wall heaters. There is a common outlook porch on each level of the building. $$
Motel
Comfortable rooms in one-story units with mountain views and a common porch. $$
Stone Cottages
Six historic stone cottages perched on the Basin that can sleep up to a maximum of seven. All cottages have private baths, electric wall heaters and large porches. $$

CASTROVILLE
Landmark Inn
402 Florence Street,
TX 78009
Tel: 830-931-2133
Fax: 830-538-3858
Originally a mail stop on the old road to California and a hotel since 1870. Located in a state historical park with good bird- and butterfly-watching. The comfortable, simply furnished rooms have been taken back to their 1940s construction, a few with private bathrooms. Very good value. $

COLUMBUS
Columbus Inn
2208 Hwy 71S, TX 78934
Tel: 979-732-5723
Fax: 979-732-60084
Standard motel rooms, some with refrigerators. Amenities include pool and laundry facilities. $

CRYSTAL CITY
Casa de Lorenzo Motel
1800 Hwy 83N, TX 78839
Tel: 830-374-3483
Pleasant motel with restaurant, playground, fitness and laundry facilities. $

EL PASO
Camino Real Paso del Norte Hotel
101 South El Paso St, TX 79901
Tel: 915-534-3000
Handsome and sophisticated border hotel with some parts dating to 1912. Pool, sauna and excellent bar and restaurant. $$$
Hostelling International – Gardner Hotel
311 East Franklin Ave, TX 79901
Tel: 915-532-3661
Fax: 915-532-0302
Email: epihost@whc.net
Housed in the landmark Gardner Hotel. Amenities include kitchen, equipment storage, laundry and lockers. A few private rooms are also available. No curfew. $

FREDERICKSBURG
Best Western Sunday House Inn
314 East Highway Street
Tel: 830-992-2929
Efficient, popular hotel with clean rooms. Offers breakfast coupons for nearby Sunday Haus Café. $$
Dietzel Motel
909 W. Main (Jct. 290W and 87N),
TX 78624
Tel: 830-997-3330
Simple and well-maintained rooms 1 mile (1.6 km) west of town center. $

GALVESTON
Gaido's Seaside Inn
3700 Seawall, TX 77550
Tel: 409-762-9625
Fax: 409-762-4825
Many rooms have a seaview. There is also a tiered flower garden. $

Hotel Prices

Categories based on average cost of a double room for one night.
$ = under $65
$$ = up to $100
$$$ = up to $150
$$$$ = over $150

Reef Resort
8502 Seawall Boulevard,
TX 77554
Tel: 409-740-0492
Gulf view rooms have private balconies. **$**

HONDO
Whitetail Lodge
Hwy 90E (PO Box 110),
TX 78861
Tel: 830 426 3031
Fax: 830-426-8662
Comfortable, well-maintained lodge with restaurant nearby. Free continental breakfast **$**

HOUSTON
Sara's Bed & Breakfast Inn
911 Heights Boulevard,
TX 77008
Tel: 713-868-1130,
800-593-1130
Fax: 713-868-1160
Victorian mansion with 14 rooms; VCRs and video library available.
$$
St Regis
1919 Briar Oaks Lane,
TX 77027
Tel: 713-840-7600
US Freephone: 800-241-3333
Fax: 713-840-0616
Luxury accommodation, including 52 suites adjacent to the exclusive River Oaks neighborhood. The Astro Floor features maître d' and butler service. Interpreters. **$$$$**
**Hostelling International –
Houston International Hostel Inc.**
5302 Crawford, TX 77004
Tel: 713-523-1009
Pleasant house with tree-shaded porch, courtyard and gazebo. Close to NASA and other attractions. Facilities include kitchen, piano, laundry and bicycles. **$**

The Westin Galleria
5060 W Alabama, TX 77056
Tel: 713 960-8100
US Freephone: 800-228-3000
Fax: 713-960-6554
Stylish hotel in Galleria mall. Superb facilities, including ice rink, pool, restaurant, and gym.
$$$

JOHNSON CITY
Save Inn Motel
107 Hwy 281 and 290S
(PO Box 610), TX 78636
Tel: 830-868-4044
Fax: 830-868-7822
Tidy, well-fitted rooms fitted with coffee makers. Pool. **$–$$**

LAJITAS
Lajitas on the Rio Grande
Star Rt 70, Box 400, Terlingua,
TX 79852
Tel: 915-424-3471
Fax: 915-424-3277
www.lajitas.com
A reconstructed frontier town with spectacular mountain backdrop. On the edge of Big Bend National Park. The resort features an Old West hotel and saloon, pool, barbecues, float trips on the Rio Grande and Country and Western dancing. **$$**

MARATHON
Gage Hotel
PO Box 46, Marathon,
TX 79842
Tel: 915-386-4205
Built as a private lodge by rancher Alfred Gage in the 1920s, this charming little hotel, a Texas Historical Landmark, is replete with western antiques; a modern adobe building was added in the early 1990s. Amenities: air conditioning, restaurant, pool, shared baths, some fireplaces.
$–$$

MARFA
Arcón Inn
215 North Austin, 79843
Tel: 915-729-4826
Fax: 915-729-3391
Email: arconinn@iglobal.net
This century-old adobe home has been an inn since the

1950s. The interior is a fine blend of Victorian and southwestern styles. Full southwestern breakfast and dinner by reservation. **$$$**

NEW BRAUNFELS
Gruene Mansion Inn
1275 Gruene Road, TX 78130
Tel: 830-629-2641
Fax: 830-629-7375
Former cotton plantation home, with 25 rooms with antiques scattered in restored barns and sheds. Overlooks Guadalupe River, and is adjacent to Greune Hall, the oldest dance hall in Texas. **$$$**

PRESIDIO
Three Palms Inn
Old Hwy 67N, TX 79845
Tel: 915-229-3211
A well-kept motor inn with pool and cable television. **$**

SAN ANTONIO
The Historic Menger Hotel
204 Alamo Plaza, TX78205
Tel: 210-223-4361
US Freephone: 800-345-9285
Fax: 210-270-0761
Built in 1859 and located across from the Alamo. Several rooms have Jacuzzis and are furnished with antiques. Bar, Colonial Room restaurant, spa and fitness center.
$$$–$$$$
La Mansion del Río
112 College, TX 78205
Tel: 210-518-1000
Fax: 210-226-0389
Spanish mission architecture on quiet portion of Paseo del Río. Interpreters. **$$$**
Oge House on the Riverwalk
209 Washington Street, TX 78204
Tel: 210-223-2353
Fax: 210-226-5812
An 1857 antebellum mansion with exquisite antiques. **$$$**

TERLINGUA
Big Bend Motor Inn
PO Box 336, TX 79852
Tel: 915-371-2218
Fax: 915-371-2555
Minutes from the entrance to Big Bend National Park, this inn offers comfortable rooms with mountain

views, some with refrigerators and microwaves. Pool. **$$**

VAN HORN
Best Western Americana Inn
1309 Broadway, TX 79855
Tel: 915-283-2030
US Freephone: 800-621-2478
A welcome stop if you need a break from the road. Free continental breakfast, pool and cable TV/HBO. Some rooms have fridges. **$**

WHERE TO EAT

Don't plan on dieting while in Texas. Texans love their food, and a visit here wouldn't be complete without sampling a good portion of it. Tex-Mex food has become synonymous with the state, and it's not all fire-breathing hot, so even the most wary should give it a try. Another Texas staple is the barbecue, usually huge chunks of beef (but sometimes pork and sausage) which are cooked slowly for hours over special wood such as hickory or mesquite to add to the distinctive flavor. One of the state's celebrated barbecue joints is **The Salt Lick** at Driftwood (tel: 512-858-4959), 13 miles (20 km) west of Austin in the Hill Country.

The dish of Texas is chili con carne, and you'll find it throughout the state. On average, some 15 chili competitions are held each month. The "runner-up" to the state dish must surely be chicken-fried steak, an inexpensive steak covered with batter and fried, usually served with gravy and found on Texan menus. No matter how much you eat, leave room to try the local pecan pie.

ALPINE
Outback Bar and Grill
300 South Phelps and Avenue G
Tel: 915-837-5074
Eclectic menu featuring large portions of steak, chicken, Mexican and Italian seafood dishes. **$$**

AUSTIN
Cisco's Bakery and Coffee Shop
East 6th Street
Tel: 512-478-2420

Fiery, hangover-busting Mexican breakfasts. **$**
Scholz Garden
1607 San Jacinto Boulevard
Tel: 512-474-1958
(see page 277) **$$–$$$**
Threadgill's
6416 North Lamar
Tel: 512-459-3855
Famed Texan roadhouse café with live music on Wednesday evening. Lavish servings of southern cuisine, Cajun and vegetarian. **$**

COLUMBUS
Schobel's
2020 Milam Street
Tel: 979-732-2385
Nice range of well-prepared dishes served in pleasant, informal atmosphere. The salad bar and noon buffet are very popular. **$**

EL PASO
The Dome Restaurant
101 South El Paso Street
Tel: 915-534-3010
Located in the Camino Real Hotel. Superb, innovative seafood and wild game creations matched by the majestic surroundings. **$$**

Restaurant Prices

Categories based on average cost of dinner and a glass of wine, before tip.
$ = under $15
$$ = up to $30
$$$ = over $30

Leo's Mexican Food
5103 Montana Avenue
Tel: 915-562-5101
Reliable local favorite for authentic Tex-Mex. **$**
Smitty's
6219 Airport Road
Tel: 915-772-5876
Divine Texas barbecue accompanied by that stalwart trinity – potato salad, beans and slaw. Not very central but well worth a detour. **$**

FREDERICKSBURG
Altdorf Restaurant & Beer Garden
301 West Main Street
Tel: 830-997-7695

German music, beer and grub. **$**
Dietz Bakery
218 Main Street
Tel: 830-997-3250
Delicious breads and pastries. **$**

HOUSTON
The Brownstone
2736 Virginia
Tel: 713-520-5666
Top-notch food in opulent surroundings. **$$$**
Goode Company Texas BBQ
5109 Kirby
Tel: 713-522-2530
Fabled barbecue place. **$$**
Dessert Gallery
3200 Kirby Drive
Tel: 713-522-9999
Sara Brook's sexy desserts plus furniture as art. Lunch specials. **$**
Pappadeaux Seafood Kitchen
6015 Westheimer
Tel: 713-782-6310
Favored local Cajun spot. **$$**
Rainbow Lodge
1 Birdsall near Memorial Park
Tel: 713-861-8666
Classy fishing lodge with garden, seafood and wild game. **$$$**

JOHNSON CITY
Hill Country Cupboard
Hwy 290
Tel: 830-868-4625
Country-style lunch special. **$**

MARFA
Tumblewood Grill
500 East San Antonio Street
Tel: 915-729-4065
Well-prepared regional cuisine in attractive surroundings. **$$**

NEW BRAUNFELS
Krause's Café
148 South Castell Avenue
Tel: 830-625-7581
Great German food Texas-style. **$**

PRESIDIO
El Patio Restaurant
513 O'Reilly Street
Downtown, featuring Mexican or American entrees, salad bar. **$**

SAN ANTONIO
Casa Rio
430 East Commerce St

Tel: 210-225-6718
This enduring Riverwalk favorite serves large portions of tasty, inexpensive Mexican food. **$**
County Line
111 W Crockett, on the Riverwalk
Tel: 210-229-1941
Popular barbecue parlor. **$$**
Tower of the Americas
222 Hemisfair Plaza
Tel: 210-223-3101
Spectacular views from the revolving tower. Classy food. **$$$**

UVALDE
Haby's BBQ
529 West Main Street
Tel: 830-278-5746
Steaks and Tex-Mex dishes. **$**

SHOPPING

AUSTIN
Austin's biggest mall, **Highland Mall**, is at 6001 Airport Boulevard, but there are also numerous little specialty shops, such as the **Turquoise Trading Post**, Burnet Road at Koenig, which displays a large selection of Native American jewelry, including Zuni fetishes, Navaho Kachina dolls, medicine wheels and dreamcatchers. The more macabre-minded will enjoy the selection of skulls, hides and trophy mounts available at the **Corner Shoppe**, 5900 Lamar Street. As befits a college town – and state capital – Austin is proud of its literary leanings, pointing out that not only does it house branches of the big bookstore chains, such as **Borders** and **Barnes & Noble**, but also many independents, among them **Congress Avenue Booksellers Half Price Books** – which deals in used books and music – and three stores specializing in African-American literature: **Folktales**, **Just For Us** and **Mitchie's Fine Black Art Gallery & Bookstore**.

EL PASO
El Paso is the home of the cowboy boot manufacturer, **Tony Lama**. There are four factory outlets in the city.

SAN ANTONIO
Visitors to San Antonio's **North Star** mall (Loop 410 between San Pedro and MacCullough) are invited to begin their browsing with a visit to the information booth to pick up a free shopping bag and a coupon booklet offering discounts at many of the 200 stores. These include such big names as **Saks Fifth Avenue**, **Marshall Field's**, **Guess**, **Williams-Sonoma** and **Gap**. There are other malls, of which the most attractive architecturally is **Rivercenter**, 849 East Commerce, adjoining the restaurants and IMAX theater in the heart of downtown. **La Villita**, a recreated Mexican village, and **El Mercado** (514 West Commerce) both offer specialty shops with Mexican arts and crafts.

Hotel Prices

Categories based on average cost of a double room for one night.
$ = under $65
$$ = up to $100
$$$ = up to $150
$$$$ = over $150

NEW MEXICO

WHERE TO STAY

ALAMOGORDO
Best Western Desert Aire Motor Inn
1021 South White Sands Blvd, NM 88310
Tel: 505-437-2110
Close to White Sands National Monument. Guest rooms face onto a large attractive pool. Continental breakfasts included. Sauna, outdoor Jacuzzi and game room. **$**

CLOUDCROFT
The Lodge
Corona Place, (PO Box 497), NM 88317
Tel: 505-682-2566
One of the last remaining hotels built during the region's timber industry boom in the late 19th/ early 20th century. The Victorian-style lodge rooms are furnished

with antiques. The Pavilion rooms are more simply furnished and include full breakfast. **$$**

DEMING
Butterfield Stage Motel
309 West Pine Street, NM 88030
Tel: 505-544-0011
Basic but very clean and warm. **$**

LAS CRUCES
Royal Host Motel
2146 West Pichaco St, NM 88005
Tel: 505-524-8536
Simple and well-maintained. Pool and cable TV. **$**

LORDSBURG
Best Western American Motor Inn
944 East Railroad, NM 87701
Tel: 505-542-3591
Attractive rooms and a pool. **$**

MESCALERO
Inn of the Mountain Gods
PO Box 269, NM 88340
Tel: 505-257-5141
US Freephone: 800-545-9011
Owned by the Mescalero Apache tribe, this resort hotel is located on a lake in the Sacramento Mountains and offers a variety of recreational activities, including golf, tennis, pool, fishing and boating. **$$–$$$**

RUIDOSO
Swiss Chalet Inn
1451 Mechem Drive, (PO Box 759), Hwy 48N, NM 88355
Tel: 505-258-3333
Fax: 505-258-5325
A Swiss-style hotel located in a cool, pine-clad forest with panoramic views of Sierra Blanca Mountain. Full breakfast, pool, hot tub, restaurant and tavern. **$$**

SILVER CITY
Bear Mountain Guest Ranch
PO Box 1163, NM 88062
Tel: 505-538-2538
www.BearMtGuest Ranch.com
Great for nature lovers, large 1920s ranch house charges all-inclusive full board rates in its very pleasant rooms and offers

guided bird-watching trips plus a variety of activities including mountain biking or cross-country skiing tours. **$$$$**

Hostelling International – Carter House
101 North Cooper St, NM 88061
Tel: 505-388-5485
Light and airy older home located in the historic district with fine mountain views from the wraparound porch. Amenities include kitchen, baggage storage, lockers, cable TV/VCR and laundry facilities. **$**

WHERE TO EAT

LAS CRUCES
Nellie's Cafe
1226 West Hadley Avenue
Tel: 505-524-9982
Excellent Mexican food laced with fresh and fiery salsa. **$**

MESCALERO
Dan Li Ka, Inn of the Mountain Gods
PO Box 269
Tel: 505-257-5141
Excellent fine dining at the beautiful inn. **$$**

SILVER CITY
Drifter Motel
711 Silver Heights Boulevard
Tel: 505-538-2916
Good-value breakfasts. **$**
Silver Cafe
514 North Bullard
Tel: 505-388-3480
Pleasant mid-town cafe. **$**

ARIZONA

WHERE TO STAY

BISBEE
Bisbee Grand Hotel
61 Main St, AZ 85603
Tel: 520-432-5900
Elegantly restored Victorian hotel with period decor; in a small southern Arizona mining town. Amenities: parking, saloon, billiard room and a free breakfast. **$$**
Copper Queen Hotel
11 Howell Ave, AZ 85603
Tel: 520-432-2216

A turn-of-the century Victorian landmark built during the heyday of the Copper Queen Mine; guests in the past have included John Wayne and Teddy Roosevelt. Amenities: parking, television, restaurant, saloon, pool. **$$**

GILA BEND
Best Western Space Age Lodge
401 E Pima St, Box C, NM 85337
Tel: 520-683-2273.
(see page 310) **$**

PHOENIX
Arizona Biltmore
24th St & Missouri Ave, AZ 285016
Tel: 602-955-6600
Fax: 602-381-7600
An elegant grand hotel designed by Frank Lloyd Wright in landscaped grounds. Pools, fitness room, golf courses, biking, restaurants, bars, shops. **$$$$**
Desert Rose
3424 E. Van Buren St, AZ 85008
Tel: 602-275-4421
Modest but comfortable small hotel with pool and restaurant a short drive from downtown. **$**
Maricopa Manor
15 W Pasadena Avenue,
AZ 85013
Tel: 602-274-6302
Spanish-style home built in the 1920s furnished with antiques and art. All rooms are suites. With pool, spa and gardens. **$$–$$$**

SCOTTSDALE
Phoenician
Tel: 480-941-8200
(see page 309) **$$$**

TOMBSTONE
Tombstone Motel
502 East Fremont St, AZ 85638
Tel: 520-457-3478

Hotel Prices

Categories based on average cost of a double room for one night.
$ = under $65
$$ = up to $100
$$$ = up to $150
$$$$ = over $150

Clean, well-fitted rooms in historic 1880s building. **$**

TUCSON
Hotel Congress
311 East Congress, AZ 85701
Tel: 520 622-8848
US Freephone: 800-722-8848
John Dillinger and his gang stayed here. Why shouldn't you? Idiosyncratic and inexpensive. **$**
Lazy K Bar Guest Ranch
8401 North Scenic Drive, AZ 85743
Tel: 520-744-3050
US Freephone: 800-321-7018
Cabins in the Tucson Mountains. Horseback riding, swimming pool, spa, tennis courts, volleyball and basketball. Includes a ranch store and entertainment. **$**
Lodge on the Desert
306 North Alvernon Way, AZ 85711
Tel: 520-325-3366
US Freephone: 800-456-5634
In-town resort restored to its original casual allure. Most rooms have red-tiled patios and fireplaces. Its restaurant is recognized as one of the best in Tucson. **$$–$$$**

YUMA
La Fuente Inn and Suites
1513 East 16th Street, AZ 85365
Tel: 928-329-1814
Attractive contemporary inn with nicely landscaped gardens and pool. **$$**
Yuma Cabana Hotel
2151 South Fourth Ave, AZ 85364
Tel: 928-783-8311
Attractive little oasis. Very good value. **$**

WHERE TO EAT

BISBEE
Dot's Diner
1 Old Douglas Road
Tel: 520-432-2046
Superlative diner fare at absurdly cheap prices. Adjacent to a unique trailer park. **$**

GILA BEND
Outer Limits Restaurant
(connected to the Best Western

Restaurant Prices

Categories based on average cost of dinner and a glass of wine, before tip.
$ = under $15
$$ = up to $30
$$$ = over $30

Space Age Lodge) 401 E Pima St, Box C, NM 85337
Tel: 928-683-2273
(see page 310) $

PHOENIX
Aunt Chiladas
7330 N Dreamy Draw Drive
Tel: 602-944-1286
Although its tamed-down Mexican food compared with what you'd find elsewhere, the flour tortilla chips (available on request) and fresh salsa more than compensate. $
Christo's
6327 N 7th Street
Tel: 602-264-1784
One of the top Phoenix restaurants, dishing up elegant Italian food in a formal setting. $$
Ed Debevic's
2102 E Highland Avenue
Tel: 602-956-2760
Infamous (in a good way) for their rude staff, this 1950's-style diner dishes up excellent cafe fare. $

SCOTTSDALE
Jean Claude's Petit Cafe
7340 East Shoeman Lane
Tel: 480-947-5288
Contemporary French bistro good for a romantic night out.
$–$$
Shogun
7366 East Shea Boulevard
Tel: 480-922-8824
Good choice for sushi, tempura and other Japanese specialties.
$–$$

TOMBSTONE
Nellie Cashman's Restaurant
117 South Fifth Street
Tel: 520-457-2212
A long-running Tombstone favorite.
$–$$

TUCSON
Dakota Cafe
6541 East Tanque Verde Road
Tel: 520-298-7188
Popular café with a broad menu and vegetarian dishes. $
El Minuto
354 South Main Avenue
Tel: 520-882-4145
Spicy and filling Mexican food in a stripped-down cantina. Popular with locals. $
Janos
150 North Main Avenue
Tel: 520-884-9426
Inventive French-southwestern cuisine served in a lovely 19th-century adobe. $$

YUMA
Brownies' Restaurant
1145 South Fourth Street
Tel: 928-783-7911
Good breakfasts and very reasonable dinners. $
Crossing Restaurant
2690 South Fourth Avenue
Tel: 928-726-5551
Reliable if unexciting. $

SHOPPING

PHOENIX
The city has several large malls located to the north, as well as the **Arizona Center**, Van Buren Street, in downtown. A number of interesting shops are located in **Heritage Square**, which is also in the city center.
Heard Museum Gift Shop
2301 North Central Avenue
Exquisite Native American jewelry and other crafts.

SCOTTSDALE
Fashion Square
(see page 309)

TUCSON
Tucson is a good center for southwestern crafts. Try **Kaibab Shops**, 2841–43 Campbell Avenue or **Mark Subblette Medicine Man Gallery**, 7000 East Tanque Verde Road for Mexican and Native American crafts including rugs, blankets, pottery and beadwork.

CALIFORNIA

WHERE TO STAY

EL CENTRO
E–Z 8 Motel
455 Wake Avenue, CA 92243
Tel: 760-352-6620
Clean, standard motel rooms with free continental breakfast, pool and laundry facilities. A few rooms are equipped with kitchenettes. $

JACUMBA
Jacumba Hot Springs Spa
44500 Old US 80, CA 91934
Tel: 619-766-4501
Relaxing natural hot springs, pools and private Jacuzzis. Very good restaurant serving international dishes, and bar. $

WHERE TO EAT

EL CENTRO
La Hacienda Cafe
841 West Main Street
Tel: 760-353-8118
Very good Mexican food. $

LA MESA
Marieta's Restaurant
8949 La Mesa Boulevard
Tel: 619-462-3500
Southwestern dishes and friendly service. $$
Brigantine Seafood Restaurant
9350 Fuerte Drive
Tel: 619-465-1935
Fresh seafood. $$

Smokers Take Note

Always check, when booking a restaurant table or a hotel room, whether smoking is allowed, and where. Some hotels and motels have designated smoking floors, while some restaurants allow smoking in the bar, but not at a table. If you plan on visiting California, you might as well give up cigarettes now; the evil weed is banned even in some parks and outdoor areas.

Pacific Route

Useful Addresses

California tourist information:
(see page 426)
Oregon tourist information:
Economic Development Department
775 Summer St. NE, Salem,
OR 97310
Tel: 800-547-7842
www.traveloregon.com
Washington tourist information
(see page 406)

Hub City:
SAN DIEGO

GETTING AROUND

Public transportation
From the airport: San Diego
International Airport (tel: 619-686-
8065) is located 3 miles (5 km)
from downtown. Various shuttle
services operate from the airport to
the center and are reasonablly
priced. The Metropolitan Transit
System bus route 992 travels from
the airport to downtown.
City buses: City buses are run by
San Diego Metropolitan Transit
System (tel: 619-685-4900). The
San Diego Trolley System runs from
the Santa Fe Depot at 1850 Kettner
Boulevard, crossing into Mexico at
San Ysidro.
Intercity buses: The Greyhound
depot is at Broadway and First
Avenue.
Trains: Amtrak services run from
the Santa Fe Depot at 10850
Kettner Boulevard.

Private Transportation
Unlike Los Angeles, San Diego is a
relatively easy city to explore either
with or without a car. However, as in
most big cities, journeys are best

planned around the weekday early
morning and late afternoon crush.
Parking is generally easy to find and
for the most part moderately priced.
Most of the major car rental
agencies have offices at the airport
and in the downtown area.
Car rental companies:
Avis, tel: 800-230-4898
Budget, tel: 800-577-0700
Hertz, tel: 800-654-3131
Taxis:
American, tel: 619-234-1111
Orange Cab, tel: 619-291-3333
Yellow Cab, tel: 619-234-6161

Traveling to Tijuana/Baja
Non US citizens should bring their
passports or green cards. US
citizens don't legally need a
passport unless they're visiting for
more than 72 hours, or plan to go
beyond the Hwy 1 checkpoint below
Baja's Ensenada, but in light of
recent, heightened security
precautions, it's a good idea to
travel with a passport anyway, or
acquire a tourist visa in San Diego
from any travel agent, the Mexican
Consulate General, the Mexico
Government Tourism Office or the
Automobile Club of Southern
California. Proof of nationality must
accompany any visa application.
    US insurance is not valid in
Mexico and it is definitely a wise
move to obtain short-term
insurance, obtainable at
innumerable sales offices just
north of the border. Crossing into
Mexico is easy, with immigration
officers at both sides usually just
waving you along. There are three
major crossings: at busy **San
Ysidro**, 18 miles (29 km) south of
downtown San Diego, which is the
gateway to Tijuana; at **Tecate** off
State 94, where there is rarely a
wait, although the solitary customs
officer tends to close the border in
early evening; and at **Mexicali**
(Baja's capital), a dreary industrial
city opposite the California town of
Calexico, which is about 90 miles
(144 km) to the east.
    Because driving is not easy in
Tijuana for those unfamiliar with the
city (and the Spanish language),
many drivers park in San Diego's

San Ysidro, crossing into Tijuana
via the elevated pedestrian
walkway. Avoid leaving your car in
the parking places of merchants
unless you want to have it towed
away by police. There's an all-day
secure lot off the "Last Exit US
parking" ramp – turn right at the
stop sign to the Tijuana side. Cheap
taxis and buses are available.
Crossing Back: The return to
California can be more tense than
the entry into Mexico, as American
officers take much more interest in
who's coming into the country.
Expect long lines, especially in busy
vacation periods.

Hotel Prices

Categories based on average
cost of a double room for one
night.
$ = under $65
$$ = up to $100
$$$ = up to $150
$$$$ = over $150

WHERE TO STAY

Holiday Inn-Harbor View
1617 1st Avenue
Tel: 619-239-6171
Fax: 619-233-6228
Close to I-5. Pool, restaurant,
laundromat. Shuttle to airport, zoo,
Sea World. **$$$**
Horton Grand
311 Island Avenue
Tel: 619-544-1886
US Freephone: 800-542-1886
Fax: 619-239-3823
www.hortongrand.com
Elegant, historic Victorian hotel, in
Gaslamp District. Near Horton
Plaza, Marina Park, Seaport Village,
Convention Center. Fireplaces,
antiques. **$$-$$$**
Hotel del Coronado
1500 Orange Ave, Coronado,
CA 92118
Tel: 619-435-6611
Fax: 619-522-8262
www.hoteldel.com
World-famous Victorian-era
landmark. Tennis court, pool, spa,
nearby golf, boating, beach,
restaurants. **$$$$**

La Pensione Hotel
606 West Date Street
Tel: 619-236-8000
Fax: 619-236-8088
www.lapensionehotel.com
A wonderful little secret, San Diego's best budget hotel, in Little Italy surrounded by cafes. Easy walk to downtown and harbor. Two blocks to trolley. European-style guesthouse, 80 units. $

U.S. Grant Hotel
326 Broadway
Tel: 619-232-3121
US Freephone: 800-334-6957
Fax: 619-232-3626
www.grandheritage.com
Restored, grand old historic hotel in heart of business, shopping, nightlife. Near trolley and Convention Center. $$$

Westin Horton Plaza
910 Broadway
Tel: 619-239-2200
US Freephone: 800-643-7846
Fax: 619-239-0509
www.westin.com
In the heart of downtown. Restaurant, pool, spa, lighted tennis courts, health club. $$$$

Restaurant Prices

Categories based on average cost of dinner and a glass of wine, before tip.
$ = under $15
$$ = up to $30
$$$ = over $30

WHERE TO EAT

Anthony's Fish Grotto
1360 North Harbor Drive
Tel: 619-232-7408
Fabulous seafood served with dramatic flair. Located on the waterfront. Jackets and reservations required. Open for dinner only. $$$

Casa de Pico
2754 Calhoun Street
Tel: 619-296-3267
Located in the Bazaar del Mundo in Old Town. Reliable Mexican food and great margaritas. $

The Marine Room
2000 Spindrift Drive, La Jolla
Tel: 858-459-7222
At high tide the waves crash just outside the windows. $$

Old Trieste
2335 Morena Boulevard
Tel: 619-276-1841
Reputed to be one of the best Italian restaurants in town. Closed Sunday and Monday. $$$

SHOPPING

San Diego's **Gaslamp Quarter**, a 16-block, 38-acre (17-hectare) district recommended for arts and crafts. In addition to its **Seaport Village** and the multilevel **Horton Plaza**, San Diego is also just a short hop away from the Mexican border town of Tijuana, where there are different souvenirs (look for leather) and lower prices

CALIFORNIA

WHERE TO STAY

ARCATA
Fairwinds Motel
1674 G Street, CA 95521
Tel: 707-822-4824
Basic and clean. $$

BIG SUR
Pfeiffer Big Sur State Park
For park information, tel: 831-667-2315
Julia Pfeiffer Burns State Park
For park information, tel: 831-667-2377
Big Sur Lodge
State Route 1, Big Sur, 93920
Tel: 831-667-3100
US Freephone: 800-424-4787
Fax: 831-667-3110
Big Sur architect Mickey Muenning used the sea and the mountains as a backdrop to this lush resort. $$

Big Sur River Inn
Hwy 1 at Phenger Creek, CA 93920
Tel: 831-667-2700
Fax: 831-667-2743
www.bigsuriverinn.com
Magnificent river views and warm welcoming rooms. Heated pool, restaurant, bar and patio. $$

Ventana Inn
Highway 1, CA 93920
Tel: 831-667-2331
Fax: 831-667-2419
Quoted as America's most romantic resort, by an *LA Times*' writer. $$$

BODEGA BAY
Bodega Bay Lodge Resort
103 Coast Highway 1, CA 94923
Tel: 707-875-3525
US Freephone: 800-368-2468
Fax: 707-875-2428
All rooms have panoramic ocean view and many have fireplaces. Romantic hideaway with restaurant, pool, fitness center and sauna. $$

Inn at the Tides
800 Hwy 1, CA 94923
Tel: 707-875-2751
Fax: 707-875-3285
US Freephone: 800-862-4945
www.innatthetides.com
Impressive views from these hillside lodges featuring fireplaces and continental breakfast. $$$

CARDIFF-BY-THE-SEA
Cardiff-by-the-Sea Lodge
142 Chesterfield, CA 92007
Tel: 760-944-6674
Fax: 760-944-6841
Neat, individual seaview rooms with fireplaces and whirlpool tubs. $$$

CARLSBAD
La Costa Resort and Spa
2100 Costa Del Mar Road
Tel: 760-438-9111
A sprawling Southern Californian "total resort" well-known for its two PGA championship golf courses and de luxe facilities. The 500-room complex includes health spas, golf courses and tennis courts. $$$$

Ocean Palms Beach Resort
2950 Ocean Street, CA 92008
Tel: 760-729-2493
Fax: 760-729-0579
This full-service resort is minutes from the beach. The complex includes beachfront studios and suites with fully equipped kitchens, heated pool, and Jacuzzi. $$$

CARMEL
Cypress Inn
Lincoln and 7th streets, CA 93923
Tel: 408-624-3871

Fax: 408-624-8216
Mission-style inn, warmly furnished with a garden courtyard and a restaurant/bar. **$$**

La Playa Hotel
Camino Real & Eighth St, CA 93923
Tel: 831-624-6476
Lush, prize-winning gardens surround this historic Mediterranean-style hotel, located two blocks from the stunning Pacific coast. **$$$**

Vagabond's House Inn
Fourth & Dolores Street
PO Box 2747, CA 93921
Tel: 831-624-7738
Fax: 831-626-1234
US Freephone: 800-262-1262
www.carmelfun.com
Eleven uniquely-appointed rooms surround a tranquil stone courtyard, graced by mature oak tree and waterfalls. A short stroll to local shops. **$$$–$$$$**

CAYUCOS
Beachwalker Inn
501 South Ocean Ave, CA 93940
Tel: 805-995-2133
Fax: 805-995-3139
Warm and welcoming rooms and suites with gas fireplaces. **$$$**

ELK
Harbor House by the Sea
5600 South Hwy 1, PO Box 369,
CA 95432
Tel: 707-877-3203
Fax: 707-877-3452
www.theharborhouseinn.com
Fine early 20th-century house overlooking magnificent rock formations. The inn is fronted by beautifully landscaped gardens and pathways leading to the beach. The dining room offers Californian cuisine with Tuscan and Provençal accents. **$$$$**

EUREKA
Eureka Inn
518 7th Street, CA 95501
US Freephone: 877-275-7814
(see page 362) **$$**
Carter House Inn
301 L Street
Tel: 707-444-8062
Renovated older home with comfortable, well-appointed rooms. Breakfast included. **$$$**

A Weaver's Inn
1440 B Street, CA 95501
Tel: 707-443-8119
Fax: 707-443-7923
www.humboldt1.com/~weavrinn
A pretty Queen Anne Colonial revival c.1883 building surrounded by a pristine white picket fence and furnished in period style. The attractive grounds feature a Japanese Contemplation Garden, cottage-style garden and croquet lawn. **$$–$$$**

FERNDALE
Gingerbread Mansion Inn
400 Berding Street,
CA 95536
Tel: 707-786-4000
US Freephone: 800-952-4136
Fax: 707-952-4136
www.gingerbread-mansion.com
(see page 360) **$$**
Shaw House Inn
703 Main Street,
CA 95536-1125
Tel: 707-786-9958
Fax: 707-786-9958
www.shawhouse.com
(see page361) **$$$**
Victorian Inn
400 Ocean Avenue, CA 95536
Tel: 707-786-4949
(see page 361) **$$$**

FORTUNA
Six Rivers Motel
531 South Fortuna Boulevard
Tel: 707-725-1181
Well-maintained, good-value rooms some with refrigerators and microwaves. **$**

GARBERVILLE
Best Western Humboldt House Inn
701 Redwood Drive, CA 95542
Tel: 707-923-2771
US Freephone: 800-248-7234
Fax: 707-923-4259
An ideal base for touring the Redwoods. Spacious rooms, some with balconies and mountain views. Pool, spa, complimentary breakfast and newspaper. **$$**
Historic Benbow Inn
455 Lake Benbow Drive,
CA 95542
Tel: 707-923-2124
Fax: 707-923-2122

This Tudor-style inn has been welcoming guests for over 70 years. Three of the four spacious rooms have fireplaces and one of the three has a Jacuzzi as well. Extras include classic films in the library and afternoon tea and scones on the terrace overlooking Benbow Lake. **$$$**

GUALALA
Gualala Country Inn
47955 Center Street, CA 95445
Tel: 707-884-4343
Fax: 707-884-1018
www.gualala.com
Peaceful inn with ocean views. Several rooms with fireplaces and spas. **$$$**

Hotel Prices

Categories based on average cost of a double room for one night.
$ = under $65
$$ = up to $100
$$$ = up to $150
$$$$ = over $150

GUERNEVILLE
The Willows
15905 River Road, CA 95446
Tel: 707-869-2824
Elegant riverside inn. **$$–$$$**

HALF MOON BAY
Cypress Inn on Miramar Beach
407 Mirada Road, CA 94019
Tel: 650-726-6076
US Freephone: 800-832-3224
Fax: 650-712-0380
www.cypressinn.com
A light and airy inn featuring skylights and imaginative use of natural colors and materials. Full breakfast and dinner served by the fireside, only minutes to the fine sandy beach. **$$$$**

HUNTINGTON BEACH
Maxwell's By the Sea
317 Pacific Coast Highway
Tel: 714-536-2555.
On the famous pier with good views as well as good food. **$**

INVERNESS
Hotel Inverness
25 Park Avenue, CA 94937
Tel: 415-669-7393
Fax: 415-669-1702
www.hotelinverness.com
In the historic section of Inverness, amidst lush woods, this hotel features stylish furnishings and a vibrant color scheme. **$$$–$$$$**
Klamath
15497 Hwy 101, CA 95548
Tel: 707-483-3152
US Freephone: 800-848-2982
Fax: 707-482-2005
Pleasant motel encircled by Redwood national and state parks with the unusual Forest Cafe opposite. Spick and span rooms, tennis court, king/queen size beds and cable TV/HBO. **$**

LA JOLLA
La Jolla Beach & Tennis Club
2000 Spindthrift Drive, CA 92037
Tel: 858-454-7126
Fax: 619-456-3805.
On the beach, near Sea World. Restaurant with pool, golf, tennis, some disabled facilities. **$$$$**
Torrey Pines Inn
11480 N Torrey Pines Rd, CA 92037
Tel: 858-453-4420
US Freephone: 800-995-4507
Fax: 619-453-0691
Overlooks ocean, 1 mile (2 km) from beach, near Del Mar racetrack. Pool, restaurant, golf. **$$**

LAGUNA BEACH
The Carriage House-B&B
1322 Catalina Street, CA 92651
Tel: 949-494-8945
Fax: 949-494-8945
A Charming B&B with en-suite rooms. **$$$**
Hotel Laguna
425 S Coast Highway, CA 92651
Tel: 949-494-1151
US Freephone: 800-524-2927
Fax: 949-497-2163
On beach. Near Pageant of Masters. Restaurants. **$$$**
Inn at Laguna Beach
211 N Coast Highway, CA 92651
Tel: 949-497-9722
Fax: 949-497-9972
Located on a bluff above the beach, many of the inns offer patios with

an oceanview. Heated pool and whirlpool also on grounds. **$$$$**

LOMPOC
Tally Ho Motor Inn
1020 East Ocean Ave, CA 93436
Tel: 805-735-6444
Fax: 805-735-5558
Good facilities and well-kept rooms, some with microwaves and refrigerators. Sauna, indoor Jacuzzi, laundry facilities. Free breakfast. **$**

MENDOCINO
The Stanford Inn by the Sea
PO Box 487, CA 95460
Tel: 707-937-5615
Fax: 707-937-0305
www.stanfordinn.com
A unique hilltop inn overlooking (beautifully) landscaped gardens with marvelous open vistas across the fields to the bay. The well-furnished rooms and suites have sofas and wood-burning fireplaces. Sumptuous breakfasts, large pool, sauna, spa and exercise room. Wheelchair-accessible rooms. **$$$$**

MONTEREY
Hotel Pacific
300 Pacific Street, CA 93940
Tel: 831-373-5700
Fax: 831-373-6921
Elegant adobe-style hotel. All rooms have deck and gas fireplaces for relaxing and free newspaper and breakfast for waking up in the morning. **$$$$**
Monterey Plaza Hotel
400 Cannery Row, CA 93940
Tel: 831-646-1700
US Freephone: 800-631-1339
Fax: 831-646-1339
Large hotel (285 rooms) with bellman, concierge and two restaurants in the heart of Cannery Row. **$$$**
Old Monterey Inn
500 Martin Street, CA 93940
Tel: 831-375-8284
US Freephone: 800-350-2344
Fax: 831-375-6730
www.oldmonterey inn.com
This English Tudor-style inn is surrounded by oak-wooded grounds and fine, beautifully tended gardens. First-rate service and attention to detail. **$$$$**

MORRO BAY
Baywood Bed and Breakfast Inn
1370 Second Street, CA 93402
Tel: 805-528-8888
Fax: 805-528-8887
www.baywoodinn.com
Lovely suites with fireplaces, bay views and full breakfast. **$$**
Embarcadero Inn
456 Embarcadero St, CA 93442
Fax: 805-772-1060
This peaceful inn features luxury rooms with private balconies and attentive service. A good base for relaxing or touring local attractions. All rooms with bay view, many with balconies and fireplaces and two with hot tubs as well. **$$$**

NEWPORT BEACH
Newport Classic Inn
2300 W Coast Highway, CA 92663
Tel: 949-722-2999
US Freephone: 800-633-3199
Fax: 949-631-5659
On bay, half a mile (1 km) from beach. Restaurant, pool, sauna. **$**

OJAI
Rose Garden Inn
615 West Ojai Avenue, CA 93023
Tel: 805-646-1434
Comfortable accommodation and a friendly atmosphere. Sixteen rooms or cottages with fireplaces nestled in over an acre of lawns. Pool, spa and redwood dry sauna. **$$**

PESCADERO
Hostelling International –
Pigeon Point Lighthouse
210 Pigeon Point Road, CA 94060
Tel: 650-879-0633
Housed in an active 115 ft (35 meter) 19th-century cliff side lighthouse. An ideal vantage point for observing gray whales on their annual migration. Amenities include kitchen, outdoor hot tub, on-site parking and equipment storage. Wheelchair accessible. **$**

PISMO BEACH
Edgewater Inn and Suites
280 Wadsworth Avenue, CA 93449
Tel: 805-773-4811
Fax: 805-773-5121
These spacious rooms and

suites with fully equipped kitchens, heated pool and Jacuzzi are ideal for families. Situated on the beach. Free continental breakfast. **$$–$$$**

Spyglass Inn
2703 Spyglass Drive, CA 93449
Tel: 805-773-4855
Fax: 805-773-5298
www.spyglassinn.com
Stylishly refurbished with panoramic ocean view, dining room and lounge. **$$$**

REDONDO BEACH
Best Western Sunrise Hotel
400 N Harbor Drive
Tel: 310-376-0746
Fax: 310-376-7384
At the marina. Pool, spa, restaurant. **$$$**

Portofino Hotel & Yacht Club
260 Portofino Way
Tel: 213-379-8481
US Freephone: 800-468-4292
Fax: 310-372-7329.
Pool, restaurant, views over the marina and access to Gold's Gym nearby. **$$$$**

REDWOOD NATIONAL PARK
Hostelling International
14480 California Hwy 101
at Wilson Creek Road,
CA 95548
Tel: 707-482-8265
Email: redwoodhostel
@mail.telis.org
Set in the Redwood National Park with grand views from the porches. Other features include an inviting common room, pellet stove, bicycle rack, laundry facilities and on-site parking **$**

SAN CLEMENTE
Hostelling International
233 Ave Granada,
CA 92672-4029
Tel: 949-492-2848
www.hostelweb.com
Within walking distance of the beach and close to local amenities such as the Farmers' Market. Good atmosphere. Facilities include kitchen, patios, laundry, courtyard and lockers. **$**

SAN FRANCISCO
The Archbishop's Mansion
1000 Fulton Street, CA 94117
Tel: 415-563-7872
US Freephone: 800-543-5820
Fax: 415-885-3193
Exquisite French chateau mansion in Alamo Square built in 1904 for the archbishop of San Francisco. An historical landmark. Complimentary breakfast and wine are served. **$$$**

Hostelling International – Downtown
312 Mason Street, CA 94102
Tel: 415-788-5604
One of the largest hostels in the country includes about 200 beds and community kitchens in its downtown location. **$**

Hotel Boheme
444 Columbus Avenue, CA 94133
Tel: 415-433-9111
Fax: 415-362-6292
An abundance of bohemian charm and bags of history. Wonderful black and white photographs line the hallway **$$**

Red Victorian Inn
1665 Haight Street, CA 94117
Tel: 415-864-1978
Perfect for the budget traveler. Friendly and casual with each room reflecting a different theme. **$**

York Hotel
940 Sutter Street, CA 94109
Tel: 415-885-6800
US Freephone: 800-808-9675
Fax: 415-885-2115
The setting for the Hitchcock movie Vertigo is both sophisticated and comfortable. The Plush Room Theater, which was once a Prohibition-era speakeasy now known for its cabaret, is also located here. **$–$$**

SAN LUIS OBISPO
Apple Farm Trellis Court
2015 Monterey Street, CA 93401
Tel: 805-544-6100
Cozy rooms with fireplaces and pleasing decor. There is a good restaurant serving cider produced on-site by a water-powered apple press. **$$**

Hostelling International
1617 Santa Rosa Street, CA 93401
Tel: 805-544-4678
Fax: 805-544-3142

http://internetcafe.allyn.com/SLO
Convenient location for downtown shops, restaurants, theaters, farmers' market and Amtrak station. Amenities include kitchen, bicycle rental, laundry, lockers, fireplace and piano. **$**

Madonna Inn
100 Madonna Road, CA 93405
Tel: 805-543 3000
Fax: 805-543 1800
Well known for its eccentricity and bizarre decor. The 109 rooms come dressed up in color-themed Western, Hawaiian, Austrian, etc. **$$**

SANTA BARBARA
The Chesire Cat B&B
36 W Valerio Street, CA 93101
Tel: 805-569-1610
Fax: 805-682-1876
Ironically smoke free, this restored Victorian home offers a relaxed and pampered stay in the heart of Santa Barbara. **$$$$**

Hotel Prices

Categories based on average cost of a double room for one night.
$ = under $65
$$ = up to $100
$$$ = up to $150
$$$$ = over $150

Simpson House
121 East Arrellaga, CA 93101
Tel: 805-963-7067
US Freephone: 800-676-1280
Fax: 805-564-4811
www.simpsonhouseinn.com
A meticulously restored Victorian estate set in an acre of English gardens yet only a short stroll away from the downtown historic district and the beach. **$$$$**

The Upham
1404 De La Vina, CA 93101
Tel: 805-962-0058
US Freephone: 800-727-0876
Fax: 805-963-2825
Built in 1871, this is Southern California's oldest continuously operating hostelry. Charming garden cottages and main building furnished with antiques and period furniture. **$$$**

SCOTIA
Scotia Inn
Main and Mill, CA, 95565
Tel: 707-764-5683
Tidy rooms; breakfasts. **$$**

SEAL BEACH
Seal Beach Inn and Gardens
212 Fifth Street, CA 90740
Tel: 562-493-2416
Fax: 562-799-0483
www.sealbeachinn.com
Refined and sophisticated with
peaceful public areas, library,
swimming pool, tearoom and
courtyard with French
Mediterranean flavor. **$$$$**

SONOMA
Sonoma Mission Inn and Spa
18140 Sonoma Highway,
CA 95476
US Freephone: 800-257-7544
www.sonomamissioninn.com
Pricey European-style spa in
the heart of the wine country.
Romantic, rooms and suites
with marbled baths and plantation
shutters. Acclaimed fine dining
and attentive service. **$$$$**

WESTPORT
Howard Creek Ranch
40501 North Hwy 1,
CA 95488
Tel: 707-964-6725
Fax: 707-964-1603
Quiet rooms in historic farmhouse
surrounded by beauty. **$$–$$$$**

WHERE TO EAT

BIG SUR
Big Sur River Inn Restaurant
Tel: 831-667-2700
Relaxed and informal with river
views. **$$**

CARMEL
Pacific Edge
Highlands Inn, Hwy 1
Tel: 831-622-5445
Best view, best regional. **$$**
Papa Chano's Taqueria
462 Alvarado Street
Tel: 831-646-9587
Good value, filling and flavorful
Mexican food. **$**

Restaurant Prices

Categories based on average
cost of dinner and a glass of
wine, before tip.
$ = under $15
$$ = up to $30
$$$ = over $30

CASTROVILLE
Giant Artichoke Restaurant
11221 Merritt Street, CA 95012
Tel: 831-633-4259
(see page 348) **$$$**

ENCINITAS
Cilantro's
3702 Via De La Valle, Del Mar
Tel: 619-259-8777
Good southwestern food. **$**
Jake's Del Mar
1660 Coast Boulevard, Del Mar
Tel: 619-755-2002
Outdoors and romantic. **$$**

GUADALUPE
Western Tavern
899 Guadalupe Street
Tel: 805-343-2211
Top-quality steaks. **$$**

HALF MOON BAY
Joe's on the Coast
2380 Cabrillo Highway
Tel: 650-560-9260
Savor the feeling of being out of
San Francisco, but not too far away
in case you need to return to the
city soon. Joe's is open for
breakfast, lunch and dinner serving
hardy portions of American classics
like hamburgers and roast beef. **$$**

LA JOLLA
The Cottage
7702 Fay Avenue
Tel: 858-454-8409
The promise of a Cottage breakfast
should be enough to coax even the
worst sleepyhead into the daylight.
The fragrant, sweet pastries,
aromatic coffee and soothing
atmosphere revive gently. **$$**
George's at the Cove
1250 Prospect Street
Tel: 858-454-4244
Fresh, seasonal Californian cuisine
and marvelous views of La Jolla

Cove. The top floor is open-air and
casual; the first two floors are more
formal. **$$–$$$**
Laguna Beach
Las Brisas, 361 Cliff Dr,
Laguna Beach
Tel: 714-497-5434
Beside the sea. Mexican cuisine. **$**
La Jolla Beach & Tennis Club
2000 Spindthrift Drive
Tel: 858-454-7126
Fax: 858-456-3805
On the beach, near Sea World.
Restaurant, pool, golf, tennis, some
disabled facilities. **$$$$**
Torrey Pines Inn
11480 N Torrey Pines Road
Tel: 858-453-4420
US Freephone: 800-995-4507
Fax: 858-453-0691
Overlooks ocean, 1 mile (2 km)
from beach, near Del Mar racetrack.
Pool, restaurant, golf. **$$**

LOMPOC
Sissy's Uptown Café
112 South I Street
Tel: 805-735-4877
A local favorite for baked goods and
desserts. Soup, sandwiches and
salads are also available. **$**

MENDOCINO
Café Beaujolais
961 Ukiah Street
Tel: 707-937-5614
Upscale Californian cuisine. **$$$**

MONTEREY
Fandango
223 17th, Pacific Grove
Tel: 831-372-3456
Italian, Basque and Spanish flavors,
with many seafood dishes, and a
mesquite grill. Paella from fresh
local catches. **$$$**
Fresh Cream
Heritage Harbor Building 100
Tel: 831-375-9798
Frequently listed as one of the top
100 restaurants in the country,
Fresh Cream's French/American
cuisine has rack of lamb and crisp
duck as specialties, as well as
many vegetarian dishes. Every table
with ocean view. **$$$**
Sardine Factory
701 Wave Street
Tel: 831-373-3775

Get in here if you can. Reservations are required at this semi-formal restaurant serving the health conscious and lovers of fresh seafood and pasta. **$$$**

MORRO BAY
Bayside Cafe
State Park Road
Tel: 805-772-1465
A nifty little cafe situated in Morro Bay State Park serving well-cooked Californian and Mexican dishes. The char-broiled fish sandwich is very popular. Bay views. **$**

NEWPORT BEACH
Crab Cooker
2200 Newport Blvd
Tel: 949-673-0100
Grilled seafood on paper plates, reasonable prices; no reservations. **$$**

ORICK
Palm Café and Motel
21130 Highway 101, CA 95555
Tel: 707-488 3381
(see page 364) **$$**

PACIFIC BEACH
Ichiban P.B.
1441 Garnet Avenue
Tel: 828-270-5755
Cheap and cheerful sushi and noodle house. **$**

SAMOA
Samoa Cookhouse
Off Hwy 101 across the Samoa Bridge
Tel: 707-442 1659
Breakfast includes orange juice, scrambled eggs, pancakes, sausages, hash browns and coffee. Hefty lunches and dinners start with soup, salad and plenty of bread, and end with hot apple pie.
(see page 362) **$**

SAN FRANCISCO
A. Sabella
2766 Taylor St, Fisherman's Wharf
Tel: 415-771-6775
Dungeness crab, a stunning Bay view, old-world hospitality and a renowned wine list combine with 110 years of experience. **$$**

Restaurant Prices

Categories based on average cost of dinner and a glass of wine, before tip.
$ = under $15
$$ = up to $30
$$$ = over $30

Greens
Building A, Fort Mason in the Marina district
Tel: 415-771-6222
Organic produce, seasonal specials and a mesquite grill are the cornerstones of this vegetarian restaurant. Plus spectacular views of the Golden Gate Bridge. **$$$**
House of Nanking
919 Kearny Street, Chinatown
Tel: 415-421-1429
The city's most popular and acclaimed Chinese, where the cramped seating and pushy service are part of the charm. Avoid weekend evenings. **$**
Masa's
648 Bush St, north of Union Square
Tel: 415-989-7154
Perhaps the most expensive and critically lauded restaurant in all of San Francisco. The perennial winner in the city's restaurant lists. **$$$$**
Rose Pistola
532 Columbus Avenue, North Beach
Tel: 415-399-0499
The ambiance and wood-fired oven have made this one of SF's hottest restaurants. Small dishes served family-style allow a wide variety of flavors. Do not pass up dessert. Heated sidewalk dining is perfect for watching the North Beach crowds stroll by. **$$**
Tadich
240 California St, Financial District
Tel: 415-391-1849
The oldest restaurant in San Francisco, Tadich has been serving fish, crab and oysters for a century and a half. **$$**

SAN LUIS OBISPO
Big Sky Cafe
1121 Broad Street
Tel: 805-545-5401
A breakfast favorite. **$**

SANTA BARBARA
Acapulco
1114 State Street
Tel: 805-963-3469
Artfully prepared and spiced Mexican food provided for almost three decades. **$**
Brophy Brothers
119 Harbor Way
Tel: 805-966-4418
Fried, sauteed, grilled and chowdered seafood, with marine views. The 1950s jukebox and the popularity of their hand-shaken *margueritas* combine to make it a very lively spot. **$$**
La Marina
Four Seasons Biltmore Hotel, 1260 Channel Drive, Montecito
Tel: 805-969-2261
Swanky hotel restaurant offering a weekly 5-course menu that includes such entrees as roast Chilean sea bass, grilled pavé or lobster with sweet corn risotto. Also sample five specially selected wines. **$$$**
Montecito Inn
1295 Coast Village Road
Tel: 805-969-7854
(see page 340) **$$**
The Wine Cask
813 Anacapa Street
Tel: 805-966-9463
Hundreds of wines from the adjoining shop to go with Californian cuisine served in a lovely room with painted ceilings. **$$$**

SANTA CRUZ
Gabriella Cafe
910 Cedar Street
Tel: 831-457-1677
Tasty seafood and pasta and pleasant atmosphere. **$**

VENICE
Rose Café and Market
220 Rose Avenue
Tel: 310-399-0711
(see page 336) **$$**
Wine tours
For details on winery tours contact: Napa Valley Vinters' Association PO Box 141, CA 94574
Tel: 707-226-7459
Fax: 707-255-2066
Most tours include free tasting and the chance to buy a few bottles – or a few cases.

SHOPPING

Santa Barbara
La Arcada shopping paseo is a cheerful Spanish-style courtyard adorned with tile, ornamental ironwork and bright flags.

San Francisco
From elegant malls to farmers' markets, Northern California offers a wide array of shopping opportunities. In San Francisco alone, there are 20 distinct shopping areas. You might want to start by exploring some or all of the following:
Union Square: perhaps the most famous shopping area in San Francisco, the square includes the charming **Maiden Lane** with boutiques, galleries and a building designed by Frank Lloyd Wright (currently home to **Xanadu Tribal Art Gallery**).
Chinatown: between Stockton, Kearny, Bush and Broadway. Good for fresh produce, fish and poultry. Traditional herbalist, antiques, jewelry and souvenir shops vie for attention. The crowded streets flow into North Beach.
North Beach: this area offers a mix of book shops, Italian restaurants and delicatessens, cafés, vintage clothing and designer boutiques.
Fisherman's Wharf: shopping extends from **Pier 39** to **Ghirardelli Square** in **The Cannery**, a remodeled Del Monte peach canning plant; **The Anchorage**, a colorful, modern complex; and Ghirardelli Square itself.
Along with unusual shops and galleries, each complex offers individual landscaping, live entertainment, open-air walkways and breathtaking views. Look for validated parking in marked structures if you're driving.
Sacramento Street: considered by locals to be a "secret" shopping district. Here, between Broderick and Arguello, the streets are often quiet and there's a concentration of upscale consignment and thrift stores, unusual children's and infant's clothing and toy stores, designer men's and women's

clothing, furniture, fine linens and antiques for the house and garden. Bring your credit card as it's pricey.

OREGON

WHERE TO STAY

ASTORIA
Clementine's
847 Exchange Street, OR 97103
Tel: 503-325-2005
www.clementines-bb.com
A classic Italianate Victorian building with pretty English cottage gardens and a small library. The inn has five rooms with queen-sized beds, private bathrooms. One room has a gas fireplace. **$$**
Crest Motel
5366 Leif Erickson Dr, OR 97103
Tel: 503-325 3141.
Exceptionally nice motel with superb river views, hot tub on lawn under the gazebo and continental breakfast. **$$**

BANDON
Hostelling International – Sea Star
375 Second Street, OR 97411
Tel: 541-347-9632
Fax: 503-363-5304
www.SeaStarBandon.com/hi-sea.html
An attractive hostel located in the historic Old Town Waterfront District. Private rooms, skylights, exposed wood beams, cozy wood-burning stove and deck with harbor views. Also on the premises is the **Inn at Face Rock**
3225 Beach Loop Road, OR 97411
Tel: 541-347-9441
Fax: 541-347-2532
Good-sized rooms with restaurant, lounge and spa. Close to area attractions. Disabled access. **$$**

BROOKINGS
Pacific Sunset Inn
HWY 101N, OR 97415
Tel: 541-469-2141
Basic motel accommodation. **$**

COOS BAY
Best Western Holiday Motel
411 North Bayshore Dr, OR 97420
Tel: 541-269-5111
Fax: 541-269-7111
Well-appointed rooms convenient

for local attractions. Cable TV/HBO, fitness center, guest laundry, pool, spa and continental breakfast. **$**

FLORENCE
Johnson House
216 Maple Street, OR 97439
Tel: 541-997-8000
www.touroregon.com/thejohnsonhouse
Very reasonable accommodations in this restored Victorian house in the old town Waterfront district. **$$**

GOLD BEACH
City Center Motel
94200 Harlow Street, OR 97444
Tel: 541-247-6675
Comfortable, well-maintained motel. **$**
Tu Tu' Tun Lodge
96550 N Bank Rogue, OR 97444
Tel: 541-247-6664
Fax: 541-247-0672
www.tututun.com
A contemporary lodge in tranquil riverside setting offering gourmet dining, white-water rafting trips, guided fishing and more. **$$–$$$$**

LINCOLN CITY
Salishan Lodge
PO Box 118, Glen Eden Beach, CA 97388
Tel: 541-764-2371
Full service, four season resort set in 750 wooded acres (304 hectares) with golf, tennis, pool fitness centers, attic lounge, and an excellent restaurant. **$$$**

NYE BEACH
Penny Saver Motel
710 North Coast Hwy, OR 97365
Tel: 541-265-6631

Hotel Prices

Categories based on average cost of a double room for one night.
$ = under $65
$$ = up to $100
$$$ = up to $150
$$$$ = over $150

Well-fitted rooms, some with kitchenettes. Free continental breakfast. **$**

PORTLAND
The Benson Hotel
309 SW Broadway, OR 97205
Tel: 503-228-2000
Fax: 503-226-2709
www.citysearch.com
Kitchenettes, in-room spa, exercise room, tennis, restaurant. **$$$$**
Gedney Gardens B&B
2651 N.W. Cornell Rd, OR 97210
Tel: 503-226-6514
Fax: 503-228-8134
Three attractive rooms, full breakfast included. **$**
Hawthorn Inn & Suites
4319 N.W. Yeon Ave, OR 97210
Tel: 503-497-9044
US Freephone: 800-528-1234
Fax: 503-497-1030
Pool, spa, sauna. **$$**
Mark Spencer Hotel
409 SW 11th Avenue, OR 97205
Tel: 503-224-3293
US Freephone: 800-558-3934
Fax: 503-223-0522
www.markspencer.com
Rooftop garden deck, some kitchenettes. **$$$**
Shilo Suites Hotel
11707 N.E. Airport Way,
OR 97220
Tel: 503-252-4300
Pool, spa, exercise room, sauna, restaurant. **$$$**

REEDSPORT
Tropicana Motel
1593 Highway Ave 101,
OR 97467
Tel: 541-271-3671
US Freephone: 800-799-9920
Good-sized rooms with cable TV. Rooms with refrigerators, microwaves and kitchens are available. Free continental breakfast included. **$**

ROCKAWAY BEACH
101 Motel
530 Hwy 101, OR 97136
Tel: 503-355-2420
Well-fitted, good value motel rooms with nice views, fireplaces, kitchens and cable television. Hot tub. Wheelchair accessible. **$**

Restaurant Prices

Categories based on average cost of dinner and a glass of wine, before tip.
$ = under $15
$$ = up to $30
$$$ = over $30

SEASIDE
Hostelling International – Seaside
930 North Holladay Dr,
OR 97138
Tel: 503-738-7911
Email: HISeaside@Transport.com
On the Necanicum River, four blocks from the ocean. Amenities include kitchen, outdoor decks and lawn on river, barbecue, laundry, kayak and canoe rental, espresso bar. **$**

TILLAMOOK
Tillamook Inn
1810 Hwy 101N, OR 97141
Tel: 503-842-4413
Pleasant motor inn, some units with kitchenettes. **$**

YACHATS
Fireside Motel
1881 North Hwy 101, OR 97498
Tel: 541-547-3636
Older, well-maintained motel. Some ocean-view rooms with balconies and a few with gas fireplaces. **$$$**

WHAT TO EAT

ASTORIA
Columbia Cafe
1114 Marine Drive
Tel: 503-325-2233
Buzzing atmosphere and gloriously fresh seafood. **$$**
The Ship Inn
1 Second Street
Tel: 503-325-0033
Decent English pub-style grub. **$**

BANDON
Bandon Boatworks Restaurant
275 Lincoln Avenue SW
Tel: 541-347-2111
Excellent fresh seafood and lighthouse views. **$**

BROOKINGS
Wharfside Seafood Restaurant
16362 Lower Harbor Road
Tel: 541-469-7316
Best casual. **$$**

CANNON BEACH
Lazy Susan Cafe
126 North Hemlock
Tel: 503-436-2816
Excellent, filling breakfasts with a few lighter alternatives. **$**

FLORENCE
Blue Hen Cafe
1675 Hwy 101
Tel: 541-997-3907
Homely place dishing up generous servings of lovingly prepared food. Highlights are the crepes and the large, hot baking powder biscuits. **$**

LINCOLN CITY
Bay House
5911 Southwest Hwy 101
Tel: 541-996-3222
Popular seafood restaurant. **$$**

MANZANITA
Blue Sky Cafe
154 Laneda Avenue
Tel: 503-368-5712
Eclectic menu featuring fresh local produce, much of it organic. **$$**

NEWPORT
Canyon Way Bookstore and Restaurant
1216 Southwest Canyon Way
Tel: 541-265-8319
Best lunch. **$**

PORTLAND
Bijou Café
132 SW Third Avenue
Tel: 503-222-3187
Popular downtown café. Great breakfasts. **$**
Bread and Ink
3610 Hawthorne Boulevard
Tel: 503-239-4756
Food cooked with fresh ingredients and cheerful service justify this café's popularity. Eclectic menu. **$**
Café des Amis
1987 NW Kearney Street
Tel: 503-295-6487
French bistro. Good wine list. **$$**

Broadway Coffee Trader
2130 NE Broadway St
Tel: 503-281-3882
No frills – just dependable, satisfying
breakfasts and lunches. **$**

Jake's Famous Crawfish
401 SW 12th
Tel: 503-249-8486
Mouthwatering seafood. **$$**

YACHATS
The Adobe Resort and Restaurant
1555 Hwy 101
Tel: 541-547-3141
Good-quality, well-prepared steaks
and fine views. **$$**

SHOPPING

PORTLAND
Saturday Market
Food, arts and crafts stalls.
Bustling, lively atmosphere. From
March to December on Saturdays
and Sundays.

Powell's City of Books
1005 West Burnside Street
Browse for hours.

Old Town district
Specialty shops in lovely setting.

Portland Pendleton Shop
900 South West Fourth Avenue
A good stock of the famous Oregon
Pendleton shirts.

WASHINGTON

WHERE TO STAY

ABERDEEN
Flamingo Motel
1120 East Wishkah, WA 98520
Tel: 360-532-4103
Clean, functional motel with 20
comfortable units. **$**

CHINOOK
**Hostelling International –
Fort Columbia**
PO Box 224, WA 98614
Tel: 360-777-8755
www.washingtonhostels.org/
Spectacular river views from this
hillside hostel. Good spot for
whale watching. Amenities include
kitchen, laundry facilities,
fireplace on-site parking and
bicycles. **$**

ELMA
**Hostelling International –
Grays Harbor Hotel**
6 Ginny Lane, WA 98541
Tel: 360-482-3119
Email: ghhostel@techline.com
Located halfway between Olympia
and Aberdeen. Amenities include
kitchen, library, hot tub, self-
service bicycle repair shop and
storage. **$**

GRAYLAND
Walsh Motel
1593 Hwy 105, WA 98547
Tel: 360-267-2191
With 24 standard units some with
wheelchair access. **$**

OLYMPIA
Cavanaughs at Capitol Lake
2300 Evergreen Park Dr. SW,
OR 98502
Tel: 360-943-4000
Fax: 360-357-6604
With a beautiful natural setting on
the outside, the rooms inside offer
whirlpools, balconies and all
modern conveniences. **$$$**

Hotel Prices

Categories based on average
cost of a double room for one
night.
$ = under $65
$$ = up to $100
$$$ = up to $150
$$$$ = over $150

RAYMOND
Maunu's Mountcastle Motel
524 Third Street, WA 98577
Tel: 360-942-5571
Spotless rooms, some with
microwaves and refrigerators. **$**

WHERE TO EAT

ABERDEEN
Bridges Restaurant
112 N G Street
Tel: 360-532-6563
Fine dining in a relaxed setting
of brass, glass and dark wood.
Menu features steak and seafood.
$$

Smokers Take Note

Always check, when booking a
restaurant table or a hotel room,
whether smoking is allowed, and
where. Some hotels and motels
have designated smoking floors,
while some restaurants allow
smoking in the bar, but not at a
table. If you plan on visiting
California, you might as well give
up cigarettes now; the evil weed
is banned even in some parks
and outdoor areas.

CHINOOK
Sanctuary Restaurant
794 SR 101
Tel: 360-777 8380
Avoiding all innuendo's of sinful
desserts and heavenly starters, you
can pull up a pew to dine in this
restored Methodist church. **$$**

OLYMPIA
La Petite Maison
101 Division Street
Tel: 360-943-8812
The French-country decor is quiet
and will relax you so you can fully
enjoy the menu of fresh seafood
and decadent desserts. **$$**

Santosh Restaurant
116 Fourth Avenue
Tel: 360-943-3442
Serving the best north Indian
cuisine in Olympia, Santosh also
claims one of the trendiest
settings in the city. **$$**

Saigon Rendez-Vous
117 Fifth Avenue W
Tel: 360-352-1989
Vietnamese and Chinese menus
plus vegetarian specialties. **$$**

Further Reading

General

American Diner: Then and Now by J.S. Gutman. (Harper Perennial, 1993).
Another Country by James Baldwin. (Dell, 1988).
The Book of the American West ed. Jay Monaghan. (Julian Messner Inc, 1963).
Great Plains by Ian Frazier. (Farrar, Straus and Giroux, 1989).
In Search of America by John Steinbeck. (Viking, 1962).
Legends of the American Desert by Alex Schoumatoff. (Knopf, 1997).
National Park Ranger: An American Icon by Charles R. Farabee. (Roberts Rinehart Publishers, 2003).
Native America, by Christine Mather, photographs by Jack Parsons. (New York: Clarkson Potter, 1991).
The Oxford Illustrated Literary Guide to the United States by Eugene Ehrlich & Gorton Carruth. (Oxford University Press, 1982).
Redwood Pioneer: A Frontier Remembered by Andrew Genzoli & Wallace E Marin. (Schooner Features, 1970).
Skid Road: An Informal Portrait of Seattle by Murray Morgan. (University of Washington Press, 1988).
Smithsonian Guide to Historic America, Henry Wiencek, New York: Stewart. (Tabori and Chang, 1989).
Still Life in Harlem by Eddy L. Harris. (Henry Holt and Company, Inc, 1966).
War So Terrible, Sherman and Atlanta, by James P. Jones and James L. McDonough. (WW Norton and Co, New York, 1987).
Webster's American Biographies (G & C Merriam Co, 1974)

Fiction

Always Outnumbered, Always Outgunned, Walter Mosley. (W.W. Norton & Company, 1977).
Black Cherry Blues by James Lee Burke, New York, (Random House, Inc).
Bonfire of the Vanities by Tom Wolfe. (Farrar, Straus, Giroux, 1987).
The Border Trilogy by Cormac McCarthy. (Alfred A Knopf, Inc. 1994).
The Bostonians Henry James. (Knopf, 1993).
Brokeback Mountain, Annie Proulx. (The New Yorker, October 13 1997; London, Fourth Estate Limited, 1998).
Death Comes to the Archbishop, Willa Cather. (Alfred A Knopf, 1927).
The Friends of Eddie Coyle by George Higgins. (Viking Penguin, 1987).
Gone With The Wind, by Margaret Mitchell. (MacMillan, 1936).
Lake Woebegon Days by Garrison Keillor. (Viking Penguin, 1985).
Midnight in the Garden of Good and Evil, by John Berendt. (Random House, 1994).
My Antonia by Willa Cather. (Houghton Mifflin, 1918).
Only Revolutions by Mark Z. Danielewski. (Knopf, 2006).
Riders of the Purple Sage, by Zane Grey. (New York: Penguin, 1990).
The Scarlet Letter by Nathaniel Hawthorne. (Knopf, 1992).
Tales of the City, by Armistead Maupin. (Chronicle Publishing Company, 1978).
Tortilla Curtain by T Coraghessan Boyle. (Bloomsbury Publishing, 1995).
Where I'm Calling From, Raymond Carver. (New York: Random House 1986).
The Wrong Case, James Crumley. (New York, Random House Ltd. 1975).

On the Road

Blue Highways: A Journey into America by William Least Heat Moon. (Little, Brown and Company, 1982).
The California Highway Book by Rick Adams & Louise McCorkle. (Ballantine Books, 1985).
Drive They Said: Poems About Americans and Their Cars edited by Kurt Brown. (Milkweed Editions, 1994).
Driving to Detroit: An Automotive Odyssey by Lesley Hazleton. (The Free Press, 1998).
Fear and Loathing in Las Vegas by Hunter S Thompson. (Random House, 1972).
The Lost Continent: Travels in Small Town America by Bill Bryson. (Secker and Warburg, 1989).
Lost Highway: Journeys and Arrivals of American Musicians by Peter Guralnick. (Vintage Books, 1982).
The New Roadside America by Doug Kirby, Ken Smith and Doug Kirby. (Simon and Schuster1992).
Open Road: A Celebration of the American Highway by Phil Patton. (Simon and Schuster, 1986).
Out West: American Journey Along the Lewis and Clark Trail by Dayton Duncan. (Viking Penguin, 1987).
An Overland Journey by Horace Greeley (Knopf, 1963).
The Ride of Our Lives by Mike Leonard. (Random House, 2006).
Traveling the Oregon Trail by Julie Fanselow. (Falcon Press, 1992).
Travels with Charley: in Where the Road and the Sky Collide: America Through the Eyes of its Drivers by K.T, Berger. (Henry Holt, 1993).

Other Insight Guides

For more detailed information about particular cities, states and regions, Insight Guides publishes a comprehensive range of titles.

Companion titles to the present book include **Western United States, American Southwest, Arizona and the Grand Canyon, Boston, California, Southern California, Chicago, Florida, Las Vegas, Los Angeles, Miami, New England, New Orleans, New York City, New York City Museums, New York State, The New South, Orlando, Pacific Northwest, Philadelphia, San Francisco, Seattle, Texas** and **Washington DC**. Thematic titles include **North American and Alaskan Cruises** and **US National Parks West**.

ART & PHOTO CREDITS

INSIGHT GUIDE US on The Road

Cartographic Editor Zoë Goodwin
Production Linton Donaldson
Design Consultants
Carlotta Junger, Graham Mitchener
Picture Research
Hilary Genin, Natasha Babaian
Proofreading Lisa Cussans
Indexing Elizabeth Cook

Trip/Viesti Collection 59, 137, 253
Universal Studios Florida 85BR
US Postal Service 301T
Joe Viesti 28, 32
Walt Disney Company 85TL
Greg Ward/APA 252, 256T, 259T, 267T, 270T, 278T, 300, 303T, 304, 311T, 312, 312T, 315T
Andrea Wells 50, 111, 131B, 166
Randy Wells back cover center right, front flap top, 46/47, 73, 74T, 75, 84, 94/95, 108, 109, 110, 127, 135, 136, 138, 145, 154, 156, 158, 161, 167, 167T, 169, 196TR, 205T, 256, 265, 329
Jan Whiting 349
Marcus Wilson-Smith 90T, 289T
Martha Ellen Zenfell 344, 345T

Picture Spreads

Pages 52/53
Top row, left to right:
Mockford/Bonetti/APA, Tony

Perrottet/APA. *Center row:* Nigel Francis/Robert Harding Picture Library, Ellen Rooney, Catherine Karnow. *Bottom row:* Richard Berenholtz/The Stock Market.
Pages 92/93: *Top row, left to right:* Catherine Karnow, Andreas M. Gross. *Centrer row:* Andreas M. Gross, Mark Read/APA. *Bottom row:* both Catherine Karnow.
Pages 100/101: *Top row, left to right:* Mark Read/APA, Marcus Brooke. *Center row:* all Mark Read/APA. *Bottom row:* New England Picture Agency/Bachmann, Mark Read/APA, Mark Read/APA.
Pages 172/173: *Top row, left to right:* Catherine Karnow. *Center row:* Andreas M. Gross, Dave G. Houser, Dave G. Houser. *Bottom row:* Andreas M. Gross, Dave G. Houser
Pages 180/181: *All Photography:*

Catherine Karnow, except *bottom left* : Richard Nowitz
Pages 236/237: *Top row:* both Catherine Karnow. *Centrer row:* Glyn Genin/APA. *Bottom row:* Catherine Karnow, Maxine Cass, Maxine Cass.
Pages 244/245: *Top row, left to right:* Andreas M. Gross. *Centrer row:* both Andreas M. Gross. *Bottom row:* Bob Krist, Greg Ward/APA, Margaret Mitchell House & Museum.
Pages 322/323: *Top row, left to right:* Andreas M. Gross. *Center row:* Trip/N. & J. Wiseman, Andreas M. Gross, Trip/Malcolm Lee, Mark Downey. *Bottom row:* San Diego Zoo.

Map Production Colourmap Scanning Ltd.

© 2007 Apa Publications GmbH & Co. Verlag KG (Singapore branch)

Index

Atlantic Route

	New York, NY	Baltimore, MD	Roanoke, VA	Savannah, GA	Orlando, FL	Miami, FL	Key West, FL
New York, NY	—	202	543	811	1170	1597	1761
Baltimore, MD	202	—	341	609	968	1395	1559
Roanoke, VA	543	341	—	268	627	1054	1218
Savannah, GA	811	609	268	—	359	786	960
Orlando, FL	1170	968	627	359	—	427	591
Miami, FL	1597	1395	1054	786	427	—	164
Key West, FL	1761	1559	1218	960	591	164	—

Central Route

	Washington DC	Memphis, TN	Joplin, MO	Amarillo, TX	Gallup, NM	Flagstaff, AZ	Los Angeles, CA
Washington DC	—	940	1371	1850	2270	2452	2922
Memphis, TN	940	—	431	910	1330	1512	1982
Joplin, MO	1371	431	—	479	899	1081	1551
Amarillo, TX	1850	910	479	—	420	602	1072
Gallup, NM	2270	1330	899	420	—	182	652
Flagstaff, AZ	2452	1512	1081	602	182	—	470
Los Angeles, CA	2922	1982	1551	1072	652	470	—

Northern Route

	Boston, MA	Buffalo, NY	Chicago, IL	Pierre, SD	Cody, WY	Seattle, WA	Cape Flattery, WA
Boston, MA	—	872	1419	2309	2891	3961	4095
Buffalo, NY	872	—	547	1437	2019	3089	3223
Chicago, IL	1419	547	—	890	1472	2542	2676
Pierre, SD	2309	1437	890	—	582	1652	1786
Cody, WY	2891	2019	1472	582	—	1070	1204
Seattle, WA	3961	3089	2542	1652	1070	—	134
Cape Flattery, WA	4095	3223	2676	1786	1204	134	—

Southern Route

	Atlanta, GA	New Orleans, LA	Houston, TX	San Antonio, TX	Lordsburg, NM	Phoenix, AZ	San Diego, CA
Atlanta, GA	—	473	825	1070	1989	2213	2572
New Orleans, LA	473	—	352	597	1516	1740	2099
Houston, TX	825	352	—	245	1164	1388	1747
San Antonio, TX	1070	597	245	—	919	1143	1502
Lordsburg, NM	1989	1516	1164	919	—	224	583
Phoenix, AZ	2213	1740	1388	1143	224	—	359
San Diego, CA	2572	2099	1747	1502	583	359	—

Pacific Route

	San Diego, CA	Los Angeles, CA	San Francisco, CA	Eureka, CA	Crescent, OR	Newport, OR	Seattle, WA
San Diego, CA	—	124	504	785	867	1108	1399
Los Angeles, CA	124	—	380	661	743	984	1275
San Francisco, CA	504	380	—	281	363	604	895
Eureka, CA	785	661	281	—	82	323	614
Crescent, OR	867	743	363	82	—	241	532
Newport, OR	1108	984	604	323	241	—	291
Seattle, WA	1399	1275	895	614	532	291	—

Atlantic Route
New York (NY) - Key West (FL)

Northern Route
Boston (MA) - Cape Flattery (WA)

Central Route
Washington, DC - Los Angeles (CA)

Southern Route
Atlanta (GA) - San Diego (CA)

Pacific Route
San Diego (CA) - Seattle (WA)

Interstate Route Marker

Even numbers indicate east-west routes; odd show north-south routes.

US Highway Marker

Four-way Stop Sign

Traffic from all four directions must stop. The first vehicle to reach the intersection should move first.

Yield Ahead

Reduce speed and allow vehicles crossing your path right-of-way.

One-w
trav

Traffic Merges (from right)

Traffic flows merge from indicated direction.

2-Way Traffic

Traffic flows in both directions.

Traffic Lane Joins

Traffic enters carriageway with new lane.

Yield Ahead

A yield sign is ahead.

Divi

Divid
adja

Dead End

Not a through road, no access to other streets.

Crossing Traffic

Highway is crossed by road. Look to left and right for cars.

Stop sign ahead

Stop sign ahead, prepare to stop.

Slippery Surface

Road surface is slippery when wet. First half-hour of rain is most hazardous.

Be
cro

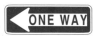

Construction Ahead

Distance given until construction begins. Watch for further signs.

Railroad Crossing Ahead

Slow and prepare to stop at crossing ahead.

Left Turn

All traffic must turn left.

Keep Right

Traffic is required to keep to the right of medians or obstructions.

The la
pu
Re
us

One Way

One-way traffic in direction of arrow.

School Zone

Follow speed limit displayed when lights above sign flash.

Camping

Roadside park and rest area.

School

Children crossing road.

Rest Area

Roadside park and rest area.

Hospital

Watch for pedestrians and emergency vehicles.

No p

Lane Control

Travel in lane.

Lane Control

Clear the lane. If flashing, left turn is permitted.

Lane Co

Don't use lan
approach